Milarepa and the Art of Discipleship I

THE COMPLETE WORKS OF SANGHARAKSHITA
include all his previously published work, as well as talks,
seminars, and writings published here for the first time. The
collection represents the definitive edition of his life's work as
Buddhist writer and teacher. For further details, including the
contents of each volume, please turn to the 'Guide' on pp.707–11.

COMPLETE WORKS $\mathrm{I}8$ COMMENTARY

Sangharakshita
Milarepa and the
Art of Discipleship 1

EDITED BY VIDYADEVI

Windhorse Publications
169 Mill Road
Cambridge
CB1 3AN
UK

info@windhorsepublications.com
www.windhorsepublications.com

Cover design by Dhammarati
Cover images: Back flap and front: Detail of Marpa (1012–1096) and Milarepa
(1052–1135), Tibet, 16th century, courtesy of the Rubin Museum of Art
Typesetting and layout by Ruth Rudd
Printed by Bell & Bain Ltd, Glasgow

British Library Cataloguing in Publication Data:
A catalogue record for this book is available from the British Library.

ISBN 978-1-911407-02-7 (paperback)
ISBN 978-1-911407-01-0 (hardback)

CONTENTS

FOREWORD

> The turquoise flower is killed by frost;
> This is an example of change
> (This is an example of change);
> It is after the manner of transitoriness.
> Ponder upon this truth
> (Ponder upon this truth)
> And practise the noble teaching.

As we sang these words in harmony and they echoed around the atrium, an immense silence seemed to surround the sound. There was a mingled sense of something ancient and immediate, as far off as stars and as close as breathing. It was as though the whole world had stopped to listen. The choir paused for breath and began the next verse, and the listening audience seemed to play a part in a revelation, as though we were sharing, or creating, a real, if fleeting, insight into the truth.

It was a special moment on a special occasion – Sangharakshita's ninetieth birthday – in a special place, the atrium of the Sangharakshita Library at Adhisthana. The version of 'Milarepa's Eight Wonderful Examples' we sang was adapted by the composer, Vipulakirti, from a translation by Sir Humphrey Clarke published in 1958 as *The Message of Milarepa*.[1] In the preface to that work, the translator, saying that in his view 'Milarepa is the St Francis of Tibet', explains that 'the style adopted in this translation is deliberately archaic in order to give the same impression that the language of the songs themselves does to the Tibetan of today'.[2] Perhaps that was what gave the melody its archaic feeling, the sense of words floating across almost a thousand years from the yogi who first sang them among the Tibetan mountains.

Clarke's slim volume was not the first translation to bring Milarepa to the English-speaking world. In 1928, the American Walter Yeeling Evans-Wentz, who settled in Darjeeling just after the First World War, worked with the translator Lama Kazi Dawa-Samdup to produce Milarepa's life story, *Tibet's Great Yogī Milarepa*.[3] A version of this found its way into a book which the 20-year old Dennis Lingwood, not yet ordained as Sangharakshita, came across in 1945, in a library in Singapore. His account of the chance discovery shows what it meant to him:

> In Dwight Goddard's *Buddhist Bible*, which I borrowed from the Lodge library, I found an abridged version of *Tibet's Great Yogī Milarepa*. It would be difficult to find a more powerful incentive to the leading of the spiritual life than this masterpiece of religious autobiography. As I read it my hair stood on end and tears came into my eyes. If I had any doubts about the nature of my vocation they were now dispelled, and from that time onwards I lived only for the day when I would be free to follow to its end the path that, as it seemed, had been in reality mine from the beginning.[4]

His path took Sangharakshita to the Himalayan region and then eventually back to England, where, in the period 1976–1980, he chose to give a number of seminars on Milarepa's songs. When recently asked the reason, as well as recalling his first encounter with Milarepa all those years ago, he said simply, 'Their teaching is direct and relevant, besides having an element of poetry and human interest.' The seminars were based on the 1962 translation by Garma C. C. Chang given the poetic title *The Hundred Thousand Songs of Milarepa*. (The more literal title would simply be *The Collected Songs of Milarepa*.) In the foreword, Peter Gruber reported that Mr Chang was Chinese and, in the late 1930s, travelled to Tibet 'to search for Dharma and Enlightenment'.[5] Gruber met Chang in 1947 in Darjeeling, where he and Sangharakshita must surely have crossed paths. As Chang explained, he was given editorial assistance and suggestions by, among others, Gerald Yorke, whom Sangharakshita knew and who had in his younger days, as Sangharakshita reports in his memoir *Moving Against the Stream*, 'been a disciple of the black magician Aleister Crowley, the "Wickedest Man in the World".'[6] At the time Sangharakshita met him, Yorke was working for the London publisher Rider & Co., and helped to bring out the first edition of Sangharakshita's *The Three Jewels*. His involvement with the *Songs of Milarepa* may partly explain why the text, though readable and poetic, is evidently in places quite far adrift from the original Tibetan. It seems that now is the time for a new wave of interest in the text. This year (2017), an authoritative new translation by Christopher Stagg is to be published by Shambhala Publications, a successor to Chang's version, which Shambhala have faithfully kept in print for more than fifty years. A commentary on Milarepa's songs by Chögyam Trungpa, compiled from seminars he gave in the 1970s, has also just been published. Trungpa, while expressing his deep appreciation for Chang's translation, also had reservations about it, expressing a hope that 'subsequent translations would have a less religious tone and a more direct and earthy feel, in keeping with the tone of Milarepa's own speech and poetry'.[7]

Whatever its limitations, Chang's translation has given access to an aspect of Milarepa's life that was previously little known outside the Tibetan-speaking world. The story of Milarepa's early years – the ill-treatment at the hands of his uncle and aunt that led him to learn sorcery as a means of revenge, and his tough, life-or-death apprenticeship in Dharma practice as a disciple of Marpa – is so well known that it was even made into a film in 2006, and I vividly recall a dramatic perform-ance of the much-loved story in Kathmandu. Less well known is the next phase of Milarepa's life, when he himself became Dharma teacher to many men and women, as well as demons and demonesses, and even *devas* in pigeon form. Given that he spent his life meditating in solitude in the mountains as his guru Marpa had instructed, it may seem strange that he managed to acquire so many disciples but, as we will see, people often sought him out, however remote his location, and he himself, out of compassion, never missed any opportunity to communicate the Dharma to anyone he happened to meet.

It is this Milarepa we meet in this two-volume commentary, which is based on eleven study-seminars. In the 1970s and 1980s Sangharakshita gave dozens of seminars on a wide range of texts and themes. In order that these teachings could one day reach a wider audience, a massive tape recorder was always present, and members of the small sangha of those days devoted themselves to transcribing the recordings, to be produced in printed form (all now available in digital format on the website freebuddhistaudio.com). The transcripts have great charm, some transcribers' style including hints at atmosphere ('laughter', 'rattle of teacups') and occasional uncertainties; I am still grateful to whoever, hazarding a guess at the obscure title of a wonderful Dharma book, transcribed 'Kindly Bent to Ease Us' as 'Kindly Bent Tweezers(?)'. It was rather wonderful for bookish types to discover that even if their talents didn't run to plastering walls or whatever their local Buddhist centre needed, they could still do something useful. Whether they knew it or not, they were following in the footsteps of Buddhists from the very beginning, one of the main activities of the very earliest sangha being to record the teachings, or rather to commit them to memory, using song, or at least chanting, to help them remember.

Whatever the ostensible subject of study, seminar conversation was sure to turn from time to time to matters that had nothing to do with the text. Occasionally observations were made that are best forgiven and forgotten (sometimes it helps to bear in mind that many of the participants were very young at the time), and sometimes priortiy was given to matters vital to the development of the young Buddhist movement (just over a decade old at the time of the Milarepa seminars). A number of seminars have been edited and published over the years and now appear in these *Complete Works*.[8] It being impractical to include all the rest, at least we have added as many excerpts of Pāli canon commentary as could be squeezed into volume 15 and the whole collection of Milarepa seminars. The first three stories in volume 18 have been published before, in *The Yogi's Joy*, here reproduced in the elegant and succinct version edited by Jinananda and Pabodhana, but the rest are published here for the first time. Sangharakshita has been unable to read through the edited version in the way he used to, but he has given his wholehearted blessing to the project and has been most helpful in answering queries. I am also very grateful to Vessantara, who was present at the very first of these seminars (in the hot summer of 1976), for finding the time to read through a substantial part of the text and suggest some adjustments on the basis of his expert knowledge of the Tibetan tradition. Thanks also, as ever, to Kalyanaprabha for all her help, and to Kalyanasri and Dharmottara for their thoughtful comments. The questions and answers of the seminars have been edited here into continuous text for ease of reading, but although the individual voices of the seminar participants have been blended, the questions and observations they ventured played a vital role in drawing forth Sangharakshita's insights into the text and guiding the flow of the narrative, which is therefore very much a joint effort.

Seminar-based commentary is different from systematic written study. One verse of source text may catalyse pages of discussion while an entire song may slip by almost unnoticed, sometimes for an arbitrary reason like an approaching tea break. Also, the seminar focuses on the needs of those present – in this case young men most of whom were new to Dharma practice. (The Milarepa seminars happen to have been attended by men; Sangharakshita led other seminars attended by women – for example, an insightful series on *The Jewel Ornament of Liberation*, the classic text by Milarepa's disciple Gampopa.) While information about the Tantric practices Milarepa mentions is sometimes given, not much is said about how they are performed, this having been at the time beyond the scope of those present and in any case being best learned not from a book but from personal contact with a teacher. The commentary also sometimes analyses in detail (and to useful effect) an inference of the translation which a more accurate rendering might show to be misleading; though Sangharakshita sometimes comments that the translation may be adrift and suggests other possible readings. Endnotes have been added to locate references to the Buddhist canon and other sources, and to suggest links to other passages in the *Complete Works*. Also, to help with navigation around these volumes, a brief synopsis and a list of themes is provided at the start of each story.

In the first of the sequence of stories told in these two volumes, 'The Tale of Red Rock Jewel Valley', we find Milarepa on his own in the mountains, beset by doubts and demons and desperately missing his teacher and the sangha, but finding his own way to overcome his difficulties. That's really the last time we see him alone: all the subsequent stories are about his meetings with other people, though he returns to solitary meditation whenever he gets the chance. In the second story he sings joyously of the solitary life, and the third describes what happens when he meets a young nobleman about to cross a river. In the previously unpublished fourth story, 'The Shepherd's Search for Mind', there are two contrasting encounters, the first with a married couple who try to convince Milarepa of the joys of conventional life, and the second with a young shepherd who is full of questions about the nature of his own mind and is encouraged to investigate for himself.

The seven stories which fill the rest of volume 18 and the whole of volume 19, under the title 'Rechungpa's Journey to Enlightenment', follow the development of Milarepa's relationship with his disciple Rechungpa, from their first meeting, when the young man goes to investigate a voice he hears singing in the mountains, to their final parting. An introduction to the sequence, including some reflections on how Rechungpa is presented in *The Hundred Thousand Songs*, and a brief account of the stories in the original text which feature Rechungpa but are not part of this commentary, appears at the start of the sequence. Needless to say, his progress towards Enlightenment is not without incident, and the ups and downs he experiences, surely recognizable to anyone who has ever seriously tried to live a spiritual life, are told with humour, irony, and pathos, revealing the all too human nature of the disciple and the wisdom and compassion of his patient teacher.

Rechungpa is credited with having written Milarepa's biography, having one day been inspired to ask his guru to tell his life story.[9] The text not only tells Milarepa's story but gives us an idea of Rechungpa's interview technique. Having heard all about Milarepa's grim experiences and seeking a little light relief, he says,

'The Jetsün's deeds are in truth amazing and wondrous beyond compare. [Jetsün or Jetsun means something like "revered one".] But these episodes of your life inspire only tears and not laughter. I pray, please describe the episodes of your life that inspire laughter.' The Jetsün replied, 'The episodes that inspire laughter are those in which, by virtue of practising with perseverance, I established fortunate humans and non-human disciples on the path of ripening and liberation, thereby benefiting the teachings of the Buddha.'[10]

Milarepa's methods of 'establishing disciples on the path' are as varied as the dsiciples themselves. One can see what Sir Humphrey Clarke meant when he compared Milarepa to St Francis, but it's hard to imagine a

Christian saint engaging in a frank discussion with a party of visitors who ask him please to cover up his nakedness as it embarrasses them,[11] or, when asked for a song expressing the key for obtaining Enlightenment in this lifetime, exposing his buttocks, which are covered in callouses from long periods of sitting meditation, and declaring that this is his ultimate precept.

This latter incident is mentioned in a section called 'Milarepa's personal style' in *Drinking the Mountain Stream: Songs of Tibet's Beloved Saint, Milarepa.*[12] In his foreword to that work, Lama Kunga Rinpoche remarks frankly, 'If the reader is expecting something like a magical and instantaneous reward from this book, I would say that it is rather difficult – do something else.' But, he adds, 'The book, the reader, and the teacher together might produce something of value, something useful.' This thoughtful statement brings to mind a famous and outrageous episode in which Milarepa burns the books of teachings which Rechungpa has travelled all the way from Tibet to India to acquire. Why? How could he? And what happens next? I will leave you to find out in the story called 'Rechungpa's Repentance'.[13] But the question of the value of words, much explored here, is entwined with irony. Here you are, on the brink of this extensive collection of words overheard in conversation about the long-ago songs and stories of an almost legendary figure, mediated through an impressionistic translation and an idiosyncratic editorial process. What do you hope to gain from it? How are you going to recognize whatever you personally need to help you on your own journey towards Enlightenment? Sometimes it may shine out from the pages like a gift, or a kind of bibliomancy, and sometimes you will need help to see it, because you 'can't see for looking', as the homely English phrase has it. Hence the immeasurable value of collective Dharma study and the specific advice only a friend or mentor can give, the 'Pith-Instruction', to use a term frequently encountered in this commentary. Among all the anecdotes and reflections, challenges and reassurances in this text, some things will make a world of difference to you while others will pass you by, maybe because they don't apply to you, or because you don't yet see that they do. As Sangharakshita advises, it is crucial to notice what we find genuinely interesting (which may be quite different from what we think we should find interesting) and use that as our way in to genuine understanding.[14]

The basic question is: what can we learn, spiritually speaking, on our own and what do we need help to discover? Many of the themes of this commentary – some of which are allowed to return more than once, because they seem important enough to bear repetition – circle around a crucial subject: the art of discipleship. In his talk 'Is a Guru Necessary?' given in 1970, and twenty years later, in his talk 'My Relation to the Western Buddhist Order',[15] Sangharakshita considered the complexities of the term we have inherited from the spiritual traditions of the East: 'guru'. The Western term 'disciple', whose simple origin is in the Latin verb *discere*, 'to learn', has become just as complex, and has also been the subject of much discussion in our sangha. But the two terms don't mean anything on their own; they only make sense in relation to each other, and here we see and feel that, in the interactions between Milarepa and his disciples, and in Milarepa's devotion to his own guru, Marpa. Not that, even if we accept the terms, the roles of 'guru' and 'disciple' are fixed. As Sangharakshita makes clear, for a Dharma tradition to continue, it is vital that students do better than their teachers;[16] and, as well, individual relationships are part of a wider network of spiritual friendship, the golden net which Sangharakshita urges us to recognize in his poem 'Four Gifts'.[17]

Part of the golden net is the network of many people responsible for the funding and production of these *Complete Works*, which you will find described and appreciated elsewhere in this volume. Here, I can't resist extending particular thanks to Shantavira, the faithful and indefatigable copyeditor of these volumes. Shantavira has worked on the publication of Sangharakshita's writings longer than anyone and deserves all our praise. May all blessings be his, especially for his long hours of work on this commentary.

Embedded in its prose are many songs, diamonds among precious coal. I am remembering again the voices singing in the library, seventy years after the author of this book found his eyes full of tears on his first meeting with Milarepa, and many centuries after the songs were first given voice in the clear air of the Tibetan mountains. We don't know what they sounded like then, or whether the verses we read now in our own language bear any resemblance to the words Milarepa sang, having been passed down to us through so many generations, so many sensibilities. I can't help hearing in them something of the haunting sorrow and earthy joy of the songs of the medieval troubadours, although, thrillingly, they may have been sung in a style similar to the Tibetan folksong of today. What is remarkable is that even when they reach us as bare words on the page they are still alive, perhaps even – if we give them our heartfelt attention – enlightening.

Vidyadevi
Herefordshire,
August 2017

The Yogi's Joy

I

MILAREPA'S WORLD AND PHILOSOPHY

A SINGING GURU

The stories we are going to consider here are taken from a work known as *The Hundred Thousand Songs of Milarepa*, which records the inspired poetic utterances of the famous, revered, and much loved eleventh-century Tibetan yogi and poet. The figure of 100,000 is a considerable exaggeration, of course, but the episodes I want to discuss do each include a number of songs which convey the distinctive flavour of the work as a whole: they are very approachable and often quite light-hearted, even humorous, while at the same time they express the very essence of dedicated spiritual practice.

They were composed almost a thousand years ago. At the time Milarepa was alive, the Normans were conquering England, and in continental Europe the Holy Roman Emperors were quarrelling with the papacy. In the Americas the Mayas were establishing a new empire in Yucatan, while in China the Northern Sung dynasty was appeasing the Mongols by surrendering territory. And in India a 1,500-year period of Buddhist culture was coming dramatically to an end – for this was the time of the Muslim invasion. Buddhist monasteries were being destroyed, monks were being murdered, gurus were being scattered, and as a result the teachings were being speedily lost. In Tibet, by contrast, Buddhism was enjoying a long-awaited renaissance. The arrival from India of the master Atiśa had coincided with a period in which centralized political control had broken up. As a result local fiefdoms were flourishing, presided over by regional nobles, and this helped to bring about a corresponding diversity of cultural and religious custom.

It is generally thought that the songs of Milarepa were compiled and written down by a yogi of the Kagyu school of Tibetan Buddhism in the fourteenth century, but we cannot be sure how many of them were passed down from Milarepa himself and how many of them were composed by the inspired compiler. It may well be that having put together the songs that had come down to his time, the writer felt there were gaps that needed to be filled and wrote extra songs where they seemed to be required. Which of the songs were sung by Milarepa himself is therefore a matter for scholars to research and debate, and we cannot take them as records of actual meetings at specific times and places. At least some of them may be composites of a number of occasions, people, and locations, but they have the fresh and vivid sense of actual events, and also communicate spiritual teachings of a high standard. From a literary point of view, the fact that the compiler may have put some of his own verses into the mouth of Milarepa hardly seems to matter. If he did, he was a great poet himself, with a considerable gift for narrative. From a spiritual point of view, if he composed some of the songs, he must have been a person of advanced spiritual development.

In Tibetan scroll paintings (called *thangkas*), Milarepa is often depicted as green in colour. This is because for many years he lived a solitary mountain existence, subsisting only on nettles, and apparently this had the effect of turning his body green. He is usually shown naked except for a small cotton cloth, his only covering in the bitter snows of the Tibetan mountain ranges. But he is remembered chiefly for his songs – and they really are songs, not just lyrical poems. In fact, we can get a pretty good idea how Milarepa's songs would have sounded. Singing and chanting are still popular and widespread among Tibetan people. I lived in the Himalayan town of Kalimpong in the 1950s, when it was starting to fill up with Tibetan refugees, and I would often meet Tibetan beggars, whether ordinary people or monks, who used to sing. They would come to the door and chant verses of blessing on the house, accompanying themselves on a little drum and setting the verses to a distinctive and pleasant melody.

Most of us are familiar with the kind of sound produced by Tibetan monks chanting pujas, but it is not only monks who chant in this way. Wherever there is a group of Tibetans working together, perhaps in the fields or building a house, you will hear a traditional song with very similar cadences, though without the complex overtones to be heard in the monastery. These are not sophisticated melodies; Tibetan songs are rather like those of village India, or Christian hymns, with each verse sung to the same simple tune. In the Tibetan folk tradition you sometimes have not even a melody but a simple succession of notes to which each group of two or four lines is sung. Many Tibetans could come up with a song like this more or less spontaneously, making it up as they went along. This is fairly easy because of the structure of the Tibetan language: Tibetan is largely monosyllabic and it is therefore not difficult to string words together in lines of eight or twelve syllables and chant them to a simple tune picked out on a single-stringed instrument. Anyone with a dash of ingenuity and inspiration can keep this up for a long time.

The 'hundred thousand' songs have been translated into English by Garma C.C. Chang. Here is an example of the way his translation sometimes comes close to the original verse form, with its repeated rhythm of more or less eight syllables, taken from the verses called 'Complimentary Song to the Deities of Red Rock Jewel Valley'.

> This lonely spot where stands my hut
> Is a place pleasing to the Buddhas,
> A place where accomplished beings dwell,
> A refuge where I dwell alone.[18]

The Tantric song form – the *vajra-gīta* – can be traced back to the songs of the wandering musician yogis of medieval India, who practised yoga, meditation, and other forms of spiritual training while supporting themselves in a variety of ways. Many lived a solitary life in hermitages or even cremation grounds, while others lived as householders, but they all had something in common: their uncompromising dedication to spiritual practice.

Milarepa is associated above all with inspiration, both lyrical and spiritual, and this is reflected in the poetic form in which it is expressed. The same is true of the Buddha himself, many of whose more exalted utterances are gathered in a collection of discourses known as the *Udānas*, teachings expressed in verse form suggesting heightened inspiration, a communication from an even higher level than is normal for an Enlightened one.

The songs of Milarepa have significance for us because they express the truths and experiences of authentic Buddhist practice. They have an immediacy that resonates even today, so many years after they were first uttered. The songs are about not only the harshness and remoteness of the Tibetan mountain ranges, but also the peaks and valleys of an inner terrain – the inner world of the Tantric yogi.

FIRST STORY
THE TALE OF RED ROCK JEWEL VALLEY

In which, while collecting wood, Milarepa realizes that he is still not rid of ego-clinging, and is struck by the utter futility of the world and all its affairs. Alone, he longs for his guru and his Dharma brothers, but learns to trust his own experience and is reassured that his solitary practice will bear fruit. Finding that five Indian demons with eyes as large as saucers have made themselves at home in his cave, he eventually discovers that there is nothing to be afraid of.

Themes:

2

FINDING THE SANGHA

MILAREPA'S MINDFULNESS

Once the great Yogi Milarepa was staying at the Eagle Castle of (Red Rock) Jewel Valley, absorbing himself in the practice of the Mahāmudrā meditation. Feeling hungry, he decided to prepare some food, but after looking about he found there was nothing left in the cave, neither water nor fuel, let alone salt, oil, or flour. 'It seems that I have neglected things too much!' he said, 'I must go out and collect some wood.'

He went out. But when he had gathered a handful of twigs, a sudden storm arose, and the wind was strong enough to blow away the wood and tear his ragged robe. When he tried to hold the robe together, the wood blew away. When he tried to clutch the wood, the robe blew apart. (Frustrated,) Milarepa thought, 'Although I have been practising the Dharma and living in solitude for such a long time, I am still not rid of ego-clinging! What is the use of practising Dharma if one cannot subdue ego-clinging? Let the wind blow my wood away if it likes. Let the wind blow my robe off if it wishes!' Thinking thus, he ceased resisting. But, due to weakness from lack of food, with the next gust of wind he could no longer withstand the storm, and fell down in a faint.

When he came to, the storm was over. High up on the branch of
a tree he saw a shred of his clothing swaying in the gentle breeze.
The utter futility of this world and all its affairs struck Milarepa,
and a strong feeling of renunciation overwhelmed him.

In 'The Tale of Red Rock Jewel Valley' we encounter Milarepa at a
comparatively early stage in his career, when his practice is still quite
a struggle and he is still more or less clothed. As we shall see, he also
still possesses some books. Even so, he has evidently been practising
meditation in solitude, following the practice of *mahāmudrā* – the union
of bliss and emptiness – according to his guru's instructions, for a long
time. And in this episode his practice suddenly bears fruit through an
unexpected, if apparently trivial, turn of events, of which Milarepa is
able to take advantage by means of a very basic practice: mindfulness.

It is clear that his practice of mindfulness is very effective because
he is so quick to observe his instinctive reaction when his robe blows
apart, and to realize what that reaction implies with regard to his
spiritual development. The incident is so trivial that most people,
even most practising Buddhists, wouldn't think twice about it, beyond
perhaps noticing their momentary frustration at trying to do the work of
three hands with two. But Milarepa is keeping a close and unremitting
watch over himself, and it is the brief conflict in his mind that draws
his attention to the deeper issue. Seeing beyond his frustration to the
fundamental delusion underlying it, he realizes that while he is literally
clinging to his robe, he is clinging to his ego just as tightly. As the wind
snatches his robe from him, he observes himself possessively clinging
to his meagre property and says to himself, 'What is making me cling
to my robe in this way? It is because I feel that it is *mine*, it is *my* robe,
my body needs it for covering. *I* need it.' At once recognizing this as
evidence of a still active ego, he gives up his robe to the importunate
tugging of the wind.

One of the best known accounts of the Buddha's teaching of
mindfulness is the *Satipaṭṭhāna Sutta*,[19] the discourse on the four
foundations of mindfulness. As one of the most important of the Pāli
suttas, or discourses, this text is part of the bedrock of modern-day
Theravādin practice, and its theme of mindfulness remains integral to
all traditions of Buddhism. Of particular relevance here is the practice
of recollecting what are known as mental objects, especially the six

sense bases and their objects. This aspect of mindfulness involves maintaining a continuous awareness that, as objects impinge upon consciousness via the sense bases or sense organs, various unhealthy mental states arise to intrude on that simple awareness. These unhealthy states, known collectively as the hindrances, include moods and thoughts of lust, ill will, sloth and torpor, restlessness and anxiety, and doubt. Each in its own way clouds the essential lightness and clarity of perception.

These deep-seated states of mind are a product of our karma, our deluded actions, and they form the very fabric of our self-view, our sense of who we are and hence what the world is. They are consequently extremely subtle and hard to detect. Mindfulness of one's mental processes is, for this reason, a particularly demanding practice, one that calls for every bit of striving one can muster.

Milarepa's sustained awareness of these subtle mental processes has enabled him to detect the arising of the fetter of self-view, the delusion that he is a fixed, separate entity, even as he is grasping desperately at his few remaining possessions, his robe and a few sticks of firewood. Indeed, it is at such a moment of instinctive reaction that this fetter will force itself into view, even though it is also at just such a moment that mindfulness is most likely to be lost.

Milarepa's mindfulness consists in seeing how, when the senses come into contact with their objects, any one of the hindrances may arise. Once we are able to refine consciousness to the extent that we can be aware of these subtle mental comings and goings, we then have only to understand deeply enough the significance of what we see to take the appropriate action. This calls for vigilant and unremitting practice. The hindrances do not arise with any great fanfare; on the contrary, they are extremely subtle. It is the very small things that give them away, and it is these we have to look out for, in other people and in ourselves.

This is as much as can be asked of anybody. We cannot be expected to be perfect all the time, or even much of the time. All we are invited to do is to stay awake, to keep watch over ourselves, especially with respect to small, seemingly insignificant things that we do or say or think or feel – and to take in the implications of what we notice. The task is to recognize what your observation tells you about yourself, and then to do whatever you need to do to adjust your attitude and bring it more into line with the way things really are.

The importance of mindfulness is reflected in the fact that – at least according to one tradition – the Buddha's last words to his disciples were, 'With mindfulness, strive' (*appamādena sampādetha* in Pāli).[20] It is as though just these two things are expected of us and encapsulate everything we need to do. Know what you are doing – pay attention to every last detail of your existence as it occurs. Take note of every detail of your experience as it impinges upon your consciousness – especially those details that others will probably miss. And if you notice any vestige of anything unskilful, any attachment, any impulse that 'that is mine, this is due to me,' take immediate action to change your attitude. The whole procedure is less complicated than it may sound. Milarepa manages to do it in the moment between his brief tussle with the elements and his blackout. But though it is simple and quick, its effects are truly momentous.

Near the end of this story, Milarepa comes to the conclusion that a demon was behind the storm. But why does he infer this? It may be difficult for us to imagine the power of a storm in the mountains of Tibet. When I lived in the Himalayan town of Kalimpong, there was once an earth tremor that made the two-storey house in front of which I was standing actually jump a couple of inches. It was as though the whole mountain jumped. When we are exposed to the elements in this way, we get a salutary reminder of the insignificance of human intentions as far as those powers – however we interpret them – are concerned. One has only to experience the full force of such elemental powers, whether of storm, volcano, or earthquake, to begin to see the traditional belief that demons are behind those natural phenomena in a different light. Unprotected by the paraphernalia of modern civilization, we realize that we are at the mercy of natural forces beyond our control.

But here the storm is not to be taken entirely literally. Demon-created and apparently out of control, its fury and clamour are metaphors for the raging whirlwind of ego-clinging that makes our progress through this brief life of ours so very difficult and painful. Yet unlike the storms of the physical world, this tempest can be stilled if we know how to go about it. By bringing the subtle, almost imperceptible practice of mindfulness to the storm of our ego-clinging, we can eventually tame this demonic force. In Milarepa's case, just one moment of insight into the true nature of mind has caused the storm to abate, the demon of worldly clinging to vanish.

His practice of mindfulness and insight continues when he comes round and finds himself lying naked on the ground. He has evidently been unconscious for a while because the storm is over, but the first thing he sees is a shred of his robe in the branches of a tree, fluttering in the now gentle breeze. Again, he is able to see the situation with clarity and creativity.

What strikes him is its absurdity. It is as though that shred of clothing, the last thing he possessed, represents all worldly attachments. In a mere shred of cloth he sees all worldly things, everything that one could cling to – wealth, possessions and pleasures, friends, family and connections, appearance, status and achievements. He sees that they are all liable to be taken away from us at any time. They can all just blow away.

Milarepa's practice of *mahāmudrā* is quite closely related to Zen, and his moment of insight is a little reminiscent of some of the stories of the Zen masters in which a very simple, apparently insignificant incident sparks off a deep realization. A monk, say, is meditating in the middle of the forest when he sees a single yellow leaf fall, and in that one moment gains insight into the transitory nature of all conditioned things. There is even a *Jātaka* tale in a similar vein (the *Jātakas* are the traditional folk tales about the Buddha's previous lives). A king is having his hair and beard trimmed when he notices that the combing and snipping stops for a moment while the barber plucks out a hair. 'What are you doing?' he says, and the barber replies, 'It is your first grey hair, sir, look.' The king gazes at that one grey hair, and then he gets up from his comfortable chair, throws off his fine clothes and walks straight out of the palace into the forest to become a wandering monk. In that single hair he saw everything: old age, disease, and death, the end of all his worldly possessions.[21]

SONG OF SPIRITUAL FRIENDSHIP

Milarepa's response to this realization is to sit down and meditate. As he does so, a cluster of white clouds rises from the valley to the east, above the temple of his guru, Marpa, whom he imagines teaching there his other disciples, Milarepa's 'brothers'. There seems to be a suggestion here that with the appearance of the cluster of white clouds something is happening – whether in physical form or as a vision – as the fruit of Milarepa's practice of the guru yoga, the formal visualization and veneration of his teacher. The clouds certainly serve to connect Milarepa's thoughts to his guru.

Milarepa desperately misses his guru. The profound spiritual connection between them is not enough for him in his present mood. What follows is a song of devotion to Marpa, and of longing for human contact with him. Milarepa wants to see his guru, face to face, in the flesh. He also misses Marpa's wife and his fellow disciples.

> Though limited in reverence, I wish to see you;
> Though weak in faith, I wish to join you.
> The more I meditate, the more I long for my Guru.
>
> Does your wife, Dagmema, still dwell with you?
> To her I am more grateful than to my mother....
>
> How happy I would be could I join the gathering,
> At which you may be teaching the Hevajra Tantra....
>
> Though short my diligence, I have need for learning;
> Though poor my perseverance, I wish to practice.
> The more I contemplate, the more I think of you;
> The more I meditate, the more I think of my Guru.
>
> The brothers from Weu and Tsang may be there.
> If so, I would be joyful and happy.
> Though inferior my Experience and Realization,
> I wish to compare mine with theirs.

Devotion to the guru is fundamental to Tantric practice. Indeed, this episode begins, as do all the episodes of the collected songs of Milarepa, with an expression of devotion and worship – 'Obeisance to all gurus' – which is meant to remind us of the source of the teachings. This salutation asserts the primacy of personal, oral teaching over mere book learning within the school of Tibetan Buddhism that takes its name from this overriding emphasis, the Kagyu or 'whispered transmission', the lineage to which Milarepa belongs. In other words, we are being warned that a text – any text – is not enough for our practical spiritual purposes.

The 'brothers' for whom Milarepa longs are his '*vajra* brothers', his fellow trainees who have received initiation from the same guru. The term signals the importance of the relationship between them. Having the same *vajrācārya* or Tantric path and the same *vajra guru* or Tantric guru creates an especially close bond with special responsibilities. Harmony is of tremendous significance in such a close-knit spiritual community, and to dispute with your *vajra* brother is very damaging, spiritually speaking. As each of you has dedicated yourself to the same ideal and the same path, if you quarrel with a Dharma brother, you are quarrelling with your own commitment.

Milarepa naturally entitles his song 'Thoughts of my Guru'. However, there is a suggestion that he feels his separation from his *vajra* brothers even more intensely. The language in the final verse is painfully strong. If he misses his *vajra* brothers more than his guru, it is not because of any lack of devotion to Marpa; it is because they are more on his level. They are able to offer a kind of straightforward human companionship that he cannot get from someone he reveres so much. As he says, he can compare his experience with theirs, measure himself against them.

He may be in some spiritual contact with his *vajra* brothers through keeping them in mind, but it is clearly not enough to overcome his sense of isolation. Milarepa can at least practise the guru visualization as a means of getting close to his teacher, but as far as I know there is no Tantric practice in which you visualize your *vajra* brothers. But even if there were such a practice, it still wouldn't be enough. You would still want to meet up with them, to talk with them, to have tangible, personal contact. And this is Milarepa's experience. He still feels the physical separation, the acute and pressing need for simple, straightforward human company, and he prays to his guru to relieve him of the pain this need gives him.

LONELINESS IN THE SPIRITUAL COMMUNITY

It is easy to lose heart at a time like this, when you have put in a lot of work and get nothing but pain and loneliness in return. Having been sent into the mountains to meditate on his own, Milarepa misses a sense of the spiritual community's support of his individual endeavour. Marpa and his disciples no doubt do comprise a true spiritual community, but it seems that in his darker moments Milarepa cannot always see them in that light. For all his conscious aspiration to the contrary, at least for the time being he is seeing the spiritual community not as a spiritual community, but as a group from whose warmth and companionship he feels excluded; and he is seeing himself not as an individual, but as a member of that group.

Samuel Johnson, the great eighteenth-century English critic, lexicographer, and conversationalist, once said that the reason for his attachment to human company was his fear that the melancholy that descended upon him when he was alone would drive him mad. In this sort of state it isn't exactly a friend you seek – even if a friend will serve your purpose – but simply someone to distract you from your experience of separateness. Not that the presence of another person will necessarily do this. After all, it is not physical solitude that engenders loneliness, but mental isolation, which the mere physical proximity of others can never completely eradicate.

To some extent such loneliness is inherent in conditioned existence. The very fact of one's subjectivity – that one has a sense of ego, or separate self – means that one will always feel to some extent cut off from others. The mere fact that others are *others* means that you are isolated and therefore experience loneliness. If you are sufficiently mindful you will notice that subtle sense of loneliness in your experience all the time, even – perhaps particularly – when you are with a good friend. The better you know someone and the more time you spend with them, the more you realize they are fundamentally different and ultimately separate from you. They think differently from you: they don't really penetrate into your thoughts, nor do you ever quite succeed in seeing things from their point of view. In the end you don't understand how it feels to be them, and nor can they understand how it feels to be you.

So, although you may live for years side by side with someone who is very dear to you, your very closeness may help you to see that you are really on your own. This is the kind of insight that can emerge from being aware and mindful when you are with another person. There can be warmth and companionship, but no amount of good friendship can – or should – alleviate the existential loneliness of conditioned existence. If companionship does help you to forget it, that isn't really a good thing. We should not expect from others more than they are able to give.

True spiritual fellowship fosters communication in its most mature sense: mutual responsiveness across a chasm. Even though you share a heartfelt ideal, you are both aware that as long as there is a sense of separate selfhood, you will always feel an element of loneliness, when you are on your own and even when you are with a friend. Indeed, it is your shared ideal that reminds you of that chasm between you. The more that knowledge is implicit in your communication, the more effective the communication will be. If you are in a reasonably positive state of mind, such an insight will be exhilarating rather than depressing. A good friend is someone with whom you can be alone.

COMPETITIVENESS IN THE SPIRITUAL COMMUNITY

> *Though inferior my Experience and Realization,*
> *I wish to compare mine with theirs.*

In expressing a wish to compare his experience with that of his *vajra* brothers, Milarepa makes reference to an aspect of the spiritual community that might seem inimical to harmony: that of comparing one's progress with others. Competition, however, is not always a bad thing, even in the spiritual community. Measuring yourself against others, testing your strength of body or brain against theirs, is a healthy impulse. It is important not just for the individual but for the social group, and it is good for everyone, even those who come off worst in the contest.

Competitiveness drives you to strive for as high a place as possible within the hierarchy of the group to which you belong, and through that struggle you find not only your place in the hierarchy but also your natural level of competence. You need to compete in order to discover how to make the best use of your abilities. If you have the ability to be a leader, you will naturally work your way up the hierarchy to occupy that position. Indeed, it is essential for the survival of the group and the species as a whole that you do so. Power hierarchies seem to have arisen originally in hunter-gatherer societies, primarily among the males, and their survival value is obvious. If the group is to be organized to defend itself from attack by other groups, it is in everyone's interests that the strongest and cleverest members should take the lead.

A normal healthy male thus has a drive to find out where he stands in relation to other men, and when you get a lot of men together there is invariably a tendency for the young bulls to challenge the old bull. What you end up with is a power structure, and ideally, if this structure is established by open competition, it will reflect the comparative strength and skill – as well as the shrewdness and cunning – of the individuals within it.

This basic drive has little to do with the spiritual life, except that any spiritual development has to begin with a healthy human individual. Maintaining the hierarchy of power through competitiveness is useful for many practical purposes and in any situation where a clear objective needs to be achieved. In large projects in particular, it may be impractical to give everyone an equal voice in forming every decision. But a hierarchy of power should not be confused with the spiritual hierarchy. Someone who is physically weak, and not particularly bright or ambitious in an ordinary way, may still have the drive to keep going on the spiritual path when strong men fall by the wayside.

Confusion can easily arise because a hierarchy of power is readily apparent to everyone, whereas a spiritual hierarchy is not. Moreover, there are always practical, organizational goals to be achieved even within the context of the spiritual community. It may be that some people like to get things done through hierarchical structures, while others prefer working in close cooperation on a more or less equal basis. This may mean that certain people end up taking charge of large spiritual institutions while others tend to be involved in smaller situations. Such arrangements do not imply any spiritual superiority or inferiority on the part of the individuals concerned. Within the context of the spiritual community, the hierarchy of power is to be regarded as instrumental and provisional only. Someone who occupies a higher place within the structure is not thereby more integrated, more developed as a person, more of an individual.

For some people being first in line, or being the centre of things, is so important that they can be thrown into a very negative mental state when that petty ambition is thwarted, and the spiritual community is by no means exempt from this. This is why the usual Buddhist convention is that when a number of people are to be ordained or initiated they line up in order of natural seniority, the eldest or the longest-standing disciple going first. This avoids any dispute.

So long as there is genuine friendship, competitiveness within the spiritual community is generally harmless and even sometimes useful from a practical point of view. But it should be competitiveness of a playful kind. And the more spiritually developed you are, the less you will mind where you find yourself in the hierarchy. You will just step quietly and unobtrusively into the position that your qualities – or lack of them – warrant.

In Milarepa's case, his qualities have led him to this desolate spot, many miles away from his companions in the spiritual life, although he is not yet quite reconciled to this state of affairs. But that is about to change.

TRUSTING IN ONE'S OWN EXPERIENCE

Milarepa's sincere faith in his guru finally brings him the answer he seeks. Although they are physically separated, his guru reveals himself in a vision, riding a lion. Mañjuśrī, the archetypal bodhisattva of wisdom, is sometimes depicted riding a lion, so the fact that Marpa appears in the same way suggests that he is a manifestation of the wisdom aspect of the Dharma. In any case, his message is entirely reasonable. Rather than reminding Milarepa of what will happen if he doesn't pull himself together and of what rewards await him if he does, Marpa simply reminds him how far he has come.

> Have you not continually offered service to the Guru and to the
> Three Precious Ones above? Have you not dedicated your merits
> to sentient beings in the Six Realms? Have not you yourself
> reached that state of grace in which you can purify your sins and
> achieve merits?

He draws Milarepa's attention to the positive aspects of his own experience, to the progress he knows he has already made. If his practice has had any beneficial results, then Milarepa has the firm basis he needs for faith in his continuing path.

Marpa's appearance in this way is reminiscent of the earth goddess who, according to the traditional accounts, appeared at a similarly critical moment in the Buddha's life, when the Buddha-to-be (Siddhartha) is being assailed by Māra. Māra doubts Siddhartha's right to sit on the *vajrāsana*, the diamond throne that only a Buddha-to-be can occupy. But the earth goddess arises to bear witness to the depth of Siddhartha's practice, to remind him of the long road he has travelled over many lifetimes to arrive at this place.[22]

Becoming conscious of the positive outcome of his dedicated practice of mindfulness and devotion, even though it appears to have led him only to this lonely and desolate mountain, Milarepa has the intelligence to see that on the basis of what he has already experienced, the practices will eventually bear fruit. They will support you if you will commit yourself to them. If you will only jump into the air, the force of gravity can be relied upon to work. The Three Jewels will do their bit if you do yours. They are always there; that is why they are called Refuges. When you go for Refuge to them they will never fail.

MILAREPA'S SONG OF RESOLVE

My earnest song, called 'Thoughts of my Guru',
Must surely have been heard by you, my teacher;
Yet I am still in darkness.
Pray, pity me and grant me your protection!

Indomitable perseverance
Is the highest offering to my Guru.
The best way to please Him
Is to endure the hardship of meditation!
Abiding in this cave, alone,
Is the noblest service to the Ḍākinīs!...

Guru mine, pray grant me your protection!
Help this mendicant to stay ever in his hermitage.

The song shows Milarepa's mettle even in his moment of weakness. He is effectively saying, 'What else have I got?' He is still, as he says, in darkness, but he does not entreat Marpa to be gentle with him, to indulge his simple and innocent human yearning for the company of like-minded people. Instead, he asks his guru to help him persevere on the path set out for him. He sees that he must seek inspiration in the very hardship that seems to be drying up his inspiration. There is no way back, and he does not ask for one. This resurgence of faith in the path is enough to lift his flagging spirits. His inspiration returns, and his energies are again aroused.

Exalted, Milarepa adjusted his robe and carried a handful of
wood back to his cave. Inside, he was startled to find five Indian
demons with eyes as large as saucers. One was sitting on his bed
and preaching, two were listening to the sermon, another was
preparing and offering food, and the last was studying Milarepa's
books.

Following his initial shock, Milarepa thought, 'These must be
magical apparitions of the local deities who dislike me. Although
I have been living here a long time, I have never given them any
offering or compliment.'

From this passage it would seem that Milarepa has retrieved both his
robe and the wood he has collected. But here is another shock, perhaps
even more disconcerting than the storm. His cave has suddenly become
a little crowded. Five demons have arrived, apparently for an extended
visit. They are Indian demons, rather than the home-grown Tibetan
variety, so they are all the more strange and terrifying.

Milarepa's initial thought is that these demons are the local gods or
spirits, irritated at having been ignored and appearing in malevolent
form in order to frighten him into offering them some respect. He has
overlooked the need to pay homage to them, make them offerings, show
appreciation of their prior claim on the place where he wants to practise.
He needs to placate them so that they do not disturb his meditation.

A local deity is the power of a particular area – literally the spirit
of the place in a personalized form. It isn't just a mental response to
the place; it is a perceptible presence. This is the difference between
a modern experience of place and a traditional view. It is a universal
human trait even today to personalize inanimate objects like ships and
cars. People often have a kind of relationship with such things, involving
affection and respect. We can also find ourselves reacting with irritation
to the apparent malevolence of a gust of wind that blows away a hat, or
a chair that gets in the way, or a car that won't start. But for modern,
urban, rationalistic people, that is as far as our personalizing tendencies
go. We tend to see the environment as an arrangement of more or less
inanimate objects, interrelated by various physical processes.

But we should not regard this modern attitude as in any sense normal. In a pre-modern culture one's surroundings were always straightforwardly alive. Local deities are the literal personification of the psychic atmosphere of particular locations and natural objects like trees. In Pāli texts, for example, one comes across tree divinities who start speaking to one or another of the monks, perhaps rebuking him or encouraging him in his meditation. Such spirits are common in the folklore of primitive cultures. It is as though primitive people (I don't mean to imply any disparagement by the use of the term 'primitive') have a great sensitivity to the psychic atmosphere of a particular spot and a tendency to experience it in personal terms, as a spirit or divinity of some kind.

Many primitive peoples establish their whole religious culture upon these perceptions. Wherever they are, whether in the middle of a desert or forest, or by a stream or gully, they sense someone there, and regard this being or entity as the local deity. If you want to refer to a particular local atmosphere, the general effect that a region or place has on the psyche, you speak of the god or goddess of that tract of land or forest or cave or shrine. A certain numinous atmosphere becomes concentrated into a particular form or figure, so that the atmosphere of a place is *someone* rather than *something*. Without necessarily seeing or hearing anything, you feel a kind of presence.

My friend and teacher Yogi Chen (a Chan and Vajrayāna practitioner who used to live in a little bungalow near the bazaar in Kalimpong) used to tell me endless stories of his own encounters with gods and goddesses and other such beings, including these local deities. When I went to see him he might say, for example, 'Just before you arrived, such-and-such a deity came and told me what I was to say to you.' This sort of remark used to give me food for thought. I knew him well enough not to doubt his sincerity, and it was not a decision on his part to express his experience in these terms. This was the truth of his experience, however one might try to evaluate it. These beings were completely real to him, as real as the people who came to see him, if not more so. His was perhaps the most extreme case of this way of seeing that I have been closely associated with, though I have known other people whose experience was similar. It is as though such people are psychically organized to experience things in this way. It's rather like the way children experience things. They literally see forms and figures – not physically, but with an inner eye – and they may even hear voices. This is how they experience what most of us would describe in more impersonal terms as the atmosphere of a place.

Modern Westerners who find themselves susceptible to this way of experiencing the influence of a place tend to get on well with meditation, especially meditation of a visionary or devotional kind. But there are some places in Britain – Glastonbury, for example – that retain such a strong atmosphere that most people can feel it. Explain it how you will, you can feel an unusual quality in the very air of the place, and to speak of the local deity is probably the simplest and most straightforward way of referring to this. If you are receptive enough you can pick up some unseen quality in many places, perhaps particularly in woods and ancient forests.

Nor is the psychic atmosphere of such places always benign. At a place in England where I used to go on retreat, I noticed a distinct atmosphere among the trees nearby. Other people noticed it too, and found the forest a frightening place to be. The trees seemed angry and resentful, perhaps because they were planted so close together. Like people stuck on a congested train, they didn't have enough space. A nearby airfield may also have contributed to their discomfort; the noise from planes flying low overhead cannot have been good for their nerves. But whatever the reason for this unpleasant atmosphere, it was not just a poetic fancy on my part. I felt it quite directly. Those trees didn't like human beings; they weren't pleased to see me. By contrast, the woods near our retreat centre in Norfolk, Padmaloka, seem very happy.

It must have made quite a psychological difference to the monks of the Buddha's time that they lived out their lives under trees. Northern India was one great forest at the time, and is referred to as such in the Pāli texts (the Pāli term is *mahāvana*). The monks slept in the forest, they walked along narrow tracks through it, and they begged for alms in villages surrounded by it. Of course, since the Buddha's time many forests have been cut down and humanity has lost the company of very many trees. One can only speculate as to the effect of this loss on the human psyche, but perhaps it is significant that even in the most industrial of cities, the city planners have felt the need to plant trees along the streets and in the parks.

One can imagine that the effect of living in an environment populated by large numbers of animals would be similarly noticeable. On the plains of Africa the presence of enormous flocks and herds must give one a strong sensation of being a member of a single species among many, many others, part of a whole complex of living beings, the vast majority of which are non-human. Where humans do not dominate, we perhaps become aware of different psychic forces than those we are used to, and aware of ourselves as belonging to just another species of animal. At the same time, we see the gulf between ourselves and these other forms of life, and the specific significance of human life, and we feel our need for the companionship of other human beings. In the end, the experience of other forms of life may bring us back to an appreciation of our own kind, of those with whom we can communicate most fully.

It is not, after all, as if there is an absence of nature in towns and cities; it is more that nature is present in a particular form, that of an overwhelming preponderance of human beings, producing an extraordinary range of psychic energies. Even towns and cities have their local deities. In the *Mahāparinibbāna Sutta*, for example, the Buddha is described as arriving at a certain spot (Pāṭaligāma, near the modern Patna) and prophesying that one day a great city would be built there.[23] Apparently he detected the kind of powerful deities that incite men's minds to build cities (rather than, say, meditate). Even today, at the feet of the high-rise apartment blocks of modern Hong Kong or Bangkok, you will find shrines to the local gods, with incense burning and perhaps a few flowers as offerings. Our usual experience of nature, the countryside as we call it in England, is another thing altogether. Domesticated and cultivated, the countryside is less intensely stimulating, less inhabited in this sense of psychic presences, than either the city or nature in the wild.

SUBDUING DEMONS

The significant point to be drawn from Milarepa's encounter with these demons, however, is that the Buddhist ideal is to adopt a friendly attitude towards all such deities, whether they appear as benign spirits or as malignant demons. It is true that the teacher who is credited with establishing Buddhism in Tibet, Padmasambhava, is commonly said to have achieved this by subduing the local demons. But this terminology may be a little misleading, suggesting as it does an aggressive suppression of malignant spirits. In fact, 'demon' in the sense of 'devil' is a purely Christian usage of the Greek *daimon*, meaning a presiding genius or tutelary deity. Far from suppressing these powerful forces, Padmasambhava harnessed their energies, putting them at the service of the Dharma.

The Buddha himself always insisted on respecting the local gods and religious traditions, and when the figure of the Buddha first became an object of worship, he was depicted with major gods from the Hindu pantheon waiting upon him. One image, for example, shows him descending from the *devaloka* or heaven realms attended by Indra and Brahmā. The old gods are thus not excluded but given their place in a greater scheme. The ethnic is integrated with the universal, the lower religious ideal with the higher spiritual and transcendental ideal.

If this integration does not take place in some way, trouble will ensue, for these strange forces are not as alien as they seem. Their existence is to some extent bound up with our own. The energies that find their expression in the form of the spirits and demons that appear in the folklore of indigenous culture also emerge as aspects of ourselves, and these basic energies cannot just be put to one side and ignored. You could perhaps do so if you were Enlightened – the Buddha's Enlightened disciple Śāriputra famously managed to ignore the violent attentions of a malignant demon completely on one occasion (as observed by his friend Maudgalyayāna and recorded in the Pāli canon).[24] But if we are not Enlightened, these energies have to be harnessed, directed, assimilated, absorbed, which may mean bringing local deities into line. In folkloric terms, the demons have to be subdued.

So if you are going to build a Buddhist temple in England, it is probably a mistake to build a replica of a Tibetan or Japanese building. You would first need to find a location that already had a positive atmosphere. Then you could introduce into the construction of the temple certain motifs or decorative touches with an indigenous significance. In place of bodhi leaves carved into the wooden beams you could have oak leaves, with all the associations that they embody for the English – druids, mistletoe, the protective 'wooden walls' of the Royal Navy, hearts of oak, strength, stability, and so on – and in this way you would to some extent incorporate the energies of the local culture into your spiritual purposes. All those associations would contribute their energies to the ideals to which the temple was dedicated, and gradually more and more features of the local culture could be brought in to support your spiritual aims.

So Milarepa sings a complimentary song to the demons in an attempt to charm them into leaving him alone. He lets them know that he has taken a bodhisattva vow, and that therefore he wishes them well.

> Ye local demons, ghosts, and gods,
> All friends of Milarepa,
> Drink the nectar of kindness and compassion,
> Then return to your abodes.

But the Indian demons did not vanish, and stared balefully at Milarepa. Two of them advanced, one grimacing and biting his lower lip, and the other grinding his teeth horribly. A third, coming up behind, gave a violent, malicious laugh and shouted loudly.

Clearly the demons are not inclined to avail themselves of Milarepa's offer of the nectar of kindness and compassion. They are certainly not at all charmed. Realizing that this attempt to appease them has failed, Milarepa tries a different tactic. Delivering a powerful incantation, he calls on his higher energies to confront these dark forces that have invaded his practice. In doing this he is flexing his spiritual muscles, as it were. Why, after all, should a fervent devotee of the Buddha himself have anything to fear from mere demons? The demons must surely acknowledge that they have been beaten in a straight fight. But no. They remain unmoved.

Seeing that he is on entirely the wrong tack with them, Milarepa tries to put things right with a 'compassionate' lesson in Buddhist doctrine. Nonetheless, the demons obstinately stay put. In hindsight it is obvious why this ploy fails. It fails because it is a ploy. His motive in preaching the Dharma is not the spiritual welfare of the demons. The Dharma may indeed involve great compassion, but in this case it is not his own. As he has recourse to great compassion only when the wrathful Buddha meditation fails, it is not even ordinary compassion. He tries to get rid of them by force, and when that fails he tries to get rid of them by kindness, but his attitude remains the same.

The demons seem to have made themselves quite cosy in Milarepa's cave. But why do they present a scene of such studied domesticity? It seems an odd way for Indian demons to behave. The answer is that they are a particular kind of demon, best described not as spirits of place but as *pretas*, 'hungry ghosts'. *Pretas* are embodiments of craving or neurotic desire – hence their eyes like saucers – and the scene they are enacting is a kind of ghastly parody of the spiritual community for which Milarepa has been yearning.

Suddenly Milarepa realizes what is going on. He has misread the nature of these demons, taking them to be unfriendly local spirits, the neighbourhood thugs of the spirit world, when they are in fact something much closer to home. They are a kind of emanation of Milarepa's state of mind, of his *preta*-like longing to be supported in his weakness, to be distracted and comforted by the warmth and companionship of his *vajra* brothers. His craving turns the spiritual community in his own mind into a collection of hungry ghosts gathered together out of neurotic craving. In his heart of hearts this is what Milarepa wants, perhaps what we all want, but until now he has not understood that this is the case, so the demons have remained.

There is nothing wrong with the positive human group. One needs the support and encouragement of like-minded companions. But the true spiritual community is more than that. It means more than sharing a psychologically healthy lifestyle, more than satisfying the simple human desire for contact and warmth under the guise of engagement in spiritual practice. The demons represent aspects of Milarepa's own unsubdued ego, which takes the form of a subtle clinging to his identity as a member of the religious group. And you cannot get rid of ego with ego, even if that egotism takes up a wrathful Buddha meditation or gives a teaching on compassion to do it. He has been trying to rid himself of these unpleasant manifestations by force of will, when all he had to do was see their true nature.

In Biblical language, it is like trying to cast out Satan with the fire of Satan.[25] As long as you are wrestling with the devil you will not get rid of him. If you fight against the forces of evil as if they were really out there ranged against you, you will only magnify your egotism. But if you recognize the devil in Buddhist terms, as Māra, you just have to see through him, to see him as a state of your own mind. After all, Milarepa says to himself, I am supposed to have seen through to the essential reality common to all things. I am void, the demons are void. Who is trying to get rid of what? So he sings his 'Song of Realization'.

Father Guru, who conquered the Four Demons,
I bow to you, Marpa the Translator.

I, whom you see, the man with a name,
Son of Darsen Gharmo,
Was nurtured in my mother's womb,
Completing the Three Veins.
A baby, I slept in my cradle;
A youth, I watched the door;
A man, I lived on the high mountain.

Though the storm on the snow peak is awesome,
I have no fear.
Though the precipice is steep and perilous,
I am not afraid!

I, whom you see, the man with a name,
Am a son of the Golden Eagle;
I grew wings and feathers in the egg.
A child, I slept in my cradle;
A youth, I watched the door;
A man, I flew in the sky.
Though the sky is high and wide, I do not fear;
Though the way is steep and narrow, I am not afraid.

I, whom you see, the man with a name,
Am a son of Nya Chen Yor Mo, the King of fishes.
In my mother's womb, I rolled my golden eyes;
A child, I slept in my cradle;
A youth, I learned to swim;
A man, I swam in the great ocean.
Though thundering waves are frightening,
    I do not fear;
Though fishing hooks abound, I am not afraid.

I, whom you see, the man with a name,
Am a son of Ghagyu Lamas.
Faith grew in my mother's womb.
A baby, I entered the door of Dharma;
A youth, I studied Buddha's teaching;
A man, I lived alone in caves.
Though demons, ghosts, and devils multiply,
    I am not afraid.

The snow-lion's paws are never frozen,
Or of what use would it be
To call the lion 'King' –
He who has the Three Perfect Powers.

The eagle never falls down from the sky;
If so, would that not be absurd?
An iron block cannot be cracked by a stone;
If so, why refine the iron ore?
I, Milarepa, fear neither demons nor evils;
If they frightened Milarepa, to what avail
Would be his Realization and Enlightenment?

Ye ghosts and demons, enemies of the Dharma,
    I welcome you today!
It is my pleasure to receive you!
I pray you, stay; do not hasten to leave;
We will discourse and play together.
Although you would be gone, stay the night;
We will pit the Black against the White Dharma,
And see who plays the best.

Before you came, you vowed to afflict me.
Shame and disgrace would follow
If you returned with this vow unfulfilled.

Distracted first by the storm, then by the demons, Milarepa comes
each time to himself again, as he reconnects with his realization of the
mahāmudrā teaching. On each occasion, as a result of remembering his

practice, he recognizes himself, and sees that his frustrating experience and the demons are not separate from the process of integrating his energies. In introducing himself as 'the man with a name', Milarepa is effectively recollecting himself. By his name he is known, recognized, recollected.

The golden eagle, the snow lion, and the king of fishes are traditional images and they often appear in Milarepa's songs. Here they serve to elaborate a basic theme, ringing the changes on his original statement. The principle they illustrate is his embodiment of Enlightenment, the idea that he has taken on Enlightenment as his essential nature, allowing him to live and move in the transcendental realm as they do in their natural environments. He can no more be frightened of demons than the eagle can fall out of the sky.

Not only this. Just as the eagle is an eagle even in the egg, so Milarepa is who he is even in his mother's womb, surrounded by the 'three veins' around which, according to Tibetan tradition, the embryo develops. His faith is not some alien growth. His realization of the Void emerges in the process of his natural development; it is integral to what he is, not grafted on later.

It seems that when we are quite young – before we get involved in the world socially, economically, and sexually, when we are still fairly innocent, still a spectator – we see the simple reality of things quite clearly. Then for a few years we are led away from that knowledge. We listen to other people and get entangled with them, and we lose touch with our own vision and insight. It may be only in our early twenties, or much later, that it all starts to come back to us, perhaps slowly and painfully. Indeed, for a long time we may not get far beyond the knowledge we had when we were much younger.

There is perhaps a connection between this kind of experience and the Tibetan teaching on the intermediate state or *bardo*. It is generally understood in Tibetan Buddhism that when we are in the *bardo* state following physical death (*bardo* means 'in between'), we have opportunities for spiritual attainment that we are not able to assimilate. We have no way of contextualizing them, so we go bouncing down from level to level until we find some experience with which we are familiar and to which we can respond. Thus we arrive at our next rebirth, back in this world again. However, we have had that vision of reality in between, and there may be some vestige of this, however vague and obscure, lingering on in the early years of our next life.

There is an example of this in the life-story of the Buddha himself. The traditional accounts describe how one day he went to rest in the shade of a rose-apple tree while his father, the king, conducted a ritual first ploughing of the fields in springtime. As the boy rested in the cool shade of the tree, his mind progressed quite naturally through states of increasing clarity and joy into the meditative state known as the first *dhyāna*. At that time he had no context in which to place his experience, and he forgot it. It was only much later in his life, having left his spiritual teachers and gone to seek Enlightenment at the foot of the bodhi tree, that he found himself recollecting that incident from his boyhood.[26] Regaining a flavour of the spontaneous bliss he had experienced then, he thought, 'Is this the way?' And the rest, as they say, is history.

One important aspect of this story is that it appears to show that meditative experience is not gained by the forcible application of a particular technique, but unfolds as a process of natural growth and development. Techniques and practices are necessary to assist and guide this process, but it is as though one has to proceed by letting things grow naturally and by encouraging and coaxing that growth, rather than forcing one's development by sheer effort of will.

The common-sense view of personal development is that we begin life in ignorance and gradually learn more about the nature of things through experience and various kinds of training. The Buddha's experience under the rose-apple tree, however, suggests that from a spiritual point of view, important knowledge goes hand-in-hand with innocence and is lost with experience, at least with experience of a certain kind. In going out into the world with the aim of gaining wisdom, we are liable to get tangled up in all kinds of things and end up not wiser but more deluded. Even in the pursuit of spiritual training it is possible to entrap oneself further in time and place and personality and in doing so move still further from true wisdom, the understanding that is altogether beyond time and place and free from personality.

Milarepa rushes at the demons and they shrink back in fear, then swirl together and vanish. He is successful in dealing with them this time because he has realized what they really are. He rushes at them not because he has decided to act aggressively, but as an expression of his spiritual power, which in turn expresses his realization that in the ultimate sense there are no demons. There is nothing to be afraid of and therefore no need to get rid of them. It is nothing to him if they choose to stay.

'This was the Demon King, Vināyaka the Obstacle-Maker, who came searching for evil opportunities,' thought Milarepa. 'The storm, too, was undoubtedly his creation. By the mercy of my Guru, he had no chance to harm me.'

It seems that Milarepa's *mahāmudrā* practice and his realization of the mind as a transparency of voidness momentarily deserted him under the shock of being haunted by these hungry ghosts. But the earlier vision of his guru is what eventually recalled him to his experience of the truth of things, enabling him to disarm his visitors. This is presumably what he means by 'the mercy of my Guru'.

In retrospect it seems significant that Marpa earlier addressed Milarepa in that vision as 'Great Sorcerer', reminding his disciple of the powers of which he had made use before his conversion. Was Marpa giving him an implicit warning, in anticipation of the demonic challenge to come, not to fall back into his old habits? Perhaps he was saying, 'You have been meditating all this time in that cave, but aren't you still just a sorcerer trying to gain your ends by forcible means? Are you going to carry on imposing yourself on your situation, applying the powers at your disposal, just as in the old days you worked your will by force of magic?'

In the early stages of any spiritual career there has to be a struggle, and Milarepa evidently struggled hard and well. But he has reached an advanced stage where will-power is not the most positive quality to develop. He did fall briefly into his old habits when he attempted to use the Dharma in a kind of power game with the demons in order to rid himself of them, but then, drawing on the depth of his accumulated mindfulness and understanding, he finally saw through them.

GUARDING THE JEWELS OF BUDDHIST PRACTICE

How do we safeguard the essential wisdom of the Dharma? It may seem as though Milarepa's answer is to avoid human contact at all costs and hide himself away in the mountains to pursue a life of meditation and abstinence. But the example of his life is not quite what it seems.

It appears extreme, outstandingly austere, and solitary, perhaps more so even than that of Gautama the Buddha. But he still manages to embody the Mahāyāna ideal of compassion, of practising for the sake of others, as conspicuously as any teacher of that tradition. His songs have produced a tremendous effect on many generations of Tibetans, and the joy those songs express, with never a care for his material needs, even for basic food and shelter, must have inspired countless hermits in their own practice.

Milarepa's practice and way of life – his solitary, comfortless, but joyful life – is his teaching. He has attained the goal, but that is no reason to abandon the path, because the goal is not in the end separate from that path. Milarepa benefits people by exemplification, by living out the teaching he espouses without any compromise at all. His strength as a practitioner is in his commitment to his chosen path. Even though in principle he could have continued to practise under other conditions, settled in a monastery or even out in the world, he would not have done so by choice.

Milarepa sets an inspiring example of transcendental faith and joy, determination and mindful vigilance, but he does not offer a realistically practical lifestyle for us to follow. He lived in a society in which the Buddhist tradition was well established and where its doctrines and practices were widely understood and appreciated. He may have completely disregarded mundane, material matters himself, but there were faithful people who would certainly have made his life a little easier, at least from time to time. They would get to hear about him and appreciate the value of what he was doing enough to trudge up the mountain to supply him with with food and drink.

Unfortunately, such supportive conditions for the life of a hermit are very hard to find in the world today. For one thing, even ostensibly inaccessible places are much busier than they used to be. If you tried to follow Milarepa's example and meditate in a cave in the mountains, or in some relatively uninhabited region, you would be unlikely to find yourself alone for long, given the presence of backpackers and hikers, mountaineers and skiers, explorers and scientists, fossil-hunters, naturalists, and all the rest. And would all those people, or the local people, appreciate the significance of what you were doing? It may be a weakness of faith on my part, but I'm afraid I would not personally want to rely on the ravens to feed me,[27] or the locals for that matter.

They wouldn't be likely to think, 'Here's a yogi doing something important,' and come trotting along with food and drink. Indeed, if they took any interest in you, they might well report you to the authorities and recommend your detention on the grounds of impaired mental health.

So we cannot get away from the world in quite the way Milarepa did. Escape is no longer possible. Escapism, yes, but not escape. Modern societies are not prepared to leave anyone or anything alone. Through our practice of mindfulness we can go some way towards creating our own internal refuge, but we still have to deal, all the time, with surroundings that are not conducive to stillness, simplicity, and contentment.

For most of us, therefore, Milarepa's example presents not so much a lifestyle to follow as a warning against over-confidence, and the danger of abandoning the safeguard of positive conditions prematurely. When you have been on retreat, it can seem very tempting to throw yourself back into worldly life, because you feel so full of energy and positivity. You cannot see the threat to your practice from the world around you. You don't see it coming; it just smothers and seduces you until your retreat seems like a distant dream.

The message of Milarepa's solitary life is a little reminiscent of a parable in the Pāli canon. The Buddha says that the deer are safe as long as they feed high in the mountains, but when they come down to the fields to nibble the crops, they are liable to be shot. In the same way, he goes on, if monks stray from their ancestral grazing grounds, the pastures of meditation and the solitary life – if they start nibbling at the fringes of worldly life – then Māra is likely to take a pot-shot at them.[28] As Buddhists, we need to stay on our own home ground, and that means moving decisively away from the lower pastures of the mountain, where our ideals and aspirations are continually curbed and compromised by the worldly values that surround us.

We need to try, even in the midst of the world, to carve out a specifically Buddhist way of life, a kind of miniature Pure Land where people can work together, live together, and practise together in ways that do justice to their spiritual aspirations. It might take the form of residential communities, or right-livelihood businesses, or Buddhist centres dedicated to practising, communicating, and celebrating the Dharma. They would be places in which spiritual values could be nurtured and allowed to grow, sheltered – at least to some extent – from the inhospitable winds of the mundane world.

We cannot expect the situations we set up to offer perfect conditions for practice, any more that those who set them up will be perfectly accomplished practitioners. You cannot bring into existence the perfect Buddhist culture, or the mature individuals to nurture it, at a stroke. Especially at the beginning, they will be working with the limitations of the group mentality they have inherited. But it will be a start, a necessary beginning. And as those who are able to enjoy such conditions grow and develop spiritually, the conditions will get better, providing greater opportunity for further progress.

The very presence of such spiritual oases will have an effect on the surrounding culture. Newcomers will be attracted and inspired and will want to join in, and in this way spiritual values will gain ground within worldly society and be able to sustain a presence there. So the process can go on indefinitely, both in a structural, social sense, and in the sense of new levels of individual progress.

However, the spiritual community is not just a structure in which to live and work. It is also concerned with the ways in which individuals associate with each other. Ideally, the social structures we create among ourselves will provide a basis upon which to develop individuality in the truest sense, and certainly not to hold it back. After all, as human beings we are social animals. The Buddhist path is all about overcoming ego, and collective situations are very good places in which to bring this about. The essential context for spiritual progress is thus the sangha or spiritual community. This is the companionship that helps you grow rather than the group with which you must conform. The sangha, if it is a real sangha, provides a collective situation in which you can be honest about your thoughts and feelings, even though sometimes you may need to restrain yourself from acting on them. The 'middle way' of individuality avoids both individualism in the sense of disregard of others and a timid, mindless social conformity.

Decision-making is the central issue in any collective situation. All too often in everyday life we are faced with decisions that have been made for us, and this is bound to create inner conflict. In the spiritual community, however, you will ideally feel that you can talk about your conflicted feelings. You don't have to pretend you are keen to do something when you are not. If it is a question of preference rather than moral principle, you can even say, 'Well, to be honest I'd prefer to do something else – though I don't mind going along with what you want if it's important to you.' The principle here is to refrain from insisting on your preference while feeling free to be honest about what you prefer. In that case you can go along with what others want in spite of your own feelings. There is no pretence in that conformity, especially in view of the fact that feelings are evanescent and can change swiftly and genuinely. In the end, you can honestly want to do what the others want to do, even though you originally wanted to do something different. But whatever happens, the collective context has not held you back from the honest expression of your thoughts, nor coerced you into behaving in a certain way in order to avoid condemnation.

In this way our incipient individuality – our willingness to take responsibility for ourselves in self-motivated spiritual endeavour – begins to grow deeper roots. We will be able to protect Buddhist ethical and spiritual values from becoming institutionalized, from serving and perpetuating worldly values rather than dissolving and transforming them. In time, as the spiritual community develops, contact with wider society will not be as costly to the individual's progress. We will be in a stronger position to deal creatively with the wider world, on our own terms. Perhaps eventually genuine hermits will be able to follow Milarepa's inspiring example, supported by the wider sangha. At that point we will have achieved something closer to the supportive conditions enjoyed by the cotton-clad yogi Milarepa in old Tibet.

Traditionally, the going forth from worldly entanglements is an integral part of the 'Going for Refuge' to the Buddha, his teaching, and the spiritual community. In our own case, the question is not so much whether we can establish a certain preconceived way of life or work but whether we can surround ourselves with conditions that support our spiritual aspirations. When you step away from the conditions you have inherited, when you go forth, to use the traditional phrase, to pursue the spiritual life, this is not just a shift in your external circumstances. Renunciation as an external act is significant only to the extent that it reflects an inner experience. If you go forth, in whatever way, with a genuine spiritual motivation, into a more avowedly Buddhist context, you are moving in the direction of Enlightenment.

The reaching of this decisive point is a turning away from the group and a turning towards the spiritual community. In the highest sense the spiritual community is represented by the whole Buddhist tradition, a lineage of gurus and teachers leading all the way up to the bodhisattvas and the Buddhas. But in a more everyday sense, and this is where we begin to transform our lives, the spiritual community consists of ordinary men and women who are prepared to struggle with their demons – just as even Milarepa had to do.

SECOND STORY
THE SONG OF A YOGI'S JOY

In which Milarepa, delighting in meditating in the tiger's cave, is visited by five novices to whom he sings of the joys of his way of life. Nothing can extinguish Milarepa's joy, which is rooted in bodily experience – the precious human body. He shows how fear is overcome through equanimity.

Themes:

3
BEYOND FEAR

Here I have used David Snellgrove's translation,[29] in which this episode is called 'Mila Repa and the Novices'. At the time I gave the seminar on which this chapter is based, this seemed to me the best version available. Chang's better-known version, in which this episode is called 'Song of a Yogi's Joy', had yet to appear.

BEAUTY AND FEAR

The opening section of 'Song of a Yogi's Joy' brings us immediately into a remote, often terrifying elemental world. Milarepa is in a high and isolated mountainous region on the sparsely inhabited border between Nepal and Tibet, and judging by the name given to his temporary residence, the tiger-cave of Singa-dzong, he has chosen to occupy a fearsome place of shelter. But it soon becomes apparent that this rather alarmingly named cave is not as unsuitable for meditation as it sounds. Milarepa finds its atmosphere peaceful and tranquil; and then he sees something – or someone. He is visited by the radiantly beautiful figure of the local deity of Yolmo. Consequently, his meditation is calm and full of energy and joy.

This visitation suggests that Milarepa has a vivid sense that the atmosphere of the place is fully in harmony with his meditative mood and spiritual aspirations. It's as though the atmosphere of the cave is entirely attuned to his purpose, and ready to cooperate with his aspirations. Milarepa's attitude is simply to make the best use he can of this beneficial environment. Of course, this is very much in contrast to the atmosphere created by the demons of the previous chapter, and we can conclude that Milarepa's own mental state is quite different.

As it happens, Milarepa is not to be allowed to continue to enjoy his meditative time in the tiger's cave undisturbed; some other visitors are on their way. News evidently travelled fast even in the remotest parts of medieval Tibet, and as a result, Milarepa is visited by a group of five novices who comment on the perilous and isolated nature of the place and speculate rather intelligently as to whether it will benefit his meditation.

Incidentally, these novices are referred to as nuns in Chang's translation. Certainly, Tibetan Buddhist nuns are always technically novices, because women were not given full ordination in the Indo-Tibetan tradition, the original Buddhist order of nuns having died out within about a millennium of its inception. However, in this context it seems more likely that the novices visiting Milarepa are male.

Milarepa responds with his own impressions of his habitation – which has been chosen for him, it seems, by his teacher – and his observations come as a bit of a surprise. If we have had any kind of mental picture of this remote place up to now, it has been bleak, barren, and inhospitable. The tiger's cave offers nothing in the way of comfort, and appears – even to the eye of medieval Tibetan trainee monks, who would be used to levels of hardship that we would not contemplate – eerie and dangerous.

But Milarepa himself is full of praise for it. He talks in terms of colour and light, flowers and birdsong. There is even a suggestion of some human presence, or at least flowering meadows, even if they are so far from habitation that they are visited only rarely.

The novices' impression of the place is an example of the way negative emotions get in the way of our appreciation of things and reduce our ability to see the world around us. They see the loneliness of the location and the almost unbroken solitude of Milarepa's existence, and this is what makes the place frightening to them. Being overpowered in this way by the sense of solitude, they don't see the beauty.

This is a common reaction, of course. Some people find even the ordinary English countryside terrifying, seemingly happier to congregate in places where any disconcerting encounter with terror or beauty can safely be avoided. In places like art galleries, too, we are used to going around in a crowd, and some people are perhaps more comfortable with that than being left alone with all that beauty. But someone who is sufficiently absorbed in the collection will hardly notice the absence of other people in the gallery – and if they do notice, they will be only too happy to enjoy the art undisturbed.

Milarepa's whole life is like this. He is not oppressed by solitude – he does not feel lonely – and he is therefore free to enjoy the natural beauty of his surroundings. He knows this place is lonely, but he is glad of it and doesn't experience the loneliness as a threat. One might say that Milarepa is in harmony with the local deities, in a way that the novices are not. Where others experience loneliness and fear, Milarepa sees only beauty and joy. This is due to his attainment of what he calls 'the Clear Light of Realization of the Void'. The 'Void' is śūnyatā, the Mahāyāna and Vajrayāna term for ultimate reality. But why does he call it the 'Clear Light'?

THE CLEAR LIGHT OF THE VOID

It is in such a lonely place as this,
That I, the yogin Milarepa,
Am joyous in the Clear Light of Realization of the Void,
Joyous exceedingly at its many ways of appearance,
Joyous at its greatness of variety.

Milarepa's use of this expression, which is very common in the literature of the tradition, signals a clear parting of the ways between the Yogācāra school of Buddhism and the rationalistic philosophizing of any tradition, referring as it does to the actual experience of the Void, not to some abstract theoretical construct. But why 'Clear Light of the Void'? What kind of light is it?

The voidness or emptiness of this realization is not null and void, but a state of utter freedom. It is intensely positive, beautiful, lucid, and bright – such that one can really compare it only to the purity and energy of brilliantly clear light. Of course, this is a metaphor. It is certainly not light as we commonly understand it. For one thing, ordinary light has a source, whereas the pure light of the Void doesn't come from anywhere – and it doesn't go anywhere. Śūnyatā is free of any duality such as subject and object, time and space, or even light and dark.

When we think of something we think of it as being this or that, or that rather than this, and we naturally think of ultimate reality in the same way. Certainly the expression 'Clear Light of the Void' suggests that we are to think of it as having the nature of light rather than darkness. But this is only a manner of speaking. In fact, reality cannot be fixed to, or in, any one thing, or tied down in any way. Not of course that it is itself any kind of 'thing'.

The followers of the Yogācāra were concerned to follow a progressive path: first reduce all phenomena, all appearances, to the One Mind, and then realize that the One Mind is perfectly void of any distinction between subject and object. For the Yogācāra, mind is no more real in an ultimate sense than anything else. It is not any kind of universal substance from which everything ultimately derives. It must be seen to be void. There is mind, consciousness, awareness – completely pure, completely illuminated and bright, but within it there is no absolutely existent subject and object, or even a notion of a self in the ordinary sense. Of course, it is almost impossible for us to see this, to leave behind the idea of duality without seeing in its place some kind of unity, however subtle. This is why reality is sometimes referred to as 'not-two' or 'non-dual', thus avoiding the risk of a return to a fixed and final conception of what reality is like.

To speak of the Void is perhaps as near as we can come to a description of the yogi's state of complete openness and freedom. We cannot fix down a clear description of the Void, because its nature is not to be a particular thing with a fixed identity. 'It' is mobile, constantly changing, flowing, forever assuming different forms. Knowing the true nature of the Void, we should not be surprised if it demonstrates its void nature by changing into something else. The Enlightened mind does not try to pin reality down to any particular manifestation and insist on experiencing it only in that way.

When you see things from this perspective, the very idea of the attainment of a goal becomes absurd, because the goal is ultimately to transcend the duality that is necessarily involved in the attainment of a goal. You let go of any sense that you are realizing some separable, distinguishable attainment that you didn't have before and that others do not have. On the contrary, you realize that you were unknowingly a Buddha from the very beginning – like the beggar in a parable from the

Lotus Sūtra (*Saddharma Puṇḍarīka*) who didn't realize that a priceless jewel had been sewn into the corner of his robe.[30] You have not left the world of impurity behind or come into possession of the pure realm of Nirvāṇa. Your own ordinary thought is confirmed in the Buddha state. The 'attainment' is outside time, and when you come to it, you realize that you have been there all the time. So when you gain Enlightenment you realize that you always were Enlightened. Your original possession has simply been confirmed. The absurdity of the situation is often, apparently, what first strikes the newly Enlightened person – hence the laughter that is so often reported in the Zen tradition as the natural reaction to the event. How ridiculous to think that one had ever been anything but Enlightened! How silly to have suffered so much and so unnecessarily!

Free from *saṃsāra*, the round of mundane existence, you become free within *saṃsāra*. You are able to return to the world of suffering without taking that world of distinctions for absolute reality. The laughter therefore also arises from intense relief. It is as though, having spent your whole life deeply anxious about something, you suddenly see the truth of the situation, which is that there was never anything to worry about. 'How absurd all that anxiety and struggle was!' you say to yourself, 'What a fool I've been, thinking I was this and thinking I was that! I was just barking up the wrong tree.' And at that point you can afford to laugh. 'What a silly Buddha I was!'

FEAR AND CONFUSION IN THE CLEAR LIGHT OF THE VOID

> Joyous with a body free of harmful karma,
> Joyous in confusion of diversity,
> Joyous midst fearful appearances,

Even that which appears confusing and fearful cannot extinguish Milarepa's joy. His assurance and confidence are not subject to external conditions. He feels no compulsion to impose any kind of logical order on the true nature of things. He doesn't insist on understanding the ultimate reality of things. He doesn't try to fit reality to any idea – even the idea of its variety. If its variety were suddenly to resolve itself back into a unity, he would be joyous in that too. Let reality be as it wishes. He doesn't hold on to it in any form. Let it be one, let it be many, let it be empty, let it be full – he doesn't mind, he remains joyous. He has no fixed ideas about reality to which he insists that his experience of it should conform. He is 'joyous in the Clear Light of Realization of the Void'.

In his meditations, too, though he may be visited by fearful apparitions of deities of various kinds, he sees them as just that – apparitions. All fear is ultimately fear of annihilation, and you gain courage by accepting that possibility, transcending the threatened self and going beyond it to a new self – at which point the process starts again. Milarepa can no longer be fooled by any sense of annihilation, and now he experiences only a deep fulfilment where fear used to be.

Milarepa's experience is not abstract or theoretical. His joy is rooted in bodily experience – the precious human body that Tibetan Buddhism traditionally prizes as the ideal vehicle for the attainment of Enlightenment. So he takes joy in the blessing of 'a body free from harmful karma', of being able to meditate without hindrance in the form of bodily pain or weakness. Not being dependent on the positive conditions he enjoys makes it easier for him not to take them for granted.

DISTRACTION AND PAIN IN THE ENLIGHTENED MIND

> Joyous in my freedom from that state where distractions rise and
> pass away.

The implication of this line is that with regard to distractions in meditation there are three distinct states of mind. There is, first, the state of mind in which distractions are experienced as arising and just hanging around. They may be recognized as distractions or hindrances, but they are not considered impermanent, and they are therefore difficult to deal with decisively or effectively.

Secondly, there is the state of mind in which a certain degree of understanding has arisen with regard to the impermanence of things. Distractions are experienced as transient, passing through the mind like clouds. Knowing that there is no need to turn an itch into a studied interest, you don't allow yourself to get involved in it, and the same goes for all distractions. Just because you feel an occasional hankering for certain worldly pleasures when you are on retreat, or for things in your day-to-day life that you have forsworn for a certain period or even for life, you don't have to take such yearnings seriously. They are just momentary hindrances of craving or restlessness arising from previous conditioning.

Both these states of mind call for vigilance and effort. But being Enlightened, Milarepa does not need to deliberately redirect his mental and emotional energies towards Enlightenment. It is at least questionable whether the fully Enlightened mind will encounter distractions in the usual sense at all, because an Enlightened person will be able to see potential distractions for what they are even as they arise, without falling under their spell.

> Joyous exceedingly where hardship is great,
> Joyous in freedom from sickness,
> Joyous that suffering has turned to be joy,

Milarepa clearly endures extreme physical hardship – cold, hunger, and so on – but note that he is joyous *exceedingly* in these circumstances. This is because it is in such adverse conditions that his joy shines out as not being dependent on his circumstances. For Milarepa, even misfortune is a source of delight. He still experiences painful feelings of body and mind, but he finds joy in them, because every misfortune becomes another opportunity to experience the unconditioned nature of his joy. Note also that he is joyous not that suffering has turned *into* joy, but that suffering has turned to *be* joy. That is, suffering and joy are not experienced as separate. He continues to experience the suffering, but the suffering is now joy. He's hungry: it's a joyful experience to be hungry; he's cold: it's a joyful experience to be cold. For Milarepa every setback is a reminder of the impermanent, unpredictable nature of *saṃsāra* and the sheer pointlessness of holding on to things and experiences as though the world were anything other than a product of mind.

This is an aspect of the Enlightened mind that it is important to get right. As long as it is associated with the physical body, there must always be the possibility at least of physical suffering, and even of the emotional suffering associated with life as a human being. But even though you suffer – whether the suffering is bodily pain or the emotional pain of losing someone close to you – your reaction to that pain, and your experience of it, will be entirely different from that of the unenlightened person.

Joyous in the treasure of triumphant songs now uttered,
Joyous exceedingly at the sounds and signs of multitudinous
syllables,
Joyous at their turning into groups of words,

As an Enlightened being, Milarepa enjoys the complete equanimity of his mind in all circumstances. He enjoys the pure creativity of its response: whatever he experiences, his mind does not react by clinging to the experience or cutting off from it; his response is always one of further positivity, further skilful activity. Whether in songs or in other kinds of spontaneous expression, he enjoys the playful and inexhaustible manifestation of the Enlightened mind.

Like any hermit, Milarepa obviously relishes silence, but here he announces his enjoyment of singing and speaking. He enjoys watching the syllables coming out of his mouth and forming themselves into words and sentences. We can take it that his speech is not the expression of his ego, not 'self-expression' as we understand it, but more like the chanting of mantras and puja recitation. It is the spontaneous expression of the non-dual state.

TRANSCENDING FEAR

After his initial paean to the joys of the yogi's way of life, Milarepa gives his visitors various teachings before concluding their meeting with a song that returns to his original theme of fear and the spiritual life. He begins the song by calling down the blessing of his teacher to help them come to firm knowledge, i.e. irreversible insight,

In the divine fortress of your own body.

Chang, in his translation, makes this a more modest prayer for firm knowledge but, either way, the emphasis on the body is significant. Of course, one is most naturally fearful on behalf of the body or, if one is at all religious, for the state of one's soul, or one's 'merit', which the body, far from protecting, is perceived to put at risk through sense cravings. The idea of the body as a fortress therefore challenges some deeply rooted assumptions. Milarepa is reminding us that firm knowledge can be attained only within the psychophysical organism, the precious human body. The body is indeed the citadel of awakening.

> Frightened by fears, I built up a castle.
> The voidness of absolute being, this was that castle,
> And of its destruction I now have no fear.

The protection afforded by the voidness of absolute being is clearly not against the vicissitudes of life, or even against feeling exposed to them. It will not replace the need to take appropriate steps to minimize the effects of life's misfortunes. But it does protect one's positive state from being affected by those misfortunes or dependent on the outcome of events. If in its non-duality Milarepa's joy is a transcendence of joy, it is also a transcendence of fear. There is no attachment to the experience of joy, and thus no fear of losing it.

Fearlessness or *abhaya* is one of the fruits of spiritual practice and its development is a particularly important aspect of Buddhism. It is linked to the traditional description of the ultimate objective as a refuge. A castle is the ultimate material refuge, the securest place possible. It is also the ultimate expression of fear, and of the distinction we draw between self and other, us and them. The 'voidness of absolute being' means the ultimate non-reality of the very distinction between subject and object, self and other, and it becomes a castle because it protects us against fear itself. Fear indicates attachment to the self, in whatever way we conceive of it, and that in turn implies duality. We fear any threat to the self from what we perceive as not self, as the other. As long as that distinction is perceived as absolute, we can never protect ourselves absolutely, and we will always be subject to fear.

Milarepa goes on to consider the various kinds of ordinary human fear, making the way we assuage each of them into a symbol for some spiritual or transcendental quality or set of qualities. This quality, instead of temporarily assuaging the need that gives rise to fear, cuts across the whole cycle of dependency, and thus removes the fear.

For instance, Milarepa's protection against the cold is the 'warmth within', which is a reference to the practice of *tummo*, 'psychic heat', by which spiritual means you can generate actual bodily heat. Less literally, we could take the experience of cold as representing loneliness, the chill of emotional deprivation. The producing of warmth within then becomes contentment or emotional positivity, a radiance that comes not from some external source but from one's own spiritual resources. It is a glow of inwardly generated well-being.

As for the fear of poverty, this is overcome by means of the 'seven inexhaustible jewels'. Traditionally these are of gold, silver, crystal, ruby, coral, agate, and cornelian. Again, we can look for a symbolic meaning here. The Buddhist tradition has two well-known sets of seven 'jewels'. There are the seven jewels of the *cakravartin-rāja*, the righteous or wheel-turning king: the elephant, the horse, the councillor, the woman, the commander-in-chief, and so on, and there also is a list of seven positive mental events called the 'seven jewels'. Either of these could be meant here. Milarepa is saying that by virtue of the spiritual qualities over which he has attained mastery, he has all the wealth in the world at his disposal. Far from being the impoverished beggar he appears to be, he is like a wheel-turning king, the world-governing monarch whose laws and decrees are based not on tradition or selfish ambition but on the Dharma. Material poverty holds no fear for him, because the wealth he values is not material but springs from a renunciation of material wealth. The seven jewels can never be taken away from him by circumstances. As positive mental events, they are inexhaustible and endless.

Inexhaustible too is the rapture and bliss of the concentrated mind attained through meditation.

> Fearful of hunger, I sought for some food,
> Absorption in the absolute, this was that food,
> And from hunger I now have no fear.

One is reminded here of the aspiration of a verse from the *Dhammapada*: 'Feeders on rapture shall we be.'[31] This is something that any regular meditator will be able to appreciate. Meditative absorption can be so tangibly and immediately beneficial that it is experienced as a sort of sustenance. Rapture (Sanskrit *prīti*, Pāli *pīti*) is an inner nourishment that keeps the concentrated mind in a self-sufficient state of spiritual well-being. More generally, positive mental states, especially the state of mindful awareness, nourish the whole psychophysical organism. When attachment and aversion to things and experiences are abandoned, fear of hunger is nowhere to be found.

Next in Milarepa's list of fears comes fear of thirst. This is the most frequent and immediately pressing of the physical appetites, and a powerful and seamless practice is needed to relieve the burden of fear associated with it: the nectar of mindfulness, as Milarepa calls it.

Finally, Milarepa evokes the fear of losing one's way.

> Fearful of straying, I sought for a way,
> The practice of two-in-one, this was that way,
> And of straying I now have no fear.

The 'practice of two-in-one', which translates the term *yuganaddha*, is a specifically Tantric reference to the non-duality of wisdom and compassion at the highest level. Once you have accomplished this, you have at last achieved, or embodied, the Middle Way. Until that point you have to keep asking yourself whether or not what you are doing is really the most skilful thing to be doing at that moment. Are you on the straight and narrow, or have you strayed a little off the path? Are you on the path of *nirvāṇa* or the path of *saṃsāra*? Are you making progress or are you stuck in dry intellectual understanding, barren concentration of mind, or uninspired if apparently skilful activity?

With the practice of non-duality, there is no distinction to be made between path and non-path. There is no right path or wrong path, and therefore no possibility of going astray. You no longer have to wonder if you are still on the right path. There is no path. The 'path' is one of no longer following a path. There is no question of choosing between alternatives. By uniting wisdom and compassion in your own experience you have also gone beyond the archetypes of the right and wrong paths: *saṃsāra* and *nirvāṇa*, the conditioned and the Unconditioned. Milarepa's conclusion is that he is happy under any conditions whatsoever – and the next verse reveals the kind of conditions he has in mind.

> At Yolmo in the tiger-cave of Singa-dzong
> One trembles with fear at the roar of the tigress
> And this sends one involuntarily to strict seclusion.

Towards the end of the song Milarepa adopts a more obviously literary tone as he notes the sights and sounds of his solitary hermitage and the emotions that these evoke. Whether or not this elevated style is responsible for an element of ambiguity in the meaning is debatable, but Chang's translation transfers the trembling from Milarepa to the tigress, whose 'roar' becomes a 'howling', a 'trembling cry'. But it would seem quite possible that even Milarepa would tremble with fear, having placed himself in close proximity to a tigress and her cubs. It is important to remember that being fearless does not mean that you never feel fear. The point is that even while he doesn't suppress his natural human reactions, he is able to be happy in the experience of fear. It is as though he relishes the roar of the tigress. His fearlessness does not exclude the experience of fear; he actually enjoys the fear that, as an embodied being, he naturally feels.

There is a kind of terror that is so invigorating as to be strangely pleasing; the proximity of danger makes you feel stronger, more courageous and heroic. Thus, trembling with fear can put heart into your practice and positively drive you to practise harder, with the awareness that whatever fearful experiences arise are finally no more than that – appearances, not fixed realities. You are the one element in the equation that can open up and release your tight hold upon objects – whether you crave them or fear them.

Together with this seclusion from the world comes the arising of compassion, which Milarepa then – as he sings in the next verse – feels for the tiger-cubs. This combination of withdrawal and compassion is very important in the teaching of the great founder of the Gelug school, Tsongkhapa: the withdrawal from the conditioned, accompanied by the arising of the *bodhicitta* – the will to Enlightenment for the sake of all beings – produces Enlightenment. It is not enough to withdraw; you must go out to the world in kindness as well. And, conversely, it is not enough to be compassionate; the element of withdrawal is also needed.

WORKING WITH REFLECTION

The cries of the monkeys cling to one's mind,
And this causes involuntarily a feeling of sadness,
But at the chattering of their young one just wants to laugh,
And this produces involuntarily an elevation of spirit.

References to the cries of monkeys feature prominently in Chinese poetry, in which they are intended to convey an impression of touching melancholy, associated with evening shadows and soft rain. To hear a monkey calling through the mist seems naturally to produce a sort of pleasing mournfulness; the haunting sound clings to the mind.

Milarepa shares this common emotional reflex and, as with his natural reaction of fear, he does not suppress it. But he doesn't wallow in it either. He doesn't allow his mind to drift from this keen responsiveness to the sadness of the world around him into a self-regarding melancholia. His solitary situation is one in which loneliness can quite easily turn into depression, and here he shows us how to work creatively with the moods that we might experience on solitary retreat, directing this initial response of sadness towards a broader appreciation of the situation in which we find ourselves.

Attending to the comical chattering of the young monkeys, his initial reflectiveness turns into happy laughter, bringing an access of energy and an elevation of spirit. This positive result of a simple but creative shift of attention suggests the beginning of the spiralling process outlined in the traditional formulation of the *bodhyaṅgas*, the seven factors of Enlightenment.[32] The upward spiral begins with mindfulness, continues with investigation of mental states, energy, joy, and so on, and culminates in an exalted state of insight and equanimity.

> Sweet to the ear is the sad song of the cuckoo with its
>   tremulous note,
> And one is caused to hearken involuntarily,
> And the varied cries of the raven are cheering to his neighbour
>   the yogin.
>
> Happy is the state of one who lives in such a spot as this,
> Without the presence of a single companion, and even in this
>   one is happy.
> And now by the song of this rejoicing yogin
> May the sufferings of all beings be removed.

Milarepa's attitude is never self-referential in the narrow sense. His equanimity is a state of mind free from fixed views, from one-sided reactions both to external physical events and to emotional or mental events. He does not see or feel things from just his own point of view. He is always able to take in the whole situation. His awareness is thus essentially appreciative in tone. The colour and vibrancy of these verses illustrate the fact that Milarepa's poetic sensibility is attuned to beauty wherever and whenever it may be discerned. His freedom from partial, self-referential, fixed views means also that he is not ascetic in the traditional sense of refusing to take pleasure in things.

Nonetheless this is more than just aesthetic appreciation – it is a practice, even if in Milarepa's case it has been perfected and is second nature. Whatever emotions arise, he shifts effortlessly in a continually more positive direction. He turns to good account all those lonely sights and sounds that could be, if one allowed, distracting or even dispiriting.

The fact that this elevation of mind is involuntary is characteristic of Milarepa's sublime mental state. The perceiving mind is, after all, impermanent, and for Milarepa impermanence is a source of delight. If your experience of 'yourself' is not separateness but the blissful Void, you have transcended the duality of self and other that is the ultimate basis for loneliness. You are no longer an ego and therefore no longer distinct from other egos. How can you feel lonely if you don't experience the ultimate reality of yourself – even when absolutely alone – as separate from others?

What this closing section conveys is a sense that the world around Milarepa supports him in his practice. It does so because his practice is intimately concerned with that world. He expects to be uplifted by the cries of the raven because he feels he is the raven's neighbour. He sees himself as sharing the place where he lives with the wild natural forms – both animals and spirits – that have always occupied it and will continue to do so when he has moved on.

So it is not that Milarepa is happy *despite* his isolation. He is happy *in* it. He isn't trying to hang on to his joy; in fact, he is letting go of it. He isn't doing his best to be positive in a challenging situation; he actually sees his situation in positive terms. He is happy that he is without a single companion even as he offers up his happiness to the welfare of all beings. In his remote mountain hermitage, Milarepa renounces attachment to human community, to property, to any sense of separate self. And he does this not for the sake of a miserable, deprived existence, but the more fully to enjoy the freedom of the blissfully clear light of the Void.

THIRD STORY
THE MEETING AT SILVER SPRING

In which, after a dream about a green *ḍākinī* and a lotus with eight petals, Milarepa realizes that the flower represents eight heart-disciples and that he is about to meet one of them. Sure enough, by a silver river he meets a young nobleman on a horse. The young man refuses to give the yogi a ride across the river and is astonished to see Milarepa walk past him across the water. Milarepa tells his life story at the young man's request, and explains how his practice has enabled him to perform such a miracle. Milarepa refuses to accept whatever material gifts the young man can offer, the yogi being well supplied with the spiritual equivalents, down to his boots, which he says are made of the leather of awakening. Through this exchange the relationship between pleasure and renunciation is explored, and the relationship between guru and disciple is created.

Themes:

4
A MAN OF THE BEYOND

THE ULTIMATE RELATIONSHIP

If 'The Song of a Yogi's Joy' offers an account of the Enlightened state in isolation, 'The Meeting at Silver Spring' shows what happens when that Enlightened state comes into contact with unenlightened humanity; when this sublime, seemingly incommunicable realization of ultimate truth or reality encounters someone who, at least initially, has not the slightest inkling that any such truth exists, much less that it could be communicated to him.

This really is a problem, and one that even the Buddha Śākyamuni had to solve once supreme Enlightenment had been attained. The Buddha's resolve to teach the Dharma arose, the legends say, from his response to the pleading of the god Brahmā Sahāmpati, whose intervention helped the Buddha see that there were at least some beings who had 'but little dust' to obscure their vision and who might be receptive to the highest truth.[33] In Milarepa's case, a similar impetus would seem to require him to practise 'for the benefit of all beings', even while he lives out of easy reach of any of those beings.

The central issues upon which this group of songs focuses are broadly twofold. First, there is the problem of the vast gulf that separates the worldly mind from the Enlightened mind. How can something that lies beyond the reach of language be communicated? As we shall see, effective communication relies in large part on the pre-existing familiarity of both parties with the thing being described. Yet, for the unenlightened being, the non-dual state is utterly unknown. The issue here is essentially one of perspective.

The second issue provides the solution to this problem, at least in the tradition in which Milarepa practises. Enlightenment never arises in isolation from beings. There is no such thing as Enlightenment; there are only Enlightened beings. The question of communication has to be answered in the sphere of human receptivity, not in the abstract terms of philosophy. The issue here is one, therefore, of the personal relationship between guru and disciple, and every relationship must begin with a meeting.

THE YOGI'S DREAM: *ḌĀKINĪS*

The story begins one day in early autumn, when Milarepa goes on his almsround. He has spent the summer months in solitary retreat at North Shri Ri, dedicating himself to meditation. But now it is harvest time, and he sets off through the mountains. On his way, the great yogi stops to take a rest, and falls asleep. On the face of it, it perhaps seems odd that an experienced yogi, practised in mindfulness, should just drop off, but there is, as it turns out, a deeper process at work, to which he is sensitive enough to respond, for he not only sleeps; he dreams.

He sleeps, that is to say, only to dream. It is as though he senses that something is ready to come through, and he is sufficiently highly developed to allow that dreaming state to come over him. He is able just to let it happen, in the confidence that by so doing he is opening a channel of expression for positive forces that can come through in no other way.

In his dream Milarepa is visited by a mysterious and beautiful girl, green in colour, with shining golden hair. She is leading a youth who is about twenty years old. Turning to Milarepa, she tells him that the lotus of his heart is destined to have eight petals, and that the youth is one of them. So saying, the girl disappears.

When he wakes, Milarepa is quick to identify this figure as a *ḍākinī*. The Sanskrit term is the feminine and more familiar form of the word *ḍāka* and means, basically, 'she of space'. The Tibetans translate it as *khandroma*, commonly translated into English as 'sky-dancer' or 'celestial maiden'. So a *ḍākinī* is one who dances or flies through space, and is therefore free and unimpeded. At the same time, space represents mind in its absolute aspect. She does not so much move within space as embody the vast untapped store of emotional energy that can arise, as if from nowhere, from the very depths of the mind. More specifically – the sky being a symbol of *śūnyatā* or emptiness – the *ḍākinī* or sky-dancer is one who dwells in the consciousness of the conditioned nature of all things – that is, in the knowledge of their ultimate emptiness. In everyday life, we rarely experience passionate energies that are also positive. It may be only in our dreams that we come in contact with them at all. What the ḍākinī represents is the irruption of such energies into consciousness.

The 'great *ḍākinīs*,' as they are called, are no less than Buddhas in female form. At the other end of the scale, a *ḍākinī* may be no more than the kind of very attractive woman who has a certain almost magical quality – not just sex appeal – about her. A *ḍākinī* can be a sort of siren, fascinating and stimulating. In psychological terms she may be recognized as the anima; for the artist, she appears as a muse; but at the very highest level she is the inspirational aspect of Enlightenment itself.

In Milarepa's dream, the *ḍākinī* appears as a force of spiritual inspiration, welling up from unconscious depths. Her appearance suggests emotional energies in a pure, intensely refined form: one might say that she is midway between the *ḍākinī* as simply an exceptionally fascinating woman and the Ḍākinī with a capital Ḍ, the Ḍākinī as Buddha, as the moving spirit of Enlightenment. Her green colour makes it clear straightaway that she is quite out of the ordinary – certainly non-human. Green is also naturally associated with the earth, and suggests something springing up with a fresh energy. It is the colour of nature in its most restful, tranquil, and harmonious aspect, but it is also the colour of action, growth, and even inspiration.

As for the gold of her hair, fair hair would have been quite extraordinary to medieval Tibetans, so it indicates something rare and precious, not materially but in the sense of spiritual riches. Gold is in any case the colour of richness and abundance, suggesting the inexhaustible wealth of the Enlightened mind, overflowing to the delight and benefit of living beings.

MILAREPA'S KARMA

Milarepa goes on to contemplate the *ḍākinī*'s words and the image they have conjured up of his heart as a lotus with eight petals. He realizes that these must represent 'eight superlative, destined, heart-like disciples', that is, disciples who are very close to the heart of the guru, who are, one might say, the guru's very heart. Milarepa concludes that he will soon come across a disciple who is what he calls 'Karma-exhausted'. This, more than any aptitude for scholarship or Buddhist devotion, is what will mark him out as a prospective 'heart son'. Such a person may not even be interested, at least initially, in becoming any kind of disciple, but he will nonetheless be in an ideal state of readiness to set out on the path of higher spiritual training.

Karma literally means 'action', and it is axiomatic to Buddhism that actions have consequences. Clearly some of these consequences will be spiritually positive, but some of them will be negative. Some of our actions, particularly those that have become habits, whether of body, speech, or mind, will get in the way of our progress towards insight, throwing up obstacles to prevent our carrying out even our best intentions. We may have resolved to lead a thoroughly spiritual life, for example, but find that there is something that hinders us from carrying out that resolution. There may be external circumstances set up by our past actions which now stand in the way of our present aims and aspirations, or we may be subject to habits and tendencies that are the result of ways in which we have repeatedly acted in the past. In all likelihood, our karmic obstacles will arise as a combination of factors, both external and internal. According to Buddhism, it is our karma that has caused us to be reborn in the human realm at all. For this reason alone, it is highly unusual to encounter someone without any karmic traces. However, in the case of this 'heart-like disciple', nothing will be left over from the past to get in the way if he decides to take up the spiritual life. He has no previous unskilful actions hanging over him in the form of a karmic debt; he is free of any such burden.

This was by no means the case for Milarepa himself. Milarepa came to the Dharma encumbered by some very weighty negative karma indeed, but he worked through it with the help of his teacher Marpa. Marpa was a tough character who reared his disciples the hard way, so he was exactly the guru Milarepa needed. Having committed a number of serious misdeeds, even atrocities, including the murder of a whole group of people using sorcery, Milarepa was in need of strong spiritual medicine.

Milarepa's is in some ways the classic Vajrayāna career. When he was a young child his father died and his uncle not only stole Milarepa's inheritance, but proceeded to mistreat him and his sister in abominable fashion, beating them, starving them, and forcing them to carry out menial tasks night and day. To prepare himself to take his revenge, Milarepa apprenticed himself to a sorcerer and became an adept himself. Making use of his supernormal powers, he brought down a great storm on his uncle's house, killing a large number of those inside, including the wicked uncle himself.

According to Buddhist doctrine, the karmic consequences of this act threatened considerable and protracted future suffering for Milarepa, and when he realized this, he knew there was only one option open to him: he had to gain Enlightenment in his present lifetime. His situation was so urgent that only the most intense spiritual practice and the highest Tantric teaching would be of any use to him. If he was not to go straight to hell after death, there could be no halfway house.

With this single aim in view, Milarepa sought out Marpa as his teacher, and endured under him the harsh training that his lamentable karmic situation demanded. In accordance with Tantric custom, Milarepa submitted himself completely to Marpa's will. The Tantric teacher – or *vajra guru* – has a single aim: to introduce the disciple to the direct experience of their own essential nature, in other words, to the true nature of mind. In bringing the disciple to experience authentic reality, the guru has to disentangle him from words and theories, from his own conceptions and ideas about what he is. Sometimes this involves uncompromising and dramatic, even harrowing, tests of patience and resolve. In Milarepa's case, Marpa pushed him to the limit and beyond. As Milarepa recalls in the first of the songs in this chapter, 'I reduced my body to powder in his service.'[34]

The story of their relationship is a story of frustration, disappointment, torment, and extreme physical and mental hardship. But as Marpa pointed out to his disciple, if you offer yourself – body, speech, and mind – to your guru, you cannot very well complain about how he treats you, and if you feel upset, that means you are still holding something back. Indeed, Marpa tested his faith in him by behaving in an outrageously unreasonable manner, telling him several times to build a tower, then telling him to pull it down again. All this was to purify Milarepa sufficiently to be able to practise the *mahāmudrā* – the union of bliss and emptiness – effectively, and of course in the end, he succeeded in doing so.

But the disciple whom Milarepa is about to meet is in a very different situation from that of the young Milarepa: he is already open and receptive to the Dharma, and in a position, karmically speaking, for him to begin to put the Dharma into practice immediately.

MILAREPA'S DRY FEET

After waking from his dream, Milarepa again sets out on his way. He labours up the steep track leading to Bong, and eventually comes to a river whose clear waters glisten like silver. For a second time, the yogi lays down his head to sleep. Some time goes by, and when he wakes up, he is confronted by a young nobleman mounted on a handsome black horse. The expected meeting, it seems, is about to happen.

The young man would perhaps not have paid him any attention if Milarepa had been doing what a yogi is expected to do on the road – just walking along or perhaps sitting in meditation. But as it is, he asks him why he has been sleeping there. Milarepa engages the young man in conversation, and asks him to give him a ride across the river, explaining that wading through water is difficult at his age. The young man does not want to trouble himself, however; all he can think of is the good time he is going to have with the friends he is on his way to meet, and he is also concerned not to put his horse under unnecessary strain.

The youth has none of the humility or piety one might associate with someone destined to be the heart-disciple of an Enlightened yogi. One would not immediately recognize him as religious material. Yet it is precisely this unaffected and straightforward quality that marks him as well suited to the Tantric training. Indeed, it is a quality shared by many of the Tibetans I knew during my years in Kalimpong. They were hardy people, fond of what luxury and pleasure they could find, and keenly curious – all in all, good material for the Dharma. Many of them had an unspoilt, sincere, slightly naive quality which very few Westerners, nowadays at least, seem to have. I am reminded particularly of one of my Tibetan students, one of five brothers who were minor aristocrats from Kham in eastern Tibet. They did quite well as merchants and were well-to-do, bluff, and hearty fellows. As was customary, they divided their income into three equal parts: one third went to business and household expenses, another third was laid out for pleasure – picnics, parties, gambling, and so on – and the remainder was for the Dharma, and was donated to the monks. I once saw these brothers encountering a steam engine for the first time. It was a tiny mountain train, but as the wheels began to turn and the whistle hooted they displayed the kind of unaffected astonishment, wonder, and interest that is in many ways the ideal response to the Dharma. This sort of healthy, full-blooded attitude is rarely to be encountered in the more sophisticated cultures of the West.

So the young man's response to Milarepa is the straightforward answer of an ordinary, well-adjusted human being. There is no indecisiveness, no neurotic anxiety about what the yogi will think, no prevarication or shame. He might seem a little selfish, but it is the natural and even healthy selfishness of youth; he wants to enjoy life, not worry about decrepit old yogis. He is not unfriendly; he says quite candidly that he doesn't want to perform this small favour, and straightforwardly explains why. Then he rides on without looking back – without, that is, feeling any irrational, neurotic guilt.

At this point, Milarepa enters the 'Samādhi of Guru-Union', uniting himself with the unbroken Kagyu lineage. Having entered that state of concentration, he does something even more remarkable. Holding his breath, he walks on the surface of the river, gently and mindfully moving across the stream to the far side, whence he looks back to observe the young man who is still only half way across. The young man sees Milarepa gliding past him and cannot believe his eyes.

What the youth has seen, after all, cannot be explained by ordinary means. Milarepa's walking on water would appear to be a display of supernormal ability, a miracle, in other words. But if its only function was to be a marker of Milarepa's psychic power, it would be no more than a highly accomplished magic trick. In the present context, we need to look more deeply. Just as with Milarepa's dream of the ḍākinī, we need to understand what this miracle symbolizes, rather as we would a dream image. Milarepa has presented the young man with something impossible. He seems to be showing that, for the yogic adept, the normal order of physical reality can be turned upside down easily and effortlessly, that the heavy and solid can be made to rise above the apparently fluid and ungraspable and find a firm foundation there. Understood symbolically, Milarepa's feat represents the manifestation of a different realm of being, a higher metaphysical plane of existence.

The young man, we learn, has a fairly sceptical turn of mind, and he does not accept the evidence of his senses without testing it. When he arrives at the bank, he takes a careful look at Milarepa's feet and finds that not even his soles are wet. He considers the possibility that he has been hallucinating, and looks for clues as to how Milarepa might have crossed the river. Only when he has exhausted the naturalistic possibilities does he embrace the supernormal explanation. His reason having been allowed full rein, faith then arises very readily and spontaneously.

The first thing he does is apologize and express regret for not having given Milarepa a ride. In a way this is odd, because of all people Milarepa was evidently the least in need of help in this respect. But of course the boy's regret is largely for himself, having missed an opportunity to do what an accomplished lama has asked of him. He realizes that what appeared to be an appeal for help was actually Milarepa's desire to do him a good turn, and he has frustrated that compassionate impulse. He has let Milarepa down, and in so doing he has let himself down. But he does not berate himself or wallow in regrets, and once he has bowed down to Milarepa many times, his natural inquisitiveness asserts itself. He asks him a whole series of questions – where is he from, who is his teacher, what meditation does he practise, where did he come from that day, and where is he going – which Milarepa answers by way of a song.

MILAREPA'S SONG OF THE TANTRIC PATH

First of all, Milarepa announces that he has travelled far in his pursuit of higher knowledge, and then he goes on to describe his spiritual path. This includes learning the 'fierce exorcism of the Black and Red Planets' – that is, the darker arts of the Tantra. However, his teacher in these arts, for all his expertise, was not able, as Milarepa puts it, to clear his doubts. These doubts are not simply intellectual, but arise from a more fundamental emotional and existential perplexity.

As he goes on to say, Milarepa's career culminated in his initiation under his root guru, Marpa the Translator, who 'had experienced the mother-like Essence of Mind'. In the Vajrayāna it is sometimes said that the aim of one's practice is the meeting of the mother-mind with the son-mind, the mother-mind being the original, primordial mind and the son-mind being the phenomenal but Enlightened mind as it reunites with its original source. So Milarepa is declaring his faith in the depth of Marpa's realization.

Nor is he in any doubt about the need for this guru-disciple relationship. There is no question of making a choice of guru, or of weighing up one against another. Marpa was his guru even before he met him. 'Just to hear his name caused my skin to tingle and my hair to rise.' And when he finally did meet Marpa, his heart was changed – that is, his faith was deepened – 'just by glancing at his face'.

Marpa initiated Milarepa into the Hevajra Tantra and 'Nāropa's skilful path' – that is, the six yogas of Nāropa. These are (1) the cultivation of inner heat or *tummo* as a means of controlling the subtle energies of the psychophysical organism; (2) the visualization of the illusory or subtle body created out of the six perfections; (3) controlling dreams and becoming conscious in the dream state; (4) realizing the mind as the clear light of *śūnyatā*; (5) training in the after-death experience of the *bardos*; and (6) training in the transference of consciousness at the moment of death.

After this, Milarepa 'took the vows and won the Four Initiations of the blessed Dem Chog'. Dem Chog (Sanskrit *saṃvara*: 'great bliss') is a specifically Tantric deity, shown in *yab-yum* form at the centre of the mandala. The four initiations are: the initiation with the jar; the secret initiation; the wisdom initiation; and, finally, one simply known as the 'fourth initiation'. They are also called the initiations of body, speech, mind, and the unity of the three, and together they amount to full Tantric initiation. So Milarepa has been initiated into the full practice of the Tantric path.

All this leads up to the realization of the 'essence of Mahāmudrā'. This is the highest teaching according to the Kagyu tradition, referred to here by Milarepa as the 'Whispered Succession', of which in a sense Milarepa is the founder in Tibet. *Mahāmudrā* literally means great symbol, great attitude, or great seal, and its purpose is the realization of the true nature of mind as beyond subject and object, resulting in what Milarepa describes (in his next song) as 'illuminating Self-Awareness'.

The prefix *mahā* means great, and in any Mahāyāna context refers not to size or extent but to *śūnyatā* – that is, to Enlightenment as the realization of emptiness. The term '*mahāmudrā*' thus suggests a unity of form (*mudrā*) and emptiness that is beyond conceptualization. As a practice, it is an expedient means of realizing this unity. For the

Yogācāra, *śūnyatā* is the nature of reality, which may be described as the non-duality of self and other, subject and object. Its subjective counterpart, the wisdom that realizes the nature of reality, is called *prajñā*. The experience itself is of course neither subjective nor objective; whether *śūnyatā* or *prajñā*, it is the sky-like realm of the *ḍākinī*. When Milarepa sings, 'I am a yogi (who can) dwell in the sky,' he means that his life is spontaneous and free of obstruction.

He also puts it here in terms of a total transcendence of thought and language. He has, he sings, 'realized in full the ultimate "Beyond-all-Playwords"'. The term *playwords*, meaning 'concepts', is found again and again in Milarepa's songs. By calling concepts 'playwords', he means he no longer takes them as referring to fixed or absolute realities. He has realized the nature of reality as unmediated and unbound by concepts in a way that echoes the perfection of wisdom teachings of the Mahāyāna. We can now perhaps begin to see more clearly the significance of his miraculous walking on the surface of the water.

Milarepa explains to the boy:

Having united the Four Elements,
I have no fear of water.

He is able to walk on water because he is no longer threatened by the separateness of the elements, whether within or without. He has fully accepted that he himself is composed of elements, and that death will return those elements back to the world. By no longer resisting the separate qualities of the elements even within himself, he has integrated them into non-dual awareness.

At the same time, by taking the everyday world and radically rearranging its material elements before the young man's incredulous eyes, he is demonstrating the depth of his understanding. He knows that the very idea of an element – like that of a self – is an entirely fictitious mental construct. He knows it in his bones. He is fully integrated not just emotionally, not even just physically, but in the sky-like non-duality of the *mahāmudrā*. In this state, there is no here or there, no self or other, and therefore no reliance on the separate qualities of the elements.

Freed at last from the burden of dualistic thinking, Milarepa lives without the illusory security of imagining that he knows for sure where he is going to sleep that night.

Where I shall go this evening, I am not certain,
For mine is the yogi's way of life.

He ends his song by briefly suggesting the basis of the young man's own values, exposing their ludicrous poverty and narrowness by comparison with those extolled in the inspiring account of his own quest.

Have you heard what I have sung,
My happy boy who seeks nought but pleasure?

THE YOUTH'S SALUTATION AND OFFERING

As a result of his contact with Milarepa, the boy begins to realize that he is quite a different person from who he thought he was. He has been thinking of himself as a young playboy, but his meeting with Milarepa has made him aware of something much more fundamental, much more real, in his nature. And this tremendous upheaval, this bursting through into consciousness of something that was unconscious, is accompanied by weeping. The boy experiences his true nature, or something near to it, in the form of an unshakeable faith, a faith that amounts to an experience of transcendental insight. There is a tremendous release, not just of emotion but of energy, expressed in freely flowing tears.

This is the kind of overwhelming effect that meeting the Tantric guru can have. A guru is someone who activates your dormant energies by bringing his own more integrated and freed-up energies into contact with yours. In the Tantric sense, therefore, the guru performs the same function as a Buddha. The guru is the Buddha principle active within the field of our own experience.

For many of us, the Buddha himself may be no more than an idea, a distant figure. But through the guru – should we happen to be in contact with one – we are in a position to receive the spiritual influence of all the Buddhas, and in this sense he is our point of contact with them. This is not to say that the guru is necessarily Enlightened, but simply that, through his personal knowledge of his disciples, he can present the teachings of the Buddha in the way that is most effective for each person.

The guru is an interpreter, a translator, rather than a Buddha or even a teacher. His primary role is to activate dormant energy, although he may teach as a secondary function of that role. The guru may be said to stimulate the disciple's energies in a highly positive way, but he may also be said to stir up those energies in such a way as to make it impossible to ignore or deny them. The energies having been aroused, the disciple must then learn to work with them.

The boy declares:

You are the Sage unrecognized, a man of the beyond!
You are the Buddha whom one meets so rarely.

The boy is saying that he had not realized who Milarepa really was, but what he says also suggests that it is in the nature of the sage to be unrecognized. A sage doesn't necessarily have the kind of characteristics that will impress an ordinary person. Indeed, whatever charisma or conceptual wisdom he may emanate or dispense is more or less incidental in comparison with the reality of his attainment. 'A man of the beyond' is the kind of ascription one might find in the Pāli canon, placing the Enlightened being as it does firmly outside all ascriptions. He doesn't belong to this world; he belongs to the beyond; he is a new kind of man – indeed, he is a Buddha.

Your instructions are the preaching of the Nirmāṇakāya.

The *nirmāṇakāya* is the body of reality or truth as it manifests within the mundane world – that is, it is what we conventionally think of as a Buddha. We gather, then, that the boy knows enough Buddhism to be able to appreciate quite precisely who Milarepa really is – he has the technical terms at his fingertips. In fact, as we learn later in the text, he is a student interested in Buddhist scholarship, as well as a playboy.

The young man then discloses a strange sense of having heard Milarepa's name before, and even of having seen him before, though he knows that he hasn't done so in the historical sense.

It seems that I have heard your name before,
But yet I am not sure.
It seems that I may have seen you before,
But again, I am not sure.

That he recognizes Milarepa's *name* is very significant. 'Name' here is not a label attached in the memory to a particular set of characteristics. Milarepa's name signifies his unique nature as an individual, indeed, his unconditioned nature. The boy's recognition of it suggests that Milarepa has made a profound impression on him, in a way that echoes Milarepa's own account of hearing the name of *his* teacher for the first time.

This recognition is therefore not only of the teacher but also of something deep within the young man himself. The meeting with Milarepa has confronted him with something he hadn't known was there – except that, at some level, part of him must have known that it was there all along, which is why it is not totally unfamiliar.

It is a moment of insight, a recognition of his true nature. And inasmuch as it is contact with Milarepa that has put him in touch with that deeper level of himself, it is as though he has known Milarepa before too. The two recognitions are inextricably connected in the young man's experience – Milarepa in some sense *is* that deeper level of himself. But what does this mean? The only way to put it is to say that it is an encounter outside time – that it takes place without before and after, without past, present, and future – although the young man does not quite see this clearly. It is not a discovery of the new so much as a recognition of the very, very old. This is what you experience when you come into contact with someone who is outside time. The temporal mind is trying to make sense of non-temporal reality, in which there is no before or after or now. You have an intuitive knowledge of having seen or known that person before, but you are unable to say how or when. You feel that you have always known them – 'always' not in the sense of taking place from the beginning and going on within time, but in the sense of coming from a dimension in which there is no present, past, or future.

It is thus not surprising that the youth is confused. Milarepa has put him in contact with a level of his being that is still very obscure to him. He has sparked off a veiled realization, an intuition of something beyond the parameters of a world conditioned by time. The young man encounters Milarepa outside time – at least, he experiences what Milarepa *is* outside time – that being the only way Milarepa as he really is can be experienced. His realization consists in his contact with Milarepa's innate or intrinsic Buddha nature, and thus in a sense with his own Buddha nature. But he continues to question his grip on his experience. His security in the present has been shaken, opened up, and he is no longer quite so self-assured.

> Whether the obeisance that I made you
> Was sincere enough, I do not know.

A few minutes earlier, when he had made his obeisance to Milarepa, he would have been certain of this. But now he has been introduced to new levels of himself, and he doesn't know where he's coming from, what level he is speaking from. The continuity of his experience has been interrupted. Though before he bowed to Milarepa many times, and asked his questions 'with great sincerity and faith', he is no longer the person who bowed a few minutes before, nor, he now realizes, is Milarepa the man to whom he thought he was bowing.

A MAN OF THE WORLD

Any auspicious meeting in Tibet involves the offering of gifts, and the young man now proceeds to offer Milarepa a whole series of them. He begins by making an offering of his horse, which runs, he says, like the wind. The horse's features and accoutrements are described in loving detail.

> On his neck hangs a wondrous bell;
> On his back of well-known pedigree
> Is a saddle cloth, most warm and smooth;
> On it rests a strong wooden saddle.
> The girth is fashioned of steel from Mon....
> His forelock curls like a tiger's smile,
> Shining brightly like a mirrored star.

These things are valuable in a way that is perhaps difficult for us to understand today, because they are symbolic of an attitude to material things that is very unusual these days. All these objects have been individually made by individual craftsmen; they each have their own character, to be appreciated and cherished. We might wonder what could possibly be special about an ordinary thing like a saddle-cloth, but the boy has a good word even for a humble object like that.

We find the same respect for objects in Homer's epic accounts of the ancient Greek world. We read not of a wooden bowl, but of a well-carved wooden bowl; likewise, a cauldron is strongly forged, and a sword is smoothly and expertly fashioned. Everything in this world stands out, everything has a presence. Objects have a clear provenance: you know where they have come from, from whom they have been passed down to you, where and how they were made – and all this makes a difference to your attitude to them.

In our age of mass production, in sharp contrast, there is a confusion of objects in our lives that inevitably blunts awareness. The disposability of objects, our knowledge that most things can be replaced, means that we don't feel we need to care for them or attend to them. When we see a factory-made object, we might appreciate the design, but a single example of that design is never unique. We can hardly conceive of how things have been made, or even where they were made, apart from the ubiquitous label saying 'Made in China'.

The young man is thus offering far more than we can really imagine. As for the horse itself, it represents the only form of transport in Tibet. There can be little doubt that a beautiful horse with all its fine equipment is tremendously valuable. This is no ordinary gift. Moreover, as the young man reminds Milarepa, a horse signifies a certain social prestige: 'To a man of the world, a good horse is his pride.' He is therefore unambiguously sacrificing his worldly pride – at least, that is his intention, although as we shall see, worldly pride is not to be so easily disposed of. And it is interesting to see why he is prepared to be so generous. It is out of a very proper spiritual fear.

Praying that you may keep me from the hell
Into which I else would fall.

He does not know, of course, that he is 'Karma-exhausted'. He does not realize how hopeful his situation really is. But it is in his intense awareness of spiritual danger that his best hope lies. It seems, in fact, that the depth of insight that has produced his fear of hell has also given him the faith that will prevent him falling into hell. We can see in his prayer a plea to Milarepa to help him make use of the merit he has, so that he can avoid the inevitable reversal of his karmic situation that would ensue from allowing that merit to go to waste.

As well as being his most valuable possession – as a fast car might be for a young man today – a horse is also a powerful symbol. The young man is placing at Milarepa's disposal not simply his prized horse, but – on a symbolic level – all his energies. Milarepa certainly points the youth in the direction of this symbolic interpretation of his offering. He acknowledges the young man as his patron or lay supporter, but he says he has another, better horse, with better accoutrements. He then lists the teachings and attainments of his tradition as the accoutrements to the central Tantric goal of mobilizing the psychic energies of the whole being, and directing them towards the experience of non-duality.

> A horse of Prāṇa-Mind have I;
> I adorn him with the silk scarf of Dhyāna,
> His skin is the magic Ensuing Dhyāna Stage,

If *dhyāna* is meditation in the sense of the experience of higher, superconscious states, the 'Ensuing Dhyāna Stage' is the after-effect of the successful practice of meditation, the very positive state that continues even when you are engaged in ordinary activities afterwards. The same kind of thing happens after a retreat: you continue to experience the positive effects of that experience for weeks afterwards.

> His headstall is the Prāṇa of Vital-force;
> His forelock curl is Three-pointed Time,

Time is the devouring tiger of the boy's original image for his horse's forelock curl. But when past, present, and future are integrated, it becomes, as it were, a three-pointed star, reflecting the image the boy chose to describe his horse's forelock, 'shining brightly like a mirrored star'. (The translator surmises that three-pointed time refers to the three favourable times for meditation.) But now there is a curious contradiction.

> Tranquillity within is his adornment,
> Bodily movement is his rein,
> And ever-flowing inspiration is his bridle.
> He gallops wildly along the Spine's Central Path.

The external and inessential nature of adornment is in direct contrast to the contained and self-sufficient nature of inner tranquillity – yet here they are set out as equivalent to each other, just as, paradoxically, bodily movement is given the function of holding back bodily movement, and untrammelled inspiration the function of constraining and controlling the head.

Milarepa is saying that he no longer needs any adornment, anything inessential, or any self-control. His action and non-action combine to create a perfectly balanced – yet dynamically energetic – practice. If ever-flowing inspiration is his bridle, this suggests that in the Enlightened state, even though there is no holding back, everything is in its place. This is not chaos, but the dynamism of unfettered energy perfectly attuned to reality, in harmony with all that is positive, all that is free. Nothing holds Milarepa back because there is nobody to be held back. It is the bridle of no bridle, the restraint of no restraint. His energy enables him to gallop at full pelt even along the most obscure of routes and within the narrowest of confines – that is, the 'Spine's Central Path' (the central channel or median nerve through which the yogi trains himself to contain and channel his physical and psychic energies). All aspects of his being – body, mind, feelings, emotions – are engaged in this wild and beautiful release of energy.

In recognizing Milarepa as the 'Buddha whom one meets so rarely', and in renouncing his pride, the young man has already come a long way. But he still has much to learn. So, having proclaimed his mastery of his own energies, and his freedom from dependence on external sources of energy, Milarepa tells the young man that he doesn't need his horse. Refusing the gift, Milarepa concludes by throwing down a challenge: 'Go your way, young man, and look for pleasure!'

5
FREE FROM EGO

ENERGY AND THE SPIRITUAL LIFE

The Tantra is concerned above all with energy, an emphasis which offsets in the most direct way possible the tendency to view the central concept of the Perfection of Wisdom teachings – 'voidness' or *śūnyatā* – as featureless, colourless, and without content. According to the Tantra, the Void is alive with unleashed energy. It is attained not when the yogi has thought very hard about it, but when it illuminates the whole of his consciousness. The experience of the Void is entirely bright and beautiful with fully experienced energy – a bright white light, containing within itself all the colours of the rainbow.

Philosophically, the counterbalance to the abstract teaching on *śūnyatā* is the Yogācāra view of 'Mind Only', which is shared by both Mahāyāna and Tantric schools of Buddhism, and open to being understood at a merely philosophical level. In the end, any philosophy can lose touch with its practical applications, and it is at the level of specific practices that we find the main difference, from the Vajrayāna point of view, between the Vajrayāna and the Mahāyāna teachings. The Vajrayāna is concerned with transforming the entire psychophysical organism, with refining, manipulating, and redirecting its mental and physical energies into increasingly subtle, concentrated, and refined states.

The Vajrayāna concretizes the highest teachings of the Dharma in a direct experience of the body, but its conception of the body does not stop with the material substratum of physical experience. The Tantric practitioner works with the subtle body, which resembles the physical body in every respect except that it is 'mind-formed' rather than simply an animated material form. Experienced at this level, the body manifests not as matter but as energy.

The avowed goal of the Vajrayāna is the direct experience of one's own essential nature, and the work of the Tantra is to bring this about through a radical transformation of energy. To begin this process, one's energies must be activated, indeed decisively stirred up, from their sleeping earthbound state. The significant moment at which these energies are roused is the point of initiation, or what is sometimes referred to as Tantric empowerment.

My friend Yogi Chen, a Chan and Vajrayāna master whom I visited quite regularly when I lived in Kalimpong in the 1950s, used to make the point that although one might realize certain truths at a deeper than intellectual level by means of Mahāyāna meditation, such realization remained essentially mental and emotional. It did not involve the whole being, it did not incorporate all one's energies; according to him it was the specific function of the Tantra to bring even one's physical energies into that higher spiritual realization, to transform the body as well as the intellect and the emotions.

There is nothing really revolutionary about this Tantric perspective. Throughout the Buddhist tradition, including the Theravāda, it is emphasized that the experience of meditation is of the body as well as the mind. In the *Saṃyutta Nikāya* of the Pāli canon, for example, we find the following account of the Buddha's meditative powers.

When, Ānanda, the Tathāgata immerses the body in the mind and
the mind in the body, and when he dwells having entered upon
a blissful perception and a buoyant perception in regard to the
body, on that occasion the body of the Tathāgata rises up without
difficulty from the earth into the air. He wields the various kinds
of spiritual power: having been one, he becomes many; having
been many, he becomes one.... he exercises mastery with the body
as far as the brahmā world.[35]

The Pāli texts are therefore no more in favour of a bloodless and dis-embodied practice than are the tantras. In all Buddhist traditions the spiritual has to be 'incorporated'. However, practitioners of the Vajrayāna place particular emphasis on this aspect of spiritual practice, primarily through teachings known as the 'inner yogas'. These are based on an understanding of the body that differs radically from modern western notions of the physical. In the inner yogas, one works to transform the subtle energies of the illusory body, as it is called, which closely follows the physical structure of the human organism. By means of a system similar to that of the ancient Indian Tantra, the Vajrayāna maps out the illusory body in a network of energy channels and energy centres that correspond to certain areas of the 'gross' physical body. This is what Milarepa is referring to when he sings (in the first song of this episode) of his mastery of the practice of manipulating the *nāḍīs, prāṇa,* and *bindu.*

Prāṇa, sometimes translated as 'breath', refers to these psychophysical energies, while *bindu* refers specifically to masculine sexual energy. *Nāḍī,* sometimes translated as 'vein', means something more like 'nerve' – though not in the sense of the term as it applies to the ordinary nervous system. The *nāḍīs* are something more like a subtle network of vital forces. Different texts say different things about the subtle body, but the Tibetan tradition presents it as a subtle counterpart of the physical body, and as coextensive with it.

According to the Tantra, the nerves of the subtle body correspond with the median nerve running down the physical spine. On the left of the spinal column is the *lalanā,* coloured white and corresponding to the moon and to water, while on the right is the *rasanā,* which is red and corresponds to the sun and to fire. Tantric practice consists in bringing the 'breath' (*prāṇa*) into what is known as the central channel – the *avadhūtī* or subtle median nerve. This involves mobilizing the various bodily and mental forces and channelling them through one or other of the centres of psychospiritual energy – known as chakras – that lie along this subtle median nerve. The result is the liberation of these forces as they are brought together into a consciously experienced single flow of subtle energy. There are said to be seven chakras in all. The lowest chakra, the *mūlādhāra,* is at the perineum. The second is a few fingers' breadth below the navel, the third at the navel, the fourth at the heart, the fifth at the throat, the sixth between the eyebrows, and the seventh at the crown of the head. The Tantra symbolizes the chakras in the form of lotus flowers of varying numbers of petals, the thousand-petalled lotus being the topmost.

In this way the solar and lunar energies are brought together in an ever more subtle yet increasingly concentrated synthesis. Reason combines with emotion, meditation combines with action in the world, and working on one's own development combines with working for the welfare of others. Wisdom and compassion are unified in the direct experience of reality, free from any obstruction or delusion.

The method of the Tantra is based on the idea of correspondence between higher and lower manifestations of energy, familiar in the West from the old axiom of European alchemy, 'As above, so below.'[36] The Tantric sage's engagement with the elemental nature of the material universe is intimately involved with the transformation of consciousness – the inner world of the mind. For example, certain of the chakras are associated with one or another of the elements: earth, water, fire, air, and space. The degree of refinement of the material elements relative to one another corresponds to the varying degrees of integration and refinement of consciousness or psychophysical energy achieved through the opening of different chakras.

Enlightenment is dependent on energy being totally available on all levels, and within the Tantra this becomes the main focus of one's practice. Nor is this an exercise in abstract wish-fulfilment. It is worked out in the concrete details of everyday existence. If there are energies that are not going along with what you are essentially trying to do, even though they may not actively hold you back, they will nonetheless tend to sit like a dead weight on the energies that are actively trying to take you forward. The Tantra is designed to address this fundamental problem of the spiritual life: that you can make quite a lot of effort and still get nowhere.

Liberation is essentially about liberating energies, which means experiencing them more fully. One of the ways we repress energy or lock it away is in habitual patterns of thought, feeling, and behaviour. If Buddhism is concerned with bringing about the direct experience of oneself in the very depths of one's being, it does so by bringing into consciousness this submerged energy of which we are usually unaware.

This is easier said than done. Ideally, you want to get rid of the negativity but retain the energy tied up within it. There is a lot of energy in anger, for example – you might even say that anger *is* raw, crude energy – and you can't afford to throw it away simply because it is tainted with ill will. Unfortunately, this is what often happens. The energy is thrown away with the negativity – which is perhaps why so many religious men and women, although they are good people, seem rather weak and bloodless and incapable of saying boo to a goose. It would seem that, in order to purge themselves of what they see as their human weakness and wickedness, they have also repressed their energy. This inevitably sets up further trouble later on. It is notable that people who could never be described as 'good' often have a lot of zest for life, which makes them a lot of fun to be with.

This is a major theme in the work of the poet and painter William Blake. His thesis is that we identify goodness with the faculty of reason that restrains energy, and the forces of evil with the energy that needs to be restrained. In *The Marriage of Heaven and Hell*, which is where this aspect of his ideas is most clearly to the fore, he asserts that 'The tigers of wrath are wiser than the horses of instruction' – that is, energy itself is good, and it is only the curbing of energy that is truly negative. In a note to this work he remarks, 'The reason Milton wrote in fetters when he wrote of Angels and God, and at liberty when of Devils and Hell, is because he was a true Poet, and of the Devil's party without knowing it.'

This is not to say that if you have lots of energy, you are bound to be wicked. Your energies should be accepted as essentially positive even if you may need to change how you express them. Energy can always be transformed. But if you clamp down on energy generally, positive energies like joy don't get the opportunity to arise at all, because they are locked in along with more negative energies, and the only outcome will be frustration. It's important to bear in mind that truly positive energy, whether one's own or someone else's, is often more difficult to deal with than negative energy. You know where you are with negative energy, whether you indulge it, clamp down on it, or react to it. But what do you do with joy, for example? It doesn't follow the comfortable cycle of unconscious reactivity that is the experience of negative emotions.

If we are to reclaim and integrate all our energies in the Tantric spirit, we have first to happily accept our cruder energies, however muddied they are with old, unhelpful karmic patterns, as the raw material of life. One good way of working with turbulent, difficult, and uncomfortable energies, and of keeping energy flowing while dissolving the negativity in it, is to chant mantras. You could do some mantra chanting to dissolve anger, for example, using the practice to coax energy out of the angry emotion and release it in the form of the chanting voice. However, one of the dangers of what could be called a pseudo-Tantric approach is that, on the pretext of transforming negativity, you end up, consciously or otherwise, using the practice to indulge negativity. In the case of chanting, you would need to be careful that you were truly transforming the energy and not simply transferring the negativity into the tone and quality of your chanting. You might find yourself chanting the mantra with an oppressive, constraining energy that not only reinforces your angry mood but communicates it to whoever else is present. One has to be receptive to the positive content of the mantra, putting the *energy* of one's negativity into the chanting, not the negativity itself, and always looking for a brighter, lighter, and more vital energy to come through.

For the Tantra, energy is primary, and one's ethical practice needs to be configured to take this into account. It is not enough simply to hold back from unskilful action. While unskilful action is always unskilful, holding back energy is unskilful too. From a Tantric perspective, if you don't put as much energy as you can into whatever you are doing, it isn't really worth bothering to do it. And according to Tantric ethics it is unskilful to block energy – whether your own or someone else's – and unskilful to misappropriate or exploit energy, misuse or abuse it, subvert or misdirect it, pollute or muddy it.

MILAREPA'S SONG OF PROTECTION

It is clearly difficult psychologically to offer something to someone who doesn't want or need the thing you're offering. Having turned down the horse, Milarepa is certainly not going to need spurs or boots. But the young man is not put off, and offers his boots anyway. They are evidently the best money can buy, made from elk, wild yak, and crocodile skin, embroidered with silk and decorated with brass spurs. He knows that the Tantra involves making offerings, and he is certainly doing the right thing in making them. Moreover, he prefaces his offering by correctly observing that 'there is no attachment in your heart'.

Having made that observation, however, he seems to challenge Milarepa to prove it, suggesting that Milarepa may need boots to protect him from dogs with sharp teeth, brambles, and so on. It is as if he is trying to sell the boots to Milarepa, to tickle his fancy, to awaken in him a sense of dissatisfaction with a life without boots. Finally, however, he reverts to an attitude of personal sacrifice, of giving up something in which he invests his identity, and he concludes by asking for Milarepa's compassionate blessing. Even so, Milarepa refuses the offering.

What Milarepa needs is what he already has: the inner boots of renunciation and mindfulness. The point he makes in the song is essentially the same as in the previous one. But what he says here is strangely reminiscent of an image from a work called the *Bodhicaryāvatāra*, by the eighth-century Indian Mahāyāna poet Śāntideva. In a verse from that work Śāntideva points out that in order to protect your feet you could try to cover the whole earth in leather or, more economically, you could fit two small pieces of leather to your feet and get the same protection.[37] He says that while most of us choose the sensible option in this respect by wearing shoes, we fail to protect ourselves against enemies by recourse to the same principle. You can gird yourself to kill your enemies whenever they try to prevent you from getting what you want; but this is a ridiculous policy when there is the alternative of practising the *mettā bhāvanā*, the meditation through which one develops loving-kindness. In the cultivation of love for all that lives, you can protect yourself from thoughts of enmity arising in the first place.

If there is a need to weigh the concern to protect one's body from without against the concern to protect the mind from within, Milarepa is very clear about which he thinks is more important. Indeed, the kind of external situations in which a pair of stout boots provide protection have become so unimportant to him that they can be appropriated as metaphoric features of his inner landscape – Craving Meadow, Jealous Swamp, and the land of darkness and blind views. The dog of Hate and the steep hill of Pride are also to be avoided. All these names seem to anticipate in a curious way the language of John Bunyan's seventeenth-century classic of Nonconformist spirituality, *The Pilgrim's Progress*, with its Slough of Despond, Valley of Humiliation, and Doubting Castle. This song uses the same potent metaphor of the inner life as a journey towards a distant goal.

Obviously, the features of the spiritual landscape are produced by the mind of the individual negotiating them, and they keep reappearing, over and over again, so the journey is daunting to say the least. So what kind of footwear is required for such frustrating terrain? The answer is plain. There is no point in slipping your feet into something stylish and cosy. You need tough boots. They will hurt a bit to begin with, but they will last, and give you protection and a sure grip in whatever terrain you encounter.

I cut my boots from the hide of the renunciation of Saṃsāra
And with the leather of awakening from transiency and delusion.
I made my boots with the craftsmanship of deep faith in Karma,
With the dye of Non-clinging to the Myriad Forms,
And with the thread and rope of Devotion;[38]

To give up the untrustworthy protection offered by self-interest, to awaken to absolute insecurity, to accept that your unskilful actions of the past will have unforeseen consequences, these are the hard tasks of the spiritual life. But at some point one has to put these boots on. Devotion is of course the function of binding oneself to one's ideals with vows of dedication, so it is appropriately compared with bootlaces.

Buddhist practice is presented here as a source of protection which allows the practitioner to go unscathed through the world. It is quite a common conception, found also in the idea of the armour of śūnyatā and even in the image that traditionally illustrates the fourth level of meditative concentration or dhyāna, which is likened to a man who emerges from a pool on a hot day and wraps himself from head to foot in a white sheet.[39] (The Bible uses the same language in expressions such as the 'whole armour of God' and the 'shield of faith'.) Positive mental states are the best protection not only against the vicissitudes of material existence but, more importantly, against one's own tendency towards ego-centred thought and activity.

These are my boots, the boots of a yogi;

These boots are what enable Milarepa to navigate Craving Meadow, to scale the steep hill of Pride, and, one presumes, to resist the biting teeth of the dog of Hate. However, Milarepa's primary aim here, getting rid of ego-clinging, should not be confused with a kind of feeble self-effacement. It does not invite us to throw a wet blanket of self-admonishment over any feeling of pleasure at having done something well, with the thought, 'Oh dear, that's the ego.'

A friend of mine from my very early days back in England in the 1960s used to write me long letters every few months with lots of good advice, and she would constantly undercut any trace of self-assertion by apologizing for her ego. She would write, 'I was sorry not to hear from you for such a long time – but that's just my ego,' or 'I felt quite pleased when someone came to see me and said how nice my paintings were – but of course that's just my ego.' When one trips over oneself at every step in this way, I'm afraid it is just the ego saying, 'That's just my ego,' probably as an automatic ploy to forestall criticism. It is an inverted form of conceit, dressed up as non-ego. What one is apologizing for may well not be one's ego at all. One should not be too ego-conscious in this sense.

In fact, the Tantra, and the Mahāyāna generally, is careful to identify a positive form of pride which it calls Buddha-pride. It is unconnected with ego-clinging, and starts with an honest satisfaction with what one is doing. In traditional texts, the practitioner is encouraged to reflect, 'Having taken the bodhisattva vow, I belong to the family of the Buddha which I must never disgrace. How can I consider committing an unskilful act that might bring shame to that name?'

We need not be thinking in terms of the bodhisattva ideal to apply this to our own lives. If, for example, you are going to cook a meal for your friends and you want to do it to the best of your ability, your ego-centred motivation would be to prove that you are better than others, to win appreciation and acknowledgement of your efforts and skill. But a positive Buddha-pride attitude would be, 'How could I even think of neglecting to do this as skilfully as I can? Not to give of my best would be unworthy of the ideal to which I have committed myself, and of the regard I have for my friends. Indeed, it is a matter of pride to prepare the meal with *mettā* as well as skill. Otherwise, I would be letting myself down, letting my friends down, and letting the Buddha down.'

This is the kind of healthy self-respect of which the youth is eminently capable, given the straightforwardness of his general approach to life. But as yet he has not been able to transform his worldly self-respect into genuine Buddha-pride. He remains oblivious to the momentous shift in attitude that he will have to make if he is to become Milarepa's disciple.

MILAREPA'S SONG OF THE *BARDO*

The young man addresses Milarepa now as a teacher.

> Precious and accomplished Guru,
> Freed from Ego-clinging,

Evoking the bleak hardship of Milarepa's wanderings, he offers his jacket against the cold – and again the offering is clearly of the highest quality. Being 'freed from ego-clinging', Milarepa is not likely to appreciate owning such a covetable garment, but this does not stop the young man from describing it in meticulous detail, from its lining and silk facings to its lynx fur trim and its collar and hem made of otter skin.

However, Milarepa refuses to acknowledge the claims to his attention of passing bodily discomfort when he has much more crucial matters to address. He puts up with material hardship to sharpen his concentration on the real issue: the teaching here is about ethical practice.

> O'er the cities of the Six Realms in Saṃsāra,
> With fury blows the evil, Karmic wind.
> Driven by the senses and deprived of freedom,
> One wanders between life and death, roving in Bardo!...
>
> For my part, I aspire to the Realm of Reality,
> And adorn the cloth of pure mind and heart
> With the embroidery of immaculate discipline.
> Mindfulness is the tailor...

In this powerful song Milarepa presents the essence of our predicament in any of the six realms of conditioned existence,[40] whether as gods or demons, animals or human beings. In any mundane situation we are in some kind of *bardo*, that is, an intermediate state. The word '*bardo*' is most often used to refer to the state between death and rebirth, but there are other *bardos* too, including the *bardo* of the dream state, the *bardo* of meditation, and the *bardo* of everyday life.

When we are in a dream, it seems entirely real. It is usually only when we wake up from it that we understand we have been dreaming. Similarly, to one who is Enlightened and has woken up to the reality of things, everyday life will appear as it really is: transient and subject to ever-changing conditions. In other words, a *bardo*.

Seeing ordinary life as an intermediate state reminds us that we are involved in something we do not fully understand. We do not see the whole picture, although our worldly habits of mind conspire to hide this reality from us. Wandering the *bardo* in our confusion, we are buffeted, as Milarepa says, by the furious winds of evil karma – that is, by the effects of our past moral mistakes. We are usually not aware that our actions of body, speech, and mind will have ramifications in terms of our future experience. Hence the need to remember, to be mindful, and Milarepa produces a telling image of mindfulness as the tailor who puts the garment of our practice together.

Milarepa also offers here a neat reversal of what may be our usual way of thinking. We might normally regard ethics as a worthy but dull base material which we can embroider with more colourful practices, but Milarepa adorns the cloth of *samādhi* or meditation with the embroidery of *śīla* or ethics. Seen as embroidery, the practice of ethics becomes a matter of delicate and sensitive craftsmanship, the delightful flowering of one's practice rather than just its roots.

Milarepa's is an advanced practice of ethical discipline, which in the Kagyu tradition is sometimes understood to follow three stages of development. At the first stage, you are able to work effectively at behaving skilfully and cultivating positive mental states, given the right supportive conditions around you, or at least regular contact with others who are practising in the same way. The second stage of ethical development is the maintenance of the purity of your practice even among people whose beliefs and habits are in opposition to your values and principles and way of life, perhaps even people living evil lives. To continue to practise effectively in a hostile environment represents a higher level of development. You are like a lotus flower growing from the mud.

With the third level, which Milarepa has reached, you are not only able to practise effectively under adverse conditions; you are unaffected by them. *Saṃsāra* and *nirvāṇa* – the state of worldly life and the state of Enlightenment – are not separate, although they appear so to the unenlightened mind. With the realization of the true nature of mind, you understand that both are the products of human consciousness, and you are not personally attached to any one form of human consciousness over another. All forms are void. It is a fundamental Buddhist teaching that things have no *svabhāva*, no 'own being', no ultimate, individual, unchanging essence. Everything is fluid, unfixed, open.

So does Enlightenment take you beyond the working out of karma altogether? Having gone beyond conceptions of self and other, pleasure and pain, good and evil, do you no longer separate out cause and effect as absolute distinctions, and do you therefore no longer recognize and respect the operation of karma? The Enlightened mind sees the conditioned and the unconditioned as non-dual – i.e. as an unreal distinction – but the distinction must be very real and clear for those of us who have not transcended it, if we are to have any chance of doing so. If we are going to think of changing our present state, if we have any notion of making progress, we have to discriminate between suffering and joy, confusion and clarity, fear and confidence, self and other, *saṃsāra* and *nirvāṇa*.

If you are Enlightened and therefore 'above' duality, you still see that skilful actions on the mundane level produce happiness and unskilful actions produce pain. In other words, your realization of *śūnyatā* does not cancel out your respect for the law of conditionality as it operates on the mundane level. So an Enlightened being does not ignore the law of cause and effect; in fact, one aspect of Enlightenment is the ability to see it with absolute clarity. Absolute truth does not negate relative truth on the level at which relative truth operates.

There is a famous Zen story that illustrates the danger of misunderstanding this aspect of Enlightenment. It concerns a 'spirit fox', a sort of haunted or spirit-possessed fox. A monk eventually exorcises this creature and then asks him how he came to be a spirit fox. It seems that the spirit fox was originally a Zen master, and that he became a spirit fox as a result of his wrong answer to an apparently simple question. The question was, 'What becomes of the law of karma when you become Enlightened?' and the answer he gave was, 'When you become Enlightened you go beyond the law of karma.' For that terrible mistake he had been reborn as a spirit fox for five hundred rebirths. So he asks the monk what he should have said. 'What I should have said,' the monk replies, 'is that when you become Enlightened, you do not get in the way of the law of karma.'[41]

> I brighten the shoulder padding
> With the Great Light (which shines at the time) of death.
> I cut the hem of Bardo Enlightenment
> To the 'measurement' of pure Magic-Bodies.

Finally, Milarepa introduces the theme of gaining Enlightenment in the *bardo* state between death and rebirth. When released from the physical body with which it has identified itself throughout life, the mind has a brief opportunity to realize its true nature. If you realize the Clear Light in the intermediate state after death, you become Enlightened, and in doing so, you realize the 'pure Magic-Bodies'.

Here Milarepa is referring to a complex doctrine which was developed in the Buddhist tradition over many centuries. There is much that could be said about it, but in this context we will just try to get a basic sense of what he means by 'Magic-Bodies'.

THE TRIKĀYA DOCTRINE

The Tantric conception of Enlightenment is based on the perception that to be any kind of being, even an Enlightened one, you always have to be embodied in some way. If there is no ultimate duality between conditioned and unconditioned, an Enlightened mind must always come with an Enlightened body. The question is: what kind of body?

The figure of the Buddha presents Buddhism with a paradox. The Buddha was a human being – albeit an Enlightened one – who lived at a certain time and place. But he was much more than that. The Buddha is the manifestation in time and space of something that is beyond personality, beyond time and space, certainly beyond any conceptual designation on the part of the unenlightened, dualistic mind.

A distinction therefore emerged in the earliest days of Buddhism between the physical body of the historical Buddha and the non-dual Enlightened state from which his teaching emanated. References in the Pāli canon to the *dharmakāya* indicate that the early understanding of this 'body of truth' was that it was the totality of the truths taught by the Buddha. However, as the Buddhist tradition developed into the Mahāyāna, the conception of the *dharmakāya* began to be understood in metaphysical terms rather than simply in doctrinal terms, and the body of truth came to be regarded as identical with reality itself in all its non-dual formlessness.

It is in the later phases of the Mahāyāna, particularly in the Yogācāra, that we find a third conception of the Buddha – a third body – which is neither abstract and beyond thought nor concretely historical. This is the *sambhogakāya* (literally 'body of mutual enjoyment') – the archetypal Buddha or bodhisattva, the ideal being. This, rather than the conception of the Buddha as a historical personality, came to be the focal point of the Mahāyāna *sūtras*. The *sambhogakāya* inhabits the vast reaches of time and space in a way that renders the Buddha ever present, always accessible. The physical body of the Enlightened mind, meanwhile, came to be known as the *nirmāṇakāya*, or 'created body'.

These, then, are the three Buddha bodies. First there is the *dharmakāya*, the body of truth, of ultimate reality. Secondly there is what became known as the *nirmāṇakāya*, the historical, flesh-and-blood Buddha, a 'created body' or 'magic body', as Milarepa calls it. And thirdly, forming a bridge between the historical and the literally inconceivable, we find the *sambhogakāya*, the archetypal embodiment, which manifests in the forms of Buddha and bodhisattva figures. These figures represent the ideal of the Buddha considered in the most elevated terms of myth and symbol, and are the basis of the visualization practices of the Vajrayāna.

It must be emphasized that the *trikāya* – the three Buddha bodies – are not to be understood as being separate from each other (although the translation of *kāya* as 'body', being somewhat over-literal, doesn't really help us to understand this). The three 'bodies' do not stand side by side or on top of each other; they are more like different dimensions of the Buddha-nature. Penetrate deeply into the historical Buddha and you encounter the *sambhogakāya*; penetrate more deeply still, and you reach the *dharmakāya*.

Another way of thinking of the *trikāya* doctrine is that it represents Enlightenment as the transformation of all aspects of being, the three *kāyas* of the Buddha corresponding on the transcendental level to body, speech, and mind on the mundane level. The task of the guru is to make the truth manifest in the disciple throughout his or her whole being by initiating and instructing him or her in a Tantric *sādhana*. The ensuing Enlightenment is said to consist in the transformation of one's body into *nirmāṇakāya*, one's speech into *sambhogakāya*, and one's mind or heart into *dharmakāya*. According to the Tantra, this transformation is a fuller, richer, and more complex realization than the kind of insight accessible to non-Tantric Buddhists.

For the Vajrayāna the route to the *dharmakāya* is through a direct encounter with the *sambhogakāya*, the archetypal realm. This is the basis of the visualization practices of the Tantric path; one goes for Refuge to one's *yidam*, the archetypal Buddha or bodhisattva to whom one is introduced at the moment of Tantric initiation. The visualization practices of the Vajrayāna are based on the pragmatic understanding that the *sambhogakāya* is as far ahead as we can see. Whatever lies beyond that must be left alone for the time being.

In any effort to understand the images, myths, and symbols of the Vajrayāna, we are inevitably held back by our natural tendency to literal-mindedness. The imagination is of far greater use in this context than the ordinary rational mind, because the reality represented by the *sambhogakāya* and manifested in the form of archetypal Buddhas and bodhisattvas is accessible only by means of a visionary faculty. But what is required here is more than just imagination in the sense of an ability to build up images in the mind, or even a creative artistic faculty. Whatever mental images one creates must be infused with at least some sense of the Buddha's teaching that the true nature of conditioned things – including visionary experience – is impermanent and provisional. This meditative visionary faculty is not *above* the imagination; it is another dimension of imagination: Imagination with a capital I. It is essentially the same faculty.

From another point of view, one can also say that the formless is not necessarily closer to reality than that which has form. One could say that the *dharmakāya* is Buddhahood without form, the *sambhogakāya* is Buddhahood with form, and the two are non-different. In fact, transcendental insight can be developed with regard to any conditioned object – even through contemplation of a matchbox if that matchbox is experienced as conditioned and empty of inherent existence. Realizing that because it came into existence it must therefore go out of existence, and that all apparent 'things' are like this, you can develop insight. The reason we are not likely to develop insight through contemplating a matchbox is simply that we are not likely to have very strong feelings about that particular object, so it would be hard for us to concentrate on it very powerfully. However, if you have an experience of the *sambhogakāya*, a vision of a realm of archetypal forms, if you actually see a bodhisattva, all your most refined emotional energies will be aroused and unified behind your contemplation of the aspect of reality that the figure symbolizes, and this may catapult you into insight.

One could think of the *nirmāṇakāya* and the *sambhogakāya* as two veils hung before the *dharmakāya*, understood as reality in its pristine, unmediated form. The *sambhogakāya* veil is thinner, more diaphanous, and perhaps more brightly coloured than the *nirmāṇakāya* veil, but through both – whether through the personality of the historical Buddha or through the brilliant form of a visualized Buddha or bodhisattva – the transcendental may be glimpsed.

Famously, some contemporaries of the historical Buddha, although they met and talked to him, had no idea of the transcendental reality he represented. Likewise, one can have a purely visual experience of a Buddha or bodhisattva without any sense of that figure's true significance. In other words, it is quite possible to see either the *nirmāṇakāya* or *sambhogakāya* at face value, oblivious to the *dharmakāya* shining through. But to allow these forms to take us closer to an experience of the unconditioned nature of pure reality, we need not consciously strive to read significance in them or explain them in words. They can be left to speak for themselves, to have their own effect upon us. We just have to be receptive to them.

MILAREPA'S SONG OF PSYCHIC HEAT

Nothing if not persistent, the young man continues his guide to medieval Tibetan men's tailoring. Over his reddish-green jacket he is wearing a coat in grey-green wool hemmed with maroon fur, and this too he offers to Milarepa, who declares that, like all the other offerings, it is surplus to his requirements.

> With the cloth of Ah Shea Vital Heat
> Is the lapel of Four Cakras made.
> My tailor is the inner Prāṇa-Mind
> Who warms Thig Le and makes it flow;
> The merged Bliss-Void experience
> Is the needle used for sewing;

Milarepa's theme in the song with which he refuses this gift is *tummo*, psychic heat, a practice that assumed a great importance in the Vajrayāna traditions. Like the meditation on the *bindu* and the *nāḍīs*, the *tummo* practice works by means of special breathing practices and yogic postures designed to bring one's energies to an intense pitch of concentration. One then begins various visualizations of the inner fire, and these are said to have certain physical effects, in particular that of raising the body temperature regardless of external conditions. This is how Milarepa, the cotton-clad yogi, could withstand the bitter cold of his mountain hermitage.

Tummo is the 'cloth' that keeps him warm. This effect is a well-attested phenomenon associated with meditative concentration: you naturally generate physical heat when you meditate, heat that others can feel. It can sometimes even seem as though you have a feverishly high temperature – except that you feel not ill but happy and comfortable. Some yogis make a particular practice out of this experience of *tummo*.

However, the idea of psychic heat should not be taken only on a literal level. The pleasurable experience of heat in the body is the psychophysical counterpart of the intense bliss which, according to the Tantra, has to be conjoined with a mental apprehension or intuition of voidness in the non-dual *samādhi* state. Bliss and emptiness are complementary aspects of what is actually a single experience. We find the same idea expressed in the traditional Mahāyāna notion of Enlightenment as the supreme union of *samādhi* and *prajñā*, of transcendental insight and supremely positive emotion. The Tantra simply emphasizes in more concrete terms that these two factors must always go together. The Void is not just a clear mental experience, and *tummo* is not just a warm physical experience. They come together in an experience of intense bliss.

This idea that Enlightenment is blissful may seem to be in clear contrast to the cool, emotionally astringent Nirvāṇa which Theravādin Buddhism is popularly supposed to envisage. In fact, though, the blissful element of Nirvāṇa is emphasized throughout the Buddhist tradition; after all, the well-known expression *nibbānam paramam sukkham* ('Nirvāṇa is the highest bliss') comes directly from the *Dhammapada* of the Pāli canon.[42]

In deep states of meditation, the vital energies of the body become concentrated in an experience of profound stability. This process of the intensification of bodily energy and emotional and cognitive clarity can be traced in the formulation known as the seven factors of Enlightenment, or *bodhyaṅgas*, which is found throughout the Pāli canon.[43] As one's bodily energies become increasingly concentrated and refined, they are transformed – via the state of *prīti*, or rapture – into *sukha*, serene joy. The vital energy remains, but it is integrated into a succession of increasingly positive mental states, and consciousness becomes permeated with a blissful lightness and energy.

The producing of inner warmth then becomes contentment or emotional positivity, a radiance that is not stimulated by some external source but comes from your own spiritual resources. Wisdom's diamond-like clarity is utterly suffused with the blissful heat of inwardly generated well-being and contentment. The bliss gives content to the experience of voidness, while the voidness gives clarity to the experience of bliss. So you experience blissful inner heat and, at the same time, the illuminating Void, like fire and ice together.

The four higher chakras are 'made of' this vital heat; in other words, the *tummo* practice of *caṇḍāli* yoga involves heating the *bindu* or 'Thig Le'. This is a reference, literally speaking, to semen, but we can also take it to mean energy in its grosser form, which is gradually sublimated and made more and more subtle and refined. The 'inner Prāṇa-Mind' warms this energy and causes it to flow. In the course of being heated, the energy becomes sublimated and refined, and rises up, guided by the inner *prāṇa* mind, through the central channel or median nerve to awaken the four major psychic centres or chakras of the heart, the throat, the third eye, and the crown of the head.

This process is guided by cognitive insight into the clear void of *śūnyatā*, which engages all the vital energies in the form of a steadily intensifying bliss, finally to unite them with that clear experience of the Void. To put it another way, the process of gathering one's energies is inherently and increasingly blissful, until that bliss is so intense that it unites with the clear void. And at this point the inborn vital heat manifests.

The cloth is Inborn Vital Heat.
Now summer and winter are for me the same!

When Milarepa says that summer and winter are the same for him, he means not only that he is impervious to extremes of climate, but that he has gone beyond all distinctions. This is the inborn vital heat, *sahajiya*, or inherent Buddha nature. It is a transcendental heat, which is coterminous with reality. It is not artificially produced; it needs only to be released. It is there from the beginning.

MILAREPA'S SONG OF THE GURU

The young man's next song follows the usual pattern of salutation and praise of Milarepa's non-attachment, followed by solicitous but facile conjecture as to his material needs, and an offering of something that will supposedly meet them. He seems not to have heard what Milarepa has just been saying about his practice of *tummo*, because he surmises that 'you must sometimes feel the cold'. He therefore offers his hat, a heady confection of crocodile hide, vulture skin, and gaudy feathers around an intricate frame of precious metal. He recommends it to Milarepa not on aesthetic or practical grounds but on account of its exchange value, which is apparently that of a big yak. Rather than asking for some kind of blessing in return, he makes his first commitment.

> In summer and in winter,
> I will follow and pay homage to you!

Milarepa tells him not to be too rash; to keep his hat – and his head.

> My dear young man,
> Do not lose your head!

Milarepa is no longer at the mercy of the elements. Just as he has no fear of water,

> I fear not the element of air within,
> Nor do I depend on falcon's flesh.
> I feel gay and joyous in a biting wind.

He has no need for wealth. Nor does he need a hat, as the crown of his head is already occupied – by his guru, Marpa, visualized above his head as part of the practice of guru yoga.[44]

The guru yoga differs from lineage to lineage, but it usually begins with imagining your guru above your head. Then you go on to imagine your guru's guru above his head, and that guru's guru in turn above his head, and so on, through the whole lineage. Next you imagine the blessing of the gurus coming down through the lineage to you. And then you feel your mind united with your guru's mind, and his mind united with his own guru's mind, going back in this way to the Buddha, the original transcendental source of inspiration, usually visualized not as the historical Buddha Śākyamuni but in an archetypal or *sambhogakāya* form, perhaps Vajradhara or Amitābha.

As a devoted disciple you are supposed to be aware of your guru above your head all the time. This is because, according to the Vajrayāna, the guru does not just stand for the Buddha but *is* the Buddha, at least so far as the individual disciple is concerned. The guru is the master who helps you to transform your crude, mundane body, speech, and mind into the unconditioned body, speech, and mind of a Buddha. Consequently, you see your guru not only as the *dharmakāya*, the embodiment of the ultimate truth or ultimate reality, but also as the *sambhogakāya*, the manifestation of Buddhahood in time and space.

The exercise is a simple matter of cultivating, experiencing, and expressing gratitude. Gratitude opens us up to the fact of our interconnectedness with others. Whenever we enjoy or achieve something, it is salutary to recognize and acknowledge the work and kindness of all the individuals who have contributed to it. But gratitude to the guru has an extra dimension, because what we are grateful for is beyond valuation. There is no hope of repaying the debt, except by passing the gift on to others. Another way of looking at this is to say that gratitude is a way of opening ourselves up to the merit accrued by the guru, which becomes inextricably linked with our own, as he passes it freely on to us.

The guru yoga is a formal version of something that should happen anyway in the spiritual life. We should all be grateful to whoever it was who first introduced us to the Dharma. There is a very famous example of this: the Buddha's most eminent disciple, Śāriputra, made a point of prostrating in gratitude every day of his life to Aśvajit, the disciple who gave him his first contact with the Dharma. Although Śāriputra quickly outstripped Aśvajit in spiritual attainment, Enlightened as he was, he continued to prostrate himself to the still unenlightened Aśvajit.[45]

> He is the Wish-Fulfilling Gem, Buddha's Transformation Body.
> If you see him with the eye of veneration,
> You will find he is the Buddha Dorje-Chang!

The guru is the manifestation in the present time of the current of spiritual energy that has come down from the Buddha through the lineage of one's own tradition. The lineage, or line of transmission, is like a spiritual chain reaction. It is not the actual handing down of an object or thing. Even though the idea of transmission suggests that the disciple gains something which he or she did not previously have, the role of the guru is primarily to activate the disciple's energies. He (or sometimes she) enables the disciple to tap the vast source of inspiration and energy that lies hidden and unconscious in their own being.

Nor does transmission consist in a certificated process whereby a kind of spiritual management role is passed on from one generation to another. For one thing, a guru may have had many teachers and all the transmissions he has received through all of them are focused through him on the disciple. The lineage is not a sort of spiritual family tree that the interested disciple might like to trace back to the Buddha. It represents a direct experience of awakening, a living truth that has been stimulated again and again through the guru-disciple relationship.

Dorje-Chang is the Buddha Vajradhara, 'bearer of the *vajra*'. He is depicted with a *vajra* standing upright in his palm (the *vajra* being a symbol of ultimate reality), and sometimes a *vajra* bell as well, and he is considered to be the primordial originator of the whole Kagyu lineage, and thus their adi-guru or Adibuddha. (The term *adi* means primordial, i.e. from the beginning.) But Vajradhara is the primordial guru or Buddha not in the sense of initiating the lineage in time, or even at the beginning of time. He symbolizes its origin as being outside time altogether, as being transcendental, and in that sense, without origin. Thus, *adi* really means 'without origin', and the Adibuddha symbolizes the timeless nature of Enlightenment or Buddhahood. Buddhahood in its essence has no beginning. It cannot be said to arise, because it is always there. It represents a dimension beyond time, into which you break through on the attainment of Enlightenment, at which point you realize that you have always been there.

MILAREPA'S SONG OF THE TREASURE OF CONTENTMENT

The youth next offers his most treasured possession:

This white translucent six-edged jade

The youth is evidently quite well off. It should not be assumed, however, that these offerings are what he just happens to have about his person at the time. They almost certainly constitute most of his wealth. This is characteristic of traditional, pre-industrial societies, particularly nomadic cultures such as those of medieval Mongolia and Tibet. Your wealth is not kept in the bank, or in stocks and shares, or even in bars of gold under the bed. It is in your hat, your coat, your horse, your sword. You wear it – or your wife wears it in the form of gold ornaments. The womenfolk of nomadic tribal societies are like walking banks; in time of need they can sell a gold ring or a bangle. As the young man points out, 'With this jade you can never be poor.'

Of course, farmers and peasants hold their wealth in land and cattle, but the nobility traditionally carry their fortunes in the form of personal adornment. Even in England, as recently as the reign of Elizabeth I, young men would come to London from the country having sold large tracts of land in order to appear at court dressed in fabulously expensive clothes of silk and jewel-encrusted satin, hoping to catch the queen's eye and win preferment. They were, it was said, 'wearing their estates on their backs'. A sensible young man would invest a great deal of money in a gold hilt for his sword or a jewelled feather for his cap, in the hope of a good return in terms of advancement to fame and fortune, power, and prosperity. Tibetans who have not been urbanized and modernized still maintain this sort of attitude to anything they wear or carry. A nomad from the far-flung valleys of the Tibetan plateau would never think of wearing something fake or artificial if he could avoid it, especially on a trip to Lhasa or on pilgrimage. He would be sure to wear real gold, real jewels, quality leather and cloth.

As usual, the young man prefaces his offering with a statement of faith in Milarepa, particularly in his non-attachment. He is able to acknowledge that there is no point in trying to seduce or buy Milarepa with his gift. But it is as if he has still not really taken in what he understands in theory. He cannot help pointing out that with this jade Milarepa can never be poor, so his lack of insight betrays itself.

Moreover, having offered his most precious possession, he can't help asking for a teaching instead of just a blessing. There is an unspoken assumption that the value of the offering calls for an equivalent spiritual reward. But Milarepa is still not prepared to accept the implication that he himself has any need or desire for anything. He replies according to the terms in which the offering has been made.

> There is no end to human greed.
> Even with hoarded wealth head-high,
> One cannot reach contentment.
> I do not envy you your wealth and goods.

The greatest treasure is contentment in my heart;
The teaching of the Whispered Lineage is my wealth;

Here Milarepa's teaching is completely continuous in principle with that of the historical Buddha. There is a verse in the *Dhammapada* that says just the same: *santuṭṭhiparamaṃ dhanaṃ* – 'Contentment is the greatest wealth.'[46]

My devotion to the Dharma is my ornament.
I deck myself with Retaining Mindfulness;

We adorn whatever we value or love, whether it is ourselves or someone else, or the Three Jewels. Milarepa prefers to adorn his breast only with the devotion of his heart to the Dharma. If he does wear any kind of decoration, it is what he calls 'retaining mindfulness', by which he means the recollection of meditative experience, especially *dhyāna*, through his daily life.

Milarepa is saying that by virtue of his spiritual attainments he has all the wealth in the world at his disposal. As a continuous stream of positive mental events, the spiritual qualities over which he has attained mastery are inexhaustible. They can never be taken away from him by circumstances. Material poverty consequently holds no fear for him. The wealth he values is not material – in fact it springs from a renunciation of material wealth. His wealth is the Dharma, and more specifically, the Dharma as expounded by his teachers. And this of course is very much the focus of the Kagyu tradition, the Whispered Lineage.

The lineage is whispered in the sense of being taught confidentially, that is to say, not in books or public talks, but in a very personal exchange. Other factors being equal, the greater the number of people one is speaking to, the more generalized, even approximate, is the teaching. When someone gives a teaching to many people at the same time, it is up to each listener to decide for themselves how it applies to them individually, which makes it much more difficult for genuine transformation to occur. The smaller the number of people, the more specific and therefore, in a sense, the more true the teaching can be. Even if you are addressing just two people, you have to direct what you say to what is common in them both, rather than what is individual and unique in each of them. The best situation for spiritual teaching is thus one-to-one communication, when what is truly individual in you makes contact with what is truly individual in the other person. When a guru does speak to just one person, he doesn't have to say much. One sentence may do. You can cut straight through all the general theory, the broad principles, and the full range of teachings designed to meet the needs of any conceivable kind of individual.

In the Tantric tradition generally, and in the Kagyu lineage in particular, it is usually said that any guru will find only a few disciples to whom he can communicate the teaching. In Milarepa's case, these are the eight 'heart-disciples'. Each of them receives his own unique transmission of the Dharma, which is not necessarily a conceptual or verbalized teaching. The Zen tradition has a similar kind of transmission. It is this individual, unique teaching, 'whispered' into the ear of one person at a time, which makes the greatest impact.

THE YOUTH'S SONG OF GOING FOR REFUGE

Undeterred by Milarepa's refusal of his gifts, the young man now takes a new tack.

> It is natural for a supreme being like you not to want these illusory possessions. I now offer you my Three Companions. From now on I will never carry a weapon or kill sentient beings. I beg you to grant me the Ordination. I pray you to protect me with your compassionate grace!

As this offering makes especially clear, every time Milarepa turns him down the young man offers something more, and puts more of himself at stake. To begin with he was simply anxious to be saved from hell. Then he asked for Milarepa's compassionate blessing. Then he requested the teaching. And with this offering comes a glimmering of something not hinted at before: he realizes that the worldliness of his way of life is standing in the way of a deeper meeting with his teacher. He is no longer going to try to offer Milarepa material possessions in some expectation that he is going to find a use for them. Having acknowledged that the gifts he offers have no value for the cotton-clad yogi, he now takes a huge step forward. A far more profound ideal has begun to reveal itself to him and he is ready to reorganize his life in order to attain it. He is beginning, in other words, to take responsibility for his own spiritual life, a decision marked by his asking for ordination, presumably lay ordination as an *upāsaka*. Having done so, the youth throws himself under Milarepa's care, asking for the protection of his 'compassionate grace'.

The concept of grace appears quite frequently in the Songs of Milarepa. The Tibetan term is *cheno* or *chinlap*, which in his translation of *Tibet's Great Yogī Milarepa* Lama Kazi Dawa-Samdup renders as 'grace-waves'.[47] The Pāli term is *anubhāva* – *anu* meaning 'after', and *bhāva*, 'being', or 'becoming'. It's rather like an echo: somebody is in a certain state of mind, a certain mood, and an echo or reflection of that mood is produced in somebody else. It is a traditional Buddhist belief that all those of high spiritual attainment emit this kind of influence.

Of course, there is nothing special or exceptional about having an influence or impact on others. All living beings emit an unseen and often unnoticed influence; we all generate an aura of some kind, with varying degrees of power. But what is being spoken of here as grace is something exceptional. The more deeply your insight has penetrated, the more positive and powerful becomes your aura or influence, and in the case of the Buddhas and bodhisattvas, it is without limit. They are always sending out these grace-waves, and we just have to open ourselves to them.

Contrary to popular belief, the strictly Buddhist understanding is that this *anubhāva* does not offer material protection from material misfortune. It is quite easy to slip into talking about the Buddhas and bodhisattvas protecting beings in a literal sense, particularly in the context of popular Buddhism, but such notions are not in accordance with all aspects of the tradition. Some would say that you are helped, supported, and even protected by 'grace-waves' only in the sense that being more open to positive influences puts you in a more positive frame of mind, psychologically and spiritually. It is this that enables you to make progress. Exactly what the young man means by asking for protection we have no way of knowing. Perhaps he isn't quite sure himself; perhaps he is not clear in his own mind whether he is asking for mundane or spiritual protection, or some combination of the two.

What we may be sure of is that in renouncing the physical protection of his weapons for the spiritual protection of the guru, he is taking a huge step forward, especially given the time and place in which he lives.

His weapons are part of his identity – hence his name for them: his Three Companions. They never leave his side, for without them he will feel powerless to respond to attack. Medieval Tibet was a dangerous place, with very little law and certainly no police to enforce it, and much depended upon your ability to defend yourself.

WARRIORS OF TIBET

In trying to picture this young warrior and his attitude to life, I am again reminded of my Khamba student in Kalimpong. Khamba men are very distinctive, even among other Tibetans. There is something decidedly swashbuckling about them, with their big boots and cowboy hats, their swords tucked in their belts, and their jacket sleeves nonchalantly knotted around their waists. Looking at Khamba mule-drivers swaggering down the street in Kalimpong, you would think they owned the place, and people thought it best to get out of their way. I remember on one occasion going into a bank – a place of sober composure, even in India – and finding one of these Tibetans stretched out asleep on the floor. No one had dared to ask him to get up and move along; that would have been asking for trouble.

The Khambas' fondness for a good fight also influenced their choice of entertainment. Kalimpong had its own cinema, and you could count on a full house when the programme featured a western. Romantic films were just so much silly nonsense as far as the Khambas were concerned, but a cowboy film was a different matter, and the more shootings, fist-fights, and mayhem, the better they liked it. In short, they are a proud and defiant people, and a good deal less sophisticated than the city-dwellers of Lhasa, who tend to look down on them as rather barbaric and bellicose. But their bravery is legendary. The Khambas were the last Tibetans to surrender to the Chinese, continuing to harry them in guerrilla raids from the mountains even after the invaders had taken over their country.

At the same time the Khambas are very religious, and in the early days of the invasion, when they used to ambush caravans, they were careful to avoid robbing those of Buddhist lamas. My Khamba student once told me a story that epitomises the attitude of the Khamba warriors. It happened that a caravan belonging to one of the larger and more prestigious monasteries was passing though the land. It belonged to a *tulku*, an incarnate lama, for whom the Khambas are known to have tremendous respect. The usual custom with Tibetan caravans is for the leading horse to wear a special decoration, usually a red plume on its forehead, and to be trained not to allow any other horse or mule to get ahead of it. A caravan belonging to an incarnate lama would be made instantly recognizable by a distinctive variation of this form of decoration. However, in this case the manager of one of the big monasteries had decided that the leading horse should not wear its special insignia, so as not to advertise the caravan as being in any way unusual. If people knew that it belonged to an incarnate lama, the manager thought, it would be more likely to be attacked and robbed of the precious goods it could be expected to be carrying.

Unfortunately, this stratagem had the opposite effect to that intended. The Khamba men saw the unmarked caravan approaching in the distance and, considering it fair game, ambushed it and even killed a number of people in the process. When the guerrillas discovered in the course of their looting that it belonged to an incarnate lama, they were mortified and gave back all that they had taken, and begged the manager to convey their deepest apologies to the lama. They wished they could have restored the lives of those they had killed, but as for that, they said, it was the manager's fault for disguising the caravan.

This is very much the style and spirit of the Khambas, and we can be sure that the young nobleman whom Milarepa meets in 'The Meeting at Silver Spring' is more than a little like them. For him, life would have been a simple matter of protecting himself from real enemies who were in a position to do real and perhaps murderous harm. Your weapons and your willingness to use them would have had an important part to play in your protection by instilling fear into others. With his weapons, the youth says, 'I was like a ruthless bandit.'

In giving up his weapons the youth places himself under the protection of spiritual rather than material power. He surrenders them because they are the means of taking care of his interests through violence, through breaking the precepts. So he is moving from the practice of *dāna*, generosity, the first of the six perfections of the bodhisattva path, to the practice of *śīla* or morality, the second perfection.[48] Having offered more and more of his possessions until he has nothing left to give, he is now ready to sacrifice his whole way of life in so far as it breaks the ethical precepts. He is ready to commit himself, to go for Refuge to the Buddha, Dharma, and Sangha, and as part of this process he has to think about how he lives his life and make the changes necessary to bring it into line with the ethical ideals of the Dharma. So the meeting at Silver Spring has started to bite. He is beginning to think seriously about what being a disciple really entails. Now will Milarepa be satisfied?

MILAREPA'S SONG OF THE CONQUEROR

No, is the answer. Milarepa is still unmoved, refusing to believe that the youth can keep his vow. He knows full well that there is a world of difference between intending to follow the ethical precepts and being able to put your noble aspirations into practice, especially when the going gets tough.

> He who does not renounce the 'all-important' combat
> Will be imprisoned and lose his chance for freedom!
> Battles and armies are not for the yogi.

'All-important' is in quotation marks here to signify that it refers to something that is accorded huge significance by social convention and popular assumptions but which just a little thought will reveal to be fairly trivial. For the young man, as for most males of any social standing in pre-industrial cultures, the all-important thing is combat. It used to be the same in Europe: to be a man of honour or, in England, a gentleman, involved being prepared to defend that honour when it was impugned. It may seem obviously absurd to have to wager your life on a duel because someone has insulted you, but it was all-important at the time.

Similar values persist in any culture where violence and aggressive competition prevail, such as urban gang culture. Membership of the group involves being prepared to defend the honour of being a member. In giving up his willingness to fight, the youth is giving up his allegiance to the collective values of his group. This is why his gift of weaponry represents a far more significant gesture than most of us can imagine.

In the industrial age, 'respectability' became all-important. Today, high status within one or another social grouping is dependent on a variety of signifiers that can be gathered under the general heading of 'success', usually linked to material prosperity. Today, the false value that imprisons us is the importance we give to being a successful person, by whatever criteria we judge success.

> The world without is my quiver,
> The Non-clinging Self-Illumination within
> Is my sheath of leopard skin,
> My weapon is the sword of Great Wisdom.

> The Two-in-One Path is my rope,
> My thumb-guard is the merit of meditation.

The two-in-one path is that of wisdom and compassion. The path of compassion or skilful means is pursued within the sphere of external activity, among other living beings, in *saṃsāra*. The path of wisdom, on the other hand, is followed, in a sense, in the world within. But there is no real distinction to be made between external and internal, mundane and transcendental, *saṃsāra* and *nirvāṇa*. To follow the two-in-one path is to integrate the outer world and the 'Non-clinging Self-Illumination within', seeing them as one, seeing *saṃsāra* and *nirvāṇa* as perfectly interwoven in a living vision of non-duality. The two-in-one path is the path of the Mahāyāna, which sees the non-duality of form and emptiness, *rūpa* and *śūnyatā*.

> Upon the bow-string of Ultimate Unborn Voidness
> I set steady the notch of Bodhi-Heart;
> I shoot the arrow of the Four Infinities
> At the army of the Five Poisons.

In Mahāyāna and Vajrayana Buddhism, Enlightenment is inseparable from the heartfelt desire to rescue all beings from the sufferings of *saṃsāra*. This is the bodhi-heart, the *bodhicitta*, the will to Enlightenment for the sake of all beings, which is the main spiritual faculty to be cultivated by the Mahāyānist. Withdrawal from the mundane, accompanied by the arising of the *bodhicitta*, produces Enlightenment. The traditional conclusion to any Mahāyāna practice is therefore to transfer any merit accruing to oneself through that practice to benefit all beings. (Of course, in doing so, one makes it possible for the practice to contribute to one's own liberation.)

As for the ultimate unborn voidness, this is the goal of Enlightenment itself. So why is it the bow-string and not the target? Well, as the verse reminds us, the ultimate voidness is unborn. As absolute reality, it is outside time, so it does not exist as a target in time and space. Nor should we forget that an arrow is a lethal weapon, and that one aims an arrow to destroy a target. It is therefore more appropriate that the target should be something we do seek to destroy through our spiritual practice: the 'army of the Five Poisons'.

The 'Four Infinities' of the arrow with which the poisons are to be pierced and brought down are the four meditation practices called the *brahma vihāras*, the 'illimitables', or the 'divine abidings'. As this verse tells us, they are steadied and powered by their connection with ultimate reality through the *bodhicitta*. The *brahma vihāras* are *mettā* or universal friendliness, *karuṇā* or compassion, *muditā* or sympathetic joy, and *upekkhā* or equanimity. The five poisons are usually listed as craving, hatred, pride or conceit, ignorance, and distraction – though sometimes jealousy is substituted for distraction. These are our states of mind most of the time. Greed, resentment, vanity, envy, and shallowness are like an occupying army, attacking our peace and happiness minute by minute, hour by hour, day by day.

Without taking the imagery too literally, it is perhaps noteworthy that while usually each *brahma vihāra* meditation is meant to target one poison in particular, they are here directed collectively at the poisons together. That is, the positive emotions are seen as different aspects of essentially one and the same emotional attitude or direction, just as the poisons are seen as inextricably tangled up in each other.

The song is unequivocally martial in tone and intent. Milarepa is saying, 'Be a warrior by all means, but use your warrior's strength to fight the inner, spiritual battle.' In this way he is trying to transpose the young man's energies, martial as they are – and thus in a sense the tough young man himself – from the worldly plane to the spiritual plane. He wants to make him a spiritual warrior.

A battle is a telling and perennial metaphor for the spiritual life, suggesting an intensity of focus, a sense of something all-important at stake, and the need to make a choice between values that are set in eternal opposition to one another. It is familiar enough in the Christian tradition, of course; one thinks of hymns like 'Onward Christian Soldiers', and Blake's 'Jerusalem':

Bring me my bow of burning gold:
Bring me my arrows of desire:
Bring me my spear: O clouds unfold!
Bring me my chariot of fire.

I will not cease from mental fight,
Nor shall my sword sleep in my hand,
Till we have built Jerusalem...[49]

The tradition of the warrior persists in other ways too. Even today, the aristocratic ideal of the medieval knight or the samurai warrior is a potent one, with its challenges to honour that are not to be refused, and its tests of courage and generosity, loyalty and purity. For all its unequivocal commitment to the principle of causing no harm to living beings, Buddhism also makes use of military metaphors and images to denote the heroic warrior-like spirit that is a vital spiritual quality. Weapons of one kind or another are wielded by bodhisattvas to signify certain transcendental qualities. For example, Mañjughoṣa, the bodhisattva of wisdom, wields in his right hand a sword with which he is said to cut through ignorance.

The military metaphor has its dangers, most obviously in the tendency to turn an inward and spiritual struggle to realize one's highest ideals into a conflict with external forces that are seen to oppose those ideals. However appropriate or otherwise it may be to engage in some kind of external conflict, this should not be confused with the real spiritual struggle, which takes place within. The military analogy also suggests a high price will be paid for failure or defeat, but this does not apply to the spiritual battle. Those who do not commit themselves to the struggle cannot be said to have been defeated, while those who do so are guaranteed to triumph. As Milarepa sings in conclusion,

There is no doubt I shall win the battle;

Another risk associated with the idea of the spiritual warrior is that you become too ascetic, and under the pretext of 'fighting the good fight' force the pace of your practice, allaying your neurotic guilt by punishing yourself. And there is an even greater risk of being too hard on other people, of expressing hatred and ill will under the pretext of encouraging others to take on the heroic ideal. In view of this, it is especially significant that the practices mentioned in this context are those specifically concerned with the cultivation of positive emotion, of kindness towards all that lives, including oneself.

That battles and armies are perennially fascinating and awe-inspiring, even for monks, is illustrated by the presence in the Vinaya, the rules of monastic conduct, of a rule prohibiting *bhikkhus* from 'looking at armies'.[50] As Milarepa says, 'Battles and armies are not for the yogi.' Even today, people can develop quite an unhealthy interest in the progress of war as it unfolds in the news. But the energy of that interest can be harnessed in the service of the very different kind of battle that is the spiritual life.

The combative approach to the spiritual life is of course by no means the only way to describe the Buddhist path. It is not a literal description of the spiritual life but a metaphor, and another metaphor will do just as well, especially if it holds more appeal. Instead of the ideal of the knight-errant, you may just as fruitfully be inspired by the ideal of the gardener, or the healer, say, not destroying the poisons but nurturing positive qualities or alleviating suffering, engaging in a cooperative process rather than a counteractive one. If the warrior is basically a masculine ideal, the complementary ideal is more feminine – receptive and cooperative rather than confrontational. You might even be inspired by a childlike ideal of innocence and openness, like that exemplified by the much-loved Japanese poet, Ryōkan. Or you might prefer the image of the flower, imagining yourself growing in a garden, opening your leaves and blossoming in stillness and silence, just unfolding your petals, sending forth your perfume, and gazing up at the face of the sun. Again, there are well-known Christian references to such models – one thinks of Mary, the 'handmaid of the Lord' and Jesus' tribute to the 'lilies of the field'.

In taking inspiration from these metaphors, you're not thinking in terms of acting like a warrior, or a gardener, or a flower. Your aim is to transpose mundane qualities into spiritual ones, seeking to be a spiritual warrior, a spiritual healer, a spiritual flower, a spiritual handmaid, a spiritual gardener. However effective the healer, however beautiful the flower, however innocent the child, and however nurturing the gardener, such an ideal is a model of the spiritual life, not the spiritual life itself.

By the same token, calling one ideal masculine and another feminine is not to say that as spiritual ideals these have anything to do with how masculine or feminine you are in the ordinary sense. Warriors may almost always be men, but spiritual warriors can be of either sex, and so can spiritual flowers and even spiritual handmaids. As so often in the spiritual life, one has to be very careful not to be literalistic.

We may say that the warrior ideal represents *vīrya* – energy in pursuit of the good – while the flower represents the opposite or complementary spiritual faculty, *samādhi* – meditation and contemplation. As so often in the spiritual life, there is a paradox here. Milarepa speaks to the young man's real interests in order to harness and transform the energy engaged with them, and the effect should be to internalize the young man's combativeness, to turn it against itself, so that he is fighting his own aggression. The effect of the warrior ideal on this young man will thus be to turn him into more of a spiritual flower. The warrior type of person needs to be encouraged to sit still, to be quiet and patient, to be a warrior in meditation; he or she will still be intensely active, but in an entirely different way. Conversely, if you are inspired by the ideal of nurturing or healing or blossoming, you have to be encouraged to internalize these qualities so that they express themselves with the vigour and heroism that real growth requires.

The opposite way of looking at these ideals can also work. If you tend to be slack and sluggish, you might still be able to find inspiration in the warrior ideal, while if you are a restless, aggressive type, you may be able to cultivate a yearning to be more contemplative, to be a spiritual flower. Either way, it is important that we do not simply carry our ordinary habits over into the spiritual life. And for this, the warrior ideal is always needed – at the service of, or in the context of, the ideal of the flower.

6

PLEASING THE GURU

> You Yogi, who are the living Buddha,
> Although many know the Dharma,
> Few can practice it.[51]

Aware of his great good fortune in finding Milarepa and of this tremendous opportunity, the young man is now even keener to place himself under Milarepa's instruction, if the master will only accept him. In the opening lines of his song, the would-be disciple puts his finger on a crucial – if apparently rather elementary – point: that while intellectual understanding is relatively common, actual practice and ultimate realization is very rare. But to dismiss this point as elementary would be to miss it altogether. It is easy to take the point; it is much more difficult to apply it to our own situation.

We tend not to realize how much we identify with what we think we know rather than what we actually know from our own experience. Entranced by theory and perhaps rather alienated from our experience, we find that trying to put spiritual principles into practice has none of the alluring charm of the play of ideas, but that, as the youth quite rightly observes, it is simply hard work. We almost inevitably imagine that if we know something in conceptual terms we really do know it. The amount of knowledge one can amass about Buddhism can become very impressive, without necessarily leaving any impression in terms of practice even at the most elementary level. Even the ability to write books about Buddhism can make a formidable contrast with what is put into daily practice. But the young man values Milarepa's teaching as arising from, he says, 'hard work'.

It is not only that very few people try to put the teachings into practice. The youth says that few people have the *capacity* to practise. The implication seems to be that in view of our knowledge of the clear benefits of practising the Dharma, the fact that we fail to do so must be acknowledged as a kind of disability. It is a disability that can be overcome, but it runs very deep.

> One in hundreds is hard to find
> Who can give proof of his accomplishment.

The young man goes on to say that it is hard to find one among hundreds (presumably hundreds of those who practise the spiritual life) 'who can give proof of his accomplishment'. This calls to mind Sri Krishna's famous observation in the *Bhagavad Gītā* that 'among a thousand people, perhaps only one searches for me; and out of a thousand who search for me, perhaps only one finds me.'[52]

But how is it possible to give 'proof of accomplishment'? There is no way to prove beyond doubt that someone has reached a given level of spiritual attainment. This is one of the themes of the *Diamond Sūtra*: that even if you have the thirty-two major and sixty-eight minor marks of a great man, this does not prove that you are a Buddha.[53] A yogi may be leading a life of great simplicity and self-denial, but someone unsympathetic to what the yogi is trying to do will see only a destitute beggar. This is exactly the view taken by Milarepa's own sister: she is quite scathing on the subject of his status as a yogi. The only evidence she is prepared to recognize is what she can see: temples and numerous disciples, and the financial rewards that come with them. She remarks derisively that Milarepa is so wretched that he hasn't even a blanket with which to cover his nakedness.[54] And even if one is disposed to be rather more impressed by outward signs of spiritual ability than Milarepa's materially-minded sister, one must bear in mind that even his ability to walk on water shows only either that he has supernormal powers or that he can provoke hallucinations. It doesn't prove transcendental insight. Yet the young man shows complete faith in Milarepa, due to his own readiness to follow the spiritual path. Come what may, he knows that Milarepa must be his guru.

The only 'proof' of someone's transcendental attainment is one's own intuitive conviction. Clearly this is what has led the young man to make his decisive commitment to follow Milarepa. There is nothing provisional about his decision, no question of making do with Milarepa until the next guru comes along. From what he says, he isn't wondering whether, if this doesn't work out, he might find a guru who suits him better or who can work bigger miracles.

Flitting from guru to guru is a weakness that is not confined to the West. The closest friend I made in my time in Kalimpong, Dhardo Rimpoche, who was also my teacher, told me that the Tibetans are as prone to it as anyone else. When he arrived in Kalimpong in the late 1940s, as the only incarnate lama in the town he was the object of great respect and devotion. It was Rimpoche this and Rimpoche that, and he received offerings and invitations, and performed ceremonies and blessings for people morning, noon, and night. A few years later another incarnate lama arrived, and almost overnight Dhardo Rimpoche was dropped in favour of the new lama in town. As more and more lamas turned up – and by the time I settled there dozens of lamas had crossed over the mountains to Kalimpong as refugees – the townsfolk became quite dizzy with indecision. They were unable to resist the temptation to sample the latest spiritual sensation, be it a head lama or the chief abbot of a great monastery, or the incarnation of this bodhisattva or that *siddha*. And when they heard that the Dorje Lamo, the one and only female incarnation, was on her way, everyone naturally wanted to be among the first to get her blessing.

Of course, the eminent gurus didn't play along with this cupidity on the part of their disciples. For example, there were three great Nyingma gurus in Kalimpong who, because they were closely connected in terms of their common tradition and knew each other quite well, were the subject of considerable speculation with regard to their comparative status. Eventually, a disciple of all three summoned up the nerve to ask one of them, very politely, to satisfy everyone's curiosity. Was one of them greater than the other two, and if so, which of them was it? The guru thought for a moment, and then he said, 'Well, I'll tell you how things stand. As a matter of fact one of us is much more developed than the others, but as for which one it is, none of you will ever know.'[55]

The type of teaching offered by a guru might not suit one's temperament, and this might be a good reason for seeking out another. A little shopping around might be appropriate at the initial stages of one's spiritual career. But there are people who spend their whole lives drifting from one teacher to another. Why? It often has to do with a half-conscious expectation that the guru can somehow do it all for you. When you have been with a particular guru for a while and nothing much seems to have happened, it is often the guru whom you find wanting rather than your own efforts, and if you find yourself in this position, the sheer novelty of a new guru, with a new set of teachings, new practices, even new jokes, all promising a new beginning and fresh hope, is very appealing. So instead of refreshing your spiritual practice by digging deeper into it, you trade in your stale old guru for an exciting new one.

Milarepa himself, as he says in the opening song of this episode, called off his search for a guru as soon as he heard Marpa's name. After that, his path was one of complete submission to his guru's wishes. Even though Marpa himself led a householder's life, with a wife and family, when he insisted that Milarepa should follow the solitary life of a hermit, Milarepa did not question his decision. This is not to say that Marpa could literally order Milarepa to do anything; that is not how a spiritual relationship works. There can be no desire on the part of any follower of the Dharma to exert power over anyone else. Power has no place in the spiritual community, and that includes the relationship between a Tantric guru and his disciple. But the nature of the guru-disciple relationship is such that a guru's quietest hints or gentlest recommendations have the force of commands for his heart-disciples.

As it happens, Marpa is unlikely to have expressed himself with reticence. It was not his way. By all accounts he was a rather peppery character, and one can't imagine him saying, 'This is just a suggestion, but I think it would be a good idea for you to spend the rest of your life in solitude up a remote mountain.' He would just have barked at Milarepa, 'Off you go!' and Milarepa, being Milarepa, would have obeyed instantly – but not because he was under Marpa's thumb. It is the receptivity of the disciple that gives the force of a command to the guru's suggestions or orders. However loudly Marpa barked at him, Milarepa was free to do as he pleased; his obedience sprang entirely from his supreme receptivity to his guru.

Without this unquestioning attitude, the relationship between a guru and his disciple will not work, because any such relationship is naturally volatile, being based – in a sense – on a conflict of interests. For example, if you obey a guru in order to win his approval, he is more than likely to withhold that approval. You might appear to be doing all sorts of good and virtuous things when in fact you are just looking for recognition from the guru, and when he spots this he will not pat you on the back. After all, it is the ego in us that wants praise from the guru, but the guru's role is to knock the ego on the head – so to speak – not pat it on the back.

So if the guru is doing his job, your grasping after approval will not be satisfied but possibly give way to resentment and disappointment in your teacher. Feeling let down, thinking he doesn't appreciate you, you may become sullen and uncooperative. This is particularly unfortunate. Your relationship with the guru is, after all, more than just ordinary friendship. He embodies your highest aspiration, so if you reject him, you lose your connection with your own guiding ideals. He will of course remain open to you, but you might close off the channel of communication from your side, and even start to find fault with him.

Looking for faults in the teacher or guru can be a way of unconsciously evading one's spiritual responsibility. If one consciously accepts certain principles, one should feel a responsibility to put them into practice. If one then fails to do so, finding fault with the teacher is a convenient way of explaining away one's failure. One might find oneself blaming the teacher or even the whole sangha. To the extent that the spiritual community as a whole represents a sort of collective guru figure in relation to oneself, one may come to see it in an entirely negative light.

There is a broader principle here, which can be applied to the way we see anyone. We may well be aware of other people's behaviour as skilful or unskilful, but we must try not to pass narrow moral judgement on them. Never mind whether the judgement is negative or positive; the principle is that we shouldn't judge people simply in terms of virtues and faults.

So how should we see other people? We can't help seeing them in some way or another, and we will certainly see both their faults and their virtues. But we shouldn't see them exclusively in those terms; we shouldn't reduce them to good or bad or a combination of the two. The best way to see them is as living, growing, developing human beings. If we are to do justice to others, we must always consider what they do in the context of the person doing it; their deeds shouldn't be seen in isolation from the overall growth and development of the individual. In short, we should always try to see the person, not what he or she does.

The more carefully you try to look at someone, the more difficult it seems to be to know and judge them. Naturally their actions do express something of their character. But as well as understanding the person in the light of their actions, you have to understand their actions in the light of the person. The same goes for what they say: to understand someone's words fully, you have to relate them back to the person speaking them. Suppose someone repeats to you something that a friend of yours has said, or describes something your friend has done, without knowing your friend very well. As you know your friend better than they do, you will probably understand what they said or did rather better than them, and you may be able to explain that there has been a misunderstanding. Sometimes the person behind the action or words is bigger than the actions or the words, and sometimes of course he or she is smaller. But you cannot arrive at any real knowledge of a person simply through knowing what they have done or said, without reference to who they are as a whole.

Tibetans, and Tantric practitioners generally, make a great deal of the point that the disciple cannot really understand the actions of the guru. While this can be made the basis of a lot of humbug and even exploitation, in principle it is true. You cannot fully understand the words or the actions of someone more developed than yourself any more than a dog can fully understand the words or actions of its master. If this analogy seems brutal, it might help to reflect that while a dog can never become a human being, as a disciple you can equal, and surpass, the spiritual attainments of your guru – if you want to. Once we start passing moral judgement on people, our tendency is to see faults rather than virtues; at least, it is the faults that seem to stand out. But there is a particular danger in passing judgement on the character of our teacher, as we will then lose faith in him and his advice, and we will no longer be able to commit ourselves wholeheartedly to the ideals to which he has introduced us. Indeed, to the extent that we are out of communication with him, we are cutting ourselves off from our inspiration and undermining our practice.

Your teachings spring from much hard work,
And so I dare not ask without paying first....
I now offer you this knife and belt.
Later, I will ask you for the Teachings.

Milarepa had to perform all sorts of tasks for Marpa before he was given Marpa's 'compassionate blessing' and the teachings he needed. Marpa himself had to pay in gold for the teachings that he gathered in India. But Milarepa is a different sort of guru. He will not accept such offerings. So what can the young man do to get the teachings?

Traditionally the Dharma cannot be bought. Any material support received is not linked to the teaching given, because to make such a link suggests some kind of equivalence in value between the teaching and whatever mundane wealth is offered in return for it, which is crucially to misrepresent the nature of the Dharma. At the same time, one has to be prepared to make an offering of one's material wealth as a token of one's commitment to spiritual values above mundane ones. The young man certainly has a robust understanding of this attitude. When he says, 'I dare not ask without paying first,' he means he would be ashamed to do so. But he is not asking for the teachings there and then; he is now prepared to leave a decent interval between the offering and the request.

It is a question not of bargaining for the Dharma, but of putting one's money where one's mouth is. For money is what we are talking about here. Money is the easiest thing to give – it is specifically designed for ease of disbursement. All you have to do is put your hand in your pocket and take the stuff out, or sign a cheque and hand it over. Yet it is sometimes money that we find it most difficult to give. The teachings we want from the guru are the fruit of perhaps decades of determined application to meditation, of hardship and privation – and we want it all for nothing. Marpa said as much to Milarepa himself. According to *The Life of Milarepa*, when Milarepa first asked for the teachings, Marpa replied, 'Is it to reward your many crimes that I went to India at the risk of my life? You say you want these teachings which are the living breath of the dakinis and for which, disdaining riches, I offered gold without measure. I hope you are only joking! Anyone else would kill you for that!'[56]

The difficulty we experience in parting with our money is a symbolic recognition of the much greater difficulty the teacher has experienced in the course of his own mastery of the teachings. Giving as generously as you can is thus what makes a meeting between teacher and disciple possible. The meeting is based on a mutual recognition of what is truly important: that the worldly value of the offering is as nothing when compared to the value of the teaching.

The Tantra therefore traditionally insists on a significant financial outlay to signify the full commitment of your energies and resources. Originally the disciple was meant to give his entire worldly wealth. At the time of Tantric initiation you brought along all your property – usually made portable in the form of a bag of gold – and you offered it all to the guru. Later this was changed, and you were asked instead to make a substantial cash payment, however much you could manage. If you think about it, this is not necessarily a watering down of the principle, because it still exposes any lack of commitment on your part. When you are told you can give what you like, the struggle going on in your mind may be all too apparent. 'Shall I give a hundred or might I get away with fifty? Maybe I should give sixty to be on the safe side.' Someone in this position might find they were less concerned about how much they could give for the teaching than about how little they could get it for, or that they were tempted to hedge their bets in case the teachings proved not to transform their life as advertised. If you are betrayed by a loss of nerve, an unspoken admission that you are going to allow your spiritual life to be governed by mundane considerations, this is a sure sign of a lack of spiritual receptivity.

There is often a degree of misunderstanding with regard to money and the spiritual life. People think that if you are a holy person you shouldn't be concerned with anything as grubby as money; the whole subject of cash is regarded in spiritual circles as rather indecent. But money is not sordid; it's just that we tend to become sordid where money is involved. We associate money with the mean and grasping attitude that it can tend to arouse in us, rather than seeing it as a way of expressing generosity and open-handedness.

A more significant misunderstanding in this context is the idea that teachings of this nature can be given external form and placed at our disposal in the way that information can be gained from a book or a seminar, a lecture or a conversation. A guru's teaching is not a commodity.

You can't acquire it from books or special mantras. It is a meeting of minds, a communication in the sense of a mutual resonance between individuals, and it can take place only when both people are completely open and unguarded, and have no expectations in terms of the content of the communication. Even if all the communication seems to be flowing one way, it is more than that one-way flow. It is not like a file being downloaded to one computer from another. It is always an exchange.

The teacher is by definition open to the disciple. His wisdom is compassionate in nature, and he is simply waiting for an opportunity to give it. But he can do so only if the disciple is receptive. Given that the disciple is – again by definition – more restricted in his or her view of reality and of what the teaching means, the teacher must sometimes simply hold back. To use a traditional metaphor, if your pot is upside down, the guru cannot pour anything into it.

If you are expecting the teacher to give to you, you must be willing to be generous yourself. It is only when the generosity of the teacher meets that of the disciple that communication can really happen. The willingness to give is more than just a sign of receptivity. It *is* receptivity. When you give something valuable, you give up your attachment to it and show your confidence in the teacher. The fact that you get the teaching once you've paid up does not mean that you've paid *for* it. The payment is the manifestation of the openness you need if you are to receive the teaching. The willingness to give everything shows that you are fearless, and that you have complete faith in the teacher. It is also a discarding of old ideas about what is important and what is not.

Of course, it is better to think in terms of paying for the Dharma than not to give at all. A misunderstanding may be cleared up in the course of time, but if you never start giving up your attachments, you will never start receiving the Dharma. Giving is a spiritual practice in itself, and that practice is all the guru wants to see, whether or not they are the personal recipient of your generosity. Giving is a habit to be cultivated. If you are wealthy, it may be easier to make the gesture of a big public donation than to make a habit of being generous on a day-to-day basis, and you may have to work towards that kind of ongoing generosity slowly. But if you have only two coins and you give both of them, you really are giving up everything, although no one is likely to be very impressed. The quiet generosity of those who possess almost nothing is a treasure in itself.

This reminds me of an occasion during my time in Kalimpong. It was in 1956, when I was invited by the Indian government as one of fifty-seven 'distinguished Buddhists from border areas' to visit Delhi for the 2,500th Buddha *Jayanti* (birthday) celebrations. In the course of our travels we came to Benares, where, in the company of a Tibetan friend, I visited an old Tibetan lama who was living there in order to learn Sanskrit. Apparently the Dalai Lama had asked him to teach, but he had refused. Although he was about fifty, which is old for a Tibetan, he said that he had too much still to learn, and that he had to complete his studies first.

We found him in a small bare room at the top of a Hindu ashram, seated on the floor behind a tin trunk which he was using as a makeshift desk. He was very happy to meet us, and we talked for about an hour and a half. As we rose to go, he said, 'Wait, I must give you something.' He looked around the room – which didn't take long because there was nothing in it – seeming almost desperate to find something that would serve as a gift. Suddenly his face cleared. He took his *mālā*, the string of beads on which the recitation of mantras is counted, broke the cord, and gave me one of the beads. 'Please take this,' he said. 'It is all I have, but I must have said many millions of mantras with it over the years.' This gift, from this poor and humble monk, was worthless in material terms, but in spiritual terms it was immensely valuable. Through this eloquent reminder of his years of practice, he was offering the Dharma, which is the best gift anyone can give or receive.[57]

Returning to Milarepa, he probably doesn't even have a *mālā*. But he does have the Dharma, and consequently he rejects any implication that he has any need or desire for anything that can be bought or sold, given or taken away. But implicit in the young man's choice of gifts, and his manner of giving them, there is still a sense of worldly exchange, an assumption that the treasure of Milarepa's attainment and instruction has its worldly price. As each gift is offered, Milarepa counters it with a fresh restatement of his attainment, which is beyond valuation. The very basis of that attainment is, after all, the letting go of worldly objects.

MILAREPA'S SONG OF THE CLAY POT AND THE UNHIRED TEACHER

Milarepa tells the young man that he cannot yet give him the teachings, and explains why.

Listen to me, ingenuous young man!
From my hut's roof in the snow mountain
Flows the quintessence of milk and nectar.
Though it is not made of gold or jewels,
I would not pour it into earthenware.

There is a rich confusion of images here. The 'quintessence of milk and nectar' refers to the dissolving of the yogi's subtle energies into the bliss of the Enlightened mind. It also recalls meditation practices in which one imagines a bright, nourishing stream of nectar pouring down on one's head from a visualized archetypal figure above. Milarepa poetically conflates this image with the melting snow dripping from the roof of his hut. But as he develops the image and envisages pouring the milk and nectar, it comes to refer to the teaching distilled from his meditation. Although he cannot claim that his own teaching is very precious – 'it is not made of gold or jewels' – it is the most precious thing he has to offer, and he wants to be very careful where he pours it. Not only must the vessel be receptive – the pot must be the right way up – but it cannot be made of just any old earthenware. In other words, our practice is not to fill ourselves with profound and precious teachings but to make ourselves fit to receive them, to become a strong, unbreakable vessel, even a diamond vessel.

Milarepa next points to the cotton belt around his waist – which is probably the meditation band he wears round his neck and knees to keep his body upright during his hours and days of meditation practice.

Around this waist of mine, the poor man of strong will,
Is tied a cotton belt of fanatic devotion!
The absence of pretence and hypocrisy
Is the pattern of my belt.

In symbolizing 'fanatic devotion' (or perhaps 'intense' would be a better translation, for nothing that is truly Buddhist can really be described as fanatic), the belt needs no embellishments. Milarepa's devotion does not draw attention to itself. His practice is held together by simplicity of faith and direct and diligent honesty of purpose. The image is reminiscent of the Biblical phrase 'gird up thy loins' – that is, hitch up your robe ready for work. His devotion is a practical and realistic response to the true nature of things.

Bright wisdom is my knife,
Its sheath, the confidence of the Three Measurements.

As is customary, wisdom is likened to a blade, with its associations of cutting, penetrating, and reflecting. Intellectual understanding, by contrast, is represented here by the image of the sheath. Milarepa's sheath is his confidence in his practice, based on the Three Measurements, which Chang suggests refers to the yogi's judgement of how far his experience matches his understanding of the scriptures, and whether it brings him closer to the bodhisattva ideal and deepens his insight. His wisdom, however penetrating, is thus always put in the context of his understanding of the scriptures. Like a sheath, his understanding protects his wisdom.

TAKING PAYMENT FOR TEACHINGS

Lest goddesses punish me,
I have never asked for wealth or money
When teaching in the past,
Nor shall I do so now.
Dear boy, you may go home;
I do not want your gifts.

Milarepa is not questioning the importance for the disciple of making offerings before the teachings can be received, but he is mindful of the danger for the teacher of losing sight of the subtlety of the principle involved and demanding cash for teachings. It is a little like the communist principle: 'To each according to his need; from each according to his ability.' There is no cash nexus, no bargain struck. Rather than, 'I give you this, *therefore* you give me that,' the principle is, 'I will try to give you what I can, with no relation to anything you may or may not give to me.' If the guru is a real guru, he will give what he can in any case.

Milarepa is beyond being able to sell his teachings; there is no literal danger of being punished by the 'goddesses' – by which he presumably means the *ḍākinīs* representing his inspiration – because he is not separate from them. They are not external deities looking on in judgement. But he is saying that his ability to communicate the teachings is linked to his inability to sell them. The goddesses – the *ḍākinīs* and inspirational muses – are there to be served, not used, and if you try to exploit them for your own ends, they will desert you.

The same principle applies to the powers of inspiration to which people like artists, psychics, and mystics have at least intermittent access. If those powers are not honoured, they can indeed be lost. A creative artist who starts using his or her talent to produce work simply to make money is likely to find that the springs of inspiration will eventually dry up. This certainly happened to fashionable society painters like the nineteenth-century English prodigy, John Millais, who began his career as an artist with real promise and went on to turn out popular sentimental works like *Bubbles*. Likewise, spiritual teachers who are bursting with positive creative energy when they set up their own organization or ashram can find that, if they follow the lure of wealth and celebrity when they start becoming successful, their gift leaves them. Not everyone succumbs to such pressures, of course; for example, some lamas and gurus who could have expected to live out their lives quietly in Tibet have evidently adjusted to the pressures of western culture and withstood its temptations rather better than others.

Unfortunately, once someone finds they can heal people or teach people to meditate, and that they can get paid to do so, the vocation can easily turn into a profession, becoming *essentially* a money-making enterprise rather than being generated by inspiration. You might start off idealistically, but the idealism can fade away quickly if you get caught up in maximizing profits. Whether it is writing or painting, or practising medicine or alternative therapies, or even going into Buddhism and meditation, these days almost the first consideration seems to be how you are to get a rewarding livelihood out of whatever you are inspired to do. But if you embark on yoga classes or therapy simply in order to become a yoga teacher or a therapist, or if you sit down to write a 'best-selling novel', you are never going to feel the breath of the *ḍākinīs* on the back of your neck as you work.

The essence of spiritual inspiration is that it is free and spontaneous. Spiritual attainments should never be used, even for a good purpose. Even directing one's creativity towards some purely unselfish aim is to abuse it. Creativity will find its own uses, its own expression. It has its own momentum, and to try to harness it to a practical purpose is to deny its very nature. We see it as a good thing to try to put everything to good use, however trivial that use may be, and we feel uneasy if we can't put our finger on what something is *for*. But that uneasiness comes down to not knowing what we ourselves are for.

We are uneasy with the thought that we are not here *for* anything. But the truth of the matter is that we are the glorious end-product of millions of years of evolution, and we need find no further justification for ourselves. One of the less appealing legacies of Christianity is its encouragement of an unnecessarily abject view of ourselves. Charles Wesley, one of the founders of Methodism, liked to remind his congregations that they were mere grovelling worms, but the truth is that, splendid though worms are in their own way, we can safely claim to have left that species behind us by a comfortable margin. Indeed, without being unduly immodest, we can call ourselves the end-product, even the crown, of the evolutionary process. Our human existence is much more significant than we usually like to think. We can have no higher purpose than being ourselves. The only step worth taking from where we find ourselves as human beings is to evolve into Buddhas. We are not here to be useful. We don't have to justify our human status by engaging in some useful occupation. Of course there is nothing wrong with useful occupation, but we should beware of any idea that our purpose on this earth is to fill up our time with useful activities.

In this context, consider the traditional life of the Buddhist monk. Though he is supported by the laity, there is no pressure on him to make himself useful. The fact that he is a monk is quite enough. All that is expected of him is that he should wear his robe correctly, keep his head shaved, eat his food at the proper time, and that sort of thing. He doesn't even have to meditate. Just living the harmless life of a monk is considered an achievement in itself. This attitude may encourage laziness, and it must be admitted that some monks don't really deserve the respect and support they receive. But the danger is more than offset by the important message that such a radical attitude communicates, which is that the spiritual life is not to be expected to produce material results. In fact, the majority of monks in the East do take up useful occupations like teaching or caring for the sick, but ideally they do this because they are inspired to do it. It is a spontaneous activity, an expression of what they are.

Clergy in the West are impressively active and outgoing by comparison, but this seems to be at the cost of surrendering this principle. Out of concern to justify their existence in terms that the mundane world can appreciate – by engaging in social and charity work, like running youth clubs for teenagers and bingo for pensioners – they may end up neglecting their central function, so that people start to wonder what they are really for, beyond providing a kind of social service.

One can say perhaps that the job of religious full-timers is to demonstrate that the most useful thing you can do is to be. The spiritual life is an end in itself and doesn't have to be justified in worldly terms. In the work and profit-driven culture of the West, we should do more than pay lip service to this ideal; we should do what we can to support at least a few people simply to live a Buddhist life, without any expectation that they should earn their keep in some way, whether by teaching or writing or study or even by working especially hard at their meditation. The only way to experience the value of doing this is to do it. You have actually to experience paying for someone to do nothing in particular. Or, more demanding still, you have to experience being paid to do nothing in particular. Being supported in this way, your contribution then is simply to be happy in whatever you choose to do or not do. You might do things like giving lectures, meditating, or writing; you might do nothing much at all. You might simply be around for people to talk to – and even then your 'job' is to be happy whether anyone talks to you or not.

To do this would be to introduce into our lives a little of the fragrance, the essence, of Sukhāvatī, the Pure Land beloved of Buddhist mythology. You don't have to work there, because clothes and food appear spontaneously; all you need do is sit on a lotus and listen to the Dharma. Ideally, everything we do should have something of this spirit about it. If we work, it should be because we want to, because it makes us happy. Of course, we may sometimes be aware of the spiritual need to push ourselves through barriers of laziness or diffidence. But we should not be working just to fulfil an obligation to put in so many hours in return for pay. Too many people work on the basis of a deep-seated feeling of guilt and obligation, and people also exploit and manipulate others on the same basis.

One of the functions of a Buddhist organization should therefore be to provide material support without strings attached for those who are able to commit themselves fully to the spiritual life. It may as yet be difficult to achieve this on a large scale in the West, but one or two models of that way of going about things would at least remind us of that ideal. It would remind us that it is the human being that matters, the human being that is the whole purpose of any truly spiritual movement. Any Buddhist movement runs the risk of allowing its aspirations to sink to the level of purely organizational goals, and once those take hold, it is a small step to start to regard the human beings that make up that movement as little more than the means of realizing those organizational ends. We need always to remind ourselves of our real aim, however inconvenient and impractical it may be to do so. If a human being is a means to anything, it is to his or her development as an individual, and if an individual is a means to anything, it is to Buddhahood.

Imagine the 'job' of doing nothing in particular, not out of laziness but as a practice of embodying the sheer enormity of a reality that exceeds any mundane notion of occupation or utility. Paradoxically, it would be quite challenging. People do not always take cheerfully to being left to their own devices. The devil, as they say, finds work for idle hands to do, and at the very least you're likely to get bored and restless and start to seek distraction. But imagine having someone around who has nothing to rush off and do, who is not tired or busy, who is cheerful, peaceful, yet full of energy, and available to respond to the call of the *ḍākinīs* in whatever form it might take. Such a 'duty' could be taken up successfully only by someone who was spiritually committed.

After all, how would you employ a Buddha? Does he have to justify his Buddhahood? No. The mere fact that he is a Buddha is enough. By the same token, we can cultivate the vision of Buddhahood by resisting the impulse to make a commodity of ourselves. Our highest aspiration should be to take freely and give freely, acting spontaneously in everything we do, rather than out of a sense of obligation or even responsibility. As far as we can, we should abjure all coercive attempts to make us justify our existence by paying our way and working for our keep.

7

LISTENING FOR THE TEACHINGS

MILAREPA'S SONG OF THE YOGI'S TEMPLE

The young man's offers now become extravagant, even desperate. He proposes building Milarepa a temple, although he introduces the proposal with an almost self-defeating air.

> You are a real yogi, an ascetic worker,
> Disgusted with mundane things
> And indifferent to the world....
> Although one thing to you is as another,
> A permanent home may help your inspiration.[58]

The young man is not planning to skimp on materials, scale, or design features, and he goes on to conjure up a splendid vision of tall pillars, a large floor decorated with a mandala, a well-adorned pagoda, and a shrine. No doubt most spiritual practitioners would be only too glad to accept free use of a place in which to practise undisturbed. Even the Buddha, while advocating a wandering life for his disciples, accepted offers of land and shelter during the rainy season.

The all-important proviso is that gifts should come with no strings attached. Although truly to give means renouncing all rights in respect to what you have given, someone who gives often has a barely conscious expectation that they are going to get something, however intangible, in return. If you find yourself in the position of being presented with a gift, especially a substantial one, you need to do what you can to make sure that the person who wants to give it is capable of doing so freely, so that there will be no subsequent regrets, resentment, or recriminations. If you get any sense that they have made their offer in a burst of enthusiasm that they are going to regret, you should turn it down.

But Milarepa turns this offer down for other reasons. Having chosen a wandering lifestyle, he is determined to avoid even the slightest occasion for the worldly attachment that is likely to accompany any kind of settled situation. His response to the suggestion that a permanent home might be inspiring is scathing.

> My confused young lad!
> Do you not know that this world is transient and unreal?
> When you come before the King of the Dead
> Your rich man's money is of no avail.
> There your wealth can never buy you off;
> There you will find no place to swing a strong man's sword,
> No place to dance or strut about the stage.
> Your flesh will be as dust....
> The temple wherein I dwell is the inner unborn Mind;

Whatever the boy says to try to convince Milarepa that a temple would be useful and convenient, and would promote his spiritual values, from Milarepa's point of view it would be nothing but a compromise and a snare. The very expression 'a permanent home may help your inspiration' gives the game away. To take possession of property in perpetuity, to use a legal phrase, suggests that one is going to get from that property something more than the temporary accommodation that in reality is all we can expect from the world, however much money we have. How can Milarepa take possession of a temple intended to proclaim values that are diametrically opposed to materialism and possessiveness? How can he accept a permanent home in an impermanent universe?

Milarepa reverses the symbolic process. A temple is designed to symbolize in concrete terms various as yet unrealized spiritual ideals, but Milarepa has already realized those ideals and has no need to refer to them symbolically, through external forms. Instead, he refers to the temple of his direct spiritual experience, which is more solid and real than stone and wood.

> I erect the pillars of the Real
> On the foundation of immutability....
> On the ground of the Dhyānic Warmth
> I draw a Mandal of Clear Observation.

The offering of the mandala is one of the foundation yogas of the Tantra. In this practice, the mandala is visualized as a symbolic representation of the whole universe as it is described in traditional Buddhist cosmology. In offering a mandala, you are symbolically offering the whole world, the universe itself – everything mundane. You are saying in effect that you have recognized the true value of the teaching. It is so precious to you that in order to receive it you are willing to give everything you have or could possibly have. When you offer the mandala, your happiness and gratitude for what you have received expresses itself in your desire to offer everything you have, everything you experience, everything you could ever experience, to the Buddhas and bodhisattvas. Nobody could ever make such an offering literally, of course, but one can do it symbolically, and it is the motivation which is the most important thing. Finally, in case you are carried away by any feelings of elation or inflation, you reflect that all these offerings are ultimately empty. You cannot even hold on to whatever you may hope to gain from your actions.[59]

As well as being a symbolic offering of the world as it seems to us to be, a mandala can also symbolize a vision of the world, a pattern of reality that lies beyond what is apparent in everyday life and thought. One can meditate on a mandala as a visualized circle of forms, with a particular Buddha at the centre and other Buddhas or bodhisattvas arranged around the central form. This kind of mandala is the archetypal image of concentration, of energies gathering around a central point.

Milarepa's 'Mandal of Clear Observation' – his insight – is inseparable from the 'ground of the Dhyānic Warmth' upon which it is inscribed. What this means is that he is not just concentrating on the mandala as an object of meditation. Having harmonized his cruder elemental or base nature, he has absorbed within himself all the qualities which the Buddhas and bodhisattvas of the mandala embody and symbolize. It is as though, in his realization of non-duality, he *is* the mandala, and all the Buddhas within it, and all the *ḍākinīs* and goddesses who come to make offerings to it. They are all aspects of his Enlightened experience. This mandala or sacred space is not an inner realm as opposed to an outer or objective realm. Milarepa finds a sacred mandala in the world around him wherever he is, and sees whatever visions come to him as the activity of his own mind. Consequently, he has no fear of error or going astray, and no need of any kind of sacred space, let alone a temple.

MILAREPA'S SONG OF THE YOGI'S MATE

Throwing caution to the wind, the young man now offers Milarepa his sister's hand in marriage. Again, he is aware that Milarepa is hardly likely to look favourably on this idea, and initially he offers her services as a kind of nursemaid before describing her more seductive attractions with his usual hyperbole.

> She is heiress to a royal tradition.
> Do not mistakenly regard her as of common stock;
> She is the heart-taker among the crowds,
> Radiant as a rainbow, she is more beautiful than angels.

Milarepa does not mince his words.

> Do not talk like a fool. I have already renounced family ties. I am
> not interested in an ego-clinging woman. The so-called faith of the
> common people is most unstable and liable to change. I am an old
> beggar with no family and no relatives. People will laugh at you,
> if you give her to me. Afterwards, you will regret what you have
> done. I have no desire to become your brother-in-law.

In turning down the boy's offer, we can take it that Milarepa is not concerned with any spiritual danger to himself that might arise from taking a consort. However, he is happy with the results of having renounced family ties, and he knows that other people, even those who support and admire him, do not have the strength of faith to see a change of lifestyle as only that. If he was to take a wife, they would lose whatever faith they had in the Dharma and their respect for its practitioners, and he would become in their eyes simply an old beggar. Besides, he is not at all interested in making wealthy connections by joining the boy's family, and with just a little mockery he addresses his devotee as 'young lord'. He remarks mildly on the lust and attachment that women generally arouse in men – which, as it happens, is the effect that the 'young lord' has just been attempting to produce upon Milarepa himself – before going on.

> A qualified Illumination-Woman is indeed most rare.
> To have angelic company on the Bodhi-Path
> Is a wonder and a marvel;
> Yet you a little have exaggerated.
> This is why the Mudrā Practice is so very hard.

Milarepa doesn't rule out the possibility of finding a genuine spiritual consort, but such 'angelic company' is a marvel precisely because it is so rare. The boy's use of the conventional exaggerations of romantic language to describe his sister simply shows how very hard it is to practise the Tantra with a consort; one so easily becomes intoxicated.

Milarepa's song continues in the usual way to extol the joys of the spiritual life in terms of the various characteristics of the offering that have been extolled by the young man. This particular offering gives him the opportunity to present his relationship with the nature of reality in fervent, even passionate terms. There is certainly no nihilism in his evocation of *śūnyatā*. *Śūnyatā* is realized on the basis of a full engagement of the emotions, and its realization expresses itself in kindness. Conversely, if you do not love the Dharma passionately, the life of sexual renunciation or *brahmacarya* will be a real struggle. Indeed, it is a struggle that you will lose, one way or another, if you do not find the means to arouse strong feelings within your practice.

> My wonder woman is the lust-free Śūnyatā.
> There is compassion on her face,
> And kindness in her smile....
>
> She is such a charming witch –
> The realization of Truth is her origin!
> This is my wife, the yogi's mate.

The youth seems to imagine that Milarepa is in need of companionship. But in fact, coursing in non-dual two-in-one-ness, Milarepa experiences no delusive separation between 'self' in here and 'world' out there. In this blissful union of unreal opposites, everything is available to him. It is the delusive view that one is separate from others that lies at the root of fear and loneliness and the yearning for companions.

PLEASURE ON THE PATH OF RENUNCIATION

In Buddhism, the abandonment of worldly attachment is regarded as a prerequisite for spiritual development, and for this reason there are many practices designed to help us break out of the ways in which we are attached to objects of the senses. The recollection of the loathsomeness of food, for example, is meant to help us overcome our attachment to the pleasures of eating. In similar fashion, the recollection of the impurity of the thirty-two bodily substances – hair, fat, phlegm, pus, and all the rest of it – is supposed to help us to overcome sexual craving. And the recollection of death helps us to see that all the things we set our hearts on will eventually cease to be.

These examples of the Buddha's teaching seem to suggest that the path to Enlightenment is a process of cutting ourselves off from the mundane, leaving the world behind, disengaging from the impure. The sober recollection of the unpleasant qualities of worldly things is a traditional means of focusing the mind on that which is beyond the world. It is an approach to practice that is to be found throughout the Pāli canon, and it is said to appeal to a particular kind of Buddhist practitioner: the 'doctrine follower', the disciple whose immediate response to Buddhism is predominantly intellectual rather than emotional. Rather than being encouraged by the thought of attaining the unmitigated bliss of the Unconditioned, the doctrine follower is spurred on by the knowledge that all objects of the senses are inherently impermanent and must be given up at death. This type of practitioner tends to see the goal of his or her practice as attaining freedom from the disappointments and hardships of conditioned existence and the sufferings of repeated rebirths. Milarepa himself was famously driven in his practice by the fear of future suffering. Having committed so many evil deeds, there was only one possible option open to him: if he didn't gain Enlightenment in this lifetime, he would go straight to hell when he died. His situation was so urgent that only the most intense spiritual practice would be of any use to him.

The danger of that motivation for those of lesser spiritual capacity than Milarepa is that the spiritual life becomes associated only with fear and revulsion. While such a motivation may provide a necessary spur to practice, in the longer term it will be counter-productive without a correspondingly powerful faith in the positive outcome of that practice. In contradistinction to the doctrine follower, therefore, we find the 'faith follower'. Rather than recoiling from the evils of the world, the faith follower feels drawn to the joy and beauty of Enlightenment. Such a person does not feel inspired by the thought of their precarious and unhappy lot in this world, and it would be useless to talk to them about the unpleasantness of conditioned existence. They need to hear about the positive qualities of the Unconditioned.

Milarepa lives not just an ascetic life but a life dedicated to joy. He is as much a faith follower as a doctrine follower, seeing that the spiritual life is rewarding in its own right, and that Nirvāṇa is as attractive and fascinating as *saṃsāra* is unpleasant and disappointing. We can be positively drawn even to the ineffable emptiness of *śūnyatā*. And after all, there is pleasure in conditioned existence alongside the pain, and not all of that pleasure ties us to the wheel of repeated rebirth. As well as *kāma-chanda*, desire for worldly pleasures, we also experience *dharma-chanda*, the desire for the pleasures of the Buddhist path.

Human beings are ruled to a great extent by pleasure, and we can't function well without it; it has a tonic effect that is important for our overall health. If you haven't enjoyed anything for a long time, if you haven't experienced some thoroughgoing happiness and delight recently, you will tend to feel listless and drained of energy. So if you give up the 'pleasurable things' of this life, you will have to replace them somehow. If you don't replace them with pleasures that will draw you towards a higher purpose, your energy will get stuck and may even force its way out in disagreeable ways. Unless you enjoy what you're doing, you can't do it in a very positive spirit for long.

At the same time, if we are eventually to appreciate the limitless pleasure of Nirvāṇa, we have to develop our sensitivity and discernment by cultivating a more refined enjoyment of the objects of the senses, crude as these may be when compared to the bliss of the transcendental. To begin with, we need to bring our higher aspirations to bear upon our habitual sources of pleasure, and see where they can be refined. Innocent and harmless pleasures like those of nature, music, art, and even food and drink enjoyed in good company are to be relished.

It is usually in childhood that our capacity for delight in simple pleasures of our own making is most evident. As we get older it seems to fade away, and we find we are unable to enjoy things in the way a child does. We no longer play or absorb ourselves unselfconsciously in some innocent activity, and what we call our pleasures become dull routines, almost a matter of duty rather than spontaneous enjoyment. Of course, children also get upset very easily, and experience unhappiness and even misery to a degree that adults usually manage to avoid. We should aim to experience the spontaneity and capacity for happiness of a child while bringing an adult's perspective to setbacks and small catastrophes.

When it comes to Dharma practice, it is important to take delight in our study, our meditation, our practice of ethics, and, like Milarepa in the tiger's cave, even our renunciation and the difficulties we encounter. The key to this is practice, which means a gradual but steady and determined shifting of perspective in the way we live, not just passively accepting whatever happens to drift into our lives but engaging with life more actively. We need to take responsibility for our enjoyment, not just relying on external supports but generating well-being from our own concentrated attention, experienced through the practice of meditation. We can also learn to share our pleasures, and to put them into the perspective of a hierarchy of values.

The important thing is to learn to find pleasure in a way that is in harmony with your higher aspirations or ideals. Otherwise, like everyone else, you are going to be caught up in what passes for pleasure in the ordinary world – in other words, an endless cycle of superficial pleasures and nagging frustrations, petty likes and dislikes, habitual and unconsidered preferences. If Buddhahood is the state of non-duality at the highest level, attachment to worldly pleasures is the complete opposite: a product of the reactive or dualistic mind at the lowest level which constantly reinforces our need to define ourselves according to our likes and dislikes. The quickest and easiest way to gain Buddhahood in one lifetime is thus not to make much of your likes and dislikes and thereby to free yourself from attachment to them. Conversely, the easiest way to block your progress towards Buddhahood is to be picky: 'I like this but I don't like that. I'll do this but I won't do that. I'll have coffee but I won't have tea.'

Having likes and dislikes is not the problem. The problem is insisting on them, making them absolute rules that are not to be transgressed. It is this that strengthens the dualistic mind. There is nothing wrong with preferring coffee, but if it upsets you to be given tea instead, and particularly if you feel that you have to make a fuss about it, then clearly you are tightening the bonds of duality around your mind. Our most obvious likes and dislikes are connected with food and drink and they are usually left over from childhood. It is fair enough for a child – a developing individual trying to establish a healthy, separate ego – to insist on personal preferences, but as we mature we should ideally outgrow all this, though unfortunately we tend not to. Our daily lives become enmeshed in a constant succession of petty likes and dislikes which make up a kind of network of reactivity, and this fixes our sense of ourselves and grows stronger every time we allow our preferences to dictate our state of mind.

But the creative mind slices through this neat web of personal predilections and antipathies. Recognizing that pleasures are inherently impermanent, it responds accordingly, never attaching so much importance to likes and dislikes that it is thrown into a state of vexation when they are disregarded. As Śāntideva says in the *Bodhicaryāvatāra*, 'What essence has remained mine from things I once enjoyed, now perished, for which my infatuation led me to ignore the advice of my teachers?'[60] Seen in this light, the objects we crave are illusory, and so are the subjective bodily senses that perceive them.

Of course, preferences and tastes are not all equally subjective. Some are matters of principle – not drinking alcohol or eating meat, for example – though if these really are about principle, your state of mind will not be unduly affected when they are not catered for. Aesthetic likes and dislikes may also have a degree of objectivity, although a discerning taste is not stuck in fixed preferences but is capable of changing and responding to new experiences. The aesthetic criterion also applies to one's tastes in food and drink; some people's palates are clearly more cultivated than others.

With both artistic taste and culinary taste, liking or disliking is different from aesthetic discernment, the one being subjective while the other is a response to objective degrees of value. Unfortunately, most of us proceed most of the time on the basis of purely subjective likes and dislikes, not attempting any more objective evaluation of our tastes, and this is inimical to the development of the creative mind and the spiritual life generally. We do so, moreover, with the support of a commonly held but mistaken view that denies the objective component of taste and holds that it is always a purely personal matter. According to this view, one person's taste in music, say, is no better than anyone else's; it's just different.

To continue with this example, it is true that any assessment of music's spiritual quality is subjective in the sense that it is related to a particular kind of sensitivity. But music is not just a series of pleasant – or unpleasant – sensations; it also has a mental or emotional and spiritual content. In my view there is an objective hierarchy of degrees of aesthetic development, and therefore of spiritual sensitivity. This is not to advocate the enforced appreciation of high art at the expense of other forms of culture or to demand uncomprehending worship of the creative icons of the European past. The principle of a hierarchy of value is more important than any specific judgement. It's a question of the degree of development in terms of consciousness, creativity, awareness, responsibility, and all the other qualities that make up human individuality, that a work of art communicates. The better the art, the more fully it communicates these qualities.

From a spiritual point of view, the important thing to acknowledge is not that one person's taste in the arts is better than that of someone else, but that some human beings really are better than others in certain respects. The terms of reference vary greatly. Some individuals are better than others in terms of physical attainment, others excel in terms of mental skills; some are superior in terms of artistry while others are pre-eminent in terms of moral and spiritual development. There is a passage in the Pāli canon which makes this point beautifully. The Buddha praises each of his disciples for his special qualities: one of them is best at meditation, while another is especially sensitive in the way he collects alms, another stands out for his ability to explain the Dharma, and so on.[61]

To sum up, likes and dislikes have an element of objective validity, and in as much as pleasure is essential to the spiritual life, we can say that refining our tastes is important. On the other hand, any tastes and habits that we allow to become a burden to others, and that we cannot happily put aside when we need to, do not deserve any respect. But the main point is that enjoyment is not a luxury, something peripheral to the main business of practising the Dharma; it is not an element to introduce if there's time. It is central to the whole exercise. Only joy will keep us going in the spiritual life. You can only practise the Dharma if you have the energy, the spark, the zest for it. You need to be able to relish it for what it is – a feast for the famished heart and mind.

If you do not love the Dharma passionately, even if you are a doctrine follower, you cannot live the life of renunciation authentically. It may take some effort before you enjoy your Dharma life, but enjoyment has to be on the agenda somewhere. There is a Hindi proverb: 'Bitter in the mouth but sweet in the stomach.' The Dharma is like that for some people. It may taste rather bitter at first, but you taste the real sweetness of it as you start to digest and assimilate it. In the end, the methods of doctrine and faith converge in the same goal, a complementary union of insight and bliss.

MILAREPA'S SONG OF SELF-RESPECT

The boy finally wants to offer Milarepa a pair of trousers with which to protect his modesty. As before, he begins by showing his clear grasp of Tantric theory, and his understanding of Milarepa's nature, by admitting that Milarepa has nothing left to hide, being free from all ideas of disgrace and shame. However, he follows this with an argument that challenges Milarepa's chosen path.

> We worldly men are shamed by indecent exposure.
> Even the perfect Buddha, the fully enlightened Being,
> Discreetly follows worldly customs.

Following this preamble, the young man runs through what is for him a fairly cursory description of his trousers – which he says have been tailored by his uncle – before making an offering of them. But, leaving fashions in Tibetan trousers aside, what is behind the offering is the suggestion that Milarepa should abandon his eremitical Tantric lifestyle for one that accommodates conventional social propriety. The boy's critical attitude towards Milarepa's lifestyle is all too common. Many people, perhaps especially those whose own spiritual practice is rather desultory, have decided views with regard to the way of life that should be followed by more serious practitioners. It is as if they believe that the practice of the Dharma should be regulated according to mundane standards of propriety.

Milarepa replies by challenging the boy to explain what he finds so strange about his penis being visible, hanging there as nature intended. He points out that he came from his mother's womb naked, and that death will not spare his clothes any more than it will spare his body. He then begins a brief disquisition on the difference between mundane discretion or shame and spiritual dignity or self-respect. The question is: of what should we be truly ashamed?

That is merely the nature-born male organ;
I cannot understand this so-called 'shame' of yours...

Look at sinful, evil, and meaningless deeds;
You are *not* ashamed of them.

In offering up his weapons, the youth has renounced the 'all important combat' that has been so firmly a part of his identity as a member of the clan or group, but he is clearly holding on to some group values, and here he shows it in his conflation of self-respect with respectability. This is very common. I remember that when I was a small child, most children were not allowed to run about and play when they were dressed in their Sunday best. They were made to sit at home so that they would stay neat and tidy. This was nothing to do with religion; it was all about social niceties. Even during my youth, if a man didn't wear a tie or a hat, he was considered not to be fully dressed, while wearing a coloured shirt was an act of flagrant recklessness. Those particular signs of respectability have changed, but the concern to display the appropriate marks of submission to group norms is still very apparent. In an age of consumerism, respectability is less a matter of a rigid dress code and more about a carefully maintained range of purchases and recreational activities that will ensure peer acceptance. You need to have the right sort of job and live in the right part of town, go on holiday to the right ski resort, drive the right kind of car, and even follow the right religion.

The perception of things as all-important when they are nothing of the kind is reinforced by vulnerability to group disapproval, and also by lack of imagination, an inability to contemplate stepping outside the range of possibilities that society thinks acceptable. Unfortunately, Buddhists have all too often succumbed to this kind of failure of nerve and vision. When you get a narrow and rigid monasticism, when the monastic rules and even the way you dress and shave your head have turned into a kind of Buddhist respectability, or when it becomes all-important to spend the right number of years studying Buddhist philosophy in the right monastic universities, then what is really all-important is to re-emphasize what is really all-important. It was for this reason that some Tantric yogis originally set out to flout convention, to challenge what other people considered important, even within the Buddhist world.

When I first came back to England in the early 1960s, after some twenty years in Asia, it was impressed upon me as all-important that Buddhism should be respectable. I soon realized that what the people who were trying to influence me meant by this was that Buddhism should be made as acceptable as possible to the values of the English middle classes. But if Buddhists agree to such a thing, Buddhism ceases to be Buddhism. The same may be said for the versions of Buddhism that are peddled to the consumer society these days, and the way that Buddhism is profiled to appeal to different niche markets, to fit in with whatever that society considers to be all-important. It may well find acceptance in this way, but it ceases to be Buddhism.

Of course, if you want to communicate the Dharma to a lot of people, you cannot afford to alienate them by causing offence, especially by breaking their taboos. At the same time, you need to be careful not to lose sight of what you are trying to communicate. It is easy to forget that the Buddhist message is a subversive one, that its values run counter to mundane or worldly norms, and that your commitment to its ethical principles may lead you on occasion to offend conventional notions of morality. If the Buddha 'discreetly follows worldly customs', he does so only in so far as these do not compromise the ideals of the Dharma and the integrity of the lifestyle he has chosen through which to express those ideals.

It is normal to be ashamed of anything that excludes one from the group, and social inclusion is fundamentally predicated on the respect given to taboos, whether one observes them or breaks them. Milarepa speaks from a position that is not in opposition to social convention, but simply beyond it. That is to say, it is not a position at all. He avoids any fixed position, whether of conformity or individualism. In other words he is not a conformist or an individualist, but an individual. He does not define himself in relation to the group, whether by joining it or by setting himself apart from it.

A true individual is someone who has developed self-awareness, through one discipline or another, and on that basis a confidence and self-respect that does not depend upon convention or fashion. If you are a true individual, your sense of identity and purpose in life does not rely on your social identity – whether you are a citizen, family member, worker, rebel, or iconoclast. As a mature human being, your self-awareness transcends human social groups of all kinds. Your defining relationship is an inner relationship with the deeper reality of things, the truth behind appearances. One might even say that the true individual is one through whom that deeper reality of things functions and is present in the world. If you are a true individual you can stand on your own two feet and at the same time maintain a harmony with the way things really are.

Milarepa is an individual in the true sense because he is free of the power of social conventions. He doesn't need to conform to other people's expectations of how a spiritual practitioner should look; it doesn't matter to him how he is seen. We tend to be most ashamed of matters over which we have no control, like our social background or what we look like. Milarepa, by contrast, is ashamed only of 'sinful, evil, and meaningless deeds'. The things that preoccupy the vast majority of people are quite simply of no concern to him at all; and conversely, he sees how important it is to feel real shame about deeds and activities about which most people would feel no compunction.

Milarepa concludes by describing how he maintains his self-respect.

> My fine wool is the Heart-for-Bodhi
> With which I spin the thread of Four Initiations;
> The cloth I weave is the liberation Path of Samādhi;
> The dye I use is made of virtues and good-wishes.

All the initiations of the Tantric path are spun from the same stuff: the *bodhicitta*, the will to Enlightenment for the sake of all beings. Weaving the thread of the teachings to which one is introduced into cloth is a good metaphor for spiritual practice, suggesting a harmonious and steady labour resulting in a strong fabric. As for the practice of ethics and *mettā*, it is appropriate that these are the dye in Milarepa's account of the production of what he calls his 'dignified and altruistic trousers'. *Mettā* and the practice of ethics gently soak in to transform the deepest fibres of one's being.

MILAREPA'S SONG OF FEARLESS HONESTY

Finally realizing that he isn't going to be able to secure a link with Milarepa by offering gifts on the spot, the young man wants to know where he can find him again, hoping to be able to invite him to his house. Milarepa tells him that at harvest time he goes to Din Ri, then after the threshing to Nya Non, and in winter he retires to a remote retreat. The youth tries to discourage Milarepa from taking his chosen route, saying of Din Ri that it is a place of the damned, where flour is like gold and the people are mean and impoverished by famine. As for Nya Non, it is a paradise for bandits and murderers, inhabited by packs of lepers, and littered with cremation grounds and cemeteries. He is no more complimentary about the regions beyond. The border with Nepal is high and cold, with snow and blizzards, while Nepal itself cannot be recommended on account of heat and disease and 'dangerous rope bridges'. Further south one cannot make oneself understood, and the trees are stiff like corpses. He ends by begging that Milarepa will 'visit my country for a fortnight'.

The young man is obviously trying to appear solicitous for Milarepa's welfare, warning him against dangers and inviting him to his own part of the world, with the clear implication that he will see to it that Milarepa is well looked after while he is there. What Milarepa hears, however, is his complacent condescension. It is as though the young man is really saying, 'Here am I, a young man of noble family graciously inviting this poor yogi to my home; he ought to be pleased and grateful.'

Milarepa is quick to put him in his place. He is no doubt already familiar with this patronizing attitude, as are most Buddhist monks in the East today. It is usually the rich man of the village who tends to harbour the presumption that the monks are indebted to him as one of their more generous supporters. He assumes that they are under an obligation to him for helping to rebuild their vihara, or supplying them with robes, or providing them with a feast on regular occasions through the year. It is an understandable assumption, but the monks are usually quick to detect it, and equally quick gently to take their generous patron down a peg or two.

> You arrogant young man with strong desires,...
> It is hard to meet an immaculate man of merit,...
>
> I am a yogi who thinks and says whate'er he likes,
> But I have never caused malicious gossip....
>
> I am an abandoned yogi, who eats for food
> The inner Samādhi of Non-discernment....
> Cheerful and comfortable am I in times of famine.
>
> Though the paths are perilous and dreadful,
> My prayer to the Gracious One will never fail me....
> My inseparable companion is the Bodhi-Mind;...
>
> Since I have no possessions, I have no enemy.
> Cheerful and at ease I meet the bandits.

Milarepa rebuts the young man's very terms of reference. He flies in the face of all common-sense perceptions of self, home, security, happiness, and even good and evil. It must come as quite a shock to the well-meaning boy. Milarepa exposes the direct link between craving and hatred, attachment and fear, thereby turning his would-be patron's assumptions inside out.

The young man's fears for Milarepa's welfare are in fact a measure of his own desires. What he offers as protection and security is no such thing. It is not for Milarepa to go for protection to wealthy patrons. It is for them to go for Refuge to what he embodies. The youth begs Milarepa to avoid hardships, and Milarepa responds by pointing out to him that the hardships are for the young man himself to face. With his strong desires it is going to be hard for him to locate men of virtue, because men of virtue are not going to choose the easy life towards which those strong desires incline him. The yogi chooses hardship because it enables him to see how much of his experience is not 'out there' but his response to his perception of what is happening. A comfortable life does not provide this possibility of freedom for the mind.

So far as the young man is concerned, his warnings about the dangers of Din Ri and the inhabitants of Nya Non represent good, well-meant common-sense advice. But Milarepa sees them merely as calumny. Fear and condemnation of alien places and peoples goes with a blind attachment to our own community. To take people as we find them would be a threat to our sense of identity. As soon as we find safety in a place, a group, or even a self, we fear all the more any threat from what we perceive as not self but 'other'. As long as we cling to a self, we will always have to deal with fear. What the youth offers as protection and security is therefore no such thing. The young man's fears for Milarepa are his own fears. Milarepa is able to take people as he finds them because he has renounced his group identity in favour of the freedom of absolute emptiness. That is all the protection he needs, and no stranger can ever be a threat to him.

This goes even for bandits. We get a sense of the relaxed nature of Milarepa's relations with bandits from an incident in his biography which concerns a nocturnal visit to his cave from a robber. As Milarepa hears the robber stealthily rooting around, he calls out, 'I don't think you'll be able to find anything there in the dark. I've never found anything even in daylight!' At this, the robber cannot help laughing, and goes on his way.[62] Milarepa has nothing to fear from the intruder, after all. He has nothing worth stealing, and he is as unconcerned about getting anything from him in the way of apology or revenge as he is about clinging to his few possessions.

The youth is false and misleading in his speech, not because he means to be, but because his very experience of himself and of the world is false. If he is to practise truthful speech, he may need to be more circumspect and keep his prejudices to himself, even if this means being less candid. Milarepa, on the other hand, can speak his mind without fear that his speech will betray negative emotion. It is not that he is shameless, but that he has no more need for shame. His thoughts are not subject to craving and hatred, so he does not need to guard them. It is one thing to be guarded in your speech; to be guarded in your thoughts requires another level of mindfulness. Milarepa no longer has to be careful even about what he is thinking, so he can be completely open.

I was once teaching a class at our very first Buddhist centre, called Sakura – this must have been in the late sixties – when one of our regular friends arrived looking quite shaken. He said that on the way there, as he was walking along the street, he had cast a casual glance into a passing baby-carriage. As he did so, the baby turned towards him and fixed him with a look that was utterly unnerving in its directness and honesty. The impact of simple, straightforward truthfulness – delivered without premeditation or artifice – was in an obscure way quite terrifying, he said; and he realized that adults rarely look at one another in that way, that they have lost that direct gaze.

In childhood, honesty comes first, and prevarication is learned as part of the process of socialization, as a way of adjusting to the needs and expectations of others. As a very small child, you don't have to be told that truthfulness is a virtue; you have a natural, effortless directness. But after a while you become aware that other people have perceptions different from yours, and that you can therefore hide what you know from them. The question for the rest of your life is how much use you make of this discovery.

It is a rare individual who can stay honest, straightforward, and open in adult life; most of us live with a kind of background dishonesty. Our words are almost constantly at some degree of variance with our thoughts; accompanying almost any conversation we have is a rather different conversation going on in our heads, in which our unvoiced feelings, reactions, and desires seethe and multiply. Clearly we do this partly to avoid maligning or insulting those around us, but the price we pay is living with this almost constant – and therefore virtually unconscious – gap between our words and our thoughts.

Milarepa singles out the quality of open-hearted candour in the people of Nya Non, so colourfully maligned by the young man. They may be rough, but they are entirely without artifice.

Though Nya Non may be of bad repute,
The people there are candid and ingenuous.

As in the days of old, they are straightforward and outspoken.
Easy-going and carefree,
They eat and drink without pretension;
They keep things as they are,
And groves and forests flourish.

In the eyes of a sophisticated young nobleman they may be uncultured, uneducated, even savage and backward, but Milarepa is able to see the same qualities much more positively, because he has nothing to fear from them. He has nothing worth stealing, and he is unconcerned about getting anything from anybody. So what he sees are people without airs and graces, who enjoy a good time and don't go chasing after novelty.

The boy's dire warnings about bandit country and its unsavoury inhabitants and awful dangers remind me of the reactions of some people when they heard that we were proposing to establish a Buddhist centre in Bethnal Green, in the East End of London. 'You won't survive in such a tough neighbourhood,' they said. 'Bethnal Green is gangland territory; the local roughs won't take kindly to a bunch of effete Buddhists arriving in their midst.' But in the event, those who came to build the Buddhist centre there found that the local people, while perhaps being rather rough and ready, were also old-fashioned, straightforward, and unpretentious.

> As for me, I take no interest in worldly wealth,
> Nor am I attached to food and drink.
> Contented, I care not for loitering and amusement.
> When, therefore, I meditate, my Samādhi deepens.
>
> This is why I go to Nya Non.
> Having mastered the art of Dumo's Fire,
> I have no fear of cold or heat;
> Cheerful and in comfort I meet the falling snow.
>
> Today I see no reason to delay my journey,
> But I shall not go to your country;
> Proud and haughty patrons are distasteful to me.
> How can I ingratiate myself with those I do not know?

Milarepa makes the important point that you cannot become friends with people who are proud and haughty, because in putting on such airs they are refusing to let themselves be known as they really are, and can have no hope of being receptive to others. Whether or not they are aware of it, their pride is a mask. An implicit connection is made here between lack of pride and openness to the Dharma.

Milarepa's way of life provides a clear prescription for deepening meditation. He has found from his own experience that if you put aside your desires – for worldly attainments, for sensual pleasures, and for distractions – your *samādhi* deepens. It is as simple as that. Furthermore, he is not troubled by heat or cold. It is with a little kindly irony that at the end of the song he addresses the boy as 'my dear, contented youth'.

> My dear, contented youth, it is time for you to go.
> May your health be good and your life long.

Milarepa's intention is to make it clear to the young man that he has to make up his mind. Which is he going to choose, worldly attachments or the guru? He can't hold on to both.

THE YOUTH'S SONG OF JOYFUL DESPAIR

At this, the young man finally gives up all his cajoling and bragging and tendering of gifts. He has done all he can, and he has still failed to convince Milarepa of his faith. And he has begun to see how his own mind has been working. He has been priding himself upon being the serious object of attention of a great, wonder-working yogi. In his desperation, he draws out his knife and turns the point towards his heart.

> Proud and happy I was, conceit arose within me;
> I thought that I was a well-gifted person,

This sort of inflation often happens to spiritual practitioners, especially beginners, when they become too elated by their early successes. As a result of some genuine experience within meditation, or perhaps an access of faith such as the boy has had, you start to fantasize about your spiritual prospects. You think, 'Well, it looks as though I have some real aptitude for this that others don't have. My prospects for becoming Enlightened are looking good.'

When things are going well and you are pleased with your progress, it is easy to become not just pleased, but pleased with yourself. You lose your mindfulness and get carried away, falling under the sway of what the Greeks called hubris, the sort of overweening pride that makes you forget your limitations and with them the decencies and duties of life. For the ancient Greeks, this was a deadly sin, to think that you are untouchable, to fancy that you have the virtues of the gods and forget that you are a mortal human being.

The young man is of course right in thinking that he is special. Indeed, though he doesn't yet know it, he is one of the eight destined heart-disciples of Milarepa. The trouble is that until now he has thought that being such a disciple is a privileged or prestigious position. He is right to realize that he is not subject to habitual negative mental states and that his motivation is pure. His mistake has been to see this as proof of his spiritual grade or rank.

The young man's next observation seems quite extraordinary, in view of the fact that he is so overcome with dejection that he is preparing to commit suicide.

> Since the day that I was born,
> I have never been so happy as today.

To feel and express two contrary emotions at the same time, though it sounds contradictory, is an entirely coherent and authentic response, as most of us know from our own experience. It is possible to feel utterly broken, to feel that one's grasp on reality has gone completely, and at the same time to feel supremely happy, even rapturous. Though Milarepa has apparently rejected him as a disciple and is not going to give him any teaching, the young man is ecstatically happy to have met someone in whom he can have faith. It is not even as though he feels he has derived any kind of clarity or understanding from the encounter. He has given all he can of himself and has been rejected anyway. His humiliation is absolute. But he has faith – faith in the intuitive awareness that Milarepa speaks from a position far deeper than anything he has ever experienced himself. This at once undermines and unsettles his sense of identity while also offering a glimpse of a far more profoundly satisfying truth. This is the source of his happiness. His meeting with Milarepa has introduced something radically new into his consciousness – the first glimmering of awareness of the essentially unconditioned nature of reality. The natural consequence of that faith is joy.

> I feel that I am most ignorant and pitiful....
> With a feeling of frustration, I have lost my way.
> I am beginning to believe I have no capacity for Dharma!

In fact, in losing his false confidence in his capacity for understanding and practising the Dharma, he has developed a real capacity for doing so. Understanding just how ignorant he really is, and seeing that he is no match for the situation, his decision to commit suicide is made in a very positive spirit. His situation is, he feels, as good as it is ever going to get. He has had his chance; he has met an Enlightened teacher, although he was evidently not up to the challenge of being his disciple.

'Tis better for me now to die,
To die before such an accomplished saint,
When my heart is full of Dharma.

Up till now, he has tried to tell Milarepa what Milarepa himself needs and what he should do. But now, at last, he leaves it up to Milarepa to make up his own mind. He realizes that all his firmly held ideas count for nothing with someone who is in touch with reality. He surrenders.

After hearing such a sorry tale from this poor lad,
With your omniscient mind, you know what should be said.

A MEETING ACROSS LIFETIMES

Milarepa is now convinced by the prophecy of the goddess in his dream. Concluding that there must have been a mutual vow between himself and the young man in a previous life, he completely changes his attitude towards him. Previously he has been dismissive; now he offers praise. Thus far he has been ruthlessly deflating the young man's pretensions (or so it appears – there is really nothing ruthless about Milarepa). Now his harshness has reduced the young man's egotism. The time has come for encouragement, kindness, and appreciation of his good qualities.

This change of approach, and its timing, is obviously important. If gurus are always encouraging and sympathetic, their students start imagining that the spiritual life is easy. On the other hand, if the guru is relentlessly critical, the same students can become so discouraged that they give up. It is generally best to err on the side of encouragement (if only to reduce the risk of students becoming suicidal), though as a guru one should consider one's own temperament and attempt to compensate for its natural propensities.

The balance of qualities making up the ideal type of personality for a teacher is exemplified in Milarepa's own guru, Marpa, who is a classic example of what Carl Jung termed an extraverted thinking type. He was a scholar, but he did more than just translate texts from Sanskrit into Tibetan. He earned his appellation 'the Translator' by his great feat of bringing Buddhist texts and teachings from India to Tibet in the course of three long and perilous journeys. He was as far from the model of the withdrawn and retiring scholar, what Jung terms the introverted thinking type, as one can imagine.

Marpa is an example of someone who is both very learned and a great teacher, but not all scholars can do both. Someone who is an introverted thinking type may become a teacher on account of the depth of his knowledge and understanding of a subject, but he may be totally unsuited to teaching. A person of this type tends to get bound up with his own thoughts, and is correspondingly remote from the objective world. Such people make bad teachers because they are too interested in their own ideas, getting absorbed in the material for its own sake and developing that interest at the expense of the needs of the people they are supposed to be teaching. Jung mentions a famous chemist who admitted in his biography that he consistently failed to answer students' questions because they would spark off trains of thought in his own mind that he could not force himself to ignore. Engrossed in his own thinking, he would forget about the question that initiated it and would wave the student away, saying, 'I'll let you know next week.' The students would be left in the dark, not knowing how to proceed with their work, and they would receive in due course a long and abstruse note that took their problem as a starting point but had no constructive bearing on it.

By contrast, if, like Marpa, you are of the extraverted thinking type, you will be sufficiently aware of the students' needs and why they are asking their questions to give them at least a provisional answer. Instead of losing yourself in your own reflections, you will allow your students to get on with *their* thinking. If you are yourself somewhat introverted and find yourself in the position of teaching, you need to be careful to apply yourself to the actual questions and the real needs of the person in front of you. You will then at least be *acting* like an extraverted thinking type, and this will have the effect of gradually altering your conditioning. One's personality is not set in stone. It may seem as though there is nothing you can do about who you are, but if the Dharma is about anything it is about our capacity to change our conditioning.

> It seems our hopes in bygone lives arranged the meeting;
> It was our destiny to meet before the Silver Spring.
> You must be one whose Karma is unstained,

As the fruit of good karma, i.e. ethically skilful action, the young man's spiritual aspiration is an aspect of his *karma vipāka* which, being positive, is known as *puṇya* or merit. Negative karma, on the other hand, is unskilful action which bears fruit as negative *vipāka*. When we speak of our karma catching up with us, we mean that our immoral or unskilful behaviour has borne fruit, *vipāka*. Sometimes one can be aware of these karmic effects from previous unskilful actions as they arise in one's day-to-day experience. You may have made some kind of good and creative resolution, but some combination of factors – perhaps habitual tendencies or external circumstances that you have set up through your actions – prevents you doing as you intended.

There is nothing mysterious or mystical about the law of karma. The principle behind it is that all actions of body, speech, and mind have an effect, not that everything that happens is the result of karma. It is only when all other avenues of explanation have been explored that we should begin to look to karma for the root cause of anything. This is what we have seen Milarepa do in this episode. While he took the dream vision of the green girl seriously and was on the lookout for what it might prophesy, he did not jump to conclusions. He tested the young man to the very limit, and only then did he consider that there must be a mutual vow between them.

The idea of a mutual vow refers to the kind of very positive karma associated with being able to give some kind of conscious direction to one's rebirth. For example, it is certainly feasible to aspire to rekindle a special connection with another person in a future life. It is a general Indian understanding of the workings of karma that one can make a vow or resolution to sustain a link made in one life through to a succeeding life. As a disciple, you could vow to be reunited in future lives with your teacher or with a spiritual companion, a fellow disciple, even a number of spiritual friends. The idea of a band of individuals being spiritually connected down through the ages, lifetime after lifetime, is both resonant and romantic.

Of course, the link that people want to continue in this way is often romantic in a more prosaic sense, and one might be tempted to use as an example the Pāli legends which suggest a connection over lifetimes between the Buddha-to-be and his wife, Yaśodharā. This spiritualizing of what is essentially a social and romantic contract is perhaps best seen as part of the process of idealizing everything about the Buddha's life, even before he became Enlightened, and all his previous lives as well. The essential point, as far as Buddhism is concerned, is that the connection should be spiritual, not a mundane link based on sense desire.

It is also traditional to vow to be reborn into a future life that doesn't have the limitations of one's present existence. Of course, this is rather a different way of thinking about life than the one favoured by our own society, in which emphasis is placed on the capacities of all of us, whatever our circumstances. In many ways it is a very good thing to seek equal opportunities for all, but we all owe it to ourselves to be honest about the limitations we need to overcome if we are to make spiritual progress.

If you say, 'I refuse to accept that my particular situation is a limitation, and to see it that way is just to take a view of my circumstances that has been imposed upon me by ancient prejudices,' you might feel better, but that doesn't necessarily mean that no limitation exists. For example, you might hold that it doesn't matter whether you are rich or poor, and in a way that is true, but it must be admitted that it is a disadvantage to be poor in a society that places value on material wealth, and that the struggle of dealing with that disadvantage can make practising the Dharma more difficult.

Sometimes we acknowledge our limitations but disclaim responsibility for them by saying that they have been foisted on us by external forces. If you are prone to a bad temper, you might throw up your hands and say, 'I admit it, but there's nothing I can about it. My grandfather had a bad temper, my father was also thoroughly unpleasant, and I am merely the victim of the trait he has passed down to me.' From a spiritual point of view, this attitude is not at all conducive to progress. All you are saying really is that you don't want to be bothered with the realities of the spiritual life. If your conditioning puts you at any kind of disadvantage, you need first to recognize the fact, secondly to put aside the question of who might be ultimately responsible, and thirdly to do something to go beyond that conditioning. You have to acknowledge that when you get angry, you yourself are flying into a rage, not some other person. You have to take responsibility for who you really are.

It is a disadvantage to live in a country in which you do not have the opportunity to become a Buddhist monk in the traditional sense and live the wandering life supported by the lay people. We have to recognize that. The West has advantages too, of course, but there is no point in saying that our opportunities to practise the Dharma are just as good as those of people in traditional Buddhist countries, with their temples, Buddhist universities, and a well-established sangha. In certain respects we are at a disadvantage and we owe it to ourselves to recognize that. Likewise, if a woman has certain disadvantages because of her gender – whether those disadvantages are inherent or imposed – let her recognize that. And if a man suffers disadvantages due to his being a man, then let him recognize those limitations and set about going beyond them.

The real issue about making vows or aspirations for future lives is trying to see honestly which circumstances of your life are truly advantageous from a spiritual point of view and which are not. Instead of pretending to yourself that your situation is just as good as any other, you may need to acknowledge that you have drifted into an unsatisfactory situation that you now take for granted, and that, if you really wanted to, you could move forward from it in this life, never mind a future one. On the other hand, you may need to accept that some limitations cannot be changed here and now, and accept that they are limitations. None of us has to identify fully with whatever circumstances we are born with or have had imposed upon us. According to the Dharma, whatever limitations we face can be transcended, but we are more likely to transcend them if we recognize them as limitations to start with.

This is precisely what the young man has done in his song of joyful desperation. Up to now he has not been able to acknowledge the bankruptcy of his views. Having done so, he can at last begin to make progress, and Milarepa can begin to teach him.

Milarepa now gives his new disciple a set of basic precepts upon which to found his practice. His first precepts challenge the young man's very sense of identity.

> Know that kinsmen are the devil-planned hindrances of Dharma;
> Think not of them as real, but quench your craving for them.

The term 'devil' as a translation of 'Māra' is in a way too strong, suggesting – at least to people brought up in the Christian tradition – an awe-inspiring and omnipresent power of evil. Theologically speaking, no such absolute and ubiquitous principle of evil, corresponding to the absolute and ubiquitous principle of good in the figure of God, is accepted within the Christian tradition, but from an emotional point of view, this is how the devil tends to be perceived. Buddhism, by contrast, emphasizes conditionality, cause and effect, rather than the simple conflict of good and evil. Māra, the 'devil' of the Buddhist tradition, is just a hindrance, a silly, blundering, psychic nuisance or trickster who is easily seen through with even a modicum of extra awareness and mindfulness, and who disappears the instant he is detected.

It is in this sense that Milarepa describes kinsmen as 'devil-planned hindrances of Dharma'. Kinsmen are singled out to head the list of emotional ties that the boy has to break because in any relatively primitive and unorganized society, with no centralized government and no administration or police force, you have to rely on your kinsmen. You stick by them and they stick by you, and you may on occasion have to fight together against outsiders, whether invaders or bandits. So one's kinsmen are much more than the members of a modern nuclear family. They are a whole clan or tribe. The Mafia is perhaps the most notorious modern-day example of such a close-knit social grouping. To belong to such a group involves you in an often complex network of responsibilities and reciprocal duties, with a strong sense of loyalty and solidarity binding you together in a group and against others.

For a young man there is therefore no question of not fighting to protect the group when it is attacked or threatened. Likewise, a young woman might feel she was going against her own nature if she were not to look after the group's sick and elderly. It is expected of you, and you expect it of yourself. But if you are to grow towards Enlightenment, all your actions should be in pursuit of self-determination, not collective duty. You have to take full responsibility for your actions of body, speech, and mind. While this might mean continuing to fulfil your duties in the family and the wider community, you do this through personal choice, not group pressure, however subtle or self-imposed. When Milarepa enjoins the young man not to think of such a group as real, he is not denying the fact of kinship but warning him against identifying too exclusively with the duties incumbent upon him as a member of a group.

This young man is, moreover, a nobleman, and the higher you go up the social scale, the more important become the ties of blood and family. The strong group mentality arising out of this status-enhanced identification with the clan is a particular hindrance to the practice of the Dharma, and this is what Māra represents in this context. As long as your identity consists primarily in your membership of a particular group, and your principal loyalty is to that group, your practice of the Dharma is going to be limited.

For this reason it is common in many religious traditions to take on a new name when you commit yourself to the spiritual life. The idea is to put your old identity with its attachments behind you, and take on a more spiritually productive one. In the Buddha's day there was no change of name upon ordination, but in Sri Lanka, China, Japan, Tibet, and Thailand new monks all take up a Buddhist name – though in Thailand some monks retain their lay name after ordination and simply prefix it with the title 'Reverend'. In Tibet, lay names are also usually Dharma names, Tibet having been a Buddhist country for centuries. A child might be called Dorje, for example, this being the Tibetan translation of the Sanskrit *vajra*. However, although the *vajra* is an important Buddhist symbol, the name Dorje is so common that people do not immediately think of the Dharma when they hear it. As we find out later on, the young man in our story is called Dharma Wonshu, but this name is unlikely to have had any particular spiritual significance for him, at least until now.

Similarly, one does not associate the name John with the Evangelist; but when England was being converted to Christianity, one's Christian or baptismal name did have a spiritual significance, while one's surname registered one's place in the world. Of course, some Christians today do feel the true significance of their names. And new members of the order I founded, the Western Buddhist Order (later Triratna), are given new names, usually in Sanskrit or Pāli, to recognize that their going for Refuge to Buddha, Dharma, and Sangha is what ultimately defines them.

> Money and dainties are the devil's envoys;…
> Association with them is pernicious.
> Renounce them and all other things that bind you.

> Delight in pleasures is the devil's rope;
> Think, then, of death to conquer your desires.

We don't like to have to remember that one day we will have to leave behind all that we enjoy, but this fact is the only aspect of what we possess and enjoy of which we can be absolutely sure. Many people follow the injunction of the poet to 'Gather ye rosebuds while ye may,' imagining that the only sensible option in the face of impermanence is to grasp frantically at life's pleasures. But the poem by Robert Herrick from which this famous line comes is about taking your opportunities while they are there, which is slightly different from being waylaid by the 'devil's envoys' and finding yourself in thrall to them. Pleasure in itself is a good thing, and Milarepa is the first to proclaim the joys of life. But if something is so pleasurable that you are unable to be mindful while you are enjoying it, it binds you and will certainly lead to suffering.

> Young companions are the tempting devil's snare;
> Knowing they are delusive, watch them carefully.

> One's native land is the dungeon of the devil;

Attachment to one's kith and kin, and to those with whom one shares a broader identity, whether national or linguistic, can also be bound up with attachment to a geographical location. Hence 'one's native land is the dungeon of the devil'. To make sense of this pronouncement, we could think of the dungeon as a locality with which we are comfortably familiar rather than a whole country or nation, which may be too large and varied for us to be very much attached to it.

Milarepa extends this admonition to any sense of group identity, even that arising out of the companionship of friends. He especially has in mind the friends the young man was on his way to meet. His point is not that friends who aren't interested in the spiritual life are 'evil'; it is more that one can unwittingly allow the assumptions of one's constant companions to seep into one's consciousness. Their ideas and attitudes rub off on you, and it becomes difficult to avoid conforming to their expectations. Without noticing what is happening, you can start, little by little, thinking as they think, behaving as they behave. And if their ideas and attitudes are conventional and materialistic, if they don't appreciate or understand the spiritual dimension of life, the perspectives and ideals that fuel your spiritual practice will tend to fade away when you are with them. It is in this sense that their companionship is delusive.

This is plain, straightforward advice that can be taken quite literally to refer to one's immediate friends and companions, but it also has a more general application. Milarepa is saying, in effect, that if you are not yet a bodhisattva, worldly people will have a greater effect on you than you will have on them. This seems to be a golden rule for people trying to live a spiritual life. If you can, avoid living apart from other Dharma practitioners for too long, or at least avoid settling in too comfortably with people who do not share your ideals, however amiable they may be in other respects. Your dealings should be friendly and concerned, but they should have a clear cut-off point. When you are observing a particularly strict or intense form of practice, you have to be especially careful about whom you associate with. If you want to get on with your practice, you have to protect it and the conditions on which it is based. This might seem antisocial, but in the spiritual life one has above all to be practical. In any case, when one considers what passes for a social life in the case of a great many people, this policy is less antisocial than it might seem. The reality of modern social life – all those dinner parties and evenings in the pub – is that it doesn't really involve very much in the way of friendly and enjoyable communication.

A common misapprehension among religious practitioners of all kinds is to imagine that in order to communicate with people you have to be able to speak their language, catch their cultural references, be in touch with the latest trends and jargon, and go along with whatever activities and diversions are currently popular. This is certainly not my experience. When I came back from India to England in 1964, I was completely out of touch with everything that had happened between the war years and the early sixties. Televisions and supermarkets, mods and rockers, night clubs and pop music, were all quite new to me, while other things, like steam trains, were rapidly disappearing.

In any human exchange, references to the transient features of the cultural landscape are useful only for establishing the most superficial initial contact, and if you wish to communicate yourself more deeply to others, you will need to be able to fall back on something more solid. It is your sincerity and commitment that should come across, and you will only be undermining this by trying to be relevant or up-to-date. People who are themselves blown by the winds of fashion can still respect the integrity of someone who does not appear to be subject to such vagaries. There was a time, for example, when magistrates used to affect ignorance of pop stars and other manias of the day whenever these were mentioned in court proceedings. They would interrupt the questioning of witnesses to say crustily, according to one urban legend, 'And what, pray, are the Beatles?' to which the barrister would reply, 'The Beatles, m'Lud, is the name of a popular singing group.' At that time the public was genuinely impressed by this evidence, as it seemed, of a sort of judicial remoteness. The magistrate's appearance of being above the ups and downs of fashion seemed to be a reassuring sign that even-handed justice would be done. (Things are rather different now, of course.) But, as spiritual practitioners, we needn't hide our ignorance of the latest fashions, or slavishly try to keep up with them for the sake of being able to talk to other people. Communication shouldn't depend on the cultural flotsam that happens to be passing at the time. It should be based on the human qualities that are common to all of us, whatever our generation. People respond to clear-cut principles, lived out and expressed with conviction, and to a person who knows clearly what they stand for. After all, if you are not sure you quite believe in what you are talking about, why should anyone else take it seriously?

Milarepa has not finished with Māra, and concludes with an exhortation not to waste time.

Put all aside and strive for Dharma.
Only by instant action can you succeed!

By 'instant action' Milarepa means that whatever you need to do, you must make it your spiritual practice. If you think to yourself that you will 'do some practice' when you have finished doing whatever you are doing now, then – even if you do get round to 'doing some practice' – it will not be true practice. Whether you are meditating, reflecting, studying, talking to someone, working, or just being mindful while you are doing chores, even when you are simply doing nothing and enjoying the view, you should put all thoughts of anything else aside and do what you are doing wholeheartedly.

In time your body of illusion will decay.

Here we find a poetic conflation of two strands of reflection on impermanence: illusion and decay. It is when we see objects change that we conclude that the 'objects' observed are ultimately illusory. One's 'body of illusion' is of course illusory only in the sense that it is not a fixed, unchanging entity. It is illusory *because* it is in the process of decay. We can say that the body we perceive to be in the process of change is illusory because there is nothing in it that is not part of that process. Change is all there is. There is nothing that changes.

The darting bird of mind will fly up anyway;
'Tis better now to wing your way to Heaven!

The 'darting bird' refers to the Tibetan belief that at death your consciousness passes out through the top of your head. Get on with it now, is Milarepa's advice; let it rise up in meditation. Here we are reminded that meditation is a preparation for death, and that death is a state of enforced meditation. Milarepa is always concerned as a teacher to instil a sense of urgency in his disciples, bringing the consciousness of death into the present moment and thus bringing the present moment to life, clarifying everything.

This is very helpful for the doctrine follower, but a faith follower may prefer to contemplate impermanence from another angle. Once you see something as illusory in the way I have described, there is no need to reflect that it will decay. Instead, you can begin to experience the freedom that comes when worldly attachments begin to fall away. Instead of considering the uncertain time of your death, you can remind yourself that if you commit yourself wholeheartedly to your practice, you do not know when insight, and even Enlightenment itself, might arise.

At the very least, things would be much better here and now if you could only bring awareness of impermanence and conditionality into the present moment. By the same token, if you notice you are relaxing the effort to be mindful, just think of the wonderful opportunity you are letting slip. In worrying about how much money you have left in the bank or becoming irritated at being given the 'wrong' kind of breakfast cereal, are you missing the possibility of Enlightenment here and now?

The song ends with Milarepa accepting the young man as his disciple and for the first time calling him 'my son'. Even though as a yogi he is accustomed to maintaining an even mind through all the ups and downs of life, he says he feels a particular joy at this juncture.

My son! This is the start of your journey on the Bodhi-Path.
Even I, the Yogi, rejoice at your success.
You too, young man, should be glad and joyful!

8

LAYING DOWN YOUR DOUBTS

BEAUTY ON THE SPIRITUAL PATH

Bubbling over with happiness and inspiration at being accepted as a disciple, and vowing to return, the young man bows to his new teacher and circumambulates him many times before going on his way. Four months later he returns in the company of his nephew and offers Milarepa a piece of white jade, while his nephew offers half an ounce of gold. But Milarepa tells them to take their offerings to the translator Bhari, who is building a stupa at Drin, and to ask him to give them some preliminary initiations.

It might seem strange that Milarepa should send his heart-disciple to another teacher, but we have to remember the young man's character. He is a young nobleman who until very recently took great pride in his possessions, which were of the finest quality. Although thoroughly sincere in his devotion to Milarepa, he is still at a comparatively low level of consciousness, and his mind is still attuned to the world of sensuous desire. If we compare him with Milarepa, the solitary yogi who has no possessions, not even a robe to cover his naked body, we see that there is an enormous gulf between them.

Milarepa could have given the young men the pith instructions himself, initiating them into the highest yoga there and then. But that would have been all he had to offer. He has no ritual implements, no lamps and images, no shrine or offerings. His shrewd assessment is that this prosperous young man, with his appreciation of fine things and his healthy temperament, is going to find the highest teachings of the Tantra rather colourless, bleak, dry, and remote. So he sends him and his nephew to Bhari Lotsawa (which means Bhari the Translator). He was a well-known figure among the Tibetan Buddhists of those days, renowned as a great teacher and yogi, but with a very different lifestyle from that of the ascetic Milarepa. As far as we can tell, he lived not in a cave but in a temple or monastery, surrounded by a large number of disciples, and with plenty going on around him.

I have myself witnessed the way in which some Tibetan lamas still function, with hundreds of disciples gathered together for round-the-clock ceremonies – the wail of conch shells piercing through the chanting, and butter lamps illuminating awe-inspiring images through billowing clouds of incense – and it is very impressive and elevating. Even if it does not represent the very deepest level of spiritual practice and experience, it is a profound and crucial intermediate stage.

Milarepa has weighed up the spiritual needs of his new disciple and decided that he will benefit from sharing a monastic situation with many other practitioners. Even though he may have been impelled towards the Dharma by a powerful degree of initial visionary insight, the young man still needs to establish a positive foundation by learning to enjoy his practice of the Dharma at a fairly ordinary level. He needs to be inspired by rich, colourful devotional ceremonies and initiations and fascinating teachings; he needs to handle delicately designed ritual implements and meditate on beautifully painted thangkas.

One of the qualities that makes Tantric ritual so effective is its strong aesthetic appeal. It appeals to the senses while replacing the kinds of things that naturally tend to arouse our interest with objects of more refined beauty, through which our emotional energies are directed towards objects of perception which transcend the senses altogether. Milarepa knows that for his young disciple, purifying and refining his sensuality in this way is a necessary intermediate stage.

What we are trying to do in all our practice, whether of ethics, meditation, or ritual, is to refine consciousness, to draw it away from grasping, attraction, and aversion, and make it subtle enough to begin to appreciate reality itself, which is neither pleasant nor unpleasant. The idea is to try to cultivate a sense of uplift, a feeling of joy in the contemplation of beauty appreciated for its own sake rather than as an object of possession.

In this, of course, the arts can play a part. By exposing ourselves to works of art, we allow them to lead our relatively unrefined, even gross, feelings and reactions in the direction of greater awareness and delicacy of feeling. Thus beauty becomes an intermediary between unreality and reality, an agent of transformation, whether in the form of the arts or through the aesthetic aspects of Tantric rituals and visualizations. This is why in the *Symposium* Plato refers to Eros as a daemon or intermediary, neither man nor god but a demigod, linking earth and heaven. You cannot pass from earth to heaven – from being human to being a god – directly. It is a process, represented by the daemon, of being attracted and inspired towards making progress. Particularly at the beginning of the spiritual life, there must be something for the lower emotions and the senses to latch on to, some enjoyment, some beauty – otherwise they will simply go back to their old objects. We tend to imagine that the objects of our senses are what give us pleasure, but in fact it is the engaging of our energies that is the real source of that pleasure. And the corollary of this is that if we are to engage our energies in the spiritual life, this must be a pleasurable exercise. We cannot transfer the engagement of our energies from one object to another by force of will; they have to be coaxed. This is the value of religious art – that it leads one's energies, one's feelings and emotions, quite naturally and gently upwards. And the lack of it perhaps accounts for the dry, joyless, or even lifeless impression given by the more extreme puritan sects that abjure all ornament.

Some people don't need the arts or colourful ritual to transform their emotional energies, but most of us do, unless we live in very beautiful natural surroundings, which may have the same effect. I certainly felt this when I lived in Kalimpong. The whole landscape was jewel-like in the brilliance of its colours. The sky was bright blue, the clouds were pure white, and the sunrise on the snow peaks displayed a shifting spectacle of colours – pinks, violets, greens, and golds – like a Pre-Raphaelite painting. There was something about the place and the landscape that inspired awe. Perhaps because the town had no history, one felt the presence of nature looming over it, and the mundane world didn't seem to hold sway there. In Tibet itself, due to the high altitude, the air is even clearer, and the colour of natural objects stands out vividly, even though sometimes one can see nothing but the dark brown vastness of the mountains and the intense blue of the sky, without even so much as a flower or a tree to soften the view. Such beauty, however austere, transforms the mind.

If you can redirect the sense-oriented emotions onto objects of beauty or wild nature, it becomes much easier to engage them with even more subtle objects of perception, such as those experienced in meditation. If you can go from sense desire to appreciative, contemplative delight, you know you can go further and leave behind even that enjoyment for something more beautiful still. The trouble is that we take the beauty around us for granted. It doesn't provoke wonder, gratitude, or worship, because we don't live from day to day, so we don't discover things anew. It's the same old sun and moon, the same old people, the same old world. But if you look with a fresh, new mind, you will experience everything as if for the first time. According to an ancient Indian definition, the beautiful is that which from moment to moment is always new. That is to say, it removes the mind from the world in which things grow old. It is fresh at every successive moment – except that the moment is not connected with the previous moment or the succeeding one. It is timeless, because every moment is unique. There is no question of tiring of such beauty. And the same can happen in one's relations with people. If you see someone aright, if you see them objectively in the contemplative sense, and appreciate and delight in them for what they are, you will never find them boring.

CONVERSION

We are not told how long the young men spend with Bhari Lotsawa. It could be months, perhaps a year or two, or even longer. We are told that while they are with him they are given the initiation of Dem Chog, which is quite elaborate and would have taken weeks or even months to complete. Our young man then returns to Milarepa, remaining with him for five years. He is initiated into the six yogas of Nāropa and the *mahāmudrā*, and then Milarepa finally imparts to him his own 'pith instructions' and gives him the name Repa Shiwa Aui, which means 'cotton-clad light of peace'.

The contrast between the young man's former persona and his new dedication to a life of renunciation could hardly be more marked. We are told he was a great sensualist before, but that he now completely renounces the world. In fact, he exemplifies a classic spiritual phenomenon. It is often the kind of person who is most full-bloodedly involved with worldly life who most full-bloodedly enters the spiritual life. The great sinner becomes the great saint. St Augustine of Hippo is the Christian example that comes most immediately to mind, though he was rather different by temperament from the young man in our story. When he was young, Augustine was certainly a sensualist, but he was a tormented, dissatisfied, and guilt-ridden one; and when he became a saint he was still quite guilt-ridden and tormented. It seems that even when he was at his most worldly he had reservations about worldly life, and that he had reservations throughout his spiritual life as well; whichever direction he took, there was always an element of strain and unease.

By contrast, the young man in our story seems thoroughly to have enjoyed his life. He has enjoyed his horse, his saddle, his boots, and all the rest, and without any sense of guilt he has happily given them up in order to plunge headlong into the spiritual life. His is an untroubled progression from the healthy, happy human being towards a state of being that is more than healthy, more than happy, and even – in a sense – more than human.

If it is not altogether appropriate to compare St Augustine with such a minor figure as Repa Shiwa Aui, a comparison with Milarepa is instructive. The great Tibetan yogi is most commonly likened to St Francis, on account of his complete renunciation of all worldly things combined with his kindly and imaginative appreciation of the world around him. However, the real motive force for Milarepa's spiritual life was his thoroughgoing wickedness as a young man, and in this sense he rather resembles St Augustine. On their conversion, each made a complete moral turnaround – although Milarepa was a different sort of sinner and, consequently, a different sort of saint. St Augustine was 'guilty' of little more than sensuality, yet he never seems to have achieved peace of mind. Milarepa, on the other hand, having repented heartily of his murders and sorcery, and accepted a great deal of hardship in order to purge himself, was then apparently free of any residue of guilt. The difference between these two seems to expose the inherent problems of a spiritual life conducted within the context of Christianity, certain aspects of whose doctrine, considered from a Buddhist point of view, would seem to be inimical to a healthy spiritual life. The words 'sensuality' and 'sensualist' both carry an element of moral condemnation in English – a language soaked in the values of Christianity – a condemnation that is entirely absent from Buddhism.

VOWS

Finally, the young man takes certain vows: not to wear leather shoes or more than one piece of cotton clothing, never to return to his native land, and never to secure for himself more food than he can consume in two days. Taking vows or undertaking obligations of a spiritual nature – for example, that you will perform a practice three times a day – is customary at the time of Tantric initiation, and is naturally a part of spiritual conversion. Within the Buddhist tradition great importance is attached to the strict observance of these solemn pledges. Taking a vow you know you can honour builds your confidence in your spiritual capacity, and through that you grow.

By the same token, breaking a solemn vow is held to be extremely damaging karma. It is for this reason that it is best to take a vow that specifies a definite period of time. If you take a vow for life, you can't be sure that you will be able to keep it until the moment of your death, and the result may be an underlying sense of self-doubt rather than self-confidence. Moreover, if you break the vow, your confidence may be undermined, you might experience a lingering sense of guilt, and – at worst – you might not feel able to commit to anything again.

The great vows of the cosmic bodhisattvas, found in Mahāyāna sūtras such as the *Avataṃsaka Sūtra*, the *Vimalakīrti-nirdeśa*, and the *Lotus Sūtra*, are rather different. They can hardly be taken for a limited period of time because they specifically involve not setting limits on one's altruistic aspiration. The motivation behind the bodhisattva vows is to bring about the arising of the *bodhicitta*, which has nothing to do with time, indeed it defies description in terms of time or place. In an advanced bodhisattva, the *bodhicitta* will already have arisen anyway, so the vow is more symbolic than literal.

At his own level, presumably short of the arising of the *bodhicitta*, the young man's vows likewise represent an achievement in terms of depth of understanding and strength of determination. Intense spiritual practice requires a powerful commitment to persist through the challenges it inevitably throws up, if one is to make any real progress.

To take a vow, the disciple's commitment must be beyond question, and this requires a high degree of self-knowledge and integration. It is this stability that Repa Shiwa Aui's time with Bhari Lotsawa gave him.

DROPPING ALL TALK OF ENLIGHTENMENT

After all his wonderful Tantric initiations, Repa Shiwa Aui is now brought down to earth with some straightforward, almost Theravādin-style, practical instruction. It's certainly a far cry from the colourful Tantric ritual of Bhari Lotsawa. It is as though, for all their profound meaning, for all that they adorn the essential structure of the Dharma so beautifully, those rituals are the externals, the glittering surface of the Dharma. Most ordinary Tibetans are clearly uplifted and inspired by these elaborate and profound ceremonies without feeling that they are incompatible with a life that lacks much in the way of spiritual commitment. But Milarepa is getting to the bare bones of the teaching now, the solid framework which is the basis of all the inspiring ceremonies.

As we have seen, the master-disciple relationship is intensely personal, a fully developed human being speaking to the mature spiritual aspiration of one who is less developed, so the teaching that arises from it is directly relevant to the particular circumstances and individual needs of the disciple. From his own practice and realization, Milarepa has extracted a personalized application of the Dharma which he gives to Shiwa Aui in the form of a number of precepts.

The song of instruction that follows is straightforward, simple, and direct in its presentation and structure. There is nothing complicated or intellectually abstruse about it. Its significance lies in its transformative power, now that the young man is in a position to take in the instructions fully and thus to be able to put them fully into effect.

> Dear son, if you want to consummate your meditation,
> Restrain yourself from bigotry and empty talk;
> Think not of the noble glories of the past;[63]

Milarepa's first admonition concerns speech. This is where we waste so much of our energy and time, where we lose our mindfulness, and also where we express and thus reinforce our fixed views, our blind spots, our narrow, one-sided, and limited opinions. Through speech we preen ourselves, bask in our achievements or in the reflected glory of our social status, and play up to others' perceptions of us. One imagines that Milarepa has identified this self-important young man as particularly liable to be drawn into a discussion of the noble glories of the past.

More importantly, this first point is about taking the Dharma seriously, not just talking about it emptily. This is a less obvious point than it might seem. I know from my own experience that it is possible to give a wonderfully well-received talk about the importance of giving and generosity, and simple acts of kindness and self-sacrifice, and to see that the audience is thoroughly inspired by this compassionate vision. One may follow the talk with a rousing puja which everyone joins in, evoking and espousing one spiritual aspiration after another. But then try asking for volunteers to help wash up the cups and stack the chairs, and you can find that the enthusiasm stops flowing as if someone had turned off a tap. On the occasion I have in mind, of perhaps fifty-odd people who had evidently liked the idea of the bodhisattva ideal well enough to sit through a whole evening devoted to it, not a soul stirred in response to a request for ten minutes' help with the washing-up. In short, even when we appreciate the Dharma enough to talk about it, even when we feel truly inspired, we are not necessarily receptive to it.

The Danish existentialist philosopher Kierkegaard famously wrote that the whole of organized Christianity is based on one great assumption: that God is a fool.[64] He gave as an example his observation that every Sunday people go to church and listen dutifully to the preacher telling them to love their neighbour and so on while they know that he doesn't expect them to take him seriously, and he knows that they know this. They all assume that they can fool God in this way, that God will accept this foolishness as something real, as real Christians practising real Christianity. It is a big farce, and one can only feel sorry for clergymen who have to stand up in the pulpit week after week and speak earnestly about matters to which they give only limited credence themselves, and which anyway leave no discernible impression on their dwindling congregations. It must be literally soul-destroying.

Of course, no religion is free of this kind of self-delusion. The danger is that it becomes accepted, even institutionalized. When Buddhist teachers concern themselves exclusively with the social and institutional functions of 'respectable' religion – births, deaths, and marriages – it spells the end for the transmission of a radical spiritual perspective worthy of the name. The danger for any spiritual movement is that its institutions, its practices, even its language and terms of reference, become ends in themselves rather than means towards the transcendence of all mundane preoccupations.

> Stay in the valley to which no men come;
> Keep from bad companions, and yourself examine;

'An unexamined life is not worth living,' said Socrates, and Milarepa would no doubt have agreed. His disciple is warned to keep out of the way of society in general and unsuitable companions in particular, and to examine himself. Clearly, the two injunctions are connected: the unexamined life is usually the indiscriminately sociable life. Going to the local bar, for example, remains a popular way of avoiding experiencing one's mental states. But at this level of practice, the influence of 'bad companions' can come from the unlikeliest of quarters. The very spiritual community that exists to serve and support spiritual practice can simply support complacency, or perhaps a lack of care. In the end, you have to be able to be alone.

> Yearn not to become a Guru;
> Be humble and practice diligently;
> Never hope quickly to attain Enlightenment,
> But meditate until you die.

It might seem strange for a Buddhist to be told not to hope to attain Enlightenment quickly – even more so for a Tantric practitioner; the Tantra is, after all, meant to offer a quick route to Enlightenment. This advice is intended to help its recipient with a particular problem: that we can end up concerning ourselves so much with the end product – or what seems to be the end product – that we lose our appetite for the process of getting there. We make the mistake of separating the end from the means, when the goal is in fact implicit in the path.

For instance, if you are trying to write a book or paint a picture, it is fatal to the creative process just to want to get the thing finished and done with. Even if you feel under pressure to finish it, you still have to create some space in which to be devoted to and immersed in the process for its own sake. It is the same for the practising Buddhist. To practise properly, you have to be so immersed in your meditation, so devoted to your practice, that you are not really bothered about gaining Enlightenment. Even though you know that meditation leads to Enlightenment, you find the process itself so satisfying that you don't mind being in it indefinitely. You just want to meditate. It is something you are going to do until you die. You are in no hurry to get somewhere else. You don't hope to attain Enlightenment quickly, because it's such fun getting there.

This explains the emphasis in the spiritual life on mindfulness, on recollecting and fully appreciating what you are doing at the present moment. Of course you have a goal, but your awareness of it should occupy you only to the extent that it gives purpose or direction to what you are doing here and now. It's the same with any task; at some point you will have to complete it, but you won't do that satisfactorily unless you forget about completing it and concentrate on what you are doing. It's a matter of identifying yourself with the process rather than the achievement. Don't be too eager for recognition and acknowledgement of your commitment and experience. Be happy getting on with your practice. When your inherent momentum simply carries you forward, that is the time to shoulder new responsibilities or take on new commitments. Don't think too much about becoming a Buddha; just get on with trying to be a bodhisattva.

And with regard to whatever you do achieve, Milarepa reminds his aristocratic new disciple, be humble. If you make a lot of noise about your skilful action, its skilfulness is of course vitiated. The ego will never be satisfied with performing a skilful action for the sake of it. It wants to claim a kind of commission, recognition, a pat on the back. Looking for praise reveals a lack of confidence in what you have done, and this comes down to a lack of confidence in yourself. If you cannot feel you have done something right until someone else recognizes what you have done, your actions will never feel adequate. The consequences of such lack of confidence can be serious. You will perhaps find yourself doing something not because you think it is the right thing to do, but in order to get approval. And skilful actions performed for approval pave the way for unskilful actions.

Forgetting words and studies,
Practice the Key-Instructions.
If you would benefit yourself,
Renounce talk and words;
Concentrate on your devotions.

The emphasis here is on personal devotion, the 'Key-Instructions' being personal precepts for practice rather than universally relevant teachings for general discussion. These admonitions are of significance for Buddhists in the West because we have so many books to read – on Zen, on Mahāyāna, even on the *mahāmudrā* – and so little time, it seems, for actual practice. If any Westerner practises even a hundredth part of what they read, they are probably doing pretty well. This is of course a situation that runs entirely counter to tradition.

Suppose we put aside all we had learned from books and gave an account of the Dharma based entirely on our own experience. What could we say that wasn't hearsay? At some point we may consciously have practised a precept or two – but all of them? We could talk a little about our efforts in meditation, about our experience of puja, of being on retreat, about friendship, even, if we had actually experienced spiritual fellowship as opposed to just hanging out with our Buddhist friends. Most of us would be hard put to give detailed descriptions of Buddhas and bodhisattvas, because we wouldn't ever have seen any of them. As for *śūnyatā*, virtually all of us would draw a blank there, and the same would go for perfect wisdom. But even the most elementary and fundamental truths of Buddhism – like 'Hatred does not cease by hatred; hatred ceases only by love'[65] – are, for a good many of us, untested maxims. How many of us have found out through our own experience that this is the way hatred ceases? How much Dharma do we really know for ourselves?

It seems that it is human nature that once someone has learned one thing, however superficially, they want to move on to something different, something more advanced, even something more esoteric. They see a book that promises to impart secret teachings that have never before been divulged to anyone but a small band of trusted disciples, and they think, 'This is just the thing for me.' Anyone, they think, can understand the basic stuff; *they* want something that will take them further, deeper, beyond the ken of ordinary folk. The Tibetans as I knew them in Kalimpong were just the same as Western people in this respect. If word went round that a great lama had arrived in town with some very special teachings, some secret and advanced initiations, they would flock to hear him. A discourse on the five precepts, on the other hand, would never draw a crowd because they'd heard it all before. Of course, it was true enough that they knew the precepts backwards, but as for practising them, that was quite another matter.

There is nothing wrong with a wide-eyed fascination with the world of human knowledge, nothing wrong with the healthy curiosity of the child who just wants to find out things for their own sake and is forever asking questions. Clearly we don't want to lose that kind of fresh inquiring mind. But here Milarepa is deprecating the appropriation of knowledge as a means of reinforcing the ego. This kind of acquisition is no different from acquiring material possessions, except that it may offer even greater social and cultural respectability.

Such an acquisitive attitude to the teachings is bound up with a purely intellectual approach to them, together with an idea that one is equal to what one understands intellectually, that if one understands the words one has mastered the meaning. But as the great English poet Samuel Taylor Coleridge said, you cannot reverence what you understand, and this is certainly true when it comes to the Dharma. If you think you've mastered the Dharma, how can you reverence it? Reverence can only be offered to what you do not understand, to what you are able to acknowledge you haven't mastered. The Dharma is by definition something very far beyond where you are, and if you have no reverence for it, you cannot possibly get any closer to it in terms of your actual experience. This is the great danger of theoretical understanding: that the basic egotism behind it will cut you off from real experience of the Dharma.

You don't need a lot of initiations or shelves groaning with Dharma books and Sanskrit dictionaries to make your practice effective. Just reflect on what it really means to go for Refuge to the Buddha, the Dharma, and the Sangha, and do your best to live in accordance with that. Perform the puja and try to absorb and really feel what you are chanting and saying. Reflect on the five or ten precepts and use them as the touchstone to see how your practice could be improved. Cultivate spiritual friends. Meditate regularly. Just one or two practices are enough: the mindfulness of breathing to develop clarity, and the *mettā bhāvanā* for positive emotion. Perhaps you could reflect on the Noble Eightfold Path, and specifically on how to put it into practice. You might have a string of *mālā* beads and one or two pictures, plus a few books, including one or two anthologies of sayings of the Buddha, and a few favourite lectures on tape or disk. That is all you really need by way of intellectual equipment to take you as far as you want to go. If your practice does not keep pace with your theoretical understanding, if what you read is not being put into action, all that reading is probably hindering your practice. Milarepa goes on to explain that 'in the teaching of Marpa's Line' – the Kagyu or 'Whispered' Lineage – special emphasis is placed on actual practice as opposed to any kind of verbal proliferation.

MILAREPA'S SONG OF DANGERS AND FALLACIES

> Listen to those high-flown words, and pompous talk;
> Look at those charlatans, madly engaged in fervent argument.

Milarepa goes on to make a blistering attack on the plausible charlatans of the spiritual community, and the self-delusion and conceit that creep into any tradition that is over-reliant on conceptual argument. He begins by castigating the scholastic monks of his time and their hobby of public disputation. This was very popular in India during the latter days of Indian Buddhism, and subsequently in Tibet. The tradition of public debate continues to this day in the Gelug school of Tibetan Buddhism, although it is rather frowned on by the Nyingmapas and rejected completely by the Kagyupas, as Milarepa rejects it here.

But the dangers of intellectual conceit are not confined to Tibet. In the West the academic world, even the Buddhist academic world, may present a cool, cultivated façade, but behind it – just as in any sphere of human life – seethe all the passions of the ego, especially envy, jealousy, and malice. The memoirs of academics make sobering reading in this respect. As far as the study of Buddhism is concerned, this civilized kind of conceit manifests especially with regard to the more esoteric or advanced aspects of Buddhism – anything that is presented as being too difficult or demanding for most people, and as requiring special training or study. It is easy to imagine that you are a real authority on the subject because you can talk knowledgeably about it, and to assume because of all your subtle understanding that you are a cut above ordinary Buddhists, who seem to you to practise without knowing what they are doing or what Buddhism is really about. A practitioner who starts to study the scriptures and finds they have some academic talent should be careful not to let this talent turn their head. Once you enter that world, it is hard to avoid being drawn into its petty vanities and disputes.

Milarepa is not objecting to the constructive exchange of ideas and views. He does not object even to the adoption of definite positions. What he warns against is the adoption of *fixed* positions to be tenaciously defended, and the use of arguments to crush one's interlocutor, to thrust one's point of view on them in an overbearing manner. Even if you are right – even if your position is based on a degree of personal experience and even insight – there is no excuse for insisting that you are right, and belabouring someone with your view in the face of their refusal to accept it. If there is any truth in your position, it will come across in the openness of your communication, not by fighting tooth and nail. Whatever insight or realization you have will be conveyed in the quality of your communication, not the force of your argument.

It is natural to want sometimes to shake someone out of their complacent false position. You certainly don't want to spread a superficial agreement over your differences, and it may be skilful to want to open their eyes to a perspective to which they offer initial resistance. The question is how to do this. There is an Indian story that suggests an answer. It is about a lad from the city who is walking through flooded rice fields on one of the narrow raised footpaths that criss-cross the cultivated land. He comes across a calf blocking his way and tries to push it to one side, but it won't budge. However hard he pushes, the calf pushes obstinately back. After a while, a girl comes out of a nearby shelter, looks him up and down, and says, 'You look like an educated man, but you don't seem to have much in the way of common sense.' And so saying, she puts her finger in the calf's mouth and leads it gently away, the calf happily sucking on her finger as it follows after her.

You can influence people more by listening to what they are trying to say, seeing why they want to be where they are and gently drawing them towards your vision of things, than by meeting their views head on and just browbeating them. As Buddhists, the basis of our communication with others should be just that – communication, not point-scoring or verbal kung fu. The most important thing is to be open to the other person. Once they see that it is the truth you are looking for, not victory, they may well begin to listen to what you have to say. Try to experience them as a living, feeling, thinking human being, not just a mouthpiece for a set of views with which you may or may not agree. If your approach is genuine, if you have a real desire to find the truth of the matter, you may even find that you are not quite as well informed as you thought you were.

> In talk they seem intent to frighten you;
> In sleep, they slumber, pompous men;
> They walk like haughty Mongols.
> Dangers and obstacles encompass them.

Milarepa paints a vivid picture of those who argue – whether on behalf of right view or not doesn't matter – without the basic desire really to communicate. Despite all the noise of their fervent wrangling they are asleep. They are unaware, spiritually completely unconscious, even as they are relishing their mastery of the Dharma. They think they are engaged in discussing the finer points of doctrine, but that isn't what is happening at all. Although they don't know it, they are just like rutting animals competing for dominance. If you want to have a contest of wills, that is quite healthy at its own level, but if you imagine that in doing so you are discussing the Dharma, you are in trouble.

If you listen carefully you can usually hear if there is an ego pushing behind someone's words. When you realize that this is what is happening, you have to be careful not to be drawn into the game they want to play, and be clear in your own mind that your aim is different from theirs. Your aim is not to win the argument but to communicate the truth as you see it. If you fail to establish communication, you have lost right from the start, however watertight your argument might be. If you come up against an ego-propelled argument, you are better off withdrawing from that particular topic and re-establishing friendly communication about something else.

When you listen very carefully for the ego that is inflaming an argument, you will sometimes find that ego to be your own. You can be as urbane as you like, but if your ego is tied up with your argument, you will not really be open to the other person and you will therefore fail to communicate with them. It is not the form of words you use that counts so much as the spirit informing them. If you have a clear and orderly mind, you will want to put your point across in the form of a logical argument, and you may even feel the need to press your argument vigorously, but you can be vigorous without being crushing.

Another source of conflict to look out for is any expectation that other people should be rational. It is not reasonable to expect people to be reasonable, and you should never be surprised when they are not. If it upsets you to be met with an unreasonable reaction to a rational argument, you yourself are being unreasonable. It is inevitable that people will be unreasonable even when they are trying to be rational. Of course they will react emotionally – what else does one expect? Why be hurt and taken aback? People aren't rational, and in some ways it is good that they are not – good that they aren't *narrowly* rational, at least. In the long run we need to have access to other, non-rational aspects of ourselves, and to do that we may need to put up with each other's unreasonableness from time to time.

Disputes will therefore occur regularly, even in the spiritual community. Sometimes they may even seem like profound disagreements as to the nature of the commitment that you share. However, the problem is usually a misunderstanding, and this in turn often comes down to a difference in temperament, which is what needs to be addressed. For example, those with a more extrovert temperament tend to interpret their commitment in terms that involve the assumption of a need for structure and organization. Those with a more introverted disposition, by contrast, tend to the opposite view, feeling that their commitment is leading them in the direction of being unstructured, even unorganized. Some apparently profound disagreements can arise out of such contrary perspectives, but they would be much less damaging if those opposing perspectives could be recognized as coming from differing psychological propensities.

The Three Kingdoms and Six Realms are jeopardized
By desires forever leading sentient beings into danger.

The three kingdoms are the three planes of mundane existence: the *kāmaloka*, the world of sensuous desire, the *rūpaloka*, the world of pure or archetypal form, and the *arūpaloka*, the formless world. The six realms are those of the gods, jealous gods, hell beings, hungry ghosts, animals, and humans, as depicted on the Tibetan Wheel of Life. So Milarepa is saying that the whole of conditioned existence, even in its most pure and elevated aspects, is subject to the danger of desire.

If the desire is to overcome one's opponents in debate about the Dharma, the danger is all the greater. It is always dangerous to allow your mindfulness to evaporate in the fervour of wanting to be right and to prove the other person wrong. But if you are making the Dharma the occasion for your unmindfulness, you are making the route to liberation into yet another mundane trap, and that will leave you really stuck. There is nothing more dangerous than pseudo-Dharma. If you cling to your idea of right view as if it were a fixed thing that you can fight for and win, you are making a fundamental mistake.

DANGEROUS PATHS

Milarepa goes on to elaborate on the kinds of danger to which his new disciple is likely to be exposed.

There are seven dangers you should watch:
Falling into the blissful Hīnayāna peace;...

In the traditional Mahāyāna view, the blissful Hīnayāna peace was the 'incomplete' Nirvāṇa of what it called the Hīnayāna, the 'lesser method', following which the disciple aimed to become an *arhant* – that is, to gain Nirvāṇa for himself or herself alone. The bodhisattva ideal of the Mahāyāna schools – the vow to save all beings from the sufferings of conditioned existence – was meant to stir a deeper spiritual ambition. In certain Mahāyāna *sūtras*, especially the *Lotus Sūtra*, the term '*arhant*' refers to someone bent on Nirvāṇa only for themselves, with the implication that they are unwilling to take the last great altruistic step of commitment to the bodhisattva ideal – to become not just an *arhant* but a Buddha. However, the Buddha himself made no explicit distinction between the attainment of an *arhant* and that of a Buddha; the rather more narrow and restricted use of the term *arhant* developed only later in the Mahāyāna tradition.

The term 'Hīnayāna' is best understood not as part of the lexicon of sectarian polemic but as referring to the kind of limited ideal of personal salvation or emancipation that may be espoused by any practitioner of any school. As far as Milarepa is concerned, the Vajrayāna represents, by contrast with this limited model, the most practical, direct, experiential approach to the Dharma, especially through meditation. This is the way of practice, the way of experience, the way of actual self-transformation. In this context, the 'blissful Hīnayāna peace' can be understood as providing a counterpoint of limited spiritual ambition against which to emphasize the dynamic and other-regarding quality of the Mahāyāna goal.

The blissful Hīnayāna peace is that of a subtle, pseudo-spiritual ego; it is Enlightenment envisaged as being 'for me' and as closing the door on other people and their problems. It is pseudo-spiritual individualism in all its forms, whether or not it speaks the language of compassion. Milarepa is pointing out that transcendental experience gained on the basis of the merit accumulated through effective practice is not enough. When some sort of spiritual experience comes out of the blue, you might be tempted to think, 'Well, that's it, I'm there, I've reached the goal,' but Milarepa says, 'Not so. You still have to keep working at your practice, even then.' You may have had the vision, but you still have to work at transforming yourself in accordance with that vision. As long as even the subtlest ego persists, there can be no true state of Enlightenment.

This pseudo-spiritual individualism is the first of Milarepa's seven dangers. As far as we are concerned, it is our tendency to approach our practice from the point of view of our own interests. The next danger occurs on a much cruder level of consciousness.

Using your Buddhist knowledge to get food;…

Milarepa is concerned that Shiwa Aui and his cousin could end up like so many priests, debasing Buddhism from a purely spiritual teaching – a universal truth and a training for the individual – into an ethnic religion, a means of giving people what they want in return for a livelihood. They might have had a real experience of the Dharma, and their perception of things might have undergone a genuine shift, but they haven't yet attained any firm realization. The breakthrough into a new way of perceiving that they have experienced, real and valuable though it may be, is not enough to safeguard them against this danger once they go back to practise in the midst of the world. They will have to be mindful of the spiritual lie of the land. It is all too likely that they will find themselves inclined to feather their nests and ingratiate themselves with the villagers for the sake of their patronage.

This is a common error. You attain some genuine spiritual experience, but then your ego intervenes to appropriate the fruits of your practice and attainment for selfish ends. A degeneration of the ideal with which an individual may have embarked on their spiritual career happens in all religions. Indeed, it can happen in any career in which one is motivated by devotion to some ideal of truth or serving others. In the end you may stop giving yourself to that ideal, your only real concern having become to make money and to be respected as a professional middle-class person.

By Milarepa's time, the Dharma had been the religion of Tibet for some four hundred years, but it need not take that long for a quiet corruption to establish itself. The rot can set in almost immediately, as is evident from the records of events towards the end of the Buddha's own lifetime, which suggest that by no means all his followers even then were truly striving earnestly for the goal.

As the Dharma has spread into different cultures it has tended, unlike Christianity, to merge with pre-existing spiritual traditions rather than simply replace them, converting the whole culture rather than drawing converts out of it. This inevitably meant there was a danger that the spiritual ideals of the Dharma might be contaminated by the more mundane considerations of the ethnic rituals with which it merged. In Tibet, as in India, the Dharma sprang up amidst a rich variety of magical rites that were originally employed in pre-Buddhist cultures for mundane purposes, like destroying enemies, making money, arousing love, and so on. The Tantra took them over and turned them to spiritual use by giving them a symbolic meaning. You would perform the ritual not in order to gain something from it for yourself or your 'client', but in order to meditate on its symbolic significance. The rite of destruction, for example, was used in this contemplative way as a means to destroy one's egotism and defilements. But the sublimation process can easily slip into reverse; the vivid ethnic use of these rites can seem a lot more compelling than the subtleties of their Dharmic symbolism.

Thus the initiate could easily be drawn into exploiting the rites and practices commercially, by performing them as magical rites in return for a fee. As a village priest in Tibet or India, you could set up in business in this way, offering to fulfil the worldly ambitions and desires of local people through magical rites. You ceased to be a living embodiment of the Buddha's teaching and became instead little more than a fortune-teller, or even a beggar. 'Using your Buddhist knowledge to get food' is to see the Dharma as a thing that can be exchanged for worldly advantage.

It is often said that ordinary Indian people are deeply religious and spiritually minded. However, this is true only if you conflate religiosity, or a belief in the efficacy of magical means of securing material or egotistic objectives, with the truly spiritual life. In the case of the average Tibetan too, at least in old Tibet, any Tantric initiation was taken as a general blessing to help one gain prosperity and well-being. It is only a short step from accepting this perception of the rite to accepting money for it.

So how does the authentic spiritual community sustain itself? The economic principle of the sangha may be summarized in terms that set it apart from the principles of modern capitalist society. Each member gives according to his or her ability and takes according to his or her needs. In Buddhist cultures, the monk is given what he needs by the lay community in the way of food and clothing. For the lay people this is *dāna*, giving for its own sake, as a virtue in itself. As far as the monk is concerned, he is happy to give whatever he can, but not by way of exchange. He gives teaching, but he doesn't turn it on like a tap. Ideally he teaches simply by communicating himself as best he can. If there is teaching in that communication, that is fine, and if there isn't much on a particular occasion with a particular person, that is fine as well.

In the 1950s, when the Buddhist conversion movement in India was just beginning, I came across one or two cases of people who had been ordained as monks after a fashion and were going round administering the Refuges and converting people for a price. This is the kind of thing that Milarepa is warning against. One is turning something that is meant to diminish the ego into something that reinforces it, and this is particularly unskilful. It is one thing to take the mundane path rather than the spiritual path, but to turn the spiritual path into the mundane path leaves you with no way out of your corruption.

So Milarepa warns against using the Dharma as a means of support, that is, against being a professional Buddhist. The principle here is that you should not teach the Dharma in *exchange* for something else. You should not turn the holy Dharma into a consecrated meal ticket. It has to be given freely, to be communicated as something beyond price.

Making your communication of the Dharma your livelihood inevitably tends to turn the teaching into a commodity.

Inflating yourself with pride of priesthood;...

By priesthood is meant technical monastic ordination within the Tibetan tradition, which Milarepa insists is not an achievement that in itself sets you above other Buddhists. Ordination is essentially about going to the Buddha, the Dharma, and the Sangha for your refuge; it is about taking the Buddha and his teaching and his Enlightened disciples as your point of reference in everything you say, think, and do. Public ordination is a recognition of this commitment on the part of the Buddhist community, and an expression of their confidence in your ability to carry it out. In this sense, we might concede that those who have been ordained are quite special individuals, and even in certain respects on a higher level than others. But therein lies a danger. Ordination can become a matter of pride and personal satisfaction, of status. When an ecclesiastical ceremony is taken as entitling you to deference and respect, then it has nothing to do with going for Refuge, and everything to do with ego. The danger of such 'pride of priesthood' is real throughout the Buddhist world, especially in cultures where Buddhism is tied in to the wider social establishment and where spiritual status is denoted by ecclesiastical rank. The danger comes when the monks themselves take this socio-spiritual hierarchy literally; when they do so, they join the professional classes, rather in the manner of a nineteenth-century English vicar taking tea with the gentry and offering platitudes to the parish poor. It is always possible to adopt a particular lifestyle out of hypocrisy, hoping to acquire the reputation that goes with being a serious practitioner without the trouble of really committing yourself to practice. Of course it is also possible to live the kind of simple existence associated with the spiritual life while having no aspiration whatsoever.

There is no Buddhist priesthood in the strict sense of the word. However, in all Buddhist countries there are those who have received ordination as monks and there are also individuals who have committed themselves wholeheartedly to the practice of the Dharma without any formal rite of ordination. In the Kagyu tradition, of which Milarepa is part, the renunciation of worldly attachments and the wholehearted commitment to Dharma is strong, but nonetheless the Kagyupas do not bother about monastic ordination. The same is true among the Nyingmapas, although followers of both schools often lead very ascetic lives.

But regardless of one's chosen lifestyle, whether one is living as a monk, a hermit, or a householder, *saṃsāra* is always present, and always operational. It is always there because *saṃsāra* is nothing more or less than our own reactive mind. We bring it with us wherever we are. It never lets up; it never takes a holiday, even if we do. Our habitual grasping for worldly things is like a gravitational pull; if we are not vigilant, it will quite easily overcome the much more remote force impelling us towards Enlightenment.

Hugh Latimer, the sixteenth-century English martyr who in the end was burned at the stake by Queen Mary, once gave a famous sermon in which he made much the same point in a rather striking fashion. He warned idle bishops that the Devil was the busiest bishop in the land, always active in his diocese, never taking a holiday or even stopping to rest.[66] And Māra is no different in this respect. He is much readier to let us go off on retreat than he is to let go of our minds once we are there. It might seem that all we have to do to be at peace is get away from our distractions – but this is not so. In his enthusiasm, Shiwa Aui may go to live far up in the mountains, but Māra will have no trouble finding him there and prattling to him of the entertainments of the town: the singing, the dancing, the fairs and the festivals, the processions and the celebrations, the drinking parties, all the fun and frolic of eleventh-century Tibetan social life. And if he fails to get through to him with that kind of message, he will try to fill him with 'pride of priesthood'.

> Falling into yogic-madness;...

Many different kinds of practice fall under the general heading of the Tantra, and some of these, especially those concerned with the arousal and channelling of subtle energies – for example, through *prāṇāyāma* or breath control – can be psychically destabilizing. Without the guidance of an experienced teacher, the psychophysical energies that such a practice is designed to stir up can run out of control. They can 'heat the brain,' as it is said, so that you become psychologically unbalanced.

This would seem to be the yogic madness Milarepa is referring to here, a state of psychic disturbance brought about by uncontrolled vital energies being released in yoga and meditation practice. Understood in this way, the ignorance that lies behind this danger is not so much a case of subtle ego-clinging as a lack of understanding of the practices. There is also the possibility that Milarepa is referring not to a real madness triggered by one's practice but merely to zaniness. Even in Milarepa's time, wild and wacky behaviour, more self-indulgent than truly spontaneous, was sometimes adopted by people who wanted to impress others with their 'crazy wisdom'. As with the 'charlatans, madly engaged in fervent argument', a studied spiritual unconventionality is usually a mask for a superficial understanding and practice of the Dharma.

Indulging in empty speeches;...

The danger here lies in airing one's knowledge, especially knowledge that is not based on personal experience, in order to impress. It is the tendency to pronounce your opinions and views on the Dharma not for the sake of whoever might be listening but simply to hear your own voice authoritatively holding forth. The danger is not just vanity, but misusing the Dharma. If you are airing your own views rather than making it clear what the Dharma has to say, your communication is just an empty noise, however impressive your command of rhetoric. That is to say, your *ḍākinī* will desert you. The *ḍākinī*, remember, is the third Tantric Refuge, representing spiritual inspiration as it becomes available to you. When you are in touch with the *ḍākinīs*, you will find forces of inspiration welling up within you – but of course what can well up can also dry up. Let yourself become arrogant or glib, and the forces of inspiration will slip away. You will be so busy listening to the sound of your own voice that you won't be able to hear the voice of the *ḍākinī* within.

Anyone who has ever given a talk on the Dharma will have experienced this from time to time. After a while you become aware that the spirit in which you prepared your material or in which you began to teach has left you, and that what you are saying is coming out in a rather dead, mechanical way. You no longer feel in touch with it. Nothing is coming up from within; the *ḍākinīs* have taken flight. When this happens, you need to allow time for the forces of inspiration to well up again. The *ḍākinīs* are easily disturbed, and to stay in contact with them you have to listen very carefully. Theirs is a subtle and refined form of energy, and you can't take it for granted. In other words, you need to know where your inspiration comes from and make sure that you keep the channels to that source open.

Falling into the trap of nothingness.

Milarepa balances his caution against falling into the blissful Hīnayāna peace with a warning about a danger inherent in the perfection of wisdom teachings of the Mahāyāna. This danger is that the central concept of śūnyatā or emptiness can easily be misunderstood. The unwary student is likely to interpret it nihilistically, thinking of Nirvāna as the cessation of the conditioned and nothing beyond that, a state of nothingness. But śūnyatā is not nothingness. All things are empty, but this does not mean they do not exist; it means they are empty of anything fixed or permanent.

It is true that nothing has any unchanging essence. Everything, including you, is in constant flux. Things may be said to exist only in dependence on conditions. So everything is composite, conditioned, and nothing that the conceptualizing mind tries to pin down exists in quite the way the mind thinks it does. But the way the mind does perceive things is still useful, indeed necessary, in helping us communicate and understand things on a mundane level. Indeed, we cannot make any progress on the spiritual path without the distinctions the mind makes – without, for example, being able to make a distinction between samsāra and nirvāna. Ultimately we may have to realize the emptiness of that distinction, and that nothing at all exists as a separate entity. But it is better, as Nāgārjuna puts it, to cling to a self-view as big as Mount Meru than to get caught up in a wrong view of śūnyatā. The idea of śūnyatā is strong medicine, but it becomes strong poison if it is taken the wrong way. On the other hand, if we apprehend śūnyatā correctly, even if our understanding is limited, we will be able to appreciate our experience even as we let go of it, and act for the welfare of others without thinking of the distinction of self and other as ultimately valid – that is, without making a big fuss about it.

Thus, ignorance is the cause of fallacies and dangers.

The seventh danger is the cause of the preceding ones. It is ignorance, the mistake of believing you are a fixed entity, a self or soul, that you are marked out as special and separate from other living beings. Ignorance permeates the whole of *saṃsāra*, and is the root of all hindrances and obstacles to the spiritual life.

Milarepa is referring here not just to general ignorance of the mundane world, but specifically to ignorance in the sense of misunderstanding the Dharma, losing touch with the real significance of Tantric practice. Ignorance of this kind is immensely dangerous, and leads even the most sincere practitioner astray. Because the Dharma is the way to emancipation, if you use it for mundane ends while imagining you are practising correctly, you really are in trouble. The Dharma has to be approached warily, with respect. As the Buddha himself said, getting it wrong is like grabbing a snake in the wrong way: you are going to get bitten.[67]

The teaching of the Whispered Lineage is the Ḍākinīs' breath.

The *ḍākinīs* represent untrammelled energies whose natural medium is the openness of reality, and their breath is inspiration; appropriately, the English word 'inspiration' literally means the drawing in of breath. So the *ḍākinīs*' breath is the very inspiration of inspiration itself. The Whispered Lineage is pure inspiration. It is not the inspiration you get from books, from thinking, from intellectual understanding; it is not the inspiration that comes from the Freudian – or even the Jungian – unconscious. It comes straight out of the open space of reality itself, straight from the Enlightened mind. You could say that the Dharma itself is the *ḍākinīs*' breath, the Buddha's breath. And if the Dharma doesn't inspire you, then it isn't the Dharma – at least not for you at this time. It may perhaps inspire you later, but that inspiration has to be there for the Dharma to operate as the Dharma. You may lead a good life without inspiration, but you won't get far with your spiritual life.

Milarepa is asserting that it is not enough to take your stand on books or accepted teachings or tradition, or on conventional religious life, with its ordination, its monasticism, its robes, Tantric rites, and ceremonies. No – there must be that pure inspiration from the experience of reality itself. This is the only valid basis for a spiritual tradition or school of practice. This is what the Kagyu school stands for: actual practice as opposed to any kind of verbal proliferation. To put it in an extreme way, if you can't feel the *ḍākinīs*' breath on your shoulder, whatever you do spiritually speaking is just hypocritical posturing. So a good motto to carry with you through the spiritual life is: don't forget the breath of the *ḍākinīs*.

Never doubt this truth.

The chief protection from the seven dangers comes from one's relationship with the lineage, which stretches all the way back to the Buddha. In particular it comes from one's relationship with the guru as the embodiment of the Buddha in this life. It is faith, in other words, rather than wisdom, that will be your lifeline when your Tantric practice begins to go off course. Effective Tantric practice relies, above all, on energy, on positivity and inspiration, and the chief enemy at this level is the insidious fetter of doubt, whether it is doubt in oneself or in the practices.

We have already seen how crucial this personal transmission of the Dharma is, especially in the Tantra, and even more especially in the Kagyu tradition, the Whispered Lineage. A slightly cynical, worldly impulse will very easily throw into doubt the idea that this Tibetan Buddhist school is the *ḍākinīs*' breath. Shiwa Aui is inspired enough at the moment, but when his inspiration deserts him, he will need to know how to guard his faith. Now is the time when he must be mindful of the conditioned nature of his inspiration, and be alert enough to anticipate occasions when it may be lost, and his faith along with it.

This danger is very real. If he does come round to thinking that the lineage is not in fact experientially based, that its conclusions are merely the result of thinking about reality, then Shiwa Aui will lose faith in Milarepa himself. More importantly, he will lose faith in the unique bond that has been created by the whispered transmission. If he were ever to think that the teachings Milarepa had given him were just so much repetition, just book knowledge, a product of conjecture and supposition, his Dharma practice would be in tatters. This is why Milarepa emphasizes the breath of the *ḍākinīs*, and the fact that his teaching is based on his own experience – based, that is, on reality. Only by safeguarding his faith in the authenticity of Milarepa's teaching will Shiwa Aui be able to make progress in his practice.

Shiwa Aui, how can you ever go astray
Since you are near me, the great Cotton-clad One?

When he says 'since you are near me', Milarepa does not mean that his new disciple should necessarily stay with him physically. Our teachers do not always appear to us in the form in which we originally met them, or indeed in any human form at all, and there is no need to be afraid that in the absence of your teacher you are going to stop learning, or even stop receiving new teachings. You can receive guidance or instruction in all sorts of other ways. It can be from your own mind, from the mental states that reveal themselves to you in your practice of meditation and mindfulness, ethics and reflection. It can be from your study of the Dharma, from the sparks struck by the formulated teachings as your mind applies itself to them. It can be from nature itself; you may find, with Shakespeare's exiled Duke in *As You Like It*, 'Tongues in trees, books in the running brooks, sermons in stones, and good in everything'.[68] Being 'near the teacher' means remaining open to the teaching that is all around you, wherever you are.

It is not healthy to rely on the guru to such an extent that you are closed to the possibility of receiving instruction from other sources. If you do want to surrender yourself entirely and devotedly to your spiritual teacher, at least avoid seeing him or her in too literal and limited a way. You can listen out for your teacher even when he is nowhere near in geographical terms, and hear him speaking to you through all sorts of situations in which he plays no part at all in any literal sense.

Don't turn your faith and devotion into a limiting factor. The aim of education is to enable you to develop your own understanding and capacity to learn. The teaching does not come just from the teacher, it comes from the pupil too, and from the material taught. The qualities needed in oneself as an aspirant, together with the goals to which one aspires, are also teachers, especially in the form of bodhisattvas. All these different teachers represent the communication of different facets of one reality, and they may equally be regarded as the communication of the guru.

> Lay down your doubts and meditate.
> He who relies on the true Teachings will never go astray.

Individual doubts may be dealt with by effective argument, but in the end, the doubting mind can never be laid to rest outside of practice. The 'true Teachings' are true in the sense that one can verify them for oneself, and one can obviously have full confidence in following this principle. This explains the emphasis, in the Kagyu tradition, on renunciation and unstinting spiritual practice. If there is one thing for us to take to heart from Milarepa's teaching, it is this: more and more of less and less. Concentrate more and more on those things that are simple, capable of being expressed in a few words, yet of basic importance. Make 'back to the beginning' your watchword. Keep going back to what you think you understand, what is so straightforward that you never think twice about it, and consider it, reflect on it and on how it bears on your experience of life and practice as a Buddhist. Very often we do not realize the extent to which we understand but do not practise. We think we understand a spiritual teaching because we can follow its logic, but to put it into practice, day in and day out, involves a very different kind of knowledge.

What, for example, does something as basic as the first of the five precepts really mean? Is it enough to say that it is an undertaking not to take life? It literally means 'abstain from violence to breathing beings', but what are the implications for us in terms of changing the way we relate to others? This is the way the precepts work; practising them is supposed to change us. Conversely, if you harm others you are committing two breaches of the precept at the same time: you are harming others as well as yourself.

If the first precept seems straightforward, if you think you can more or less forget about it, you are completely misunderstanding the nature of basic practices. They are basic not in the sense that they are something to leave behind, but in the sense that they are to be constantly maintained. Not hurting or harming living beings is a good start, but if you leave it at that, you are going to be applying the precept in a fairly crude and unthinking way. It should be much more creative than a self-imposed restriction on your violent and destructive impulses. It means letting go of hatred and developing respect and friendliness towards people and animals. It also includes the quality of mindfulness in one's relations with others.

More specifically, the first precept is an undertaking not to hinder or trespass on the individuality of another. What, after all, is that 'breathing being'? At the heart of the precept is the awareness that a living being is essentially a growing being, a developing being. This is the *raison d'être* of that being's existence: not only to live but to grow, to evolve. The precept asks you to consider what any living being's process of development consists in, where their energy is moving, and how to avoid getting in the way. If you see that you can assist in this process of development, then the first precept demands that support from you as well. It also involves your duty to your own development. If you hinder another, if you fail in your duty to them, you are also failing in your duty to yourself; you are hindering your own growth and development, blocking your own positive energy.

Why does this precept come first? What makes it the basis of all Buddhist practice? The answer is simple. It is the first principle of ethical and spiritual living because it allows people the space to grow in their own way. D. H. Lawrence said that the first principle of good parenting was to let the child alone – and that the second and third principles were the same. Obviously you have to stop the child falling into the fire or running into the road, but, other than that, a parent's duty is to support a child's growth rather than interfere with it. The same thing goes for the way we respond to other people and support their growth.

It can be good to share our experience with someone who wants to talk things through, but sometimes we are too quick to follow this or even replace it with advice and subtle pressure, however friendly. Do we really know what is truly best for someone? Do we really know what constitutes growth and development for them as an individual? It is remarkable how sometimes a person who has only the vaguest idea of the direction their own life is taking can be quite definite in their analysis of the practice of others. So this is the first precept: just stand clear. Of course, don't harm beings in the obvious sense, but also allow them to evolve according to their own individuality. If we leave people unharmed but cannot resist interfering with and checking their growth, our practice of this precept still needs a lot of work.

The first precept alone therefore gives us quite a lot to be getting on with. It is perhaps surprising how little we need to know in order to practise the Dharma, and even to communicate it. It is no use trying to beat the intellectuals at their own game, but people – even intellectuals – will always be convinced by basic honesty and sincerity, by simple clarity of purpose and friendliness of demeanour. Showing that you are trying to practise one precept, and that your heart is in it, may be more impressive than being able to discourse learnedly on all the schools of Buddhist philosophy. If you can communicate the fact that practising the Dharma makes you happier and less selfish, that is more than enough.

Think not, my son, of meaningless word-knowledge
But concentrate on your devotions.
Then you will soon attain the great Accomplishment.

Meaningless word-knowledge is conceptual understanding that is not put to the test of experience. Faith based on book learning is always vulnerable to being challenged and negated by more book learning, but this is the wrong way round. The purpose of learning is to support the faith and inspiration that comes from actual practice. We should not of course forget that Milarepa's teacher, and the founder of the Kagyu lineage, Marpa, is celebrated for his book knowledge. Not for nothing is he known as Marpa the Translator; he spent much of his time making long trips to India, where he gained initiations and collected Tantric texts, bringing this wealth of literary material back to Tibet. However, Milarepa warns Shiwa Aui that theories, views, and reflections are only a guide to the truth. The experience of the truth is found in practice.

SHIWA AUI'S SONG OF RENUNCIATION

Milarepa's vehement warnings against the dangers of book learning are evidently heeded. We are told that from this time Shiwa Aui gives up his search for intellectual knowledge and concentrates on his devotions, to the neglect of his diet and appearance. It would seem that Milarepa has seen Shiwa Aui in the early years of his discipleship poring over texts, getting to know them and fiercely debating over the finer points of Buddhist logic. Perhaps he has expressed ambitions to become a scholar of Buddhism. Anyway, his worldly ambition clearly lingered in this form beyond his initial conversion. But now he cuts a wretched figure. As a result of his total devotion to practice he has, like Milarepa, become an emaciated and ragged-robed yogi. One day an old friend comes across him and commiserates with him over his fall from being 'a gay spark from a rich family' to his present sorry condition. In reply, Shiwa Aui sings a song that indicates how far he has come.

Oh my Father Guru, the Jetsun, the real Buddha,
The Field-of-Offering for my parents!

Just as a field is where you sow seeds and harvest the crop, a holy person is traditionally regarded in Buddhism as a 'field of merit' where the offerings you plant will ripen into *puṇya* or merit. Shiwa Aui's parents have, so to speak, made an offering of their son to Milarepa. The offering being so valuable and Milarepa being such a holy person, the merit that will accrue to them in future will be correspondingly abundant. Far from being the wretched failure of a rich family, as his friend is suggesting, Shiwa Aui has brought an immeasurable source of wealth to his parents. Having pointed out that he has provided well for his family's prosperity, Shiwa Aui goes on to declare his independence, indicating exactly why he is much better off without his family.

> Brothers, sisters, and all (relatives) give rise to Saṃsāra:
> But I have now renounced them.
> The Jetsun is my sole companion and comrade in the Dharma.
> Alone he is my source for the Buddha's Teaching;
> With him, the real Buddha, I remain in solitude.
>
> A group of three or four leads but to empty talk, ...
>
> Books and commentaries bring one nought but pride,
> But the authentic Buddha gives
> The one-sentence Pith-Instruction.

Gone now is any regard for outer appearances, for his bookish, garrulous, socializing and clannish old self. Gone is any regard for worldly accumulation or the sense of group identity bound up with it. His family ties him to the saṃsāric realm of likes and dislikes, of empty habit and empty talk, whereas his guru offers him true communication with a true individual.

Here we find the characteristic emphasis of the Kagyu, which is to avoid too much study, group discussion, and even ritual or anything like highly organized religious practice. Instead, you have just two people living in close proximity – the Enlightened teacher and the faithful disciple – with this simple but direct communication between them: 'the one-sentence Pith-Instruction', the most intensive teaching one can receive.

The more one has, the more one craves.
So I forsake my home and renounce my native land.

The country with no boundary-posts is the place near Buddha
Wherein the faithful one can practise virtuous deeds.

Associates and servants cause more anxiety and craving,
So I renounce them for all time.

According to the rules of conduct originally established by the Buddha, monks should not live near a frontier if they could avoid it, because of the border disputes that made such regions dangerous and disturbing. This is the most obvious sense in which the 'country with no boundary posts is the place near Buddha'. Shiwa Aui refers to this obscure rule of the Vinaya to highlight the deeper issue represented by boundaries: the more you possess, the more you have to defend; and the more you identify with those possessions, the more entrenched becomes your view of yourself, and the more fixed the boundary between self and other.

Shiwa Aui is not afraid to state the obvious fact that getting what we want does not provide a lasting solution to any of our problems. It is the wanting itself that is the real problem, the erroneous view that we can 'fix' reality by reorganizing the world of people and things to suit our aims and preferences. In Shiwa Aui's case, he has learned that even his most valued possessions, his family, his entourage, and all the privileges and protection that derive from being a member of a clan, cannot protect him from impermanence and death.

After this, Shiwa Aui served Milarepa until he died, and he eventually became Enlightened himself. By contrast, it seems that his nephew, Sang Jye Jhab, turned out 'foolish and powerful', presiding over a small temple near Nya Non, and 'the Jetsun was slightly displeased with him'. One can imagine how this unsatisfactory disciple would have set himself up as the disciple of the great Milarepa, and lived off the offerings of the laity by performing weddings and funerals, baby-namings and crop-blessings. We can imagine him perhaps in the end becoming a married yogi with lots of disciples, and tending his little garden. Milarepa was not of course troubled within himself over this spiritual capitulation, just a little disappointed.

The meeting between Milarepa and this young nobleman at Silver Spring has archetypal qualities. It began with a normal, happy, healthy young man with a fine family, wealth, and education, riding out to have a good time with his friends. He meets a yogi, a strange, shamelessly naked figure lying by the roadside. He doesn't much like the look of him, but he is jerked out of his initial contempt by something that doesn't make sense to him. Faith arises, faith which the yogi Milarepa tests until the young man is reduced to despair. But his joy in his faith remains, and Milarepa finally accepts him, teaches him, and trains him. The young man spends a lot of time with Milarepa, and eventually gains Enlightenment. No doubt there were many ups and downs during the five years of the young man's apprenticeship about which we are not told, but the main outlines of his story are clear and straightforward.

Its main theme is the impotence of a bargaining attitude with regard to the Dharma. The Dharma cannot be bought. The young man makes his series of offerings in a spirit of real devotion but also with a degree of egoism. Above all, he assumes that what he possesses, his 'valuables', have some kind of absolute value, and that they must count for something even in exchange for the Dharma. The unspoken assumption is that if he makes these offerings, Milarepa will feel obliged to offer him some of his own valuables in return. However subtly the young man dresses this bartering for the Dharma as 'offerings', his imperfect motivation cannot be hidden from Milarepa, and the offerings are therefore rejected as unacceptable.

Because the Dharma can only be given, not bought, in a sense the young man is trying to take the not-given (to use the words of the second precept). He wants to keep hold of his ego, to get hold of the Dharma for himself, but as long as that ego is there he is not going to be able to receive the Dharma. This will, this grabbing, this ego, has to be broken down. He has to realize his complete spiritual impotence. Only then, when he starts doubting whether he has any capacity for the Dharma at all, does faith arise, and he can move forward.

In the end, the young man has to offer *himself*, and when he does this, when he no longer keeps anything of himself in reserve, there is no one left behind to expect something in exchange. When he says, 'You know what should be said,' there is no further presumption that he can tell

Milarepa anything he needs to know. He knows he cannot buy Milarepa. This is when Milarepa starts to give him encouragement and teachings.

The moral of the story seems to be that you get results only after you have put all your energy into something, failed, and given up, or given in. Having tried over and over again to achieve something (in fact, to grab at it), you are eventually forced to accept defeat, to recognize that you are powerless, that your egoistic will can achieve nothing in this situation. Then something within you shifts. To take a superficial example, you might enjoy arguing, and you might try to argue various points of view with someone; but as you try one argument after another, in the end you may just have to accept that the other person has a keener intellect than yours. Only having tried your utmost do you realize your intellectual inadequacy, at least as regards reasoned argument. Whether in this or in some other way, it is good for us to try very hard, fail, and accept what that means.

At a much higher level, the Zen koan works on the same principle. You are presented with a puzzle of some kind: 'What is the sound of one hand clapping?' or 'How do you get a goose out of a bottle without breaking the bottle or injuring the goose?' You turn a riddle like this over and over in your mind, trying to work it out, thinking about it so intently that it dominates your every waking moment. You think and think and think, perhaps for years on end, until finally your reasoning powers let go their grip and your rational mind gives up – really gives up. It isn't that your mind is at a loss while it casts about for another approach, or that it simply loses interest; you experience the total impotence of the thinking mind, and that is your breakthrough, your flash of transcendental insight wit. The ego has to exhaust itself against some impenetrable object.

This object may be a person, as in the case of Milarepa, or a problem, as in the case of the koan, or some situation in ordinary life, like having a strongly held view demolished by argument, or being turned down by the lover you'd set your heart on, or failing to get the qualification you'd set your sights on. Whatever it is, you find yourself unable to step forward or back. You are right up against it, and in the end you can only surrender – and this is very good for you in terms of stripping bare your egoistic will.

The whole process is much more radical when you confront not just a situation involving other unenlightened individuals, but someone like

Milarepa. Someone who is Enlightened knows exactly what they are doing, they can see your unenlightened egoistic will all the way down to its roots, and they are determined to root out every last fibre of it. They will close every loophole and leave you with nowhere to go, no leg to stand on, no straw to clutch. They will bring you to rock-bottom, even to despair. Only then, when you are thoroughly purged of your egoistic pride, will you get a single word of encouragement. And that is how you become a heart-disciple.

The Shepherd's Search
for Mind

THE SHEPHERD'S SEARCH FOR MIND

In which two contrasting encounters are described. In the first, a married couple try to convince Milarepa to accept their generous offer to set him up in worldly life, but he explains his determination to refuse their offer in no uncertain terms, and in the end convinces them to follow the spiritual path. In the second encounter, a young shepherd wants to know the nature of mind and is encouraged to find out for himself.

Themes:

I

NO NEED OF THESE THINGS

HERE COMES THE WONDERFUL YOGI!

In 'The Meeting at Silver Spring' we found Milarepa in communication with a youth who to begin with had no notion of the Dharma at all, and was led by Milarepa through a process of transformation by the end of which he had become a heart disciple. In this chapter we find Milarepa in two more versions of the same situation: a meeting with someone, seemingly by chance, and an interaction which in the end bears great fruit. But these two situations couldn't be more different, although as we shall see there is a definite connection, a definite relationship, between the two parts of the chapter. They form a sort of diptych, one could say, contrasting one with the other.

> One day, Jetsun Milarepa descended from the Great Light Cave to the Happy Village of Mang Yul for food and alms. Seeing many people in the center of the village, he said to them, 'Dear patrons, please give me some food this morning.' They asked, 'Are you the much-talked-about yogi who formerly resided at Ragma?' He replied, 'Yes, I am.' Then a great respect for him arose within them and they cried, 'Oh, here comes the wonderful yogi!'

So Milarepa is living up on the mountainside, meditating in Great Light Cave, and every now and then he comes down to the village at the foot of the mountain. Perhaps it's a market day, because there are a lot of people around in the centre of the village. He approaches them and says, 'Dear patrons, please give me some food this morning.' This would be unconventional behaviour for a monk – according to Buddhist tradition you're not supposed to ask for alms, but just to stand with your begging-bowl – but Milarepa isn't a conventional monk. In fact, he isn't a monk at all. According to the Kagyu tradition he may have received a *śrāmaṇera* ordination, but certainly he never became a monk in the technical sense, a *bhikkhu* or *gelong*; he was 'just' a yogi. He didn't bother about the formalities of monastic life; he didn't even have a begging-bowl. When he sees all these people gathered in the centre of the village he just approaches them and says, 'Please give me some food.' He is a very simple, direct, almost childlike person. They can no doubt see that he is rather unusual. He is probably virtually naked – just about covered up with a piece of cloth, but not much more than that. He apparently never wore monastic robes or anything of that sort. That's why he was called Milarepa, *repa* meaning one who wears a piece of cotton cloth.

Although he's been living up in the mountains, the people in the village have apparently heard about him. He was quite well known in that part of Tibet, and they've heard that there is this crazy yogi living in a cave above the snow line, virtually naked and singing songs when people come to see him, so when they see this wild, bizarre-looking figure, they suspect that it might be the much-talked-about yogi. In Tibet in the old days there wasn't much to talk about. Nothing much happened. If you had a yogi living in your neighbourhood, that was at least a topic of conversation, especially if he was someone rather eccentric and strange like Milarepa. They ask, 'Are you the much-talked-about yogi who formerly resided at Ragma?' and he replies, without false modesty, 'Yes, I am.'

At Milarepa's time the Dharma had been the state religion in Tibet for about three hundred years, so Buddhism is established among these people – otherwise what significance would a yogi have? He would just be some mad naked fellow living in a cave. They seem to have an innate respect for yogis, and he addresses them as 'dear patrons', which suggests that in that part of Tibet the Dharma is fairly well established and people know what a yogi is. They therefore know, presumably, what meditation is, and they're sufficiently interested in the whole idea of yogis to be talking about this one. There may even be a little *gompa* (a temple) in the village, and a Nyingma-type priest or performer of ceremonies; we are not told. But, anyway, they are Buddhists, they are familiar with the idea of yoga, and they're quite prepared to welcome Milarepa, they're glad to see him, and 'a great respect arose within them'. Their spontaneous response is significant. They don't say, 'What a crazy looking fellow!' or 'How stupid to pass your time like that!' so they must have some idea of what yoga (in the sense of meditation) is all about. The ground is prepared, so when he turns up and asks for alms they say, 'Oh, here comes the wonderful yogi!' One can't imagine that sort of thing happening nowadays, even in India. They'd think you were wasting your time and you ought to be working, or at least engaging in social work.

We know that Milarepa didn't go begging for alms very often, so this is a special occasion. Maybe he felt drawn to that village; maybe there are people living there who are ready to hear more of the Dharma. Perhaps asking for food is only a pretext. As we have seen, in the story called 'The Meeting at Silver Spring' Milarepa meets a young man on a horse and asks for a lift across the river. Actually, as it later transpires, he is able to cross the river by his magic power, but he asks the young man to give him a lift just to get into conversation with him, and then he can start talking about the Dharma. Something of that sort might have happened here.

WHERE ARE YOUR HOME AND RELATIVES?

> Among them was a married couple who had no children. Inviting Milarepa to their house, they served him and said, 'Dear Lama, where are your home and relatives?' Milarepa replied, 'I am a poor beggar who has disavowed his relatives and native land and has also been forsaken by them.' Then the couple cried, 'In that case we would like to adopt you into our family! We have a good strip of land which we can give you; you can then marry an attractive woman, and soon you will have relatives.' Milarepa replied, 'I have no need of these things, and will tell you why.'

It is not unusual in Tibet that a married couple should have no children, and perhaps they invite Milarepa to their house because they feel a parental interest in him, or feel sorry for him. He looks very poor and perhaps to their eyes very miserable – he hasn't any proper clothes, and he's begging for food. They invite him to their house and serve him – presumably they offer him food – and then they say, 'Dear Lama, where are your home and relatives?' This is a question I was asked repeatedly in my own wandering days. Indian householders used to ask me, 'Where are your mother and father?' I'd say, 'Oh, they're thousands of miles away.' And they'd always say, 'Oh, how can you bear to be separated from them? They must be weeping for you.' Family feeling is very strong, and it puzzled people to see someone living apparently happily in a non-family situation. This seems to be a universal human thing. Milarepa tells them that he has disavowed his relatives and native land and has also been forsaken by them. In other words, the separation is complete: he's left them and they have left him. He's just a beggar without family, without native land. He's not even living in his own part of Tibet. Tibet in the old days was divided into not exactly independent kingdoms, but certainly independent areas. There wasn't much contact between them, and you were loyal to your particular area.

The couple immediately say, 'In that case we would like to adopt you into our family.' Milarepa is perhaps quite a bit younger than they are – he took up the spiritual life rather late, apparently when he was about forty, but they might be fifty or sixty. Maybe they're thinking, 'The gods have sent us a son!' They go on to offer him 'a good strip of land' on the strength of which he will be able to marry an attractive woman and soon have relatives of his own – heirs, a family, a home. Everything will be complete. He won't be on his own any more. How wonderful! In other words, they've got an initial respect for him, they feel devoted towards him and think he's a wonderful yogi, but they haven't grasped anything about the spiritual life at all. Their first instinct is to incorporate him into their way of life. They do it naively and straightforwardly, with a good heart. There's no idea of undermining his spiritual commitment. They just don't know, they can't see, that their offer is incompatible with his way of life. But of course Milarepa does. He says, 'I have no need of these things and will tell you why.'

As soon as someone who is committed to the spiritual life comes into contact with the group, this tends to be what the group tries to do. It tries to incorporate you into itself, in this case into the family. This couple haven't got any children, they see Milarepa, they like and admire him, and their first thought is to make him their son. It is not that they want to do him any harm, or be untrue to Buddhism; they just don't see that their offer is incompatible with what he is trying to do in his life. This is the sort of thing that one always has to be on one's guard against. Of course you've got to keep up a relationship with the group, you can't just break off from it entirely, and that is shown by the fact that Milarepa came down from the mountain and asked for food. There's that connection even in the case of the ascetic. But one has to be very careful that that doesn't develop into something else.

That reminds me of a story about a guru who left his disciple meditating under a tree. He said, 'You just stay there and meditate. Don't do anything else at all. I'll come back later and see how you are getting along.' The disciple had absolutely nothing at all except a *kaupin*, a small strip of cloth which is all that some yogis in India wear. People would come and give him food, apparently. He meditated for some days, got on quite well, and then he felt the need to wash his *kaupin*. He didn't have a change of *kaupin*, so he just washed the one he was wearing in a nearby stream and hung it up on the tree to dry. Then, naked as he was, he went back to meditating while his *kaupin* was drying. But while the *kaupin* was hanging there, a rat crawled up the trunk of the tree and nibbled the cloth, and when the disciple opened his eyes after meditating he saw that quite a hole had been nibbled out of the *kaupin*, which was small enough to begin with. Rather displeased, he thought, 'Well, we can't have that. If this rat goes on nibbling my *kaupin* every time I wash it, I won't be very decent.'

The next time someone came from the village with food, he said, 'Look, I've got a problem. There's a rat that comes and gnaws my *kaupin* when I wash it. Could you please get me a cat which would keep an eye on the rat? Then my *kaupin* will be safe.' The next day they brought him a cat, and the rat never came back. But after a couple of days the cat started getting hungry. It mewed so piteously that the next time people came with food, the disciple asked them, 'Please could you bring some milk for my cat?' So every day a villager had to come with milk for his cat. One day the villager who was bringing the milk said, 'Look, we come every day with milk for your cat. We don't mind, we're happy to do it, but sometimes it's a bit troublesome. Would you mind if we gave you a cow? Then you can milk the cow and give the milk to the cat.' The disciple thought that was a sensible idea, so a cow was brought and tied to the tree.

Now he had a cow, of course, he had to spend his time cutting grass for it to eat. In India there is no grazing; you go and cut grass, dry grass usually, for your cow. So now the disciple was spending several hours a day cutting grass for the cow, and he couldn't get on with his meditation. He thought, 'This is no good. My guru told me to meditate.' The next time a villager came along he explained the problem, and the man said, 'OK, I'll arrange for someone to come and cut grass for you; there will be no problem then.' So a man was sent from the village to do the grass cutting. This went on for two or three days, and then the man who was cutting the grass said to the yogi, 'Look, I'm quite happy to do the grass cutting every day for you, but I have a wife and children at home and I really need some money.' The disciple said, 'I'm spending all my time meditating. I haven't got any money.' The grass-cutter said, 'Well, the cat doesn't need all the milk from the cow. You can sell some of the milk and out of the proceeds you can pay me for cutting the grass.' The disciple thought that was rather a good idea, so the grass-cutter let it be known that there was milk for sale. So now the disciple was selling the milk from the cow, paying the grass-cutter, looking after the cat, and carrying on with his meditation.

In the end so many people were coming for milk that it started becoming troublesome, and then the cow produced a calf. He had another chat with the village folk, and they said, 'You need someone to take the whole responsibility off your hands. There's a very nice girl in the village. Marry her and she'll take care of everything. She's a very good, well-trained girl, she'll manage the business' – because the selling of milk was developing into a business by that time – 'and you can get on with your meditation.' To cut a long story short, he married the girl, she came to live there, there were more and more cows, and she built up a big business. In the end, there was so much to do that he had to help. They built a house and it developed into a farm. Three years later his guru came back to see how he was getting on with his meditation. Instead of just a tree he found a dairy farm with several dozen cows and calves, and a woman moving around the farm, and several servants and grass-cutters and helpers, and one or two children, and lots and lots of cats. He just didn't know what to think. When he saw the disciple, he said, 'What on earth happened?' The disciple's eyes were opened and he fell at his guru's feet, 'Oh, guru-ji,' he said, 'It was all for the sake of a *kaupin*!' This is the sort of thing that happens if you aren't very careful.

So Milarepa says, 'I have no need of these things, and I will tell you why.'

> Home and land at first seem pleasant;
> But they are like a rasp filing away one's body, word, and mind!
> How toilsome ploughing and digging can become!
> And when the seeds you planted never sprout, you have worked
>   for nought!
> In the end it becomes a land of misery – desolate and unprotected –
> A place of Hungry Spirits, and of haunting ghosts!
> When I think of the warehouse
> For storing sinful deeds,
> It gnaws at my heart;
> In such a prison of transiency I will not stay,
> I have no wish to join your family!

> *Home and land at first seem pleasant;*
> *But they are like a rasp filing away one's body, word,*
>   *and mind!*

Isn't Milarepa being unduly negative? Are home and land really like a rasp filing away body, word, and mind? When you take a rasp to a piece of wood, little by little the sawdust drops away, and likewise home and land are having an effect on you all the time. This metaphor is really expressive; you're being worn away, worn down. Whatever your occupation you're being worn away in the sense that you're getting older all the time, but in some ways it seems as though your whole being is being rasped away. I notice this sometimes when I go to London and travel on the Underground. When you look at people's faces, you can see that they're being rasped away. They've spent the day at the office or in a factory, and it's had a wearing effect on them. They're tired not in the way you feel tired when you've done a good positive day's work, but just exhausted. It's been a dull, boring day, and their body, speech, and mind have been rasped away by it.

How toilsome ploughing and digging can become!

An occupation like this is just sheer hard work. It's all right to go and spend a weekend in the country to help with a bit of milking, or pick a few flowers or even a couple of cabbages, but that's not a farmer's life. People often have romantic ideas about life in the country, but farming, even modern mechanized farming, is grinding hard work. In India – and Tibet is probably even worse – you can see how hard people have to work to win a living out of the land. Tibet is not a fertile country – it's rocky, stony, and there's a lot of snow. You have to work really hard, and presumably Milarepa had had some experience of that. Every Tibetan has, practically, except those who live in monasteries. Everybody ploughs and sows and digs. 'How toilsome ploughing and digging can become!' It's not a question of just doing it when you feel like it, or when the weather is fine. You have to do it out of sheer necessity every single day. You're never free from it, whatever the weather is like, and your life depends upon it. If you don't work you'll starve. It's as simple as that. And even if you do the work, you sometimes starve. You may lose your crop. I don't think we always realize what a difficult life most of the people in the world have had throughout history until recent times, and what a difficult life many people still have.

And when the seeds you planted never sprout, you have worked
for nought!

A farmer sweats his guts out ploughing, digging, cultivating, looking after his crops, and then he loses the whole lot. There can be a hailstorm, there can be a flood, the crop doesn't get enough water or gets too much sun, and he loses the lot. You might think that at least it's a healthier way of living than life in the city, and a way of life that unites people because they're all undergoing the same difficulties, but I'm not so sure about that. When I went from village to village in India, the predominant impression was of stagnation. Country folk are in a way healthier than people living in towns – they're well built, they usually get enough to eat, they get a lot of exercise – but life is stagnant, and there's little intellectual interest or any real spiritual life. Dr Ambedkar, the leader of the ex-Untouchables, used to say, 'Don't idealize the villages. They're sinks of superstition and backwardness.'[69] Under certain conditions, in a country with a good climate, you could have a very attractive farming life, but that's not typical, certainly not in India. Even in England, life in the villages, while it may be solid and safe, can be very dull. In his book *The Buddha* Trevor Ling points out that in the Buddha's lifetime, Buddhism made its greatest appeal in the urban areas, and that was where the Buddha went.[70] You find still in India today that it's very difficult to stir things up in the villages. There is a sort of togetherness, but it's very group-orientated, very restricting. You can't do what the group doesn't approve of, or go against it even in very small matters. And then of course you've got the caste system, which is very divisive. There's not just one village community; there are a number of separate castes that have very little to do with one another. It's true that there may be more individual contact and recognition than you usually get in the cities, but in the city you usually get greater freedom of choice and action. We have to be very careful not to idealize village life.

I'm very doubtful whether a full-time farming life would be compatible with the spiritual life. Farming as a full-time occupation is very demanding and difficult. You probably wouldn't have time for meditation, and you might be so tired you didn't feel like meditating. There could perhaps be a spiritual community that engaged with farming activity, but it could not involve full-time work. You would have to have enough people to be able to distribute the work so that no one had to exhaust themselves working. That's true of life in general, of course – even building a Buddhist centre.

> In the end it becomes a land of misery – desolate and
>   unprotected –
> A place of Hungry Spirits, and of haunting ghosts!

Can Milarepa mean that literally? And if not, what does he mean by it? Well, what do ghosts represent? They represent the past. When you're at home it's as if you can't get away from the past. Somebody's always saying, 'When you were a little boy you did this or you did that.' There are all these ghosts around and you're not allowed to get away from them; in fact people think that you still are that ghost. I went to see someone not so long ago whom I've known for a number of years, and she offered me a particular kind of jam. I said, 'No thank you,' and she said in quite an injured tone, 'Oh, you always used to like that kind of jam,' as if to say, you haven't got the right to change. If you liked it twenty years ago, you just have to go on liking it. You're always being confronted by these ghosts. There is perhaps the suggestion in this verse that when you're at home you're among ghosts, because people are always thinking about how things used to be, and how you used to be. They're not living in the present.

When I met my sister for the first time after twenty years away from England, within a matter of minutes she was recalling an incident when as a small child I pushed her down the stairs, or so she alleged. She still seemed to have a grievance about it. That was a ghost, as it were. Home is the place where you are not allowed to get away from the past. This is one of the reasons why it is good to leave home, to encounter people who see you and know you and experience you as you are now, not as you were fifteen, twenty, or thirty years ago. We drag along enough of the past as it is in the form of our conditioning. We don't want that to be continually stimulated and reinforced by other people referring to us as we were twenty or thirty years ago, or even five years ago, even last year, even yesterday. Today is today. Getting away from home means getting away from the past. Home is the past congealed, and if it congeals around you, you're stuck. It's not that your relatives mean to do you any harm. In their own way they're quite fond of you, but they can't help functioning in that sort of way and having that sort of effect. If they're not seeing the person you are now, it's like being a ghost going back to the old haunts; no one sees you as you are.

The younger you are, the more quickly time passes in the sense that you experience more within a given period of time. The older you are, other factors being equal, the less you experience. If when you're young you go away from home for five years, or even a year, a lot will have happened to you, and you're a very different person when you get back. But to the old folks at home not much time may seem to have passed. Perhaps they've gone on in the same routine – the same annual holiday in the same place. The changes that have happened are so minor – green curtains instead of pink, a new pussy cat, or a new cover for the settee. In the meantime you could have revolutionized your whole life, but they may be oblivious to that. Of course, some people are more perceptive than others. Also, the kind of change taking place in you may manifest in your behaviour. If you go home and say, 'I'm a vegetarian, please don't give me meat or fish,' that's a change they can recognize and either agree or disagree with. But if it's a subtle inner change that doesn't show externally in your behaviour, the chances are that they won't notice anything at all, especially if you go along with their way of life.

It isn't only parents, it's everybody. We don't like change. We like things to be as we're used to them being. We may accept in principle this idea of change and development, but if within the sangha someone whom you have known in a certain way suddenly changes so rapidly and to such an extent that he goes right out of your ken, as it were, you might not be very happy about that. It's the same principle. 'We used to have such jolly times together, taking classes and organizing retreats, but he's not into those things any more. All he wants to do now is go and meditate.' I'm not suggesting that revolutionary change necessarily takes that particular form, but you might feel that he was out of your reach now and you might not feel very happy about it. Not that you begrudge him his progress, but you would prefer that he remained the person that you used to know. Parents often provide a conspicuous example of that kind of thing, but everybody is prone to it, perhaps even including ourselves. We just have to be on the lookout. We always do like to settle down in what is familiar.

Sometimes you leave behind your old friends and relations, and you find that the people you can really relate to are those who are as it were keeping pace with you. There's a wonderful Sufi story about a guru and his disciple. They had spent quite some time together and they used to have very deep spiritual discussions, but the disciple had to go to join his parents in their tribe miles and miles away. The disciple was very unhappy, thinking that that was an end to the discussions he found so inspiring. But the teacher said, 'Beget the man you need.' That is, produce someone to whom you can relate, someone of the same degree of awareness as yourself. This is what you have to do. If you go off somewhere and find yourself on your own, you have to get into contact with someone and develop the communication between you until you can communicate on your own terms. This may benefit the other person, of course, but you need to do it for your own benefit too. It's so important to be able to communicate that you have to work on communication with whoever is around, even if it's your grandmother. You're forced to do it, or die of boredom.

One can understand why Milarepa is being a bit hard on home life. He certainly doesn't think in terms of home sweet home.

> *When I think of the warehouse*
> *For storing sinful deeds,*
> *It gnaws at my heart.*

Oh dear. Now he's calling home a warehouse for storing sinful deeds.
That's pretty strong. What can he mean by that? Well, a warehouse is
somewhere where you store things, accumulate things. And likewise, you
just go on multiplying whatever is unskilful at home. You just go round
in circles. You don't get anywhere. And just to think of this 'gnaws at
my heart'.

> *In such a prison of transiency I will not stay,*
> *I have no wish to join your family!*

He's already left his own family. Why should he join theirs? It's just like
a prison, a sort of upholstered cell.

A HEAVENLY ANGEL?

> The married couple said, 'Please do not talk like that! We will find
> you a fine girl from a prominent family, who is fit to be your bride
> and who will suit your taste. Please consider this.'

They think he's just holding out, or just shy, so now they promise to find
him a bride to suit his taste, and beg him not to reject their offer out of
hand. But he says:

> At first, the lady is like a heavenly angel;
> The more you look at her, the more you want to gaze.
> Middle-aged, she becomes a demon with a corpse's eyes;
> You say one word to her and she shouts back two.
> She pulls your hair and hits your knee,
> You strike her with your staff, but back she throws a ladle.
> At life's end, she becomes an old cow with no teeth.
> Her angry eyes burn with a devilish fire
> Penetrating deep into your heart!
> I keep away from women to avoid fights and quarrels.
> For the young bride you mentioned, I have no appetite.

Setting aside the hideously unflattering description as best we can – Milarepa is going to extremes to make a point – the key point here is in the second line: 'The more you look at her, the more you want to gaze.' The point is that you can never be satisfied. Neurotic craving is wanting something that the situation can't give you. If you blunder into a certain situation and you realize after a while that it can't give you what you really want or need, if you're healthy you just withdraw from that situation. But if even though you don't get what you want you go on trying harder and harder to get it, that's neurotic. Why on earth would you do that, sometimes even after it's pointed out to you? Perhaps it's just a habit. You know it's bad for you, and you're not even enjoying it, but you still go on. Here *kalyāṇa mitratā*, spiritual friendship, is very important, just to get you into another mood, onto a different wavelength, into a different environment, thinking different thoughts. But it would seem to be the nature of every unskilful thought to be self-perpetuating.

According to the Abhidharma a distinction is made between *citta* and *caittas*. *Citta* is mind and *caitta* can be translated as mental function. Mind attends to the mental object in a general way, and the different mental functions associated with mind attend to and become involved with the mental object in various specific ways. These mental functions, these *caittas*, are divided into categories: there are *caittas* which are present only in mental states of a certain kind and *caittas* which are present in all mental states. For instance, there are certain *caittas* – usually eleven are listed – which are present in all *kuśala*, skilful, states of mind. If any one of those eleven factors is not present, you're not in a *kuśala* state of consciousness.[71] The different schools – Abhidharma, Theravāda, Sarvāstivāda, Yogācāra – give different lists of these *caittas*, these mental functions, which are found in all skilful states of consciousness, and first on the list of each tradition comes faith, *śraddhā*. There is no skilful mental state in which *śraddhā* does not form an element. Faith is the consciousness of something higher, the awareness that it has a higher value, and the attraction towards it. If *śraddhā* is in every skilful mental state, and if *śraddhā* is of that nature, every skilful mental state is essentially self-transcending or essentially progressive. And conversely, in any unskilful mental state there is *aśraddhā*, which is absence of *śraddhā*, absence of faith. Just as the skilful mental state has an inbuilt tendency to transcend itself, the unskilful mental state has an inbuilt tendency to degenerate. If you are in an unskilful mental state, you don't just remain in that same mental state; it gets more and more unskilful by its very nature. If you are gazing at your beloved in a neurotic way, the more neurotic, left to itself, your mental state will become.

But why should husband and wife quarrel? After all, they love each other. This is the sort of question that people ought to ask themselves. Why are some marriages so unhappy? Everybody gets married looking for happiness, believing in happiness, expecting happiness. What happens? The problem is that the expectations of both parties are unreasonable. Each thinks the other is going to give them happiness, not realising that happiness is something – if you think in those terms at all – that you must create for yourself. You can certainly have a happy communication with another person, but you must have the capacity for communication and happiness within yourself first. The other person can't give it to you. Once you've got it, then you can enjoy it together, which does give an extra dimension, very much so. But they can't give it to you, and you can't give it to them.

Finding yourself quarrelling with a lover can give you a sort of revelation about yourself. It happens because you expect so much of the other person. It's so selfish, so grasping. If they don't give you what you want, all hell is let loose. This is what love is for many people, and this is why there can be so much violence in that sort of situation. It is not without significance that, at least until very recently, before terrorism and all that, most murders took place within the family circle, especially between husband and wife, or the *crime passionnel*, the crime of passion – the lover stabbing the mistress, the mistress poisoning the lover. Obviously very violent passions are aroused. You want something. You want it very, very badly, as if your whole life depends upon it. It's an infantile demand, and if you don't get it, you become a little demon, just as you used to when you were a child and didn't get what you wanted. When the breast was denied to you, when mother wouldn't come, you'd scream your little head off, and that is what you do now, except that your head is bigger and more swollen than it was then and you've got your brain to intervene and justify everything. It's a pretty grim situation. If the situation ends up as Milarepa describes it, in a way it's your fault. There's this deep resentment because you've not been able to be free and become an individual, and neither has the other person. There's just mutual resentment between you. If there is genuine liking and real affection and reasonableness, two people can live together reasonably happily – but not with this projective neurotic passion. It's quite impossible then. So we've got the message. Milarepa sees through it all.

DON'T YOU NEED A SON AT ALL?

> The husband then said, 'Dear Lama, it is true that when one grows old and close to death he has not the same capacity for enjoying life or for being pleasant as when he was young. But if I have no son, my grief and disappointment will be unbearable. How about you? Don't you need a son at all?'

In a traditional society the desire for a son can be very strong indeed – someone to inherit your name, inherit your property, even make offerings on behalf of your soul after death. In India it is considered a terrible thing not to have a son to keep up the family line and make offerings, and some people like to have as many sons as possible to help with the work. So the husband asks Milarepa, 'Don't you need a son at all?' They've accepted that he doesn't want a wife. What about a son? But Milarepa says:

> In youth, the son is like the Prince of Heaven;
> You love him so much that the passion is hard to bear.
> In middle age he becomes a ruthless creditor
> To whom you give all, but he still wants more.
> Driven from the house are his own parents.
> Invited in is his beloved, charming lady.
> His father calls, but he will not answer;
> His mother cries out, but he will not listen.
> Then the neighbors take advantage, spreading lies and rumors.
> Thus I learned that one's child oft becomes one enemy.
> Bearing this in mind, I renounce the fetters of Saṃsāra.
> For sons and nephews I have no appetite.

Presumably Milarepa is speaking from the father's point of view. When you have a son you are tremendously happy. You feel that you're a real man, you've produced a son, and he will carry on your name, follow in your footsteps, maybe learn your trade. He'll help you in your work, and when he grows up he'll be your companion too. So at first you really idolize your son. You see this with many fathers: they think the world of their son, in some cases more than they think of their wife, and the son monopolizes their attention. But when the son is older, he doesn't think he owes his parents anything. He thinks his parents still owe something to him. Children can sometimes be so selfish, so greedy. They just go on taking and taking from their parents. And the father has perhaps got into the habit of giving. After all, when the boy is a child the father has to give him everything, and even when he starts growing up the father just goes on giving in a foolish way. Whatever the son wants, he gets. The father never gives the boy proper advice, never says, 'Look, why don't you work for yourself? Why don't you get things together for yourself?' He just gives him everything. In traditional societies you find quite a bit of this sort of thing, and it carries on even when the son is middle-aged and the father is a very old man.

In some primitive societies you get what Milarepa describes here: the son goes on living in the parental home and his parents are driven out as beggars, as if they were complete strangers. Your parents have done so much for you – they've brought you up, they've given you everything – but the first time you fall in love you forget all about your parents, and maybe sacrifice them to your partner, despite all that your parents have done for you. What's the use of having a son like that? This sort of thing happened much more in the old primitive, more enclosed communities. These days, especially in the city, you can leave home much more easily. You can get away from your parents, so you're more likely to remain on good terms with them. But suppose you had to stay in the same village, even go on living in the same house, even after marriage. You want your own place, but you can't have it. Your parents are there. It's their place in a sense, it's the family place. You might try to turn them out in the end if you're strong enough or shameless enough. This is the way things go on. This is what the father has to suffer. So why have a son? You're so fond of him at the beginning, you treat him like a 'Prince of Heaven', but in the end he turns against you. This is of course drawing a rather dark and dramatic picture. It doesn't always happen like that, obviously, but quite often it does. It's the story of Shakespeare's *King Lear*. The father wanted to divide his kingdom and wanted his three daughters to declare their love for him in return for his gift. The youngest daughter, Cordelia, didn't give the right answer, though she was the one who really loved her father. The other two said what they thought their father would like to hear, just to gain the property. As soon as they got their hands on it, as soon as the kingdom was divided between them and their husbands, they turned against their father, and this almost drove him mad. On a less grand, more commonplace scale this sort of thing happens especially after a man gets married and goes away from home. You often see a misunderstanding developing between him and his parents. But anyway, that's another rather dark picture. Let's see if we have any better luck with daughters.

LIFE IN THE RAW

> Both husband and wife agreed with him, replying, 'What you have said is indeed true. Sometimes one's own son becomes an enemy. Perhaps it would be better to have a daughter. What do you think?'

They don't stop trying! A son may be a young brute who beats his old parents and treats them badly, but surely a soft, gentle daughter would be better.

> In answer Milarepa sang:

> In youth, a daughter is like a smiling, heavenly angel;
> She is more attractive and precious than are jewels.
> In middle age, she is good for nothing.
> Before her father, she openly carries things away;
> She pilfers secretly behind her mother's back.
> If her parents do not praise her and satisfy her wants,
> They will suffer from her bitterness and temper.
> In the end, she becomes red-faced and wields a sword.
> At her best, she may serve and devote herself to others;
> At her worst, she will bring mishaps and disaster.
> Woman is always a trouble-maker;
> Bearing this in mind, one should avoid irretrievable misfortunes.
> For women, the primary source of suffering, I have no appetite.

Is Milarepa being too strong here? Has he overstated his case? Well, perhaps he is overstating it because most people don't see the situation at all, and as it were understate the case. If there is on occasions a clash of wills between women and men, it's the two coming together that creates the conflict, not the nature or behaviour of one or other of them, so it's not just women's fault, despite what Milarepa says here. If he was speaking to a young woman, he would no doubt paint the other side of the picture, talking about how undesirable it would be to have a husband and what brutes they are.

We have to bear in mind that Tibetans are a very direct and down-to-earth people. Milarepa is being very realistic. No doubt the couple have had their own experience of life and seen things for themselves. After all, they live in a village, and you see life at very close quarters in a village. In a sense you really see life in the raw. Every quarrel that goes on, every time a husband beats his wife, or a wife scratches her husband's face, you know it. If there's a little feud going on, or a little plot, you know all about it. Life in the village is intense and petty. So they see the truth of what he says. It is very hard to take, and even quite unpleasant; he's certainly not pulling his punches. But their faith gets stronger and stronger. He's being very real, he's showing them what life is really like, he's opening their eyes. That's not to say that there aren't any positive possibilities in life. There certainly are, but you can only actualize those positive possibilities if you are alive to the negative situations and can avoid them.

When it comes to the question of whether marriage is compatible with spiritual life, the principle is that you get into your meditation, your communication, your study, your right livelihood, as deeply as you can. As regards your lifestyle, whether you're married or not, you will work that out quite naturally if you're sincere in your commitment to spiritual practice. It isn't possible to lay down hard and fast rules. If you yourself find that marriage is incompatible with your spiritual development and if you're sincere, you will extricate yourself from it. If you find that you can develop spiritually in the context of being married, then you will continue to be married and continue to grow. Only you can decide. There is no guarantee that if you're not married you will automatically develop spiritually. The young single man isn't necessarily nearer to the goal than the elderly married man. He may have a better chance in some ways, but don't forget the story of the hare and the tortoise. The general principle is to evolve, to develop. It's up to you to adjust your lifestyle according to your own judgement. If you have close contact with other people who are committed to the spiritual life, they will tell you what they think, and if they think you're fooling yourself, they'll tell you that, and you have a perfect right to tell them if they're fooling themselves with their practice of celibacy, if that's what they're practising. One hopes that in the end the truth of the situation will emerge and everybody will grow in their own way. One cannot say to anybody as a hard and fast rule that of course they can't grow much spiritually speaking because they're married. That would be a very cruel thing to say and could be quite untrue. The emphasis should be on development in a positive way, and other things will take care of themselves. You will know when the time comes if you have to make a change. You just have to make the effort to evolve and ask yourself sincerely what is holding you back or not holding you back.

A FOUNTAIN OF REGRET

> The husband and wife then said, 'One may not need sons and daughters, but without relatives, life would be too miserable and helpless. Is that not so?'

They're still not giving up, but they're being gradually convinced.

Milarepa again sang:

> At first, when a man greets his relatives,
> He is happy and joyful; with enthusiasm
> He serves, entertains, and talks to them.
> Later, they share his meat and wine.
> He offers something to them once, they may reciprocate.
> In the end, they cause anger, craving, and bitterness;
> They are a fountain of regret and unhappiness.
> With this in mind, I renounce pleasant and sociable friends;
> For kinsmen and neighbors, I have no appetite.

Again, is Milarepa overstating his case, or can this be taken completely literally? One might say that he is deliberately showing them just one side of things, to show them the opposite of their view of life, but perhaps there's more to it than that. The point seems to be that if the Dharma element is not there, sooner or later there will be trouble with other people. People will one day get angry or there will be a misunderstanding. Unless you've got the Dharma as a basis, a point of reference, a standard underlying the relationship or the contact, things can go wrong. If there isn't any spiritual principle involved in your contact with your relations, sooner or later something will happen – or perhaps you will just get stuck relating to people in the same old patterns. The basic point is that without the Dharma to refer to, without some higher spiritual principle in the light of which you can conduct your relationships, human relationships of any kind tend to end in disaster. And in the light of that higher principle some neurotic relationships will just dissolve.

THE WELFARE OF ALL SENTIENT BEINGS

The couple then said, 'Indeed, you may not need kinsmen. However, since we have a great deal of property, would you like to have and take care of it?' Milarepa replied, 'As the sun and moon never stop to brighten one small place, so I devote myself to the welfare of all sentient beings. I cannot, therefore, become a member of your family. By merely beholding me, both of you will be benefited in this and future lives. I will also make a wish that we may meet in the Pure Land of Oujen.'

There's quite an important point here. It isn't that you should give up family life. It's more that you should make the whole world, the whole of humanity, your family. You can look at it in a positive way, not just dismissing the family, but including it in a larger whole which includes everybody. Giving up the family really means giving up the limitation between the family and everybody else, as when doing the *mettā bhāvanā*, you feel, or try to feel, towards everybody the same affection that usually you feel only towards your so-called nearest and dearest. Having shown them the negative side of things without any sort of compromise, he gives a hint of a more positive approach. After all, even if you 'give up your family' you're still relating to them; of course you are. How can you break that link? Your mother is still your mother; you can never undo that. Your father is still your father. Friends are still friends. But you remove the barrier. Everybody becomes like your father and mother, and your brother and sister, and your friends and kinsmen. You don't give anybody up. You only give up the limitations. It's easier said than done. It may be that you have literally to give up the family for a while before you can afford to let yourself come back into contact with them, treating them just like anybody else. There may have to be a break before you can come back to them just as people, just as members of the human race.

> As the sun and moon never stop to brighten one small place, so
> I devote myself to the welfare of all sentient beings.

I've taken the bodhisattva vow; I want to gain Enlightenment for the sake of all sentient beings – this is what Milarepa is saying. I don't want to restrict myself to one particular group of people, to a family, to the people living in one particular spot. I want to benefit everybody. The whole human race is my family. I aspire to belong to the family of humanity itself, and do what I can for everybody – not just work for the sake of a few. So Milarepa is placing his negative and ascetic attitude with regard to home and land, family, relation, kinsmen, and neighbours, within the highly positive Mahāyānistic context. It is limitation and attachment that he is against, not the people themselves. He wants to benefit everybody and work for everybody, and that should be the spirit. We have to be very careful about how we use the language of giving up. You don't give up your family. You join a bigger family in which your old family is included. You only give up your narrow, exclusive attachment.

> By merely beholding me, both of you will be benefited in this
> and future lives.

This is a reminder that knowing others is a way of knowing yourself. It's not knowing *about* others – it's direct knowledge. If you are aware of somebody else, you become more aware of yourself, because that other person is also aware of you. He may see in you something that you don't see. You may see in him something that he doesn't see. Because he sees you, you see yourself; because you see him, he sees himself. In this way you mutually enhance each other's awareness and individuality.

If you're perceptive and aware you can see someone without them having to say anything. Communication in the form of speech is a sort of bridge, a middle way between complete knowledge and complete ignorance of somebody. Through speech people reveal something of themselves. You can get to know them. But it's best in a way if you know them just by looking at them, just by seeing directly. In the case of Milarepa the couple may not see all of him, but they do see something of him, and he sees them; and the more they see him the more they see themselves. In this way they are benefited 'in this and future lives'.

Different people have different aspects. It's not even a question of level or degree, but of dimension. It may be that on the whole someone is more developed than you are, or you may be more developed, more aware, than they are, but the more developed person of the two can still gain something from the less developed, or at least he will deepen his own experience. In Milarepa's case, he is seeing his own more enlightened state just beginning to be reflected in them. What a positive experience! He must be overjoyed. After all, as a bodhisattva he wants to enlighten everybody, and he sees that these people's initial faith, though limited, is now developing into a bit of understanding. They're beginning to sympathize with him, beginning to really see him – surely that's the gain. He is experiencing other beings experiencing himself. It's like a light being reflected in so many more facets. It's not as though there's Milarepa and then there's other people. There are just these different facets. In a sense there's one person, and different aspects or facets of that one person are being progressively illuminated. It isn't as though there's a Milarepa quite separate from the husband and wife who are talking to him. It isn't that because he is more developed than them, he has nothing to gain from communication with them. That's taking it much too literalistically. Even a Buddha gains when others become Enlightened, because he sees his Buddhahood reflected in more and more people. In that sense you can even say – though this is not traditional language – that he becomes more of a Buddha than ever. One could say that this is one reason why the bodhisattva says he will not gain Enlightenment until everybody gains Enlightenment. How can he be Enlightened until everybody is Enlightened?

This is why, on a very much lower level, if you are teaching classes and courses and giving lectures at a Buddhist centre, if you're not getting something out of it yourself, you shouldn't be doing it. If you're thinking, 'Well, here I am, giving out this teaching, but of course I've already gone beyond it, so I'm not getting anything out of it myself', that's completely the wrong attitude. You may know those particular facts or have got to that particular level, but the act of communicating that to others is itself an experience, is itself a matter of growth and development for you. The facets are multiplying. You are not just one facet – you are all the facets.

> *I will also make a wish that we may meet in the Pure Land*
> *of Oujen.*

He's placing them, as it were, in a position of equality with himself, saying that they'll all meet together in the Pure Land of Padmasambhava, Ouyen or Urgyen – not a geographical location but the ideal, archetypal realm of the copper-coloured mountain where Padmasambhava lives surrounded by Buddhas and bodhisattvas and *ḍākas* and *ḍākinīs* and all the rest, a sort of mandala, a perfect world.

THE DELUSIONS OF *SAMSĀRA*

Milarepa then burst into another song:

Wealth, at first, leads to self-enjoyment,
Making other people envious.
However much one has, one never feels it is enough,
Until one is bound by the miser's demon;
It is then hard to spend it on virtuous deeds.

Wealth provokes enemies and stirs up ghosts.
One works hard to gather riches which others will spend;
In the end, one struggles for life and death.
To amass wealth and money invites enemies;
So I renounce the delusions of Saṃsāra.
To become the victim of deceitful devils,
I have no appetite.

The couple have offered him their property, or at least they've suggested that he should take care of it, but he doesn't want property, he doesn't want wealth. He comes back to the basic issue: possessions. This applies also to the home and the native land, the wife, the son, the daughter, the relations and kinsmen, friends in the ordinary sense. There is this feeling that they are 'mine', this sense of property. This becomes very tangible and concrete when it is actual houses and land, but that's just one of the most concrete forms of property. This is the source of all the troubles one experiences in connection with all these things and people. You think that they are yours. You treat them as your very own. This is the real difficulty, this business of 'mine', which is of course bound up with the sense of 'me' or 'I'. So,

> Wealth, at first, leads to self-enjoyment,
> Making other people envious.
> However much one has, one never feels it is enough,

In other words, the whole idea of possession is essentially neurotic. Possession means that you're trying to get from outside something you should be getting from inside. Outside things can give you a certain degree of comfort and enjoyment, but they can't give you any lasting pleasure or satisfaction, and the problem may be that this is what you are trying to get out of them. You can't go on trying to fill the inner void with some other thing, some other person. You've got to generate it from within yourself.

> Until one is bound by the miser's demon;
> It is then hard to spend it on virtuous deeds.

You get so much into the habit of grasping and heaping up and amassing that you just don't like to give any of it away.

> Wealth provokes enemies and stirs up ghosts.
> One works hard to gather riches which others will spend;
> In the end, one struggles for life and death.
> To amass wealth and money invites enemies;
> So I renounce the delusions of Saṃsāra.
> To become the victim of deceitful devils,
> I have no appetite.

Essentially it is the sense of possession that Milarepa is giving up. That's why he goes about naked, or at best wearing a bit of cotton cloth. He doesn't possess anything – but it's not the non-possession of external things which is so important, but not having the feeling of 'mine' with regard to anything at all. In the *Dhammapada* the Buddha says, 'The fool says to himself this son is mine, this wealth is mine. Thus the fool, the spiritually immature person, torments himself.' And then the Buddha goes on to say, 'He does not even belong to himself. How then should a son belong to him? How then should wealth?'[72] Nothing is yours because you can't keep it forever. If it really was yours you could go on keeping it, but nothing in the whole world is yours. It's this sense of possession that Milarepa is undermining.

You think of home and native land as *your* home, *your* native land. If your country is attacked or your national flag is insulted, you will feel hurt. If your wife is carried off by another man, you will feel upset, but if he carries off somebody else's wife, you're not bothered at all. Why this difference? If your son dies, you're terribly upset, but if a thousand other people lose their sons you hardly give it a thought. It's the same with a daughter, the same with friends. It's this sense of possession that Milarepa is really attacking, this sense of 'mine' and 'I' – the ego. The individual is something different. The ego is neurotic individuality, or individuality which has gone neurotic or gone mad. It's not individuality itself. It's an excrescence on individuality, a wart, a boil, always sensitive and sore.

UNSHAKEABLE FAITH

> These songs gave the couple unshakable faith in Milarepa and
> they gave away all their possessions for the sake of the Dharma.

That's very significant. They had started off with some faith, but a very limited outlook, a very conventional attitude, but they listened to song after song, and these songs gave the couple unshakeable faith in Milarepa. Unshakeable faith – not belief or blind faith, but genuine faith – is very rare. Faith can so easily be disturbed, so easily shaken. But they developed unshakeable faith in Milarepa and 'gave away all their possessions for the sake of the Dharma'. They acted upon that faith. They weren't lukewarm. It wasn't just words. They realized the import of what Milarepa was saying about property and possessions, so they put it into practice. They didn't just give their possessions away, but gave them 'for the sake of the Dharma'. We can read that in two ways, or even consider that both ways are meant. In one sense perhaps they gave them away for the sake of practising the spiritual principle of the Dharma, i.e. the principle of non-attachment, non-possession; or in another sense, perhaps they gave them away for Dharma purposes like building a monastery, making Buddha images, and so on.

> They began to practice the Jetsun's teachings and were forever
> released from falling into the three lower Realms.

The three lower realms are the *preta* (hungry ghost), animal, and hell realms, as depicted among the six realms of the Tibetan wheel of life. They started off with a little bit of faith and all those conventional ideas, and by the end of the story they are Stream Entrants. No doubt the ground was prepared, and also their lives were uncomplicated – there were very few distractions. This is one of the great differences between life today and life as it was in ancient times. In the old days you dealt with one thing at a time. You took everything seriously. There was no such thing as publicity, no mass media. In our day, in a way, everybody is much less serious. In Milarepa's Tibet people acted upon what they were taught, what they believed. They were more deeply convinced. Having become aware of the spiritual path, because of the simplicity of their life they would either follow the path or not – no half measures, no possibility of rationalizing it away.

Notice that they develop an unshakeable faith in Milarepa rather than in the Dharma. This is very much within the Tantric context, in which the guru embodies the Buddhadharma itself. The guru's mind is the Buddha, his speech is the Dharma, and your contact with him is the Sangha. It's not that you are out of contact with the Three Jewels; you're in contact with them in the form of the guru. The Dharma is what the Buddha originally taught, but the Dharma for you is what the guru teaches. In a commentary on the *Bhagavad Gītā*, it is said that the Vedas are the cows, the Upanishads the milk drawn from the cow, and the teaching is like the butter churned from the milk.[73] You need the teaching in the form of butter, so to speak.

When they died, they entered the path (of Bodhi) and step by step approached Buddhahood.

Perhaps it was 'when they died' because they were in a certain social situation and although they didn't really belong to it any more, it still affected them and it was only at the time of death that they became definitely entrants upon the path of Enlightenment. That seems to be the suggestion. The moment of death is of course regarded as very important in Tibetan Buddhism, and in Buddhism generally. It's said that you can gain Enlightenment or something very close to it at the moment of death, when the limitations of physical existence are removed, provided of course that you've practised the Dharma beforehand.

AN INSPIRED MOOD

> After this, the Jetsun returned to the Bodhi Cave of Ragma. His former patrons gave their services and offerings to him, and he remained there in an inspired mood.

I don't know what the original Tibetan word for this 'inspired mood' would be. Perhaps it's a sort of higher *samādhi* state, but very joyful and exuberant. Perhaps his inspired mood is connected with his meeting with those two people. He has gained something from it. He certainly doesn't feel as though he is just passing on the same old teachings that he's known for ages.

The impression we get of Milarepa from this episode is that he is completely uncompromising and outspoken, in some ways more uncompromising than the Buddha himself, at least outwardly. The Buddha wore robes, or at least clothes; Milarepa didn't. Milarepa stayed up in the mountains all the time, but the Buddha didn't – far from it. Sometimes that sort of example is necessary. We can't say that Milarepa was more Enlightened than the Buddha – that would be absurd – but a different kind of presentation of the ideal, an emphasis on austerity and rigour, is very much needed from time to time. Not everybody is going to be like that, but it's good to know that there is that pattern to follow. It's not possible for any one person – even a Buddha – to embody all the aspects of the ideal in one human life. You can't be a Milarepa and a Padmasambhava at the same time. You can't be a Milarepa and a Vimalakīrti at the same time. Vimalakīrti's ideal is a great ideal, and so is Milarepa's, but you can't have both at the same time, not on this human plane. You can only have all the different facets or aspects of one as it were Enlightened personality on the level of the *sambhogakāya*, which is the full manifestation of all possible aspects of Enlightened experience. On this earthly plane, the *nirmāṇakāya* is of either this kind or that kind, but not of all kinds. You have Enlightened teachers who are very learned and Enlightened teachers who are completely ignorant of books. Some people will need one kind of teacher, and some will need another. You have Enlightened teachers who live in mountains and caves and forests, and others who live at home with their wife and family. They're in contact with different people, needing different kinds of path. There are Enlightened teachers who meditate all the time and others who don't meditate at all in the technical sense of sitting and meditating.

You can't have one lifestyle which is the ideal for everybody. The ideal, Enlightenment, is the same for all, but there is no one way of manifesting Enlightenment which everybody has to accept and follow. That just isn't possible. This is one of the great beauties of Buddhism – it allows for that sort of diversity. That's why there's an instance in the Pāli canon of the Buddha praising all of his chief disciples in turn and saying what they were distinguished for. They were all *arhant* disciples as far as we know, but one was the best preacher, another was the best at collecting alms, another was best at supernormal displays and manifestations, another was foremost in wisdom, another was foremost in asceticism, and so on.[74] It wasn't that one was more Enlightened than the others. They were all Enlightened, they all had that spiritual genius, but their talents were different. The Buddha said on another occasion, 'I have disciples who practise this, that, and the other form of asceticism. I have disciples who do not practise those forms of asceticism.' It doesn't mean that they were less Enlightened, or more Enlightened. There was just a difference of temperament and approach. We have to be tolerant about these things, and not think that if someone isn't a strict vegetarian, for instance, they can't be on the spiritual path at all. One has to be very careful about things like that. Of course, we will want to encourage them to become vegetarian, but we shouldn't discount all the other efforts they are making to follow the spiritual path.

We should have a healthy respect and even admiration for all these different manifestations of the ideal. We should admire Milarepa, but admire Padmasambhava too, and Tsongkhapa, and Aśoka. We should rejoice in all their merits. We shouldn't say, 'I like Milarepa but I don't like Tsongkhapa, he's much too learned for me' or 'I like Tsongkhapa, but I don't like Milarepa, he just wasn't learned enough.' Don't say, 'I like Padmasambhava but I don't like Vasubandhu – too dry' or 'I like magical displays but I don't like asceticism.' Admire them all. You don't have to follow them. You can admire them without following them, just as if you're an artist you can admire Rembrandt's artistic genius even though you might not want to paint like him because your talent, your style, your approach, your personality is different. You can admire a great ascetic without being a great ascetic yourself, or even a small one. You can genuinely admire Padmasambhava without being the least bit interested in magic. Of course, that presupposes that you are actually following some particular ideal, that you don't just have a dilettante admiration for them all without following any of them. It presupposes that you are trying to actualize at least one aspect of the ideal, one particular lifestyle. You're not just collecting them all like cigarette cards.

2

OBSERVE YOUR MIND

FRIEND BODHI-HEART

One day, two young shepherds came to him. The younger one
asked, 'Dear Lama, have you a companion?'
Milarepa replied, 'Yes, I have.'
'Who is he?'
'His name is "Friend Bodhi-Heart".'
'Where is he now?'
'In the House of the Universal Seed Consciousness.'
'What do you mean by that?'
'My own body.'

The elder boy then said, 'Lama, we had better go, as you
cannot guide us.' But the younger one said, 'Do you mean this
consciousness is mind itself, and that the physical body is the
house of the mind?'
'Yes, that is correct.'

The boy continued, 'We know that although a house usually
belongs only to one person, many people can enter it, so we
always find a number of people living in one house. In the same
way, is there only one mind in the body, or are there many? If
there are many, how do they live together?'

'Well, as to whether there is only one mind in the body or many, you had better find that out by yourself.'

'Revered One, I will try.'

One day, presumably when Milarepa was still living in the cave, perhaps still in an inspired mood, two young shepherds came along. Perhaps they had lost their way and, noticing the cave and this strange yogi-like figure, came to ask him for directions.

The younger one asked, 'Dear Lama, have you a companion?'

These two young shepherds were together, they were companions, but they found Milarepa living alone, so this is a natural question. It's not unlike the questions put by the husband and wife in the previous section, but whereas the couple asked, 'Dear Lama, where are your home and relatives?', showing that they attached most importance to these things, the two young shepherds talk about companions. The younger one asks 'Dear Lama, have you a companion?' as if to say 'Well, I've got a companion, my shepherd friend here; we're herding the sheep together. But you seem to be living here by yourself.'

Milarepa replied, 'Yes, I have.'

'Who is he?'

'His name is "Friend Bodhi-Heart".'

Bodhi-Heart is the translator's rendering of *bodhicitta*. Immediately we notice a difference of approach – a difference of technique, almost – between the way Milarepa answered the husband and wife in the first section of this chapter and the way he answers the young shepherd. In the first case he said that he doesn't have any need of the things the couple are offering, whereas here he says that he has a companion, though not of the kind the young shepherd is perhaps imagining. The reason for the difference is presumably that the young shepherd is much more open to something like that, much less tied down by conditioning, so Milarepa can afford to make use of this sort of approach. He doesn't say, 'I've no need of a companion' but 'Yes, I do have a companion, the *bodhicitta*.' The *bodhicitta* is his companion simply in the sense that it is with him all the time. Just as the two shepherds go around together, Milarepa and the *bodhicitta* are never separated.

> 'Where is he now?'
> 'In the House of the Universal Seed Consciousness.'
> 'What do you mean by that?'
> 'My own body.'

Of course, the young shepherd doesn't actually see the companion – he doesn't see Friend Bodhi-Heart – so he asks 'Where is he now?' Perhaps at this stage he doesn't realize that Milarepa is speaking about a spiritual state of mind, not about an actual person. The Tibetan expression for *bodhicitta* is *changchub sems*, and Changchub is also a Tibetan name. The young shepherd might not be quite clear at this stage who or what Milarepa is talking about, so he asks, 'Where is he now?' as if to say 'Does he live in the cave with you, or has he gone out somewhere?' So Milarepa says that he is 'in the House of the Universal Seed Consciousness' – in other words, in the house of the *ālaya-vijñāna*.[75] 'What do you mean by that?' The young shepherd is quite curious. 'My own body.'

THE HOUSE OF THE MIND

At this point the elder boy intervenes, saying, 'Lama, we had better go, as you cannot guide us.' There's a touch of irony here. Milarepa and the young shepherd have got into this rather strange conversation which the elder boy is clearly not following at all. He says they'd better go as Milarepa cannot guide them, but the irony is that actually Milarepa *is* guiding them. He is giving them directions, but in a different way and on a different plane altogether. He isn't telling them where to go in search of their lost sheep, but in which direction to go from the spiritual point of view in search of themselves, in search of the *bodhicitta*. The younger boy, clearly the brighter of the two, says,

> 'Do you mean this consciousness is mind itself, and that the
> physical body is the house of the mind?'
> 'Yes, that is correct.'

The boy continued, 'We know that although a house usually belongs only to one person, many people can enter it, so we always find a number of people living in one house. In the same way, is there only one mind in the body, or are there many? If there are many, how do they live together?'

He's got quite an enquiring mind. He's probably quite unsophisticated, he probably doesn't know anything about Buddhism, but he's naturally very intelligent and perceptive, so he understands Milarepa's comparison at once. As soon as Milarepa talks about the house in which the universal seed consciousness lives being his own body, the shepherd gets the point, and he can start reasoning and exploring from that. He says, as it were, 'All right, I understand what you mean. The universal seed consciousness lives in the body as in a house. You've compared the body to the house, but how far can we pursue that analogy? An ordinary physical house can be inhabited by one person or by a number of people. Is that true of the body? Is there just one mind inhabiting the body, or are there a number of minds? If there are a number of minds, how do they coexist in one and the same body? What are the relationships between these different minds which inhabit or make use of one body?' We can see he's quite intelligent; he's capable of reasoning from this analogy and trying to see how far it can be applied.

According to Buddhist tradition there are different planes of existence, different worlds if you like, and the relationship between 'body' (for want of a better term) and 'mind' in these different planes differs. This is perhaps something that isn't always realized – that the possibilities of being are infinite. It's said, for instance, that there are planes where there are several minds connected with one body. There are other planes where you've got a number of bodies connected with one mind, and other planes, other worlds, where there's one mind connected with one body, as in our human world. Perhaps, by way of analogy, we can think of bee societies. In a bee colony it's as though there's one mind and a multiplicity of bodies. Apparently in the beehive the queen bee corresponds to the brain. If she dies, the whole colony collapses, just as when the human brain dies, when the person dies, the constituent bits of the physical body start falling apart, because there's nothing to hold them together. To what extent the queen bee is the 'mind' for all those worker bees, drones, and so on, is a separate question, but we can use that analogy to help us understand what Buddhist tradition means by this multiplicity of bodies in a single mind on certain planes.

So the young shepherd isn't asking such a foolish question as one might at first think. There is that possibility envisaged in Buddhist tradition that there should be a number of different consciousnesses making use of one and the same body. We seem to get some inkling of that in the case of so-called multiple personality, or even possession, as in the oracles of Tibet, where you've got what seems to be an entirely different personality making use of a physical body, descending into it, speaking through it, and then another and another and another, five or six, one after the other, apparently different personalities making use of and speaking through that particular physical body. You can say of course that they are all different aspects of one and the same personality, but they function and are recognizable as different personalities.

Anyway, that's somewhat by the way – but we can understand the way in which this young shepherd's mind is working. He's quite unusually intelligent. He grasps the point of what Milarepa is saying, and he wants to take it further. So Milarepa says,

> 'Well, as to whether there is only one mind in the body or
> many, you had better find that out by yourself.'

This suggests that Milarepa's whole emphasis is on personal experience. Don't take it from me, don't take it from books, don't take it from Buddhist tradition. You've got a mind. You've got a body. Find out for yourself. Sometimes people ask me, 'Is the mind the same as the body or is it different?' Well, you've got a body. If you don't know whether your body is the same as your mind, who else can tell you? I've got a mind and a body, but so have you; just introspect and find out. You're in exactly the same position as I am. This is the emphasis of Buddhism. You can give a bit of guidance or a few hints to another person, teach them methods of meditation and so on, but you've got no business doing for them things that they are quite able to do for themselves. Milarepa therefore tells the shepherd that he had better find that out for himself. And the boy says, 'Revered one, I will try.' That's very significant. He's a straightforward lad. He doesn't say, 'It would be much better if you could explain to me. I don't fully understand, could I have a little lecture on the subject please?' He just says, 'Revered one, I will try.'

At this point, the boys took their leave and went home. Next morning, the younger boy returned and said to Milarepa, 'Dear Lama, last night I tried to find out what my mind is and how it works. I observed it carefully and found that I have only one mind. Even though one wants to, one cannot kill this mind. However much one wishes to dismiss it, it will not go away. If one tries to catch it, it cannot be grasped; nor can it be held by pressing it. If you want it to remain, it will not stay; if you release it, it will not go. You try to gather it; it cannot be picked up. You try to see it; it cannot be seen. You try to understand it; it cannot be known. If you think it is an existing entity and cast it off, it will not leave you. If you think that it is non-existent, you feel it running on. It is something illuminating, aware, wide-awake, yet incomprehensible. In short, it is hard to say what the mind really is. Please be kind enough to explain the meaning of the mind.'

The younger shepherd apparently returned alone. The two young shepherds both met Milarepa on the first day, but the elder one drops out of the picture very quickly. He didn't understand what the talk was all about on that first occasion. He didn't understand what Milarepa was saying, or even what his companion was asking, so he doesn't come back. It's strange in a way: two people have got the same opportunity, and one makes use of it while the other just doesn't, or can't.

> *The younger boy returned and said to Milarepa, 'Dear Lama, last night I tried to find out what my mind is and how it works. I observed it carefully, and found that I have only one mind.'*

He didn't make any assumptions. He was quite open-minded about whether there was one mind or whether there were many. He just observed carefully and found 'that I have only one mind'.

> *Even though one wants to, one cannot kill this mind.*

Why should you want to 'kill' your mind? I'm not sure how faithful the translation is; this section of the chapter is comparatively abstruse, and I have a suspicion that the translator might not always quite have got the point. But taking his English version quite literally, what is the young shepherd saying? Perhaps he's referring to trying to stop mental chatter. After all, it's your mind, it's your mental chatter. Why shouldn't you be able to stop it when you want to? If you want to raise your hand, you can raise it. How is it that you can't stop mental chatter when you want to?

> However much one wants to dismiss it, it will not go away. If one tries to catch it, it cannot be grasped; nor can it be held by pressing it. If you want it to remain, it will not stay; if you release it, it will not go. You try to gather it; it cannot be picked up. You try to see it; it cannot be seen.

Suppose you want to keep your mind fixed on a particular object. It won't stay there just because you want it to. The mind is so mysteriously active. It's doing all these things, but you can't even see it. Why is that? You cannot see the mind, because it is the mind that sees. In the same way, you can't catch the mind, you can't pick it up. It's the mind that tries to or pick up the mind, so what is caught, what is picked up, is not the mind. The mind eludes you, or eludes itself, because 'you' means mind. You try to understand it, but it cannot be known. How can you understand your own mind? It is the mind that is trying to understand the mind, so what you understand is not the mind. You may understand a very great deal, but inasmuch as the understander is the mind itself, the mind remains unknown. It lurks in the background. You can never see the mind, touch the mind, understand the mind, because it is the mind itself which is doing these things. You think you've caught hold of the mind out there as an object, but it sort of whips round and becomes the subject. So you haven't seen it, you haven't understood it, it has eluded you.

> If you think it is an existing entity and cast it off, it will not leave you. If you think it is non-existent, you feel it running on. It is something illuminating, aware, wide-awake, yet incomprehensible.

The young shepherd is trying to say something positive about the mind but he's finding it very difficult. It's something illuminating, aware, wide awake, yet incomprehensible. In short, it's hard to say what the mind really is. This reminds me of a chapter of the *Dhammapada*, in the 'Cittavagga', the chapter on mind or consciousness. The Buddha says very much the same thing in far fewer words: *phandanaṃ capalaṃ cittaṃ, durakkhaṃ dunnivārayaṃ*: 'this mind, which is always quivering and vibrating, which is moving about, which is very difficult to guard and protect'.[76]

What has really happened? What has the young shepherd discovered? What is it that he has begun to see, to realize, or to get a glimpse of? You can't know the mind, but also you can't know, in a sense, that you can't know the mind. This is what he's really getting at. But why can't you know the mind? One has to look into the question of what is meant by 'know'. The assumption is a dualistic knowing, a subject and an object. If within the framework of subject and object – taking this framework as absolute – you as subject try to know yourself as object, or mind as subject tries to understand mind as object, it's impossible.

The shepherd's investigation reveals to him that the mind is something illuminating, but he doesn't say that it illuminates any particular thing. It's aware, but he doesn't say that it's aware of anything. It's wide awake, but he doesn't say that it's wide awake with regard to anything. And it's incomprehensible, because if it becomes comprehensible you make it an object, which means you're back within the subject-object framework. It is neither object nor subject, so how are you going to get at it? You can't know it, but at the same time you can't not know it. You could speak of an experience, but only by analogy. Where does that leave him? He says,

Please be kind enough to explain the meaning of the mind.

He's trying to grapple with this subject-object problem, but in a way you can't grapple with it, because if you've got a subject-object out there, subject and object are both object and you remain as subject, so you're still within this dualistic framework. You can't think about it, you can't reason about it, you can't do anything about it – you can only just stop. If you stop, there's some possibility of the natural spontaneity of the mind – which is neither subject nor object, object nor subject – manifesting. And that is the point of the Mahāmudrā.

So let's see what Milarepa says – or sings.

> Listen to me, dear shepherd, the protector (of sheep)!
> By merely hearing about sugar's taste,
> Sweetness cannot be experienced;
> Though one's mind may understand
> What sweetness is,
> It cannot experience it directly;
> Only the tongue can know it.
> In the same way one cannot see in full the nature of mind,
> Though he may have a glimpse of it
> If it has been pointed out by others.
> If one relies not on this one glimpse,
> But continues searching for the nature of mind
> He will see it fully in the end.
> Dear shepherd, in this way you should observe your mind.

What is happening here? Usually when we talk about the mind we talk about mind as subject, though by talking about it we make it into an object and we ourselves remain, or our mind remains, as subject. But the mind that Milarepa is now talking about is the mind which is neither subject nor object, the mind that cannot be spoken about. If you are to speak about the mind at all, you cannot help at least appearing to make that mind, which is neither subject nor object, into an object. But as long as you bear that in mind and are not misled by words, you may get a glimpse. Towards the end of his little speech the young shepherd has begun to get a glimpse of this mind which is neither subject nor object. But if you even say, 'I've begun to get a glimpse of the mind which is neither subject nor object', if you are not careful you at once turn it into an object. Milarepa therefore says,

> *Though one's mind may understand*
> *What sweetness is,*
> *It cannot experience it directly;*
> *Only the tongue can know it.*

Mind is, as it were, functioning dualistically – that is, in terms of subject and object. It might have an intellectual understanding, a theoretical grasp, of the fact that mind in its true nature is neither subject nor object, but it doesn't really experience it. Just as you can know what sweetness is but you don't experience sweetness – only the tongue can know what sweetness is – in the same way your mind in the ordinary sense, the subject, cannot experience mind in the true sense – that is, mind that is neither subject nor object. You need another faculty, a sort of spiritual tongue to as it were taste mind in that sense. That faculty is of course *prajñā* or wisdom, which is not a faculty in the subjective sense. *Prajñā* itself is neither subjective nor objective.

In the same way one cannot see in full the nature of mind.

Mind as subject cannot see in full – well, strictly speaking cannot see at all – mind as neither subject nor object. At the same time, one cannot say that it cannot see it at all, because if that were the case, how could your mind, even your false mind, realize that true mind? There would be no possibility of any connection. You can't realize it, but at the same time the possibility of your realizing it does exist. There's obviously a contradiction in paradoxical language, but this is the only way in which one can speak of it if one is going to speak at all.

Though he may have a glimpse of it
If it has been pointed out by others.

It is not pointed out as an object because that would be to falsify it. In connection with the Mahāmudrā tradition there is what has become a pointing-out ceremony, in which the mind is pointed out to you – not your subjective mind but the mind which is neither subject nor object. In that sense it is not pointed out. It can only be pointed out, to use the language of the perfection of wisdom, by a non-pointing out. One way to try to get some idea of this – which at the same time is not an idea you can get – is by trying to discuss it with other people. You begin to feel a bit bewildered, you begin to feel your subjectivity or your mind in the ordinary sense collapsing. At the same time, you don't see anything. There's just a sort of gap where an object would have been, a gap where the subject was, the mind was. And it's not that you see the two coalescing. Well, there's no one to see, there's nothing to see. For want of a better expression something happens, and that can subsequently be described as having had the mind pointed out to you. But one must be careful to take not even that language very literally.

> If one relies not on this one glimpse,
> But continues searching for the nature of mind
> He will see it fully in the end.
> Dear shepherd, in this way you should observe your mind.

There must be terrific spiritual potential in this young shepherd for Milarepa to be able to speak like that. In the earlier encounter with the married couple he was hammering away at quite basic things – their attachment to home and native land, their attachment to the idea of a wife, a son, a daughter, kinsfolk, and friends. There was so much conditioning to be removed. But this young shepherd is very receptive. He's got a very quick, perceptive mind, so Milarepa is taking him straight into the depths of the Mahāmudrā teaching. Perhaps he doesn't know anything about Buddhism yet. Perhaps he hasn't even heard of Buddhism, except in a very vague and general way. But he's got an enquiring mind, and that's all that you need. The mind is the raw material; the mind is the stuff, as it were, of Enlightenment. So Milarepa is pushing him quite hard.

HOW ACTIVE IS THE MIND!

> The boy then said, 'In that case, please give me the Pointing-out-Instruction, and this evening I will look into it. I shall return tomorrow and tell you the result.'

The young shepherd is quite a self-confident boy. He doesn't wait for Milarepa to tell him to come back, or even ask if he may come. He says, 'I shall return tomorrow and tell you the result.' He's very naive and childlike.

> Milarepa replied, 'Very well. When you get home, try to find out the colour of the mind. Is it white, red, or what? What is its shape? Is it oblong, round, or what? Also, try to locate where in your body it dwells.'

This is basically the same thing as he's said already, but he's asking the young shepherd to go into it in greater detail, to try to realize it more thoroughly. If the mind isn't an object, how can it have a colour? How can it have a shape? Milarepa wants the boy to see that for himself. 'Also try to locate where in your body it dwells.' Milarepa said earlier on that the Universal Seed Consciousness dwells in its house – i.e. in the body – and the boy has understood that, but now he wants him to try to see just where it dwells. In other words, he wants him to have a still more thorough grasp of the fact that the mind is not an object.

> The next morning when the sun rose, the shepherd drove the sheep
> before him, and came to Milarepa, who asked, 'Did you try last
> night to find out what the mind is like?' The boy replied, 'Yes, I did.'
> 'What does it look like?'

The boy didn't waste any time, he spent the whole night working on the problem. But he's got his sheep with him now, so he's not neglecting his work, you notice – very typically Tibetan this, that he is doing his day's work just the same. And here is what he discovered about the mind:

> 'Well, it is limpid, lucid, moving, unpredictable, and ungraspable.
> It has no color or shape. When it associates with the eyes, it sees;
> when with the ear, it hears; when with the nose, it smells; when
> with the tongue, it tastes and talks; and when with the feet it
> walks. If the body is agitated, the mind, too, is stirred. Normally
> the mind directs the body; when the body is in good condition,
> the mind can command it at will, but when the body becomes
> old, decayed, or bereft, the mind will leave it behind without a
> thought as one throws away a stone after cleaning oneself. The
> mind is very realistic and adaptable. On the other hand, the body
> does not remain quiet or submissive, but frequently gives trouble
> to the mind. It causes suffering and pain until the mind loses its
> self-control. At night in the state of sleep the mind goes away; it
> is indeed very busy and hard-working. It is clear to me that all my
> sufferings are caused by it (the mind).'

It's quite a clear, simple, straightforward reply, with no nonsense about it. 'Limpid' means clear, you can see through it. Ultimately, of course, you can see through the mind in the sense of seeing that there's no real subject-object distinction. One of the things that you notice about the mind is that it's always moving, and it's unpredictable – you just can't tell what it's going to do next. A thought will suddenly flash into your mind. You don't know where it comes from or why you're thinking like that, or feeling like that. And it's ungraspable because, of course, it isn't an object. It has no colour or shape for the same reason.

How active the mind is! How much energy it must have! It never stops. And where is all that energy coming from? You're thinking all the time – even at night you're dreaming. The mind goes on and on – thought after thought, idea after idea, feeling after feeling – year after year, day and night. How does the mind manage to keep it up? It's really quite wonderful. 'It is indeed very busy and hard-working.' Perhaps this is said a bit ironically. 'It is clear to me that all my sufferings are caused by it.' That's a rather sudden conclusion. It doesn't follow logically from what has gone before. One might think exactly the opposite – that sufferings are caused by the body. But they're not. This is what he sees. He's not being logical; he just sees quite inconsequentially that all his suffering is caused by the mind.

IT IS THE MIND THAT CAN FREE YOU

The Jetsun then sang:

Listen to me, young shepherd.
The body is between the conscious and unconscious state,
While the mind is the crucial and decisive factor!
He who feels sufferings in the lower Realms
Is the prisoner of Saṃsāra,
Yet it is the mind that can free you from Saṃsāra.
Surely you want to reach the other shore?
Surely you long for the City of Well-Being and Liberation?
If you desire to go, dear child, I can show
The way to you and give you the instructions.

Presumably the body he is referring to is the living physical body. You can't say that the body itself is conscious. It is conscious only in association with the mind. You can't say that it's unconscious, because so long as the body is associated with the mind, it reflects the consciousness or the consciousness works through it – there is after all a difference between a living body and a dead body. The body is thus between conscious and unconscious. You can't say that the body is either conscious or unconscious; it's the mind which is the crucial and decisive factor. If the mind is there, the body is as it were conscious. If the mind isn't there, the body is not conscious.

The young shepherd has begun to be somewhat interested in the spiritual life. He's begun to study the nature of his mind, begun to understand what the mind is really like. Perhaps he's even had a glimpse, by way of a non-glimpse, of his true mind, his real mind. But of course that isn't enough; he now has to follow it up systematically. So far, one might say, he's been on the path of irregular steps. He doesn't know anything about Buddhism, he hasn't even gone for Refuge, but still he's got some insight into the Mahāmudrā, virtually. So far he has followed the path of irregular steps. Now he's got to get onto the path of regular steps so that he can consolidate his understanding and his realization.[77] In effect Milarepa is asking him, 'Do you want to take this seriously? You've understood a bit about the mind. You've understood that the mind causes you a lot of trouble. In fact, it causes all the trouble of the saṃsāra. If you want to be free from those troubles, you will have to work on your mind, to understand your mind in the way you've begun to understand it, but in a much more thoroughgoing, systematic fashion. Wouldn't you like to be liberated? Wouldn't you like to completely realize your own true mind, of which you've had at least a glimpse?' The young shepherd is naturally gifted. He's had a glimpse with very little help from Milarepa. He's very receptive. But there is the possibility even at this stage that he will just go back to his village and forget all about it. So Milarepa is putting it to him: are you prepared to follow up the implications of what you've already seen to the very end? Are you ready to think in terms of Enlightenment, of really seeing the mind fully? Wouldn't you like that?

> The shepherd replied, 'Certainly, dear Lama, I have made up my
> mind to seek it.' Milarepa then asked, 'What is your name?'
> 'Sangje Jhap.'
> 'How old are you?'
> 'Sixteen.'

So the shepherd really wants to know his own true mind. And Milarepa then asks, 'What is your name?' The significance of that is surely that he is making a relationship with the boy. To ask somebody's name is not just asking for their label, it's asking for them. If you ask somebody's name in this sort of context, you're asking because you want to know the person, because you want to establish a relationship. His name is Sangje Jhap, so he's probably a Buddhist, because *sangje* means Buddha. (*Jhap* means quick or quickly.) And he's sixteen, which is perhaps not without significance, because in the Mahāyāna scriptures, bodhisattvas are always described as being like sixteen-year-old princes. The age of sixteen is regarded as the prime of life, the ideal age, when you're at your best, your most beautiful, healthy, happy, bright, intelligent. You're in the bloom of youth, as it were, before the world has touched you. Bodhisattvas are thus said to appear in the form of sixteen-year-old youths. Sixteen represents as it were the age of human perfection, so it becomes a suitable image or symbol for the bodhisattva state. This young Tibetan shepherd is at this ideal age. His intelligence is fully developed. He still has his youthful energy and vigour. Presumably he's unmarried – that's another important point, because in conventional society, as soon as you pass the age of sixteen marriage may be looming on the horizon, whereas up to that time your energies are still at your own disposal.

Intelligence has been defined – I think this is as satisfactory a definition as I've ever come across – as the creative manipulation of concepts. The emphasis is on 'creative'. The mind uses concepts, but they're not ends in themselves. You've got to manipulate them creatively, use them in an imaginative way. Intelligence is not memory, not experience, but this creative manipulation of concepts. It goes beyond perception; it's there to use creatively the concepts derived from your experience, from your perception.

If you are ever talking to a group of teenagers, it's important to remember that they're as intelligent as any adults you will ever meet. Never talk down to them. They may not be very knowledgeable – though they may be more knowledgeable than you are in some fields – and they may not have much experience of life or power of judgement, but their basic intelligence is equal to yours, and you must never forget that. You are no more intelligent than they are; you're only better informed and more experienced. Young people can pick up on non-creativity very quickly. If you're not alive, if you're just a dry old stick who has read a lot of books about Buddhism, they'll know instantly, probably before you've opened your mouth. If you're not alive, you'll get nowhere with them – quite rightly, too. You may get away with a learned spiel with older people, but not with the young. You can be forgiven slips and errors provided that you are alive. That is very, very important.

WHO GOES FOR REFUGE?

> Thereupon the Jetsun gave him the teaching of 'Taking Refuge', explaining briefly its benefits and significance. He then said, 'When you get back home this evening, do not stop reciting the Prayer; and in the meantime try to find out which takes refuge, the mind or the body. Tell me the result tomorrow.'

The significance of the fact that he gave him the teaching of Going for Refuge is surely that it is fundamental. Milarepa has put him firmly onto the path of regular steps. In Tibetan Buddhism the basic spiritual commitment is the Going for Refuge; you have to get that clear first, which is why Milarepa explains briefly 'its benefits and significance'. Presumably 'reciting the Prayer' is the Going for Refuge repeated like a mantra: you go on saying to yourself, *Buddham saranam gacchāmi*, *Dharmam saranam gacchāmi*, and so on. Presumably Sangye Jhap will recite it in Tibetan. 'And in the meantime try to find out which takes refuge, the mind or the body. Tell me the result tomorrow.'

Milarepa is doing a very interesting thing. He's combining the Going for Refuge, which is a basic and fundamental practice, with the search for mind, the Mahāmudrā teaching. He's making something basic a basis for the understanding of something very much more advanced. It reminds me a bit of one of the Zen traditions, in which if, for instance, you're in the habit of reciting the Amitābha mantra, supposing you're a devotee of the Pure Land, the Zen master asks you to find out who recites the salutation to Buddha Amitābha. In much the same way, Milarepa teaches the young man to go for Refuge, and then he asks him, continuing the quest for mind, to try to find out who is it that goes for Refuge, the mind or the body. 'Tell me the result tomorrow.' Now Milarepa is taking more initiative. By this time perhaps the young shepherd is a bit out of his depth. He needs help and guidance. So what happens? Let's go on.

The next morning the shepherd came and said to Milarepa, 'Dear Lama, last night I tried to find out which of these two takes refuge, the body or the mind. I found that it is neither of them. (I observed the body first.) Each part, from the head down to the toes, has a name. I asked myself, "Is it the body as a whole which takes refuge?" It cannot be so, for when the mind leaves the body, the latter no longer exists. People then call it a "corpse", and certainly it cannot be called a "refuge-seeker". Furthermore, when it disintegrates, it ceases to be a corpse; therefore, it cannot be the body which takes refuge in Buddha. I then asked myself, "Is it the mind that takes refuge?" But the refuge-seeker cannot be the mind, as the latter is only the mind and nothing else. If one says that the present mind is the (real) mind, and the succeeding one is the one which takes refuge, there will be two minds; and names for both, such as the "present mind" and the "future mind", should then be given them. Besides, when the act of "Refuge-seeking" takes place, both the present and succeeding minds have passed away! If one says both take refuge, then the mind will (become something immutable) which never (grows) or ceases to be. If that is so, then in all the lives of the past and future in the Six Realms of Saṃsāra, we meet nothing but this "Refuge-seeker". But I cannot remember anything in my past life; nor do I know what will take place in my future one. The mind of last year and yesterday are gone; that of tomorrow has not yet come; the present flowing one does not stay. Pray, my teacher, please give me an explanation. I submit everything to you; you know everything, you know what I need!'

The basic conclusion is that the body doesn't go for Refuge – that's pretty obvious. When we say 'body' we usually mean body in association with mind, in other words the living body. The body by itself is just a corpse, and clearly a corpse can't go for Refuge. But the mind doesn't go for Refuge either. The arguments here are a bit abstruse, but to begin with, the mind isn't just one thing or entity. It is constantly changing. It is a succession of thoughts. Can you carry over the act of going for Refuge from one thought to another? The mind of the present starts going for Refuge but it doesn't succeed in carrying that over to the subsequent mind. The mind that begins to go for Refuge just ceases. If the movement of going for Refuge can be carried over from the present thought to the subsequent thought, that would mean that they coexist, and if they coexist, mind doesn't change, mind is immutable, and the whole series of thoughts is immutable. If that were the case, you would be going for Refuge all the time, even in the past before you went for Refuge – which doesn't make sense. And if you didn't go for Refuge in the past, you couldn't go for Refuge in the present either if the assumption is that all your mental activities are one continuous immutable chain. One can only conclude that mind also doesn't go for Refuge, can't go for Refuge. This may seem like logic-chopping, but the import, or at least the conclusion, is clear.

If the body doesn't go for Refuge and the mind doesn't go for Refuge, who goes for Refuge? To simplify a little, and look at it in the light of traditional Buddhist thought, nobody goes for Refuge. There is a going for Refuge, but there's nobody to go for Refuge – neither the body nor the mind. This isn't stated explicitly, but it's an implication. There is no going for Refuge by anybody – there's just a going for Refuge. But perhaps the young shepherd hasn't come to that point yet. He's only understood that the body can't go for Refuge and the mind can't go for Refuge, so he's in a bit of a quandary. He's rather stuck. He hasn't, apparently, come to the point of realizing that there is only a spontaneous going for Refuge, which has no subject and no object. He appeals to Milarepa, 'Pray, my teacher, please give me an explanation. I submit everything to you; you know everything, you know what I need.' And in answer to his request Milarepa gives a long and comprehensive teaching:

> I sincerely pray to my Guru
> Who realized the truth of Non-ego,
> I pray with body, words, and mind;
> I pray with great faith and sincerity.
> Pray bless me and my disciples,
> Enable us to realize the Truth of Non-ego!
> Pity us and deliver us from the plight of ego-clinging!

From this verse it's clear that the whole thing is about the ego. You think in terms of the ego because you think in terms of object and subject. You think that if there's a going for Refuge there must be someone who goes for Refuge. If it isn't the body it must be the mind. If it isn't the mind it must be the body. The young shepherd has just seen that the body cannot go for Refuge and the mind cannot go for Refuge, so he's puzzled, because he assumes that someone must go for Refuge. But in this verse Milarepa comes straight to the point. It's a question of non-ego – not thinking in terms of subject and object, not thinking in terms of ego, but not thinking there must be an unchanging subject for every action that can be identified as the ego.

HOW TO SEE NOTHING

> Listen carefully, dear shepherd.
> Clinging to the notion of ego is characteristic of this
>   consciousness.
> If one looks into this consciousness itself,
> He sees no ego; of it nothing is seen!

This is quite important. 'This consciousness' means our ordinary mundane consciousness, which thinks in terms of ego, clings to ego. If you look into 'this consciousness itself' in a non-dualistic way, not just treating it as an object, look without looking, then you see consciousness but not ego. It's only the relative mind, the worldly mind, which is associated with ego. Consciousness itself, as it were – though again one mustn't think of it as an object out there – consciousness in its true nature is not associated with ego. In consciousness, in reality, there is no subject, no ego. 'He sees no ego; of it nothing is seen.' This seeing of non-ego is a sort of non-seeing; one can only say that.

> If one can practice the teaching of Mahāmudrā
> And knows how to see nothing, something will be seen.

In the same way as if you see something you don't see anything, if you know how to see nothing, something will be seen. If you see nothing – well, there's nobody seeing. And if there's nobody seeing – there's no ego – something will be seen. The wisdom, as it were, will see the Void, or the Voidness will be seen by the wisdom. The wisdom will be the Voidness. The Voidness will be the wisdom.

To practice the teaching of Mahāmudrā
One needs great faith, humility, and zeal as the Foundation.
One should understand the truth of Karma and Causation as
    the Path.
In order to achieve the Accomplishment, one should depend
    upon a Guru
For the Initiation, Instruction, and Inner Teaching.

Milarepa has shown the shepherd the goal: the Mahāmudrā. *Mahā* means great and *mudrā* means gesture or symbol or attitude, so the Mahāmudrā is the great attitude, the great symbol, the great gesture. It's the most important of the spiritual traditions of the Kagyu tradition, of which Milarepa is of course regarded as one of the founders, along with Marpa and Gampopa, and it corresponds roughly to the *ati-yoga* or supreme yoga teaching of the Nyingmapas. To practise the teaching of Mahāmudrā is to see and know one's own mind in the true sense, not that mind which is an object and not knowing it with a mind which is a subject.

In this verse we have this triad of terms: the foundation, the path, and the accomplishment. This well-known triad can be applied in various ways or within different contexts. You need first of all the basis from which you start, then the course along which you go, and then the accomplishment, the goal, the result which you achieve. In this case, as regards the Mahāmudrā, to start with you need faith, humility, and zeal. That's your foundation. Your path is an understanding of the truth of karma and causation, or rather conditionality: that whatever arises, arises in dependence upon conditions, and if you want that particular experience to arise, you must create or bring into existence the appropriate conditions. This is what you must firmly realize. It won't come about by accident or luck or even somebody's blessing. It will arise in dependence upon the conditions which you yourself bring into existence, which you yourself create. Your path here is the understanding of the truth of karma and causation. And what about the accomplishment? For this one should depend upon a guru for the initiation, instruction, and inner teaching. It's very, very difficult, though not impossible, to have a spontaneous awakening to the truth of the Mahāmudrā, to the truth of the real nature of your own mind, yourself. You need to have it pointed out to you, at least to some extent to begin with, before you can really get working on it.

Here Milarepa is emphasizing what is important if you want to practise the teaching of Mahāmudrā, if you want to see nothing and in that way see something. First, you must have faith, humility, and zeal as the foundation. Then, you should understand the truth of karma and conditionality as the path. And thirdly, you should depend upon a guru for the initiation, instruction, and inner teaching in order to achieve the accomplishment which is the realization of the Mahāmudrā itself. One shouldn't take initiation, instruction, and inner teaching in too formal or institutionalized a sense. Right here, in the course of this song, in a sense Milarepa is giving initiation, instruction, the inner teaching.

THE DEFIANCE OF DEATH

It requires a disciple possessing merit to receive the teaching;
It requires a man who disregards comfort and suffering;
It requires the courage of fearlessness, the defiance of death!
Dear shepherd, can you do these things?
If so, you are well-destined;
If not, it is better not to talk about the subject.
This ask yourself, and think carefully.

It requires a disciple possessing merit to receive the teaching.

Merit is *puṇya*, a very important conception. *Puṇya karma*, meritorious action, is usually taken simply in the sense of good deeds, but it's very much more than that. What, after all, is a *puṇya karma*? Basically, it's a skilful action of body, speech, and mind, but it is not just that. If you perform a skilful action, you set up a sort of skilful atmosphere. It's not exactly self-perpetuating because you always need to keep up the effort, but if you're constantly thinking skilful thoughts, speaking skilful words, and performing skilful actions, you set up around yourself a skilful vibration; you create a sort of skilful field. *Puṇya* is not only the skilful action that you perform, it's also this skilful atmosphere that you create around yourself, something very positive and powerful. The longer you go on performing skilful and meritorious deeds, the more there is this aura of skilfulness around you, and it is that which is *puṇya*, which influences others, affects others, and even draws to yourself some greater good. Before you can truly receive the teaching – and don't forget that Milarepa is talking about the Mahāmudrā here, a very advanced practice – you must be in this highly receptive and creatively skilful mood or state, you must have reached a very high pitch of skilfulness and merit. Only then can you be what is called a worthy vehicle of the teaching. Only then can you really receive. It requires a disciple possessing merit to receive the teaching: not just someone who's done a lot of good deeds, but one who is, here and now, in a very powerfully positive state, with this powerful aura of *puṇya* around him.

> *It requires a man who disregards comfort and suffering.*
> *It requires the courage of fearlessness, the defiance of death.*

It is relatively easy to understand that in order to receive the Mahāmudrā teaching one must be prepared to disregard comfort and suffering, but why does it require 'the courage of fearlessness, the defiance of death'? It's because the Mahāmudrā teaching is concerned with the realization of the non-egoistic nature of the mind, the fact that in the mind there is neither subject nor object. In the case of most people it's the dropping off of the physical body that they're afraid of. They identify themselves with the physical body, so it's death in this sense that is being referred to. If you're not ready to defy death, you're not ready for the Mahāmudrā teaching. Fear of death is essentially fear of loss of ego, loss of self, and unless you're ready to give up that fear, unless you're a hero in that sense, there's not much point in going into the Mahāmudrā teaching. It is sometimes said, for instance in the Zen tradition, that those who are used to being close to death can be quite close to the spiritual path, because they're ready to give up their lives, ready to give up their physical bodies, which means they've achieved some measure of renunciation of ego. This is why you sometimes find military people with a great affinity with the spiritual life. I don't mean military administrators who just press buttons at a safe distance from the battlefield, but people who are ready to go out and risk their lives. There has to be some measure of non-ego there. It's people who have got this sort of courage who are in a position to receive the Mahāmudrā teaching, not those who stay safely at home and shun risk and danger. Here we find Milarepa drawing attention to what I've sometimes called the heroic ideal or the heroic aspect of Buddhism[78] – fearlessness, being prepared to face death.

Dear shepherd, can you do these things?
If so, you are well destined;
If not, it is better not to talk about the subject.
This ask yourself, and think carefully.

There's so much glib talk, even in Tibet, about the Mahāmudrā, giving up the ego, going beyond it all, the one mind, the unconditioned. But it's all just talk. If you're not ready to give up your life you'd better just leave these things alone. Once again Milarepa is very uncompromising. But nowadays, unfortunately, who runs may read.[79] Anyone can pick up the sayings of the Zen masters or the songs of Milarepa. Of course, that's also a good thing, but there is the danger of a sort of vulgarization, of people taking these teachings too lightly and thinking they've understood them just because they've read a book and understand the words. If you aren't ready to die, as it were, Milarepa is saying, leave the Mahāmudrā alone. It's not for you, it's only for the heroes who are prepared to defy death. If you're not ready to defy death, you're not within a million miles of the Mahāmudrā, so you'd better not try to touch it.

But this young shepherd has apparently never read a book. He was presumably born into a Buddhist family, he seems to have a Buddhist name, but until now he hasn't really gone for Refuge. He is just very fresh and alive and receptive and young, and presumably he is ready to give up his life if necessary. So Milarepa goes on to sing:

When you sought the 'I' (last night) you could not find it.
This is the practice of Non-ego of Personality.
If you want to practice the Non-ego of Existence,
Follow my example and for twelve years meditate.
Then you will understand the nature of Mind.
Think well on this, dear boy!

This is a reference to the Buddhist philosophy, as we have to call it, of the twofold non-ego or the twofold *śūnyatā*, the absence of self from the subject, the absence of self from the object. These are technically called *pudgala-nairātmya* or *pudgala-śūnyatā* and *dharma-nairātmya* or *dharma-śūnyatā*, or *sarva-śūnyatā*, the emphasis on the voidness of all things, both subject and object.[80] According to the Mahāyāna, the Hīnayāna teaches only the non-ego nature of the subject, whereas the

Mahāyāna teaches the non-egohood of all things whatsoever, teaches that all things are, as it were, empty. This is called the *sarvadharma-śūnyatā*, the emptiness of all *dharmas* in the sense of things or objects or phenomena, all things conditioned and unconditioned. Milarepa says that if you want to go more deeply into this question of non-ego, if you want to realize not only that there is no ego in yourself but there is no ego anywhere in the world, no ego in any object, that they're all completely empty and void, then, as Milarepa has himself done, you must meditate for twelve years. 'Then you will understand the nature of mind. Think well on this, dear boy!' Think carefully before you commit yourself. And what does the shepherd say?

I OFFER YOU MY BODY AND MY HEAD

The shepherd said, 'I offer you my body and my head. Please make me understand my own mind definitely and clearly.' The Jetsun thought, 'I shall see whether this child can really practice,' and then he said, 'First pray to the Three Precious Ones, then visualize an image of Buddha in front of your nose.' Thus Milarepa gave the shepherd the instruction of concentration and sent him away.

The boy is instructed to pray to – that is, to invoke – the Three Precious Ones, then visualize an image of the Buddha, and then he is given the instruction of concentration and sent away. Milarepa has started him on the systematic practice of meditation, according to the path of regular steps.

There was no sign of the boy for seven days. On the seventh day, his father came to Milarepa, saying, 'Dear Lama, my son has not come home for a week. This is very unusual. Wondering whether he was lost, I inquired of the other shepherds who had been with him. They all said that he had come to you for the Dharma, and thought he had then gone home. But where is he?' 'He was here,' replied Milarepa, 'but has not come back now for seven days.' The father was deeply grieved and wept bitterly as he left Milarepa. Many people were then sent out to search for the boy. Finally, they found him in a clay pit sitting upright with his eyes wide open staring straight in front. They asked him, 'What are you doing here?' He replied, 'I am practicing the meditation my Guru taught me.' 'Then why have you not returned home for seven days?' 'I have only been meditating a little while, you must be joking!' As he said this, he looked at the sun and found that it was earlier than the time he had started to meditate. In his bewilderment he asked, 'What has happened?'

You can see how intensively, how sincerely, the boy practised. He went and got on with the meditation straightaway and lost all sense of time. He just plunged into it. Some people can do this, especially the young. Young people, generally speaking, are often more wholehearted than older people. They can give themselves more completely and more totally. The shepherd went missing for seven days. He was just getting on with the meditation and to him it seemed as though he'd been meditating for just a little while. When he checked the time by looking at the sun, it seemed as though it was earlier than when he started meditating. No wonder he was puzzled.

From that day on, the boy's family had great difficulty with him, because he had almost completely lost the notion of time. What appeared to him to have been only one day, was the passing of four or five days to others. Many times his parents sent people out to search for him. Thus both he and his family began to feel miserable. At this juncture they asked him whether he wanted to live with Milarepa for good. He said that he would like nothing better. So they provided him with food and sent him to the Teacher.

Well, that seems to be a very reasonable offer. They not only sent him to the teacher but provided him with food to live on while he was there.

Milarepa first gave him the Precepts of Five Virtues, preached the doctrine of Dharma, and then granted him the teaching of the Innate-born Wisdom. Through practice, the boy gradually attained good meditation experience and Milarepa was very pleased.

Once again it's the path of regular steps. Milarepa has given him the Refuges, he's gone for Refuge, and now he gives him the five *śīlas*, the five precepts. He 'preached the doctrine of the Dharma' – presumably the basic Buddhist teaching – then 'granted him the teaching of the innate-born wisdom', which is of course a very advanced teaching cognate with the teaching of the Mahāmudrā. 'Innate-born' presumably translates the Tibetan equivalent of *sahaja*, that is to say 'arising with' or 'born with' you, in other words non-separable from you, pertaining to your own innermost nature: not wisdom that you gain or achieve but wisdom that you realize has always been there, that is innate. So 'through practice, the boy gradually attained good meditation experience and Milarepa was very pleased'. This sentence may refer to a period of several years of practice. One mustn't be misled by the brevity and simplicity of the text. But then comes a very important concluding song.

THE TEST

(In order, however, to clarify the boy's misapprehension on the nature of true Realization), he sang:

I bow down at the feet of Marpa,
He who received grace from Nāropa and Medripa.
Those who practice the Dharma with their mouths
Talk much and seem to know much teaching,
But when the time comes for the perceiver to leave the deadened body,
The mouth-bound preacher into space is thrown.

This reminds me of a little story told in modern India about a parrot. In India they don't teach parrots to swear, they teach them to recite mantras. There's a story that a holy man had a parrot and taught it to say 'Hare Ram, Hare Ram, Hare Ram', invoking one of the Hindu gods. But one day the cat caught hold of the parrot and ran off with it, and of course the parrot completely forgot all about 'Hare Ram, Hare Ram' and let out its own natural squawk. It's said that so-called religious people are very often like that. They can talk all day about Buddha, Dharma, Sangha, Mahāmudrā, self-realization, Enlightenment, Nirvāṇa, all the rest of it. But let the cat get hold of them – in other words, let death come and catch hold of them – and they just let out their own natural squawk. They're terrified, they forget all about the Dharma.

Death is the test. What happens then? It's easy to go on talking while you're still well and comfortable and happy, but when death seizes hold of you, what will you be like then? What will be your reaction? That's the test. This is what Milarepa is saying.

When the Clear Light shines, it is cloaked by blindness.
The chance to see the Dharmakāya at the time of death
Is lost through fear and confusion.

Even though one spends his life in studying the Canon,
It helps not at the moment of the mind's departure.

If you practise during your life, if you've at least weakened the ego-sense, then the time of death can be a wonderful opportunity. According to the Tibetan Tantric teaching, at the moment of death, when you have dissociated from the physical body and the ordinary mind isn't working, you have a momentary experience of your own true mind, the *dharmakāya*. If during your lifetime you've prepared through your practice a basis on which to receive this, then you can hold that experience, you can allow yourself, your ego, to be dissolved into the *dharmakāya*, and in that way gain Enlightenment at the moment of death. But there must be a basis already prepared, and you do that by your spiritual practice, by the efforts to dissolve the ego-sense you have made during your lifetime; otherwise the opportunity is lost through fear and confusion.

This sort of test comes not only at the moment of the mind's departure but if any sort of disaster or trouble hits you. If you lose someone who is near and dear to you or maybe you lose a limb, or have a long illness, or lose all your money, or you are blamed for something, or become very unpopular, even persecuted, that's the test.

Alas! Those proficient yogis who long have practiced meditation
Mistake the psychic experience of illumination
For Transcendental Wisdom,
And are happy with this form of self-deception.

Now Milarepa is dealing with more advanced errors of the kind to which the young shepherd may fall victim. If you've been meditating for a long time you can have the experience of great luminosity, great awareness, great light. This is a psychic experience, not the light of wisdom, but you can mistake it for that, and that's the great danger.

> Therefore when at death the Transcendental Wisdom of the
> Dharmakāya shines,
> These yogis cannot unify the Light of Mother-and-Son.
> Since meditation cannot help them as they die,
> They are still in danger of rebirth in lower Realms.

The mother-light is the light of the *dharmakāya*, and the son-light is the light of your own emerging wisdom going as it were to meet the light of the *dharmakāya*. Perhaps for us in the West mother-light isn't a very happy expression, suggesting a sort of going back into the womb, which of course isn't a place of light, but a place of darkness. As an alternative, one could perhaps instead speak of the father-light and the son-light. Milarepa says that those yogis who during their lifetime have mistaken the psychic experience of illumination for transcendental wisdom will be in difficulties at the time of death. They will be unable to unite or merge, to use those metaphorical expressions, their own son-light with that mother- or father-light of the *dharmakāya*. 'Meditation cannot help them as they die' because they have not been meditating correctly, or at least have not meditated to a sufficiently advanced extent, so they're still in danger of rebirth in lower realms.

PURE AND BRIGHT AS A FLOWER

> My dear son, best of laymen, listen to me carefully!

Now he addresses him as 'son', you notice; he's become a son-disciple.

> When your body is rightly posed, and your mind absorbed deep
>   in meditation,
> You may feel that thought and mind both disappear;
> Yet this is but the surface experience of Dhyāna.

Milarepa begins with the fundamentals: sitting correctly and getting your mind concentrated, all your energies flowing in the same direction. But although 'you may feel that thought and mind both disappear, yet this is but the surface experience of dhyāna'. Don't think you've achieved anything very deep. This is always a mistake which one is liable to make: you feel prematurely that you've really got there.

> By constant practice and mindfulness thereon,
> One feels radiant Self-awareness shining like a brilliant lamp.
> It is pure and bright as a flower,
> It is like the feeling of staring
> Into the vast and empty sky.
> The Awareness of Voidness is limpid and transparent, yet vivid.
> This Non-thought, this radiant and transparent experience
> Is but the feeling of Dhyāna.

You've not even approached *prajñā* or wisdom; you're still in the region of *dhyāna*.

> With this good foundation
> One should further pray to the Three Precious Ones,
> And penetrate to Reality by deep thinking and contemplation.

Why should the Three Jewels be invoked at this stage? To remind you not only of what you're doing, but of what you're seeking. The Three Jewels represent transcendental values. You can have a good meditation, even experience all those *dhyāna* levels, without being a Buddhist. The *dhyānas* are common to all religions. But if you want to penetrate through to transcendental experience, if you want to develop wisdom, then you must think in specifically Buddhist terms, for want of a better term, so you invoke the Three Jewels, you open yourself to purely transcendental experiences. You can't maintain the *dhyāna* level indefinitely; the gravitational pull will sooner or later assert itself if you don't 'penetrate to Reality', and you try to do that through invoking the Three Jewels.

> He thus can tie the Non-ego Wisdom
> With the beneficial life-rope of deep Dhyāna.

In other words, *dhyāna* is not enough; there must be wisdom too.

With the power of kindness and compassion,
And with the altruistic vow of the Bodhi-Heart,
He can see direct and clear
The truth of the Enlightened Path,
Of which nothing can be seen, yet all is clearly visioned.

Dhyāna is the foundation, then comes transcendental wisdom conjoined
with absolute compassion, so then he can 'see direct and clear the truth
of the Enlightened path, of which nothing can be seen, yet all is clearly
visioned'. Again, there's this paradoxical language, because we're
concerned with the Mahāmudrā, with the ultimate truth.

THE PLACE OF BUDDHA

He sees how wrong were the fears and hopes of his own mind.
Without arrival, he reaches the place of Buddha;
Without seeing, he visions the Dharmakāya;
Without effort, he does all things naturally.

The fears and hopes of his own mind were wrong because they were
based on ego. There's no 'I' that arrives at the place of Buddha; and there
isn't even an arrival, because gaining Enlightenment doesn't involve going
anywhere. 'Without seeing, he visions the Dharmakāya.' The *dharmakāya*
is not an object. This point that without effort he does all things naturally,
this spontaneity, is very important as a corollary. The one mind, the mind
which is neither subject nor object, is as it were spontaneous. It's innate,
natural; it wells up or bubbles up within you. Once you've got over the
ego-sense, once you don't think or experience any longer in terms of object
and subject, you not only realize the one mind which is beyond subject
and object, but also you liberate a tremendous creativity, a tremendous
spontaneity. This is a very important aspect of the Mahāmudrā teaching.
The idea is not that you should deliberately be spontaneous, which is a
contradiction in terms, but there is a practice whereby in order to learn
to be spontaneous, even though on a lower level, you just do whatever
occurs to you. If you do this sort of practice, very often you can't do any
other. If you feel like going for a walk, you go for a walk; if you feel like
eating, you eat; if you feel like drinking, you drink; if you feel like singing,
you sing; if you feel like going to sleep, you go to sleep. You follow your

impulses, but with great awareness. This is obviously quite a difficult, dangerous practice, but it's a way of coming to realize that spontaneity is a corollary of the realization of non-ego.

When you realize non-ego, you don't become all solid and stolid and steady and reliable. You might appear to other people to be very whimsical and unpredictable and unsatisfactory. There's no effort; the spontaneity just bubbles up. The bodhisattva doesn't have to make any effort to help people, it's just fun. This is an aspect of the bodhisattva's career. The *bodhicarya* is *anubhogacarya*, which means, as Suzuki translates it, 'the life of spontaneity'.[81] You're spontaneous all the time. When you become Enlightened, if you can imagine or dream of that day, you won't become all solemn and religious and spiritual. No, you'll become very happy and carefree; you'll be bubbling over with joy all the time, at least inwardly. It isn't that when you're Enlightened you'll be bubbling over with joy always. You'll be unpredictable. You might sit quietly in a corner just for fun, or just to puzzle people a bit, so that they don't associate the Enlightened state solely with that sort of bubbly joy. But the principle is that naturalness and spontaneity are very much stressed by the Mahāmudrā.

Then Milarepa says:

Dear son, the Virtue-seeker, bear this instruction in your mind.

So he still isn't finished!

Milarepa then gave the boy complete Initiation and verbal instructions. After practicing them, the boy attained superlative Experience and Realization. He was known as one of the 'Heart-Sons' of the Jetsun, Repa Sangje Jhap.

This is the story of Milarepa's second visit to Ragma, and of his meeting with Repa Sangje Jhap.

And so the shepherd too became a 'repa', a cotton-clad one, like Milarepa. We're not told how long it took him to attain 'superlative experience', but it was probably quite a number of years.

This section of the chapter contrasts with the previous section in the sense that the story of the shepherd feels continuous and flowing and spontaneous, whereas in the first section Milarepa was having to respond to a reactive mind and keep hammering away at it, changing tack, assuming a different form every time it shifted its ground. The young shepherd is much more alive and spontaneous. In the first section Milarepa is breaking down the conditioned, reactive mind, whereas in the second section he is encouraging the creative mind. In the long run it amounts to the same thing, but there's a great difference of approach and feeling. It shows the genius of Milarepa, that he could teach such totally different people.

When Milarepa is with a disciple or when he meets somebody, he often refers to the good karmic link between them. Traditionally it would be accepted that they had had an association in past lives, and it does sometimes seem like that. Why do you take to someone when you meet them for the first time, and not to somebody else? You can explain it in other ways, maybe it's chemical or psychological, but it doesn't seem like that sometimes.

There's a saying that if you don't produce a disciple who is twice as good as you are, you have betrayed the Dharma. If in every generation the disciple is just a little bit below his teacher's standard, after a few generations the Dharma will fade away entirely. If you are a Dharma teacher, you therefore have to aim to produce someone better than you are, even twice as good as you are, just so that the Dharma may continue. You can't afford to compromise all the time and just encourage this person a little bit and that person a little bit. You have to keep an eye open for promising people who can go a long, long way. Otherwise there's no hope for the future of the Dharma. You have to keep your eyes open, or even go out and look for the brilliant disciple. That doesn't necessarily mean the flashy one who is always protesting how devoted he is, but the really solid reliable person who is going to make a real effort.

Rechungpa's Journey
to Enlightenment

EDITOR'S INTRODUCTION

In the summer and autumn of 1980 Sangharakshita led a sequence of seven seminars based on chapters of *The Hundred Thousand Songs of Milarepa* which tell the story of Milarepa's relationship with his disciple Rechungpa, from their first meeting, when Rechungpa, then a young boy, is attracted to the sound of Milarepa's voice, singing in the mountains, to their final parting, when Rechungpa leaves with his guru's blessing to begin his own Dharma teaching career. It is on these seven seminars that the following commentary – which takes up the rest of this volume and the whole of volume 19 of the *Complete Works* – is based. The story unfolds almost like a novel, and has many recurring themes – for example, Rechungpa's perpetual wish to go elsewhere despite Milarepa's advice that from the point of view of his spiritual development he would be better to stay where he is, and the disciple's struggles to overcome his pride in his achievements, especially his intellectual victories and his acquisition on his journeys of special teachings.

There are several ways in which this commentary, extensive though it is, does not quite tell the whole story of Rechungpa's journey to Enlightenment. Firstly, and most literally, in the case of two stories, 'Heartfelt Advice to Rechungpa' and 'Rechungpa's Departure', (both in volume 19), the seminar ran out of time before all the text had been studied. We have added the rest of the source text so that the whole story is told, even though the final section is without comment.

Secondly, the commentary does not cover all the chapters of *The Hundred Thousand Songs* in which Rechungpa appears. To summarize the episodes not covered, early on in the text there's a chapter promisingly called 'The Enlightenment of Rechungpa', but although the translator states in excited italics, reporting Rechungpa's response to a statement of Milarepa's, '*As Milarepa said this, Rechungpa suddenly became enlightened*', at the end of the whole episode Milarepa merely says, 'Rechungpa, this is indeed the real Experience and knowledge. You can truly be called a well-gifted disciple.' He clearly has more to learn; Enlightenment is not yet complete.[82] Another chapter, 'The Challenge from the Logicians', sheds quite a different light on the young disciple, and sets the scene for the following chapter, which is considered in detail in our commentary in the story 'Rechungpa's Third Journey to India'. While Milarepa patiently endures the verbal assaults of a pair of logicians who want to beat him in debate, and emerges victorious on his own terms, Rechungpa's main part in the story is to attempt to defend his guru by physically attacking an insolent scholar with a stick, having to be restrained by his more forbearing teacher.[83] Taking another tack, in the story called 'Milarepa and the Dying Sheep' we find Rechungpa keen to take 'some comfort and enjoyment to increase my devotion'. Shown by a dubious Milarepa the piteous plight of a dying sheep, Rechungpa is shocked into genuine renunciation.[84] In other stories Rechungpa plays a more conventional disciple's role, just being the person who with a well-timed question prompts Milarepa into singing a song or giving advice.[85] Less conventionally, in a short story, 'The Miracle of the Vase Initiation', we get an intriguing glimpse of Rechungpa as an artist: we are told that having completed a painting of the Vajra Yoginī, he brings it to Milarepa, asking him to blessing the painting.[86]

It is in chapter 41 of *The Hundred Thousand Songs*, 'The Holy Gambopa – Milarepa's Foremost Disciple', that we get a subtle hint about a third and different kind of way in which there may be more to be said about Rechungpa. Gampopa (as his name is more usually spelled in English) and Rechungpa are usually referred to as Milarepa's two chief disciples, but apparently one of them is more 'chief' than the other. In *The Hundred Thousand Songs*, just before Milarepa meets Rechungpa, a *ḍākinī* prophesies that Gampopa will be 'the sun pupil' and Rechungpa 'the moon pupil'[87] and in chapter 41's lengthy account of Gampopa's life Rechungpa is certainly eclipsed; indeed, in our only brief glimpse of him in this story, he is preparing tea.[88]

At the time Sangharakshita gave the seminars on which this work is based, no biography of Rechungpa had yet been published in English translation, and the characterization of Rechungpa given in *The Hundred Thousand Songs of Milarepa* as translated by Garma C. C. Chang went unchallenged. Now, however, a number of works are available to give us different perspectives on Rechungpa. Light is shed on him by *The Biographies of Rechungpa: The Evolution of a Tibetan Hagiography*, in which Peter Alan Roberts charts the way the telling of Rechungpa's life story was altered over a period of three centuries. This illuminating study of a number of biographies shows how, by the time of writing of *The Hundred Thousand Songs of Milarepa*, which is a comparatively late text, Rechungpa's story had become an account of a stubborn, proud, and recalcitrant disciple, in contrast to the holy Gampopa. 'In *The Hundred Thousand Songs of Milarepa*, which provides the popular image of Rechungpa, he is unequivocally portrayed as secondary to Gampopa, the Kadampa monk who merged Milarepa's teaching with the Kadampa tradition to form the Dakpo Kagyu school.... Tsangnyön [said to be the author of *The Hundred Thousand Songs*] emphasises Rechungpa's deficiencies and the superiority of Gampopa and even gives the impression that it was Gampopa alone who received the entire transmission of Milarepa's instruction.'[89]

Strange to say, whether or not the disciple we meet in *The Hundred Thousand Songs*, and consequently in Sangharakshita's commentary, bears any resemblance to the historical Rechungpa, his story is all the more inspiring and instructive because we see so graphically the struggles he has to undergo in the course of his spiritual life. He is stubborn, easily distracted, unwilling to be impressed, determined to get his own way at all costs, over-dependent on book learning, and in short altogether recognizable as the kind of disciple we ourselves may be, if we can allow ourselves to admit it – or perhaps at least he reminds us of a friend of ours who has similarly regrettable tendencies....

But this story is really about not a person but a relationship. However far Rechungpa travels, and however many sidetracks he follows, literally or psychologically, whatever the physical distance between them, his patient teacher is with him every step of the way

– sometimes to Rechungpa's intense discomfort, as we will see – and his methods of helping his heart-disciple are closely examined here. Or, one could say, on another level the story is not really about either of the two cotton-clad yogis whose activities and insights come to us from lives lived almost a thousand years ago. Neither is it about the participants in those seminars in 1980, though their curiosity and zest to learn how to live the spiritual life is what prompted the exploration of the text from which this commentary is woven. It is really about us, in the sense that the story is told for our benefit. The whole story is thus not really whole unless it includes us.

Narrative has a remarkable power to amuse and shock us, move us and even change us, if we allow that to happen – but that's a big if. Indeed, it is the basic theme of this whole commentary. Each of us is evidently up against whatever our own version is of Rechungpa's fabled resistance to the truth. We also face the challenge of a further, and most mysterious, way in which all these many words cannot tell the whole story. No words can do so, as Milarepa himself makes abundantly clear. Perhaps poems or songs can come close, can overcome our resistance in a way that prose (including this well-meaning introduction) cannot. There was a moment in the midst of finding a way through the forest of words when – in a clearing – a few lines from one of Milarepa's songs pierced me to the heart, though I can't say quite why:

> When I look back at my clinging mind,
> It appears like a short-lived sparrow in the woods –
> Homeless, and with nowhere to sleep;
> When I think of this, my heart is filled with grief.[90]

As well as staying alive to those moments when light penetrates the darkness, we are going to need other help to discern which of all these words will speak to our own condition. First, we will need our wits about us. In the words of a much-loved Perfection of Wisdom text, we will need to call forth as much as we have of love, of respect, and of faith. And we will also need our spiritual friends to help us see the wood for the trees, to discern the Pith-Instructions applicable specifically to us. We may imagine that we are better equipped than Rechungpa (as depicted in *The Hundred Thousand Songs*) to see what we need to do, but the essential truth of the situation seems to be that we are more than likely to be wrong. Time to swallow our pride and get ready to learn. Luckily for us, these stories are entertaining and funny, moving and strange, as well as having, in their own way, the power to transform us, whether we like it or not.

Vidyadevi

FIRST STORY
MILAREPA'S FIRST MEETING
WITH RECHUNGPA

In which Milarepa, after an exchange with some builders about the construction of his spiritual 'house', meets Rechungpa, a gifted young storyteller and reciter of *sūtras* who is attracted to Milarepa when he hears him singing, and stays with him to learn the Dharma. Rechungpa's family are so angry with him for taking up the spiritual life that they try to kill him by infecting him with leprosy. He opts to leave his newly found guru and go to India to seek a cure. He comes back to find Milarepa still meditating.

Themes:

I

NO TIME FOR THAT SORT OF THING

As prophesied by (Marpa), Milarepa went to the upper part of
Gung Tang. When he arrived at the Castle there, he found that
many people were building a house and asked them for some food.
They replied, 'We are working on this building. You can see that
we are very busy and have no time for that sort of thing. It looks
as though you have plenty of time to spare, so why don't you join
us in the work?'

This first song is prompted by a very down-to-earth incident. We gather
that the people who are building the house resent the fact that Milarepa
is idle when they're all hard at work. He appears to have nothing to
do – he's not a monk, just a wandering yogi with no visible means of
support – and he approaches them and asks them for food, when they
think that one should earn one's daily bread. They say they are busy and
have no time for 'that sort of thing'. What they mean by 'that sort of
thing' depends upon whether they recognize him as a yogi or whether
they think he's just a beggar. The work that they are doing is visible,
but Milarepa's work is not so obvious. To those who are preoccupied
with mundane, tangible things, it's as though those who are occupied
in some other way are not doing anything at all. It's like the story of
a maidservant who was asked to deliver a message to her mistress 'if
she isn't busy', and later said, 'Oh no, she wasn't busy. She was only
writing.' In the eyes of a person who spends all day on hard physical

work, writing is not work. Washing dishes or bricklaying is work – not just sitting at a desk writing. So even if the people building the house had recognized Milarepa as a yogi, perhaps in their eyes he would not have been doing anything. What does a yogi do? Nothing at all. He just spends his time meditating, and in the eyes of working people, to be meditating is not to be doing anything. There are plenty of people these days who hold the same view. On the other hand – the passage is a bit ambiguous – they might have just seen him as an idle beggar whom they didn't have time to feed. They're not altogether unkind. Perhaps they mean it ironically when they say, 'It looks as though you have plenty of time to spare, so why don't you join us in the work?'

> Milarepa said, 'Yes, I now have plenty of leisure, but I have earned it by finishing the construction of my 'house' in my own way. Even if you do not give me any food, I will never work on a worldly building, which I would most certainly abandon.' The men asked him, 'How did you build your house, and why do you spurn our work so strongly?'

In other words, he has finished his work. In Pāli texts, various stock phrases are used to describe the *arhant's* attainment of Enlightenment: 'He has laid down the burden', 'He has done what was to be done', 'He has finished his work', and Milarepa is in that sort of state. But does one ever reach a point when there is nothing more to do? Can Milarepa's words be taken literally? In the terms of Early Buddhism he has passed the point of no return, or in terms of the Mahāyāna he has traversed the eighth of the Bodhisattva's ten *bhūmis*, and there is no danger of him falling back from that.[91] Whatever the context, there is this notion of irreversibility, of reaching a point from which you cannot fall back into the purely reactive process. Whatever you do henceforth can only be creative. You can go only from one level of creativity to another.

One could say that Milarepa has finished doing whatever he needed to do for his own sake, but he still has a lot to do for other people out of compassion, which is of course why he approached these people in the first place. Milarepa doesn't bother about food, we know that, but he has approached them asking for food to establish contact with them, because he knows, perhaps without thinking about it consciously, that some good for them can come out of that.

Milarepa has done plenty of building work in his time, as we know. As far as we can tell from his biography, the towers he had to build, demolish and rebuild at his guru Marpa's instruction were real[92], and he had to build them with stones that he carried himself, which gave him sores on his back. But there are symbolical overtones as well, and that brings us to the symbolism of the house in this passage. They are building a material house, and Milarepa has built a house which as we will see is non-material, but before you can start building a house, you need something besides bricks and mortar. To put it in Aristotelian terms, you've got the material cause and the efficient cause, but you also need the formal cause and the final cause[93]: that is, the idea of the house and the purpose for which you are going to build it. You've got an idea in your mind; this is what comes first. You have a need which the building of the house would fulfil, and then you body forth your idea in the material world.

This suggests that everything we do is symbolical, or at least expressive. Whether you are conscious of it or not, whether the idea in your mind is very clearly formulated or not, you are all the time giving expression to something. If you need a house and you decide to build it yourself, once you've got the land and the money for materials, you will design your house in a way that is not just governed by utilitarian considerations. If you decide to have red bricks instead of grey, or circular windows rather than square ones, this will say something about you. Likewise, you can look on your life as being the working out not just of your ideas but in a way of the idea which is you.

It is significant that the process of rebirth is likened to the building of a house. In some famous verses in the *Dhammapada*, the Buddha says, addressing his own ignorance, 'Housebuilder, I have seen you now.'[94] He had seen what causes the whole process of birth and death and then rebirth to be repeated over and over again, what causes the house of this worldly life to be built again and again. In this passage we have much the same sort of symbolism, the bodying forth in material terms of something that is within you as an idea, a tendency, an impulse. At the back of all these ideas, all these tendencies, all these impulses, there is *you*, and essentially it is that which you are bodying forth. It's as though, so far as you are concerned, the world is a collection of raw materials and you are giving form to a certain amount of the material that the world contains as a means of expressing what you are. All the time we are creating a pattern, a structure, which is good or bad, positive or negative, skilful or unskilful, according to the state of mind out of which we create it.[95]

There are overtones of this sort of thing in this passage. The householders are not just building a house, but giving expression to a particular attitude, and this is why Milarepa goes on to say to them, 'Your worldly houses are delusions, mere prisons for the demons.' They are the expression of a reactive process. They build a house as a place of security, a place of refuge, maybe a place in which they can carry on all sorts of unskilful activities. That's what a house means to them. It's not just putting up four walls; there's far more to it than that.

Once Milarepa has declared, 'I will never work on a worldly building, which I would most certainly abandon', the men ask him, 'How did you build your house and why do you spurn our work so strongly?' Perhaps they still think that he's got a house somewhere else, and having built it he's not interested in helping them build theirs. But they also want to know why he spurns their work, and in his song sung in reply he explains.

> Faith is the firm foundation of my house,
> Diligence forms the high walls,
> Meditation makes the huge bricks,
> And Wisdom is the great cornerstone.
> With these four things I built my castle,
> And it will last as long as the Truth eternal!
> Your worldly homes are delusions,
> Mere prisons for the demons,
> And so I would abandon and desert them.

You can see your building materials as being not only outside you in the world but in another sense inside you, depending on what you are building. But your building materials are not going to be passive in the sense that stone or wood are passive. Your materials may be human beings, if you are trying to create something in cooperation with other people, and that's a very different matter. Stone or wood can resist you because they have a certain weight, a certain quality which you have to respect, but human beings can put up active resistance. And your own mental forces, your impulses, when they become the raw material of a subtler kind of house-building, can put up a very violent resistance indeed. They have to be won over before you can do anything with them. You can't approach them violently, although strong energy may be required. You have to approach them as Padmasambhava did the demons of Tibet and bring them under control by one means or another[96] before you can create anything with them. And to bring them under control you have to be in contact with them.

So there's not only a contrast but a clash. The house builders are building a house in the literal sense, using stones, clay and so on, and they're building it for a certain purpose, with a certain idea, but Milarepa has built a house of a quite different kind. First of all, it isn't a material house. He has built his house with himself, with his faults, his emotions, his inner energies, and he has built it with a quite different motive from that of the people building their house. Theirs is a completely reactive process, and his is a completely creative process, so how can he possibly join in with the building of their house? How can you be creative and reactive at the same time?[97] The two don't overlap. When they invite him to join in the building of their house, they're really inviting him to participate in the reactive process, which he cannot do. In a sense he doesn't have that freedom. The nearest he can get is to approach them for alms. He gave them the opportunity of establishing with him the nexus of *dāna*, giving, which is the first of the *pāramitās*, the perfections[98], the opportunity of taking that first step and establishing a link between the reactive process and the creative process, but they were not able to take that opportunity. So then he had to draw their attention to the fact that their reactivity and his creativity were completely antithetical, that there was no question of him helping them to build their house. He just refused to join in.

Faith is the firm foundation of my house

The 'house' he is talking about is his individuality, one could say. He's building himself. Yeats says in one of his poems, 'Myself must I remake'.[99] The house that Milarepa is building is in a manner of speaking his own new self. It's important not to take this too literally. When you've built a house, there it stands, it appears not to change, but the new self isn't a fixed, unyielding self that you create in place of the old one; it's more like a mode of functioning. But bearing this in mind, we can speak of it as a new self.

It's as though within the person there are three things: the raw material, which is the old self; the plan for the new self; and the architect. All of these things are you. As you evolve, there's a division: there's the you that sees the plan, the idea or the vision, and there's the you that is the raw material. There's you as passive and there's you as active. The old you is passive as it were to the emerging new you, which gradually transforms the old you, taking the old you as raw material into the new you. This is what Milarepa means by his house. Faith is the foundation of this new self, this new individuality, because faith in the ideal is a feeling for the new possibilities. You have a vision of yourself as you might be, you are very deeply moved by that, and you have the faith that you can become that. In the sequence of the positive *nidānas*, in dependence upon unsatisfactoriness arises faith.[100] You see that your present self is unsatisfactory, you experience it perhaps even as painful, but you see the possibility of a new self being created, and you have faith in that possibility.

The idea that faith is the foundation suggests that faith must be there all the time. It's not as though you have faith early in your spiritual life, and then having gone through that stage, you get on to more advanced things. Just as the foundation is always there supporting the house, your faith is there all the time supporting the growing edifice of your spiritual life. Just as the foundation supports the house all the time, at every stage of your creation of your new self you need that emotional conviction, that drive. Perhaps you need it more and more; otherwise you just slow down and eventually stop.

But it is not faith that determines the next step you need to take in your spiritual life. Faith determines the general process but it cannot tell you the specific details of what to do next. You can't have faith in the wrong thing in principle, because in principle faith is confidence in whatever is going to help you to develop; but to identify specifically what you need to do, you need not just faith but judgement. If you are reasonably positive you will have a natural tendency to develop yourself and you may not need to formulate your goal very clearly because your natural movement is in that direction. But if you haven't yet succeeded in getting emotional positivity flowing, you may need to define a goal much more clearly, to give yourself something to work towards. Some people seem to be able to manage with the minimum of intellectual formulation – the faith followers, as we say – while doctrine followers need more.[101] But you can't have a reason for faith in the sense that reason cannot create faith. It can only support it or give it a certain direction or a bit more clarity.

Faith suggests that you've got some sort of ideal, some sort of vision, and also that you have been able to respond emotionally to that ideal to such an extent that you are motivated in a new way, and that suggests that to begin with you are sufficiently emotionally positive to be able to respond to the vision when you see it. Otherwise, you may see the ideal in an intellectual way, but you will not be galvanized emotionally and faith will therefore not result. So there are two factors involved: you have to have the ideal or see the vision, and you need to be emotionally free enough to be able to respond to it. When you have both, then you have faith and then you are motivated. All the way through the spiritual life you need some kind of vision or ideal ahead of you and you also need some part at least of your emotional energies to be motivated by that. Therefore, as Milarepa says, faith is the firm foundation.

You may not generate that ideal yourself. You may not have thought of it, but you are suddenly confronted by it in a book you read or something you hear or even an image you see. But however the ideal comes to you, if you have the capacity to respond emotionally, faith arises. This is what has the potential to happen in the case of Milarepa and the builders. He is a man as they are men. There is as it were a common higher self which he has created and they are able to create: not a common higher self in a metaphysical sense, but in the sense that they are able to evolve in the same kind of way into the same kind of individual. They are not aware of that yet, but by confronting them with it he confronts them with their own potential for development.

Is a lack of faith in the presence of the ideal a psychological problem? I would say that an emotionally healthy person confronted by the ideal must respond with faith. In past times, when most people were engaged in agriculture, those who came in contact with the Dharma were usually already in a very positive and healthy state. For example, Geshe Rabten's biography describes how he was brought up on a farm in eastern Tibet, not all that many years ago, in the 1920s.[102] As a boy, he was only interested in horses, dogs, and guns. He spent the whole day out in the open air with his dogs, looking after his father's horses, taking them to graze and bringing them back in the evening. When he was a bit older, he learned to read and write a little and that was the extent of his education. From time to time he saw monks and he got the impression that they were leading a far better life than anybody else. He didn't know anything about the Dharma except in a very general way, but he started feeling that he'd like to be a monk and by the time he was nineteen he'd made his mind up. When he was 20 he was on his way, walking several hundred miles to Lhasa – the journey took him three months – to join one of the big monastic universities there. This is quite natural, and it is what one finds in ancient Buddhist literature. Someone might lead a quite ordinary life as a peasant or farmer's son, and as soon as he comes into contact with something higher, whether he sees a monk walking around or he hears a teaching, he's able to respond. His emotional positivity is transformed by contact with that ideal into what we call faith. But in modern times, life having become more complicated, people may be so emotionally exhausted that when they come into contact with a spiritual ideal there's virtually no emotional response, so there's virtually no faith. They're not moved by what they see or hear and therefore there's very little motivating energy and they don't make much progress.

Faith is only possible when self-consciousness has emerged and, in the process of reflection, has developed some awareness of something beyond, something ultimate, as an object – not that it is in itself an object but one is aware of it as an object because one is still functioning within the subject–object framework[103]. Faith spans that gap all the time, and the minute faith disappears, there's no contact between your emotional energy and the goal. If faith flags, you come to a halt, except to the extent that you are carried forward by the momentum of your previous faith. But you can't go on living on the memory of faith for very long. It might keep you going for a few days or weeks, even a few months, but probably not longer than that. You have to experience faith here and now for it to provide a fresh impetus.

> Diligence forms the high walls,
> Meditation makes the huge bricks,
> And Wisdom is the great cornerstone.
> With these four things I built my castle,
> And it will last as long as the Truth eternal!

'Diligence' probably translates the Tibetan equivalent of the Sanskrit term *vīrya*, energy, which follows upon faith. You will only work at something and put energy into it if you've got faith, if the emotional conviction is there. One could say that this emotional energy, this faith, is the driving force of the Higher Evolution,[104] because it links the goal, the end of the higher evolutionary process, with the end result of the process of the lower evolution, which is the healthy, happy, emotionally positive human being. Your emotional positivity as a healthy, happy human being has come into contact, however remotely, with that ideal and it is galvanized by it and now moving towards it, carrying you with it and creating as it goes along the whole of the rest of your being – eventually the whole of your new being, your new self, your new, more enlightened individuality.

Perhaps 'diligence forms the high walls' because just as the high walls are the most prominent part of the house, diligence, like faith, is something you need all the time. But why should meditation be the 'huge bricks'? Perhaps it's because meditation is the basic building block, as it were: very square and solid. We're probably not to imagine bricks, but great stones about four or five feet square, solidly in position, just as when people sit and meditate they don't budge.

The reason why 'Wisdom is the great cornerstone' is pretty obvious. Wisdom is said in the Mahāyāna to be the only *pāramitā*, the cornerstone of the Mahāyāna life.[105] *Dāna* is not a *pāramitā* unless it's conjoined with Wisdom, *vīrya* is not a *pāramitā* unless it's joined with Wisdom and so on. Wisdom is thus the cornerstone – Wisdom in the special sense of insight into the nature of reality, a clear vision of existence.

So, 'With these four things I built my castle.' I don't know how much significance one can attach to the words of the English translation, but the workmen are building a house while Milarepa speaks of his castle, something much nobler and grander. Castles are usually built on hilltops whereas houses are usually built down in the valley. 'And it will last as long at the Truth eternal!' I'm not sure of the Tibetan original of 'Truth eternal', which has a rather occidental ring, but one can get the general sense of it: that his castle will last for ever. Bearing in mind that his 'castle' is his new self, he can say it will last for ever because it's unconditioned – not that it is everlastingly persistent within time so much as that it transcends time and space altogether.

> Your worldly homes are delusions,
> Mere prisons for the demons,
> And so I would abandon and desert them.

In other words, far from helping them build a house, if he had such a house he would leave it as quickly as he could. He is obviously referring not just to the actual house they're building but to what it represents. There are examples of writers building a house for symbolic reasons – Yeats renovated the ancient tower at Ballylee, and Walter Scott built his house Abbotsford, clearly bodying forth his Gothic fantasies. People in the past have built follies, a folly being an architectural fantasy which has no function. It's not a church, it's not a palace, it's not a mansion, it serves no purpose. That's its utility, in a way. Perhaps these days we don't have a strong sense of the 'ancestral home' in the way people used to, because people are so much more mobile. People may still invest a lot of energy in buying their own house, but then they move somewhere else and establish themselves all over again. That's different from the old days when your family was firmly set down in one spot and remained there for centuries; you lived in the house where your parents had lived and where their parents had lived before them. It might be difficult for us to appreciate the full force and weight of the symbolism of a house nowadays.

Taking Milarepa's statement symbolically, one can look at it in two ways. These 'worldly houses' – that is, the builders themselves – confine the demons, but they also allow the demons to express themselves. The demons are the unskilful mental states that are responsible for the building of the 'house'. It's as though people set up situations of one degree of concreteness or another in order to give themselves an opportunity of expressing negative emotions. It can apply to a house in the literal sense or a more provisional or metaphorical sense: a social structure, a psychological structure, a structure of personal relationships. It has been said that there is a tendency for each individual to find himself in, or rather to set up for himself, the same situation, over and over again. You find it for instance in the case of marriage. Someone gets married, and the marriage is not a success, but shortly afterwards the person marries again. Again, the marriage is not a success, for much the same reasons that the first marriage wasn't. Nonetheless, that person may marry a third time, and even a fourth time, and the same thing happens. People set up patterns of rejection, patterns of misunderstanding, patterns of failure or success, and they repeat the same pattern over and over again. They're not able to get beyond that. They build the same house again and again, in a slightly different spot or in a slightly different way but basically the same house. In the case of a house you can see what you've built but very often we don't see what we've set up for ourselves.

One of the advantages of doing anything practical, anything that becomes tangibly embodied in the objective world, is that you can see where you have gone wrong. If things remain within one's own mind in the form of subjective impressions, ideas and so on, it's very difficult to be sure. William Blake, who attached great importance to the expulsion of error, said that it could only be cast out (the casting out of all errors was what he called 'The Last Judgement') if it was given a concrete form and could be seen for what it was. He therefore regarded writers who expressed ideas with which he completely disagreed as very valuable because once those ideas had been given concrete expression, perhaps in a very powerful and effective way, it was easier to cast them out.[106]

One can carry the idea of the creative process a stage further than writing books, painting, and all that sort of thing, by creating institutions. One can fairly easily see whether they are going in the right direction. It's very easy to have a feeling for spiritual community when you're sitting down by yourself in a nice quiet place doing the *mettā bhāvanā*, but when you're in a concrete situation having to work with other people and make a success of things, this requires a whole range of faculties. You've got to have energy, foresight, mindfulness, emotional positivity, tact, diplomacy and all kinds of other qualities, so it's a situation in which you're much more seriously tested.

In the worldly situation the odds are against you, because the people with whom you are trying to do things are likely to be basing themselves on quite negative principles, on delusion, in fact, so there's no possibility of collaboration. But if you're working with other people in the sangha and you're all building Milarepa's castle together as it were, if you're trying to embody your vision creatively in a practical way, that's the real test. You get a chance to create your new society on a tiny scale. If you can't do it on that scale, how could it possibly be done on a scale involving thousands and millions of people?

Some people think that institutions, even Buddhist institutions, are at best a necessary evil, but institutions come in different forms. Some structures reinforce negativity, and others reinforce positivity. A retreat, for example, offers a structure, created in the light of experience, designed to give a maximum of help and encouragement to the people participating in that situation. So institution is not necessarily a dirty word. The question is whether or not it is functioning in a helpful way. The majority of institutions may not be very skilful or helpful but that is because of the wrongness of the general basis of our society. It doesn't invalidate the principle of the institution itself. Institutions are essentially individuals functioning together in a particular way – that's all. Individuals can function together skilfully or unskilfully, so that anyone getting caught up in the functioning of all those individuals will be influenced either positively or negatively. One need not, one cannot, reject institutions altogether.

Much of the time we don't realize how ill-formed our thoughts are, how vague, how woolly, how unclear. Very often we're not even sure *what* we think or feel. We come to know our thoughts and feelings in the process of expressing them, because that forces us to clarify them. If you objectify what you think and feel in the process of making something, you can see better where you're going and how far you've come. This includes expressing things in words: not just being glibly articulate, not just manipulating words, but really expressing something. Until the point of expression things are usually left vague and woolly, with all sorts of ideas just drifting through the mind. Until you've expressed an idea you don't have to take responsibility for it as your idea. It just passes through your mind as a possibility. But if you say 'This is what I think' and you have to clarify that, you carry the whole thing a stage further. Some people can clarify things in their own mind without writing them down or trying to express them to anyone. It depends on your powers of concentration. There are people who can engage in quite complex mental operations without putting pen to paper. But the majority of people have to write things down so that they can trace each step of the process.

By expressing your thoughts you're opening yourself up to being told you're wrong, because what you express becomes part of the objective world, public property. Anybody can look at it, criticize it, draw attention to its shortcomings, and that is very useful because any mistake you have made can be corrected, whereas if it all remains within the privacy of your own mind there is not that possibility. To express yourself is to take a risk, and some people are reluctant to take that risk, either by speaking or by writing or by giving a talk, because they fear that they may thereby expose themselves to criticism, and they may be too sensitive to be able to stand that.

Continuing to follow the thought that the 'house building' is the expression not just of your thoughts and your feelings but of *you*, we could say that standing behind every person is a sort of psychological-cum-spiritual blueprint of which they are the expression and which they are trying to work out in the experiences and events and achievements of their life. If there is a blueprint, of course, one might think that someone must have drawn it up, conceived it, and one might even say that the conceiver (or the preconceiver) was you in your past life. But one need not think of it in those terms. If you study your own life, you may see not just a repetition of a pattern or theme but the unfolding of a certain meaning. It's difficult to see this early in one's life for obvious reasons, but it's as though one's whole life in its different stages constitutes a working out of that meaning or that pattern, that gestalt.[107] That doesn't necessarily require some kind of external agency or an external plan within which one is a function. One need not take the word 'meaning' too literally. Something can exist in a subtle form and receive expression in a grosser medium, or it can exist in a germinal form and receive expression in a fuller and more detailed and explicit manner. In a sense, everything is contained in the seed but it is fully unfolded only in the whole plant and especially in the flower.

How can a reactive process evolve into a higher process? There are two possibilities. It may be purely reactive, with no creative element at all, or it may be a mixture of reactive and creative. There is a section of the path which is part of the round but at the same time part of the spiral. Cosmologically, the higher heavenly worlds or the *dhyāna* states are part of the round, part of the reactive process, but they are at the same time part of the spiral process, though still this side of the point of no return. One can have a gestalt, to use that term, coming from a previous life which is both reactive and creative – meaning by creative in this context that part of the path where the round and the spiral overlap.

But there is another element: the ideal or the vision, which is purely transcendental. If in the process of working out your particular gestalt, which is both reactive and creative, you come in contact with the ideal or the vision and faith is generated, the pattern you were working out becomes incorporated into a higher pattern which you can think of as the mandala or the Pure Land, or whichever myth you care to choose. It can be so incorporated because there is that creative element in your gestalt already to a certain extent. Had it been purely reactive there would have been no possibility of contact between you and the ideal or vision.

Once you have come in contact with the ideal, you continue to work out your pattern and incorporate it into the pattern of which the vision, let us say, is the central point, but you also come to see more and more that your particular pattern in a sense *is* that larger pattern or it links up naturally with that pattern more and more. There are aspects on the creative path that you are trying to work out that are already transcendental, or at least they are an anticipation or reflection of that. Considering this dualistically in this way keeps things simple but if one did not want to speak in exclusively dualistic terms, when describing the awakening of faith one would speak of a reflection of the Transcendental in the mundane, especially in that as it were more creative part of the mundane. You can't metaphysically completely separate the two.

What I'm getting at is that one should not think in terms of an exclusively linear model for the spiritual life in a literal way: here am I, and I go forward stage by stage, and that's the spiritual life. That is an aspect of it, so it's not untrue, but one should not look at it exclusively in those terms. For instance, you may have a true idea of spiritual community, but it may be quite vague and germinal. Only when you get an opportunity of working it out in practice and testing it and experiencing it will you find out to what extent you really are in touch with the ideal of spiritual community. In the same way, your life itself is the practical working out of something within you, and enables you to see more and more clearly what is really there – whether it is delusion or whether it is the will to Enlightenment; whether it is something quite reactive or something more purely creative. You only find that out in the process of living your life. When you take a wide survey of your life, you begin to get an idea of what you are like because you can see what you've done and what you've worked out. Your life reveals yourself to yourself. Then the contact with the vision is the appearance of something new, as though there is an irruption of another element, which involves a total rearrangement; and the rearrangement is more or less catastrophic, depending on the pattern that existed before.

Some people feel that after they make contact with Buddhism their spiritual life seems to follow naturally, almost as if it was going to happen. One way of looking at this is that when one makes contact with the sangha it's a linking-up with or a continuation of something that had already been started. But what very often happens is that you have your natural gestalt, but for the greater part of your life, for one reason or another, you have been hindered from giving expression to it, or you've given it some sort of expression, but it has been distorted due to external circumstances. When you come in contact with the vision, you can see more clearly what has been happening, get rid of or avoid those distorting factors, and link up a more adequate expression of your gestalt with the vision.

For example, someone might from childhood want to be an artist and succeed in doing so. Then as an artist they might have an ideal which they are always pursuing, and then they come in contact with the vision presented by the Dharma, and realize that this was what they were searching for all the time through their art. This just represents the next stage: the realization that art need not be left behind, but can be carried over into the artist's new life as a Buddhist. It is plain sailing, as it were. But take another case – the case of a person who is naturally an artist, whose particular gestalt is fulfilled in that way, but who as a child was prevented from being an artist and compelled to do something else. His basic nature is there – his gestalt is trying to find expression – but it finds expression in a distorted way. Maybe he has found a job in a bank or has enlisted in the army, but whatever he's doing, he is being prevented from giving natural expression to his gestalt. Then, if he comes into contact with the Buddhist community, he's got to get rid of all the conditioning that was imposed upon him by working in the bank or being in the army, and unravel the distortions of his natural creativity brought about by being subject to that process. Perhaps he needs to become an artist with the support of the sangha, because that is his means of contacting in a real way the ideals and the vision of the Dharma. Undoing that distorting effect might be a lot of work and be quite painful.

I don't believe that anybody can have a negative gestalt. The gestalt exists on a higher level than positivity and negativity in that sense. 'Negative' lives, one could say, are the result of distortions in the gestalt. To express this in terms of Buddhist thought, one could say that the gestalt represents the reflection of the *dharmakāya* in the individual. We have to take this poetically, otherwise we get into quite deep waters metaphysically, having to consider whether this represents a 'self' and so on. The important point is that you are trying to work out an ideal in your spiritual life, or *as* your spiritual life. It is not that you have a purely rational idea about Enlightenment, and you are trying to put that into practice on a purely rational basis. Much deeper, more creative forces have to be involved if you are going to get anywhere.

This is to use the term 'gestalt' very loosely, beyond the usual psychological meaning. A gestalt is a sort of whole. Mozart used to say that before he composed a symphony he heard it instantaneously; it was all there at once, as a whole. That whole was the gestalt of the symphony, which he then proceeded to write out as a series of notes played one after another, but he actually experienced the whole thing together, out of time. Likewise, it is as though our gestalt is us, already completed, in a manner of speaking, outside time, and our life consists in the living out of that in time. That's not just a metaphysical abstraction. It's something you actually feel, a power motivating you through life. That's why the symbol of the seed is useful, because it is something that grows. The gestalt is not a metaphysical entity. It's not static or inert.

To put it in traditional Buddhist terms, the gestalt is the product of the interaction between your self over a series of many lives – that is to say births and deaths and rebirths – and the *dharmakāya*, which produces as it were a reflection in you. The gestalt is the effect of the *dharmakāya* acting upon your best, most positive, most creative part. But the action of the *dharmakāya* is limited by the material itself: in some cases more limited, in other cases less limited. The material on which it is working is you as a phenomenal being.

Why should the *dharmakāya* bother? It doesn't bother. You might just as well ask why the moon should bother to reflect itself in the water. There is no question of why, because one is dealing with metaphors. One is trying to explain something through metaphors, similes, symbol or myth which perhaps can't be explained or communicated in any other way. But if you just want to stick to the facts without any explanation, what have you got? Well, you have got your life as you are actually living it or have lived it for a certain length of time. If you look at that life, you can usually see one of two things. You either see a particular pattern repeated over and over again, or you see a pattern that is not yet complete being unfolded. Because you can see half the pattern you assume that 'somewhere' there is a whole pattern. That is the gestalt, or that can be predicated as the gestalt. That's all.

One can sometimes see this quite clearly. It isn't a matter of faith or belief, but of experience and inference. It is just like if you've got a half-unrolled Persian carpet, you can see a certain part of the pattern, and you can extrapolate from the pattern you see to the pattern you do not see. There can be varying degrees of clarity depending on your life experience. To continue the metaphor, you may only see vague blotches, or – bearing in mind that the expression of your gestalt may be distorted – there may be enormous stains on the carpet, which are obscuring the part of the pattern so far revealed, or even burns or holes. But one must realize the limitations of metaphor. The whole thing is changing all the time so that it's not a question of the pattern only being revealed by the whole life. The pattern is also revealed by every part of the life. Even though the carpet has got all these stains and burns if you think in terms of one single carpet representing your whole life, you can also think that every minute is represented by the whole carpet. The carpet that you see after it has *really* been unrolled, the carpet that represents the whole life, the carpet that represents each minute after a certain stage in the unrolling process has been reached – even that still represents the whole life – has no burns, holes or stains at all. Once you've reached a certain point of creativity, a certain point of spiritual development, every single thing you do, whatever it is, fully reveals the whole pattern.

Writing one's autobiography, or telling one's life story, can be a useful way of seeing the pattern more clearly, and also showing it to other people. Sometimes before coming in contact with the sangha people have gone through all sorts of difficult, painful and traumatic experiences. If you know that, you can understand certain things about their behaviour and make allowances for them. And from your own point of view, it's not a bad thing to run through your whole life up to the present and see whether any sort of pattern, any meaning, emerges.

Our lives don't represent just a series of chances. One can quite meaningfully speak in terms of the working out of a pattern of some kind. A pattern is almost a law of nature. Experiments show that when a musical sound is made over a tray of sand, a mandala-like pattern is produced, and likewise – human beings being essentially collections of vibrations – we create patterns as we move over the surface of things. As we act, as we do things, the pattern emerges according to the nature of the vibration, which can sometimes be disturbed or distorted. Sometimes we speak as though things were entirely random, but they are not. There is freedom, but there is a certain kind of determination as well, or at least limitation, and you get both of these in the pattern. One reason why it can be useful to think of your life as the working out of a pattern is that it helps you to realize that life is not a random thing. One has freedom, but it isn't as though anything could have happened at any time. There is a perceivable pattern or at least part of a pattern. Seeing part of it, you can imagine the rest, and the whole is the gestalt, which can be revealed not only throughout the whole of the life, but at every single instant in it more and more clearly, the more creative you become.

One could perhaps say that your natural tendency is to build a house, but you come into contact with someone like Milarepa who persuades you to build a castle instead, so that your house is gradually transformed into a castle. You modify your house or enlarge it, change the structure, so that in the end you've got not the house that you started out to build, which might have been more or less complete, but a castle like that of Milarepa. There has been a switch over, as it were, from the reactive mode to the purely creative mode. It's not that you go somewhere else and build a castle. You can't, because you *are* the place. You have to start with your present materials and modify your existing pattern in the light of the new one. Sometimes you may have built your house in such an extreme way that you have to raze it to the ground and start again, as Milarepa himself had to do because of the terrible things he did early in his life, but on the other hand, if you have built your house on reasonable lines, you can expand it into a castle without too much difficulty. And the guru can see the pattern in the individual and help you work it out. He can tell you what you need to do in order to reveal and experience for yourself that hidden part of you. Leaving aside the guru, often other people see more of you – your potential, your abilities – than you can see yourself.

It might take you quite a long time to work out what you want or need to do, even after you have committed yourself to the Buddha, Dharma, and Sangha. It's vitally important to establish contact with what you actually feel – with your own emotional energy – otherwise you'll never be able to get going. An abstract idea of what is right for you to do, or what you ought to do, is not enough to motivate you in any real way. If you have lost contact with what you really want to do, you have to re-establish contact with it, even if for the time being what you want to do is something quite unskilful. Not that you necessarily need to act on that awareness – indeed, it might well be better not to – but it is vitally important to experience it. Many people are alienated and out of contact with what they really want to do, perhaps because they've had to deny it for so long, but in many cases, if people get down below the distortions and deformations, what they want to do is quite positive.

Education has a role to play here. In a book about hospital management, Florence Nightingale wrote, 'The very first requirement of a hospital is that it should do the sick no harm.'[108] Likewise, the most important thing about education is that it does no harm to the child. If one were to establish a Buddhist school, this would be principle number one. Even if you don't succeed in teaching children anything, if you avoid doing any harm, you will have done quite a lot.

'Gestalt' is just one word to describe the interaction between the phenomenal individuality and the higher principle, the reflection of that higher principle within the individual. Perhaps it is not advisable to use any one word. One can say gestalt, one can say pattern, one can say reflection, one can say seed. It's probably better to use all of them at different times in different contexts. Otherwise one might create the false impression that one is making a philosophical-cum-scientific statement. It's really a poetic statement, a statement of a metaphorical nature, which has its own truth, but which is not truth in an objective, verifiable sense. You're not giving a metaphysical explanation. You are clarifying an idea, or illuminating it metaphorically.

When you get deeply into communication with someone, you become more and more aware of the total pattern which is them. Maybe they haven't lived out the whole of the pattern, maybe they don't see much of it themselves, but you see it more and more. In a way you can't separate them from the pattern except in thought, but you experience them in a certain way. You see certain repeated behaviour and ways of thinking. You see the same motif appearing in their lives in different ways and in different contexts. Whether they are happy or sad, whether they are doing something skilful or unskilful, it's still them. There is a common pattern behind all those different expressions, maybe distorted in some cases and in others not, and you can predict what people will do and think, to the extent that you see the whole pattern. Sometimes people are unpredictable, which can mean that the pattern is overlaid with other things or some of it is just not perceivable, or you haven't been able to understand the whole of it. It is there to be seen, but you haven't seen it. Sometimes that happens on quite a small scale – you don't see the whole of what someone is thinking about and therefore you misunderstand their actions. It explains why individuality is important. The likelihood of people having the same pattern is tiny, and even though the number of elements in a pattern is limited, they can be ordered in many different ways.

Each individual is a pattern, and to create a spiritual community those patterns have to coincide in their more important elements in such a way that they reflect a more universal pattern. We usually say we must have the same ideal, but this is putting it in quite abstract, intellectual terms. It is not so much that our ideals must overlap; *we* must overlap. However differently people express their individuality, they can still fit together in the same pattern if there are some elements that overlap, some common ideals. Or, to put it another way, each individual pattern has to be a variation on a more universal common pattern. There has to be some common element however you express it, whether abstractly or concretely. The spiritual community is the unfolding of a wider, greater pattern. This is connected with the usual definition of gestalt as a whole which is greater than the sum of its parts; and that raises philosophical difficulties. But perhaps one can just look at it in terms of Mozart experiencing the whole of the symphony before he experienced its parts consecutively. One could express it in terms of a common myth, but one has to be quite careful because it is not as though the individual is being subordinated to something outside himself.

Another example of the care we need to take when using metaphor is the idea of the pattern itself. If one uses a pattern to convey the idea of something conditioned, or even as a metaphor for one's unskilful activities, of course one has to leave it behind. But one can also use it as a metaphor for creative activities, and one doesn't want to leave them behind. They just become more and more creative; in other words, the pattern extends and extends in a way that perhaps one couldn't have imagined to begin with. It's like the contrast Milarepa makes between the house and the castle. However depraved a human being may be, however lacking in development, there is in traditional Buddhist terms some reflection of the *dharmakāya*. If people who are building a house have their attention drawn to the possibility of building a castle, they will realize that it was actually the castle that they wanted to build all the time. The castle more adequately expresses their gestalt. So one has to be careful not to think of the gestalt as something limited and fixed.

Having done what it was necessary for his own development, out of compassion Milarepa is now interested in trying to help others, interested in building a bigger castle, one might say. He has built a castle big enough for himself to live in but he now wants to build one big enough to accommodate everybody else.

One of the things I've noticed is that in thinking about individual development and spiritual life and all that, people tend to think very literally and linearly. We have to make our sense of it much more multi-dimensional and much less pinned down to specific definable ideas. It has to be in a way less graspable. In a sense, it shouldn't be too clear, and one would be justified in becoming suspicious if it became so. When you discover your pattern, that will be clear in the sense that it has a definite outline, but a gestalt can't be pinned down intellectually because the intellectual road is as it were linear, which the gestalt is not.

Plato says that philosophy begins with a sense of wonder.[109] Philosophy in the true sense should suggest extra dimensions of things – not having everything intellectually docketed and labelled: that is philosophy more in the Aristotelian sense, perhaps. Things shouldn't be too clear or too sharply defined for the thinking mind. Or one could say, yes, let them be clearly defined for the thinking mind, but let the thinking mind not think that that is everything. Get things as clear as you can intellectually, by all means – don't obfuscate or indulge in vague thinking – but even when your thinking is very clear, recognize that there are other dimensions, other ways of looking at things. Reducing things to intellectual formulas represents an attenuation of reality and an attenuation of one's own experience, a self-limitation, because you're more than that.

2

HEAVENLY FARMING

The workers said, 'What you have sung is most enlightening.
Please also tell us whether, in your way of life, you have anything
like our farms, properties, relatives, companions, wives, and
children? It seems to us that these things are worth more than you
have suggested. Please tell us what possessions you have that are
so much better than ours? Why do you look upon our way of life
as worthless?'

The workers are simply asking Milarepa to enlarge upon his original
metaphor. To their way of thinking, if you have a house, you also have
farms, properties, land, relations, wives and children. If Milarepa claims
to have a house or a castle which is better than theirs, surely he will
have these other things too, but in a better way. They are asking him to
justify his position and convince them of it by going into greater detail,
so this is what he does. This elaboration of the metaphor, the myth, is
quite important, because that enables one to experience it in many of
its different aspects, and in that way it becomes more real, more vivid,
more concrete, more graspable. He replies in song:

Milarepa answered:

The Ālaya Consciousness is the good earth,
The inner teaching is the seed that is sowed,

Achievement in meditation is the sprout,
And the Three Bodies of Buddha are the ripened crop.
These are the four lasting mainstays of heavenly farming.
Your worldly farming, delusive and deceiving,
Is merely the slave-labor of the hungry;
Without hesitation I discard it!

The Ālaya Consciousness is the good earth

The *ālaya* consciousness, the *ālaya vijñāna*, which Milarepa compares to 'the good earth', is the store-consciousness. There are eight consciousnesses: the five sense consciousnesses, then the mind consciousness, the 'soiled-mind consciousness', and the *ālaya*, which is divided into the relative *ālaya* and the absolute *ālaya*.[110] Here it seems that the relative *ālaya* is what is meant. This is a rather abstruse concept and the different schools of Buddhist thought vary widely in their understanding of it. Perhaps it shouldn't be regarded as a metaphysical concept. It's more like a metaphor. It's a store, the store consciousness – 'store' is what *ālaya* means. But how are the products of consciousness, the effects of experience, 'stored'? Conventionally, we would say that this is what memory is, but how is memory possible? If we look at it in a common-sense way, the fact that we can remember now something that happened yesterday or last year suggests to us that the thought of what happened is somehow stored in the mind. Just as you put something in a cupboard and can take it out whenever you have need of it, in the same way you put away your thoughts, your ideas, in the store-house of your consciousness and you can produce them again whenever you need them.

But the image of the *ālaya* as a store has its limitations. Milarepa gives us another picture of it when he says that the *ālaya* consciousness is like 'the good earth'. If the earth wasn't always there, there wouldn't be the possibility of any seed being sown in it, and in the same way, the *ālaya* is always there. Not that it is 'good'; in a way it is beyond good and evil, because it receives defiled seeds as well as undefiled seeds. It's up to you what kind of seeds you sow. The *ālaya* is in itself neither skilful nor unskilful; it represents the possibility of gathering the fruit of whatever seeds you sow. It stores up whatever impressions it receives, whatever seeds are cast into it, and those seeds will grow when the conditions are right. It represents, in other words, the possibility of continuity. It's sometimes called the principle of the conservation of moral effort. If you put in a certain amount of effort, if you work on yourself, the effect is cumulative. Perhaps we don't always realize that. It's not as though you do something and the effect doesn't last. It does last, especially if you keep up the effort, and the fact that it is possible for it to last is represented by the principle of the *ālaya*, the principle of continuity and the conservation of moral effort or spiritual energy.

The inner teaching is the seed that is sowed

In Buddhist tradition the idea of the *ālaya*, the store-consciousness, is applied to the whole process of rebirth. It is said that every willed action that you do sooner or later produces consequences, although those consequences aren't always apparent to you (and in fact, as we will see, not all karmas ripen). What happens, according to this metaphor, is that every time you perform a willed action, you create an impression on a certain level of your mind, the level of the store consciousness. That impression is not just a passive imprint like that of a seal – it has a certain potentiality, like a seed. So one talks of depositing seeds in the *ālaya*, and these seeds remain there and they bear fruit when circumstances allow; that is, one experiences the results of one's previous willed actions. You can sow all sorts of seed in the 'soil' of the *ālaya*. You can sow what are called defiled seeds – seeds tainted with greed, hatred, and delusion – or you can sow undefiled seeds, seeds that are not tainted in that way, and the 'inner teaching' is that sort of seed.

'Inner teaching' suggests not just a general doctrinal teaching, but something specifically applicable to your own individual spiritual needs. You hear this inner teaching and you are deeply receptive to it. It makes an impression on you, not just on a superficial level of your consciousness; it goes deeper than that. You don't just hear the teaching with your ears, so it isn't just a question of an impression on the level of sense consciousness. You don't simply understand it with your ordinary mind. It goes deeper than that. You don't even understand it with your defiled-mind consciousness – that is to say, the consciousness that is split into or distorted by subject-and-object experience. You take it into yourself on a very much deeper level, the level of the *ālaya*, where you conserve it and where it remains, to have a lasting influence upon your whole being.

The seed analogy is connected with the traditional idea of earning merit in the sense that from those seeds which are positive without being transcendental is reaped a harvest in the form of merits: positive mundane experiences in some future life. One could say that the *ālaya* is that principle which makes possible the unfolding of the gestalt. One mustn't think about it metaphysically; it is not that there is a thing called the *ālaya* – that would be to reify it and make it a sort of self. The *ālaya* is a concept that clarifies the possibility of growth. It represents the fact that the results of any action affecting the individual and the results of any action that the individual has himself performed are conserved even in a situation which does not permit the results of those actions to emerge for the time being. If you have deliberately done anything, whether positive or negative, skilful or unskilful, that leaves an imprint on a certain level of your own being, here called the *ālaya*, which conserves that. Even though your life situation does not permit the results of that willed action to emerge immediately, that action is conserved in seed form at the *ālaya* level and manifests in form of a result when conditions permit.

This is not about the action of others upon you, except to the extent that you have deliberately made them your own action, as it were. The actions of others upon you – actions which you do not accept and in which you do not cooperate – only go as far as the level of the mind consciousness or the soiled-mind consciousness. They do not go to the level of the *ālaya*, so you are not morally responsible for them. So long as you are keeping up even a mental resistance to those acts and not acquiescing in them, anything you are forced to do is not depositing seeds in the *ālaya*, and therefore not modifying you in any fundamental way. To give a very extreme example, suppose you were a prisoner and you were forced to sign some sort of confession under torture, that would not 'count', karmically speaking, as a willed action on your part. Or suppose you were forced to sign a paper ordering other people to be shot. If there was no acquiescence on your part, even if the people were shot as a result, there would be no seeds deposited by you in the *ālaya*. If it was possible for seeds to be deposited in the *ālaya* in that way – in a manner of speaking 'your' *ālaya*, though the *ālaya* is really neither yours nor not-yours – there could be no human freedom, nor any individual development. The *ālaya* is concerned with an action you originate, a willed action of body, speech or mind which you deliberately perform. It is that sort of action and no other which, according to Buddhist teaching, results in what we call *karma-vipāka*.

The *ālaya* is able to conserve these impressions or seeds from life to life. If one looks at it in Abhidharma terms, there are some seeds which can only be conserved for a certain length of time, after which, if circumstances do not permit them to sprout, they will die. There are others which are much more vigorous, almost looking for circumstances in which they can develop, even forcing their way through, insisting on finding an outlet for themselves. They don't just passively wait for circumstances to be favourable. And there are yet others where as much depends on the circumstances as upon the seed itself.

The *ālaya* does not itself condition anything. It is a condition of conditioning. It is what makes conditioning in that way – and it's a strictly limited way – possible at all. So one cannot, one must not, take it as a metaphysical principle. It's a concept which is postulated as an entity in order to clarify the sort of thing that is happening.

One cannot speak of being 'in touch with' the *ālaya*. It is more that anything that is a deliberately willed action of yours, whether expressed through speech or action or thought, affects you at a level of your being of which you may be quite unconscious, which is termed the *ālaya*, and is conserved there in the sense that it has a long-lasting effect on you, even if it is not immediately evident. It will work itself out sooner or later as conditions permit.

There is no agreement between the different Yogācāra schools about the *ālaya*. It's one of the most obscure questions in the whole of Buddhist thought, maybe because people have tried to treat it metaphysically rather than metaphorically. One could say that the relative *ālaya* is within time, because it is a principle of conservation, of continuity between successive human existences, whereas the absolute *ālaya*, which is synonymous with the *dharmakāya*, is outside time altogether. But one must be careful not to make too literal a distinction. One could say that the relative *ālaya* is that aspect of the absolute *ālaya* which can be regarded as underpinning the whole process of the Higher Evolution – underpinning in the sense of conserving and maintaining the continuity of moral and spiritual effort.

Achievement in meditation is the sprout

Having been deeply impressed by the teaching on that level and having retained traces of that influence, you are able to keep up your practice of meditation and eventually experience some results from it. Or perhaps one can say that it is because one has been deeply influenced by the inner teaching in the past that when one gets the opportunity one is able to practise meditation in the present, in the sense of at least sitting for meditation. That seed deposited in the form of the inner teaching is then able to sprout in the form of an actual meditation experience.

And the Three Bodies of Buddha are the ripened crop.

By these three bodies Milarepa means the *trikāya*: the *nirmāṇakāya*, *sambhogakāya*, and *dharmakāya*. These are transformations of one's ordinary body, speech, and mind. Body, speech, and mind are the product of reactivity, part of the reactive pattern, but the three *kāyas* of the Buddha are the product of supreme creativity. They are part of the positive, creative, transcendental pattern, the mandala – or they make up the mandala. The body, speech, and mind, the three constituents of the unenlightened personality, contain within themselves in seed form the three *kāyas*. These three seeds are represented by the three syllables *oṃ āḥ hūṃ*. The white *oṃ*, which is usually located either in the forehead or at the crown of the head, is the seed of the *nirmāṇakāya* and represents the body. The red *āḥ* at the throat is the seed of the *sambhogakāya* and represents potentiality of speech. And the blue *hūṃ* at the heart is the seed of the *dharmakāya* and represents the potentiality of the mind. One speaks initially of the teaching as the seed, which sprouts in the form of meditation, and the fruit you gather in the end is that of the three *kāyas*. In other words, the result is that your body, speech, and mind, your whole unskilful being, is transformed into something totally skilful, totally transcendental. The house is rebuilt as the castle. So this is Milarepa's farming – he extends the analogy in this way.

> *These are the four lasting mainstays of heavenly farming*
> *Your worldly farming, delusive and deceiving.*
> *Is merely the slave-labor of the hungry;*
> *Without hesitation I discard it!*

This is Milarepa's verdict on worldly farming, and perhaps worldly work generally: it's 'delusive and deceiving', 'merely the slave-labour of the hungry'. But what does he mean? He suggests that the motivation for work is hunger. You want food or clothing, and you only work to get those things; it is purely utilitarian. It's 'slave-labour' because you sell your labour, sell yourself, for the sake of those things. You're no better than a slave. You're doing something in order to get a certain reward. You are not working freely and creatively. This comparison of spiritual development with farming is found in the Pāli texts, in the *Bhāradvāja Sutta* of the *Sutta-Nipāta*, where the Buddha says much the same thing to a Brahmin farmer who challenges him.[111]

Next, Milarepa tackles the builders' question as to whether he has property:

The fine warehouse of Śūnyatā,
The Supramundane Jewels,
The service and action of the Ten Virtues,
And the great happiness of Non-outflow –
These four jewels are the lasting properties of Heaven.

Milarepa says he has four jewels, four things that are precious to him. First of all there is the 'fine warehouse of Śūnyatā'. 'Warehouse' is perhaps not quite the right term. I don't know what the original Tibetan is, but if one is talking about farming, perhaps it's more like a great barn which contains everything. But why might *śūnyatā* be described as 'the fine warehouse'? *Śūnyatā* is sometimes translated as voidness or emptiness, because it is empty of the conditioned, and also, in a higher sense still, empty of the very distinction between conditioned and unconditioned. Guenther rather interestingly translates it as 'the open dimension of being',[112] though it might be better just to say 'the open dimension'. *Śūnyatā* represents the principle of unrestrictedness, the principle that anything is possible, that there's no fixed or final limitation. One thing can change into another, can be transformed into another. *Śūnyatā* is what makes everything possible. It is the principle that says that there is nothing that is not possible. In that sense, everything is in *śūnyatā*, so *śūnyatā* is the warehouse. Or one could say that *śūnyatā* is that principle in accordance with which there are no conditions that make anything impossible for ever or under all circumstances, whatever the present situation may be.

Perhaps one should restrict this definition a little by saying that any *conditioned* thing can be transformed into any other conditioned thing. Without that limitation, there could be no such thing as irreversibility or Stream Entry. And it does not mean that any conditioned thing can be transformed *immediately* into any other conditioned thing. There may have to be an intermediate series of stages. The given conditioned situation is not final; it can be succeeded by any other set of conditions, whether immediately or not. But if you've got *śūnyatā*, you've got everything. If you've got the warehouse, you've got everything you need because it's all there, so to speak, within it.

A footnote to the text says that 'Supramundane Jewels' is 'a symbolic term which denotes the transcendental merits and virtues of Buddha', but I would say that Milarepa is referring to the Three Jewels themselves, all of which have a supramundane, that is to say *lokuttara*, transcendental, aspect.

The Ten Virtues are the ten *pāramitās*. These are Milarepa's jewels, these are what he values. The jewel here represents the whole idea of value. The first of the ten *pāramitās* is *dāna-pāramitā*, the perfection of giving – 'service and action.' But why this distinction between service and action? Presumably the ten *pāramitās* are to be practised by oneself, and that is active. Maybe 'service' is more encouraging other people to practise, or being supportive in regard to other people's practice of the ten *pāramitās*. You could look at it in that way. You are of service to the practice of the *pāramitās* even when not actually practising them yourself. In any case, that is one of Milarepa's jewels, one of his properties.

Next comes 'The great happiness of Non-outflow'. This strange term 'Non-outflow' translates *anāsrava*. The *āsravas*, usually translated as biases, taints, drugs, intoxicants, are the defilements, the most negative forces impelling the individual. There are three, sometimes four in early texts: the bias towards sensuous experience; the bias towards conditioned existence; the bias of ignorance; and sometimes there is added the bias of false views.[113] The *arhant* is usually defined as the one who has completely destroyed these *āsravas*. With their destruction, therefore, one attains Nirvāna. All the *dharmas*, all the states or experiences that make up the transcendental path and the goal, are called *anāsrava dharmas*. *Dharmas* are classified by the Sarvāstivādins into two groups: those that are connected with the *āsravas* and those that are not.[114] In referring to 'the great happiness of Non-outflow', the great happiness that is experienced through those states and experiences, those *dharmas*, that are free from the biases, as one of his four jewels, his properties, Milarepa is simply referring to the happiness he experiences by following the transcendental path. So he is again extending the metaphor in the way that the builders asked him to.

> Your worldly jewels and possessions are deceiving and delusive;
> Like deceptive magic spells, they lead you astray.
> Without any hesitation, I discard them.

The magician conjures up a mirage, an illusion, of an oasis in the desert, perhaps, and people move towards it. But when they get there they find there's nothing there. Ordinary jewels and possessions are like that. You go after them but when you've got them you realize that there's nothing to them, there's no real satisfaction to be obtained from them. So, 'Without any hesitation, I discard them'.

> The Father and Mother Buddha are my parents,
> The immaculate Dharma is my face,
> The assembly of Sangha are my cousins and nephews,
> And the guardians of Dharma are my friends.
> These four are my lasting, heavenly kinsmen.
> Your worldly kinsmen are deceitful and delusive;
> Without hesitation I throw all ephemeral associates away!

The Father and Mother Buddha are my parents

The 'Father and Mother Buddha' refers to the *yab-yum* symbolism of the Vajrayāna, in which Enlightenment is conceived of as a total interpenetration of wisdom and compassion, compassion being personified as a male Buddha figure and wisdom as a female Buddha figure. These are spoken of as the *yab* and the *yum*, the father and the mother. So Milarepa is saying that he has been born from the union of wisdom and compassion. But there is more to it than that. The *bodhicitta*, the will to Enlightenment, is described as the product of transcendental wisdom and transcendental compassion. When parents come together and conception takes place, even at the very instant that the sperm fertilizes the ovum, in a sense a human being is there, because the potential for a fully developed human being is there. In the same way, the instant that transcendental wisdom and transcendental compassion come together in the individual in a single experience, the *bodhicitta* is there. And to the extent that the *bodhicitta* is there, the bodhisattva is there, even the Buddha is there, only not yet developed. So because the coming together within him of transcendental wisdom and transcendental compassion produced the *bodhicitta* and because the *bodhicitta* grew and developed until wisdom and compassion were fully developed and he gained Enlightenment, he says, 'The Father and Mother Buddhas are my parents.' After all, you grow up to be like your parents. If your father and mother are wisdom and compassion, you too will grow up to be wise and compassionate. And just as the father and mother are together in *yab-yum*, wisdom and compassion are not separate. Iconographically the father and mother can be separated, but within you as an actual experience they are not to be separated. Milarepa is identifying himself not with the physical body but with his new spiritual personality, his transcendental individuality, and he is saying that that is not born of earthly parents as his physical body was. It is the product, so to speak, of the coming together of wisdom and compassion. That is what has brought him, in the higher sense, into existence.

The immaculate Dharma is my face

One almost suspects some mistake in the translation here, but perhaps this refers to the way he communicates to other beings through the Dharma, the way they see him. But how does this fit into a list of his 'kinsmen'? Perhaps the meaning is that just as kinsmen have a common appearance, what he has in common with others is the Dharma. It is the Dharma that gives him his family features.

The assembly of Sangha are my cousins and nephews.

All those in the Sangha – the Āryasaṅgha, that is – are related in the sense that the same transcendental experience flows through their veins. So there's a whole family of many branches, all sharing the same experience. They make up the Sangha in the highest sense.

And the guardians of Dharma are my friends.
These four are my lasting, heavenly kinsmen.
Your worldly kinsmen are deceitful and delusive;
Without hesitation I throw all ephemeral associates away!

He's saying that it's spiritual relationships that are valuable, not worldly ones.

The Blissful Passing is like my father,
The Blissful Illumination in well-done work is (my background),
The Two-in-One is my glossy, lustrous skin
The Experiences and Realization are my glorious clothing.
These four are my heavenly and lasting wives.
Delusive and deceiving are your worldly companions,
They are but temporary friends, inclined to quarrel;
Without hesitation, I throw them all away.

The Blissful Passing is like my father

A note on the 'Blissful Passing' says, 'This may be otherwise rendered as "The Blissful Manifestation or Becoming." When one reaches a higher level of consciousness, even the contacts with outer manifestations becomes Blissful.' But why should the 'Blissful Passing' be 'like my father'? What is this 'Blissful Passing'? It links up with the idea of the house being transformed into the castle, the reactive pattern being modified by, even incorporated into, the creative one. It's a question of your experience, or what otherwise would have been your experience, being transformed by your present state. Everyone has had the experience of waking up in the morning and feeling in a really happy positive state, in which everything seems different and you can enjoy everything that happens to you, all your ordinary experiences. It's a bit like that, as the footnote says, when one reaches a higher level of consciousness. Even the contact with outer manifestations (that means worldly events) can become blissful. The 'Blissful Passing' seems to refer to that kind of experience, and one can begin to see why it is described as being like a father, because presumably contact with a father – remember this is Tibet in the old days – is assumed to be a positive, happy experience. When you're in a certain state of mind, everything that you come into contact with, everything that you experience, is just like your own father, the assumption being that you regard your father as someone reliable, a source of protection, reassurance, safety. When you're in that state of mind, nothing that you come into contact with is hostile; everything is experienced as positive and friendly and reassuring, just like your own father.

> The Blissful Illumination in well-done work is (my
>   background).
> The Two-in-One is my glossy, lustrous skin.

The 'Two-in-One' probably translates the Tibetan equivalent of *yuganaddha*, the experience of wisdom and compassion together, or the voidness and bliss together. In other words, it's an experience of unification, a complete reconciliation and harmony of all opposites, and this experience is extremely blissful. When you're very happy your face seems to shine and you have a glossy lustrous skin, and Milarepa's glossy lustrous skin, metaphorically speaking, is his blissful experience of the Two-in-Oneness of existence, in other words his experience of the complete integration of wisdom and compassion, or the voidness and bliss, or the relative and absolute, whatever you like to call it.

> The Experiences and Realization are my glorious clothing.

The note here says: 'These two words, Nyams and rTogs, are difficult to translate into adequate English. Nyams is the indirect, incomplete, imperfect, and 'half-opaque' experience and understanding that the yogi attains in meditation; while rTogs (Realization) is the direct, complete, clear, and perfect experience. The former is *similar* to Enlightenment, while the latter is the *real Enlightenment*.' In other words, they correspond more or less to *śamatha* and *vipaśyanā*. So *śamatha* and *vipaśyanā*, or higher meditative experience and insight, 'are my glorious clothing'.

> These four are my heavenly and lasting wives.
> Delusive and deceiving are your worldly companions,
> They are but temporary friends, inclined to quarrel;
> Without hesitation, I throw them all away.

There's a mixed metaphor here because one of the wives is compared to his father, another to his work, another to his skin, and another to his clothing, but they're all, as it were, wives. Perhaps the significance here is that a wife is a source of intense experience. It's as though Milarepa is saying, 'I have my own experiences, and they are my wives. I don't need to look to any wife outside myself for intense experiences, or bliss, or whatever. I have it all within.' There is quite a lot that could be said about this. Spiritual experiences can be sparked off, or enhanced, by contact with other individuals, by way of *kalyāṇa mitratā*. But you've got to have something to be sparked off first. The contact with the other person can't do it all for you. Maybe in the early stages of your spiritual life you do need some sparking off, being yourself already positive, by another person who is even more positive than you are. But this is different from emotional dependence of a neurotic kind, relying upon some outside source for something that you ought to be developing within yourself.

Milarepa is saying that his wives are all, as it were, within, in the form of intense blissful transcendental experience. He doesn't have to look outside. That is the aim: that you should have all those things within, so that any contact with other individuals, whether simply positive individuals or Enlightened individuals, is an enhancement of what you already have. It doesn't give you anything that you are unable or unwilling to develop for yourself.

> Mind-Awareness is my new-born babe,
> Experience of Meditation is my infant,
> Understanding-and-Realization is my child,
> And the grown youth who can keep the Doctrine is my
>   young companion.
> These four are my lasting, heavenly sons
> Your worldly offspring are delusive and deceitful;
> Without hesitation I throw them all away.

So Milarepa has not only got wives, he's got children. 'Mind-Awareness' is his 'new-born babe.' I am not sure how literally we should take this expression 'Mind-Awareness'. Maybe it's just awareness, especially at the mental level. But the idea that 'Mind-Awareness' or mental awareness is the new-born babe suggests that it's the first fruit of one's development.

One's development as an individual begins with awareness. It's something you bring into being, not something that you are handed, as it were, from the process of the lower evolution. And then, 'Experience of Meditation is my infant'. That's the intermediate stage. And 'Understanding-and-Realization is my child, and the grown youth who can keep the Doctrine is my young companion'. He's imagining children of four different ages representing various stages in the development of the individual. He has developed these stages within himself, given birth to these sons within himself, and they're the only children he has, or wants. It's a bit reminiscent of Socrates, who is spoken of as the 'Great Midwife', bringing ideas to fruition,[115] except that Milarepa is midwife to his own ideas rather than to those of other people, and not just to ideas in the abstract intellectual sense but to actual spiritual experiences.

> I wish sincerely that I and you, the good folk of Gung Tang,
> Through the Karma-affinity of this conversation,
> May meet once more in the Pure Land of Oujen.

> The villagers, strongly moved with faith, then made obeisance and offerings to Milarepa. Later, they all became his sincere disciples.

It may seem surprising that this song, which is about profound things like the *ālaya* consciousness, the inner teaching, the three bodies of Buddha and *śūnyatā*, has such a strong effect on these people, because we would assume that they haven't previously had much knowledge of the Dharma, but we don't know that. One gets the impression, reading *The Hundred Thousand Songs of Milarepa*, that knowledge of the Dharma was quite widespread at that time. People had often heard various teachers and preachers without understanding much or thinking any more about it, but when they met someone like Milarepa, it all came to life. Perhaps that is what is happening here. Of course, the whole way of life in Tibet was very different to ours. In Kalimpong I met many people newly arrived from Tibet, and it was quite evident that they had a very different attitude to the Dharma even from that of the Indians. The Indians, especially the Hindus, regarded themselves as very religious-minded, but the Tibetans regarded the Indians as irreligious. They took the Dharma extremely seriously, there's no doubt about that. It seems that where a society is based to a very great extent on religious values, even if those values are not always acted upon, if people are psychologically uncomplicated and reasonably positive, and live a straightforward life, then the Dharma can have a tremendous impact quite quickly. One gets that impression reading the Pāli scriptures too.

If people are reasonably receptive and haven't been too damaged by the way in which they have been brought up, their response to the Dharma when they initially encounter it can be very powerful, and a lot can happen in a short time – and that's what seems to happen here. 'The villagers, strongly moved with faith, then made obeisance and offerings to Milarepa.' Before, they were insisting that he should work and weren't very willing to stop and feed him, but now their attitude has completely changed. They have been convinced, apparently, that his type of house-building and his whole way of life is superior to theirs. It's a reminder that one should not only criticize people's existing way of life, but offer something better, some higher alternative.

This little introductory episode is a precursor to Milarepa's meeting with Rechungpa, and perhaps offers us a glimpse of what is to come in that relationship. In speaking in terms of building, Milarepa takes up what the builders are doing as a metaphor of what he is doing, but he enlarges upon it in order to make it clear that he is doing something radically different. The point is underlined that Milarepa, in his own way, is as active as they are. He is as much a worker as they are; the spiritual life means spiritual work. Perhaps one can also say that the activity of those villagers in building their house and Milarepa's activity in building his transcendental castle represent the two extremes, but for a lot of people there has to be something in between. Milarepa's activity is purely internal; he's only meditating and having experiences and realizing. No doubt it comes to that in the end, but the majority of people can't do that immediately. They need something which is, not so much in terms of skilfulness and unskilfulness, but in terms of relative degrees of objectivity and tangibility, halfway between the villagers literally building a house and Milarepa being absorbed in meditation.

One could make an analogy with the four grades or levels of tantras.[116] It's said that on the first level of Tantric practice one is engaged only in ritual activity. It is all external; one is engaged in making offerings and things of that sort. The second level of Tantric practice is half external and half internal; that is to say, it consists half of making offerings and other external ritual activities, and half of meditation.

Then, when you come on to the third level of Tantra it is only internal, only meditation. And the fourth is even more internal, still expressed in terms of meditation. So it's as though the villagers are completely externalized in an unskilful way, and Milarepa is completely internalized in a highly skilful way, but to begin with you need something in between the two. You need to be externalized in a skilful way, with some internal skilful practice. The average person can't engage immediately only in this internal 'castle building' through meditation and so on; you need the opportunity to participate in positive skilful external activities and structures. As well as the possibility of working on yourself directly through meditation, you may also need things like yoga, retreats, right livelihood businesses, and communities. Milarepa could do without those things, at least during the latter part of his career, but that's not true for most people.

Milarepa wishes that he and the 'good folk of Gung Tang' may meet again through 'the Karma-affinity of this conversation'. What is this karma-affinity? To begin with, what is affinity? In the literal sense it means blood relationship, but more metaphorically it means a certain mutual sympathy and attraction. It's more than shared interests; it's that you naturally and instinctively get on well and easily with somebody. And karma-affinity would be an affinity which is continuing from previous existences. The conversation they are having on this occasion is itself a karma-affinity – that's what Milarepa is saying. They've come together, they've developed an affinity, and he's expressing the wish that, as a result of this, they may come together in the future in the Pure Land of Oujen, that is to say, the Pure Land of Padmasambhava. In other words, his wish is that as the culmination of this communication, they may come together in a completely ideal state of affairs. The implication is that for that to happen, they will need to act on what he has been telling them. The Pure Land of Padmasambhava represents a very high level of experience indeed, so to meet him there they will need to reach that sort of level. But they have the opportunity; an affinity between them has been set up by the fact of this meeting. Having met once, they can go on meeting, so to speak, on different levels until their meetings culminate on that highest level of all.

If one is careful not to take it literally, one can say that the Pure Land generally, including the Pure Land of Padmasambhava, represents Enlightenment as a 'social experience'. It's a number of people's experience of their own and one another's Enlightenment in mutuality. The Pure Land, the Pure Field or *kṣetra*, expresses that in objective rather than subjective terms. It can be expressed subjectively as a number of people attaining the same Enlightenment, or objectively as a number of people living in the same Pure Land. You can't express it ultimately in either exclusively subjective or exclusively objective terms because it transcends that distinction.

So Milarepa is hoping that they will all continue on the path that he has travelled to the very end. If that happens, wherever they are, they will be together, whether that is to be taken literally, metaphorically, or in any other way. The Pure Land of Padmasambhava is a symbol of that togetherness at the very highest conceivable level. If they are travelling on the same path, they'll arrive at the same goal, wherever or whatever that may be. He calls it, for his present purpose, the Pure Land of Padmasambhava, Uḍḍiyāna or Urgyen (which Chang unusually spells 'Oujen').

There is considerable debate among scholars as to the location, geographically speaking, of Uḍḍiyāna, but probably the majority would say that it was the Swat valley in modern Pakistan. Padmasambhava is often called Urgyen Padmasambhava, although in a different tradition, he also has a Pure Land called the Copper-Coloured Mountain; that is where he's supposed to be living even now, preaching to the *rākṣasas*. Like Sukhāvatī, the Pure Land or Buddha-field of Amitābha, it isn't just an assemblage of favourable conditions; it goes beyond that. Enlightenment conceived of as a social experience is probably the best way of expressing it. It's the point of convergence of all individual aspirations, where they transcend their individuality.

3
SOMEONE SINGING

After this, Milarepa went to the upper part of Goat Hill (Ra La)
where he found Silk Cave (Za 'og Phug). Now, there was at Goat
Hill a youth, who in his early infancy had lost his father. He was a
fine, intelligent boy, whom his mother and uncle jointly supported.
Having an excellent memory, he could recite a great many stories
and sermons from the Buddhist Sūtras. Thus he always received
many gifts from the people. One day, while herding oxen on his
donkey in the upper part of the valley, he came upon the cave
where Milarepa was meditating. Thinking that he heard someone
singing, he got off the donkey, left the oxen, and approached
the cave. As soon as he saw Milarepa, an ineffable experience of
Samādhi arose within him, and for a moment he stood transfixed
in ecstasy. (Afterwards he became a Heart-Son of Milarepa – the
renowned Rechung Dorje Dragpa.)

This is our first meeting with Rechungpa – and *his* first meeting with
Milarepa, whose singing voice he hears when he is out herding oxen.
We are given a little of his background: as a boy he used to recite stories
and sermons from the Buddhist *sūtras*, in return for which people used
to give him gifts. It's said he was a fine, intelligent boy, so perhaps he
had learned to read or perhaps he'd heard the stories from wandering
monks and had a very good memory. However he learned them, he was
in the habit of reciting these stories and teachings to people, and they

appreciated that and gave him gifts. At the same time he was leading quite an ordinary life, herding oxen on his donkey in the upper part of the valley, and it was on one such occasion that he came upon the cave where Milarepa was meditating, and was curious to find out who was there and what they were singing. Maybe he thought there would be something more for him to learn by heart.

When he heard Milarepa singing, he was just curious, but when he actually saw him, he had a quite different experience. It's as though the voice could have been almost anyone's. It was just a voice. But when he *saw* Milarepa, he had an ineffable experience of *samādhi*. Why? The next paragraph suggests that there was a previous karmic connection between them:

> Awakened thus from Karma, an immutable faith toward the Jetsun arose within the boy. He offered Milarepa all the gifts that he had acquired for his services. Then he stayed with him to learn the Dharma, completely forgetting his mother and uncle. Because of this, he naturally received no income, and his mother and uncle thought, 'what has happened? (Where is he?) Have people stopped paying him?' With misgivings they began asking the patrons whether they had duly paid Rechungpa. Everybody said that he had been paid. It then dawned upon the uncle and mother (where the boy must be, and) that all the gifts must have been offered to Milarepa. They tried in every way to stop Rechungpa from continuing in this course, but to no avail. The young lad remained with Milarepa and learned the Dharma from him. Before long, the Experience and Realization of meditation grew within him. By virtue of mastering the art of Heat Yoga he was able to wear merely a single piece of cotton clothing, and thus earned the name of Rechungpa.

The phrase 'Awakened thus from Karma' is a bit ambiguous. Perhaps Rechungpa's faith in Milarepa was awakened as a result of some previous karmic connection or perhaps the experience itself awakened him from his existing karma in the sense of his existing conditionality. Either way, 'an immutable faith towards the Jetsun arose within the boy' and as the expression of that 'he offered Milarepa all the gifts that he had acquired for his services. Then he stayed with him to learn the Dharma, completely forgetting his mother and uncle.' This doesn't necessarily imply that he wasn't very attached to his mother and uncle. But even if his attachment to them was strong, the faith he developed towards Milarepa was so strong that he was able to overcome whatever attachment he had to his relatives. Sometimes if one gives up something that other people are very attached to, they say, 'Well, you couldn't have cared very much about it', but that isn't necessarily the case. You might have been very attached to it, but now an even more powerful interest has arisen. But the main thing this episode shows us is how wholehearted Tibetan Buddhists are. As soon as this boy made the contact, he had a very strong, in fact ineffable, experience and then an immutable faith arose in him towards Milarepa. He offered Milarepa all the gifts that he had acquired and stayed with him to learn the Dharma. We're not told how long this took but one gets the impression that it was pretty instantaneous. This is quite characteristic of the Tibetans.

An immutable faith is one that can't be lost or diminished, but can only increase. This is quite important because normally people's faith is quite fleeting. As we shall see later on, Rechungpa's spiritual life went on to have many ups and downs but he always had faith in Milarepa and it was out of this faith that on this first meeting he offered Milarepa all the gifts that he had acquired for his services, not keeping anything back. And then he stayed with him to learn the Dharma.

'Because of this' – because he was not going around and reciting what he knew by heart – 'he naturally received no income'. Perhaps his mother and uncle didn't like the fact that all the gifts had been given away because formerly they were on the receiving end of some of them. So 'they tried in every way to stop Rechungpa from continuing in this course but to no avail. The young lad remained with Milarepa and learned the Dharma from him. Before long the Experience and Realization of meditation grew within him. By virtue of mastering the art of Heat Yoga he was able to wear merely a single piece of cotton clothing, and thus earned the name of Rechungpa.' *Re* means 'cotton cloth', and a *repa* is one wearing the cotton cloth as a sign of proficiency in the Heat Yoga. *Chung* means small or little, so Rechungpa's name means the 'little cloth wearer'. The note tells us that he was so called because he was the youngest of the disciples. The Heat Yoga is a form of yogic practice which does actually produce a sensation of physical heat in the body. There is an increase in the bodily temperature which can be perceived by other people, and this is considered to be a sign of success in that practice.

In the case of the stories and discourses from the *sūtras*, Rechungpa's contact with the Dharma was second-hand. When he meets Milarepa there is direct contact with a spiritually developed personality, so that affects him still more strongly – but the spark of interest could already be seen in his being drawn to the stories and *sūtras*. It's a bit similar to what happens in the modern context in the West. People may be drawn first of all to reading books about Buddhism, but when they come into contact with an actual Buddhist movement, they are far more strongly attracted by that than they were by the books they read.

The stage of his spiritual career Milarepa has reached at the time of this story isn't clear. He's staying in a cave, he's meditating, and he's already had a few words with the lay people in the local village; then this is the next thing that happens. We may take it that, if not fully Enlightened at this stage, he is very far advanced on the path and much more experienced than Rechungpa. Maybe one doesn't need to say more than that. The chapters of *The Hundred Thousand Songs of Milarepa* are arranged not in chronological order, but in categories: meetings with non-human disciples, and now meetings with human disciples.

It seems to say quite a lot about the state that Rechungpa must have been in that he responded to the Dharma so naturally. There is the karmic factor, though one can't say anything much about that, certainly not dogmatically. But there's no doubt that he was leading a very simple life, like Geshe Rabten hundreds of years later. Life was very uncomplicated. He was quite a healthy person as far as one knows. His emotional reactions were quite straightforward and unsophisticated. He had natural intelligence and a good memory, so when he came in contact with something highly positive it wasn't difficult for him to respond. He had no psychological problems or anything of that sort. We are not told how old he was, but perhaps he was just sixteen or seventeen. Occasionally one does come across youngsters of this sort even in the West, even in the present day and age, so it was surely even more likely in medieval Tibet where life was very simple and strenuous, very uncomplicated.

One might say that Rechungpa was a *saddhānusārin*, a faith follower, rather than a doctrine follower. He was healthy, he was emotionally positive. He had that encounter with Milarepa, who made a profound impression on him, and he immediately started meditating, whereas a doctrine follower presumably would have got much more into the study and understanding of the doctrine, especially the philosophical aspect of it.

> Meanwhile, Rechungpa's mother and uncle became very angry. They sent him a pot on which a curse had been placed. As a result, Rechungpa contracted leprosy. Hoping to be cured, he confined himself (in the hermitage) for meditation.

The anger of Rechungpa's mother and uncle might have been at the loss of income, but perhaps a stronger factor was their own attachment and jealousy. After all, they'd brought this boy up, they'd looked after him, he was doing quite well and earning some money, and suddenly he meets this yogi living in a cave and forgets all about them. Perhaps they felt hurt and rejected, perhaps they felt that Rechungpa didn't care for them any more, as in a sense he didn't. So they became very angry. Whether or not one can bring about leprosy by sending someone a cursed pot, the important point is that they believed that they could harm him in this way, so that is what they tried to do, because they wanted to harm him. It seems that their love for Rechungpa very quickly turned to its extreme opposite. One can understand their being a bit upset and disappointed, but they go so far as to try to inflict harm on him. A curse is a very serious thing, especially among primitive peoples. When love, or so-called love, turns into hate the consequences can be very terrible indeed. It does seem extraordinary that at one time you should be very attached to somebody and supposedly love them but then something happens and it isn't just that you lose that love but it changes into its opposite and you try to harm or even kill that person. What happens when someone that you've been attached to changes or goes away and your reaction is of wanting to destroy that person? What is the mental state behind this crime of passion? It's all about revenge and craving and projection, but it's easy to use these words glibly. What is really going on?

It's almost – if such a thing is possible – as though you've projected the whole of yourself, so that you don't exist any more. It's as though you exist only in the other person. If they go away, you go away. If you don't experience them, you no longer experience yourself. Their going away is experienced as a threat to your very existence, and therefore your reaction is a violent, convulsive one. You feel that they are trying to kill you by going away and you retaliate by trying to kill them. It's a paradoxical situation because if you succeed in killing them, they will go away for good, so you are no better off than you were. But of course when you're in that sort of state you're not rational so you can't give any weight to such considerations.

It's as though Rechungpa's mother and uncle not only lived for Rechungpa in a very unhealthy way, they also lived through him. When he went away, the whole purpose of their lives was lost and they felt so angry and threatened that they had to retaliate by trying to do him a serious injury, even kill him. Not all crimes of passion are committed on the spur of the moment, as you discover if you read the newspapers. Of course at a trial for murder, one of the things that is taken into consideration is whether or not preparations were made, which suggests foresight and planning. If the accused goes and buys a revolver, then practises shooting and after a few weeks shoots his wife's lover, that is considered to be a premeditated crime, and the case goes much more heavily against him. But the psychological process is the same. Some people are quick and hasty, others are slower in the way that they do things, but there isn't any real difference of principle. Some people may think it over and become more and more angry, and then take action. Society may consider the hot-tempered person not to be so much at fault as the plotter, but they're equally dangerous, because if someone can fly off the handle you don't know what he's going to do. And if you are the type to postpone your revenge, the chances are that some factor will intervene and make it impossible for you to carry out your intentions. The crucial point is the way in which the frustration of this neurotic identification of oneself with another person, the investment of one's being in another person, can result in violent actions.

'As a result Rechungpa contracted leprosy.' Most primitive peoples believe that you can influence others by your thoughts, for better or for worse, either directly or indirectly through some material object. Be that as it may, Rechungpa contracted leprosy and he, and no doubt others, believed that it was due to the curse his mother and uncle had placed on the pot they had sent him. So, 'hoping to be cured, he confined himself in the hermitage for meditation'. It's as though he thought that since the leprosy had been caused by the unskilful mental state of his mother and uncle, it could also be cured by mental means. And perhaps he was right. A friend of mine was ill recently and he tried all sorts of treatment but nothing did him much good, so he decided in the end to fall back on traditional remedies and recite the mantra of the 'Tārā of Healing', as he said. (One of the set of twenty-one Tārās is especially associated with healing.) After two or three days he started to feel much better. No doubt there are quite a few things that are psychosomatic in origin and can be tackled in this sort of way.

One of the things that might make a difference is the fact that when you treat yourself by reciting a mantra you are active, whereas if you just swallow a pill you're completely passive. Maybe the fact that you are doing something has a positive effect on your system, and perhaps mobilizes certain resources within you. Usually people feel more positive, more alive, more healthy, when they are active, so perhaps it's a more positive and healthy approach to say to yourself, 'I'm doing this to cure myself', rather than just swallowing medicine.

> One day, five Indian yogis arrived, to whom Rechungpa offered some roasted barley which had been sent by his mother and uncle. While the Indians were eating they exclaimed, 'What a deadly disease! What a deadly disease!' They knew that Rechungpa had caught leprosy. Rechungpa then asked them whether there was any cure. One of the yogis said, 'You are indeed a pitiful person deserving of sympathy, and I feel for you. I have a Guru called Wala Tsandra who may be able to relieve you. As he will not be coming to Tibet, you will have to go to India.' And so Rechungpa asked the Jetsun for permission to go.

The fact that these yogis knew that Rechungpa had caught leprosy tells us that they had psychic powers, or at least a sort of psychic sensitivity. They were aware that the roasted barley they'd been given was contaminated in some way. They felt some impure vibration, and they knew perhaps that this had been meant for Rechungpa. At the same time, the fact that they could pick up on this suggests that it has a quasi-objective existence. It is rather like when there's something unpleasant going on between the people you're with; you can sometimes pick up on that even though it isn't directed at you. So something like that happened. The yogis ate this roasted barley – it might even have come in that same pot that the mother and uncle had sent – and although the curse wasn't meant for them they picked up something because of their acute psychic sensitivity.

Most people who practise meditation notice that they become more psychically sensitive to other people's thoughts, but how does that affect food? Some people say they can tell the mental state of whoever cooked the food, but is that due to inference or direct perception? If you see that the food hasn't been well cooked or the table hasn't been nicely laid, you can guess that the person has done it in a hurry or hasn't done it properly, but that's different from detecting it directly. One mustn't be precious about these things. If you are leading an ordinary life the chances are that you would feel such things very slightly if at all because there are so many other more powerful influences affecting you. If you're in a not very wholesome mental state, you can't just blame it on to the food. But if you are meditating regularly and you're quite careful about your way of life, you could be affected if food had been prepared by someone who was in a very negative state. This is why in India there is a tradition that if you're doing intensive meditation you should eat food either prepared by your own hand or by a fellow disciple of the same teacher, assuming that he is practising in the same sort of way that you are.

I once heard someone say that the birds still don't sing in Belsen, which, if it's true, suggests that when a lot of people in distress are concentrated in one area, it leaves an objective vibration. I certainly felt this myself at the Coliseum in Rome – something very strong and unpleasant. It wasn't just my own conscious mental associations; it was something I directly perceived. Even if one had not known, one could certainly have believed that people had been executed and tortured in that place. But even if mental states can be picked up by other people, can that be done via food? There is a widespread belief that if you eat food that has been blessed, this has a positive effect. Hindus call this *prasad*, literally 'sacred gift' – food which has been offered in puja to a god or teacher. It's all very marginal but no doubt there is some effect. In Zen monasteries they consider the correct preparation of food so important that they usually have an old, experienced monk in charge of the cooking. This is something to which we could also pay attention, making sure that the preparation of food doesn't become routine and impersonal, but is done with care.

Rechungpa asks the yogis whether there is any cure for leprosy, and one of them recommends that he should go to a particular guru in India, Wala Tsandra, to seek a cure. It's quite interesting that there's this possibility of a disease being healed by non-physical means. It has been suggested by some writers that spiritual healing doesn't play such an important part in Buddhism as it does in Christianity; there is no Buddhist equivalent of the healing miracles of Christ. But a book has recently been published on the medicine or healing Buddhas, and it seems that there was a whole tradition of spiritual healing in Buddhism, both in the Theravāda and the Mahāyāna, even in the absence of any healing miracles on the part of the Buddha.[117] This reference to Wala Tsandra seems to confirm that these yogis knew that their guru was in a position to cure diseases through meditation – not by just saying 'disease be gone!' but by teaching a meditation that cured the person of the disease.

Milarepa agreed and sang as a parting gift:

I pray my Guru to whom I owe immense gratitude,
I pray you to protect and bless my son, Rechungpa.

Son, you should renounce the world,
And work hard at the Dharma.
To the Guru, Patron Buddha, and the Three Precious Ones,
You should pray with sincere heart and not just words.
Bear this in mind when you travel in India.

By taking the food of Perseverance in Samādhi,
By wearing the clothes of Ah Tung,
And by riding the horse of the magic Prāna-Mind,
Thus, my son, should you travel in India.

You should always keep the non-defiled mind clean
You should always remember the silver-bright mirror of the
    Tantric Precept,
And observe it without vexation.
Bear this in mind, my son, as you travel in India.

If you are followed and captured by bandits,
You should remind yourself how worthless are the Eight
    Worldly Claims.
Conceal your powers and merits.
With a humble and merry mind travel in India.

My son, with my sincere prayer and blessing,
May you recover from your illness and enjoy long life.

> *I pray my Guru to whom I owe immense gratitude,*
> *I pray you to protect and bless my son, Rechungpa.*

Milarepa's guru is Marpa, so one has the impression of a lineage in the true sense. Milarepa is not himself blessing Rechungpa but praying to Marpa to bless him. The suggestion is that Milarepa sees himself as a vehicle. He sees it as his job not to obstruct anything that might pass through him from Marpa, his teacher, to Rechungpa, his disciple. One has to be cautious when using this language of transmission. It's not that something is transmitted; one can speak of a spark going from one generation to another, but one has to be careful that one doesn't give that spark any particular form which is just dependent on the accidents of one's own personality. This is perhaps what Milarepa is suggesting. He doesn't say to Rechungpa, 'I bless you, my son, off you go.' He says, 'I pray to my guru to bless my son Rechungpa.' It's as though he's trying to make himself completely transparent to the guru's influence so that it may pass through him to Rechungpa. And then Marpa will likewise pray that his guru Nāropa's blessings may come to Milarepa. Presumably you can't go back and back indefinitely. You have to come to a stop somewhere, even if you go all the way back to the Buddha. But if you're already fully Enlightened, why should you even go back to the Buddha? If Nāropa is Enlightened you might as well stop at him. If Marpa is Enlightened you might as well stop at him. If Milarepa is Enlightened you might as well stop at him.

The suggestion is that Enlightenment is non-personal, in the sense of non-egoistic. It's not as though anything can really come from Milarepa or Marpa. It can't even 'come from' the Buddha. By speaking of Milarepa or Marpa or Nāropa or the Buddha as Enlightened beings, one doesn't mean anything of the nature of an Enlightened ego. Enlightenment is not anybody's personal possession, whether you refer back to somebody else or not. Even when the Buddha Śākyamuni says, 'I am the Enlightened one', he doesn't mean it in the sense that he possesses something called Enlightenment which other people don't possess. One has to steer a middle way. There has to be some glimmer communicated of what Enlightenment is like, but at the same time it can't be claimed as a personal possession in the ordinary sense. Within the context of the Kagyu tradition Milarepa gets over that by referring back to his guru and suggesting that he is just a channel, a medium for the transmission of the guru's blessing.

> Son, you should renounce the world,
> And work hard at the Dharma.

You notice he calls Rechungpa his son. The sense in which the term is used is obvious, but there's a danger that negative associations might attach to it for some people in the modern Western context. It depends what your relationship with your father was like. If you are trying to get away from the home situation and you go along to a Buddhist centre, the last thing you want to hear is 'Hello, my son!' It's as though you've just come home again. There's also the Christian connotation – the priest is the father and the pope is the Holy Father. So perhaps one should be a little careful about using this sort of terminology. I've known Western Buddhist monks who liked to be addressed as Father this or Father that, which seemed to smack of Roman Catholicism, but in the Buddhist tradition one doesn't address monks as father. You might imagine that lay people, especially in Theravāda countries, might address *bhikkhus* as 'father' because the laity occupy a quite subordinate position as regards to the monks, but actually they don't use that form of address. The word 'Bhante', which is used, doesn't mean father; it only means reverend, venerable.

It's true that when priests are called 'father', it's a term of reverence rather than there being any suggestion that the priest really is your father. Everybody knows that the priest is not literally your father; you are looking on the priest as though he was a father in another sense. The danger is that instead of transposing the meaning of the term father to a higher level you're just duplicating in one way or another the meaning that the term had on the old level. You might end up expecting the same sort of support and consolation from the priest whom you call father as from your own father, instead of looking for something higher.

I don't know what the original Tibetan expression is for renouncing the world; perhaps it's the equivalent of Going Forth. But the English idiom 'renouncing the world' or 'giving up the world' is quite ambiguous. In what sense does one give up the world; in what sense *can* one give up the world? I found when I came back from India that many English Buddhists, especially those inclined more to the Theravāda, but even those inclined to Zen as well, thought and spoke very much in terms of giving up the world. If you were a monk you were supposed to have given up the world, and they seemed to understand by that having nothing to do with anything they considered worldly. You were literally quite separate and apart. There is a certain sense in which this is true, but they seemed to take it very literally, as in fact some people do in the East, especially in the Theravāda countries. But it would be better to think in terms of recreating the world, a new world, a better world. A reporter who came to interview me asked, 'Are you allowed to speak to people?' as though having contact with people was one of the things I was supposed to have given up. So the idiom is rather unfortunate. One can perhaps speak of Going Forth, but 'giving up the world' seems to have the wrong sort of connotation. It's a question of defining what one means by 'the world'. No doubt there are certain specific things that one needs to give up, but giving up the world is quite a sweeping statement. The world means everything! Are you going to give up eating and drinking? So 'the world' is meant at least to some extent as a metaphorical symbol.

At the same time, you shouldn't go to the other extreme and say you don't have to give up anything literally, because if you give it up in your mind that's good enough. I used to find people of that sort too, even monks. For them it was OK to give things up in their minds. They were superior to you, some of them thought, because they were able to do it mentally whereas you, being less developed spiritually, had to do it literally.

I'm not sure what the exact Tibetan idiom is here, but 'work hard at the Dharma' is quite a good expression in this context: not just 'practise the Dharma', which sounds a bit anaemic, but 'work hard at the Dharma', like working hard at your grammar or your gardening. It's something concrete and tangible. What you're really working hard at is yourself – that's where the Dharma differs from a mundane subject of study. But what does working hard at the Dharma really boil down to? Milarepa gives his version, but what does it mean in more general terms? Does it mean learning texts by heart? 'Working hard at the Dharma' suggests something objective, something outside yourself, a subject of study almost. But is that what it is? We need to try to see the precise significance of this phrase. How does one work at the Dharma? In what sense or to what extent is the Dharma a thing, as it were, that you're working at? The term Dharma is rather broad. Perhaps you never really work at 'the Dharma'; perhaps you just work at certain specific things. They are the Dharma for you. Maybe this is what Milarepa is getting at.

> To the Guru, Patron Buddha, and the Three Precious Ones,
> You should pray with sincere heart and not just words.
> Bear this in mind when you travel in India.

The Three Precious Ones are presumably the three exoteric refuges, and the first two esoteric refuges are mentioned: the guru and the yidam, translated here as the patron Buddha, though of course it can also be a bodhisattva. The third esoteric refuge, the *dakini*, isn't mentioned.[118] In view of what happens to Rechungpa later on in his life, one could perhaps surmise that Milarepa felt that he might misunderstand if that was mentioned at that point.

In any case, to work hard at the Dharma, if one thinks in terms of the esoteric rather than the exoteric refuges, means working hard at one's relationship with one's guru, working hard at the particular practice, that is to say the visualization/mantra recitation practice relating to a particular Buddha or bodhisattva that you have been given, and cultivating your relationships with fellow practitioners of the Dharma – as well as cultivating a positive attitude towards the Three Jewels in the more general, exoteric sense.

Is this language of working hard at the Dharma different from the kind of inner unfoldment represented by the gestalt? 'Working hard at the Dharma' sounds objective, whereas thinking in terms of personal myth and uncovering a pattern may sound more subjective. But in some ways both are objective. One's personal myth is more than inner unfoldment in the ordinary psychological sense, because the myth is experienced as something outside oneself, at least to a great extent.

It's true that in the case of the myth something more is involved than the conscious, active, willing self, but that is also true when you are working at something, whether the Dharma or something else. The myth seems to belong more to the greater mandala.[119] You could say that there was a series of concentric circles. In the middle you've got the mandala of usefulness in the ordinary, practical everyday sense, and then a somewhat wider and bigger circle, the mandala of working on yourself and working at the Dharma. Whether you work on yourself or whether you work at the Dharma, the language still derives from that of the mandala of usefulness. Then, outside the circle of working on yourself or working at the Dharma you've got the still wider circle or mandala of myth. Outside that, one might say, is the purely spiritual, the formless, and outside that, the Transcendental.

So the mythical is more removed from the utilitarian, whereas working on yourself and working at the Dharma seem to come in between the utilitarian and the mythical. In other words, through the mythical material you contact a 'self', in a manner of speaking, which is a larger self than the one that is involved in working on yourself or working at the Dharma. At the same time, when you realize that you are part of this myth, you are working on yourself, you are working at the Dharma, though in a rather different way, in a wider and deeper sense, not on the old utilitarian model. You are working without working.

Working on your relationship with the guru in practical terms means working on your openness or receptivity to anybody who is more experienced spiritually than you are yourself, and especially to someone whom you regard as a guru in the more specific sense. It's the same with regard to the *ḍākinī* – it's being open and communicative (that's a better word in this context than 'receptive') with those at approximately the same level of development who spark you off, and with whom you can have a spiritually stimulating exchange. It's not that you necessarily or consciously limit yourself to one particular spiritual friend, though there may be one person to whom you are much closer than anybody else; you are open to that sort of mutually stimulating relationship with anybody who is roughly on the same level as you are yourself, spiritually speaking. At the very least it means keeping in touch about your plans. Passing on information is the lowest form of communication, but it's a start. Even if all you say is, 'I'm going away to Greece for a month,' at least there's the beginning of communication.

And there's an example of that here, with Rechungpa asking Milarepa if he can go to India.

The choice of the word 'pray' is perhaps unfortunate in this context. It's not that one is to ask for anything; it's more an attitude of not only openness and receptivity, but of very positive thoughts and feelings directed towards the esoteric and the exoteric refuges. It's not just words. It's a question of inner feeling. It's very easy to pray with words and to be relatively devoid of feeling. That is a form of *śīlavrata-parāmarśa*, dependence on rules and vows in a purely external manner.[120] In the case of the puja, especially the Sevenfold Puja, you need to be aware of what you're saying. The temptation is to reel it off mechanically, because the words are so familiar and you've said them so many times before, but you've got to pay attention to the meaning. Don't just recite away without thinking; put some emotion into it. Ask yourself, 'What do these words really mean?' If you can repeat them with a genuine awareness of their meaning, the chances are that there will be some feeling there too.

Some ex-Christians feel that, having thrown out God and divine beings, they're reluctant to think that the Buddhas are external to themselves, because they think they're just reproducing God again. But others take to devotional practice immediately and feel devotion from the moment they step into a shrine-room or see a Buddha image. Perhaps like Rechungpa they are more of the faith follower type, whose emotional and devotional response is almost instantaneous and relatively uncomplicated.

The English word 'prayer' implies getting in touch with something outside of oneself, and there are equivalents in the Buddhist tradition: there's the Sanskrit term *prārthana*, and the Tibetan *monlam*, which means something like 'the path of speech'. But there's a difference between invocation and evocation. Both words are partly from a root which means simply to call, as in the word 'vocal'. To invoke is to call upon. It's as though you feel that somebody is there even though you can't see them, and that if you call upon them, they will respond. When you evoke, by contrast, it's as though they are not 'there'; you are calling them up. Conze and Snellgrove use the word 'evocation' in connection with the visualization of Buddhas and bodhisattvas, as though the figure is not already present, but has to be called up.[121] You call upon him or her so that he or she may emerge from the depths – not from the depths of your mind in a purely subjective sense, but just from the depths. Invocation is more like saying what one could call prayers – though unlike 'prayer' invocation doesn't have the connotation or even the denotation of requesting, which is perhaps the advantage of using the word invocation. There's no suggestion of asking for anything. You are asking whoever you're calling upon to let you know that they are there, and calling upon their influence, their power. It's not just something static that you're calling upon. If you call upon it and it responds, you will have called on it also in the sense that you can call on the bank for money. It's not just a presence that you call on but a power, and when the presence responds to your invocation a power is available to you, using the word power in a very broad sense.

Traditionally you call up, you evoke, the Buddhas and bodhisattvas not from within your own mind but from the Void, from the purely transcendental dimension, because they are a form of that. And then you invoke them, now that they are present. It's not only calling upon them but calling upon their power. It's like a magical rite: magical ceremonies are the model for the Tantric puja and even for the meditations. Theravāda and Mahāyāna pujas are not quite like that. There the model is 'social'; the Buddha is envisaged as the honoured guest who appears in the world and is received as such. It's not magical except to the extent that there's something magical about this visitor, this stranger, this unexpected person who suddenly appears.

To visualize Buddhas and bodhisattvas is to evoke them. It may not be a genuine evocation from the Void, from the metaphysical dimension, but even if you visualize those forms in your own mind, at least you've evoked them from your mind, and you can then invoke them. One might say that evocation gives you a more static end result and invocation is more dynamic; your calling upon is a drawing upon. Evocation is strictly your production, and that is how it is traditionally described: the *utpatti*, the production of the form. Invocation suggests that the process is carried a stage further. You have not only evoked the figure; you establish some contact. It suggests almost a tapping of energy. The energy is the energy of the Void, if one can use that expression, and the particular figure that you evoke and invoke determines the particular form that that energy takes. It may be an energy of love and compassion or an energy of wisdom or an energy of purification or whatever. When doing a puja it's important that one realizes that one is not just in contact with an idea in one's own mind in the ordinary sense, though perhaps that's quite a difficult thing to realize.

What's needed is a touch of magic. It's easier to explain symbolism in a purely rational way but that usually doesn't help much. It keeps the rational mind satisfied and stops it making too many objections but it doesn't do anything very positive for the puja itself. You can explain that when you offer a candle it represents the light of wisdom and so on, and all that is quite true, and keeps the rational mind quiet, but that sort of explanation doesn't play a very positive or creative part; it's not enough in itself.

It isn't quite right to think of approaching the puja like playing a piece of music, unless you're thinking of it as a performance for somebody else to hear, not just for your own enjoyment. Reflecting that you're doing the puja for the sake of your own spiritual development isn't really effective either. For a puja to be truly beneficial for your spiritual development you've got to do it for or to the Buddha. It isn't an exercise you're doing to develop your emotional muscles just as you might use weights in the gym to develop your physique. There has to be an objective reference, an objective orientation.

Anyway, Milarepa says, 'Bear this in mind when you travel in India,' – that is, Rechungpa should bear in mind that he should renounce the world, work hard at the Dharma, and pray with sincere heart to the Refuges. Presumably he should particularly bear this in mind when travelling because a lot of external changes take place when you are seeing a lot of new things, and it's very easy to forget things that are relatively internal, relatively spiritual.

> By taking the food of Perseverance in Samādhi,
> By wearing the clothes of Ah Tung,
> And by riding the horse of the magic Prāṇa-Mind,
> Thus, my son, should you travel in India.

Just three practical things are necessary when you travel: food, clothing, and a means of transport – in Rechungpa's case, a horse. Presumably Rechungpa has got all of these, but Milarepa advises him to take metaphorical versions of them as well. The food he is advised to take is not just *samādhi*, but perseverance in *samādhi*. Just as one meal isn't enough, because you have to eat every day, in the same way one good meditation isn't enough; you have to keep on meditating. According to the translator's note, Ah Tung means the small seed syllable *āḥ*, which is visualized at the navel centre in the heat yoga practice. If you attain success in this practice you don't need clothes. Even in the cold climate of Tibet a thin cotton garment will be sufficient.

With reference to 'the horse of the magic Prāṇa-Mind', the translator's note says, 'According to Tantric teaching, mind and Prāṇa manifest as two aspects of a unity. Mind is that which is aware. Prāṇa is the active energy which gives support to the awareness. He who masters the mind automatically masters the Prāṇa, and vice versa. The aim of any system of meditation is to control or master the Prāṇa-Mind.' This is not a particular kind of *prāṇa* called Prāṇa-Mind but *prāṇa* and mind together, forming an inseparable unity. The steed that really enables the yogi to go, to function as a yogi, is the unification of energy and awareness. The awareness has got to be perfectly pure and bright, and the energy has got to be freely flowing and positive and flowing in the right direction, providing the support, the body if you like, for the awareness.

In Tantric Buddhism it isn't just a question of clarifying the mind. It's also a question of sorting out the energies. The energies find expression in the body; awareness finds expression in the mind. It's in this sense that work is the great Tantric guru – because it's one of the things that enables one to bring one's energies into harmony with one's awareness. It's quite easy to have an awareness of things or to understand things, but to bring your energies into harmony with that understanding is quite another matter. This is an important aspect of spiritual life: not only to see clearly but to function smoothly. The aspect of clear seeing is represented by mind, the effortless, energy-full functioning is represented by *prāṇa*, and one can't neglect either. And of course what Milarepa is talking about here is working in meditation with the subtle energy system.

In this song, Milarepa is transposing the whole thing to a different level. It's not a question of food, it's a question of perseverance in *samādhi*; it's not a question of clothing, it's a question of the heat yoga; it's not a question of riding a horse, it's a question of *prāṇa* and mind. In the same way, it's not really a question of travelling to India. If you're able to do these other things, what spiritual value does travelling in India have? It's just restless wandering. However, although one doesn't want to provide material for rationalizations, perhaps Rechungpa 'needs' to travel for a while. It may seem strange that he wants to go, when Milarepa has had this tremendous effect on him, but he wants to cure the leprosy, and apparently this famous teacher, Wala Tsandra, has a special cure. Maybe he could have cured it by staying with Milarepa, but he doesn't think so. He may have an urge to travel – his particular turbulence or restlessness may take that form – and he may want to indulge that, so he is just not prepared to listen to Milarepa. If Milarepa was to say that it's not a wise thing to do, he might react strongly. So Milarepa doesn't say anything about it.

It does seem that Rechungpa has seized the opportunity very readily once he has asked for permission to be off. According to this account, he doesn't seem to have had any conflict about it at all. He doesn't seem to have thought, 'I'd really like to go to India; what a pity it means I have to leave Milarepa!' He doesn't even ask Milarepa whether he thinks it would be a good idea. He seems to have enough feeling for Milarepa to ask if he can go, but not to wonder whether he should go at all. But even if this is something that Rechunpga needs to do, I'm not so sure that this sort of restless energy is necessarily to be indulged with travel, which is a fairly new development in the world. The way some people talk it's as though they've got to travel all round the world before they can really get on with any spiritual practice. Even people who are keen to set up Dharma centres seem to think that they can't go to a nearby town to set up a centre – it's got to be in some distant part of the world. It reflects a purely subjective attitude: 'What effect is it going to have on me? Am I going to like it there?', not 'Are there people there who could get interested in the Dharma?' People may put it in terms of how it will affect their spiritual development, but it sometimes boils down to 'Would it suit me?' There's a certain lack of bodhisattva spirit.

You should always keep the non-defiled mind clean

Doesn't this seem paradoxical? If the mind is non-defiled, well, it's non-defiled. You could take it quite literally, that it is undefiled as yet so you must keep it that way, but you don't in fact start off with a non-defiled mind in the ordinary sense. Perhaps the meaning is that the surface mind should be kept as clean as the mind essentially is in its depths. It is the general Mahāyāna/Vajrayāna view that the mind in its depths is pure. It may be dusty, but the dust is only on the surface of the mind. That may or may not be a helpful analogy, but perhaps the surface must be kept clean, so that it is undefiled just as the depths are undefiled.

In a sense this is a reference to the need to keep up effort all the time, to resist the 'gravitational pull', as one might call the pull of the conditioned. Only in a sense, because there is a level of the mind where the gravitational pull is not felt, but one should so exert oneself that eventually no gravitational pull at all is felt. Then, and only then, the mind will be quite pure. There's not only the question of mind, there's also the question of energy; there's got to be not only awareness, but practice and functioning in accordance with that awareness. It isn't enough just to remind yourself that the mind is pure in its depths. You have also got to make an effort to keep it clean on the surface, so long as you continue to be under the influence of the gravitational pull. Dust is settling moment by moment, and moment by moment you have to wipe it away. If you aren't making progress at any given moment, the chances are that you are slipping back. You don't stay just where you are. You either go forward or you move back – maybe only a little, but you never stay completely still.

If Rechungpa's faith is immutable, as the text says, it must be a transcendental faith and he must have entered the stream, to use the terms of Early Buddhism, but Milarepa is presumably not satisfied that Rechungpa will have to wait another seven lives for Enlightenment. He wants him to gain Enlightenment in this life itself. So he doesn't let him off lightly.

> You should always remember the silver-bright mirror of the
>   Tantric Precept,
> And observe it without vexation.

The precept is called a mirror because it reflects your actions. You can see quite objectively in the mirror of the precept just where you are. There is the potential for this to be misinterpreted, of course. It's not conformity to an external standard. It's like looking into a mirror to see whether there's a spot on your face. If there is a spot, then when you look in the mirror you will see it and you can do something about it. Likewise, when you look at yourself in the mirror of the precepts, as it were, you can see what needs to be done. But it isn't a question of external, almost mechanical conformity. It isn't that if you draw up a long enough list of dos and don'ts and stick to that, spiritual progress will be assured. It's a rough and ready guide, no more than that.

I'm not sure in what sense 'precept' is meant here. It could mean a vow: the *samaya*, the undertaking, the oath, something you undertake to observe in consequence of a Tantric initiation. It is not imposed upon you but you see quite clearly and definitely that a certain mode of behaviour is inseparable from, or necessitated by, the initiation that you've received, to support it or to make it effective. You take that vow at the same time that you receive the initiation, seeing that the practice into which you've been initiated requires the observance of certain things.

> If you are followed and captured by bandits,
> You should remind yourself how worthless are the Eight
>   Worldly Claims.
> Conceal your powers and merits.
> With a humble and merry mind travel in India.

In those days travel was quite dangerous, and this verse reminds us of that. The 'Eight Worldly Claims' are the pairs of opposites: gain and loss, fame and infamy, praise and blame, pleasure and pain.[122] These four are the pairs of things that affect the mind in different ways: people become elated if they experience one and depressed if they experience the other. You should remind yourself not to allow yourself to be affected by these changing conditions. You shouldn't be perturbed whether you gain something or lose it, whether you suffer or not. If you fall into the hands of bandits, in whatever way that occurs, it will help you to reflect in this way. After all, if Rechungpa was captured by bandits and became upset, it would show that he wasn't very firmly established in his practice.

By advising him to 'conceal your powers and merits', Milarepa is reminding Rechungpa not to show off his learning or any psychic powers he may have. There's no need to try to impress people with how good you are or how highly developed you are spiritually. Just travel 'with a humble and merry mind'. I'm not sure how literal this translation is. It might be better to translate it 'with a lowly and contented mind' or something like that, to make sure we don't think of humble in the Uriah Heep sense,[123] or merry in the Father Christmassy sense.

> My son, with my sincere prayer and blessing,
> May you recover from your illness and enjoy long life.

We don't know what Milarepa really thought. He may have thought, 'This foolish young man is going off to this guru when he could just as easily have stayed here and I would have shown him how to cure his illness, but never mind, let him go.' On the other hand, it may be that this other guru had some special technique that Milarepa didn't have. We don't know, but I'm rather mistrustful of special techniques. I tend to think that if one kind of meditation could have cured his illness, any kind of meditation could have done so, because the effect is the same in the long run.

> Milarepa then resumed his meditation in the cave. Rechungpa closed the cave's mouth with clay, and set out for India with the yogis. (Upon arriving) there he met Lama Wala Tsandra, who (consented to give) him the complete teachings of the Wrathful Thunderbolt Holder with Eagle Wings. By practicing this for some time Rechungpa was cured.

So Milarepa then resumed his meditation in the cave. Well, there was nothing else to do. Rechungpa had gone away, so he might as well get on with some meditation.

The main theme that emerges here is travel. Rechungpa goes off to India and Milarepa reminds him how important it is to maintain the inner connection, not to forget his spiritual practice, not to become lost in his external experiences. At that time new teachings and teachers were still coming from India, so there was a tendency all the time on the part of Tibetan Buddhists to go to India, to the source, to get teachings that weren't as yet available in Tibet. But we can take 'India' in a symbolic sense too. Just as food is equated with *samādhi*, clothes with Ah Tung, and riding a horse with control of the magic *prāṇa*-mind, so travelling in India could be equated with moving in some higher sphere, some higher dimension, though Milarepa doesn't explicitly say so.

Travelling in those days had a quite different significance from the travel of our own day. First of all Rechungpa had a definite objective – he was going to get a particular teaching to cure his leprosy. He wasn't just wandering aimlessly. And, of course, he was having to go on horseback, maybe part of the way on foot. He would be going slowly, experiencing things as he went along in a way that people nowadays very often don't do. Travel today is usually much more superficial, more alienated.

4

IS MY GURU DEAD?

> When he returned to Tibet and reached Happy Valley, he inquired
> of the whereabouts of the Jetsun from a native of that valley who
> said, 'Some time ago, I heard that there was a yogi called Mila, but
> I have heard nothing about him recently.'

We are not told how long Rechungpa was away. It must have been
months, and it could have been a year or two. But anyway, when he
returns to Tibet, reaches Happy Valley and asks after Milarepa, it seems
as though the yogi has almost been forgotten. At the beginning of the
story we found Milarepa making quite an impression on the local people
and they all became his sincere disciples, but it seems that by now there's
no more than a vague recollection that there was 'some time ago a yogi
called Mila'. This suggests that people very quickly lose interest, and this
is indeed what happens. Certainly in India, a yogi or holy man of some
kind may create a great sensation on his first arrival, but after a while
people seem to forget about him. They don't know what he's doing, they
don't know whether he's still there or whether he's gone away. They're
quite vague about it. Something of this sort seems to have happened in
Milarepa's case.

> Hearing this, Rechungpa became very disturbed. He thought, 'Is
> my Guru dead?', and in great distress he proceeded to Silk Cave.
> He saw that the clay wall with which he had blocked the entrance

was still there. Thinking, 'I wonder if the Jetsun is dead inside,' he tore down the wall and entered. Seeing Milarepa sitting upright in meditation, he felt extremely happy and relieved. He asked the Jetsun about his health and welfare. In answer Milarepa (arose from meditation and) sang.

Apparently Milarepa had simply been meditating the whole time Rechungpa was away. But is such a thing possible? It's quite difficult to determine how long a yogi can go without food and exercise just sitting meditating in his cave. In my memoir *The Rainbow Road* I mentioned a female yogi who lived in a little room in the floor of a cave in South India and emerged once a day for an hour.[124] It isn't quite the same thing, but it does go to show that people are capable of more than one would have expected. If a yogi stays in his cave, as Milarepa is supposed to have done, without food, this suggests that he's in a cataleptic state of some kind, a sort of suspended animation. There have been examples even in quite recent times of hatha yogis being buried for anything up to a month. There are some yoga institutes that have carried out tests of this sort. If one could do it for a month, perhaps one could do it for three months or even a year. But this need not signify a high state of meditation. After all, animals hibernate. Evidently the human being can set up some sort of process which results in a virtual suspension of the metabolic process, so that the body is using a minimum of energy and using up existing fats, just as hibernating animals do, and it could be that some hatha yogis have mastered this technique. It is said that the body of someone who attains a very high level of meditation and remains there automatically lapses into this state, and it would seem that something like that has happened in the case of Milarepa.

Anyway, Rechungpa unsealed the cave and found Milarepa still alive, so naturally he was very pleased, asked him how he was, and in reply Milarepa sang this song.

I bow down at the feet of Marpa, the Gracious One.

Because I have left my kinsmen, I am happy;
Because I have abandoned attachment to my country, I am happy;
Since I disregard this place, I am happy;
As I do not wear the lofty garb of priesthood, I am happy;

Because I cling not to house and family, I am happy;
I need not this or that, so I am happy;
Because I possess the great wealth of Dharma, I am happy;
Because I worry not about property, I am happy;
Because I have no fear of losing anything, I am happy;
Since I never dread exhaustion, I am happy;
Having fully realized Mind-Essence, I am happy;
As I need not force myself to please my patrons, I am happy;
Having no fatigue nor weariness, I am happy;
As I need prepare for nothing, I am happy;
Since all I do complies with Dharma, I am happy;
Never desiring to move, I am happy;
As the thought of death brings me no fear, I am happy;
Bandits, thieves and robbers ne'er molest me,
So at all times I am happy!
Having won the best conditions for Dharma practice, I am happy;
Having ceased from evil deeds and left off sinning, I am happy;
Treading the Paths of Merits, I am happy;
Divorced from hate and injury, I am happy;
Having lost all pride and jealousy, I am happy;
Understanding the wrongness of the Eight Worldly Winds,
    I am happy;
Absorbed in quiet and evenmindedness, I am happy;
Using the mind to watch the mind, I am happy;
Without hope or fear, I am ever happy;
In the sphere of non-clinging Illumination, I am happy;
The Non-distinguishing Wisdom of Dharmadhātu itself is happy;
Poised in the natural realm of Immanence, I am happy;
In letting the Six Groups of Consciousness go by
To return to their original nature, I am happy;
The five radiant gates of sense all make me happy;
To stop a mind that comes and goes is happy;
Oh, I have so much of happiness and joy!
This is a song of gaiety I sing,
This is a song of gratitude to my Guru and the three
    Precious Ones –
I want no other happiness.

Through the grace of Buddhas and the Gurus
Food and clothes are provided by my patrons.
With no bad deeds and sins, I shall be joyful when I die;
With all good deeds and virtues, I am happy while alive.
Enjoying Yoga, I am indeed most happy.
But how are you, Rechungpa? Is your wish fulfilled?

Rechungpa has asked Milarepa about his health and welfare, so he's replying to that question. One might have thought that, having been shut up in that little cave, even if only for a few months, he'd be glad to get out, but apparently it isn't so. He tells Rechungpa he's happy and he explains why – for various reasons, not all of them being things that would make most people happy.

Because I have left my kinsmen, I am happy

I suppose he mentions this first because it's the first thing an ordinary person would think of. Most people are attached most of all to their family: not just their wife or husband and children but the whole family group, the tribe. Perhaps his statement that leaving his kinsmen is a reason for his happiness is a hint to Rechungpa: 'Look at all the trouble you had staying with your mother and your uncle. Look what they did to you. Look how you suffered. Look how you had to go to India and be separated from me for such a long time. It was all because of your kinsmen. But I have left my kinsmen. I have nothing to do with them, nothing to do with my mother and sister – or with my aunt and uncle' (because Milarepa's aunt and uncle gave him a lot of trouble) 'so I am happy.'

In family life there is often a lot of conflict, so many tensions and tussles, very often under the surface, but people still don't find it easy to leave. People go home for Christmas even though they're not in the least looking forward to it and would rather not go. They don't dare not to; it would create such a lot of trouble, they think. But you've got to be around to get into trouble. What can your family do to you? If things are really bad, don't let them know where you are. It's simple, but people don't see it like that. It's as though mother and father have got eyes and ears all over the place. They will know what you are up to. They will get to you. They will write to you. They will phone you.

Not that they really love you perhaps, but they don't want you to get away. That's the impression one sometimes gets.

Attachment isn't necessarily positive. When people have got these quite blind, selfish desires it's natural that they should come into conflict. If two people are very attached to each other, when one of them wants to do something, he or she wants that they should do it together, but the second person may want them both to do something else. One of them says, 'Let's go for a walk,' and the other says, 'No, let's go to the cinema.' They can't just agree that one of them will go to the cinema and the other will go for a walk. One of them has to give in, or else there's a long argument and they end up not doing either thing, or they do one of them and the person who doesn't get his or her own way ends up feeling resentful, and that's stored up for the future. No doubt there are some reasonably happy families but even in the best of them there seem to be tensions, suppressed conflicts. One can't be surprised at that. The situation is inherently such.

> *Because I have abandoned attachment to my country,*
> *I am happy.*

Now he is going quite a bit further. It's not enough to leave your kinsmen. You have to abandon attachment to your country, to the whole way of life that you've been brought up in. This is one of the reasons why living abroad for a while is very valuable spiritually. It's not so valuable, obviously, if you go to a foreign country but carry your familiar environment with you: your language, your customs, your food. You need to go to a country which is completely unfamiliar, where they don't speak your language, where you don't see people from your own country and where everything is quite different, and stay there for some time. That's the real test.

> *Since I disregard this place I am happy.*

He's not even attached to that particular valley, or that particular cave. He appreciates them, he enjoys the beauty of the place, but he doesn't cling, he isn't attached. I think that people nowadays have to be a bit careful about this question of attachment. Detachment has meaning only when there is feeling. It's easy enough not to be attached to people if you've got no feeling for them. Nowadays people are very mobile – it's very easy to move from place to place, and to say, 'Oh, I'm not attached to my house, I can move any time.' That may be true, but the reason is that you haven't developed any feeling for your country or your locality, or your house. It's because you're alienated, not because you're non-attached. By contrast, the Tibetans of Milarepa's day, whether rooted in one place or nomadic, had a strong feeling for their family, their animals, their whole way of life, never having known anything else. For such a person it's meaningful to speak in terms of becoming detached. But if from the age of two you've been dragged around from place to place by your parents and been sent off to school somewhere, if you've holidayed in different parts of the world, if you've lived in all kinds of different places and never put down any roots, all this talk of detachment is pretty meaningless.

In some circumstances, it might even be good for people to put down roots. You can't speak in terms of detachment from a place or from people unless there is feeling there in the first place. Otherwise you are merely indifferent, merely alienated, which is quite different. We experience that when we travel by air. We go so quickly from place to place that we have no time to experience anything. There's just one airport and one hotel after another, all furnished in pretty much the same style, and you can phone home any time you like wherever you are in the world. So have you really gone away? In a way you haven't, because you were never there in the first place. You've got nowhere to go away from. Only if your family has lived in the same place for a long time and you really have got roots there is it meaningful to speak in terms of detachment, going forth, widening your horizons. And one should certainly see going forth in terms of widening one's horizons, not a violent uprooting.

My friend Dr Mehta in Bombay[125] sometimes said some quite sensible things, and one of the things he said was, 'Nowadays people, especially holy men and swamis, talk a lot about detachment but that's all wrong. One shouldn't try to detach, one should try to attach. One should try to attach to the right things, not just think in terms of detaching from the wrong things.' Psychologically that's quite sound. Don't think so much in terms of detachment from your native place and your own home; think of attaching yourself to the whole world, to the whole human race – that is more positive. It's easy to be detached if you haven't got any feelings. One must be careful not to make a virtue out of one's weaknesses. You may say, 'I'm very detached' when the truth is that you just don't care about anybody. For some people it would be quite a step forward if they were to become attached to a place or a person.

As I do not wear the lofty garb of priesthood, I am happy.

Here he's referring to the yellow robe. He wasn't ordained as a *bhikkhu*. He probably wasn't even a *sāmaṇera*.[126] It would seem that in Tibet by Milarepa's time, being a monk had become almost a profession, as it is in quite a few parts of the Buddhist world today, and status and position and prestige and honour went along with it. But Milarepa was free from that. It seems he didn't want to be ordained because it would have put him in a false position. At that time it apparently had more a social or socio-ecclesiastical than a spiritual significance and he therefore wanted nothing to do with it, because it would raise the question of rivalry and position in relation to others, and he didn't want anything to do with that.

I'm reminded of an occasion soon after my ordination as a *bhikkhu* when I went down to Calcutta and bumped into the chief monk at the Maha Bodhi Society's headquarters. I happened to be wearing an old robe and he was most upset and said, 'Haven't you got anything better than that to wear?' I said, 'No, this is the only robe I've got.'[127] So he said, 'Well, we can't have you wearing that. What on earth will people think of us?' This wasn't in accordance with my ideas of what a *bhikkhu* was supposed to be like, but he was quite upset, and on the spot he gave me a brand new bright yellow robe to wear. He didn't want people in Calcutta, especially Bengali Hindus, to think that *bhikkhus* were a shabby lot. I afterwards came to realize that among *bhikkhus*, to be a poor *bhikkhu* was a real disgrace. I thought *bhikkhu* meant 'beggar', but apparently not at all. So this is the sort of thing, clearly, that Milarepa didn't want anything to do with.

Because I cling not to house and family, I am happy;
I need not this or that, so I am happy

'This or that' suggests an almost deliberate seeking for something to distract oneself. It doesn't matter what it is, but there must be something you want, something you need, something you're attached to. Any little thing will do. And the reason for that is that when you have a strong need, at least you experience yourself to some extent. If you have no needs, you're just empty and dull and bored, so you go looking around for something you can need, so that you can experience yourself. You need to have a need. You're not able to experience yourself in a positive, happy way. You turn on the television, or you flip through the colour supplements, just to see if there's something you could need.

Because I possess the great wealth of Dharma, I am happy.

This is quite simple and straightforward but often people don't realize its significance, don't realize that they've got the wealth of the Dharma. They feel as though they are poor, they don't appreciate what they've really got. They don't realize that the Dharma is in fact wealth.

Because I worry not about property, I am happy.

If you have ever owned property, you will know that you certainly have to worry about it. You've got to look after it, you've got to keep it in repair, you've got to guard it against encroachment. Whenever you get one thing finished, something else goes wrong. Either it's falling down or it needs repair or it needs painting. Milarepa's statement might suggest that it's possible to have property and not worry about it, and presumably there are some people who can, but I would think they are relatively rare.

Because I have no fear of losing anything, I am happy.

He doesn't possess anything, so he's got no fear of losing anything. If you possess something, there's usually the fear of losing it. Again we must strike a note of caution, because you can't be afraid of losing something unless you feel that you possess it. In modern times it sometimes happens that people have lost the sense of possession. They don't worry about losing something because they take it for granted that it will be possible to replace it immediately. People are like spoiled children with their toys; they just smash them, they don't bother about looking after them. People sometimes have that attitude towards their marriage too: they don't bother to get on with their wife or husband because they are replaceable. Very often people don't take trouble with their friendships or relationships, feeling that if things don't work out for one reason or another, that person can just be replaced with somebody else. This means again that there can be no question of detachment or giving up, because there is no real attachment or feeling of possession in the first place.

It's well known, for instance, that public property is nobody's property. People treat it carelessly because they don't feel that it's theirs. To misuse things because you have no sense of ownership is not a positive thing. But what do you gain by considering something as yours in a positive way? Is it really a virtue to look after things and make them last a long time? To take a concrete example, when people on a retreat break cups, from a subjective point of view it's unmindfulness, but objectively it means that those things have got to be replaced, and that means using other people's energy and money. In society in general, if people misuse public resources, other people have got to replace those if a certain level is to be kept up. (It could be, of course, that the level is too high, in which case too many things are being produced and people are having to put too much time and energy into those things.) The argument against misusing things is that other people have got to put time and energy and money into replacing them, and they might be able to use that time, energy, and money more positively. It's shameful to read of vandals burning down schools, doing in one night hundreds of thousands of pounds' worth of damage. That has all got to be paid for by the tax payer, and that money could certainly be used more positively, even if it was just sent to some other country that was in need. Of course, vandals aren't unmindful of the effects of their actions; their aim is to inconvenience people, to make people suffer. It seems to stem from an alienation from society, the propagation of a wrong ideology. In the UK the welfare state ideology is that you've got a right to everything, whereas in communist countries you're taught to respect public property. If you damage what belongs to the whole community, you are severely punished and you have to make it good, so there isn't much in the way of vandalism. People are educated to value public property, and damage to the property of the people is an offence that is taken very seriously. But in the UK, damage to public property is a very insignificant offence, because private property is what is considered important. We think, 'What does it matter? The government will pay.' But it's the people who really pay.

From a psychological point of view, to have everything readily replaceable, and therefore disposable, including even people, isn't good. People used to work for the same firm all their lives, and perhaps that had a negative aspect, but the positive side was that if you worked for a small firm for many years, you had time to build up a relationship with the people you worked with. If you're just in and out, there's no time to build up any relationship, even if the company is small enough for you to be able to do so. The quality of work deteriorates as well, because you don't feel any responsibility, or any pride in your work.

So it would seem that our mobility has some disadvantages. When I moved from India to England after twenty years, though I was glad I did it and I did it for a certain reason, it was very disruptive personally because it meant that a whole network of relationships that I'd built up in India was disrupted, and at the age of forty I had to start all over again. It's only looking back that I realize what a big disruption it was. One should avoid that sort of thing. It's all very well to be non-attached, but to disrupt positive relationships which have been developed over a long period of time is quite undesirable. For instance, I now think that the chairmen of Buddhist centres need to spend quite a long time in a particular place, maybe in some cases all their lives. I used to say that one shouldn't spend more than two or three years in one place, to avoid getting into a rut, getting attached. But perhaps the danger nowadays is the opposite: not getting involved enough to start becoming attached. Perhaps we've had enough of keeping moving; we need to put down our roots and expand from that point. Not that we shouldn't travel, but we should do it from an established centre – I mean a personal, even geographical centre.

Apart from anything else, if one has a network of relationships, one can get so many more things done. Even if one moves from one place to another, one should be careful to keep up old relationships, at least to the extent of writing, or sending cards, or phoning occasionally or meeting up when possible – unless you've outgrown those relationships or feel it would be harmful to continue them. Otherwise, you find that every few years you have to begin a whole new round of making friends, and you have no long-standing friendships. What was a virtue in medieval Tibet runs the risk of almost being a vice now. You have to be very careful in evaluating what is skilful and what is unskilful, especially when talking in terms of non-attachment, because in the ears of the modern person this might suggest indifference or just not caring, absence of feeling, virtually alienation. T. S. Eliot is not a poet I like very much, but I appreciate what he says in one of his poems: 'Teach us to care and not to care.'[128] It's not enough to learn not to care; you've got to learn to care as well. Not caring has no significance unless you're able to care. Non-attachment has no meaning unless you're full-blooded enough to be capable of attachment and all that it involves.

The nature of travel has changed drastically since Milarepa's time. In the past you travelled mostly on foot, so there was a very slow change of scene, but now you can go so quickly, by air especially, or even by car, that travelling means hurrying, and to the extent that you are hurrying, even if unintentionally, that is conducive to alienation. Travel can be good, but it has to be real travel, not simply being transported from place to place. In the old days, to get from Norwich to London would have taken several days, whereas now it takes a couple of hours. We've got used to it, but it can't be good for us. To get to Holland in half an hour or to find yourself in India in seven or eight hours is terrible. You fly over all the intervening countries, but you don't experience them, and in a few hours' time you have to deal with a complete change of scenery, climate, food, people, and culture. How wonderful it would be if you could walk instead! We don't really travel in modern times: we're just lifted up and plonked down somewhere.

Another aspect of modern life is seeing so many people with whom you don't have any relationship. In Milarepa's time, in this village where he was meditating and where Rechungpa met him, there were perhaps a few dozen people at most, and you would spend your whole life in communication with a relatively small number of people. It had its limitations, but it did mean that you were really in contact with those people. Looking back on my days in Kalimpong, I knew everybody in the town: all the officials, the shopkeepers, the schoolteachers, the doctors, the students, the coolies, everybody. I didn't have to make any special effort; it just happened, because one was part of the community and included in everything, at least when it was appropriate, which almost every occasion was.

What we have to watch out for is, in a word, alienation. We have to keep a very close eye on those qualities that are traditionally considered to be virtues like detachment or non-attachment, but which in our case may conduce to further alienation. The precepts almost have to be rewritten bearing things like that in mind. It's like advising someone to leave home who has been brought up in an orphanage, or by their ex-stepfather's ex-wife or something like that.

Since I never dread exhaustion, I am happy.

Why does he not dread exhaustion? Well, he's been doing nothing but meditating. There's no question of exhaustion: he's not expending energy, but taking it in. Exhaustion is a typically modern complaint. People may have felt tired in ancient times, but no one is ever described as having 'nervous exhaustion'. Nervous exhaustion is due to constant wear and tear and a constant succession of impressions that never impress you, or feelings that you are never able to feel. You can feel exhausted being swept from place to place at high speed, with impressions constantly impinging on you and having to take in far too many of them. You reach a point where you can take in no more and you feel exhausted. You haven't done anything – you've just been subject to a constant bombardment.

Having fully realized Mind-Essence, I am happy.

Mind-Essence (Tibetan *sems nyid*) is the open, ungraspable nature of mind; it corresponds to the Sanskrit term *cittata*.

As I need not force myself to please my patrons, I am happy.

The patrons are the lay supporters, but why bring up the idea of forcing himself to please them? Someone living a monastic or hermit life might become dependent on lay people for economic support, but at the same time the lay people might become dependent upon the monk or yogi for psychological support. They thus come to depend upon your being the sort of person they expect you to be, or would like you to be, or think you ought to be, and that means you have to conform to their expectations. You can't lead your own life; you have to please your supporters. One certainly finds this in Buddhist countries; the monks are economically dependent on the lay people, and in many cases the lay people expect something in return – very often a wholehearted endorsement of their existing attitudes. They expect a monk to be a pillar of the established order. You find this, for instance, in Thailand, where the sangha is under the control of the education department, and the monks are not permitted to do or say anything that would displease the government, on the grounds that monks are not supposed to meddle in politics. If any monk is thought to be meddling in politics, even to the extent of expressing an opinion, the ministry of education instructs his abbot that the miscreant must disrobe and return to lay life. He may not have done anything against the Vinaya; he may be a perfectly good monk. Some years ago there was a notorious case of a well-known senior monk in Bangkok who was found by the police to be in possession of Marxist literature. There was no question of his being a Communist sympathizer – he just thought he ought to inform himself of what was going on – but he was arrested and forcibly disrobed in jail. Some years later, with a change of government, he managed to get himself reinstated. I met him in Calcutta when he was quite elderly, and I can vouch for the fact that he was a quiet, respectable monk, very scholarly and studious; he just kept and read the 'wrong sort' of books. They had a sort of McCarthyist attitude in Bangkok at that time, as a result of which he had suffered, but he stuck to his guns and would not recognize that he had been disrobed. He insisted that he was still a *bhikkhu*. My Thai *bhikkhu* friends were outraged, but they couldn't say anything: any protest from them would have landed them all in jail. They were expected absolutely to toe the government line. They weren't even supposed to read books that the government didn't approve of. It's Erastianism, pure and simple:[129] the complete control of the church by the state, the church being considered a sort of department of the state, and the priests and ministers as civil servants. The *bhikkhus* in Thailand receive a state allowance according to the grade of Pāli examination they have passed; it's just like the Civil Service. Innocent Western Buddhists think that these *bhikkhus* are living like *bhikkhus* in the Buddha's day, just because they are wearing yellow robes, but that is far from being the case. In the Buddha's day the kings listened to what the Buddha and the monks had to say; it's the other way round now.

The only way you can avoid this sort of thing happening is to set up your own economic basis. If you've got patrons, a sort of *quid pro quo* is understood, and you have to please them to some extent. Even the best of monks do it. When I lived in Kalimpong I got into a great deal of trouble because I spoke my mind to some of the local Buddhist notables. I did get certain things changed, but that was because I'd built up a network of relationships. I can't do that sort of thing in England, because that network doesn't exist here.

Having no fatigue nor weariness, I am happy.

I suppose he has no fatigue or weariness for the same reason that he never dreads exhaustion: because there is a perpetual source of energy bubbling up within him, because he's doing nothing but meditating.

As I need prepare for nothing, I am happy.

The kind of preparation he means is presumably planning, scheming, looking ahead, making provision for this and that. He has no need to worry about any of that, because he has no needs to satisfy and he isn't worried what happens to him. Very often people worry about what is going to happen, and then it doesn't happen, and they realize they might just as well not have worried. Sometimes you objectively need to plan ahead, but that's different from worrying about the future, and even having to plan ahead is sometimes quite bothersome, so it would be better if you were free from that, unless you've got the sort of mind that needs that sort of exercise. In Milarepa's case he is able to live completely in the present.

Since all I do complies with Dharma, I am happy.

Everything that he does, says, and thinks is a natural, spontaneous expression of the Dharma. He is the living embodiment of the Dharma, and there is no question of his ever doing anything that is not in accordance with it – so he is happy. It's not that he has to think 'What is the Dharma?' and then, laboriously and with great effort and difficulty, comply with it. He has become completely attuned to the Dharma, so everything that he does, everything that he says, everything that he thinks, is a natural expression of the Dharma.

Never desiring to move, I am happy.

Rechungpa has been to India and back, the enterprising young disciple, but the old guru has just stayed in the same spot, not moving or even opening his eyes, apparently. Why do you move? It's because you're not happy where you are. Why do you fidget when you meditate? It's because you are not comfortable. In the same way, why do you go out of the door? It's due to some dissatisfaction. If you are completely happy where you are, why should you move? You only move in order to remove a discomfort. The bodhisattva neither comes nor goes, we are told, but that's getting rather metaphysical. Never desiring to move – maybe that is the point. Milarepa has no neurotic craving to move. Of course, there might be an objective need – you might need to go to the toilet, or someone might need something – but there is no inner restlessness, dissatisfaction or discomfort that impels you to move. Sometimes people get into a mood of just wanting to go out – not that they particularly want to do anything, but they just don't want to stay where they are.

As the thought of death brings me no fear, I am happy.

People are often afraid of death, especially as they get older. They start thinking about it more and more, and it makes them feel quite uncomfortable, or even miserable. But Milarepa isn't worried. The thought of death brings him no fear, so he's happy. But here again, one must be careful. One has to be capable of being afraid of death, and of being attached to life. Sometimes 'lack of fear of death' is just a lack of imagination, an inability to even imagine yourself as dead.

Bandits, thieves, and robbers ne'er molest me,
so at all times I am happy!

Milarepa was famous for this. He had nothing for anyone to take away, so of course thieves didn't molest him. There's a story in his biography about an incident when he was staying in a cave and at night some thieves came groping around for something they could steal. To the thieves' surprise, Milarepa burst out laughing and said, 'Well, I couldn't even find anything by day, so I don't suppose you'll find anything at night!'[130] The robbers themselves couldn't help laughing, and they went away. It was well known that he was only an old yogi sitting in a cave, so there was no point in trying to rob him. He didn't have any money hidden away. But when you have a lot of possessions, it's not just a question of looking after them, but preventing people from taking them.

> *Having won the best conditions for Dharma practice, I*
> *am happy.*

That sounds a strange statement. All he's got is a cave and nothing to eat, yet he says he's found the best conditions for Dharma practice! Some people think you need a lot of things for Dharma practice: a beautiful well-furnished place and a band of disciples to look after you, and someone to cook your food, and someone to run your errands, and all the rest of it. So often people think that in order to practise the Dharma they need a lot of equipment, like needing special gear when you take up a sport. People are very concerned about getting the right sort of robe, the right sort of cushion, or the right books, or exactly the right meditation, and they think that without these things they won't be able to meditate at all.

> *Having ceased from evil deeds and left off sinning, I am happy.*

There's not much scope for evil deeds when you're all alone in a cave and meditating all the time. But it's quite a consideration: that you don't even have to be meditating. If you are just sitting still and doing nothing, at least you are doing no harm. That's a considerable achievement. At least you're not breaking any precepts, so long as you're just sitting there. The chances are that as soon as you get up and start doing something, or as soon as you open your mouth, bang will go a precept, in one way or another. But if you're just sitting there, especially with your eyes closed, even without meditating you're not, overtly at least, breaking any precepts.

This draws attention to the importance of non-action. So often we tend to think in terms of 'doing good', but before we think about that, we could just stop all the mischief we're doing. Likewise, very often the best thing you can do for other people is just to leave them alone. Just don't get in their way – that's quite an important contribution to their welfare.

> *Treading the Path of Merits, I am happy.*

This is the path of skilful actions that results in *puṇya*, in merit, but in what sense is Milarepa treading it? He's not doing anything at all, sitting in the cave, so how can he say he is 'treading the path of merits'? Well, he is constantly producing highly skilful mental states, and what could be more meritorious than that? The merit is derived from the mental attitude with which you perform the so-called skilful action, or speak the so-called skilful word. Skilful thought is the essence of what is skilful and meritorious. Meditation is an uninterrupted flow of positive mental states. What could be more productive of merit than that?

Divorced from hate and injury, I am happy.

It's not clear whether this refers to his own mind being free from hate and injury, or the fact that alone in his cave he is free from the hatred and injury that might be inflicted by others.

Having lost all pride and jealousy, I am happy.

If you're living on your own, there's not much scope for pride or jealousy, both of which involve a comparison with other people.

Understanding the wrongness of the Eight Worldly Winds,
    I am happy.

These are the same eight worldly winds that were mentioned earlier. Understanding the wrongness of them presumably means understanding the way in which the mind oscillates between them, or is affected by them, the way it is happy when it experiences pleasure, unhappy when it experiences pain, and so on.

Absorbed in quiet and evenmindedness, I am happy.

Often people think that being quiet and evenminded is a dull, wretched state to be in – no fun, nothing stimulating – but actually that isn't so. Absorption in quiet and evenmindedness – that's the true happiness.

Using the mind to watch the mind, I am happy.

Obviously this is not an alienated awareness, not just standing aside, isolating oneself from one's own mind; the point is that he is completely aware.

> *Without hope or fear, I am ever happy.*

Here's another pair of opposites. People are often thinking in terms of hope and fear, hope representing something positive that they would like to have, and fear something negative that they would like to avoid.

> *In the sphere of non-clinging Illumination, I am happy.*

The suggestion is that this is a state of awareness, a state even of Enlightenment, in which there is no distinction between subject and object. Where there's no distinction between subject and object, how can there be clinging?

> *The Non-distinguishing Wisdom of Dharmadhātu itself*
> *is happy.*

It is non-distinguishing in the sense that it doesn't see any absolute distinction between this and that. It sees everything equally as void.

> *Poised in the natural realm of Immanence, I am happy.*

Immanence seems to translate *sahaja*, which means that which is innate or congenital. One has an experience of poise and balance and at the same time an experience of spontaneous action, and these are expressive of a state that is natural not in the ordinary sense of the term but in a metaphysical sense. They represent what belongs to you in the deepest sense; they're an expression of your ultimate nature. If you give expression to your real nature in the deepest sense, you're very poised, very balanced, because you're established on your deepest foundation, and at the same time you have complete freedom and spontaneity.

> *In letting the Six Groups of Consciousness go by*
> *To return to their original nature, I am happy.*

Presumably he's referring to the five sense-consciousnesses and the sixth sense, the mind-consciousness. By 'allowing them to return to their original nature' he must mean not giving them any attributes. The information just comes in. and the senses function in a completely natural, objective way. The eye is simply seeing, the ear is simply hearing. There's no subjective reaction. The mind is thinking, but there's no worrying, no evaluating.

> *The five radiant gates of sense all make me happy.*

There's nothing wrong with the senses, nothing wrong with seeing colours or hearing sounds. The damage is done when the mind, the defiled mind-consciousness, starts thinking in terms of attachment: this is mine, that is yours and so on.

> *To stop a mind that comes and goes is happy.*

To stop the mind that comes and goes, the restless, clinging mind that tries to find satisfaction, the mind that is now here and now there, is happy.

> *Oh, I have so much of happiness and joy!*
> *This is a song of gaiety I sing,*
> *This is a song of gratitude to my Guru and the Three*
> *   Precious Ones –*
> *I want no other happiness.*

So that is all he wants. He's quite content with his guru and the Three Jewels.

> Rechungpa said to Milarepa, 'I am well again. I have obtained what
> I wanted. From now on I would like to remain in solitude and stay
> near you. Please be so kind as to grant me further inner teachings.'

So Rechungpa would now like to stay near Milarepa. He might as well have done that in the first place! Maybe he would have been cured anyway if he had – we don't know. But anyway, he is well again now, he asks for 'further inner teachings' – teachings about meditation – and Milarepa gives them to him.

Milarepa then imparted to Rechungpa additional instructions and stayed with him in the Silk Cave. Through the continued practice of meditation Rechungpa attained the perfect Experiences and Realization.

This is the story of Milarepa meeting his Heart-Son Rechungpa in the cave of Za 'og.

I'm not sure that we are to take Rechungpa's 'perfect experiences' completely literally, because quite a lot of things happen to him after this, as we will see, but at any rate he had quite a deep experience of meditation under Milarepa's guidance at that time.

So Rechungpa meets Milarepa, is inspired by him and practises with him, but then is cursed by his mother and his uncle, becomes afflicted with leprosy, meets the five yogis, goes off to India, gets cured, returns, finds Milarepa still meditating, is afraid he is dead, enquires after his health, hears that song from Milarepa, and then meditates with Milarepa for a while. It seems quite typical, in a general way, of the whole spiritual life. You know that in a sense all you've got to do is sit down and get on with your practice, but there are always things that assail you, that make you a bit restless and want to go off and do something else, and then come back. Things come back from the past too, as represented by the mother and the uncle. It wasn't so easy for Rechungpa to get away from them. Whereas Milarepa's spiritual life was so smooth once he got on to the right path, Rechungpa is rather like a young horse that needs to be got into harness. Well, he was very young, probably just a teenager, when he first met Milarepa. It's as if he had to prepare himself before he was able to sit down and meditate – because Milarepa never forces him to do anything. He doesn't scold him. Whatever he might think, he lets him go off, and lets him come back. While he's away, he just gets on with his own meditation. He doesn't send him anxious messages: 'How are you getting on in India? Are you cured yet?' He just sits there. If Rechungpa hadn't come back, presumably he would have just gone on meditating.

As I've said before, the guru doesn't have to teach anyone.[131] That's why Milarepa said 'I need not force myself to please my patrons'. Some patrons expect you to give little sermons every now and then. They might not listen, but it's your duty to give them, because they are giving you financial support. When I was at the Hampstead Buddhist Vihara, one of the complaints some people made about me was that I wasn't there all day every day. They seemed to expect me to be what in India is called a *chokidar*, a sort of glorified watchman on duty on the door. I had a duty to be there, and they had the right to be annoyed if I was not, as though they were employing me. It was really very strange. One of the things they charged me with when they decided not to renew my invitation to stay there was that I had absented myself from the vihara, almost like absenting yourself from the army without leave. They didn't seem to appreciate that I was a free agent staying there for their benefit, totally of my own free will, and perfectly free to come and to go when I wished. It was as though I was a truant schoolboy. If anyone rang up, I had to be there to answer the phone and tell people whether there was a lecture on Sunday and what the title was, whether there was a meditation class on Thursday and so on and so forth. This was the attitude of quite a few people. It wasn't even as though they paid me! They had taken on the view that the lay people literally control the *bhikkhu*, as though he was a sort of domestic chaplain in the eighteenth-century sense, to say grace when required and keep quiet at other times. That attitude was crowned by Christmas Humphreys' famous remark that I should consider myself – he thought this quite a high ideal for me to aim at – the Buddhist equivalent of the vicar of Hampstead.

What surprised me was that there were people who regretted having invited me when they found I wasn't a strict Theravādin. They had reviewed my *Survey of Buddhism* – not only reviewed it but praised it – but it was as if they didn't take seriously what I wrote in criticism of the modern Theravāda. They seemed not to dream of the possibility that I was going to act upon it, or take my own words seriously. They hadn't taken seriously my very strong expression of faith in the Mahāyāna, or at least the Mahāyāna attitude. This is something that people find very difficult to appreciate: that one means what one says. The great English writers, and poets especially, don't just spout flowery words or highfaluting sentiments – what they write is what they actually think and really believe. It was like that with D. H. Lawrence; people didn't always take seriously what he said, but he meant it. He may have been wrong sometimes, but he meant what he said. I found the same thing, that people didn't take seriously what I said. They thought I was just making the usual conventional gestures in the direction of the bodhisattva ideal.

SECOND STORY
RECHUNGPA'S THIRD JOURNEY TO INDIA

In which Rechungpa wants to go to India again, to learn logic, so that he can defeat scholars in argument. Milarepa advises him not to go, but he insists, and also insists on receiving the guru's blessing for the journey. Milarepa finds a compromise: he can go, but for the purpose of bringing back the Formless Ḍākinī Dharmas. It is important to bear in mind that this story in *The Hundred Thousand Songs* immediately follows one called 'The Challenge of the Logicians', in which Milarepa manages to convince one of the two scholars who challenge him without resorting to logic; Rechungpa, however, still wants to beat the scholars at their own game.

Themes:

- logical argument and skilful communication 352
- discipline and training 357
- intellectual understanding 359
- motive is all-important 361
- the quality of your own being 362
- what really produces results, power mode or love mode? 363
- giving advice 363
- wanting the guru's approval and your own way 367
- we don't need all the teachings to gain Enlightenment 369
- what are transcendental *ḍākinīs*? 370

I
THE ART OF DEBATE

Obeisance to all Gurus.

Through his miraculous powers the Jetsun Milarepa had
conquered the scholar-priests in their ill-intentioned debate and
had won the argument. However, his heart-son, Rechungpa,
was not satisfied with this victory, for he thought that the Jetsun
had not answered the monk's questions in a scholarly manner.
'The only way,' Rechungpa thought to himself, 'to conquer
these scholars, who cannot even be convinced by the evidence of
miracles, is through logic and argument, or by black magic and
curses. I might ask the Jetsun to teach me black magic, but it is
not likely that he would. Oh, confound it! These damned scholars
who belittle genuine miracles as sorceries! They certainly deserve
to be dealt with! But the Jetsun will never do it. Well, it is true
that my Guru is well-versed in the Pith-Instructions for attaining
Buddhahood in one life, but in order to beat these scholars, I shall
go to India to learn logic and science.' He then went to Milarepa
and told him of his intention. The Jetsun said, 'Rechungpa, if we
had been defeated in the debate, how could the scholars have
credited us with pure (thoughts)? If you go to India merely for
the purpose of learning the art of debate, you are then doing
something wrong and worthless. (That also means that you will)
forsake meditation practice. In learning 'semantics,' you may

acquire some knowledge about words, but still you will not be able to win all the debates, nor can you master the whole study of letters. Only Buddha can answer all questions and challenges, but to achieve Buddhahood one must practice. Therefore, the best way is to abjure the world, renounce all thoughts and wishes of this life, and devote oneself to meditation. One may slay people by black magic but if he cannot deliver the victims (from Saṃsāra) both he and the victims will be damned. Formerly I used black magic to curse my enemies, but because of this sinful deed I had to go through many painful trials under Marpa. Life is very short, no one can tell when death will fall upon him. Therefore please forget everything else and concentrate on your meditation.'

What are we to make of Rechungpa's statement that the only way to beat the scholars is 'through logic and argument or by black magic and curses'? He seems to want to meet the logicians on their own ground, but why? After all, apparently Milarepa has already conquered them, so why is Rechungpa so concerned that they should be conquered through logic and argument? It's possible that he himself needs convincing on those grounds; perhaps he isn't satisfied with Milarepa's approach. On the other hand, he is blaming the scholar monks for belittling genuine miracles of sorcery, as though he has great faith in those genuine miracles whereas they do not. But his basic mistake goes deeper than all this. It seems that he has got a fixed idea about how things are to be done, and in particular how people are to be 'conquered'. The scholar-priests have been defeated in debate and Rechungpa acknowledges that, but apparently that is not enough for him, because he is over-attached to doing things in a particular way, attaching too much importance to a particular means and not giving enough recognition to the end. Even though the logicians have been defeated already, they've got to be defeated all over again in the way to which Rechungpa himself attaches such great importance, namely logic and science. This seems to be quite a common attitude. Very often people can't find it in themselves to be happy that something has been done, even if they agree that it needed doing, if it hasn't been done their way.

> *Rechungpa, if we had been defeated in the debate, how could the scholars have credited us with pure (thoughts)?*

If the priests didn't have any appreciation of sorcery, one might wonder how they could be defeated in that way rather than on their own grounds, the grounds of debate. Milarepa's statement refers to what happened in the previous chapter, at the end of which the chief logician says, 'I am convinced that what Milarepa has said is true and that we logicians have little sincerity, faith or devotion; nor do we have the pure thoughts and spirit of renunciation.' So the logicians have admitted defeat. What is important, Milarepa is saying, is that they should have recognized the genuineness of our motivation, the purity of our thoughts, the correctness of our attitude. The fact that they did so, and incidentally recognized the wrongness of their own attitude, is the real defeat – nothing to do with logical argument or science, or scoring this or that particular point. Maybe Milarepa could have won an argument on their own grounds but according to him that is not the true victory. They are really defeated when they acknowledge their fault as they have done and recognize the purity of Milarepa's attitude, in other words when they adopt a genuinely open attitude towards him. It's not really a contest between opposing points of view or opposing doctrines. It's a conflict between two people – in this case between Milarepa and the leading logician – so the victory is a victory not in terms of argument but in terms of individuals. Milarepa conquers his opponent when the opponent recognizes that he himself is insincere in his approach and Milarepa is sincere. That's what the debate is all about. Milarepa is thinking in terms of human communication, one could say, whereas Rechungpa is thinking in terms of technical debate. Milarepa is telling him to forget about the logical rights and wrongs. What interests him is that the other person has renounced his stubborn opinionated attitude and has opened himself to Milarepa, recognizing Milarepa's superior spiritual attainment.

But Rechungpa is obsessed with this idea of defeating the logicians by logical means, which suggests that he is preoccupied with victory in the narrower, more superficial sense. He's not concerned with human communication, he's not impressed that the logician has now opened himself to Milarepa. He wants him to be defeated. He wants to rub his nose in the dust, which indicates a revengeful attitude.

We can look at Rechungpa's mistaken attitude from several points of view. To begin with, he is not satisfied that the logician should have conceded defeat, he wants him to be defeated in a particular way. He thinks that 'the only way to conquer these scholars, who cannot even be convinced by the evidence of miracles, is by logic and argument or by black magic and curses'. That gives the game away, because black magic and curses represent, in a word, power, and within the spiritual context you can never defeat people by power. Trying to defeat people by reason and argument is a way of using power, and maybe that sums up Rechungpa's whole attitude. He wants to deal with the logicians in one way or another by the exercise of power, while Milarepa is content to deal with them by means of love, in the sense of *mettā*, or more than that, in the sense of *mahā karuṇā*, great compassion. So far as Milarepa is concerned, the fact that the logician has acknowledged his mistake is enough. He doesn't want him to be humiliated in the way Rechungpa apparently does.

When you're engaged in discussion with somebody, you need to be clear that what you're trying to do in putting across your point of view or your attitude is to get the other person to open himself up to you, which means of course that you must open yourself up to the other person. In other words, you must be careful to make sure that you are really trying to communicate with the other person, not just trying to beat him or her down in argument. Sometimes that may be necessary, if the other person's attitude is intensely competitive or overbearing or arrogant, but you have to be quite sure that you are able to argue skilfully; otherwise, however right you may be, you will end up looking rather foolish and then you may even start feeling angry and frustrated. But apart from that, you have to be concerned that you are doing your best to create open communication, that you're not just trying to score technical debating points and win an argument. There is a saying, 'Win an argument and lose a friend,' but it's better to lose the argument and win the friend. You can have an argument, even quite a strong one, and you may be logically defeated in everything that you say, but if you keep a positive, open attitude, the other person may go away quite impressed and think things over seriously. You haven't really lost, if you've maintained your openness and your willingness to communicate. All the time you must be concerned, even when you are right, that you are not just pushing an opinion, even a right opinion, but genuinely trying to communicate. This is what Milarepa seems to be emphasizing. He is concerned with converting people to the right path but Rechungpa is just concerned with enjoying a victory over them, regardless of what happens to them.

In the course of discussion we should be very careful to ensure that our own attitude doesn't subtly change. If people are being argumentative in a foolish, subjective way, if they're wriggling on the hook but not admitting it, and obviously closed to whatever you have to say, you can start getting a bit impatient, frustrated that they're not recognizing your point of view, and then you may want to start beating them down in the argument. But if you do that, you're functioning on the same level as them even though in a sense you are in the right, and that doesn't help. Just as in a general way there is a point at which you can either go in the direction of creativity or in the direction of reactivity, in the course of discussion you can either go the way of trying to communicate and be open or the way of trying to crush and defeat the other person in argument. In other words, there's always the danger that we can be tempted to switch from the love mode to the power mode. We have to watch for this all the time, especially those of us who are young and convinced that we're absolutely right about everything. The way some people try to put across Buddhism doesn't sound like Buddhism at all, but like something completely different. The fact that Rechungpa thinks in terms of convincing the scholar-priests by black magic and curses gives the game away, because to curse someone is to try to bring evil and harm upon them, which means that your attitude is the exact opposite of what it needs to be.

So Milarepa says to Rechungpa:

> If you go to India merely for the purpose of learning the art
> of debate, you are then doing something wrong and worthless.
> (That also means that you will) forsake meditation practice.

Again Milarepa is saying that it's not a question of words or logic or argument; it is a question of being. It is your being that convinces the other person, so you must as it were cultivate your being; and you do that through meditation. If you meditate, you will transform yourself. If you transform yourself, you will impress the other person whatever you say, whether you know logic or not. You needn't mind being defeated in argument, or exposed as ignorant of this or that. What really matters is the state of your own being, and if the other person becomes open to this as the logician became open to Milarepa's state of being, that's all that you need. You have won the argument. It's the quality of your being that is important, and the study of logic and reasoning is not going to improve that. Milarepa is saying, don't think that by going to India and learning logic and debate you're really going to be able to defeat other people. What is more, in order to study logic and debate you'll be giving up the practice of meditation, and that is what is going to transform you, that is what in the long run is going to help you to conquer other people if you want to think of it in that way.

But if Milarepa had been able to convince the scholar also on the basis of logical argument, would that not represent a more total victory? Yes and no:

> In learning 'semantics' you may acquire some knowledge about words, but still you will not be able to win all the debates, nor can you master the whole study of letters.

You can never reach a final conclusion by means of logical argument. You may be much more spiritually advanced than your opponent, but he may be much more adept at handling logical weapons than you are. Sometimes you can have the experience of arguing with someone who is better at arguing than you are and he defeats you in argument, but you know or you feel that he's not right, that you've not been defeated. I'm not referring to the sort of situation in which you refuse to acknowledge defeat out of mere stubbornness, but to the times when you know that you've been bamboozled with some apparently logical arguments but you don't know enough about logic to be able to point out the flaws in the argument. Milarepa is saying that you may have all the tricks of the logical trade at your fingertips but, even so, you won't win all the arguments. You may well meet someone who is cleverer at arguing than you. You know their arguments are sophistical but you can't answer them on logical grounds, because you're not sufficiently skilled. But suppose you were. Suppose you did defeat the other person but he wouldn't acknowledge defeat. What would you do then? You've used all your arguments, you've defeated him logically, he's unable to reply, but he doesn't change his opinion, he doesn't come over to your way of thinking, because there's a very deep conditioning in him which goes beyond logic. You may have defeated him logically but he has still not been defeated. So we come back to Milarepa's point that you defeat someone in this sort of situation only when he opens himself to you.

Sometimes you may have a discussion with somebody and that person may wipe the floor with you logically but nonetheless you've come across so positively that that person is impressed despite themselves. So who has lost and who has won?

> *Only Buddha can answer all questions and challenges, but to achieve Buddhahood one must practice.*

By this Milarepa does not exactly mean that the Buddha is the best of all debaters. It's not that the Buddha can answer all questions on their own level to the perfect satisfaction of the questioner, but he knows what is best to say whatever the circumstances, whether the listener is satisfied or not. Some of the arguments that the Buddha uses in the scriptures that convinced the people he was talking to don't convince us, but we don't 'drop' the Buddha, so to speak, because of that, because we recognize that the quality of the Buddha's being transcends particular arguments, transcends whatever he says, just as we know within ourselves on a much lower level that we can't often communicate all that we think, all that we feel, all that we understand or all that we've experienced. Our power of expression falls far short of that. Sometimes we wish we could communicate to people what we actually feel, what we actually experience, but it's very difficult. The fact that we can't communicate it, however, doesn't mean that it isn't there. Perhaps we can communicate it only under rather special conditions, especially when the other person is really open. Some people expect you to communicate and at the same time they destroy the very means of communication. They say, 'Come on, we've got two minutes – tell me all about Nirvāṇa! I'm giving you your chance! Convince me.' When they lay down conditions of that sort, they are in effect removing any possibility of communication. You can't communicate with anybody against their will; even a Buddha cannot do that. So logic is out, black magic is out, curses are out, because they are all forms of power, and you can't lead anyone onto the spiritual path through power but only through *mettā* and *karuṇā*, loving-kindness and compassion. You can't compel anybody.

This raises the whole question of imposing discipline on people. You can threaten someone in some way to stop them misbehaving and make them a more positive member of the group. That works – you see it in the army, for example – and you can produce quite positive, healthy people through the fear of punishment in one form or another, but you haven't produced individuals. A good healthy group member is a candidate for individuality, but you can't make someone an individual by using the same methods in a more refined form. You can force someone to come and sit in the meditation room when the bell rings. You can force them to sit without moving for an hour, as they do in Zen monasteries, and it may help to produce a healthy group member; but you can't force anyone to meditate. You may force him to perform concentration exercises through fear, just about, but that's all. You can't raise the level of his consciousness by force. If he's a more positive member of the group, that can be a good basis for becoming an individual, but you cannot make him an individual by means of discipline forcibly imposed. You have to let him go his own way; his development has to be as a result of his own volition. You can't make anybody develop. You can help create the right conditions, give advice, suggestions, inspiration, but that's all you can do.

Accounts of Zen Buddhism in Japan give the impression that very often the Zen monasteries, especially when they took in boys and very young men, were not so much spiritual communities as positive groups run in a semi-military way. As a result of his individual practice the occasional person may have become an individual after a number of years, but the situation as a whole was that of a positive group at best. It's all very well to talk about a spiritual community but first of all you've got to be sure you've got individuals. If they're not individuals, at best you can have a positive group, and a positive group needs discipline, which means you've got to have someone to impose the discipline. Ideally that should be someone who is himself an individual and who is imposing the discipline to prepare the way for individuality. In residential spiritual communities people need to be very clear that they are usually not yet true spiritual communities. Sometimes people will claim that because it's a spiritual community they ought to be free to do as they like – after all they're individuals, they're responsible – but the question is whether or not they really are individuals. If they're not, they cannot be truly responsible; there must be a line and they must be made to toe it. An individual doesn't need a line except a very provisional one which maybe he chalks out himself, but those who are not individuals need definite lines, as children do. Otherwise you can't create a spiritual community.

Society as a whole should really be so structured as to give this sort of training, with or without national service (which might in some ways be a good thing), so that people progress from that society which is a positive healthy group to the spiritual community. In practice, though, society is not like that. People do not usually become positive group members, and if they do, it's more by luck than by judgement. When people become interested in Buddhism, they are not necessarily positive healthy group members who have started to get some glimmerings of individuality and want to develop in that direction. They can be reactive, even neurotic people who have got a theoretical idea about being individuals, their notion of individuality perhaps being closer to individualism.

Therefore, the best way is to abjure the world, renounce all thoughts and wishes of this life, and devote oneself to meditation.

This is not just a putting down of scriptural study. The Kagyupas emphasized meditation above all else and still do, but from various songs of Milarepa's we can see that he was quite well versed in the scriptures. We might say that by 'meditation' here Milarepa means all those practices that raise the level of consciousness, that heighten the quality of one's own being. Meditation is the most important and the most direct, but it's not the only one. But even if Milarepa is referring to all those practices and pursuits that help you to evolve and develop, clearly the science of reason and debate is not among them.

An intellectual understanding of the Dharma is needed for *vipaśyanā*, but your intellectual understanding of things need not be perfect. It may be upset by somebody who is more logical than you, but it doesn't matter. You can go on happily meditating and using your provisional intellectual structure as a basis for the development of insight nonetheless and it will still work, even though it has been pulled to pieces by somebody who is a more capable thinker than you. If you yourself are convinced that it has been pulled to pieces, then of course you've got to reconstruct the whole thing all over again, taking into account the objections that have been raised. You may modify your intellectual structure as the result of debate and discussion, or feel a need to develop your intellectual faculty to some extent. You may develop your abstract logical thinking, and as a result you may come to certain conclusions upon which you may base your development of *vipaśyanā*, but somebody else with a more powerful capacity for logical thinking may come along and upset all that. Somebody with a still more powerful logical capacity might then come along and upset *his* thinking. There is no finality on that level; this is one of the things that Milarepa is getting at. In fact, usually we don't follow logic and reasoning implicitly. As Samuel Butler says in *Hudibras*, 'He that complies against his will is of his own opinion still'.[132] We very rarely change our views for purely logical reasons; we merely elaborate them further to meet the objections that have been made.

The intellect, the rational logical process, can clarify your thinking and give you a basis for reflection, but it cannot be ultimately decisive. What matters is the quality of your being, not the technical correctness of your thinking. When asked 'What is Buddhism?' Bodhidharma replied to the Chinese emperor, 'Cease to do evil, learn to do good, purify the mind.'[133] There are people who go on arguing pro and con indefinitely and all their energy goes into that and they never get on to purifying their own being. They don't seem to think that that is relevant, even if one of the things they are arguing about is the importance of actually purifying one's own being and not just arguing about it. They will argue about that and not realize that they're still just arguing.

This doesn't mean that one should shun discussion or refuse to enter into debate, but it's best to enter into it in a very provisional way. It's like a game. Even if your argument is defeated, *you* are not defeated, and what you are is the really important thing. Sometimes a person who is intellectually not very developed will 'defeat' someone with a more powerful intellect because he has more strength of character, more genuine solidity, more openness, a greater capacity to communicate. If you are talking about Buddhism with someone who is enquiring and probing, sometimes it is better to put all your cards on the table and say, 'Look, I can't meet your arguments, I find it difficult to justify my position in terms of abstract thought, but I have practised certain things which have benefited me as a human being, and I'm convinced that if you were to practise in the same way you too would be benefited. I can't justify it logically but this is my experience. I'm like a man who switches on the electric light. I can't explain how electricity works because I've not studied that subject, I just know that it works. It's just like that with Buddhism. There are clever people who understand how it works, who have studied the Madhyamaka and the Yogācāra, but I'm not one of them. I've just pressed the switch and turned on the light. But I'm not going to deny that the light is shining because I don't know how electricity works.' One can adopt some such approach, and if something of that light is reflected in your whole attitude they cannot but be at least a little bit impressed.

> One may slay people by black magic but if he cannot deliver
> the victims (from Saṃsāra), both he and the victims will be
> damned.

Milarepa doesn't rule out the use of black magic altogether as a skilful means because in that case it's only apparently black magic. You know what you are doing. In extreme cases – this is at least hypothetically postulated – you can even kill someone by black magic, as long as you know what you are doing and can accompany their consciousness and help it after death. The Vajrayāna doesn't rule out even that possibility; obviously it's open to great misuse and misunderstanding, but nonetheless the theoretical possibility is acknowledged. Perhaps even the Mahāyāna wouldn't agree with that, and certainly Theravāda Buddhism would not, though it's only an application of the principle that it is the mental state, the intention, that really counts. You can't ensure that something is right by defining it in terms of a certain way of behaving, because there's nothing that you cannot do with the wrong motive. Motive is all-important. Putting it the other way round, if the motive is wrong it doesn't matter what you do. If the motive is right it doesn't matter what you do either, but you have to be very careful how you apply that. But Milarepa isn't adopting a dogmatic attitude here. In a way, anything goes; it depends upon your state of mind.

In the same way, although we know that one of the ten precepts enjoins us to refrain from harsh speech, one could say that it is not entirely ruled out. Sometimes the Buddha spoke a little harshly, at least in a sense. You can use rough words, strong language, with a basically positive intention. You must be quite sure that you know what you're doing, but if you can handle the situation, sometimes a few rough words can produce a very positive effect. You need to make sure that you really are speaking with a positive intention, not just out of irritation or a desire to hurt the other person. The basic principle is that it's the mental state, the intention, the volition, that is all-important. Milarepa is underlining that here. He is discouraging Rechungpa from going to India to learn logic and black magic, but he is not taking the opposite point of view. It's not as though logic and black magic can never be useful. Under certain circumstances they may work, though you need to know what you're doing. But the best way is to abjure the world, renounce all thoughts and wishes of this life and devote yourself to meditation – or as we might say, to your own spiritual development. In the long run you will defeat people – if it is a question of defeating them – by force of personality. It's that which really counts.

> Formerly I used black magic to curse my enemies, but because of this sinful deed I had to go through many painful trials under Marpa.

We read about this in the life of Milarepa.[134] In that case it was not Vajrayānic black magic, which is black on the outside but white on the inside. It was magic which was black on the outside and black on the inside too.

> Life is very short, no one can tell when death will fall upon him. Therefore please forget everything else and concentrate on your meditation.

Rechungpa is concerned about debating with and defeating others, presumably in order to convert them, but what about converting himself? This is what Milarepa is saying. If you yourself are converted – that is, if you have changed yourself through your Dharma practice – you will be able to convert others. But if you have not done that work on yourself, and just try to convince others of the merits of Dharma practice with the weapons of logic and debate, you won't succeed. It all comes back to the quality of your own being. There are no short cuts. Sometimes we might be tempted to think that our Buddhist movement would expand really rapidly if we could have millions of pounds to spend on advertising and have our own radio station, our own television channel, and so on, but it wouldn't do much good. At the very best it would bring Buddhism to people's notice. It wouldn't communicate very much about it. What you have to do is get hold of people and work with them individually.

That's a long, slow process, and there's no way of speeding it up except by increasing your own efforts.

In short, Rechungpa is too much concerned with results in a quite superficial sense. Milarepa is concerned with results too, but in a much more genuine way, because he is able to see what really produces results, and he's pointing Rechungpa in that direction, although Rechungpa is quite unwilling to go that way. This opening paragraph gives us a good picture of these two different attitudes. Milarepa is concerned with the quality of the individual being, Rechungpa is more concerned with the intellectual equipment. Rechungpa is prepared to use the power mode, while Milarepa is concerned to use the love mode. Rechungpa is thinking in terms of victory and defeating people, but Milarepa is thinking in terms of encouraging openness. One could see Milarepa's attitude as more creative, Rechungpa's attitude more reactive.

When I was in India I knew some young Hindu monks at the Ramakrishna Mission who were absolutely fascinated by the life story of Swami Vivekananda, the founder of the Mission, who went to America and conquered everybody with his oratory. They were very concerned to practise their own oratory, with the idea that they too would go to America – it was usually America – and make impressive speeches about Hinduism and the Vedanta. They imagined that people would be absolutely bowled over by that and in that way they'd be conquered by the Vedanta. Maybe you get some Buddhists thinking in that sort of way too, and perhaps Rechungpa did, but it's not a genuinely spiritual attitude.

(In spite of his guru's advice), Rechungpa pressed the Jetsun to grant him permission to go to India.

Rechungpa knows that Milarepa doesn't want him to go to India but all the same he wants Milarepa to say he may. He wants Milarepa's permission to do the very thing that Milarepa is advising him not to do. He wants to do things his own way but he still wants the guru's approval of his rejection of the guru's advice. This is what he's really asking: please give me your blessing to do the very thing that you have advised me not to do. This suggests that for Rechungpa the guru has become an approval-bestowing father-figure. Rechungpa does not wish to follow his advice, he is going directly against it, but he still wants his approval.

He doesn't say, 'I know that I'm going against your advice but I'm sorry, that's what I've got to do.' He's not really concerned with following the guru's advice or instruction, or opening himself to the influence of the guru. He just wants the guru's blessing on whatever he wants to do. That's the guru's function, in his view: to approve.

So how does Milarepa deal with this? Quite skilfully, as one might imagine. He is not blind to the situation and he's not going to allow Rechungpa to remain blind to it either. He says:

> If you insist upon ignoring my advice, you may go to India, but I am not sending you there to study logic and science.

It's a sort of compromise. Rechungpa wants to go to India to study logic and science, and he won't listen to Milarepa's advice not to go, so Milarepa says, all right, I give you my permission to go to India, but not to study logic and science. Going to India is not necessarily wrong, though it may well be the wrong thing for Rechungpa, but to go to learn logic and science is definitely wrong, and Milarepa is not giving his permission for that. He says:

> When I was with Marpa I received from him only four of the nine complete teachings of the Formless Ḍākinī Dharma Series. He said that the other five were still available in India and also prophesied that a disciple in our Lineage would later secure them from (a teacher of) Nāropa's Transmission. Thereby many sentient beings will be benefited. I am now old and sick, also I have fully realized my own mind – there is no need for me to go. I think it fitting that you go to India to procure them. You will, however, need some gold for your journey.

So if Rechungpa wants to study logic and science, he will have to do so without the guru's blessing. As far as Milarepa is concerned he can go to India but for another purpose: to obtain the remaining five of the Formless Ḍākinī Dharma Series. This refers to an esoteric Tantric teaching, formless here meaning absolute, transcendental. In the *Sūtra of Huineng*, Huineng says to his disciples, 'I shall give you a formless *gāthā*' – that is to say, an infinite *gāthā* (a *gāthā* is verse), a *gāthā* dealing with transcendental realities, not with mundane truths.[135] In the same way, the

Formless Ḍākinī Dharma Series is a series of Tantric teachings in nine parts imparted by the *ḍākinī* and dealing with transcendental realities. Of those nine parts, four have already been imparted to Milarepa by Marpa, but the remaining five have not been retrieved, so Rechungpa may make it the business of his journey to obtain those. In this way Milarepa tries to give a different kind of orientation to the trip.

If someone were to say to you, 'I want to go to India,' and you wanted to encourage them to make the most of the journey, you might say, 'All right, but don't make it just a sightseeing tour. Go on pilgrimage, go to Sarnath, go to Bodh Gaya.' In that way you wouldn't be completely opposing what they want to do but you would be trying skilfully to give it a more positive direction. Sometimes that is a better way of handling people. Don't directly oppose what they want to do. If it's completely unskilful of course you have to oppose it, but if they insist on doing what they want to do, try to make it into a more positive experience for them, just as Milarepa has done here.

At the same time, he obliges Rechungpa to face up to the fact that he is ignoring Milarepa's advice. Rechungpa is trying to create a situation in which he can feel that he has been given permission, that the guru has agreed, but Milarepa is reminding him that that is not the situation. 'You are ignoring my instructions. You are going in spite of what I say; at least recognize that. Don't try to extract a purely formal permission from me and then say that you are going with my blessing. That is not the situation. You are going in defiance of my instructions, or at least ignoring them. All right, go, but I'll give you something else to do when you're there. So far as I'm concerned you are going to obtain these five Ḍākinī Dharmas, not to study logic and science.'

Milarepa doesn't want there to be a complete conflict between himself and Rechungpa. In a sense he is in a difficult position. Rechungpa wants to do something that Milarepa is convinced is not in his best interests, and he's told him that, but he won't listen. Milarepa could break off contact completely and say, 'All right, go your own way, I've finished with you.' In a sense he would be justified in doing that, but he doesn't. He adopts a compromise which is in a sense not a compromise. He meets Rechungpa halfway, even though Rechungpa is in the wrong. He won't agree to his studying logic and science but he agrees to his going to India and he adds something else of a more positive nature for him to do when he is there. In that way Rechungpa ignores his advice, but there is no breach between them. The contact is maintained, which is of course the important thing.

There could be circumstances, perhaps, in which Milarepa would feel compelled to cut off contact; that can't be ruled out. Milarepa would not willingly create that situation, but Rechungpa might make it impossible for him to do anything else. If Rechungpa went to India and studied logic and science, it could be construed that Milarepa was sending his disciple to learn black magic, and no doubt Milarepa is fully aware of that. Rechungpa might even be telling himself that he's got permission to study logic and science, and that in the end the guru has agreed, but he doesn't like to go back on what he said before so he hasn't said so outright. One mustn't underestimate the degree of rationalization that people are capable of in order to justify doing what they want to do while retaining the approval of the appropriate authorities. On the one hand there is the fear of authority, on the other their wish to do what they want to do, and by hook or by crook they will reconcile the two.

Perhaps you have found this yourself on some occasions. If you advise people not to do something they will try to qualify the statement or make exceptions in such a way that they are able to ignore in effect the advice that you are giving them. If you warn people about the danger of dependent or neurotic relationships, they will fully accept that, but they will make all sorts of exceptions – the exceptions applying to them and not to other people. There is this desire to reconcile accepting authority with continuing to do what you want to do, and thus avoid admitting that there is any conflict. If you are a theist you may convince yourself that you are doing the will of God all the time. In effect you make your will the will of God. Likewise, the disciple convinces himself that his will is the same as the guru's. It suggests that you're not able to stand on your own feet and say, 'I think this is right so I'm going to do it.' You want to do what you want to do but you want the guru, the higher authority as you see him, to approve of what you do, to give you permission. You are sufficiently free to rebel but you're not sufficiently free to be independent. If Milarepa had definitely said 'no', one would imagine that Rechungpa would have gone to India anyway and would have broken off contact with Milarepa because he would know that he had openly disobeyed him and that would mean that he would regard the link between them as broken at least for the time being, or he might feel very guilty. He might not be able to face going back to Milarepa because he had disobeyed him so flagrantly. Clearly there was a great risk of something of that sort happening, otherwise presumably Milarepa would have insisted on his not going.

There's a parallel passage in the Pāli scriptures. The Buddha is travelling in the company of a certain *bhikkhu* who, in the course of their travels, sees a rather attractive grove of mango trees and says to the Buddha, 'Let me stay here and meditate.' The Buddha says, 'No, there is no other *bhikkhu* available to accompany me, so don't go.' The *bhikkhu* – his name is Meghiya – says, 'But I want to go and meditate. There can't be any harm in that.' The Buddha still says, 'Don't go', but Meghiya insists, saying, 'O honoured one (or whatever expression he uses), you have done what you had to do, you have gained Enlightenment, but I haven't.' What can the Buddha say to that argument? Meghiya has put the Buddha in a cleft stick, almost accusing him of being selfish because, having gained Enlightenment himself, he's not considering the needs of someone who also wants to gain Enlightenment. When he puts it in that way, what can the Buddha do? He says, 'Do as you think fit,' – that's all he can say. So off Meghiya goes, thinking to himself, 'Here I am in my mango grove – now I'm going to get on with my meditation and gain Enlightenment just like the Buddha', but it's not so easy. He starts being assailed by unskilful thoughts. He is attacked by Māra, because he isn't strong enough yet to be on his own. When he comes back to the Buddha, the Buddha explains to him that for someone as immature as he is, spiritual friendship, *kalyāṇa mitratā*, is very important. He hadn't realized that, even though he was with the Buddha himself. Maybe he thought he was achieving spiritual progress completely due to his own efforts; he didn't realize the extent to which it was due to the fact that he was with the Buddha. He's like the fly sitting on the chariot and saying, 'My! Aren't I kicking up a dust!' So he learns that lesson.[136]

Rechungpa is very much this sort of disciple. He is always wanting to go off on his own somewhere – India, Weu, or wherever it is – and Milarepa is always advising him not to go, but he always insists on going and in some cases he gets into difficulties. The disciple thinks he knows best and he wants the guru's approval for what he is doing. So he is dependent on the guru without relying on him, and he is rebellious without being really independent; and that is the situation of many people. It seems to be something inherent in ego structure. However well you've been brought up and however positive and healthy your ego is, it will start reacting and kicking in this sort of way sooner or later. When a disciple is close to the guru, and he is genuinely being brought up against himself, he is very likely to react. After all, Rechungpa did get there in the end; he did become Enlightened. But that doesn't mean that in ignoring Milarepa's advice he wasn't in the wrong. It's only because Milarepa is sufficiently skilful to be able to deal with that situation that Rechungpa is enabled to gain Enlightenment eventually. It would presumably be better if he followed the guru's advice and gained Enlightenment more quickly and with less trouble.

It isn't necessarily wrong for the disciple to want to go away from the guru. The Buddha himself said on many occasions to the *bhikkhus*, 'Here are the roots of trees, sit and meditate.' He didn't say, 'Stay with me all the time' – in fact he sent disciples away quite often. But whatever the appropriate course in any instance, the point is that the guru is more likely to know what is good for the disciple than the disciple himself. If the guru says go away and the disciple wants to stay, that is equally wrong. There was the famous case of one of the *bhikkhus* who followed the Buddha around gazing upon him all the time, and the Buddha said that that was not a very skilful thing for him to do and sent him away.[137] The point is not whether a particular line of action is right, but that the guru knows better than the disciple, and whatever the guru advises, the skilful thing for the disciple to do is to follow that advice.

In Rechungpa's case, wanting Milarepa to say yes may be a formality in one sense – it's just the words of permission he wants – but from a psychological point of view he wants his approval as an authority figure. He isn't seeking his permission as a guru because as a guru Milarepa has refused his permission and if Rechungpa regarded him as a guru he would accept that. But if Milarepa doesn't think he should go, he's hoping at least to get from Milarepa the words which he can interpret as giving approval to what he wants to do.

One therefore has to be very careful about giving advice. People may try to twist your words into some kind of approval, and in doing so they change the subject matter. You have advised them to do such and such, and they take that as meaning your approval to do something seemingly subtly different which is actually very different. Then they turn round and say, 'But you said I could do it,' and you have to say, 'I didn't mean that. You're taking my words, not my real meaning.'

Anyone giving advice needs to know the person to whom he is giving it quite well. It's not enough just to repeat general principles. You have to be able to see the situation of that person and relate the general principles to their position. It's not enough to hand out platitudes or general advice. Milarepa surely knew Rechungpa's mind, his position and his attitude, and he gave advice which Rechungpa should have followed. Anyone seriously trying to live a spiritual life needs more than general principles. That's why they need a good friend, a *kalyāṇa mitra*, who can see them more clearly than they can see themselves and help them to apply those principles specifically and concretely. That assumes that you trust that your *kalyāṇa mitra* really sees you and your situation more clearly than you see it yourself. Otherwise there's no point in asking his advice. If you just want to talk things over with someone and then make up your own mind, that's different, and sometimes it's appropriate to do that in matters which aren't of great importance.

> *Thereby many sentient beings will be benefited.*

Having told Rechungpa about the five Formless Ḍākinī Dharmas which are still available in India, Milarepa adds this remark, thus calling on Rechungpa's compassionate side. Of course any Buddhist teaching of whatever school will benefit sentient beings, but in making the point to Rechungpa, Milarepa hopes to awaken his compassion, to set his journey in a much broader, more altruistic perspective. After all, his interest in logic and science is very narrow, even selfish and egocentric – not really very spiritual. So first Milarepa tries to broaden the significance of his visit to India by asking him to obtain those particular teachings while he is there and then he adds that those teachings will be for the benefit of many sentient beings, trying to awaken more of the bodhisattva spirit in Rechungpa.

> *I am now old and sick, also I have fully realized my own mind*
> *– there is no need for me to go.*

Putting this statement together with the last one, what we learn is that we don't need all the teachings in order to gain Enlightenment. What seem to be different teachings are not really different. They are different ways of putting the same basic truths. You don't have to study all the scriptures in order to understand Buddhism; they don't represent different parts of a single whole. The same teaching is repeated in different ways from different points of view in different scriptures. Milarepa may not have learned those five extra Dākinī Dharmas, but he has learned other Vajrayāna teachings and practised the essence of them, and thus he has gained Enlightenment.

It's quite important to realize that the Buddhist scriptures are alternative formulations rather than additional teachings. You don't have to work your way systematically through all of them. The Gelugpas tend to have the attitude that you need to study all the teachings, all the scriptures, all the different systems of philosophy, before you can master Buddhism, but in the Buddha's day people gained Enlightenment by hearing, understanding, and practising a few *Dhammapada* verses. There were no scriptures and no extended teachings. A single verse could be the whole teaching so far as a particular person at a particular time was concerned. From a spiritual point of view you just need one *sūtra* perhaps, or even a few verses, or the teaching of a particular school, or a particular method of meditation. If you want to study the history of Buddhist philosophy that's another matter, but you don't have to study that in order to gain Enlightenment, unless you're one of those intellectual people who can't approach even Enlightenment except in that particular way, but then you've given yourself quite a difficult task. Quite a lot of people will try to learn something more about Buddhism without having yet put into practice what they have already learned. They spread themselves more horizontally instead of deepening or elevating their experience of Buddhism.

So there's no inconsistency in Milarepa's saying that these particular teachings will benefit many sentient beings, and saying that he doesn't need them. They will benefit the particular people to whom that particular approach is suitable.

If the Formless Dākinī Dharma Series are transcendental teachings and if those teachings are given by the *dākinīs*, those *dākinīs* can only be transcendental *dākinīs*. So what are transcendental *dākinīs*? Here *dākinī* can't just mean feminine quality in the ordinary sense. It's more like the Transcendental appearing in a feminine form. So when you get teachings from the *dākinī* aspect of reality, what is the particular significance of those teachings? These *dākinīs* aren't historical characters, they're not embodied in human form. It's different from Enlightenment, which isn't something abstract, but is actually realized by an individual human being. We sometimes think of Enlightenment as though it's something that exists apart from Enlightened beings, but actually outside sentient beings there are no Buddhas. Enlightenment is only a concept, an abstract idea, a word, but there are Enlightened beings, there are Buddhas: historical Buddhas and what we call archetypal Buddhas, for want of a better term – Buddhas like Amitābha, Amoghasiddhi and so on, who are not and never were historical characters, but exist on a different level altogether. They give a reflection of Enlightenment, so to speak – not on a historical level but on an archetypal level. When you think of Amitābha, or when you think of Amoghasiddhi, you get a particular impression; each of them reveals a particular aspect of the archetypal Buddha (the *sambhogakāya* Buddha, to use the Sanskrit term).

The Formless Ḍākinī Dharmas are specific wisdom teachings – they still exist today – but of course the association with *ḍākinīs* is suggestive. The *ḍākinī* could be said to represent that which arouses your passion for the Dharma, your desire to gain Enlightenment, so by association the Ḍākinī Dharmas could be said to be those Tantric teachings that have an exciting, exhilarating, and impassioning effect upon you. *Ḍākinīs* are represented in female form, and some are depicted in the form of naked, passionate women, which obviously allows a great deal of room for misunderstanding. Just as on the intellectual level the teaching of *śūnyatā* is meant to undo all attachment, but if you become attached to the idea of *śūnyatā* there is no hope for you,[138] similarly the figure of the *ḍākinī* is meant to energize all your spiritual, even your transcendental, energies, but if you misuse that and think of the *ḍākinī* as some particular person who excites you in a quite different sort of way, you're going to get into difficulties. The danger is that you're going to project those feelings onto a particular living female form, especially if you've only got an idea, a theory, about the *ḍākinī*. If you're genuinely meditating on a *ḍākinī* form you're much less likely to do that. It's just like the Buddha's cousin Nanda being taken to Indra's heaven by the Buddha and seeing the heavenly nymphs. All his attraction to the girl he left behind ceases.[139] So it is very much a matter for practice, not for philosophizing about. But the Vajrayāna is very much concerned with energies because while it is very easy to understand things theoretically, to arouse your energies and apply them to what you accept theoretically as your goal is a very different matter.

Ḍākinīs exist, so to speak, on different levels; the word is used in different senses. On a lower level, you can have a psychological idea of feminine qualities that you try to develop within yourself rather than projecting them on to some other person, but that is still quite mundane. Here we are concerned with a symbol for an aspect of transcendental reality. The Vajrayāna is saying that it's not enough to have the correct philosophy about the Transcendental. You've got to imagine the absolute or Enlightenment or the Buddha in such a way that you are energized and inspired. Ḍākinī Dharmas are inspirational Dharmas – not flat, dull teachings, but teachings that energize and inspire and fire you, and that is really necessary. We mustn't think too literally or technically in terms of Tantric teachings being given by *ḍākinīs*. It's really that we must see or experience the goal of Enlightenment in such a way that it's inspiring and invigorating. Tibetan Buddhist art has something of these qualities. You can get at least a feeling for what the teachings are really about through the art.

After all, Milarepa is a very skilful person. Rechungpa wants to go off to India in search of instruction in logic and science, and Milarepa has said, 'OK, go to India, but I'm not permitting you to go there for the sake of logic and science. So far as I'm concerned, you're going for the sake of the Formless Ḍākinī Dharmas.' Surely there's some significance in the fact that he is talking about those Dharmas that issue from or emphasize the inspirational, experiential aspect of reality to a person like Rechungpa. He is suggesting that Rechungpa needs balance. He's too intellectual, too concerned with logic and science. He needs to be energized with more inspiration, more colour, more life, more imagination. He's still too dull and dry and intellectual and argumentative and competitive and egoistic and narrow and self-centred. Milarepa sees him quite clearly; he sees he needs those Formless Ḍākinī Dharmas. Well, he needs the Transcendental. Everybody needs the Transcendental, but he needs that particular quality of the Transcendental, the inspirational, colourful, vibrant, exciting, arousing aspect – not just mundane, psychological excitement but something purely spiritual, even transcendental. The Formless Ḍākinī Dharmas are Dharmas that really hit you, that you can't ignore, that produce a definite creative response in you. You may find that you read a Buddhist text and think, 'This is very worthy, I agree with it, I accept it', but it doesn't move you, it leaves you cold; but other things really stir you. For you, those are Ḍākinī Dharmas, even the Formless Ḍākinī Dharmas perhaps. Milarepa himself of course has these qualities – there's nothing dull, dry or abstract about him.

In a sense a trap has been laid for Rechungpa. If he really does obtain those missing Formless Ḍākinī Dharma teachings, he's going to be a very different person. He's presumably not going to just get the texts and learn the meaning intellectually; he's going to have to practise them and that's going to make a tremendous difference to him, and also it's going to affect his communication with Milarepa, because communication is another aspect of the *ḍākinī*.

If, by contrast, you are someone who is already quite imaginative and full of colour, perhaps you need to study the Abhidharma, or Yogācāra and Madhyamaka philosophy. Ideally one should maintain balance at every level. There is also such a thing as a disciplined imagination. Being imaginative isn't necessarily following a more inspirational approach – you may just be letting your imagination run riot. You mustn't imagine that because you fantasize quite easily you've got a good imagination and don't need to develop that. Fantasy is the near enemy of imagination, one might say.[140]

The *ḍākinī* has a complementary figure in the form of the *heruka*. If you think of the Enlightened state in male/female, feminine/masculine terms, it's the *ḍākinī* on the one hand and the *heruka* on the other, and sometimes you get the *heruka* with the corresponding *ḍākinī* clinging onto him in sexual union. This is the expression of the union of that basic polarity at all the different levels, at the highest possible pitch. In terms of Enlightenment it's wisdom and compassion united and inseparable. There is a danger in this sort of approach, though, because the symbols are so tangible, so concrete – that is their advantage as well, of course – that we can confuse them with quite mundane things. You might hazard a guess that the *heruka* represents wisdom and the *ḍākinī* compassion, but actually it's the other way around: in Buddhist iconography, when you get the two together, the male or masculine always represents compassion and the female or feminine represents wisdom. But in a way you can't separate them. It is said that the male represents compassion and the female represents wisdom but at that level they interpenetrate each other and the one has the qualities of the other, if you look deeply enough. How can there be compassion without understanding? Compassion means giving people what they need, and how can you give them what they need unless you understand what they need? So how can you have compassion without wisdom? And similarly, how can you have wisdom without compassion? How is it possible to see what people need and not want to give it to them?

The common thread running through the story so far is communication. Rechungpa is out of communication to quite a considerable degree with Milarepa, and also with the people that he's supposed to be converting, as is shown by the fact that he wants to use forcible methods like logic and black magic. The question of communication also comes up when Milarepa reminds Rechungpa that the Ḍākinī Dharmas are beneficial to many sentient beings. In other words, he reminds him that he is a follower of the Vajrayāna and therefore at least in principle a follower of the bodhisattva ideal. This brings in the question of communication in a very extreme form, because the bodhisattva vows to communicate the Dharma to all living beings. So running through the two paragraphs is this thread of communication and openness and not being wrapped up in one's own narrow concerns and interests. Milarepa is suggesting to Rechungpa that he could be more open to the people with whom he is debating, more open to Milarepa himself, and more open to all sentient beings.

2

NEVER GIVE YOURSELF
TO STUDYING WORDS!

> Thereupon, the Jetsun and Rechungpa collected all the gold that
> people had offered them, which totaled quite a large sum. Then
> Shindormo and Lesebum, together with many patrons, prepared a
> sacred banquet as a farewell party for Rechungpa. In the assembly,
> the Jetsun presented his disciple with all the gold, and said,
> 'Rechungpa, my son! Listen to my song and think about it. You
> should try to secure the teachings in India in this manner.'

One point that immediately catches the attention is that the Jetsun
and Rechungpa 'collected all the gold that people had offered them,
which totalled quite a large sum'. That suggests that the people don't
just venerate Milarepa; they value him and his teaching in a very
concrete, practical way. This is one of the noticeable things about
Tibetan Buddhists: their almost materialistic way of thinking about the
Dharma. My Tibetan friends and pupils never used to say, 'The Dharma
is wonderful' or 'The Dharma is sublime' or 'The Dharma is the highest
truth'. They'd always say, 'The Dharma is very useful.' They looked at
it in that very down-to-earth way. When the sacred relics of Śāriputra
and Maudgalyāyana were brought to Kalimpong and then taken up to
Gangtok,[141] the Sinhalese and Indian *bhikkhus* who accompanied them
mentioned how very much more generous the Tibetan Buddhists were
than the Indians, who were mostly Hindu anyway. This generosity
seemed to come quite naturally to the Tibetans. They seemed to have a

sense of the solidity and tangibility of the Dharma, that it was as solid as meat in the butcher's shop or cloth in the cloth merchant's shop. It was useful and it lasted a long time and it did you a lot of good, like a bottle of medicine, so of course you paid for it. To some extent their sense of the concreteness and tangibility of the Dharma meant that for them it wasn't just a matter of words and ideas. It was something that really helped you in your life, something you really got down to. For people living in rural areas of Tibet there were magical overtones, the feeling that having a lama around reciting *sūtras* helped ripen the crops and kept away the hail, so it was useful in that sort of way too. Their overall attitude seemed to be that the Dharma was of great practical use so of course it was something you paid for, just as you would pay for the services of a doctor or a lawyer. You didn't even pay; you just gave, because you were so happy to have received it.

And this is what we see here: people are giving good gold because they find the Dharma so useful. Their generosity shows that if you really value something, you'll be prepared to pay in order to get it. Or – to reverse the statement – if you're not prepared to give money for something, you probably don't value it very much. People are only prepared to spend money on something to which they attach true value. Sometimes people say they haven't enough money to go on retreat, but the next week they buy a new record player or fly off on holiday somewhere. If people value something, they'll always find some money for it. But if there's a new book, even if it's a translation of a *sūtra* that's never been translated before, and maybe the price is ten pounds, they'll think, 'That's a lot of money!' They may genuinely think that ten pounds for a translation of a *sūtra* that they've never read before is a lot to pay but three hundred pounds to pay for a record player isn't very much – which gives an idea of their scale of values.

Perhaps people don't think they can use the Dharma practically, whereas they can use a record player, but it's perhaps not so much that they think that they *can't* use the Dharma; it's more that they *don't*. There is such a thing as investment. Maybe you can't get much from a Dharma magazine immediately, but it can be useful little by little as you understand it better. If you think buying a newspaper would be more useful, ask yourself how useful a newspaper really is. Once you've learned all about the war in Iraq or Syria or wherever it is, and all about the latest accidents and divorces and squabbles in the Labour Party, how useful has all that been to you really? It has only served to enable you to pass the time in an unmindful manner.

People often seem unwilling to pay to support the teaching of the Dharma, even though they say that they are getting a tremendous amount from it. Usually the unwillingness to pay takes the form of putting a tiny amount, or nothing at all, in the *dāna* bowl. People don't mind paying a few pounds to see a film but they seem to think that paying a few pounds to spend the evening at the Buddhist centre is outrageous. Maybe a rough and ready index of the value you attach to something is how much you're prepared to pay for it. Not that you're really 'buying' the Dharma, but at least the payment makes it available to you, just as when you buy a book it doesn't mean to say you can understand it but at least the possibility of reading and understanding it is there. These people seem to have really appreciated Milarepa and his teaching, hence the gift of gold. There is sometimes some disquiet about charging for Dharma classes, but one must think about this clearly. The charge is not for the Dharma but for the facility, because you need a place to meet, and that costs money. You can't charge for the Dharma. What price could you put on it? Here Milarepa isn't charging people; they give him gold out of natural generosity. Likewise, if people visiting a Buddhist centre are naturally generous, there is no need to charge.

But why have a farewell party for Rechungpa? Why not just let him go? One might say that it is because the Vajrayāna is not just the *yāna* of experience and energy; it is the *yāna* of expression. It attaches importance not only to mind and to speech but to body, and it is through the body that things are expressed. In that way there is a reinforcement of the original understanding. You act things out. You don't merely think, 'Well, I hope that Rechungpa gets to India all right, I'm sorry to see him go.' You don't even just say that to Rechungpa. The whole thing is brought out into the open and performed, and in that way it is experienced by everybody more intensely, and whatever positivity is felt is enhanced. It becomes a more powerful communication than just saying it. You act out your rejoicing in somebody's merits, your sorrow at seeing them go, and your appreciation of what they've done. One of the weaknesses of modern life is that we aren't able to do this sufficiently or at least not in the right way. It's as though people need a structure or an occasion to enable them to show their feelings.

This is why in our own Buddhist movement we have an ordination ceremony. We don't just give someone a certificate quietly; we have a ceremony to bring the whole thing out into the open, to embody it, to express it more fully and thereby experience it more intensely. It's the same with wedding ceremonies and name-giving ceremonies. These things should not be just formalities, and if they become so, they've ceased to fulfil their true function and they should be discontinued. If everybody thinks they're a nuisance and they don't mean anything any more, stop doing them and find new ceremonies – or give up celebrating that thing at all if it's not longer important to do so. The point is to have a ceremony for everything that you consider of importance. If you consider that somebody leaving a community is important, have a ceremony, or a farewell party at least. If you consider ordination important, make it into a ceremony. If you consider becoming a Mitra important, let there be a ceremony. We don't want meaningless rituals and ceremonies; we have ceremonies because we consider something important. The ceremony is an enhancement of what is happening, enabling us to experience it more intensely and realize its significance more fully.

One might even ask what are the important things for which we don't yet have ceremonies. It might even be important to have a ceremony for a painful occasion like divorce. After all, we have a ceremony for death. When people are divorced the position is supposed to be that they no longer consider themselves husband and wife, but usually they haven't really finished with each other; there are lots of feelings left over. Just as a marriage ceremony ties the knot, a divorce ceremony would untie it. It would allow the two people involved to say, 'We have lived together for such and such period of time, there have been good times and bad times, but we have decided now to part. Each is free to go his or her own way and there are no hard feelings. Maybe we felt some resentment or maybe there was some incompatibility that we couldn't overcome, but never mind, we wish each other well.' Surely that would help them, and everybody else would then understand the situation. One might even ask why one should consider it a painful occasion. Here are these two people, but actually they weren't two people, they were just two halves, and instead of trying to become whole they tried to make a whole out of two halves, but now they've realized that they should not be dependent upon each other in that way. They want to be true individuals.

Leaving aside domestic or mundane ceremonies, we also have a *kalyaṇā mitra* ceremony, of course, because that is an important occasion, and we are learning how to celebrate festivals in a wholehearted way. The important point is that you enact something; you don't allow it to remain just in your own mind. We tend sometimes to think that if something remains just in our own mind it's more real or even more sincere. We forget that we are body, speech, and mind, so things should be given utterance and bodily expression, and in that way we experience them more fully. It's an antidote to alienation, one could say. One could even celebrate the seasons, have a spring and autumn festival; why not? There's nothing wrong with the pagan element so long as it is kept in its proper place and doesn't get out of hand.

> I bow down to Marpa, the Translator.
> Pray bless us that we keep to your Tradition.
>
> This uninformed son of mine, the loser of debate
> And full of doubts, has stopped his meditation
> And is about to wander far away to study.
> This is the very thing a yogi should avoid!
>
> Rechungpa, when you arrive in India,
> Try to secure the Formless Ḍākinī Dharmas
> Of the great Pandita Nāropa's Succession;
> But never give yourself to studying words!
>
> In the beginning I met the right person,
> I put myself in the hands of Marpa.
> In the middle, I practiced the right teaching,
> Meditating on the White Rock Mountain.
>
> At the end, I asked for alms in the right places for alms;
> I beg here and there without friends or kinsmen.
> Since I have disposed of Saṃsāra and Nirvāṇa
> And have nor hope nor fear in my mind,
> I shall ne'er regress in my meditation.

I bow down to Marpa, the Translator.
Pray bless us that we keep to your Tradition.

The prayer is addressed to Marpa, and Marpa's tradition is the Kagyu lineage, which literally means the lineage of the oral transmission. The Kagyupas attach much less importance to the study of the texts than to the oral teaching of the guru, which is of course an oral transmission in as much as he has received that teaching from his guru by word of mouth and so back to the beginning of the line, which is traced back to the Buddha Vajradhara. But when Milarepa says, 'Pray bless us in that we keep to your Tradition', he is not giving expression to a narrow sectarian attitude. The remark is probably aimed at Rechungpa. The Kagyu is a tradition of oral transmission, and Rechungpa has become over-preoccupied with books. He's very concerned with going to India to study logic and science. He's got caught up in an intellectual approach, one could say, and this represents a departure from the Kagyu tradition. He's abandoning his meditation. So Milarepa begins by saying, 'Pray bless us that we keep to your Tradition' as if to say, 'I'm afraid this is not what Rechungpa is doing. He's becoming too interested in logic and science and he's giving up his meditation.'

There does nonetheless arise the whole question of identifying oneself with a particular form of Buddhism. In the East Buddhism exists in a number of forms and people identify with 'their' form quite strongly, usually because they happen to have been born into that branch of the Buddhist tradition, just as in the West people are born into Catholic families or Methodist families or Anglican families and so on. So what should be our attitude towards particular Buddhist traditions? You can read a number of different books and listen to lectures by a number of different people, but if you want to get down to serious practice, you have to establish contact with somebody who is himself practising seriously. If you want to study the Dharma deeply, that means entering into communication with someone deeply, and you obviously can't do that with a large number of people. Can you spend all your time with more than one person? According to Buddhist tradition, especially the Vajrayāna, there needs to be the intensity that you get through close contact and communication with your teacher and your fellow disciples. That will certainly intensify your practice. At the same time, you need to be quite open to others in the sense of not being closed to anything useful that they may have to say.

Choosing a tradition isn't just about choosing a particular method that suits you. It's about a whole broad approach. Some people would say that even confining yourself to Buddhism is very narrow. Why don't you take in Christianity, Hinduism, Islam? If that sounds silly, that's because it's impossible. You might be able to do it in a vague general way, but if you're thinking in terms of your own life and practice, it's quite meaningless to think in terms of taking in lots of religious traditions. You've got your work cut out taking in Buddhism. Never mind Buddhism, you've got your work cut out taking in the Mahāyāna; never mind the Mahāyāna, you've got your work cut out taking in our own Buddhist movement. Never mind our movement, you've got your work cut out getting on with the Mindfulness of Breathing and the *mettā bhāvanā*.

> *This uninformed son of mine, the loser of debate*
> *And full of doubts, has stopped his meditation*
> *And is about to wander far away to study.*
> *This is the very thing a yogi should avoid!*

Here Milarepa, presumably still addressing Marpa, mentions three things that a yogi should avoid. He shouldn't wander about aimlessly from place to place, he shouldn't separate himself from his teacher, and he shouldn't engage in purely intellectual studies. 'Yogi' here presumably means not just someone who meditates in the narrow sense but someone who is trying to develop, someone who is trying to attain to a higher level of consciousness and being.

If Milarepa really wanted Rechungpa to stay, perhaps he could have hammered his point home a bit harder. Perhaps his reasoning is that, after all, somebody has to bring these teachings back from India. Milarepa has made it clear that he doesn't mind Rechungpa going to India; what he objects to is his going there to study science and logic. Even though Milarepa has asked him to obtain those Ḍākinī Dharmas, there's still the danger that he'll be so preoccupied with reason, science, and logic that he won't do that. Perhaps Milarepa keeps on reminding him for that reason.

One might think that Milarepa must have tremendous faith in Rechungpa; he wouldn't be likely to send off somebody who is going to let him down to bring back these presumably priceless teachings.

But he doesn't know. He may have great faith in him but that faith may or may not be justified. You can't ever be sure how somebody is going to act, but at least there is a possibility that he will bring back these teachings and he won't get ensnared in science and logic.

> Rechungpa, when you arrive in India,
> Try to secure the Formless Dākinī Dharmas
> Of the great Pandita Nāropa's Succession;
> But, never give yourself to studying words!

In this verse Milarepa points out what apparently he considers to be the great danger. The last line is the key. In *Hamlet* there is a scene in which Polonius finds Hamlet reading a book. He says, 'What matter do you read, my Lord?' and Hamlet replies, 'Words, words, words.'[142] This is very often what people read and very often what people study. They study not the meaning, just the words. It's easy to take a purely philological approach, to get caught up in words and miss the real meaning. But even to study the meaning isn't enough: you have to go beyond it to the experience that the meaning is trying to point out. In a way there are four stages: first of all the experience, then the meaning, then the idea, and then the words. You can either stay at the most superficial level, concerning yourself just with the words, or you can go from the words to the ideas. This is usually as far as a lot of people get. But you can go further, from the ideas to the real meaning that someone is trying to communicate, and from the meaning you can go even further to the experience that the meaning is throwing light on.

Sometimes people read a lot because what they read doesn't mean very much to them. It's just a way of passing the time. If you were really to take it in, really to experience it, perhaps it would be too much for you. Usually you can devour books more when you are young, not just because you're more receptive, but because you're more empty. There's scope for experience; you're still searching. As you get older and you've found a more definite path, you tend to be more sensitive to what fits in with that, so you're more discriminating.

Nāropa was a great logician and dialectician, one of the four main teachers at Nālandā University, but his biography, which has been translated by Guenther, describes how he was given a very tough time by his teacher Tilopa, who wanted to overcome his intellectualism and bring him more into contact with actual experience.[143] Tilopa was Indian too, one of the *siddhas*. Milarepa's guru was Marpa, Marpa's guru was Nāropa, Nāropa's guru was Tilopa, and Tilopa is believed to have been taught directly by the Adibuddha Vajradhara. In other words, his teaching came directly from his own spiritual experience without his having any human teacher, at least when it came to the experience that later became transmitted in the Kagyu tradition.

The real message here is: never restrict yourself to studying words. Ask yourself what the words mean; and then ask yourself what the meaning means. There is such a thing as the meaning of meaning.

> *In the beginning I met the right person,*
> *I put myself in the hands of Marpa.*

What does one learn from that? Is it a matter of chance, of karma? Milarepa just happened to hear Marpa's name one day, and he was mysteriously attracted by the mere name, without knowing anything about Marpa. Once he came into contact with him, he 'put himself in the hands of Marpa'; in other words, he gave himself totally to the Dharma. This is a great characteristic of Milarepa's life, and of the whole Vajrayāna tradition. In traditional terms, when you go for Refuge you do so with body, speech, and mind, with your whole being, your whole personality. In that way Milarepa put himself in the hands of Marpa. But is this psychologically possible any longer? Do people have that sort of faith these days?

Sometimes we do put ourselves in other people's hands, in situations where expert advice is needed. We put ourselves in the hands of doctors although we don't really understand what they're doing to us. If we have to go to law, we usually have to place ourselves in the hands of the lawyer – what else can we do? We may feel uneasy about it, but very often we don't have any alternative. But what about placing oneself in the hands of another person in this more existential way? Does it mean just doing everything the other person says? In a sense it means that you regard the other person as the expert. They know better than you; they can see further than you. Perhaps they know you better than you know yourself. So in matters of doubt you are prepared to act upon the other person's advice implicitly. If two courses of action are before you and you are unable to decide which will be better for you,

you say, 'All right, you make the decision, and whatever you decide I will follow your advice.'

Putting yourself into the hands of the other person doesn't mean that they decide for you things which you are quite capable of deciding for yourself. A person into whose hands you could put yourself with confidence wouldn't act like that anyway. Generally you do what is best as far as you can see it, but when in doubt you follow what the other person says. If you have sufficient confidence in them, even if you think you know what is best for you, if they disagree, you are prepared to follow their advice. But Rechungpa isn't prepared to follow Milarepa's advice. Milarepa advised him to not go to India but he insisted on going anyway, so perhaps Milarepa is aiming this remark at him. It's not enough to meet the right person; you've got to put yourself in his hands. Rechungpa has met the right person, he's met Milarepa, but he still wants to go on doing things his own way.

This idea of putting yourself in the hands of somebody else has to be understood properly. It is not a weaker will submitting to a more powerful will. It is not knuckling under. If it was, resentment would follow. It isn't easy to put yourself in somebody else's hands. If you go along with them or give in to them because you're afraid of offending them or you don't want to lose their regard or their affection, that is not putting yourself in their hands. You can only put yourself in another person's hands if you are convinced that they operate in accordance with the love mode and not the power mode.[144] It seems that Rechungpa does not yet have that sort of faith in Milarepa, because in another chapter he accuses him of being bitter and egoistic.[145] You can put yourself in the hands of another person only if you are convinced that they are operating in accordance with the love mode. You're not just giving them an opportunity to order you about. It's a quite different sort of relationship, a quite different sort of experience.

It may be something that develops over time. At first you may just think that that person knows more than you or is more experienced or has certain skills that you'd like to acquire. That is not putting yourself into their hands, but just making use of them, admittedly in a positive manner, in the interests of your development. Putting yourself in the hands of another person is much more existential, and you can only do it when you really feel or see that that person is operating in accordance with the love mode, not the power mode.

When you have to make a major decision about life and you can't decide what to do, you may look around for a higher authority to make it for you, but if you put yourself in the hands of somebody in this way, that's quite another matter. The higher authority represents a superior power to which you submit. A guru like Marpa is not a superior power, or a power at all. When you put yourself in the hands of someone who operates in accordance with the love mode, their advice is an expression of the love mode, and when you act on it, you go beyond your own egoistic type of functioning. You yourself are, at least passively, functioning in the love mode, in the sense that you're accepting it from another person rather than initiating it yourself, and that requires a great deal of openness. Of course, Milarepa had no choice because he was in the extreme existential situation of either having to gain Enlightenment in this life or go to hell. What could he do but put himself in the hands of someone like Marpa?

You can't really relate to a whole sangha in this way. With respect to our own Order, you could say to yourself, 'Order members as a whole, whatever individual exceptions there may be, represent a positive influence, and to the extent that the Order represents something more positive than I am myself as yet, I should open myself to it and be receptive to it.' But that is not putting oneself in the hands of the Order in the sense that Milarepa puts himself in Marpa's hands. Suppose different people gave you conflicting advice?

Putting oneself in somebody's hands requires trust. You may trust a doctor or a lawyer in their field of expertise, but when you place your trust in a guru in the Vajrayāna tradition you put yourself in his hands in a much more existential and even total manner. This does not imply any sort of arbitrariness in that person's treatment of you. Testing your faith, or telling you to do something to see if you'll do it, would be an exercise of power, not love. It is best to be cautious about trusting anybody who is too anxious or eager to tell you what to do, as distinct from just giving you a friendly suggestion.

You have to decide whether you are asking someone for his advice or whether you are putting yourself in his hands. These are two quite distinct things. You may ask the advice of somebody whom you are convinced is more experienced and wiser than you are, consider what they tell you, and act upon it if you think it's a good idea. But putting yourself in somebody's hands means deciding to act upon what they say regardless of what it is and regardless of your own feelings about it. You are not asking for advice; you are asking to be told what to do, and that is quite different. If you ask for advice, having another suggestion to consider may add to your confusion. But if you put yourself in somebody else's hands, that simplifies things considerably because you don't have to think about it any more. You just have to work out how to do what they say. It's not even a question of being told to do the right thing rather than the wrong thing. Sometimes you just need to be told to do something. In a sense it doesn't matter. You've confused yourself with so many alternatives that you end up thinking, 'All right, I give up, I just don't know. Tell me what to do.' When someone says, 'Do this,' or 'Do that,' if you have sufficient confidence in them, you will happily act upon whatever they say, and thus cut the Gordian knot.

Sometimes you don't really want to act at all, so your mind comes up with reasons why you shouldn't. Somebody else can see that and realize that you just need to do something. In a sense it doesn't matter what. They may tell you to do something you've already thought of, but you've thought about it so much that you haven't been able to summon up sufficient energy to act on it. In any case you're not sure if it's the right thing; you're considering so many other possibilities. But when they tell you to do it, you are freed from your uncertainty and enabled to act. That implies again that you really have put yourself in their hands, otherwise you might think, 'I've already thought of that, I didn't need him to tell me.' The fact that you put yourself in somebody else's hands doesn't necessarily mean that he'll tell you to do something that you've never imagined doing, something new and spectacular.

When you put yourself in somebody else's hands, it's an unconditioned relationship. You've removed all your defences; there's no possibility of your reacting. If you are in the position of being told what to do by somebody else in this way, you're very fortunate. The trouble is, there are only too many people around wanting to tell others what to do simply as an exercise in power. One has to use one's discrimination and not put oneself in the hands of people of that sort. This even applies to gurus, or rather pseudo-gurus, who give orders rather than operating in accordance with the love mode. Sometimes people who are supposed to be gurus are just group leaders who are bossing other psychologically weaker people around. It's not confined to the West; you get it in India and even Tibet.

There is unreasonable independence, reasonable independence, unreasonable dependence and reasonable dependence. Unreasonable independence is when a person insists on being independent in situations in which it would be more skilful for him to be dependent, because other people know better than he does. An example would be falling ill and saying, 'Oh, I know what's wrong with me, I know the best sort of treatment' and starting to dose yourself with different medicines instead of going to a doctor. In the same way in the spiritual situation someone may say, 'Oh, I know what's good for me, I know how to meditate, I don't need a teacher. I can understand things perfectly well for myself.' This is unreasonable independence. In fact you're not even being independent. You're being dependent on the very person you can't depend on: yourself. Reasonable independence is being independent in circumstances where you're quite able to be independent, where you have genuine understanding. You should not depend upon others when you're able to depend upon yourself. Unreasonable dependence is depending upon others to do for you things you could do for yourself. In this can be included the surrender of weak people to so-called gurus, expecting the guru to give them salvation and everything else. And reasonable dependence is when you give yourself into the hands of another person with the trust that they know better than you and the confidence that they act from the love mode rather than the power mode and that whatever they tell you to do will be genuinely for your spiritual benefit. Rechungpa is being unreasonably independent, and Milarepa is advising him to be reasonably dependent.

We encounter these four attitudes in our dealings with people even in the Buddhist community. Sometimes old people are unreasonably independent. They say, 'Oh, it's all right, don't bother to help me, I can do it myself, I've always done it myself' – CRASH! People often think they are independent when they are in fact dependent in all sorts of ways that they don't recognize. To begin with, there's dependence upon others for material things. Traditionally in Buddhism the *bhikkhu*, the monk, is dependent upon the lay supporters for four things: food, clothing, shelter, and medicine. If you are a *bhikkhu*, if you are devoting yourself entirely to the spiritual life, if you're meditating and studying the Dharma, you may reasonably expect those four things from the lay community. The modern attitude might be that everybody should work to provide for himself, but that is not the traditional Buddhist point of view. The Buddha speaks of full-time practitioners as being reasonably dependent on the lay community for material things, but *only* for material things. They are not dependent on the lay community for inspiration or teaching. To be dependent on others for material things is not necessarily unreasonable, certainly for those who are devoting themselves to full-time meditation and Dharma study and Dharma teaching. Traditional Buddhism has the Pāli term *nissaya*, which refers to the relationship of dependence between a young monk and an older monk who is teaching him. This is an official relationship; you are not supposed to leave a senior monk who is teaching you without being released from your *nissaya*, your dependence upon him for Dharma teaching and guidance.

We are usually dependent upon others for material things. Even if we earn money and buy things we're dependent on others to make them for us. We're dependent upon others for knowledge; we don't write the books that we read. We may even be dependent upon others for inspiration. These are all areas of legitimate dependence. But what about what we might call illegitimate dependence? There may be circumstances in which you are dependent on others when really you should not be. For example, you should not look to others to support your image of yourself or, even more intimately than that, your experience of yourself. Some people can't experience themselves unless a lot of people are looking at them. It is said that this is why some people become actors. But you should not be dependent upon others for your own experience of yourself – perhaps in a way that is the basic illegitimate dependence.

Emotional dependence can be either legitimate or illegitimate. There is a legitimate emotional dependence upon others for inspiration and encouragement to attain higher levels of experience, but it is not legitimate to be dependent upon others for happiness, so that you can't be happy and contented unless certain people are around; or to be dependent upon others for knowledge which you are quite able to find out for yourself; or to be dependent upon others for deciding what to do, when you ought to think it out for yourself and make up your own mind.

You can be dependent upon others for material things, for knowledge, for emotional support, inspiration, and decisions. In a properly organized state you can reasonably depend upon others – the police, for example – for protection, because that is the condition of your leading a peaceful life, a life in the course of which you can practise the Dharma. It's one of the principal aspects of real friendship that a mutual unreasonable dependence isn't fostered or encouraged. You don't bolster up each other's little weaknesses. But there's nothing to be ashamed of in a reasonable dependence. You can't be completely independent.

It may not seem reasonable to go out and work hard all day and be too tired to meditate yourself in order to allow someone else to live a meditative life. This is the situation in most Buddhist countries: there's a sort of division of labour between monks and lay people. That situation isn't necessarily healthy, but putting the most positive construction on it, one could say that you may be aware of your own limitations in a quite genuine objective healthy way. You may be aware that you can't do something but somebody else can do it, so you are quite happy to function in a supportive capacity. The important thing is that the thing is done. The unhealthy development is when there's a hard and fast division between monks and lay people and the lay people in effect pay the monks to practise the Dharma for them. If the laity believe that the monks are practising the Dharma on their behalf and that they don't have to practise it themselves, that is a wrong attitude even if the monks are actually practising the Dharma. If the monks are only pretending to practise the Dharma and living just like the laity, but the laity are supporting them under the impression that they are practising the Dharma, that is even worse.

But if you feel that somebody needs to go away on solitary retreat, for their own benefit and indirectly that of others, you might be quite happy to work to support them to go on retreat. There is a tendency for people to resent working while others are not, but I was reading about a tribe one of whose characteristics was that they didn't mind working even while others weren't. A contractor was building railways and had to hire labour from among primitive tribes who lived in the area through which the railway was passing, and he found that if he hired say a dozen men, eight of them would work and the other four would sit around. Those who were doing the work didn't mind that the others were sitting around. They felt like working so they worked, the others didn't feel like working so they didn't work, and no one minded. So we have to watch the attitude of resenting working when somebody else is not or so that somebody else doesn't have to work. We should not allow ourselves to be exploited by other people, but if we resent somebody who is not working, it suggests we're not enjoying our work, and perhaps we should question our motives for working. In Buddhist countries they're often only too happy to let the monks get on with the difficult work of meditation while they do what they think of as relatively easy work in the fields.

If you're feeling guilty for not working, either you're not taking your full share of the communal burden or else your guilt is an irrational vestige of the puritan work ethic. If your existence has to be justified in terms of work, output, money, utility, it's as though you don't have any value in yourself. In the course of having a dig at the Marxists, G. K. Chesterton says in an essay what a horrible word 'worker' is. In his view the word should be workman, a man who happens to work, but it's been made into worker as though the fact that he's a man isn't important.[146] The man has been identified completely with his function. Broadly speaking, if we speak of someone as a good worker it's because we value production above everything, like the heroes of labour who used to be praised in the Soviet Union. It's true that the *Dhammapada* appreciates the one who shakes off laziness,[147] but we must remember as well that Gampopa defines laziness as being constantly busy with politics and business, and thus neglecting the spiritual life.[148]

So far as our own Buddhist movement is concerned there shouldn't be too much of a distribution of labour, with some people doing all the spiritual work and other people doing the material work and supporting the meditators. If you are a Buddhist at all, if you've gone for Refuge, you are responsible for your own spiritual development, and you help one another. It's not that you've got a community of lay people supporting a community of monks. I have come to the conclusion that the traditional Theravādin set-up, where the monks are supported by the laity, is not a very positive arrangement. The average person needs a certain amount of physical work, and Theravādin monks by definition don't get that. There should not be a whole class of people who never do any work. According to the Vinaya a *bhikkhu* should not even kindle a fire.[149] Absolutely everything is done for the monks by lay people. To give them their due, they're not always very happy with this. I've known Theravāda *bhikkhus* who like to work, but the laity rush forward and stop them because they think it's a reflection upon their devotion. The traditional justification is that a monk gets enough exercise if he goes out on his almsround but that isn't much exercise, and usually he doesn't go out on his almsround anyway nowadays; he usually eats in the vihara.

Physical work should ideally be part of everyone's spiritual life. Not all the time: you may have a month when you go away for a solitary retreat, but broadly speaking work should be an integral part of one's spiritual life. Through physical work one experiences one's energies and therefore oneself more fully. From the spiritual point of view, especially if you are a beginner in the spiritual life, the work should be simple. It should not require a lot of paperwork or thinking or responsibility, especially responsibility for other people. It should just involve simple physical activity. Gardening is a good example – unless it's really elaborate landscape gardening.

There is also a value in working with others. You may not necessarily get to know someone better in terms of direct communication, but you will get to know more about them indirectly which may be quite important to your communication with them. If you're working with somebody day after day, in the end the real person comes out. You can see very easily whether they are sure of themselves or not, and if they drop a box on their foot and swear, it's difficult for them to maintain a pious image after that.

There's another aspect of work too: the productive aspect. Nowadays, especially in religious or pseudo-religious situations, people tend to stress the subjective much more than the objective, but there is a whole productive aspect of work which is important within the wider community. To take almost the classic example, if you were working with others on the land to grow your own food, you would get three benefits: you would experience your own energies and therefore yourself in a particular way; you'd be relating to other people through work; and you would be producing something which you need for your very existence. So there are these three interconnected aspects to work: the developmental, which includes the therapeutic; the social or community oriented; and the productive, the economic in a broader sense. Perhaps one should look at every work situation from this threefold point of view. Is it helping me to develop, is it enabling me to relate better to other people, and is it producing something (even if it's only money) which is useful to the community, especially the spiritual community?

You might think that if you had a private income, team-based right livelihood would be irrelevant. The idea that work has any significance as far as your development goes, especially working with other people, may seem like a way of dressing up the fact that you've got to work.

Such an attitude might stem from the fact that for a long time in our society we have divorced work from play. If work is not separated from play, the whole question of not working when you don't have to work falls to the ground. One might think that repetitive work cannot be play, but when primitive communities are engaged in repetitive activities like planting seeds or chopping wood, doing the same simple activity over and over again, they sing and they might even dance, and that helps to make that repetitive element more positive. The musical beat provides the foundation on which the melody and the harmony are based. Repetitive work by itself can be stultifying but if some song or other artistic or playful element is added, that repetitive quality becomes an element of something greater. There's an essay by G. K. Chesterton in which he suggests songs for all sorts of repetitive modern activities; it's a bit ridiculous, perhaps intentionally, because there are certain repetitive jobs you just can't do in that way, but it makes the point.[150]

Sometimes it happens that your work, though repetitive, takes enough of your mental energy and activity to prevent you from thinking your own thoughts while you're working. You can't put all your mental activity into the work because the work is not demanding enough, but you are prevented from getting on with your own mental processes. That is quite a negative thing. Much better is an uncomplicated job like chopping a pile of logs, which leaves you free to think your own thoughts or not to think at all if you don't want to.

> In the middle, I practiced the right teaching,
> Meditating on the White Rock Mountain.

This is where putting yourself in the hands of the right person is useful. You may be desperately in need of practising something *now*. You haven't got time, or perhaps the talent, to study all the scriptures, so you need to place yourself in the hands of someone who knows a lot of teachings, a lot of approaches, and who can select the one that is suitable for you. Very often we don't know what is best for us because we're not aware of all the possibilities.

At the same time, we mustn't be too precious. These days people are aware that there are many different kinds of meditation, and many different kinds of meditation teachers, so if they aren't getting on too well with the practice they're doing, they start saying, 'I don't think this is the right practice for me; maybe some other method would suit me better.' And this keeps happening. They try a method for a few weeks or a few days, but they don't seem to be making much progress, so they change to something else; that doesn't work very well either, so they change to something else; and they do the same thing with teachers and groups and movements. So you mustn't be too precious about finding what exactly suits you. You may not be facing up to the fact that even the right teaching, even the right practice, has actually to be practised. It's not going to work automatically.

Sometimes, therefore, I adopt the opposite point of view and say that the best practice for you is the one that you actually practise. It's not as though there is an abstract right practice, apart from simple things like if you've got a bad temper, obviously you should practise the *mettā bhāvanā*. It may not be that there is a right teaching just for you. You might make just as much progress with one as with another, it's just a question of whether you practise it or not. If you practise it, it's sure to do you good. Some people are over-precious about finding just the right community for them, just the right meditation practice, just the right kind of books to read.

There is a need of the precept in the Kadam sense – the teaching that is addressed just to you – but that's a different thing from there being an objective classical Buddhist method of meditation or spiritual practice that is the one that you've got to find. All of them, however specific they may seem, are very general when it comes to relating to the needs of the individual. The precept can only come from another individual, so if you want individual teaching, you've got to have an individual teacher. That doesn't mean glorifying one particular person and regarding him as God, so to speak; it means entering into an existential communication with someone more experienced than yourself, entering into a relationship of *kalyāṇa mitratā*. You're quite right in wanting an individual teaching, something tailored to your needs, but those needs have to be known to someone capable of describing to you the teaching that you need, and that means you've got to enter into that sort of relationship with someone. And that is not an easy matter. Are you prepared for it?

The precept in this context is the personal teaching of the guru to the disciple exactly adapted to the disciple's needs. It's a sort of digest or condensation of the teaching to meet the needs of the disciple. As a result of his study, meditation and experience, the guru puts the matter in a few simple words which he knows are going to help that particular person. He reduces the whole thing to that. That's called a precept in the sense of *upadeśa*, an individual instruction. Sometimes you can read all the *sūtras* and they don't seem to say the word that really speaks to your condition, as the Quaker phrase has it. You need something that hits the nail right on the head so far as you are concerned, and that can only come from another individual who really knows you. Sometimes you get it from the scriptures when the Buddha is speaking to someone in the same position that you are in, and the things that the Buddha says to the person apply directly to you, but that doesn't very often happen. You may feel that what the Buddha says in the scriptures is all perfectly true and wonderful, and you agree with it and accept it, but you need something more individualized than that, something that applies to the very situation you are in at this moment

> *At the end, I asked for alms in the right places for alms;*
> *I beg here and there without friends or kinsmen.*

'Asking for alms in the right places for alms' might be a technical reference to the Vinaya rules governing begging by monks. A monk, for instance, shouldn't beg for alms outside a wine shop or a brothel.[151]

So first of all he's got to meet a teacher, then he's got to practise the teaching, and then he's got to support himself while he is practising. That seems to be the sequence of beginning, middle, and end. Of course Milarepa himself didn't try to support himself for quite a long while. People used to bring him food, and for some time he did without food altogether, just living on wild nettles.

'Begging here and there without friends or kinsmen' suggests independence, non-attachment. He regards everybody equally. He doesn't make special friends among them as Rechungpa wants to do in a story we will come to later.[152] What Milarepa means here is that he doesn't enter into relations with people simply because of some common worldly interest or some tie of blood. The only basis for relationship he recognizes now is the Dharma. He certainly relates to Rechungpa, and to the lay supporters as well, but on a spiritual basis.

It isn't easy to make this kind of distinction in one's personal and social life. If you go to see your family thinking that they are just like friends, why not just go and see your next-door neighbour? The starting point is that you are related to them. Why else take all the trouble to visit and communicate with them? If one was strictly consistent one shouldn't take any trouble to see one's blood relations at all. I suppose one feels that as one has a connection, one might as well try to make something of it.

A lot of hermits express in their poetry the feeling that if they haven't got a spiritual friend, they are alone.[153] But one could put it the other way round and say that if you are with a spiritual friend you are at the same time alone. Spiritual friendship does not exclude being an individual – in fact it's based on being an individual – but you can be with a spiritual friend and still be alone in a positive sense, whereas when you are with someone on a basis of some common worldly interest, even when you are with them, you are not really with them.

In a strict sense you can't be a spiritual friend to yourself. You might reach a point where you need to put yourself in the hands of somebody else, and if there are no spiritual friends available, you have to face up to the fact that you're on your own. Even if you say you'll be a spiritual friend to yourself, don't let that prevent you from recognizing that you are on your own, you don't have any spiritual friends, and you'll have to get on without them.

> Since I have disposed of Saṃsāra and Nirvāṇa
> And have nor hope nor fear in my mind,
> I shall ne'er regress in my meditation.

Milarepa is surely making this point with reference to Rechungpa. If he hasn't regressed already, he is certainly about to regress in his meditation because he is haring off to India in pursuit of logic and science. He hasn't been keeping up his meditation very well and perhaps he won't be able to do so in India. Milarepa, by contrast, will never regress in his meditation, and he explains why. But what does he mean by saying, 'I have disposed of Saṃsāra and Nirvāṇa'? They are words or concepts which he has presumably transcended, whereas Rechungpa is still very much caught up with words and ideas, intellectual concepts, but is it easy to dispose of those concepts, or even to think of doing so? To dispose of the concepts of *saṃsāra* and *nirvāṇa* means in a sense to go beyond the whole framework of Buddhism itself, certainly beyond the framework of the Theravāda. For the Theravāda, *saṃsāra* and *nirvāṇa* are ultimate concepts. The whole spiritual life is based upon the idea that you get off that wheel of life, which represents the *saṃsāra*, and you go up the spiral path to realize *nirvāṇa*, upon the movement away from the conditioned in the direction of the Unconditioned. The whole idea of development is from a lower to a higher state, so if you think in terms of spiritual growth and development at all, you think in effect in terms of *saṃsāra* and *nirvāṇa* – a state that you get away from and a state that you move in the direction of. If you dispose of *saṃsāra* and *nirvāṇa* you dispose of the whole basis of the spiritual life. Is that an easy thing to do? How does one do that, or in what sense can one do that?

The Mahāyāna would take the view that in the ultimate analysis *saṃsāra* and *nirvāṇa* are concepts that are to be transcended if you are to reach the end of the path. But if you dispose of the concepts of *saṃsāra* and *nirvāṇa* you dispose also of the concept of a path, because the path is the means of transition from *saṃsāra* to *nirvāṇa*. To dispose of *saṃsāra* and *nirvāṇa* is something that for the vast majority of people, even those on the spiritual path, is quite unthinkable. It's cutting the ground from under their feet. Nonetheless, Milarepa is saying that if one does not wish to regress in one's meditation that is what one has to do, and that suggests that he has a very deep conception of meditation. Meditation isn't just keeping the mind concentrated. He seems to use the word meditation for the whole of the spiritual life, for the whole process of raising the level of consciousness, the whole process of following the path. It's as though he's saying you won't reach the end of the path until you get rid of the concept of path altogether. But for the majority of people on the spiritual path, it's quite impossible to realize that the path is only a concept, that *saṃsāra* and *nirvāṇa* are only concepts. They can imagine themselves realizing that, they can have a theoretical understanding, but can they really dispose of the concepts of *saṃsāra* and *nirvāṇa*, or the concept of the path?

You can't even really dispose of the thought that you can attain something. Your experience is that you are striving, making an effort, experiencing, attaining. Can you really, in actual fact, dispose of the concept of the self? Even if you think that these are just operational concepts, not ultimate realities in themselves, one could say that the idea that such terms as *saṃsāra* and *nirvāṇa* are only operational concepts is itself only an operational concept. Even the idea that they're only operational concepts isn't real for you to begin with. That doesn't enable you to dispose of them in Milarepa's terms, it only enables you to have a theoretical idea that concepts like *saṃsāra* and *nirvāṇa* are only operational concepts.

So we shouldn't think it's all that easy. It's very easy to read the passage and agree with it and say that *saṃsāra* and *nirvāṇa* are only concepts, and the path is only a concept and the self is only a concept, but we don't actually experience them as just concepts, which would mean really going beyond them. We only have a concept of their being concepts. We don't have an experience or realization of them being concepts; that is quite a different matter.

Milarepa's teaching is addressed to Rechungpa, but taking it more broadly it's addressed to people of a very high level of spiritual development indeed. If you reach the point of disposing of all such concepts, you won't regress in your meditation because you've even gone beyond the idea of progress. Regression is a concept that has significance only in relation to the counter concept of progress. If you reach the level that Milarepa is talking about, there's no question of progress, because after all, what is progress? It's going from *saṃsāra* to *nirvāṇa*. If you've disposed of those concepts, there's nothing to go from and nothing to go to. There's no path and no person travelling the path, so the possibility of regression, even the possibility of meditation, is no longer there. It isn't enough not to regress in the sense of sticking at your meditation and making progress, or experiencing yourself as making progress and believing that you're moving from a real *saṃsāra* to a real *nirvāṇa*. You've got to transcend all these concepts altogether.

Of course Rechungpa is a very long way from doing that; Milarepa is pointing out to him a very high level of spiritual experience indeed. One can't even call it a level, because if you say a higher level it supposes a lower level and that supposes a path; and that is exactly what Milarepa is denying. He denies the concept of path when he disposes of the concepts of *saṃsāra* and *nirvāṇa*. So of course he's got no hope and no fear. He's got no hope of *nirvāṇa*, no fear of *saṃsāra*, because he's disposed of those concepts, and therefore he doesn't regress. It's not that he doesn't regress in the sense that he's always making progress – he's gone beyond the concept of regression and therefore the concept of progress. In other words he's gone beyond concepts altogether. He's quite free from concepts. That isn't easy, because we need a provisional framework made up of operational concepts to provide the basis of our spiritual life and furthermore we only have a theoretical idea of the fact that they are operational concepts. We cannot but take them for real. We cannot but think there's a real *saṃsāra* and a real *nirvāṇa* and a real path and a real person who's travelling that path.

Sometimes people think they've experienced 'no thought' when they've just gone through the day with no directed thought, with woolly wandering thoughts. But even somebody who is meditating and for the time being doesn't experience discursive mental activity has not gone beyond concepts because when he comes out of that meditative state he starts thinking again and using concepts in the ordinary way. There is only a temporary suspension of the use of concepts; he has not disposed of them. If someone went through the day without thinking, he'd probably be in a sort of catatonic state, and that certainly isn't a state of transcending or disposing of concepts.

We should bear in mind that these lines come at the end of a section of Milarepa's song. In this section he has given a summary of his whole spiritual career, his biography in a nutshell: meeting his guru, his attitude to his guru, his practice of meditation, his way of life, and his ultimate spiritual realization. If there had been a *Who's Who* in his time and he'd been asked for an entry, this is perhaps what he would have written or sung.

There is a meditation practice that encourages transcending *saṃsāra* and *nirvāṇa*. In the practice of the four *śūnyatās*,[154] you reflect on the first *śūnyatā* or emptiness: that the *saṃsāra* is empty of *nirvāṇa*, and you turn that reflection over in your mind every day for a period of time, maybe years. Then at a certain point you start turning over in your mind the second *śūnyatā*: that *nirvāṇa* is empty of *saṃsāra*. This is a useful practice, because it means that one is practising *vipaśyanā* in the Mahāyāna way, and this is how transcendental insight is developed according to the classical procedure. You practise meditation in the sense of *śamatha*, the mind is calmed down, the energies are all united, and then when you are in that calm state you take up the reflection on, in the Theravāda context, the transitoriness, the painfulness, and the insubstantiality of all phenomena. From a Mahāyāna point of view you can take up one of several formulations, including the contemplation of the four *śūnyatās*. Because your discursive mental activity has been brought under control and you're reflecting in a directed, purposeful way, you develop an understanding of those teachings and they serve as a bridge or springboard for the experience of insight. They are conceptual symbols, means of transition from an intellectual understanding to an intuitive understanding. The Buddha originally had a certain transcendental experience, and wanted to communicate the means of realizing that, so he spoke in terms of impermanence and painfulness and so on, and in terms of the four *śūnyatās*. Those concepts can be used as keys to unlock the experience that the Buddha had, provided that they are contemplated by a mind that has previously been suffused by the experience of meditation in the sense of *śamatha*. This is the classical procedure. If you think about them with your ordinary wandering mind you won't penetrate very deeply into them because your mind is disturbed, your energies are scattered and divided. You need the preliminary practice of *śamatha* to make your mind one-pointed, and then with that one-pointed mind you can take up any aspect of the Buddha's teaching, but especially these formulations that give some clue to the nature of the Transcendental, and contemplate them in such a way as to develop real insight. That insight, as it is deepened, will have a transforming effect on the whole being.

People who have barely started out on the spiritual path may come across Buddhist literature and the pronouncements of lamas and Zen masters and on that basis talk quite freely about going beyond *saṃsāra* and *nirvāṇa*, and how they are only concepts and one mustn't be attached to them, and so on. Of course it is highly improbable that they have transcended the concepts of *saṃsāra* and *nirvāṇa*; they've got a theoretical idea of transcending them, which is quite another matter. For them – and for most of us too, of course – *saṃsāra* is real. They are immersed in it, they are not free from it, and for them therefore *nirvāṇa* is also real and they've got to start trying to move towards it. In other words, we must all appreciate where we are really at and guard against any conceited idea about our spiritual understanding and attainments. To be frank, you may be so much in your head, and your intellect may be so alienated from the rest of your being, that you may be able to read something like this and say, 'Oh yes, one has to dispose of *saṃsāra* and *nirvāṇa*. Of course all these dualistic concepts have only got a relative validity. I've seen through all that, so there's no question of my giving up the *saṃsāra* and realizing *nirvāṇa*; it's all one, it's all the same. My daily life is the life of the bodhisattva, the life of the Buddha.' Of course, you're just living and experiencing and suffering like anyone else, except that you have the delusion that you've gone beyond all concepts, just like Milarepa, even though your real position may be more akin to Rechungpa's in this scenario.

In short, spiritual life starts off with your own experience: you have a painful, unsatisfactory experience and you want to move away from that.

> When with my Guru Marpa on that steep hill
> He once said to me:
>
> 'The King of the Mighty Wheel holds
>   (It as) the Jewel,
> And the Bird with Five Families
> Flies in (Its) expanse of Dharma-Essence.
> Five special teachings in India still survive:
> First, the Lamp of Illuminating Wisdom,
> Second, the Wheel Net of Nāḍī and Prāṇa,
> Third, the Great Bliss of Precious Words,
> Fourth, the Universal Mirror of Equality,
> And Fifth, the Self-liberation Mahāmudrā.
> These five teachings are still taught in India.'
>
> I am now too old to go,
> But you, child of Marpa's Lineage,
> Should go to India to learn them!

There's a note after the first four lines of Milarepa's quotation from Marpa:

> The meaning of these two statements is very enigmatic. The
> translator presumes that the first statement, 'The King of
> the Mighty Wheel, (Cakravati), holds (It as) the Jewel,' is an
> expression of praise for the Teaching of the Ḍākinī. 'It,' in the
> brackets, in both the first and second statements implies the total
> teaching of the Ḍākinī.

In mentioning that he was with Marpa on that steep hill, Milarepa makes it clear that he has got a vivid mental picture of the whole scene. Have you ever noticed that when something happens to you or when someone says something to you or you read a book which makes a tremendous impression on you, you remember the whole of the surrounding scene? Maybe you read a particular Buddhist text for the first time and you remember exactly where you were – you were sitting under a tree, perhaps, and there was a sparrow on that particular branch. The whole picture is very vivid in your mind because the experience was so intense. It seems rather like that for Milarepa. He remembers the time and the place and the scene when Marpa spoke to him in that way, which suggests that Marpa's words made a tremendous impression on him.

Marpa's words on that steep hill are, as the translator remarks, enigmatic. He is presumably referring to the five Ḍākinī Dharmas that Milarepa did not obtain and which he hopes Rechungpa will now be able to bring back from India: highly esoteric Vajrayāna teachings, according to tradition the product of the transcendental forces of inspiration represented by those *ḍākinī* figures. We've just got their titles, and that doesn't tell us very much. As the translator says, the first statement is an expression of praise to the teaching of the *ḍākinī*. 'It' in the brackets in both the first and second statement apparently implies the total teaching of the *ḍākinī*. So the King of the Mighty Wheel holds the whole body of those *ḍākinī* teachings as the Jewel, and the bird with Five Families flies in its expanse of Dharma-Essence. This is very poetic but it's quite obscure. Who is this King of the Mighty Wheel who holds these teachings as a Jewel? It could be Vairocana, or it could be a guru figure, some particular teacher who has these teachings. 'He is like a king with the wish granting jewel in his hand' probably refers to the teacher or the master, the Tantric guru, whoever he may be, who has these teachings. 'The Bird with Five Families' that 'flies in its expanse of Dharma-Essence' could refer to all the many-sided spiritual realizations represented by the five Buddha families unfolding within the expanse of the Dharma essence of those teachings. In other words, by following or practising those Formless Ḍākinī Dharmas, all the Buddha bodies as unfolded in all five Buddha families are attained. It probably means something like that, or at least that may be one of the meanings.

Anyway, it would seem that Milarepa is indicating to Rechungpa the sort of teachings that he hopes he will be able to bring from India. The description is evocative but at the same time mysterious. We don't really know what Milarepa is talking about because the titles of these teachings are just like labels. They don't give us any real clue.

'These five teachings are still taught in India' refers to what was happening in the eleventh century. Milarepa lived at around the time of the Norman conquest in England – 1066 and all that. In India the Muslim conquest had begun, and it was having a very destructive effect on Buddhism. Monasteries were being destroyed, monks were being killed, gurus were being scattered, teachings were being lost. That is a disadvantage of an oral tradition, of course: if the holder of that tradition dies or is killed, the tradition is lost. I think this is why Marpa said that these five teachings are still taught in India; he is saying that these lines of gurus and disciples are still present. They haven't been cut off yet by the invaders. We know that at about that time a lot of books were burned and a lot of oral teachings were lost. Perhaps Milarepa has all that in mind. He wants Rechungpa to obtain these teachings from India before they die out altogether, because one or two hundred years later Buddhism did virtually disappear from India as a result of the Muslim invasion and conquest, in what seems to have been a concentrated and conscious destruction. Nālandā was destroyed, along with its library. Some monks sought refuge in Tibet just as in more recent times after the Chinese invasion Tibetan monks sought refuge in India.

3

THINK OF THE MEANINGS OF THIS SONG

Rechungpa was delighted. He picked up the best piece of gold, tossed it to the Jetsun as (his farewell offering), and sang:

Bless me, my teacher,
Let me risk my life to fulfill the Gurus' will.
Pray help me get the Ḍākinīs' Teachings as prophesied.
With your great Wisdom-Compassion
Pray e'er protect, and ne'er part from me.
Pray, at all times look after this, your son,
Who has no kinsman and no friend.
Pray conquer all his hindrances
And save him from going astray!
Pray safeguard him where'er he goes in India –
A land of danger, and full of bandits!
Pray lead him to the right teacher,
As he wanders on alone in that foreign land!

Rechungpa is delighted, of course, because he's getting his own way. He's going off to India to study science and logic. Of course he's also going to pick up these Formless Ḍākinī Dharmas as directed by Milarepa – he's got to do that – but basically he's doing what he wanted to do, and he seems to be a bit carried away, a bit exuberant. Maybe he's had a bit of *chhaang* to drink, who knows? (*Chhaang* is a sort of Tibetan beer.) It's a Tibetan farewell feast. He offers the best piece of gold to Milarepa as his farewell offering but not in a very respectful way – he just tosses it to him. And then he sings his song.

> *Bless me, my teacher,*
> *Let me risk my life to fulfill the Gurus' will.*

It's almost ridiculous, because he's been almost the classic example of disobedience so far. In spite of Milarepa's advice he has pressed the Jetsun to grant him permission to go to India. That doesn't suggest any great willingness to fulfil the gurus' will. It goes to show that some people can go completely against what their teacher says but at the same time they can genuinely consider themselves as the most loyal and faithful of disciples.

He seems very keen on being looked after and protected. Maybe it's in keeping with his attitude of having his own way all the time and Milarepa having to go along with him rather than him going along with Milarepa.

> *Pray conquer all his hindrances*
> *And save him from going astray!*

This is rather ironic. Milarepa has said in an earlier song, 'This uninformed son of mine, the loser of debate and full of doubts, has stopped his meditation and is about to wander far away to study. This is the very thing that a yogi should avoid.' But then Rechungpa, having got his own way, sings very piously, 'Please save me from going astray.' Again there's this sense of wanting to do what he wants to do but at the same time wanting the approval of the appropriate authority. Really he is going against that authority but he wants to keep up the pretence that he's not going against it. Maybe he doesn't dare to go against it, but at the same time he wants to have his own way, so he tries by hook or by crook to get the authority's blessing. This seems to be Rechungpa's position.

> *Pray safeguard him where'er he goes in India –*
> *A land of danger, and full of bandits!*
> *Pray lead him to the right teacher,*
> *As he wanders on alone in that foreign land!*

He could have said 'the right teacher in India', or 'the teacher who will impart to him the Formless Ḍākinī Dharmas', but he doesn't. It's almost as though he doesn't realize that Milarepa is the right teacher and that he ought to be following Milarepa's advice, which seems very strange. It's a bit like when people go from one meditation method to another. They practise a particular kind of meditation, whether the *mettā bhāvanā* or the Mindfulness of Breathing or whatever, for a short while, and they don't seem to be getting the result that they expected so they think, 'Oh well, maybe this meditation doesn't suit me', and try another one. They don't get on very well with that one either, so after a few days they want to change to yet another method. It's sometimes the same with teachers or gurus. Rechungpa doesn't seem to have great faith in Milarepa; he certainly doesn't follow his advice implicitly. People often say of a particular teacher, 'He doesn't suit me' or 'He doesn't understand me,' but what they mean is 'He's not giving me his blessing to do what I want to do.' That's the sort of teacher they're really looking for. When Rechungpa prays to be led to the right teacher, maybe he's still got the idea at the back of his mind that Milarepa is not quite the right teacher for him. Milarepa doesn't understand him. Milarepa doesn't appreciate his needs and he's not willing to let him do the things he wants to do. In other words, Rechungpa doesn't understand what finding the right teacher really means. Undoubtedly Milarepa *is* the right teacher for him.

In the West it's very difficult when this sort of situation arises because there's nothing to keep the disciple with the right teacher. In the East at least you've got the force of tradition, or maybe your parents hand you over to a particular teacher and you don't dare to go against them. But in the West if one teacher gives you advice that you don't like, you're free to say, 'he doesn't understand my needs' and go off and join somebody else. There's nothing to hold you to the right teacher, so you are in a dangerous and vulnerable position.

Take, for instance, those people who might feel that they have got the measure of the concepts of *saṃsāra* and *nirvāṇa*. If you were a little too blunt in pointing out that going beyond such concepts is not as easy as all that, they might just think, 'He doesn't understand anything. He must be a very elementary sort of Buddhist. He doesn't even understand things like transcending *saṃsāra* and *nirvāṇa*. And he doesn't appreciate me. He doesn't realize how far I've progressed. He doesn't appreciate that I am living in the world but not of it. He's got a very elementary attitude.' That could well be their attitude. As a Dharma teacher you have to devise means of dealing with that and not letting them get away with it, but you might not get the chance. They might hear you saying something of that sort and say, 'Oh well, he's not the man for me. He doesn't know anything about Buddhism. He's still taking *saṃsāra* and *nirvāṇa* seriously. He even thinks you have to meditate every day! I went beyond that long ago. I've had all these wonderful advanced esoteric initiations from all sorts of lamas.'

From this song we get the impression that Rechungpa is very naive, and also that he likes getting his own way. He's a bit blind too, and pretty stubborn, even childish, or perhaps he's just saying these things in an effort to please his teacher. He sounds like a young passionate man who hasn't thought about what he's saying. He's just copied what his teacher has said but applied it to himself. 'To fulfill the gurus' will' is the same thing that Milarepa said about himself in relation to Marpa. Rechungpa has been with Milarepa for some time at this point. The chronology is a bit obscure but from other chapters one gathers that he joined up with Milarepa when he was very young, and in one song Milarepa refers to Rechungpa as having been with him since he was a boy. It could be that he is still very young, perhaps just eighteen or so. He does seem rather juvenile.

In response, the Jetsun sang:

My son Rechungpa, on your way to India
Remember these seven Trinities of counsel:

The Skillful-Path of Tantra,
The Guru's Pith-Instruction,
And one's own judgement,
Are three important things for your remembrance!

Respect and serve the learned,
Have faith in your Guru,
Be determined and persevering.
These are three things you should remember.

Rightly to direct the Life-stream (Prāṇa),
To enter the Dharma-Essence,
And to master all the teachings,
Are three techniques you should remember.

The views of the Bliss-Void,
Of the myriad forms,
Of reasoning and following the scriptures,
Are three essentials you should remember.

A partner qualified in Mudrā,
Experience of the bliss therein,
And the 'Elephantine work,'
These are the three delights you should remember.

To instruct an idler brings misfortune,
To speak of one's experience leads to loss,
In towns to wander damages one's Yoga.
These are three dangers to remember.

To join the assembly of the Brethren,
To attend the meeting of Ḍākinīs,
And be present at the (secret) feasts,
Are the three occasions not to miss.

Think of the meanings of this song,
And put them into practice!

The Skillful-Path of Tantra,
The Guru's Pith-Instruction,
And one's own judgement,
Are three important things for your remembrance!

The Tantra is sometimes called *upāyamarga*, the path of skilful means. In other words, the path of the Tantra is not concerned with philosophy or theory at all. There is an Early Buddhist philosophy to be found in the Sarvāstivāda school and the Sautrāntika school, and a Mahāyāna philosophy in the Madhyamaka and the Yogācāra, but there is no corresponding Vajrayāna philosophy. The Vajrayāna is entirely concerned with practice, with experience. The Vajrayāna takes Mahāyāna philosophy for granted and proceeds to practise on that basis, but the Vajrayāna itself consists simply of skilful means: particular methods suited to the particular circumstances of particular individuals. This is the fundamental characteristic of the Vajrayāna. So this is an important thing for Rechungpa to remember: that he's on the Vajrayāna path, that he is concerned with the actual practice, the actual realization of the truths of Buddhism.

Then there's the guru's Pith-Instruction. The Vajrayāna path lays down certain broad practices, certain kinds of meditation and so on, but that is still too general. You need the guru's Pith-Instruction – in other words, a precept in the sense of an *upadeśa*. The guru knows Buddhism not just theoretically but from personal experience. He really knows what he is talking about with regard to the Dharma, and at the same time he knows the disciple, so he brings the Dharma into relation with the needs of the disciple by means of the Pith-Instructions. They are *Pith*-Instructions because they give the essence of the matter, the essence of the Dharma as it relates to the disciple's situation. In giving Pith-Instructions the guru takes the general principles and applies them to exactly what the disciple needs to do at this particular moment. This is why the guru is so necessary.

There is a reference in the Hindu *Bhagavad Gītā* which throws some light on this. The cow represents the Vedas, the milk is the Upanishads, which are the essence of the Vedas, and the butter made from the milk is the *Bhagavad Gītā*.[155] In the same way one could say that the cow is Buddhism, the milk is the Vajrayāna, and the butter is the Pith-Instruction.

You also need your own judgement. This is quite important. You need these three things: the general teaching of Buddhism; the guru's Pith-Instruction, which is that general teaching as applied to your specific need; and your own judgement, which you need to exercise in the carrying out of the Pith-Instruction – it's not a question of blindly following it. There's what Buddhism says, what the guru says, and what you say, and when these three things are in agreement, you can go forward with confidence. Using your own judgement doesn't mean just doing what you want to do in your own way, but genuinely and responsibly using your own understanding of Buddhism to implement the guru's Pith-Instructions.

Respect and serve the learned,
Have faith in your Guru,
Be determined and persevering.
These are three things you should remember.

Who are 'the learned' in this context? Learned in what? The word usually means intellectual understanding, and that is not depreciated in Buddhism, but a clear distinction is made between a learned man with whom you may study Buddhist texts and gain a good understanding up to a point, and a guru who is able to illuminate the real meaning of those texts. Respect and serve the learned by all means – Milarepa is saying nothing against that – but that is not enough.

How do you serve the learned? This goes back to the Indian tradition that when you study with someone you should not only learn from him but attend upon him. This is very strong in Buddhism too. Your relation to your teacher, even the teacher with whom you merely study the scriptures in an intellectual way, not to speak of spiritual teachers, is not limited to the hours of learning. You don't just go along, have your class, and go away. You also serve him, and that usually means living with him, fetching water for him, washing his clothes and bringing his food. Being a pupil even in a purely academic sense involves this in Indian tradition. One needs to establish a rapport with the teacher by serving him in this practical way as well as receiving instruction from him and respecting him, and that's even more so with the guru. It's a practical expression of your receptivity, your gratitude for the teaching. The idea of just going along to a lesson and at the end saying goodbye to the teacher and going home would be considered inadequate, even disrespectful, according to the orthodox Indian tradition.

The Greek tradition was a little like this, but not the university tradition, not even in the Middle Ages. For one thing, professors started teaching gatherings of hundreds of students, whereas in the old days, certainly in India, it was just a handful. It was like a spiritual family, whether you were learning the Dharma or things like phonetics or music or mathematics. You lived with the teacher, he taught you, and you looked after the cooking and cleaning and so on. But when the teacher has got hundreds of students and he spends an hour with one group of them and another hour with another group, the whole arrangement breaks down and the teacher lives at home with his wife.

Of course, some gurus are married too, especially among the Nyingmapas. Some of my own teachers in Kalimpong were married, but I observed that it was sometimes a hindrance to them because the wife resented the husband spending so much time with his disciples and she would be more concerned with the offerings they made than with anything else. When you have a family to support, all those considerations come in, unfortunately from the Dharma point of view.

So, 'respect and serve the learned', and beyond that, have faith in your guru. This is very similar to putting yourself in the hands of the guru. It's an act of faith. You could say that putting yourself in the hands of the guru is the volitional side of what you do, and having faith is the emotional side, so obviously the two are closely connected. Having faith in the guru is not just believing certain things about him. A lot of people who take up with oriental gurus tend to think that faith in the guru means believing all sorts of wild and fantastic things about him. They may not be practising any spiritual teaching at all. They just believe all sorts of inflated things about the guru: that he can read their thoughts or that he is an incarnation of God or that he's Enlightened, and they think that is what having faith in the guru means. But that is belief, even blind belief, not faith. Faith is an emotional attitude as a result of which you put yourself in the hands of the guru, which is quite a different thing. It's when you reach the end of your own resources. You don't know what to do, you don't know which way to turn, and unreservedly you put yourself in the hands of the guru and say, 'You decide – whatever it is, I'll do it.' You're not asking the guru to tell you what to do with regard to something about which you ought to be able to make up your own mind; you have genuinely reached the end of your tether. Having done all that you could, you put the matter to the guru and ask him what he thinks you should do.

That is the sort of attitude that accompanies faith – not just believing all sorts of extraordinary and improbable things. Some people think that they show their faith in the guru by making exaggerated statements about him, but there's a difference between on the one hand having a feeling that the guru has a higher experience and will see things in a more real way and on the other hand having a feeling of weakness in contrast to something very strong, and consequently feeling subservient, even to the point of thinking that the guru is a kind of god. They're both emotional responses: the difference can be made clear in terms of the distinction between the power mode and the love mode, provided you clarify what those terms mean. From the Buddhist point of view, the guru operates in the love mode, not the power mode. He's not someone who is more powerful than you or who is trying to control you. He's not a group leader, or a boss, an authority figure or a father figure, but something quite different from all those things.

Milarepa goes on to say, 'Be determined and persevering', and there is a point to this distinction. Determination is making up your mind, deciding definitely that this is what you're going to do; and persevering is sticking to that indefinitely or until your end is attained. It's a bit like the Buddha's last words: *Appamādena sampādetha* – 'With mindfulness, strive'.[156] Mindfulness here includes mindfulness of purpose, awareness of what you are really doing, and striving of course suggests persisting in that. To be both determined and persevering is very important. People very often don't make up their minds, and then there can be no question of perseverance.

Taking this approach to the long-term goal is one thing, but you need to do it a little all the time. Even a very long chain is made up of lots of small links. To quote a verse from a famous hymn, 'Little drops of water, little grains of sand, make the mighty ocean and the pleasant land.'[157] There's a verse in the *Dhammapada* like that: 'Just as by the constant falling of drops of water a vessel fills, so, little by little, a man fills himself with good.'[158] Or, in the Scottish idiom, 'Many a mickle makes a muckle!' Very often people are not determined or persevering because they think little things don't matter. You think, 'I'll miss the meditation just for today. It won't make any difference; after all, in the course of the next ten or fifteen years I'll be doing thousands of hours of meditation.'

> Rightly to direct the Life-stream (Prāṇa),
> To enter the Dharma-Essence,
> And to master all the teachings,
> Are three techniques you should remember.

The translator says that the Life-stream means the Prāṇa. In Tantric terms, rightly to direct the Life-stream, the Prāṇa, the energy, is to direct it into the median nerve. That is a way of saying that the energies of the being should be totally unified. The unification of energy is a supremely important point, and the Vajrayāna deals with it quite a lot. It isn't esoteric, it's quite plain and practical and down to earth. All one's energies – the energies of the conscious mind, the unconscious mind, intellectual, volitional, emotional – must be unified. According to this verse it's not just a question of directing the Life-stream but rightly directing it, unifying it by directing it towards the ideal, one could say. In every person there's a tremendous amount of energy locked up both in the physical body and in the mind – energy that either just isn't used or is blocked or is short-circuiting or leaking away. The Vajrayāna stresses the unification of all this energy. It doesn't allow you to say, 'That energy doesn't matter' or 'That energy is too gross' or 'That energy is too refined'. You need *all* your energies. They've all got to be unified. What that means in practical terms and how one does it is a big question. But the principle is clear: that the whole Life-stream, all the energies, are to be rightly directed, are to be unified. I have sometimes spoken of this in terms of horizontal and vertical integration.[159]

Before there can be any talk of rightly directing or unifying the energies, however, one has got to experience one's energies, and for many people the first task is to realize that they *have* energies. Sometimes the energy level of people at meditation classes is very low, and perhaps the reason for that is that to begin with, meditating and doing pujas is almost too refined. Perhaps the serious Buddhist practitioners of the future will come not from among those who are interested in Eastern philosophies but from among those whose energies have been aroused through their involvement with the arts or sports, and those who want to teach meditation and the Dharma will need to establish channels of communication with people like that. To be provocative, one might even say that the people who profess to be or believe they are interested in Buddhism are the ones who are least suitable to practise it.

Alternatively, if people coming along to a meditation class are into astral travel or spiritualism or other apparently wacky beliefs, there's no need to discount the possibility that they may be open to learning about the Dharma. People catch hold of whatever is to hand, and it is very difficult to contact something genuine. At least they've realized that they're not going to find it in church. Spiritualism is a widespread movement and it often draws those who genuinely wonder, 'Is there life after death?' – a good starting point for an inquiry into the Dharma. Even thinking that one is Enlightened may be a starting point for some people. They may have read a book written by a Theravāda Buddhist that says that if you think clearly and if your attitude is quite rational, you're Enlightened. Theravāda Buddhists do sometimes write a bit like that. It would be quite natural to read a book like that and in good faith think, 'I'm a clear-thinking rational sort of person. It seems as though according to Buddhism I'm Enlightened.' There is no need to be dismissive of that; such a person just needs to come to understand that there's a bit more to Enlightenment than that, so there's a way further to go.

'To enter the Dharma Essence' is in a way complementary to the previous line: unify all your energies, enter the Dharma essence. First of all you take on general teachings but as you progress, your practice becomes more and more specific, and you enter more and more into the essence of the Dharma, and see the interconnectedness of all the separate teachings. The Dharma Essence differs from the Pith-Instruction in the sense that the Pith-Instruction comes to you from the outside, from the guru, but here the suggestion is that you yourself, by virtue of your practice, are penetrating more and more deeply into the Dharma. You can perhaps visualize the Dharma as a sort of hollow cone. You enter it at the broad end at the base and as you go further and deeper into it, it narrows, becomes more concentrated, you penetrate more and more into the essence of it.

When people are new to Buddhism, the things that they want to talk about are usually so general that they've got no practical applicability at all, at least not for them. They want to discuss things like *nirvāṇa* and Enlightenment. To enter the Dharma Essence means to go from the more general and abstract to the more and more specific, the more and more individual, and therefore the more and more experienced, and that represents a unification, just as rightly directing the Life-stream represents a unification. The fact that people think it's possible to discuss *nirvāṇa* at all means they haven't even begun even to think about practising the Dharma. If you meet someone who asks you about Enlightenment or about the One Mind, you know exactly where they stand. Well, in terms of Buddhism they don't stand anywhere at all.

Why should you master all the teachings, presumably not just those of the Vajrayāna but those of the Mahāyāna and the Theravāda? It can only be for the benefit of others. You don't need to master the whole lot for the sake of your own spiritual progress. Perhaps one or two or three teachings will be quite enough. But you're not concerned only with yourself. You're concerned with helping other living beings. You need skilful means. You may have found the Abhidharma very attractive and inspiring, but other people might find it dull, and instead be attracted and inspired by the Madhyamaka teachings. You have to learn the whole array of teachings so as to be able to place them at other people's disposal. That is very much part of a bodhisattva's life, if you take the bodhisattva ideal seriously. According to the Mahāyāna *sūtras* you should not only master all the Dharmas; you should even learn all the secular arts and sciences so that you've got a wider range of means of communication and therefore can communicate with a greater number of people.

Presumably you have to balance this with actual attainment, otherwise you won't have any credibility. Mastering even one subject might take you a lifetime. The Mahāyāna perspective is that the bodhisattva's career extends over three unthinkable *kalpas*,[160] but even setting that aside the principle is clear. All sorts of odd bits and pieces of knowledge can come in handy in communicating with people. You might be in the middle of America somewhere and meet somebody who has been to Sicily. You've been to Sicily too – that's the only thing you have in common as far as you can see – so you both talk about Sicily and your experiences there, and having established a rapport, then perhaps the Dharma will enter the conversation. It's important to have a means of communication other than the Dharma itself. Don't take it literally that you're going to need to take evening classes every night of the week and learn about philately and photography and the history of Ancient Greece. It just suggests adopting a certain flexibility of approach. Everybody's got a whole rag bag of bits and pieces of knowledge, and you can use them all.

I once met somebody who had some connection with the coal trade. In my younger days I worked for about seven months in a firm that sold coal, so as it happened I knew quite a bit about it,[161] and it all came back to me. We had quite a chat about coal, and then we started talking about other things. This is the sort of thing that can happen. Use whatever bits and pieces of knowledge you've got to establish contact with people, and then perhaps you'll find a natural approach to communicating the Dharma. This is what this line is really getting at. Don't take it too literally.

> *The views of the Bliss-Void,*
> *Of the myriad forms,*
> *Of reasoning and following the scriptures,*
> *Are three essentials you should remember.*

The grammatical construction of this verse in translation is not completely clear. Presumably it means that the views of the Bliss-Void, the views of the myriad forms, and the views of reasoning and following the scriptures are three essentials you should remember. I don't think 'views' here means views in general but more like right views, the right sort of outlook.

The Bliss-Void clearly refers to a sort of compound, but what are the elements of the compound? It connects with disposing of *saṃsāra* and *nirvāṇa*. Void represents the experience of *śūnyatā*, the Transcendental, *nirvāṇa*, Bliss represents the experience of *saṃsāra* at its highest and most sublimated level, and the views of the Bliss-Void are those views concerning the bringing together, the unification, of these two. The Vajrayāna, in contradistinction to the Mahāyāna, stresses the experience of the body or with the body, through the body, the experience of energy. It stresses the fact that the whole *saṃsāra* side of things is not to be rejected or ignored, as perhaps even the Mahāyāna seems to suggest. The energies that are inherent in *saṃsāra* are to be led in the direction of Enlightenment, and these energies are to be experienced at successively higher degrees of bliss, culminating in what is called *mahāsukha*, the Great Bliss. *Mahāsukha* is that experience of bliss which is united with the experience of the Void. To speak in terms of the unification of the Void and bliss is to express in psychological, even experiential terms the same thing that one is trying to describe by speaking of disposing of or uniting or transcending *nirvāṇa* and *saṃsāra*.

It also correlates with *puṇya* and *jñāna*, the two accumulations – the accumulation of merits and the accumulation of knowledge or awareness.[162] *Jñāna* pertains to the Unconditioned, and *puṇya* pertains to the conditioned. *Puṇya* represents the highest and the most positive and skilful level of the mundane whereas *jñāna* represents the Transcendental. It's as though the Vajrayāna says that one must have a thorough experience of the *saṃsāra* at the highest level, and that experience, especially in the form of ecstatic bliss, is to be united with the purely transcendental realization of the Void. The ultimate realization which goes beyond all duality is therefore to be thought of as a unification of the Void and bliss or of *nirvāna* and *samsāra*, or of the Unconditioned and the conditioned.

In terms of practical Vajrayāna, it consists in practising, in ordinary Buddhist terms, *śamatha* meditations, which heighten the experience of bliss. Then you retain the experience of bliss while developing the experience of insight, uniting the two. The Vajrayāna does this in the highest and fullest possible sense, uniting the experience of psychophysical bliss with the purely spiritual experience of insight into the Void. It regards this as a completely balanced experience and pursues it to the limit. One could connect it with Blake's reference to 'improvement in sensual enjoyment' in the *Marriage of Heaven and Hell*,[163] and also with the visualization practice, because the Buddha's form as you normally perceive it represents the mundane in its perfection.

In the phrase 'views of the myriad forms' it's not very clear what forms are being referred to, but it would appear to mean forms in the sense of *rūpa* – the myriad appearances of things as you perceive them, especially as you see them. Presumably the views of the myriad forms refers to the fact that all these forms are *śūnyatā*, that *rūpa* is inseparable from *śūnyatā*, and *śūnyatā* is inseparable from *rūpa*, in much the same way that *śūnyatā* and bliss are inseparable.[164] One could look at it like that: that bliss is something that you experience, form is something that you see, but both the subjective and the objective, bliss representing the subjective and *rūpa* representing the objective, are to be unified with śūnyatā. The subject–object duality is to be transcended in all its forms.

In 'the views of reasoning and following the scriptures' we also have two things that are to be balanced. Reasoning cannot be discarded, but neither can the scriptures. The general Buddhist tradition holds that correct reasoning, so far as it goes, will be in accordance with the conclusions of the scriptures, and that the conclusions of the scriptures cannot be in conflict with those of true reasoning. In other words, genuine experience – and the scriptures after all communicate the Buddha's genuine spiritual experience – must be in harmony with the conclusions of valid reasoning. This is the general Buddhist position. The term 'essentials' is used for these three because they are central to the teaching.

The Tantra emphasizes the need to have an experience of *samsāra* on higher and higher levels, but other schools of Buddhism don't see it like that. One might ask therefore whether there is any other way of achieving Enlightenment than by sublimating one's basic energies. The Vajrayāna would say not – or perhaps one could say that the Vajrayāna makes this fully explicit whereas the Mahāyāna doesn't and Theravāda Buddhism certainly doesn't. Perhaps it wasn't necessary for them to do that. One gets the impression from the Pāli scriptures that although the Buddha doesn't speak in terms of energy, he was speaking to people whose energies were already fully galvanized, not blocked or leaking away, so they could take the simple teachings that he gave them and at once fully and vigorously apply them and bring their whole being into line with those teachings. It's as though the teachings of the Buddha in the Pāli canon assume that the listener is already fully in contact with his emotions and energies, that all he needs is the Dharma, because he is already sufficiently developed on the mundane side of things. Even the Mahāyāna tends to assume in its description of the bodhisattva that all you need is the Dharma. Perhaps the Vajrayāna is therefore especially applicable to people nowadays, not in the sense of needing to go off to follow a Tibetan lama but because the need to engage one's energies, which is implicit in Buddhism as a whole, is emphasized by the Vajrayāna.

The Vajrayāna developed a thousand years after the Buddha's time, and it seems that the social and cultural situation in India had changed in the meantime. In both Buddhism and Hinduism there was a very intellectual movement, especially Vedantic intellectualism, and you could even say that religion, to use that term, both in its Hindu and in its Buddhist forms, became over-intellectualized, over-academic. You had the development of the Abhidharma, and then the development of the Madhyamaka and the Yogācāra, and they all had certain highly academic aspects. From a historical point of view the Vajrayāna was a reaction against all that, emphasizing again and again the importance of practice and experience and realization. Some forms of Vajrayāna, like the Sahajayāna, quite explicitly rejected the whole academic and formal monastic routine and way of life. Some followers of that form wouldn't even be ordained as Buddhist monks because it had become too safe in a way, too formal, too stereotyped. They became freelance wandering yogi Buddhists, Milarepa being the almost archetypal example.

> *A partner qualified in Mudrā,*
> *Experience of the bliss therein,*
> *And the 'Elephantine work,'*
> *These are the three delights you should remember.*

In this context it is clear that 'a partner qualified in Mudrā' means a woman with whom one engages in yogic sexual practice, but this need not be taken literally. In the Vajrayāna there are not only exoteric but also esoteric refuges. As a more concrete and specific form of the Buddha refuge one has the guru refuge. As a more concrete and specific form of the Dharma refuge there is the *deva* – the particular Buddha or bodhisattva that one visualizes in the course of one's meditation, to whom one is devoted and who has a special significance in one's spiritual life. And then as the concrete, specific form of the Sangha refuge there is the *ḍākinī*. The *ḍākinī* can be taken to symbolize the spiritual companion, the one in whose company you practise the Dharma. That doesn't just mean two people occupying caves side by side and getting on with their practice quite separately. It suggests someone with whom you have a very positive and powerful communication, someone who sparks you off in your practice of the Dharma. Their role is not that of a teacher – they are very much on the same level and practising in the same way as you – but nonetheless you find them inspiring. There can even be an element of competitiveness. You don't try to do better than your friend, but you try to do your best, and he wants to get ahead of you not to beat you or defeat you but because he wants to do the best that he possibly can, and he uses this 'competition' to incite himself to further spiritual efforts.

Essentially it's communication in the highest form that we're able to experience it, and this is a very important aspect of the spiritual life. One might say that the relationship with the guru is the ideal vertical relationship, and the relationship with the *ḍākinī* or the 'partner qualified in Mudrā' (using the term in the symbolic sense I suggest) is the ideal horizontal relationship. But although it's broadly speaking horizontal, you're not always on exactly the same level. At one time you may be feeling a bit dull or discouraged, and then your spiritual friend will encourage you. On another occasion the position may be reversed. The difference between this and ordinary competitiveness is that you and your friend are just trying to do better than each other, so that you are stretched to your limit, and that's all you want, so it doesn't matter who 'wins'. On one occasion you may point out something that the other person doesn't see, and on another occasion he may point out something that you don't see. In the case of the 'vertical' relationship – the relationship between a disciple and his or her teacher – there may not be that kind of mutuality. On the other hand, the guru can also develop through contact with the disciples. It isn't a static or one-way relationship; it is said that you don't really start to learn until you start to teach, and that can apply at many different levels. This is brought out very strongly by Plato in connection with the educational process; in his view, the process of educating a pupil is an education for the teacher too, in a different way.

So perhaps one should think of the vertical relationship as well as the horizontal relationship in dynamic and mutual terms. A pupil who is very demanding in any subject brings out the inner resources of the teacher, resources that perhaps to begin with he wasn't aware that he possessed. Even though there is a difference between the two relationships, the horizontal and the vertical, it is not a difference in respect of dynamic mutuality, even though there is definitely a difference between the two kinds of relationship.

Perhaps we should recall the overall situation. What has happened is that Rechungpa, disregarding Milarepa's advice, is insisting on going to India even though that means giving up his regular meditation. In the end Milarepa has agreed to his going – not to study logic and science, but to obtain the Formless Ḍākinī Dharmas. But nonetheless he's not at all happy about him going, seeming to think that it represents a departure from the spiritual path, which is why he said in an earlier song 'this uninformed son of mine, the loser of debate and full of doubts, has stopped his meditation and is about to wander far away to study. This is the very thing a yogi should avoid.' So it seems that Rechungpa has become very much out of touch with the spiritual life. The fact that Milarepa asks him to remember these three delights suggests that Rechungpa must have had some experience of them previously. Perhaps if he can recall them, that will put him back in touch with a more spiritual mental state.

The second delight Milarepa mentions is the 'experience of the Bliss therein'. Again adapting this a little to consider the nature of spiritual companionship in general, this is also quite important: that the communication you enjoy with a spiritual companion is intensely blissful. That doesn't mean to say it's easy, comfortable, or sentimental – it can be quite demanding – but it can be intensely blissful, and arouse a lot of energy.

The third delight is the 'Elephantine Work', and the note says, 'The advanced yogi acts fearlessly, with great inspiration, for his own need in various unusual acts, that common people may judge him as "crazy" or "immoral".' But why should acting in this sort of way be called the elephantine work? As the biggest of the creatures, the elephant has no reason to be afraid of anything or anybody, and the yogi is like that. He's not only big, spiritually speaking, but because he's big he's fearless. He can do whatever it comes into his mind to do. He doesn't care what people think, just as the elephant doesn't mind the barking of the dogs as he goes through the village. That's the usual comparison.

Is there a connection between this fearless elephantine state and having a spiritual companion and experiencing the bliss of communication, or is the association quite fortuitous? It is stressed in the note that the advanced yogi acts fearlessly with great inspiration for his own need in various unusual acts, such that 'common people may judge him as crazy or immoral'. How does that connect with communication with one's peers? It seems to me that the connection is that the communication that you have with your spiritual peers is so radical, so no-holds-barred, so dangerous, that if you can survive that, you can survive anything. It isn't a sweet, sentimental friendship. Your friend is not going to let you get away with anything. He is going to challenge you, demand things of you, give you a tough time, perhaps, and that will free you up and make you fearless and bold and inspired in a way that maybe nothing else would. Having gone through that fierce friendship, you're ready to face the world, as it were, because the world can't give you nearly such a tough time as your spiritual friends have given you.

Here the fearlessness and unconventionality of the yogi is emphasized. With your spiritual friends, especially with your spiritual companion if you just have one special one, you're accustomed to being completely open. You're not accustomed to disguising anything. You're not afraid to say anything. And because you have become accustomed to this completely open, free, fearless communication with your spiritual companion, you can be like that when you go out into the world, if you see it as a skilful way in which to behave. You've exposed yourself to your spiritual companion. You haven't hidden anything, so you're not afraid of anything being found out; and you carry that attitude of fearlessness, openness and inspiration with you when you try to communicate with a wider audience, when you go out into the world. You're not timid, restrained, or apologetic. You're bold and forceful and confident. You're not afraid to say anything to the world, though maybe sometimes you have to consider people's reaction, not because you're afraid of it but because you don't want to scare them away.

To *instruct an idler brings misfortune*

Why would instructing an idler bring misfortune? It suggests a mistake on your part, and that might well bring misfortune. By 'an idler' is meant someone who isn't going to practise the Dharma, though he might be very busy in other ways. Someone might be motivated to instruct such a person because he might be looking for a rich patron or a powerful protector. An idler could be pleasant to be with and might even seem quite interested in the Dharma. But you would be instructing someone in the Dharma with a wrong motive and that would certainly bring about misfortune sooner or later. It certainly couldn't be a very happy relationship if you were trying to instruct them and they weren't actually practising the Dharma. There would be sure to be some unpleasantness sooner or later. To instruct an idler is thus not just a waste of time, it's almost dangerous.

To *speak of one's experience leads to loss*

The kind of experience he is referring to is presumably meditation. This sort of thing can happen quite easily. If you try to communicate your experience to someone to whom in fact you cannot communicate it for one reason or another, then communication doesn't take place and you're left just with words. That puts you out of touch with your experience, and you lose it. If, on the other hand, the other person can understand what you are saying and has perhaps had a comparable experience, talking to him can enhance your experience, because you stay in touch with it in the course of communication. This is why it is sometimes said within the Vajrayāna context that if you've received a certain initiation and you're practising a particular kind of meditation or reciting a particular mantra, you may speak of it only to fellow disciples of the same guru who have that same initiation and are performing the same practice.

One shouldn't chatter about one's meditation experience to all and sundry. If you do, you are not communicating your meditation experience; you are talking about it, which is quite another matter, and to the extent that you talk about it without communicating it, you lose it, you get out of touch with it. There was a cartoon in our recent newsletter with the caption 'So there I was sitting on my cushion twelve hours a day, knees feeling like they were about to fall off, when suddenly I started to feel this amazing feeling on the top of my head.' That's the way you mustn't talk about meditation even if you have had a strong experience, because if you start talking about it in that way you're externalizing it, separating yourself from it, alienating yourself from it, and to that extent you no longer experience it and hence you lose it.

People can be very insensitive when they ask you about Buddhism or about your experience of meditation, expecting you to be able to chat about your deepest experiences and convictions in a casual cocktail-party style. One should just refuse to do this. Say, 'If you really want to talk about this I'm quite willing to, but let's get together on some other occasion.' When someone asks over cocktails, so to speak, 'What is this meditation all about?' what can you say under those sorts of conditions? In any case, if you've had a quite deep experience, you may not have the vocabulary to do it justice. You may not even have the ideas, the conceptual framework. Then you would just have to give them an enigmatic smile.

But although 'to speak of one's experience leads to loss', that does not mean that one should never under any circumstances speak of one's experience. Obviously if the Buddha had followed that principle there would have been no such thing as Buddhism. One can certainly try to communicate one's experience if it seems a skilful thing to do, with the emphasis on communicate, not just talk about. But communication is possible only under certain conditions which have to be respected.

In towns to wander damages one's Yoga.

It's not hatha yoga that Milarepa is talking about, obviously, but meditation and spiritual practice in general. But can we take it quite literally that wandering in towns damages one's practice? Of course it's distracting, and there's the interruption to your practice, the time wasted. It suggests a passive attitude. The rather uncomplimentary comparison usually given by teachers in India is that you roam around the town like a stray dog.

This raises the whole question of one's immersion in worldly life. Does it mean that if one can avoid it one should never go into town?

For some people that might be a very good idea. The most dangerous thing about going into town, to use that as the paradigmatic situation, is that you become passive instead of being active. If you are active in the positive skilful sense you're in much less danger than when you are in a purely passive pseudo-receptive state – pseudo-receptive because it isn't genuine spiritual receptivity. You're at the mercy of all sorts of energies. If you have a strong vibe of your own which you are positively projecting, and that especially happens when you take the initiative, that is different. If you go into town to get something, you have a purpose, and that protects you slightly. If you just wander into town and drift around, lounging here and loitering there, it will have a much more deleterious effect. I've had the experience myself many times of taking the train to a particular town, being met at the station and taken to the meeting place, then giving a lecture, answering questions, having a quick cup of tea, and setting off back home, and that is a quite different experience. Even though you've gone to town, through all the traffic and the throngs of people, you are taking the initiative all the time, you are active in a highly positive and skilful manner. Because you have a definite purpose, it's a quite intense experience. If you remain positive and active and outward-going, it almost doesn't matter where you go. It's passivity that is the danger, because it allows influences to pour in upon you, and all sorts of unskilful and unpleasant energies to reach you.

Is living in a city more conducive to developing a positive, initiative-taking attitude than secluding yourself in the countryside? I'm not so sure about that. It might be better to stay in a quiet secluded spot in the country and have forays into town from time to time. Of course, you can create a quiet spot in the town itself – a Buddhist centre, or a community where you really get into your practice and from which you have your forays out, your raids as it were, before you retreat back into your lair.

Taking the initiative and being active and positive doesn't necessarily mean doing something spectacular. It is essentially a mental attitude. The great point is made in Buddhism, especially in the Abhidharma, that meditation is an active process because in meditation you are continually creating skilful mental states. It is an uninterrupted flow of skilful volitions of tremendous karmic significance. If you can go into town maintaining a highly meditative state of mind by whatsoever means, whether by repeating a mantra or in some other way, you are active rather than passive and therefore can move about in the town with less danger of damaging your yoga.

The time to go into town is definitely not when you're feeling dull and bored, because then you'll be looking for distraction. You might decide to go to a concert for a change or stimulation, though if you're bored a concert probably won't help you. If you've had rather a tiring day and you're a little out of contact with your feelings, going to a concert can be a very positive thing to do, and it's even better if you go along already in a highly positive state; then the experience of the concert heightens that.

Sometimes you may feel that going into town has a stimulating effect on you just in terms of contact with other human beings, especially after being by yourself for a while. You may see the occasional face that is genuinely positive, or people who are enjoying themselves in a quite innocent way. Too often people move past so quickly that you don't even have a chance to see their faces. To sum up, sometimes, if one is very careful, it can be mildly stimulating to spend a few minutes in town, and it's certainly an opportunity to witness the human condition. On the bus or the train you may see the 'marks of weakness, marks of woe' that Blake observed in London in his day.[165] People are so tired that they can't be bothered to pretend, and they've got no one to pretend to, so they slump, just being the way that they feel, which is tired and drained or bored and fed up or whatever.

> To join the assembly of the Brethren,
> To attend the meeting of Ḍākinīs,
> And be present at the (secret) feasts,
> These are the three occasions not to miss.

The meetings of ḍākinīs are held in cremation grounds, where there is a very heightened experience in every way. One can take the ḍākinīs literally or symbolically. Symbolically they are the upsurging spiritual energies, the energies of inspiration. And the secret feasts are the Tantric feasts. A feast, an occasion on which you all eat together, especially if you are united by a spiritual bond, is very special; there's a feeling of intimacy and harmony and communication.

However we take 'the assembly of the Brethren' (a very unlikely phrase for Milarepa to use, one might think), Milarepa is speaking in terms of a progressively deeper and more intense and more vibrant experience of spiritual community, and perhaps the 'secret feast' is the most intense of all. That is when the wine, literal or symbolical, circulates and people really enter into communication with one another. So these are the three occasions not to miss. Perhaps Milarepa is suggesting to Rechungpa that when he goes to India, even when he is busy obtaining the Formless Ḍākinī Dharmas, as Milarepa hopes he will be, he should not miss any opportunities for spiritual companionship, from the most superficial to the most profound. This applies to all of us too. If you're travelling, don't miss any opportunity for enjoying spiritual community, whether with other Buddhists or even, if possible, with members of the sangha to which you yourself belong.

The symbol of the *ḍākinī* originally belonged to Indian Buddhism, though the Tibetans have taken over the Sanskrit word and they use it quite a lot. They also use the word *khandroma*, which means 'sky-goer'. There doesn't seem to be a direct connection between the energies or passions aroused by sexual attraction and the spiritual energies symbolized by the *ḍākinī*. The great analogue for inspiration and emotional excitation is sex, so a symbol for that which is spiritually exciting, stimulating and inspiring as far as a Dharma practitioner who is attracted to women is concerned will be a young and attractive female. It's as simple as that. The *ḍāka* presumably holds the same symbolism for those attracted to the male form.

This 'secret feast', the Tantric gathering from which people not initiated into that particular mandala are excluded, raises the question of the naturally esoteric. You don't make something esoteric just by keeping people out. What makes something really secret is the fact that all the people participating are on a common wavelength or share a common experience that others are not on or do not share. The 'secret feasts' were those occasions when initiates into a particular Tantric tradition met for the purpose of ritual worship. On such occasions food would be dedicated to whichever Buddha or bodhisattva or guardian deity or *ḍākinī* was being worshipped, and then distributed among those present and sacramentally consumed as a symbol of the spiritual bond between them. These feasts were quite common in India among Tantric yogins but they started getting a bad name. There are many stories of them degenerating into orgies, especially if both male and female initiates happened to be present and if there was drinking, which might originally have been the purely sacramental drinking of a few drops of wine but eventually became a party.

The fact that members of a spiritual community eat together does add something, but you have to be careful that it doesn't also destroy something. The fact that you are eating and even drinking together shouldn't mean that you become unmindful – maybe it should be slightly formalized, as with the Japanese tea ceremony – but it can give an additional dimension. It can make the common relationship that you have very concrete. Eating together is a very basic thing, after all.

It might not be appropriate for it to occur in a shrine-room, however. The way that many people eat is so unmindful that it would be quite out of place in a shrine-room. Eating is quite a gross physical activity, associated with hunger, appetite, even greed, with the processes of digestion, assimilation, excretion, and so on. It's a pretty earthy activity associated with not very refined mental states, and you need a high degree of mindfulness to assimilate its grossness within the spiritual life. There are deities associated with gross things like eating and other physical activities. There's even one who is associated with the toilet: Ucchuṣma. In monasteries he is depicted in the toilets because he is especially associated with the flushing out of impurities from the mind as well as from the body. His name means something like 'the fiery upward blazing one'. He looks very fierce, and he's meant to deal with all the *pretas* and evil spirits that haunt the toilet.

If you have eating and drinking in the shrine-room there is the danger of a displacement of the comparatively refined atmosphere created by puja and meditation by the comparatively gross atmosphere created by eating and drinking. You have to be careful that the atmosphere created by puja and meditation transforms the atmosphere created by eating and drinking, not the other way around. It's not just a question of turning the shrine into a temporary dining room, though this is what would happen more often than not. You could try to include the eating and drinking within the ritual process so that you're eating and drinking in the same spirit as that in which you make offerings to the Buddha, but in the shrine you're trying to create a refined, spiritual atmosphere, and you do that with the help of flowers and lights and incense, and it would seem completely inappropriate to bring in cooked food with a strong smell. I've experienced this in India, in Hindu temples, and even in Buddhist ones. Sometimes the Bengali Buddhists bring in great loads of rice and curry and offer it in front of the shrine, and the smell just doesn't go with the smell of the incense.

If you do eat and drink sacramentally, you should serve small amounts of quite refined food. One might consider turning the dining room into a temporary shrine-room, rather than consecrating the activity by literally having it in a shrine-room, but perhaps we do need to do that psychologically. Perhaps it's difficult for us to really feel that kind of atmosphere unless we have some strong symbols around. The Theravāda approach is just to eat mindfully, but the Tibetans do it differently. They sit in the shrine-room with all the images there, and after they have chanted they are served with their food on the spot and they recite special food offering prayers and tea drinking prayers. An occasion like that could be 'secret' in the sense that it's probably better not to bring a guest who knows nothing about Buddhism into such a situation. He might find it very strange, as though he was being conscripted into something under pretence of being invited to a meal.

The body and the bodily energies are kept going with food, so food symbolizes all the material energies. If your spiritual communion includes taking food together, it thus represents the incorporation of the gross energies into the process of the spiritual life, and this is something that you need to try to do anyway. You don't lead the spiritual life with some rarefied part of your personality. You lead it with your whole being – body, speech, and mind. So in a way it is natural that you should not only meditate together, but eat and drink together as a spiritual activity. And work too – sacramental work – is important, though that's much more difficult to establish.

There is a difficulty, even a danger, in a sacramental approach. You mustn't sanctify everything, or spiritualize it, by superimposing upon it the symbols of religion. This is a very important point. By a sacramental approach – and I'm not altogether happy with the word sacramental – I mean the endowing of ordinary activities with a spiritual significance, or trying to appreciate the spiritual significance of those activities, so that doing them may remind you of the spiritual life. It must be a genuine process. You don't sacramentalize eating and drinking, to use that example, by rapidly and unmindfully chanting a few prayers before you eat and drink. You must genuinely eat and drink mindfully. You must genuinely feel that the energy you are getting from the food is going into your system and that this energy is being used to follow the spiritual path. It isn't enough just to chant a few mantras. You don't make a meal sacramental just by holding it in the shrine-room or having religious symbols present. The essence of the sacramental approach is a profound mental and spiritual attitude.

It's the same with the so-called sacrament of marriage. You don't spiritualize a sexual coupling just by getting a priest to pronounce some holy words over it. The sacramental cannot be mechanically made so. This is what Luther's protests against the Roman Catholic Church were about. The whole sacramental system had become mechanical and even commercialized. Instead of going to the priest and confessing your sins and being absolved from them as a meaningful process, you went along and said, 'I've done this and I've done that', paid a bit of money, the priest muttered a few words over you, and you went away with a certificate saying you were clear of the sin. That isn't a sacrament. You don't imbue something with a deeply spiritual significance by simply sticking on to the exterior of that activity the symbols of religion. But this is what happens so often, even within Buddhism. You don't make a meal sacred just by keeping an image of the Buddha on the table. And you can have a genuinely sacramental meal without any Buddha image or candles or flowers or incense or anything of that sort just because you are all eating and drinking together and are all on the same wavelength.

Likewise, doing a sevenfold puja isn't a spiritual practice if your mental state is not in tune with that. It's just attachment to rites and rituals as ends in themselves – thinking that they have significance on their own account. The Catholic doctrine, by contrast, is that the sacraments are automatically efficacious regardless of the mental state or the degree of sanctity of the person delivering them. Even if your priest is in a state of mortal sin it does not impair the efficacy of the sacraments he administers; he can still absolve you from sin. If that sounds like a con trick, that's what Luther thought too, and that was the origin of Protestantism. They threw out five of the seven sacraments and left only two: baptism and the Lord's supper, as they called it.

Of course, the church is not the only place you find this sort of thing. As I wandered round the Mind Body Spirit Festival this year I overheard various things of this sort. Someone would say, 'Let me put a few drops of this scent on your hankie – it's really powerful. It's been blessed. So many mantras have been recited over it, there are very strong vibrations attached to it.' And then there are the pills that Tibetan lamas chant over. I'm not saying that there's an absolute gulf between so-called matter and so-called mind and I'm not saying that psychical influences may not attach themselves to material objects. I'm not saying that you cannot be affected mentally by things you ingest that have had mantras or prayers recited over them. But the difference made is only marginal; you cannot attain to any degree of mental purification by such means. Wandering around the same festival, I looked at a little image and the woman who ran the stall saw me pick it up. It was quite nice but it was very expensive, and she said, 'Oh yes, it's great, isn't it? Aren't there a lot of lovely vibes all around it?' It seemed so false. I won't say that the woman was deliberately lying. Perhaps if she thought that vibes were there, she thought that she must be feeling them, and that's the patter that she was giving. You're almost buying the vibes, which justify the unreasonably high price: commercialized sacramentalism, one might even say, or sacramentalized commercialism. One must be so careful of humbug in the spiritual life. One doesn't want to exclude the element of the non-rational, the trans-normal, the magical – one doesn't want to adopt a dry, rational approach – but one must be on one's guard against humbug. When you get hundreds of people flocking to a hall in London to see the Karmapa put on his black hat, because they have been told that seeing that will assure them of salvation, is one to take it quite literally or is one to say it has a symbolical significance? And if it has a symbolical significance, what is that significance as distinct from the literal enactment of the ceremony? One is told that that black hat is quite literally woven out of the hair of *ḍākinīs*. If you're not careful, there is no end to what you're asked to swallow, and before you know what is happening you're being exploited in the name of religion, or in the name of Buddhism even.

To take another example, if you place food on the shrine and offer it to the Buddha, so that the Buddha has 'accepted' it and it comes back to you blessed, when you eat it, does it really have a special effect on your mind? This is what Hindus believe, and some Buddhists too. But if you offer food to the Buddha, is there any sense in which the Buddha accepts it? This is the essence of the sacramental meal. It's not that you simply eat it together. It is that that food is offered to whatever you worship or revere and is accepted and thereby becomes charged with a special spiritual potency, so that when you eat it, you share in that potency. You have this in many different forms both in primitive cults and in more sophisticated religions. You have it in the Mass, in which the bread and wine are changed by the magic words spoken by the priest into literally the flesh and blood of Christ, and you ingest those and share in the body of Christ. If you really believe that, clearly it has a profound psychological effect. But what is really happening? As a Buddhist do you believe that if you place food in front of the Buddha, somehow the Buddha accepts and blesses it and it becomes imbued with some sort of magical force which is then communicated to you when you eat that food, or is it just a vague feeling of uplift and magic that gives you a feeling of contentment?

It's true that when you chant mantras and make offerings, especially at festivals, something definitely gets generated, and you experience it when you bow to the Buddha. It's understandable that you should experience the effects of something that you yourself do, but it's quite different to think of the Buddha as accepting and blessing offerings of food, and that blessing changing the quality of the food, so that when you eat it, it has a special spiritual effect on you.

And how about making food offerings? It may be symbolic, but only in the sense that it reminds you of a certain spiritual truth. It is not sacramental in the strict sense. If, for instance, the image of the Buddha reminds us of the Buddha, that is commemorative and an aid to recollection. You may reflect that the Buddha comes into the world like a stranger appearing at the gate, and just as in the Indian tradition a stranger is made welcome, so you make the Buddha welcome in the world by offering the things that are offered to an honoured guest. So you lay out your seven offerings. All this is suggestive of certain meanings. But that's very different from believing that the image of the Buddha is filled with a magic force, that the Buddha is in a sense actually present in the image, and that food offered to the Buddha is actually transformed so that when you eat it you're taking in some sort of magic force.

It's a question of knowing what you're doing. Usually we're very vague and confused and do things without understanding very much about them. People aren't always clear why we have Buddha images at all. They've got accustomed to the fact that in Buddhist centres and communities you have shrines and images and they just accept it. Perhaps they've not thought about it very much. But we shouldn't forget that in India for several hundred years after the Buddha's life there were no images of the Buddha at all. If we were to open a Buddhist centre in a Muslim country we would be well advised not to have any images because the fact that 'idols' were being 'worshipped' in a Muslim country would invite immediate opposition. There's nothing in Buddhism that requires us to keep images of the Buddha, so why do we do it? Presumably because it reminds us of the ideal of Enlightenment and gives us an opportunity of developing our devotional feelings towards that ideal by making offerings to the image which, I won't say symbolizes that ideal, but tries to depict that ideal in artistic form. If that is why we do it, we need to be clear about that, not just go along with it because it happens to be the Buddhist custom.

In the concluding lines of the song, Milarepa says:

> Think of the meanings of this song,
> And put them into practice.

Putting them into practice is of course the important thing.

> Rechungpa made many obeisances to the Jetsun and then set out for India. Accompanying him were fifteen monks, their leader being a Ningmaba lama called Jidun. In Nepal both Rechungpa and Jidun had some success (in spreading the Dharma). They also met Dipupa's disciple, Bharima.
>
> (When they asked the King of Ko Kom in Nepal) for a 'Travel-Permit,' the King said, 'It is wonderful that you, the heart-disciple of the great Yogi who refused my invitation before, have now come to me.' He was delighted and granted all Rechungpa's requests. Arriving in India, Rechungpa met Dipupa and obtained all the teachings he wanted. Dipupa also had great faith in Milarepa. He entrusted Rechungpa with his gift – an aloewood staff – to present to the Jetsun upon his return to Tibet.
>
> On this journey Rechungpa also met the accomplished Yoginī, Magi, and he received from her the teaching of the Buddha of Long Life. He also learned much black magic and many deadly spells from pagan Indians.

On his way home Rechungpa again met Bharima in Nepal. As to the story of Bharima correcting the jealous translator-scholars, and Rechungpa's other adventures in Nepal and India, the reader may refer to Rechungpa's Biography, in which all is told in full.[166]

In his illuminating (Samādhi) Milarepa foresaw Rechungpa's return. He then went to Balkhu plain to welcome him. Thus, the father and the son met again.

This is the story of Rechungpa and Dipupa.

We may have gained the impression that Rechungpa was going off to India on his own, but this makes it clear that fifteen other monks went with him. And apparently he forgot all about learning the art of debate, and logic and science, or perhaps as Milarepa didn't agree to his going to India to learn that, it isn't mentioned. He did learn 'much black magic and many deadly spells', though; perhaps he decided that would be a better way of dealing with the magicians.

When I was in Kalimpong I was taught some spells by a 'pagan Indian'. He taught me love magic! He was a Bihari and he taught me all sorts of methods of charming women. I don't know why he thought I might need these, but I learned how to do it, though I've never actually employed these spells and I've forgotten most of them. I never thought they might be useful, but I was always willing to learn anything. I had that sort of attitude. So there are still these sort of people around, the repositories of black or grey magic. Maybe Rechungpa learned to do this sort of thing on a grander scale. The fact that he meets a *yoginī*, a female yogi, and receives from her the teaching of the Buddha of Long Life, shows quite clearly that at that time women did function as Tantric gurus. If this *yoginī*, Magi, is in fact Machig Labdron, Rechungpa must have met her in the Tibetan part of his journey, because she never left Tibet. She is well known because it was she who systematized the *chöd* teaching, the teaching of cutting off the ego.[167]

One may wonder whether these songs were Milarepa's own or whether they were by a later biographer who wrote them inspired by his awareness of the archetypal significance of these characters. But the story seems very real, as though it could have happened substantially as reported. Maybe they didn't sing these songs in these very words but they probably took up these attitudes and expressed these ideas.

Rechungpa was one of Milarepa's two main disciples, but Milarepa seems to have had an incredible amount of trouble with him. In other songs someone turns up, Milarepa says a few things to them, and then a few lines at the end declare that they went off and meditated for thirty years and became Enlightened. Of course one isn't told their story in full. But along with Gampopa, the author of the *Jewel Ornament of Liberation*, Rechungpa is one of Milarepa's two chief disciples.

The then incarnation of Rechung Rimpoche was a good friend of mine in Kalimpong, as it happens; he used to come to me for English lessons and I came to know him very well.[168] The idea was that he was the reincarnation of the Rechungpa in these stories, but he wasn't really like this Rechungpa. He certainly didn't profess to be of any high degree of spiritual attainment. In fact, he got involved with a young lady in Gangtok, the daughter of a friend of mine, and in the end he got married. He came to me to confess all this and was very upset about it. That may not sound too dissimilar to the Rechungpa we have met in the book, except that in the book Rechungpa does gain Enlightenment. Perhaps that's why Rechungpa is so important. Although he was up to all his tricks, he did get there in the end, which offers hope and encouragement to all of us – though that shouldn't be taken as an encouragement to backslide. The suggestion is that the good disciple is not necessarily the best or the closest disciple. There seems to be a very definite link between Rechungpa and Milarepa even though Rechungpa is at times so rebellious.

THIRD STORY
THE STORY OF THE YAK-HORN

In which Rechungpa arrives back from India, full of pride in his intellectual accomplishments and feeling that he is now more or less Milarepa's equal. Not getting the reception he feels he deserves, Rechungpa becomes angry with his guru. Milarepa conjures up a storm and miraculously shelters from it in a yak's horn. Rechungpa, too big to get inside, gets wet. After the storm, the two yogis seek alms and are given short shrift by an old woman who then dies in the night. Milarepa makes Rechungpa carry the old woman's corpse to the middle of a marsh, and teaches him the lesson that every sentient being is destined to die. Rechungpa's subsequent meditation suggests that he has learned something, though pride is still holding him back.

Themes include:

I

I AM MUCH MORE LEARNED THAN HE

Obeisance to all gurus.

Having helped Sahle Aui, the outstanding Yoginī, to further her devotion, Jetsun Milarepa went toward Balkhu to welcome his heart-son Rechungpa (upon his return from India. On the way there) he stayed at Betze Duyundzon (the Land of Pleasure) for some time. As Rechungpa was approaching from Gung Tang, the Jetsun saw in a vision that he was suffering from pride. (With this knowledge in mind) he went to welcome Rechungpa.

In the course of these stories Rechungpa goes off to India three times to study logic and other things, usually against Milarepa's advice. On this occasion, he has been away for some time, and Milarepa knows that he's on his way back, and goes to meet him. The text says, 'The Jetsun saw in a vision that he was suffering from pride,' but how could Milarepa know this? Of course, he knew Rechungpa very well. He knew that he had been away, engaging in all these advanced studies, and perhaps he knew what sort of effect that would have on Rechungpa's immature mind. On the other hand, he may have been in direct telepathic communication with Rechungpa, so that he knew his state of mind by way of direct perception. But why should he see it in the form of a vision, rather than simply having the thought that Rechungpa was suffering from pride? Perhaps he was a more visual person. He certainly wasn't an intellectual in the sense of being someone who operated mainly through concepts. Perhaps his temperament was more visual, and his experiences or intuitions or insights were spontaneously translated into visionary terms.

A mental image can vary in degrees of intensity. It can be no more than an ordinary mental picture or you can actually see it even more vividly than you see ordinary sense objects. In this case perhaps it was very vivid indeed and therefore the translator uses the term 'vision'. It's not unusual to form mental pictures, but to see visions as, say, William Blake saw them is much less common. But Milarepa seems to have had this faculty. He just saw what was going on. And in this case, he saw that Rechungpa was suffering from pride. So, 'with this knowledge in mind, he went to welcome Rechungpa'.

> When the father and son met in the center of the Balkhu plain, Rechungpa thought, 'I have now gone twice to study in India. Heretofore, I have been following my Guru's instructions to serve the Dharma and sentient beings. My Jetsun Guru's compassion and grace are indeed great, but I am much more learned in Buddhist philosophy and logic than he. Now he has come to welcome me, I wonder if he will return the obeisance to me when I bow down to him.' With this thought in mind Rechungpa prostrated himself before Milarepa and presented him with the Ahkaru staff that Dipupa had given him to offer to the Jetsun. But Milarepa gave not the slightest sign that he would even consider returning the courtesy. Rechungpa was very displeased. However, he said, 'Dear Guru, where did you stay while I was in India? How is your health? How are my Repa brothers? Where shall we go now?'

One can see the train of thought in Rechungpa's mind. It's probably true that he is 'much more learned in Buddhist philosophy and logic' than Milarepa. He's been studying these things in India while Milarepa has only been meditating. Milarepa has only gained Enlightenment, he hasn't studied Buddhist philosophy. But do you see how Rechungpa compares the two things? He is quite aware that Milarepa's compassion and grace are great, but he thinks that his greater knowledge of Buddhist philosophy and logic balances that, so that they are on equal terms now.

Rechungpa's mistake is that he doesn't understand the difference between knowledge and wisdom. He thinks of Milarepa as a kind, friendly, fatherly sort of person, but he thinks that he, Rechungpa, is the one with the knowledge of Buddhist philosophy and logic. In a way, he's seeing Milarepa as much less than he actually is. He's equating intellectual understanding with spiritual wisdom, but more than that, he doesn't even see Milarepa's wisdom, it seems. He thinks that his teacher's kindness and graciousness is counterbalanced by his own intellectual understanding of Buddhist philosophy and logic. The result is that he starts thinking that as individuals they are equal, almost as though the guru–disciple relationship between them no longer holds good. It's as though Milarepa used to be his guru, but Rechungpa has now become virtually his equal by acquiring this knowledge of Buddhist philosophy and logic. So inasmuch as Milarepa used to be his guru, he will salute him, but since they are now equals, he expects his guru to salute him back and thus recognize that they are now on the same footing.

In a way, this is natural. If you think that you are now on the same footing as your guru, surely your guru will recognize that, and will not treat you as a pupil any more, but as an equal, just as when you grow up, your father doesn't treat you as a child any more but starts treating you as an adult. The question is whether you have really become equal to the guru, whether you've really spiritually grown up.

> My Jetsun Guru's compassion and grace are indeed great. But
> I am much more learned in Buddhist philosophy and logic than
> he.

He's putting it in terms of the present, as though he doesn't appreciate the fact that he was once upon a time Milarepa's disciple. He doesn't seem to remember those days when he was very happy to be taught by Milarepa. It's as though all that is blotted out from his mind, he's so obsessed with the idea that they are equal. We find much the same thing nowadays: people being so obsessed by the idea that they are equal to everybody else that there's no question of anybody being able to learn anything from anybody else. This is probably one of the biggest *micchā-diṭṭhis* of modern times in the West. Rechungpa seems a bit infected by this sort of thing.

> Now he has come to welcome me, I wonder if he will return
> the obeisance to me when I bow down to him?

Isn't it strange that Rechungpa is thinking in this way? After all, they haven't seen each other for a long time; maybe some years have passed. Milarepa is his guru, and he is his disciple, or at least he used to be, but as they approach each other, the only thing that Rechungpa can think about is whether Milarepa is going to recognize him as an equal.

This is the sort of jockeying for position that often happens when two people meet, especially if status is at stake. There was an incident of this sort recently when the Pope went to Germany. The normal custom is that the visitor should call upon the head of state of the host country, or whoever corresponds to him or her in rank. If a reigning monarch visits Britain, he or she calls upon the Queen. If she visits his country, she calls upon him. But neither the Pope nor the Chancellor wanted to call on the other, and in the end a compromise was reached and they met in a neutral place. This is the sort of thing that happens in worldly life, and it shows that you are more concerned about your position than anything else. Rechungpa wasn't concerned with how Milarepa was. He didn't even experience happiness at seeing his guru. There's no mention that he was overjoyed to see Milarepa after such a long time. All he was concerned about was whether Milarepa was going to return his obeisance and recognize him as an equal.

So why are people, even such a spiritually gifted person as Rechungpa, so concerned about position? Why does it matter so much? Why should you try to fix the terms of the communication beforehand? Surely you don't know who is inferior and who is superior in any real sense until you are in communication. It's as though you don't want to find out how you really stand in relation to the other person. You want to have established all that beforehand and then operate from that basis. It seems that Rechungpa can't bear to face the fact that Milarepa is perhaps still spiritually superior to him and to discover that his knowledge of Buddhist philosophy and logic is not of much value. He is suffering from pride, and it's this that compels him to think in terms of his own position and prestige, and apparently prevents him even from being happy to see Milarepa and from being spontaneous. He approaches him with one fixed idea: his concern about whether his obeisance will be returned. This is a terrible state to get into. No wonder Milarepa had that vision!

But Milarepa gave not the slightest sign that he would even consider returning the courtesy.

Not the slightest! As though the very thought didn't occur to him.

> *Rechungpa was very displeased. However, he said, 'Dear Guru,*
> *where did you stay while I was in India? How is your health?*
> *How are my Repa brothers? Where shall we go now?'*

He's just going through the motions of greeting Milarepa. He is very displeased because if you want to be recognized as somebody's equal and they don't give you that recognition, you become quite frustrated and upset. We get a lot of this pseudo-equality nowadays, this idea that everybody is as good as everybody else. People fling the word 'elitism' around: if there's any suggestion that people's equality is not being recognized, there immediately follows an accusation of elitism. Nobody can be better than anybody else or more qualified than anybody else, except in some purely technical sense that doesn't really count. Maybe if Rechungpa had been alive today he might have talked in these terms.
So how does Milarepa respond?

> The Jetsun thought, 'How is it that Rechungpa has become so
> proud? He must either have been possessed by demons or affected
> by the evil influence of pagans.'

The translator is using the word 'pagans' in quite an odd way here. Presumably he's referring to the Hindus Rechungpa has met, because they hold to the idea of caste – hereditary superiority and inferiority based simply on birth, regardless of qualities. If Rechungpa has been living among these people, he may have been affected by their views to some extent. But Milarepa mentions another option, that Rechungpa 'must have been possessed by demons'. What does this tell us about Rechungpa's state? If someone seems to be possessed by some evil force, if they are behaving as though they've been taken over by something, assuming that they have not literally been possessed by a demon, what you're dealing with is a split personality. There are some kinds of negative mental states which have, so to speak, a life of their own. Rechungpa is quite a spiritually gifted person, and he's been with Milarepa for many years, but he is subject to this terrible attack of pride. It's as though there's another Rechungpa who has come into operation, as though he's a split personality. One part of him is very good, very devoted, very pious, very learned, very experienced in meditation, and there's another side which is stupid and conceited and wilful and stubborn and closed, but both sides are Rechungpa. If you think of the first one as the real Rechungpa, it's as though this one is from time to time taken over by the other Rechungpa, so that all the good qualities are in abeyance and all the negative qualities are for the time being uppermost. He may seem to be possessed, but perhaps he's been taken over not by an outside, objectively existing entity, but by another side of his own character which is deeply divided from the rest of him, so that he's in an alienated state.

There probably isn't any human being who isn't divided to some extent. It's doubtful whether anybody is completely integrated on every level. But if one is so divided that there are two quite incompatible personalities that can't coexist, that is serious, and we start speaking in terms of a split personality, or even schizophrenia. Whether or not something like that may be afflicting Rechungpa, at the moment the demon of pride has taken him over. Milarepa thinks that either he has been associating with people who are proud themselves and whose whole life is organized on that basis, or he has a split personality, he's possessed by demons. The Tibetans, in any case, believe in the possibility of literal possession by demons.

No matter what the cause, I must rescue him from this hindrance
of pride!

This is very significant. Milarepa is saying that it doesn't really matter what the cause is. The fact is that this person is suffering from 'the hindrance of pride'. Although the translator uses the word hindrance, Milarepa is really talking about the poison of pride or conceit. Pride is not of one of the five *nīvaraṇas* (the five hindrances to meditation), but of one of the five *kleśas* or poisons.[169] And the main thing is that Rechungpa should be cured. It's not necessary to be sure whether he has been possessed by demons or influenced by pagans; the fact is that he is suffering from pride and has got to be freed from it. But is that really the right approach? Surely we spend a lot of time trying to find out why we are what we are at the moment. If you realize that it's your Christian conditioning that's influencing you, or something like that, then you can work on that. Surely sometimes it's valuable to go back into the past? And if so, why is Milarepa dismissing it, or seeming to do so? Under what circumstances does one need to go back, and under what circumstances does one not need to do so?

The difference is that between a psychological problem and a spiritual one. Milarepa has described pride as a hindrance, meaning a hindrance to spiritual development, specifically meditation. If you have a spiritual ideal, if you have a vision and a desire to grow towards it, you don't need to think so much about the cause of the present unskilful state that you happen to be in. If you are preoccupied with the goal, the ideal, your energies will go into that, and they will thus be withdrawn from unskilful things. If you've got no ideal, it would seem that you need to go back into the past and find out what brought about your unskilful state of mind, but how far back are you going to go? From the point of view of psychoanalysis it seems that there's almost no end to the process of going back. They're now beginning to say that you can go back to the moment of birth, to the time you were in the womb, to previous lives. Buddhism doesn't dispute that, but even if you can go back and back through a whole series of lives, and you can understand how one thing has led to another, you still have to come back and be emancipated from your unskilful mental states in the present. Consciousness of the goal, a vision of the ideal, enables you to do that and actually to switch your energies to a more skilful direction.

However, even when you've got an ideal in front of you, if your energies are so blocked and your emotions are so alienated that the ideal is only an abstract idea, you may need to go back to try to find out how your present attitude has arisen. For instance, if you are heavily conditioned by your Christian past, even if you are involved with a Buddhist movement, you may just have an abstract idea about Enlightenment. In this case, you may have to go back a little bit, just enough to unblock your energies, and then try to get a stronger feeling for the ideal and go forward. But the general principle would seem to be to go forward, rather than back, to think in terms of the ideal that will draw you out of your present situation, rather than trying to get out of it by delving into how you got into it in the first place. If you've truly got an ideal, not just an abstract idea, you don't need to go back into the past.

Your mind might like to go back to try to find the source, but does it really matter? This is what Milarepa seems to be suggesting when he says, 'No matter what the cause, I must rescue him from this hindrance of pride!' It's very difficult to tell sometimes what the cause is, but what does it matter? What is important is that you should have enough free energy to direct towards the ideal. You may have some complex because your parents beat you when you were small. Is it really important to find out whether it was your mother who beat you, or your father, or maybe an elder brother? Perhaps it doesn't matter now. If you practise the *mettā bhāvanā* and work on overcoming all feelings of resentment towards other people, including those who may have beaten you, it doesn't matter whether you know exactly who it was. It's always a temptation to go back into the past, and it may be useful to a limited extent, despite what Milarepa says. It may be necessary to go back just a little bit and get some understanding of what has happened and how things have influenced you. But as soon as possible you should start looking forward and towards the ideal, and thinking in terms of positive growth and development.

Sometimes it may happen spontaneously. We are told that at the time of the Buddha's Enlightenment, among other experiences he had a panoramic vision of many thousands, even hundreds of thousands of past lives.[170] But he didn't need to see them, he wasn't trying to see them, it just happened. Likewise, in the course of your growth and development, it may suddenly occur to you, 'That's why I went wrong there' or 'That's why I took that particular turning'. You're not particularly anxious to know about it but you understand it spontaneously because you've reached a vantage point in your development from which you can see things more clearly. There's no need to be anxious about it or try to find out what happened. Our essential concern is with growth and development in the present and the future.

So he smiled and answered Rechungpa's questions in this song.

I am a yogi who lives on a snow-mountain peak.
With a healthy body I glorify the Mandala of the Whole.
Cleansed of vanity from the Five Poisons,
I am not unhappy;
I feel nought but joy!
Renouncing all turmoil
And fondness for diversion,

I reside alone in perfect ease.
Forswearing the bustle of this world,
Joyfully I stay in no-man's land.
Since I have left embittered family life,
I no longer have to earn and save;
Since I want no books,
I do not intend to be a learned man;
I practice virtuous deeds,
I feel no shame of heart.
Since I have no pride or vanity,
I renounce with joy the saliva-splashing debate!
Hypocrisy I have not, nor pretension.
Happy and natural I live
Without forethought or adjustment.
Since I want not fame nor glory,
Rumors and accusations disappear.
Where'er I go, I feel happy,
Whate'er I wear, I feel joyful,
Whatever food I eat, I am satisfied.
I am always happy.
Through Marpa's grace,
I, your old father Milarepa,
Have realized Saṃsāra and Nirvāṇa.
The Yoga of Joy ever fills my hermitage.

Your Repa brothers are well;
On hills remote they make progress in their meditations.
Oh, my son Rechung Dorje Draugpa,
Have you returned from India?
Did you feel tired and weary on the journey?
Has your mind been sharpened and refreshed?
Has your voice been good for singing?
Did you practice and follow your Guru's instructions?
Did you secure the teachings that you wanted?
Did you obtain all the various instructions?
Have you gained much knowledge and much learning?
Have you noticed your pride and egotism?
Are you altruistic in your thoughts and actions?

This is my song of welcoming for you,
On your return.

> *I am a yogi who lives on a snow-mountain peak.*
> *With a healthy body I glorify the Mandala of the Whole.*

Well, that's what anyone can see. It's obvious that he's a yogi who passes
his time in meditation and he lives on the peak of a snow-mountain.
But there's more to it than that. He says he glorifies 'the Mandala of
the Whole'. It's not clear what Tibetan term 'the whole' represents – it
could perhaps be the equivalent of the Sanskrit *dharmadhātu*, but it
may simply be a mistranslation. At any rate, 'the Mandala of the Whole'
is an evocative expression. A mandala is essentially a group of things
surrounding something in the centre, the things around it being aspects
of or related to the central thing, so if you think of the whole of existence
as a mandala, you are seeing everything as related to the ideal, and thus
in its true relation to the ideal and to other things. The mandala that you
might see depicted in a thangka, a Tibetan painting, is a very simplified
version. There are many forms of mandala, only one of them being that
of the mandala of the Five Buddhas, in which you have a Buddha in
the centre and then Buddhas at the four cardinal points. Then in any
mandala there are all sorts of other things – perhaps a lot, perhaps just
a few – arranged harmoniously around the central figure.

When you see the whole of existence as a mandala, it's as though
you see the whole of existence as related to the ideal and see also that
the relationship of all the aspects of existence with the ideal determines
their relationship with one another. In other words, you see the whole
cosmos as harmoniously arranged around this central fundamental
principle. That is the mandala of the whole. But the mandala has another
significance too, and it's this that is drawn out in the meditation practice
in which a mandala is offered. Mandala literally means 'circle', and the
mandala imagined and ceremonially offered in this meditation practice
is a symbolical representation of the entire world system: Mount Meru
with its oceans and encircling iron mountains and its various tiers. Each
school of Tibetan Buddhism has its own list of preparatory practices –
mūla yogas (the Tibetan term is *ngöndro*) – and one of these involves
making the offering of the mandala 100,000 times – the mandala in that
context representing the whole of mundane existence, the whole world

system according to ancient Indian ideas.[171] The offering of the mandala is the offering of the whole universe to the Buddhas and bodhisattvas, or to the guru as the embodiment of all the Buddhas and bodhisattvas. It represents a statement on your part that even if the whole universe belonged to you, you would offer it all to the Buddha, to the guru, to Padmasambhava, or whichever figure is the focus of your devotion. In this way you develop your devotion, and your capacity to give and offer. So these are the two main meanings of mandala: first, the whole of reality, and second, the cosmos, or a particular cosmos. The two meanings are clearly related, and one can take Milarepa's statement as referring to either. One could take the mandala of the whole as either being the mandala of the entire *dharmadhātu* or the mandala of our particular world system. Perhaps it means both – or something else, of course, depending on how accurate the translation is. 'Glorify' may also perhaps be a rather fanciful translation, but if we take it at its face value, if we take it that Milarepa is saying that with his body he 'glorifies the mandala of the whole', he could mean that with his healthy body he makes the mandala glorious, he adds to its beauty. By living on the snow-peak, by practising yoga, by gaining Enlightenment, he glorifies, illuminates, beautifies, the whole of existence. He has, as it were, taken his true place in it. He is not a disruptive factor; he's not out of place. He adds to the beauty of the mandala of the whole.

This is a somewhat unusual way of looking at the spiritual life, thinking in terms of finding your true place in the mandala, and through your spiritual practice adding to its beauty: being a jewel instead of a pebble, a beautiful flower instead of a heap of dung in the corner. It also suggests that gaining Enlightenment is not just a personal concern, but a way of enhancing the beauty and the richness of the whole of existence. It's thinking of the whole process of Enlightenment in aesthetic rather than in ethical terms, thinking not so much in terms of being good as in terms of being beautiful in the fullest sense. And you can't make the mandala more beautiful without being more beautiful yourself. The expression 'a beautiful person' is overused, but there is something in it. It doesn't mean tripping around in a fairy-like way; it's much more solid and genuine than that. You don't have to wear your hair long or have a beautiful golden earring – not that those things are necessarily excluded, of course.

I'm not sure whether we are to take 'with a healthy body' at face value or in a deeper sense. It could mean a skilful, wholesome being, but it certainly doesn't exclude a healthy body in the ordinary sense. In a way Milarepa is answering Rechungpa's enquiry after his health with more than Rechungpa has asked. In a sense it doesn't matter whether he's healthy or unhealthy. After all, he has realized the Truth. Perhaps as a matter of fact he does have a healthy body, but he could mean more than that. His whole being is imbued with health, with wholesomeness, with positivity. This is suggested by what follows:

> Cleansed of vanity from the Five Poisons,
> I am not unhappy;
> I feel nought but joy!

The list of five poisons varies a bit. Sometimes it's ignorance, aversion, conceit, craving, and envy, and sometimes distraction is listed instead of envy. As we've already seen, they're different from the hindrances in that the hindrances are especially related to meditation. They're the mental states that prevent you from rising from the *kāmaloka* to the *rūpaloka* and then the *arūpaloka*. You could say they represent coarse, even negative, modes of mental function. The five hindrances are craving, especially in the sense of craving for experience on the *kāmaloka* level; aversion, especially in the sense of aversion arising out of frustation in connection with enjoyment on the *kāmaloka* level; 'hurry and flurry' or 'worry and restlessness' as it's sometimes translated; sloth and torpor; and doubt in the sense of indecision. These five hindrances prevent you from attaining concentration, attaining the *dhyānas*.

But the five *kleśas*, the five poisons, are more than that. They go down to the very root of existence, one could say. It's the five poisons that stand between you and Enlightenment itself.[172] If you were to get rid of the five hindrances, you would be able to enter the first *dhyāna*, the second *dhyāna*, even the third *dhyāna*, but you would not yet have overcome the *kleśas*, which represent deeper, more existential hindrances. The poisons of craving and aversion go much deeper, and they pertain to the higher levels too, the *rūpaloka* and the *arūpaloka*, and in addition you've got ignorance itself, which is the basic *kleśa*, and conceit, which is that same basic *kleśa* from another point of view; and fifthly you've got envy or alternatively distraction. These, especially ignorance and conceit, go very much deeper than any of the five hindrances. The hindrances prevent you from achieving the *dhyāna* states, but the five *kleśas*, which of course include the five hindrances, prevent you from seeing reality itself. Those meditations which are antidotes to the poisons therefore include not just *śamatha* practices, but 'insight' practices, because it's only through transcendental insight that one can have some experience of reality and thus get rid of the five poisons.[173] It's only insight that can dispel ignorance or get rid of conceit.

The *kleśas* are related to the *āsravas*. There's the *āsrava* of craving for experience on the desire level, or in the desire-world, the *kāmaloka*. Then there's the craving for experience in the form-world, the *rūpaloka* – then the formless-world, the *arūpaloka*. And then there's the *āsrava* of ignorance and the *āsrava* of attachment to wrong views, which seems to have been added as an elaboration of ignorance.[174] These cover much the same sort of ground. The original, most primitive formula was *lobha*, *dveṣa*, and *moha*. These too can be called poisons, but in Pāli they are called the three *akuśala-mūlas*, the three roots of unskilfulness: that is to say, craving, aversion, and ignorance or bewilderment. The five poisons can be regarded as an elaboration of the three roots: craving and aversion remain the same, and *moha* is subdivided into ignorance, conceit, and distraction. In that way you get your list of five *kleśas*, though sometimes distraction is replaced by envy or jealousy. The basic point to bear in mind is that there are two main aspects, an intellectual aspect and an emotional aspect, the intellectual aspect being represented by such words as ignorance, conceit, and distraction, and the emotional aspect being represented by craving, aversion, and envy or jealousy. Both aspects are deeply negative. One could say, though this may be a bit over-schematic, that the emotionally negative aspect is overcome by *śamatha*, but the intellectually negative aspect is overcome only by *vipaśyanā* or insight. *Vipaśyanā* or insight 'fixes' the emotional positivity, one might say, in the sense of making it permanent. Until you've got that insight, you may sometimes be in a very emotionally positive state, but it may not last very long.

You only overcome the poisons permanently by gaining insight. Some of them can be suspended for the time being through the development of *śamatha*, but some can't even be suspended. The Mahāyāna identifies two *āvaraṇas* or 'coverings': the *kleśa āvaraṇa* and the *jñeya āvaraṇa* – literally, the 'covering of defilements' and the 'covering of knowables'.[175] Broadly speaking, the one represents emotional obscuration and the other represents intellectual obscuration. *Kleśa āvaraṇa* refers to all those negative emotional factors that obscure the realization of the truth, so here *kleśa* has a more emotive meaning; and *jñeya āvaraṇa* refers all those wrong conceptions of reality that obscure the realization of the truth. Running through all these terms, all these lists, is the idea of a twofold veil, or twofold obscuration. The list of five poisons to which Milarepa refers comprises both emotional and intellectual *kleśas*, and vanity or conceit is considered one of the more intellectual ones, consisting essentially in a fixed idea about oneself.

According to some of the Buddha's sayings in the Pāli canon, one should not think about oneself as either inferior, superior, or equal to other people.[176] In other words, you should not think comparatively at all. This is what Rechungpa is doing here, trying to work out who is superior, who is inferior, who is equal and so on, and this shows that he is suffering from the *kleśa* of conceit. The basic Buddhist position is that one should approach another person not thinking in those terms at all. Even to think in terms of equality means that one is still concerned with inferiority and superiority. Such thinking is quite irrelevant from the spiritual point of view. When Milarepa states, 'I am a Yogi and I live on a mountain', he's talking about himself in absolute terms, not in relation to Rechungpa. He's not saying, 'I'm a better Yogi than anybody else'; he's just describing what he does.

The emotional and the intellectual *kleśas* are interconnected, of course, because they're both aspects of you, but some are predominantly emotional and others are predominantly intellectual. When you get angry, no doubt there is some idea or concept bound up with that, but the predominant experience is emotional. In the same way, when you have certain wrong ideas in the form of *micchā-diṭṭhis*, no doubt there are feelings connected with those ideas, but it is the intellectual element that is uppermost, especially if you formulate the *micchā-diṭṭhi* systematically in the form of a philosophy. Sometimes you can deal with *micchā-diṭṭhis* on an emotional level. If somebody, as a result of their spiritual practice, dissolved the emotions that are at the root of the *micchā-diṭṭhis*, the *micchā-diṭṭhis* would vanish with the emotions. But sometimes you have to drive them back. It isn't stated in Buddhism that you can reduce the intellectual to the emotional; it isn't as though the intellectual is at root emotional. There is such a thing – at least according to the terminology – as an intellectual *kleśa*. It's as though wrong understanding is as fundamental as wrong feeling. It isn't that wrong thoughts or wrong ideas are only expressions of wrong feelings. The one is as basic as the other, it would seem. The two most basic terms in this respect are *avidyā*, ignorance, and *tṛṣṇā*, thirst or craving, and sometimes *avidyā* is regarded as the more primordial, to use that expression. It's not so much that you can reduce the emotional to the intellectual or the intellectual to the emotional with regard to the *kleśas*, but that they converge. The more deeply you go into them, the more you find a common root, which can't be described in either exclusively intellectual or exclusively emotional terms. The *micchā-diṭṭhis* are not just rationalizations of negative emotions, so it isn't enough just to reduce the *micchā-diṭṭhis* to their appropriate emotions; you still have to reduce the emotions to something more basic, you have to overcome the subject–object division, but sometimes it helps to see the emotional connections, because then you get a more comprehensive view of the problem. The emotional *kleśa* is not the root of the intellectual *kleśa*, but there is an emotional counterpart to every intellectual *kleśa*, even if there isn't an intellectual counterpart to every emotional *kleśa*.

When Milarepa says, 'Cleansed of vanity from the five poisons I am not unhappy; I feel nought but joy!' he is virtually communicating the fact that he is Enlightened. If the five poisons are no longer present, if you've developed the five *jñānas*, the five awarenesses, then you are Enlightened.

> Renouncing all turmoil
> And fondness for diversion,
> I reside alone in perfect ease.

There's much more to this than meets the eye, because 'turmoil' and 'fondness for diversion' go much deeper than we usually think, and therefore the 'perfect ease' in which Milarepa says that he is residing goes much deeper than ease in the usual sense. It's a complete relaxation which is not just physical or psychological, but existential. It's the cessation of all striving, because there's nothing to strive for. You've gained whatever there was to be gained. This ties up with the Mahāmudrā teaching, which is not a teaching about *how to* relax at the deepest level, because that would be self-contradictory, but just the teaching *of* relaxation at the deepest level of one's being. You don't even think in terms of trying to attain Enlightenment. You've gone even beyond that. This is the state of profound relaxation that Milarepa is suggesting. It might seem strange that you should need to 'renounce turmoil'. Who would want turmoil anyway? But some people find that during meditation they almost cling to the turmoil of thoughts, and if that begins to die down, they feel fear arising as a result. And even apart from meditation, some people seem to thrive on living in a way that is full of turmoil. If life becomes quiet and peaceful, they get a bit uneasy.

Presumably there is a difference between turmoil and fondness for diversion, as they are mentioned separately. Perhaps it's that the state of turmoil is painful, though better than the purely negative state of not being alive at all, whereas diversion suggests going in the direction of pleasure. But why do we give way to this 'fondness for diversion'? Why can't we enjoy just sitting quietly? Why do you find yourself thumbing through the 'what's on' pages to try to find something, anything, to entertain you? It may be that you feel you're missing out on something, but why should you feel that? Well, perhaps you *are* missing out on something, but you're just not identifying it correctly. What you're really missing out on all the time is Enlightenment, though you're just separated from it by a hair's breadth, so you rightly feel some inadequacy, some incompleteness, some insufficiency. But instead of sitting down quietly and asking yourself, 'What is it that I really need? What is it that I really want?' you go dashing off in the direction of whatever presents itself. Even if you think you want to see a film, you may not enjoy it; you just forget things for a while and then you come back to the state you were in before. Of course it might be enjoyable to see a film, but you're more likely to be able to enjoy it if you go to see it in a state of sufficiency and happiness, not just wanting something – almost anything – to fill the gap. If you are in that needy state the best thing to do is definitely just to sit and experience it. If there's something you want to see because you are interested in that particular subject, that's another matter. Then you're following up an interest, rather than giving in to a 'fondness for diversion', which suggests that you don't want to face up to the fact of your own inner emptiness. You don't want to try to find out what you really need and what you really want or need to do. You're not willing to be in touch with yourself, not willing to experience yourself.

Where does boredom come into it? If you're bored, you don't have anything particular to do and you're not seeking some diversion, but your experience of yourself is not satisfying, and there is nothing to disguise that fact from you. The usual response to boredom is to try to relieve it, but feeling bored can be quite productive. If you just sit quietly and experience the feeling, after a while you will start experiencing yourself and gradually making contact with what you really want to do. If you've tried that and nothing seems to happen, perhaps you haven't waited long enough. You might have to wait for five minutes at least, or even an hour! And if you've been sitting for a whole evening and there has been no change in the feeling of boredom, that would suggest that your feelings about what you really want to do are quite deeply buried, and that it will take quite a time to establish contact with them. It isn't an easy business. But in most cases, if you feel a bit bored and you just sit down quietly, what you will come up with after a while is an interest, a genuine interest. It's likely to be that rather than realizing what you deeply and genuinely want to do in a more existential sense.

It can help to write down how you're feeling, which may reveal how you got into the mood you're in, and what you want to do next. It speeds up the process. Very often we don't face up to the fact of how we feel. If you write it down, at least it's objectified and you see it in front of you: 'depressed', 'angry', 'miserable', 'tired', 'bored', 'lifeless', 'inert', 'dead'.... Writing it down helps to bring it more clearly and definitely into consciousness.

> *Forswearing the bustle of this world,*
> *Joyfully I stay in no-man's land.*

The phrase 'no-man's land' here doesn't mean the space between two countries or two battle lines, which is the usual meaning in English. In Tibetan there is a phrase, 'The country of the No-Men' – the 'No-Men' (the Sanskrit is *amānuṣa*) meaning those who are not human, in other words, animals. Milarepa is living high in the snowy mountains, where only animals live. In other words, he's away from human society. Before we wonder whether this has a deeper meaning, we could consider the literal meaning. What does it mean that Milarepa is living without any human contact? What sort of effect does seeing only animals have on one? You're much closer to yourself, and to nature. It's quite difficult to have this sort of experience now. I have heard it said that it's only in some parts of Africa that you can still have the experience that man is in the minority, that other forms of life are more abundant. You see it sometimes in nature films which show great herds of zebra or giraffe, or flocks of flamingos. A friend of mine some years ago went on retreat up in Scotland on a peninsula facing the Isle of Skye. During the winter he was cut off from the mainland because to get to the peninsula you have to cross mountains which are impassable in winter, so for months all he saw were seals and deer, otters and thousands of birds. It was quite an unusual experience to be surrounded by this teeming animal life. The effect of living without contact with other human beings, but seeing all this animal life around you, would surely be that you would have a much stronger sense of yourself as a human being. Here are all these living things – they're all full of life and they're very beautiful – but you can't communicate with them. You can only observe them. You have a sense of connection with them, because you are alive and so are they, but you can't communicate with them because they don't have self-consciousness in the way that you do. You can't talk to them or exchange ideas. Maybe you can tame them and train them to come to you to be fed, but you can't communicate with them in the way that you can communicate with a human being, however tame and friendly they may become. This is perhaps why in Cowper's poem 'Alexander Selkirk', describing the animals on the island where he is shipwrecked, Selkirk says, 'their tameness is shocking to me'.[177] It is shocking that they are tame because it suggests that they have had no experience of man and underlines the fact that he is the only human being there.

Also, no-man's land is land that doesn't belong to anybody. In modern times, it's impossible to find unowned land, because the nation states have extended their boundaries so that they are completely contiguous. There's no land over which no state exercises sovereignty, so you can't get away from human society, from laws, from the jurisdiction of a particular government. Formerly you could go off into the wilderness and live there, a law unto yourself, but you can't do that now. So here was Milarepa, living in this no-man's land with only the animals: no human society, no administration, no magistrate, no police. It's very difficult for us to imagine living in that state of perfect freedom, and very few people could do it, but Milarepa could.

> *Since I have left embittered family life,*
> *I no longer have to earn and save.*

Why does he speak of family life as embittered? When you say a person is embittered, it usually means that something has been done to them, or perhaps they've done something they regret, and they can't do anything about it, or they think they can't. Most people regard family life as inevitable. There's no alternative, and even if you don't like it, you've got to lump it. That can lead to an embittered attitude, if you can't imagine that there is any other way of living, or worry about how you would manage without someone there to help you with the chores of everyday life. Sometimes people don't particularly enjoy family life but they clearly need its services.

When you are in conflict about family life, what you must avoid at all costs is a feeling that you're trapped in the situation against your will. This will definitely lead to resentment and bitterness. If you are in this sort of situation in any respect, not only the family situation, you need to assess what the conflict is. Then, unless you are going to end the conflict by walking out of the situation, you must decide what weight you are going to give to the different interests that are producing the conflict. And then, having made the decision to give so much time and energy to this and so much time and energy to that, stop feeling it as a conflict, because you've taken the decision that that is what you are going to do. Otherwise you'll feel more and more resentful and embittered, and the whole thing will blow apart in the end. You feel resentful only if you feel that you're being imposed upon, that you're in a situation you can't get out of, so the very first thing you have to do is to say to yourself, 'I'm in this situation by my own choice. There's no law keeping me in it. I'm not being kept by any physical compulsion. I'm here because I want to be. So do I wish to stay in this situation or not? I'm quite free to walk out. My family will manage. No one will starve.' (At least you can think that in Britain, where we still have a welfare state.) Then, having become clear in your own mind that you are free to leave, you can think, 'Is it the most skilful thing to do, on balance?' You may well decide that it isn't, and at that point you can say to yourself, 'All right, that's my decision. I'm not under any pressure, so there's no need for any resentment. I'm doing what I want to do. I'm giving so much time and energy to my family, and so much time and energy to other things. This is my choice.'

Of course, before you can arrive at such a decision, you have to sort out any feelings of irrational guilt imposed by the group. That is part of the pressure; if one is made to feel guilty on account of doing this or that, one is still not free. So you must convince yourself that you are free, which means being free from even those subtle pressures, and then decide, so that what you are doing is the result of free choice and therefore you cannot feel resentful. Family life is 'embittered', as Milarepa describes it, in the sense that people won't face up to the situation, and feel that they are victims of circumstances. We're very often much more free than we think. Very often it's our feelings of guilt that make us think that we're not free – the guilt being induced in us by other people and their views about the situation, not the situation itself. If you're thinking of leaving your family, people are likely to turn on you and say, 'How mean! How selfish! How despicable!' You're made to feel guilty, and that guilt inhibits you from being and feeling free. But this is not appropriate to the situation; it's induced in you by other people. You're more free than you think you are in the sense that although you may think that if you did this or did that, you'd be a despicable person, that may not in fact be the case. You may just be giving way to other people's prejudices. But if you yourself come to think that whatever you're contemplating would be a despicable thing to do, you should have conviction in not doing it, and say to yourself, 'I'm going to stay where I am because that's the right thing to do.' The essential thing is to create for yourself a point of freedom from which to act, without being under any sort of pressure, because the pressure is always irrational. If somebody convinces you rationally what to do, that is not pressure, and you must be open to being genuinely convinced by someone who discusses the matter with you in a reasonable manner, not just blinding you with science or trying to overwhelm you with plausible arguments.

Never allow yourself to become passive in a situation where you are under pressure. Passivity is the complete antithesis of spiritual life, which is essentially active. I'm distinguishing passivity from receptivity; we tend to think of receptivity as passive, but it is best thought of as an active state. What we must not be in the spiritual life is passive. If you're passive, you will feel resentful, you'll feel that you're the victim of circumstances, helpless and powerless and all the rest of it. Always remember that the initiative is with you, and then do what you think best. Even your spiritual friends should never exert pressure; if they try to pressure you even in a direction that is good, they're not really acting as spiritual friends. Their task is to help you to create a point of freedom from which you can act, without any sort of pressure in any direction. If you take *any* step as a result of pressure from anybody, it can't be a spiritual step, because it isn't active. You haven't taken the initiative. 'Family life', or whatever other situation you are in, is embittered if you stay in it against your will. Perhaps you ought to stay, but if you do so, it must be because you want to, or at least because you've decided to stay out of your own free will. Perhaps it would be better not to stay, but if you choose not to, it should be because you don't want to and you've decided that is the best thing. What you mustn't do is to stay in any situation passively, as a result of external pressure of any kind.

Embarking upon family life is usually a passive thing in our society. People don't reach the age of discretion and take an objective decision to get married in the light of their own best interests. It's usually regarded as inevitable. You can find yourself slipping into it: you get involved with someone, you become attached to each other, and before long you've started talking about getting a place together, and maybe there's a baby on the way. You just slide into the situation bit by bit; you don't feel that you have taken a decision. In India most marriages are arranged, and they usually work out quite well, but if you ask young people, 'Do you want to get married?' they say, 'No, I don't.' 'So why are you getting married?' 'Well, it's not up to me, it's all arranged.' It's as though marriage is a sort of natural disaster, like a flood or a famine. There's nothing you can do about it. You can't escape because the social structure is so rigid. In the West, by contrast, we like to think that we make our own decisions. But is it really the case? For instance, say you go along to a club because your friends are going. You start dancing with someone, and even though you're not thinking about settling down, before you know where you are, you're going down that slippery slope. At no stage do you take a conscious decision that this is how you're going to spend the next fifty years of your life. Can you really say that it's a result of your free choice?

The feeling of powerlessness breeds great resentment and hostility in our society today, especially among young people, who feel they have no choice. It may not really be like that, but it seems to them that they are in a purely passive position. They feel they have no freedom and their sense of frustration sometimes finds an outlet in violence. The only action they can take is negative. A reasonably healthy human being would rather be active in a negative way than not active at all. If you're not allowed to create, you'll destroy, or at least you'll break a few windows. It's very dangerous from society's point of view to leave people in a state where they feel, rightly or wrongly, that they're just victims of the system, because there is bound to be a negative reaction. We all know that we're most miserable and angry when we feel there's nothing we can do about our situation.

As far as possible, therefore, make sure you don't get into that state, because if you do, after a while, whatever your situation, you'll start feeling embittered. If you're working in a right livelihood business and you're feeling that people are giving you more and more work to do and you can't say no, you'll end up feeling embittered, even though you may agree with the broad framework. At every stage, you must tell yourself, 'I'm quite free. I can walk out at any time. I can walk out of my home, I can walk out of my job, I can walk out of the Buddhist community if I want to. There's nothing to stop me. So if I stay, I'm staying of my own free will.' Then there's no room for disgruntlement, resentment, or bitterness.

If a situation is such that objectively you are not free, you have to come to terms with that. For instance, if you're imprisoned, even unjustly, maybe there's nothing you can do about it. But even in that situation you must be very careful not to give way to resentment, because that would just make things worse. If you have been deprived of your physical freedom, you have to be very careful that it doesn't deprive you of your mental freedom.

> Since I want no books,
> I do not intend to be a learned man.

This is a little knock at Rechungpa. If one isn't careful, reading books can be just a 'fondness for diversion', albeit of a refined, sophisticated kind. How much do we really need to read? Most people have got very busy brains, and it's very difficult to stop them from whirring away. In meditation, if you've got a very active mind, you don't try to stop it just like that; you give it something positive to occupy itself with. You may give it a mantra to focus on, so that at least it is occupied with something positive and that helps it to concentrate. In the same way, if your mind is very active, it's better that it should be busy with books about the Dharma which after all essentially deal with the same thing over and over again in different forms, from different points of view. But one mustn't become lost in that for its own sake. It's not enough to be 'a learned man'. One must read the books to remind oneself again and again about the Dharma. It's no bad thing, especially if you are a voracious reader, to go over just a few books again and again and learn them really thoroughly, rather than dipping into something new all the time. Most Buddhist books take a lot of understanding. Milarepa is not in need of Dharma books, of course. After all, he has realized the truth. A learned man is acquainted with books, but Milarepa knows from personal experience the things that the books are talking about. He has no need or intention to be a learned man.

> I practice virtuous deeds,
> I feel no shame of heart.

I'm not sure how literal this translation is, but taking it quite literally, 'shame of heart' means going against your heart. This isn't feeling shame because you haven't lived up to somebody else's expectations. It's your own heart telling you that you've fallen short of your ideal. You've not lived up to the best that is in you, and you're feeling ashamed not because of what anybody else thinks, but because of what you yourself feel. If you feel 'no shame of heart' in the positive sense that Milarepa does, it suggests that you are integrated, so there's no conflict between what you're convinced you should do and what you actually do.

> Since I have no pride or vanity,
> I renounce with joy the saliva-splashing debate!

Again this seems to be a bit of a hit at Rechungpa. He went off to India to learn logic so that he could defeat other people in debate, but Milarepa is saying that this sort of debate, even though it's ostensibly religious, is really just a competitive clash of egos, due to pride or vanity. There's a difference between discussion and argument, the difference being that discussion means communicating with people, whereas argument is just insisting on your point of view regardless of what the other person says. You're just trying to win, trying to defeat the other person, even trying to do them down. Milarepa is very happy not to have anything to do with these 'saliva-splashing' encounters.

Hypocrisy I have not, nor pretension.

Hypocrisy is pretending to be other than you are in order to get approval or praise that you're not entitled to. But why do people indulge in it? Perhaps it is sometimes justified. If, for instance, you were living in a society where unreasonable demands were made upon the citizens, and you knew that if you did not comply with those demands you would be subject to severe penalties, perhaps you would have to pretend to comply. If you lived in a totalitarian state and knew that if you did not declare your support of the system you would be whisked off to jail, you might feel obliged to be a sort of hypocrite, but that's self-protection, not real hypocrisy. Real hypocrisy involves going out of your way to appear better than you are because you crave for esteem from other people that you don't really deserve. Although you don't live up to their values, you pretend to, because you don't want to forfeit their respect. A hypocrite, one could say, is one who shares the same system of values as the people he is trying to deceive.

Happy and natural I live
Without forethought or adjustment.

Is it possible to live without forethought, without thinking about what you're going to eat or how the bills are going to be paid? Presumably Milarepa means that he lives without a neurotic preoccupation with what is going to happen. If you have a certain amount of money and you say, 'I'll spend some today and the rest I'll spend tomorrow', that is not really forethought in Milarepa's sense. But some people have a neurotic need to know what is going to happen. Full of insecurity, they want to know everything in advance so that they can be prepared for it. To give an example, someone asked me, 'How do I get from Padmaloka to London?' I said, 'You catch the train from Norwich.' 'How do I get to the station?' 'You catch a bus.' 'When does the bus come?' 'I'll give you the bus times.' 'How can I be sure that I won't miss it?' 'Just get there five minutes early.' 'But suppose the bus happens to stop up the road and the driver doesn't see me? What shall I do then? What colour is the bus? Suppose there's a breakdown that day and it doesn't come?' It's probably this sort of forethought that Milarepa is getting at. Some people like to have their lives planned out so they know exactly what is going to happen from day to day and year to year, and they get deeply disturbed when anything happens to disrupt their arrangements.

I think by 'adjustment' he must mean something like compromise – adjusting to other people's attitudes and views at the expense of your own genuine convictions.

> *Since I want not fame nor glory,*
> *Rumors and accusations disappear.*

It's sometimes said that reputation – fame, glory, a good name – is one of the last attachments to be given up. When rumours and accusations appear, one's reaction is very often to want to expose the rumours or defeat the accusations, and re-establish one's good name. But very often the more you try to do that, the more other people try to undermine your reputation, and the worse the whole situation becomes. Milarepa says that the thing to do is just not to bother about fame or glory or reputation, then there's nothing for anybody to fight about, and the rumours and accusations will disappear. If people start saying, 'Milarepa's not a real yogi!' he's not going to bother saying, 'Yes I am.' He just keeps quiet, and after a while people will start talking about something else. If he was to say, 'Yes, I am a real yogi!' and start bringing forward people to bear witness to the fact, his accusers could bring forward other people to testify against him. Then someone might write a book in support of his being a real yogi and another author might denounce him as an impostor, and it could go on for years. But it will only go on in that way if you really care about being thought a good yogi and are bothered when people say that you are not, if you try to maintain your position, so to speak, as a good yogi. If you don't bother, after a while the whole thing will just collapse, because there's nothing for anybody to fight against.

There can also be an element of self-persuasion. You may not be completely convinced. If you are, you tend not to bother what other people think. It's enough that you know within your own mind. You might think that it's unfair or unfortunate that people don't see you as you really are, but you don't feel any great desire to prove to them what you're really like. You're just sorry that there's been a failure of communication.

Where'er I go, I feel happy
Whate'er I wear, I feel joyful,
Whatever food I eat, I am satisfied.
I am always happy.
Through Marpa's grace, I, your old father Milarepa,
Have realized Saṃsāra and Nirvāṇa.
The Yoga of Joy ever fills my hermitage.

By having 'realized Saṃsāra and Nirvāṇa' he means that he has realized their non-duality, he no longer sees things in terms of pairs of opposites, and thus 'the Yoga of Joy fills my Hermitage'.

Your Repa brothers are well;
On hills remote they make progress in their meditations.

'*Re*' is cotton cloth, and '*pa*' means a person or man, so a *repa* is a Kagyu yogi, especially one who is wearing a single cotton garment as a sign that he has mastered the inner psychic heat and doesn't need any protection from the cold. These days the Kagyupas generally wear ordinary monastic dress with a white cotton garment over that. This report on the progress of his fellow disciples is another little reminder to Rechungpa, who went off to India against Milarepa's advice, neglecting his meditation.

Oh, my son Rechung Dorje Draugpa,
Have you returned from India?
Did you feel tired and weary on the journey?
Has your mind been sharpened and refreshed?

Of course what really refreshes the mind, in Milarepa's view, is not travel but meditation, immersion in positive mental states.

Has your voice been good for singing?

Singing suggests freedom of communication, and inspiration. Milarepa's hope is that Rechungpa hasn't just been studying Buddhist philosophy and logic, and debating and arguing, but that he has also kept in contact with the sources of inspiration and has sung from those to communicate it.

Did you practice and follow your guru's instructions?

He's coming a bit closer to the bone now. Basically he's asking: 'Did you remember what I said, or were you so immersed in your Buddhist philosophy and science that you forgot all about the instructions of your guru?'

Did you secure the teachings that you wanted?

Rechungpa went to India to secure certain teachings, among them of course the Ḍākinī Dharmas that Milarepa had not been able to obtain from Marpa because Marpa had not obtained them himself when he went to India.

Have you gained much knowledge and much learning?
Have you noticed your pride and egotism?
Are you altruistic in your thoughts and actions?

Now we come to the real crux. There's an antithesis between pride and egotism on the one hand and altruism in thought and action on the other. If Rechungpa had really been inspired by the bodhisattva ideal, which is the most altruistic ideal imaginable, he wouldn't have become so dominated by pride and egotism. It's not just a question of getting rid of pride and egotism, but of developing the *bodhicitta*, taking the bodhisattva ideal seriously. The bodhisattva ideal is the central teaching of the Mahāyāna, and although Milarepa follows the Vajrayāna, the Mahāyāna teaching is the essence of what is contained in the Vajrayāna. You can't enter upon the Vajrayāna unless the *bodhicitta* has arisen – that is, unless you're taking the bodhisattva ideal very seriously indeed. That is the foundation. The generation of the *bodhicitta* is one of the four *mūla yogas*.[178] Milarepa is perhaps saying that there's nothing wrong with learning Buddhist philosophy and logic, but the question is, with what intention are you learning it? What is your motive? If it is to help you spread the Dharma for the benefit of all living beings, if it's an expression of your *bodhicitta*, that's fine, but if it is simply for your own self-glorification, so that you can defeat others in argument in an egoistic way, then it's entirely unskilful. Some of the Mahāyāna texts say that the bodhisattva should equip himself with the knowledge of all the arts and the sciences, because that knowledge will help him to communicate the Dharma to a greater number of living beings. There's nothing wrong in learning these subjects if you learn them with the right motive and make good use of that knowledge.

So Milarepa hasn't given Rechungpa the welcome and the obeisance he was hoping for. This is the sort of thing that often happens: our expectations are disappointed. That's probably quite good for us, especially if we're being disappointed by someone like Milarepa, who has the situation well in hand. One gets the feeling of a tremendous and genuine concern on his part. He is not reacting at all; he's simply concerned about Rechungpa's welfare.

Have you noticed your pride and egotism?

The suggestion is that Rechungpa is unaware of himself. Pride and egotism are such big things, but you can still have them and yet not realize it. They may be obvious to everybody else but not to you. In fact, the bigger they are, the less obvious to you they are likely to be. That is their nature. 'Me?! I'm the least egoistic person I know. I just appreciate myself at my true value. Other people don't appreciate my true worth.' Very often this is people's attitude.

One way of spotting the difference between egoism and self-confidence is that if you are self-confident you don't need to know everything in advance. For instance, you might go off to a foreign country to give a lecture. If you're self-confident, you don't need to know everything in detail: what it's going to be like, what sort of people are going to come along, what sort of hall it's going to be in, because you know you've got enough self-confidence to carry you through all that. An essential characteristic of self-confidence is the ability to cope with the unknown, the unforeseen, and the unexpected. You know you can rise to the occasion, and perhaps you even feel that you are bigger than the occasion. You don't think of it in competitive terms, in comparison with other people. It's just that you know you will be able to cope; the situation won't be too much for you. The egoistic person will often search out opportunities for asserting himself, or for being overbearing. If you're self-confident, you won't do that. You just know that whatever arises, you're quite capable of dealing with it, so much so that you don't think about whether you're capable of dealing with it or not.

Of course, there is such a thing as over-confidence. 'Oh, don't worry – we'll cope with that when it comes along!' That is going to the other extreme, like when you're asked to give a talk and you're given plenty of notice, but you don't bother to prepare, so your talk isn't as good as it could have been.

Rechungpa asked after Milarepa's health, and this is his reply. Rechungpa might not think it much of a song of welcome!

2

DO NOT BE PROUD AND POMPOUS

Here is Rechungpa's song in reply to what Milarepa has been saying. He puts up a good defence.

In reply, Rechungpa sang:

Obeying my Guru, I went to India.
My journey was hazardous and full of fear,
I underwent great pain and toil –
But the trip was well worthwhile.
I saw Dipupa, the great Tantric Master,
And met Magi, the great Yoginī.
Also I saw the wondrous Patron Buddha
And witnessed fulfillment of the Dākinīs' prophecy.
I have unmistakably attained
The longed-for Pith-Instructions –
Those of the Illuminating Wisdom Lamp,
The Wheel Net of Prāṇa and the Nāḍīs,
The Universal Mirror of Equality,
The Lantern of the Great Bliss Injunctions,
The True Words on the Mirror of Self-Mind,
The Supreme Form of the Sun-like Realization,
And the Self-liberation Mahāmudrā.

As we know, it wasn't exactly in obedience to his guru that Rechungpa went to India. He really wanted to go in order to learn about debate and logic so that he could defeat the logicians in argument. Milarepa strongly advised him against going, but he insisted, so Milarepa said, 'All right, but don't go to learn the science of logic. Go to bring back certain teachings of the *ḍākinīs* which my teacher Marpa was not able to obtain when he was there.' It was on that condition, rather reluctantly, that he allowed Rechungpa to go to India. But here we have Rechungpa saying, 'Obeying my guru, I went to India'. He is making quite a virtue of it, as though he went to India in response to a direct order from Milarepa. In other words, he's playing a little game. He's trying to make out that he is a very good disciple and went to India in obedience to the guru, whereas the truth of the situation is that he wrung permission from Milarepa with great difficulty. Even then, Milarepa only allowed him to go on certain conditions which perhaps he has fulfilled, and perhaps he hasn't. The fact that his song opens with what is virtually an untruth makes one suspicious about what comes afterwards. He says, 'My journey was hazardous and full of fear', which may well have been the case. He has visited various people, and he mentions those particular Dharmas, the five teachings of the *ḍākinīs*, which he has brought back in book form. He may or may not have mastered the contents but at least he's got the books. This part of Rechungpa's song gives the impression that he's boasting a bit. 'I saw Dipupa, the great Tantric Master! I met Magi, the great Yoginī!' He's been doing a round trip of Buddhist India, seeing all these great masters and teachers and yogis, having all sorts of wonderful experiences. It seems a bit like some of the people who go off to India nowadays from the West and do the rounds. He also says, 'I have unmistakably attained the longed-for Pith-Instructions.' Perhaps he feels he has unmistakably attained them because he's got the books in his hand! So he does seem to be boasting a little.

In the next verse he sings:

I drank Nectar – the Essence of Immortality,
I received teaching on the Bardo,
The Pith-Instructions on Dhyāna practice,
On the Five Gems and Symbols Three.
I was told how to practice the Six Yogas,

And how to win what I wanted in the world.
The Mothers and Ḍākinīs gathered for me
All these wonderful instructions.
The Deities and Gurus were all well pleased,
And my mind united well with theirs.
Like a rain of flowers,
Accomplishments fell upon me.
Heavenly food was fed into my mouth,
The Pith-Instructions were put into my hand.
In farewell, the Deities wished me good luck.
My desires were met and success was won.
Like the rising sun
My heart is bright with joy.
Now I am back, my Jetsun Guru!
Now I give you the Ḍākinīs' teachings!
Please observe them,
Praise and serve them –
The holy Dharmas that have brought me my achievement.

Now he's almost trying to come across as the teacher, and he's certainly being rather patronizing. He's apparently been going from teacher to teacher, receiving this instruction and that, but one feels that he's not going very deeply into any one of these things. One does find this sort of thing even among modern Tibetans. They go from one teacher to another, and sit in on all sorts of wonderful initiations, but instead of settling down to practise any of them, they go on to somebody else and get another initiation. Some Westerners do the same sort of thing, of course. Rechungpa seems to have been doing something of that sort – seeing famous teachers and yogis and sitting in on initiations and receiving instructions – and he's got a bit carried away by it all. So now he's come back to Milarepa with these books of the *ḍākinīs'* teachings and he's even being a bit patronizing towards Milarepa himself. He's emphasizing how well he got on. It's not such an easy thing to unite one's mind with the minds of deities and gurus, but this is what he's claiming. Perhaps he did have some spiritual experiences, but clearly, at least in Milarepa's eyes, not nearly enough.

One often finds that people have some quite genuine experience, but then they start thinking too highly of themselves on account of it and instead of just carrying on steadily with their practice, they start priding themselves on what they've already achieved, and making that the basis of all sorts of claims. In this way, they don't make any further progress. Perhaps they even start regressing. The phrase 'and how to win what I wanted in the world' gives away that Rechungpa is still thinking in material terms.

'The Mothers and Ḍākinīs gathered for me all these wonderful instructions' can be taken in various ways. The Mothers or the *mātṛkās* are a bit like *ḍākinīs*, except that *ḍākinīs* are associated with the sky whereas the Mothers are associated with the earth. They also represent forces of inspiration. One could think of forces of inspiration as coming from above or below. If one thinks of them as coming from above, they're *ḍākinīs*; if one thinks of them as coming from below they are Mothers, *mātṛkās*: Mothers with a capital 'M'. There is a tradition in the Vajrayāna that certain teachings of the Buddha and Padmasambhava were not suitable for communication to people at the time that the Buddha lived or at the time that Padmasambhava lived. According to Vajrayāna tradition, these teachings were either written down and hidden away here or there or taught to non-humans like *nāgas* and *devas* and *ḍākinīs* who guarded those teachings until such time as human beings were ready for them. Rechungpa seems to be referring to that kind of thing: that the Mothers and *ḍākinīs* who had been entrusted with various teachings in the past by the Buddha himself or by great spiritual masters gathered them all together for him and transmitted them to him because he was fit to receive them.

What he is really saying is that he is a very spiritually gifted person, as demonstrated by the fact that various teachings which had hitherto been kept secret were transmitted to him while he was in India. No doubt in Buddhist circles at that time, as in Tibet even down to the present, various teachings come into circulation. They look like new teachings but they aren't really new; they have been handed down for hundreds of years but have been kept secret. Only now have they been made public. It could well be that while he was away Rechungpa made contact with people who were publishing these teachings which, according to them at least, had been kept secret for centuries, and he felt very pleased that some of these teachings had been entrusted to him and he could bring them back to Tibet in book form. It's quite possible still to have this experience when meeting Tibetan lamas in India. They may say, 'This teaching came to me from my guru, who had it from his guru. The *ḍākinīs* revealed it to him but it hasn't yet been written down. But anyway, I shall write it down for your benefit.' This is quite a common occurrence, as though there's a great reservoir of oral traditions, even now, that is being constantly drawn from. It's not always easy to distinguish the authentic from the inauthentic, but one might say that if a teaching works, if it helps you, there's no harm in taking it as authentic. In principle it's authentic because in principle it goes back to the Buddha, or to Padmasambhava.

One can see that Rechungpa is a mixture, as so many people are. There is good in him, there is genuine spiritual aspiration, but there is a sort of restlessness and impatience too. There is the pride of learning, and a sense of self-importance. There is genuine devotion to Milarepa, but at the same time he is disobedient. He has in some ways got great faith in Milarepa but he doesn't always follow his instructions. So many people are like this, neither wholly good nor wholly bad, but a strange combination of the two. But here we see Rechungpa rather carried away by his experiences and contacts and achievements in India and coming back to Tibet just a little bit inflated. As we have seen, the thing that he was really concerned about just before their meeting was how Milarepa would welcome him, whether he would return his obeisance or not. That tells us quite a lot about Rechungpa, suggesting that he may be quite puffed up on account of his various attainments and acquisitions in India, even though some of them might have been quite genuine. So let's see what Milarepa has to say to all this.

Then Rechungpa gave the books (that he had acquired in India) to the Jetsun. In order to clear up Rechungpa's pride and arrogance, Milarepa sang:

Do not be proud and pompous,
My little child, Rechungpa,
Whom I have nurtured from your teens.

In a tuneful voice I sing for you
A golden-rosary of song with meanings deep.
Keep it in your mind, if you agree with it.

Goddesses cherish the Formless Ḍākinī Dharmas,
But he who strives to become too big
Is liable to be slain by villains.
The hoarded goods of wealthy men
Provide enjoyment for their enemies;
To indulge in luxury and pleasure
Is the cause of poverty and death.
He who does not know his limit
And acts above his station,
Is stupid as a fool.
If an officer ill-treats his servants,
He harms his country.
If a servant respects not his master,
He will lose his mind
And bring misfortune on himself.
If a Doctrine-holder cannot behave,
He will destroy the Dharma.
He who does not keep the Ḍākinīs' teaching secret,
Disturbs and offends them.

> *Do not be proud and pompous,*
> *My little child, Rechungpa,*
> *Whom I have nurtured from your teens.*

With this, Milarepa brings Rechungpa right down to earth. In effect he's saying, 'Listen, don't give yourself airs in front of me. I have known you a long time. I know you very well. I know exactly where you're at. I know that all this learning that you have brought back from India doesn't amount to very much. So don't be proud and pompous.'

> *In a tuneful voice I sing for you*
> *A golden-rosary of song with meanings deep.*
> *Keep it in your mind, if you agree with it.*

So he's going to give Rechungpa some good advice in the form of a song with deep meanings. In saying, 'Keep it in your mind if you agree with it', he's still leaving Rechungpa complete freedom of choice to accept it or reject it.

Goddesses cherish the Formless Ḍākinī Dharmas,
But he who strives to become too big
Is liable to be slain by villains.

The goddesses cherish the Formless Ḍākinī Dharmas because there's something good in them, something worth preserving, but villains tend to slay 'he who strives to become too big' – and, of course, Rechungpa has put himself in that sort of danger. If you strive to become too big, if you act in an overbearing arrogant way, that may bring you into collision with people who aren't very scrupulous. You may offend and upset them, and that may be the end of you. So you've got these two different situations. Something as valuable as the Ḍākinī Dharmas will be cherished by goddesses, but someone who 'strives to become too big' is 'liable to be slain by villains'. What is positive attracts support, but that which is negative tends to attract the opposite. Milarepa is saying that if you really identify yourself with the Formless Ḍākinī Dharmas, if you really practise them and realize their meaning, you will be cherished and protected. But if you simply try to become too big, your arrogance will lead to your being destroyed, even killed.

Milarepa is also pointing out a great discrepancy between the Formless Ḍākinī Dharmas which Rechungpa thinks that he has achieved and Rechungpa's state of mind, which is not at all in accordance with those Dharmas. He's got the books, but that's about all, apparently. You can't have the fruits of the Formless Ḍākinī Dharmas without actually realizing those Formless Ḍākinī Dharmas, and Rechungpa should realize that he hasn't realized them and therefore he is unlikely to experience their fruits.

The hoarded goods of wealthy men
Provide enjoyment for their enemies;
To indulge in luxury and pleasure
Is the cause of poverty and death.

This is almost worldly wisdom: you can't take it with you when you go. What you have cherished all your life may be divided among people who are quite inimical to you. And it's clear enough that 'to indulge in luxury and pleasure is the cause of poverty and death'.

He who does not know his limit
And acts above his station
Is stupid as a fool.

By 'knowing one's limits and acting above one's station' Milarepa means behaving as though one has more spiritual attainment than one really has, and this is clearly what Rechungpa is doing. Milarepa is pointing out that it's easy to think that you've mastered something simply because you've understood the philosophical explanations. It's easy to think you've realized the Void when you've only read a book about the philosophy of *śūnyatā*. Rechungpa has come back loaded down with teachings he's gathered in India, but that means nothing. They could have all been loaded on the back of a donkey, but the donkey wouldn't have been able to understand them.

It's very important to know exactly where one stands. That may be very difficult sometimes, because one changes very much, but at least one should not think too highly of oneself or think one has achieved something that one has in fact not achieved, or understood something that one does not understand. People sometimes think that only certain special teachings are good enough for them. Just as in worldly life, when people talk as though there is one special person who is meant just for them, but really it's not like that at all, in the same way, sometimes people think there's one particular teaching that is meant just for them – the right teaching, the right mantra, the right meditation posture – and if they can just find that, it will enable them to progress spiritually very rapidly. The truth is that any old practice – any old meditation, any old mantra – will do. The main thing is that you must practise it. But some people are obsessed with this idea of getting the right practice, the right method, the right technique, the right koan, the right mantra, the right guru, the right school of Buddhism, the right monastery, the right cave, the right piece of white cloth, the right begging-bowl....

Behind this there are several *micchā-diṭṭhis*. First of all, one might suspect that such people are really avoiding the necessity to practise at all. They're putting off the day of practice. That is one element. Another element is that they're convinced that they are very special people, and therefore need a very special teaching. It's almost a form of narcissism. It also represents a faith in technique rather than in the principles of the spiritual life, the idea that if you get exactly the right combination of things, exactly the right combination of letters in a particular mantra, that will do the trick. According to this way of thinking, it is not really a transformation in oneself that is needed. One just needs to get hold of the right box of tricks.

> *If an officer ill-treats his servants,*
> *He harms his country.*

Milarepa is apparently thinking of the Tibetan-style government officer who ill-treats his servants – that is, the people who are working for him and helping him with the administration. If he ill-treats them, they don't do their job properly, the country is not well-administered, and the country suffers.

> *If a servant respects not his master,*
> *He will lose his mind*
> *And bring misfortune on himself.*
> *If a Doctrine-holder cannot behave,*
> *He will destroy the Dharma.*

The last two comparisons were leading up to this: that if a doctrine-holder cannot behave, he will destroy the Dharma. The Sanskrit word *dharmadhara* means literally a Dharma-holder or doctrine-holder, and it refers to one who preserves and transmits the Dharma. Literally it's someone who bears, carries, the Dharma. The word Dharma comes from the same root as the word *dhara*, 'to bear' or 'to support', so the *dharmadhara* is the supporter of that which supports. And you support that which supports by being yourself a supporter. In other words, you preserve the Dharma by practising the Dharma, and there is no other way to preserve it. So, 'If a Doctrine-holder cannot behave, he will destroy the Dharma.' If one who purports to maintain the Dharma does not himself practise it, he will destroy the Dharma, because the Dharma is not preserved by writing it down in books, or by giving lectures about it. The Dharma is preserved when you practise it, because the Dharma is not a book or a lecture. The Dharma is your life, your Enlightened life. There is no way of preserving the Dharma other than by practising it. You don't preserve it by writing it down and hiding the writing in holes in the ground, or by putting Buddhist literature on tape and sealing the tapes up in little cylinders and burying them in blocks of concrete. Preserving the Dharma means embodying the Dharma in your own life, and transmitting it in that way.

Rechungpa probably thinks of himself as a doctrine-holder because he has literally brought these teachings back from India, but Milarepa is saying that the doctrine can only be preserved by living it. In other words, in the long run you can only teach Buddhism out of your own experience. You can go on just repeating what you've heard only for a short time. Sooner or later you have to be able to speak from your own experience. It's very easy to think about the Dharma or Buddhism or the Sangha as something separate from yourself. Sometimes people in our own sangha talk about it and criticize it as though they didn't belong to it, apparently not realizing that if there is something wrong with the sangha, it means that there is something wrong with them and the others who are part of it, because it doesn't exist apart from the people in it. If one wants to bring about a change in the sangha, one has to bring about a change in people, including oneself – preferably starting with oneself.

> He who does not keep the Ḍākinīs' teaching secret,
> Disturbs and offends them.

What can Milarepa mean by 'keeping the *ḍākinīs'* teaching secret'? One could say, to begin with, that these Formless Ḍākinī Dharmas are rather esoteric teachings. They are Vajrayāna teachings, which pertain to quite a high level of spiritual development, so they are not to be made the subject of public exposition on the basis of a purely intellectual understanding or a knowledge of the literature. They are something to be communicated from teacher to disciple in a very genuine manner. If you don't keep the *ḍākinīs'* teaching secret, if you don't transmit it in the proper manner, if you make a public display of it, you 'disturb and offend the *ḍākinīs'*. But what does that mean? Who are the *ḍākinīs*? What are the *ḍākinīs*? They are forces of inspiration. If certain teachings have come to you as a result of some inspiration, whether your own or that of someone else, and if you start trying to communicate these teachings in the wrong way, that reverses or blocks the flow of the inspiration and the *ḍākinīs* are 'disturbed and offended'. Certain understandings might come to you as a result of your inspiration, but if you were to misuse that, if you were to talk about it too loosely or to the wrong sort of people, that would interrupt the flow of the inspiration.

It is often said that you shouldn't talk about experiences that you have in meditation, especially not with people who don't know anything about meditation or who are unsympathetic to it, because in order to talk about your experience, you'd have almost to alienate yourself from it and that would tend to inhibit the continuation of the experience. You might feel as you were speaking that you were doing yourself or the inspiration an injustice, but if you were a bit careless, you might not be able to stop yourself. Sometimes it is said in connection with Tantric practices generally that you should discuss the practice only with fellow disciples of the same teacher who have that same practice, and not talk about it in a loose way. That applies to deeper experiences of any kind, whether experienced in meditation or in any other way. You shouldn't make them the subject of general conversation. If you are in genuine communication with someone, and especially if you feel that talking about your experience would be encouraging or inspiring to him or her, then of course it's a good idea to do so. But if you try to talk about experience in public, as it were, you will find sooner or later that in fact you are not really talking about that experience, because you have had to distance yourself from it in order to talk about it. You've alienated yourself from it, and thus you've lost it; the sources of inspiration have dried up.

You might have had the experience of trying to talk to someone about something that is very meaningful to you and then realizing you've made a mistake. They're just not in sympathy with you, they can't understand, and you feel quite upset that you've even started trying to talk to them. It may even seem to have done you some harm, to have upset and disturbed you. It's this sort of thing that Milarepa means here. It isn't about the arbitrary imposition of secrecy: 'Oh no! You mustn't talk about that!' It's to do with the quality of communication. You mustn't force it. If you do, the energy and inspiration of the communication will just dry up.

It's rather doubtful that you could harm other people by telling them about such an experience. If they were in a more positive, more receptive state, you would be able to communicate your experience to them, but as they're not, you're not telling them anything they ought not to know. They don't know what you're talking about. They don't care.

It's possible that you might plant a seed in their brain that might grow in time, but it's unlikely when there is such a lack of communication. But even if you can't do any serious harm under those conditions, one might wonder what would make you want to try to communicate something when the conditions are not suitable. It could be that you have already lost contact with that inspiration, and it's only an idea about it that you try to communicate with others.

We also have to be careful not to use our inspiration in an overbearing way, trying almost to force the other person to feel inspired. If we try to do that, the whole thing will backfire on us. It points to the importance of setting up the conditions for genuine communication and not trying to force the pace on the basis of an idea of what you want to communicate. To set up the conditions, first of all you have to make sure that you have time. If you really want to communicate something of importance to somebody, arrange to spend a certain amount of time with them. Don't just catch them in passing and tell them whatever it is in five minutes when they're in a hurry and on their way somewhere else. If it's sufficiently important, make sure that you won't be interrupted. Otherwise, you might have reached a crucial point and then the door will fly open and somebody will burst in.

It's often impossible to have a proper conversation in a family situation, especially if young children are around, and you can't really talk with several people at once because each individual is so different; you can only stick to generalities. So if you want to communicate with someone who lives in a family situation, it might be best to invite him or her out to have a quiet chat somewhere else. Likewise, don't phone someone when they're at work. That's not fair. He or she may be very busy and here are you trying to talk about something important when other phones are ringing and people are coming and putting things on his or her desk.

This is what I mean, on a very basic level, about setting up the right conditions for communication. Ensure that you're going to be alone together for a certain length of time free from interruption and able to concentrate on the communication. Make sure that you don't have anything else on your mind and you're not thinking of rushing off somewhere afterwards, so that your mind is free and you can give yourself to the communication. Just as with meditation and even with puja, preparation is often half the battle. If you invite someone to your place, be prepared to receive a visitor. It's quite frustrating if someone has invited you round for a good talk and when you arrive, you find that they're in the middle of something. If they say, 'Oh, I'm so sorry, I'm in such a mess' and they have to take a pile of newspapers off the chair so you can sit down, a jarring note is struck from the very beginning. If you're going to give your guest something to eat, have the food all ready, and make the place neat and tidy, and warm and comfortable if it's wintertime. Make them feel welcome. This will make everything go much more smoothly. If the phone keeps on ringing and you keep scuttling in and out to do this and that, how is communication possible?

Taking it a stage further, you can talk about things which are of deeper significance only when a certain level of communication has been established. Broadly speaking, the greater the number of people present, the smaller the possibility of good communication. You get the most intense communication just with one person, but you still have to be sure that it really is communication. It's difficult to define real communication, but one of its characteristics is that you experience a feeling of relief that you're not having to hold anything back. Also, you feel a lot of energy flowing – not, of course, the kind of energy that sprays around when you're 'talking your head off', as they say. The energy that is generated in real communication is not like that. If you've really been communicating, you don't feel exhausted or depleted afterwards, even though you may have been talking for quite a long time. If anything, you feel an enhancement of energy and vigour. In most cases, if you keep up your communication long enough, it becomes quieter and quieter, and gentler and gentler, but not less intense. You may end up not feeling any need to say anything. Also, during real communication you are very concentrated. Your mind doesn't wander. Very often when you're talking with somebody, you start thinking about other things, but in real communication you are very absorbed, as you are when you have a good meditation. Real communication is more likely to occur when you are talking about things that are of vital significance to you.

If communication tends to be most intense on a one to one basis, what kind of communication is possible in study groups? It depends on the people. You can have twenty people in a study group and have excellent communication, though that is comparatively rare. To go to extremes, if you have forty or fifty people there's no question of discussion. You can go round the circle 'reporting in', and that can be a very positive experience, but that's just one person speaking and everybody else listening. It's very difficult to have a discussion among so many. Sometimes a 'pseudo-discussion' goes on, with four or five people discussing something and everybody else listening, but I wouldn't regard that as being a discussion group; it's only a small number of people holding a discussion and others providing the audience for that. So keeping study groups fairly small makes a certain degree of intensity possible. It doesn't automatically ensure it because if you've got five dull people, that doesn't add up to a lively study group, whatever the text may be. But you'd have a better study group with eight lively people than with forty lively people. Forty lively people in a study group doesn't bear thinking about!

If groups are too small, they're too much at the mercy of the moods of the individual members. If there are ten people in a study group, it's unlikely that all ten will be feeling dull on the same evening. There could well be two or three who feel bright and lively, and hopefully they will eventually spark everybody else off, or at least the study group leader should be able to do that. Even if there are five or ten or twenty people who are feeling dull, they should all feel energized by the end of the evening.

It was said about Mae West that 'when she was good she was very good, but when she was bad she was better', and it's the same with study groups. Obviously this is a bit of a paradox, so I'd better explain. A 'good' study group might be one where you keep strictly to the text and go into it thoroughly, where everybody is very attentive and mindful, and nobody says a word out of place or goes off at a tangent. But it's better when it's worse – that is to say, when things loosen up and people feel free to say what they're thinking and talk about what's on their mind. The purpose of a study group is not just to stick strictly to the text and go into it in an analytical way. It's also to arouse a certain kind of energy in people, to stir them up a bit. It's very important to give them the opportunity of expressing themselves, and to achieve that you may need to allow the strict study group format to relax or even break up a bit from time to time, provided you can come back to the text in the end. It's like a piano concerto with lots of elaborate cadenzas. The soloist goes on and on for minutes together, playing all sorts of musical tricks, but in the end there's a lead into the orchestra and you're back on familiar ground. In study there should be room for that sort of thing. I discovered that a study group may be better when it is worse – only technically worse, and better because it's achieving a fuller purpose – quite by accident. I was leading study and I thought one particular morning that it hadn't gone very well, but afterwards the participants said that it was the best study group they'd had for a long time and they had thoroughly enjoyed it. I started wondering why they felt like that and came to the conclusion that, because I hadn't been feeling very well that morning, I just let things have a loose rein and hadn't said as much as usual. It seems that people had enjoyed that more because they'd had a chance to get more off their chests, and stray a little bit away from the text.

Oh, my son, your pride in what you learned
Will lead you well astray!

This is really a serious admonition. Rechungpa may have learned a great deal but he has developed pride in what he has learned, and this, Milarepa says, will lead him well astray. It seems paradoxical that studying Buddhist philosophy, learning all about *śūnyatā*, all about *anātman* and all about non-ego should make you proud, but this is what happens. There's a story about a gathering of representatives of different Christian monastic orders in Paris on one occasion. A Franciscan friar got up and said, 'Everybody agrees that the Dominicans excel in learning, and as for diplomatic ability, the Jesuits are better than anybody else, but when it comes to humility, we Franciscans are tops!' Likewise, in a Buddhist context someone can be proud of his knowledge about non-ego.

3

HOW COULD A SON EVER DISRESPECT HIS FATHER?

To preach a lot, with empty words,
Ruins your good Experience and meditation.
To be swollen with pride and arrogance
Proves you have betrayed the Guru's precepts.
Nothing gives cause for more regret
Than disobedience of the Guru.
No one is more distracted and confused
Than he who ceases to meditate in solitude!
Nothing is more fruitless
Than a Buddhist who renounces not his kin!
Nothing is more shameful
Than a learned Buddhist who neglects his meditation.
Nothing is more disgraceful
Than for a monk to violate the rules.

> *To preach a lot, with empty words,*
> *Ruins your good Experience and meditation.*

Milarepa is being really severe here. He is not against preaching; what he is against is spending so much time on it that it becomes your full-time occupation and you don't ever do anything else. You don't meditate, you don't communicate, you don't spend any time on your own, you don't study. You become a full-time preacher. If you go on preaching too long, your inspiration will dry up. You might have had some knowledge and understanding to begin with, but in the end your preaching is just 'empty words'. This is quite a common experience. You can be standing in front of an audience, or even talking to someone individually, or a group of people, and you suddenly realize that what you're saying is just empty words. There's no meaning, no truth in it, there's no feeling, no experience, if for no other reason than that talking takes a lot of energy.

When we started introducing periods of silence on our early retreats – even half a day of silence, which was quite a lot in those days – people were surprised to notice how much more energy they had after a period of silence. This suggests that a lot of energy goes into talking, and you conserve energy by remaining silent or by not talking unnecessarily. If you have something meaningful to say, if you're really communicating, you don't lose energy in the same way, but if you're just talking, you lose energy, and this does not have a good effect on your spiritual experience and your meditation. When you go on talking for too long, however well you may have started, you start feeling very empty and dry and exhausted, and the same thing can happen if you're teaching the Dharma a lot. It all becomes a bit meaningless and unrelated to your own experience, just a matter of words. You can feel very depleted and the result can be that your formerly good experience of meditation is ruined for the time being. To give a talk as a genuine communication to receptive people can be a worthwhile and stimulating experience but to have to get up on a platform and spout something to people who aren't particularly interested can be exhausting. So one shouldn't get into this sort of situation. It helps to speak from your own experience, and stay close to that experience. You don't have to talk about the Four Noble Truths and Nirvāṇa and Enlightenment and so on. You can say quite a lot keeping quite close to your own experience, even though your experience may be limited. Usually it's what you're able to say from your own experience that will be most interesting and inspiring to other people. Something else that helps is really to be in communication with your audience, and ideally you should have an audience that is genuinely receptive to you – otherwise you'll just be talking to yourself.

> To be swollen with pride and arrogance
> Proves you have betrayed the Guru's precepts.

Why should this be so? Because if you followed the guru's precepts and just practised, you wouldn't feel like that. It's only because you want something other than the actual practice that you feel proud. You think you know better than the guru, and that involves pride and arrogance. Following the guru's precepts is the antithesis of 'being swollen with pride and arrogance'; it shows a kind of humility. So 'pride and arrogance' are the qualities most opposed to following the guru's instructions and observing the precepts that he has given you. 'Precepts' here means not so much the five precepts and the ten precepts, but instructions meant particularly for you. If you meet someone who professes to be following a particular teacher, if he's proud and arrogant, you can be pretty certain that he has betrayed his guru's precepts, because no guru could be giving him precepts to behave in that sort of way.

Then Milarepa says something quite striking:

> Nothing gives cause for more regret
> Than disobedience of the Guru.

This word 'disobedience' is rather ambivalent. What does it mean in relation to the guru? One must not think of the guru as an authority figure, so perhaps 'disobedience' isn't quite the right term. It's more of a question of being in harmony with the guru, being on the same wavelength. Here Milarepa seems to mean by the guru not an inner 'ideal self' but the guru in the quite literal sense – in the sense in which he is Rechungpa's guru and Rechungpa did disobey him. Although Rechungpa says that he went to India 'in accordance with Milarepa's instructions', he did no such thing. Milarepa didn't want him to go and he disregarded that. In the end Milarepa had to agree to his going and thus try to minimize the damage. So it is the guru in the literal sense that seems to be meant here. If you're out of harmony with the guru, you're out of harmony with what the guru represents, and thus you're out of harmony with the spiritual ideal, with the spiritual life, the spiritual path. In other words, you're out of harmony with the Buddha, the Dharma, and the Sangha. What could give cause for more regret than that? To be out of harmony with the guru represents an alienation from the spiritual life itself, and in the same way, to be out of harmony with your *kalyāṇa mitras*, with the sangha, with the order, would also be a great cause for regret, because you are out of harmony with what they embody.

No one is more distracted and confused
Than he who ceases to meditate in solitude!

There is an ambiguity of meaning in the English translation here: it could refer to one who interrupts his solitary meditation, or to one who, even though he is in solitude, ceases meditating. Perhaps it comes to the same thing in the end. If you give up meditation while you are in solitude, what could be worse than that? If you are in the ideal circumstances for meditation, but you don't meditate, that really is a sign of distraction and confusion. Of course, Milarepa is addressing Rechungpa, who went off to India instead of remaining in his hermitage and continuing with his meditation, so perhaps Milarepa means that 'no one is more distracted and confused' than he who goes roaming around in foreign countries, ostensibly for religious purposes, instead of continuing to meditate in solitude when that is what he really needs.

Nothing is more fruitless
Than a Buddhist who renounces not his kin!

This is a very severe statement. Does Milarepa literally mean that everybody ought to leave his relations? If you take the words literally, it suggests that if you don't renounce your kin, being a Buddhist is completely fruitless. But does he really mean that? And if not, what does he mean? Although the translator uses the word 'renounces', if we assume that it doesn't necessarily mean literally leaving, but more an inner renunciation, how would you know that you had renounced your kin in your heart, as it were, unless you put it to the test? Are not the possibilities of self-deception too great? But if we take it literally, why is Milarepa so insistent that a Buddhist, to be a fruitful Buddhist, should renounce his kin? What is so inimical to one's Buddhist life in keeping up one's relationships with one's kin?

Your kin are those people with whom you're connected by ties of blood, but that's all that connects you – you don't necessarily share the same interests. Perhaps Milarepa is saying that so long as you remain identified with the family, you are identified with a group of people with whom you don't necessarily have anything in common, and that can be a dreadful thing from the point of view of your spiritual development. Your relatives can be thoroughly unsympathetic and uncongenial sometimes, even apart from the question of Buddhism. Milarepa is perhaps saying that if you're thinking in terms of the best possible conditions for your development as an individual, you need either to be on your own or at least to be surrounded by other people who have the same ideals as you, who will be supportive to you in your aspirations.

Sometimes we don't fully understand the effect that our relations have on us, but if you've been away for a long time and then you go to see them again, you certainly appreciate it. Maybe you're fond of them and you quite like to see them, and maybe they're glad to see you, but you may find after two or three hours that the contact is beginning to have an effect on you which is not at all pleasant, positive, or skilful. And that's just after two or three hours, never mind a whole weekend. Sometimes one has to wish them well, for the time being at least, from a safe distance. Perhaps this refers most of all to fathers and mothers, brothers and sisters – people who have known you all your life. You have to bear in mind that as a Buddhist you are trying to change, and your family tend to see you as you have always been. It's not easy for them to accept the fact that you are changing, and that you're going to change some more. They themselves perhaps don't want to change, even if they think that change is possible, and they want to go on seeing you in the same old way. Very often they insist that you are still the same person, still dear old so-and-so. Whenever you encounter them, they tend to see you as you were before and treat you in that way, in effect trying to pull you back into the past and to negate the change that has taken place. Sometimes they may even say quite openly, 'You may think you've changed, but you're still our little boy, our own little Johnny!'

This is no doubt one of the reasons why Milarepa says, 'Nothing is more fruitless than a Buddhist who renounces not his kin!' It's because by not renouncing them, by staying firmly embedded in the biological group, you make it so much more difficult for yourself to evolve. The Tibetan family may have been very tightly knit because conditions of life were difficult or even harsh. Surrounded by snow and intense cold for much of the year, you would tend to huddle together for warmth and protection, so perhaps Tibetan family life was very intense and claustrophobic. In the modern West the situation is a little different. You don't have to live with your parents – most people leave home when they grow up – so maybe even from Milarepa's point of view there's no harm in going to see your parents from time to time, but to live with your blood relations all the time is almost certainly quite inimical to your development as an individual.

> *Nothing is more shameful*
> *Than a learned Buddhist who neglects his meditation.*

It's very good to know the scriptures, but not at the expense of your practice of the Dharma, especially not at the expense of your practice of meditation. There must at least be a balance between the two things. If you have to choose, it's probably better to choose meditation than book knowledge of the Dharma, but it's best of all if you can have considerable experience of both.

The use of the word 'shame' here is connected with two mental states identified by the Buddhist tradition. *Hrī* (Pali *hiri*) is usually translated as 'a sense of shame' and it is often paired with *apatrāpya* (Pali *ottappa*), 'fear of blame (by the wise)'; together they are are called the 'guardians of the world' because they are the ethical forces which keep the moral order.[179] *Apatrāpya* is shame in the sense of that feeling that prevents you from doing something because of what those you respect might say if you did it. It isn't guilt, but shame in a positive sense, consciousness of not wanting to do something of which your spiritual friends would not approve – not society in general, but those who want you to grow and develop, those who've got some degree of wisdom and insight. *Apatrāpya* is what makes you aware when you have done something that your *kalyāṇa mitras* would be sorry to know that you have done, something that would disappoint them and let them down. When Milarepa says that something is shameful, he's thinking of shame in this sort of sense. So, 'nothing is more shameful than a learned Buddhist who neglects his meditation'. He knows the Buddhist scriptures so well, he can give an excellent lecture on so many aspects of the Dharma, but he has no real experience of Buddhism himself. What a pity! He's so close to the water but he doesn't drink himself. He's so busy handing it out to other people that he doesn't realize that he himself is dying of thirst.

And then Milarepa says:

> *Nothing is more disgraceful*
> *Than for a monk to violate the rules.*

Milarepa is not very keen on rules, and he's not a monk himself, but a sort of freelance yogi and hermit, so why does he mention 'not violating rules'? The point is that it's shameful to keep up the pretence of being a monk if you're not keeping the rules. If you've committed yourself to something, it is shameful not to honour that commitment. If you say, 'I will not tell a lie,' and then you do, that is shameful, because it's like taking a vow and then breaking it, which is worse than just doing that particular thing. You've taken a vow, you've committed yourself in principle with the whole force of your being, and yet you've not adhered to that. That suggests severe disruptive forces in your own being. It's not just that you've done a particular thing; the fact that you've done it having vowed not to do it shows that you're not master of yourself. You're not integrated. You can't keep a promise – not even a promise to the Buddha, Dharma, and Sangha.

We therefore have to be very careful what we promise and what vows we take. In the Triratna Buddhist Order we take ten precepts and that's more than enough to observe regularly and permanently. The Theravāda Vinaya has 227 precepts to be observed by *bhikkhus*, which is far too many. You can't help breaking some of them, and it isn't a good thing to profess to observe precepts which you are in fact not observing. It is even more undermining if when you receive a particular ordination you undertake or are made to undertake precepts which you have no intention of observing. It is much better to undertake a small number of basic precepts which you fully intend to observe. Even five may be quite a lot. As I discovered from getting to know Tibetans in Kalimpong, some Tibetan Buddhists think of themselves as one-precept Buddhists or two-precept Buddhists. They take it very seriously. They say, 'If I can manage to practise the first and second precepts – not injuring living beings and not taking anything that doesn't belong to me – I'll be doing pretty well. Sexual misconduct? No, I don't think I can manage that one. Right speech? Well, I'm in business, I'm a trader. I'd better not take that one! As for the fifth precept, I'm a Tibetan. It's impossible for me to take that one!' They feel they've got to observe a precept seriously if they undertake it at all. Otherwise, it's better just to say *Buddhaṃ saraṇaṃ gacchāmi*, recite *oṃ maṇi padme hūṃ*, and get blessings from the lamas. If you take precepts and break them, all the devils will be after you! Even Padmasambhava couldn't rescue you! This is how seriously they take it. A lot of Tibetan Buddhists don't undertake any precepts at all. Unfortunately, they quite often recite the bodhisattva vow instead, which is a serious devaluation of the bodhisattva vow. But what Milarepa is really talking about is honouring your commitments. If you promise that you will do something, do it. A failure to do that indicates a very irresolute, unintegrated character.

> My son Rechungpa, if you agree with what I say
> You should hold it in your heart;
> If you disagree, do whate'er you please.
> I am an old man fearing death,
> And with no time for chat and gossip.
> You are young and self-conceited,
> Whoever remonstrates with you, you will condemn him in return.

> Oh, my gracious guru, Marpa the Translator,
> Pray help me, the poor beggar
> Who forever abjures all worldly desires!

Here again Milarepa is not categorical. He doesn't say, 'You've got to agree with what I say'. He is the guru, but nonetheless he is leaving Rechungpa completely free. He isn't trying to coerce him in any way; he is just telling him quite frankly exactly what he thinks. He's giving him good advice, but he's leaving him completely free to choose whether or not to follow it. This is a very important point. It is possible to coerce people into being more skilful, but this only has significance within the positive group. It has no spiritual significance; it makes no contribution to the development of the individual. The guru is not a spiritual policeman. One has to be very careful on this score. Sometimes coercion may be justified or even objectively necessary, and through it you may be able to create a positive group, but you cannot create a spiritual community through coercion. The spiritual community must be based on the free consent of all concerned. You may be able to intimidate or persuade or cajole someone into doing something, but that can never be effective in terms of their development as an individual. An action can only support their individual development if they do it because they want to do it, because they themselves are convinced or have faith that that is the best thing for them to do. A spiritual community can be founded only on the basis of complete individual freedom, and only individuals can be free. You can't be free unless you're an individual and you can't be an individual unless you're free. There's a paradox here, of course. You're not really free if you're at the mercy of every passing whim and fancy and impulse, if you simply do what you like. You're only free if you act with awareness and responsibility and emotional positivity.

Milarepa says, 'My son Rechungpa, if you agree with what I say you should hold it in your heart; if you disagree, do whate'er you please.' That's all one can say, within the purely spiritual context. You can give your advice, you can point out to someone what is best for him to do in your opinion, but if he doesn't agree, he just has to do whatever he himself thinks best. There's nothing more that you can do.

> *I am an old man fearing death,*
> *And with no time for chat and gossip.*

Milarepa is not literally fearing death, surely, but he's saying to Rechungpa that he's an old man, he could die at any time, and he is very aware of that. He's got no time to waste.

> *You are young and self-conceited,*
> *Whoever remonstrates with you, you will condemn him*
> *   in return.*

Self-conceit is not necessarily just a characteristic of the young. In fact, sometimes the old can be more self-conceited, priding themselves on their experience and belittling the young for their lack of it. Some of my young Nepalese friends in Kalimpong used to complain bitterly about the way their grandfathers spoke to them. As soon as they piped up with any remark, their grandfather would say, 'Keep quiet, you egg!' But when Milarepa says to Rechungpa, 'Whoever remonstrates with you, you will condemn him in return', it's as though he's saying, 'No one can give you any advice. You always know better. I've had my say. I've given you my advice. If you agree with it, remember it. If you disagree with it, do as you please. I'm an old man. I haven't much longer to live. I've no time for idle talk. I'm going to get on with my meditation.' Some sources say that Milarepa died aged about eighty, but he didn't turn from the 'black' path to the 'white' one until he was forty, so there's hope for us all. Most of these episodes took place quite late in his life, perhaps when he was over seventy.

> Picking up the books and the Ahkaru staff, Milarepa ran ahead with great speed by means of his miraculous power. Rechungpa could not catch up with him. He ran, gasping and panting, after his Guru as he sang this song:

> Oh, please listen to me, my Father Jetsun!
> How could a son ever disrespect his father?
> I only pray you to accept the teachings I have attained.
> I was given, beyond any doubt or possible error,
> The instructions on the Formless Ḍākinī Dharmas.
> From the profound, and the profoundest, doctrines
> I have gained conviction!
> I pray you to understand this, my dear Guru!

This chase probably represents something symbolically. Listen to Rechungpa's pleas! 'Oh, please listen to me, my Father Jetsun! How could a son ever disrespect his father?' He doesn't seem to realize that he has been showing great disrespect. He's saying, 'You don't understand me. I really have attained these things. I really am spiritually developed. Please don't continue to treat me like a little boy. It's not that I'm being disrespectful. I really do respect you, but please realize how I've developed.' He's insisting that he has attained something spiritually in India, but Milarepa is just not recognizing it. He doesn't want to be disrespectful, but he does want Milarepa to recognize that he's not the old Rechungpa. Here we come dangerously near the possibility of rationalization. People do change, they do grow up, but that doesn't mean it has happened in Rechungpa's case. And Milarepa is his spiritual father. He really does know better than Rechungpa. He's not just a biological father who cannot see when a change has taken place. If anything, he sees that Rechungpa is worse than he was before, and he doesn't hesitate to point out his faults. But Rechungpa just thinks that Milarepa doesn't appreciate him, so he goes on trying to convince him how well he has done in India.

In addition, I also attained the Yoga of Longevity,
The Ḍākinīs' Symbolic Secret Words,
The principles of the Vajra Body,
And the instructions of the Mother Buddha.
I now offer them all to you, my Jetsun Guru!
Also I have attained
The profound Tiger Protection, the Cures of Diseases,
And the Teaching of Dispersing Demons.
All these golden instructions I now offer to you.

With this great catalogue of all the teachings he has obtained, he's still thinking far too literally, not to say literalistically. He may have acquired verbal teachings and books, but that doesn't mean he's really 'got' the teachings. He thinks, 'Maybe I ought to offer these things to Milarepa. Perhaps that's where I'm going wrong. All right, out with them!', not realizing that he hasn't gained them in the true sense, and nor can he offer them. He's got nothing to give – only the memory of the verbal teaching, and the books – but he doesn't realize that yet. Maybe he has advanced a stage further, because he's thinking now that he should give whatever he has acquired to Milarepa. What he doesn't realize is that in a deeper sense he does not possess the teachings at all. He has heard about them, learned about them, got books about them, but he hasn't mastered them.

We begin to see that Rechungpa is fond of his guru – especially when the guru lets him have his own way! As we have seen, he's a mixed sort of being. He's very fond of dear old Milarepa, very devoted to him, but the old guru sometimes just gets things a bit wrong and he has to be put right. This is his attitude. He has been brought up by Milarepa since he was in his teens, so it could be that he sees Milarepa as he is to some extent, he values him as a guru, but on the other hand he is the old man who brought him up, so he is perhaps attached to him as he would be to a biological father. He shows a curious mixture of the devotion of the disciple and the rebelliousness of the son. Sometimes he loves Milarepa, sometimes he hates him. Sometimes he reveres him and does what he tells him to do, and sometimes he's wildly rebellious and does exactly the opposite. He argues with Milarepa, disagrees with him, is even disrespectful to him, but at the same time he's really fond of him, and sometimes he sees him as he really is.

Upon my shoulder I have brought back
The Medicine of Six Merits,
And the elixirs of gods and goddesses;
Now I offer them to you, my gracious Guru.
This marvellous staff made of the supreme Ahkaru plant
Was used by Ḍākinīs to rest upon.
It is a priceless and wondrous thing,
Symbolizing the Tantric teachings of Dipupa;
I now offer it to you, my Jetsun Guru.
Please appreciate these wonderful teachings
And have pity on me, the weary Rechungpa!
Please commiserate me, and give me
A chance to stop running and panting!
If you would please, please do so,
It would be the best charity.
If one can satisfy the hunger and thirst of others,
It is of the greatest merit.
To console people in distress is the best giving;
To serve people with kindness and show them the right path
Is the obligation of all Dharma-followers,
As taught by Buddha, our Lord.

What Rechungpa is really doing here is trying to teach Milarepa how to teach him. He's saying, 'I don't like being taught in this way. Please teach me in another way.' By running away from him, Milarepa is giving him the teaching he needs, but Rechungpa doesn't realize that. He wants to be taught in the way he wants to be taught, not in the way that Milarepa is actually teaching him, so he tries to tell Milarepa how to handle him.

He reminds me of the French Buddhist nun I knew in Kalimpong, who gave quite a lot of trouble to several gurus, including Dhardo Rimpoche.[180] At least two of her gurus told me that she used to do this very thing. She'd go to see them and she'd make three very respectful prostrations, but before she even got up off her knees, she'd start telling them what to do and how they were to treat her. Her rationalization was that they were Tibetan and they didn't understand French psychology, so they didn't understand what was good for her. And *she* knew, of course, what was good for her. So she used to tell them what they should tell her to do. She thought they didn't know their job as gurus and they had to be told how to do it, and she used to get very angry if they wouldn't teach her in the way she wanted to be taught. She used to complain to me very bitterly that they were supposed to be gurus but they didn't understand her psychology and they didn't listen to what she said, and so on and so on. It seems that Rechungpa was rather like that. He even tells Milarepa what would be the best charity, what would be the greatest merit, and how to console people in distress. In going so far as trying to teach Milarepa a lesson about compassion, he really must be quite blind. But this is the sort of thing that happens.

In offering Milarepa this collection of relics and religious keepsakes, he's almost accusing Milarepa of not sufficiently valuing all the wonderful teachings and objects that he has brought back from India, and not having sufficient pity on him. Sometimes people try to invest themselves with importance by being the bearers of what is important. Rechungpa has brought back from India all these wonderful teachings, and he's expecting to be received and treated as someone special on that account. When Milarepa doesn't give him that sort of treatment, he in effect accuses Milarepa of not valuing the teachings he has brought back. Of course, it's really Rechungpa himself who is not valuing them. He ends up by preaching Milarepa quite a sermon. He doesn't seem to realize that he himself is being taught a lesson by Milarepa – the very lesson that he needs. But very often people don't want to be taught the lesson they need. They want to be taught some other lesson, which may be a very good lesson, but not the one they need. They may be perfectly ready to give up certain things and they grumble that their guru doesn't ask them to give up those things. He's so unreasonable! He asks them to give up the things they don't want to give up – what a difficult guru! People say, 'Don't ask me to give that up. I'm quite ready to give up anything you ask me to, but not that!' And they honestly think they are being really open and receptive to advice.

It also seems that Rechungpa wants to be appreciated. He's been away in India a long time, and on the way he has had many hardships. He has visited many gurus, received many instructions, gathered all sorts of manuscripts and important teachings, and come back laden with relics and souvenirs, and he was expecting Milarepa to give him a wonderful reception. As we've seen, he is beginning to think that now he is virtually Milarepa's equal, and he certainly expected Milarepa to return his obeisance and appreciate all the things that he has brought back and what he has attained. But he doesn't get any such reception. Milarepa treats him quite severely, quite roughly almost. He doesn't pat him on the back and tell him what a good boy he's been; he accuses him of pride and arrogance and self-conceit. Rechungpa gets quite a nasty shock.

The reason is that he is still thinking of the Dharma as something quite external. Milarepa warned him about that when he said, 'If a doctrine holder cannot behave, he will destroy the Dharma'. The Dharma is not a thing, something that you can preserve without practising it yourself. If you do something for other people, it's natural to expect them to be grateful, just as when you speak you expect people to listen, but it becomes unhealthy if you start doing things in order to get appreciation. Appreciation should be extra, a pleasant surprise. If you do something for the sake of appreciation, and if you feel disappointed and disgruntled when you don't get it, that shows that something is wrong.

The difference between rejoicing in merits and ordinary appreciation is that one tends to appreciate someone in order that they will appreciate you in return; it's called mutual back-scratching. Also, ordinary appreciation can be a bit indiscriminate, whereas when you rejoice in someone's merits, you are rejoicing because there is now a greater amount of merit in the world. The merits in which you rejoice are for everybody's benefit, and that makes you happy. You are not appreciating that person in an indulgent way, you are just rejoicing that there is now a greater amount of good in the world, that there are more positive forces at work in the world than before.

Milarepa is clearly not very bothered about all these teachings coming from India, and one might ask how much we in the West should be bothered about these Tantric teachings. To begin with, that's assuming that these teachings have actually come down in the Tibetan tradition to the present day, which is not necessarily the case. We can only find out from experience. More and more teachings are being translated and becoming available to us, and we just have to find out what we find helpful and beneficial, whatever the source. There's quite a lot that we're not going to find useful, if only because in the course of centuries it has become so complicated. I was reading the other day a book by Alex Wayman on the forty verses dealing with the yoga of the *Guhyasamāja Tantra*, but it's so complex that I don't think it would mean anything at all to most people, or offer anything of any practical utility. The text, which summarizes a whole series of Tantric works, has been so overlaid by commentary and sub-commentary, and such technical interpretations have been given, some of them very ingenious, that it would be very difficult for most people to see where all that material connects at any point with their own experience and their own spiritual life.

All we have to do is to take on board those things that we *do* connect with in that way. There are more than enough texts for us to be getting on with. It isn't as though we've finished with the *Udāna* and the *Dhammapada* and the *Heart Sūtra* and now we're ready to go on to something else. Broadly speaking, in principle we can accept the whole Buddhist tradition, but not every part of it may be equally useful to us. Buddhism doesn't work like that. In the case of the Bible or the Koran, the whole of the text is a revelation and you have to accept all of it, but in the case of the Buddhist scriptures, you don't have to master all the scriptures in order to get the Buddha's complete message. The Buddha's message is actually very simple, but it has been expanded and elaborated in various ways, and explained from different points of view, for the sake of different kinds of people. All these versions, all these explanations, are given in what we call the Buddhist scriptures, but it may be that just two or three pages will be enough to lead you to Enlightenment. If you just confine yourself to those few pages, it's not as though there's a lot of the Dharma that you've missed. The essence of the matter, so far as you are concerned, can be contained in a page, or even in a single verse.

There's a lot of emphasis in the Tantric tradition on getting initiation, but one must ask what initiation means. One need not think of it in an external, ceremonial way. Initiation really means entering into a particular kind of relationship with a guru – a communication which is spiritually intense and within the context of which a very great deal can happen. It doesn't mean going along to a particular place and going through elaborate ceremonies and being 'given' something. That is what it has come to mean, but the essence of the matter is quite different. The Vajrayāna tradition stresses the importance of the guru because the guru is alive. You need a living Buddha, so to speak, not a dead one. The guru is not only the living Buddha but the living Dharma, the living scripture. You can read a scripture and be very inspired by it, but can that text answer your questions? Can it enter into discussion with you? No. In the same way, you can read the life of the Buddha and be very inspired, but can you stop and ask the Buddha a question? No. What he says is very general; it's not meant just for you, it's meant for everybody, at least in principle. But if you enter into direct spiritual connection with a living human being who is spiritually more experienced than you and who knows you and can reply to your questions, then you're in contact with something much more immediate, something much more oriented to your personal needs. It's the same with regard to the spiritual community. Joining a spiritual community is not a matter of undergoing some particular ceremony, but of entering into communication with people with whom you share certain ideas and communicating with them constantly, even living with them to keep the communication going.

What the Vajrayāna does is to bring the Buddha, the Dharma, and the Sangha near to you. When it says that you must see the guru as the Buddha, what it means is that the person with whom you are in direct contact and who speaks directly to your individual need is the Buddha so far as you are concerned. Likewise, the practice that you actually do, your own meditation, your own visualization practice, is the Dharma so far as you are concerned. It's not all the teachings contained in the books; so far as you are concerned, the Dharma is what you actually practise. In the same way, for you the sangha is made up of those fellow disciples with whom you are in physical contact and in whose company you practise. Śāriputra and Maudgalyāyana, Nāgārjuna and Asaṅga were great people, but you are not in actual contact with them. The sangha for you is the people with whom you practise, and especially those who are closest to you in that sense.

It is in this way that the Vajrayāna speaks of Buddha, Dharma, and Sangha in terms of guru, *deva*, and *ḍākinī*. One must beware of mystifying it. It started off in a very simple way, as a reaction against the complexity and abstruseness of monastic Buddhism, after a thousand or more years of development in India. The *siddhas*, the Indian Tantric yogis, didn't want to be monks. They didn't want to live in monasteries. It had all got too organized, too complex, too elaborate. But subsequently the Vajrayāna itself became the subject of intellectual elaboration. You had Tantric Buddhist scholars, which is very much a contradiction in terms, but it is also a contradiction in terms to have a Mahāyāna bodhisattva scholar or a Theravāda *bhikkhu* scholar. In every stage of development, whether Theravāda or Mahāyāna, Vajrayāna or Zen or whatever, you have an original creative stage in which the living ideas and images are produced and people really practise and experience the results of practice. Then you have a stage of mature development, when the whole thing is given a comprehensive intellectual framework, which is very useful. But then a stage develops where the intellectual framework becomes the subject of study for its own sake; that's the stage of scholasticism. And then you have a stage where only the outer forms are kept up. In all the *yānas* there's this process of development. The Mahāyāna started off as a creative re-expression of the spirit of Buddhism, almost in opposition to the dull, dry scholasticism of what it came to call the Hīnayāna, the 'little way'. In the end the Mahāyāna itself (the 'great way') became quite scholastic, and then the Vajrayāna arose as a protest against that. But the Vajrayāna too eventually became scholastic. Zen became scholastic, with its dictionaries of koans and their solutions. All the great forms of Buddhism have gone through this fourfold process of development and decline. It could happen to any form or tradition, including our own, because the gravitational pull is always at work. It happens when individuals no longer have individual attainments and achievements. The Dharma disappears when people no longer practise it.

This is virtually what Milarepa said in the song he sang before he ran ahead of Rechungpa. 'If a Doctrine-holder cannot behave, he will destroy the Dharma'. People ask, 'Will the Dharma eventually disappear?' as though the Dharma was something separate from the people who practise it. The Dharma will not disappear so long as people practise it. If they cease to practise it, you may have books and pictures, but you won't have the Dharma – not the Dharma as a living experience, and that's all the Dharma really is.

Likewise, you mustn't assume that just because you live in something called a 'spiritual community', it is always a spiritual community. There's no such thing as a spiritual community. You've got a number of individuals living together in the same building, and when they are relating to one another as individuals, you have a spiritual community. Some days, some weeks, it might be that people are not behaving as individuals. Communication might completely collapse, and then there is no spiritual community on the premises. But then maybe the next week, maybe for an hour or two, people are really communicating as individuals, and for that hour or two a spiritual community will be present. There isn't a thing called a spiritual community regardless of the behaviour and attitude and communication of the people who make up that spiritual community. This may seem like a very simple point but it's one that people tend to overlook.

It's so easy to get misled by labels. You can stop yourself for a while, but then after a while you forget and go back to relating to labels again. It may be inevitable that Buddhist movements will decay and others will take their place, but it's really the same movement all the time, under different labels: Theravāda, Mahāyāna, Vajrayāna, Zen. It does seem, as far as one can make out, that at all times there have been some Buddhists who really were Buddhists in all these traditions, and no doubt that is still the case. But when it is the case, it is only because people are actually practising what they profess to believe in. They are truly holders or bearers of the Dharma. They realize that you can only hold it or bear it by practising it, by identifying yourself with it.

In Kalimpong, some of the Nyingma lamas made a great thing of handing on very esoteric teachings. The Gelugpas are much stricter in the way they do everything. In the Vajrayāna, it's axiomatic that you cannot give anybody any initiation that you have not received yourself, so some of my Gelugpa friends used to say, gently making fun of the Nyingmapas, 'You know, there's a very great Nyingmapa in Kalimpong at the moment. He's got some really powerful initiations. They're so powerful that you can give them to other people even without having received them yourself!' But the essence of the matter seems to be that you can't really communicate anything that you don't personally experience. You've got to be very careful that you don't think of the Dharma or spiritual life as something external to you which you can possess or achieve or attain without yourself being identified with it. I have met people who really believed you could teach meditation without ever having meditated yourself, which seems extraordinary. I remember one occasion in London when a Theravāda *bhikkhu* presided at a meeting and said, 'We're going to start with a period of meditation. We're going to have two minutes' *mettā*!' – and I swear that after fifteen seconds he was tapping on the table to indicate that the two minute *mettā* was over. I talked with him afterwards about this, and he said, 'What is all this fuss about meditation? In Sri Lanka, we Theravāda *bhikkhus* are meditating all the time!' Apparently he genuinely believed that if you're reasonably cheerful and positive, you're meditating.

Quite a lot of people in England who say they are Buddhists don't meditate. This is encouraged, for instance, by Mrs Rhys Davids' translation of *jhāna*, the Pāli version of *dhyāna*, as 'musing'. In her translations we read that the monks used to sit at the foot of a tree musing.[181] What a feeble impression this gives of meditation! Anybody can sit at the foot of a tree and muse, and this is experiencing *dhyāna*, apparently. People like the idea that your practice spills over into your everyday life, but often it's more that your everyday life spills over into your meditation, which is not so desirable. Certainly your meditation should spill over into your everyday life in the sense that the higher state of consciousness you enjoy at the time of meditation should be prolonged into your ordinary life, but there is a great deal in modern life which is incompatible with the maintenance of that kind of dhyānic consciousness.

4

FATHER AND SON ARE IN HARMONY

The Jetsun heard Rechungpa singing this song while he was
running after him. When the song was finished, the Jetsun stopped.
He then sat down on the ground and replied to Rechungpa,
singing:

It is fine that father and son are in harmony –
Maintaining harmony with people is a great merit;
But the best merit is to keep harmony with one's father.
If one is discordant with all the people he knows
He must be a person ominous and obnoxious.
Yet even more ominous is discord between father and son.

Good it is to maintain harmony with one's father by right deeds,
Good it is to repay one's mother's kindness and bounties,
Good it is to act in concord with all.

One's wish can be fulfilled
If he is on good terms with his brothers;
To please one's Guru
Is to gain his blessings;
To be humble is to succeed.
A good Buddhist is one who conquers all bad dispositions.

Kindness is toleration of slanders;
To be modest is to gain fame and popularity;
To maintain pure discipline
Is to do away with pretense and concealment;
To live with a sage is to gain improvement;
To be indifferent is to stop all gossip;
To be good and compassionate is to advance one's Bodhi-Mind.
These are the things a wise man should do,
But a fool can never distinguish friend from foe.

Where the (actual practice of the) Path is concerned,
The Formless Ḍākinī Dharmas do not mean too much.
My relationship with you
Is much deeper and more important
Than the Tantric staff of Dipupa.
Of the accomplished Mother Magi
There is no better disciple than I.
If Ḍākinīs keep their secret teachings from me,
To whom will they impart them?

In the golden Mandala
I have enjoyed many sacramental festivals.
With the Patron Buddha, Dorje Paumo,
I have had much longer acquaintance than you.
There is not a land of Ḍākinīs and Bha Wos
That is unfamiliar to me.
Much more than yourself,
I am concerned about the things you are doing.
Oh, Rechungpa, do not be proud and go astray!
Let us go into the mountains and meditate in solitude!

> It is fine that father and son are in harmony –
> Maintaining harmony with people is a great merit;
> But the best merit is to keep harmony with one's father.

This verse suggests that maintaining harmony with people is not an easy matter. Otherwise, why speak of it as being a 'great merit'? People are of so many different dispositions, so many different outlooks. They may disagree with you. They may be engaging in unskilful actions. You don't want to compromise your own principles, but at the same time you don't want to quarrel with them. So to maintain harmony with people requires great patience, great tact, great understanding. But exactly what is meant by 'harmony' here? If by 'people' is meant people in general, harmony cannot consist in agreement. You may have to live or work with people with whom you disagree, with whom you have no real sympathy and very little in common. But nonetheless, it's good if you can maintain harmony with them. It is relatively easy to maintain harmony with people with whom you agree. It's much more difficult to maintain harmony with people with whom you don't have very much in common, or whom you even dislike. Just getting along in the world, adhering to your own point of view, your own principles, while at the same time not treading on people's toes, managing to keep up friendly relations, is not easy, and if you're able to do this, it's a great merit. It isn't easy because there are two extremes, both of which are to be avoided. At one extreme, because your principles differ from other people's, you clash with them, and at the other extreme, for the sake of so-called 'harmony', you sacrifice your principles and go along with their way of doing things. To maintain your principles and at the same time remain on friendly terms with people is really difficult.

Of course, by 'father' Milarepa means himself in relation to Rechungpa, but in more general terms we could say he means the guru, or in still more general terms, anyone who is spiritually more advanced than oneself. I have spoken sometimes in terms of 'horizontal integration' and 'vertical integration'. In the same way one could speak of maintaining 'horizontal harmony' and 'vertical harmony', horizontal harmony meaning harmony with those people who are roughly speaking on the same level as you, and vertical harmony meaning harmony with those who are on a somewhat higher level than you are. The 'best merit' is to be in harmony with one's father, that is, with someone who is more spiritually developed than you are, because if to some extent you are like him, it can only mean true harmony. If you are in harmony with all the people you meet, that is suggestive more of tact and diplomacy. You are walking a tightrope. It's so easy to upset other people, for the harmony between you and them to be disrupted. You have to be so careful. But the harmony you establish with someone who is spiritually more experienced than you is much less easily broken because it won't be broken by the other person. You've only got to think of keeping in harmony with him. You don't need to bother about his keeping in harmony with you. Because he is spiritually more developed than you, if you can attune yourself to him, that in itself will result in your own spiritual growth. Being in harmony with him isn't just passive; it doesn't mean doing whatever he tells you. It means genuinely attuning your being to his, and thus making your being a little more like his. Keeping harmony with one's 'father' is the best merit because it ensures spiritual progress.

> If one is discordant with all the people he knows
> He must be a person ominous and obnoxious.

You don't often meet somebody who is out of harmony with every single person he knows, who doesn't get on well with anybody, but you occasionally do, and of course he or she usually blames other people. Milarepa refers to such a person as 'ominous' because not only is his own future in grave danger, but he is a bad omen for anybody with whom he comes into contact, because sooner or later there will be discord. Some people get that sort of reputation. People say, 'Don't have anything to do with him, he's sure to be trouble sooner or later.'

> Yet even more ominous is discord between father and son.

That's a very strong statement. It suggests that it's more important to maintain harmony with one's father, one's 'spiritual father', than with any other person. This reminds me of something. According to the first precept, the deliberate taking of life, especially human life, is a very serious matter, and according to the Buddhist tradition there's a gradation of seriousness. The most serious offence is to wound a Buddha; the next most serious is to kill your mother or your father; and then the next most serious is to kill an *arhant*.[182] It is a more serious offence, according to Buddhism, to kill your mother or father than to kill someone who is not related to you in that way because there are natural emotional ties, so to kill your father or mother indicates a much more serious disruption of natural human solidarity; there's much more in the way of human sympathy to overcome. And it's a serious matter to kill an *arhant* because that is tantamount to attacking the spiritual ideal itself. To kill the person who embodies the spiritual ideal is to attack that ideal in the most extreme way possible. And it's the same with the Buddha. According to the scriptures you can't kill a Buddha – that is a cosmic impossibility – but you can wound him, as Devadatta wounded Śākyamuni.[183] You can cause blood to flow. That must suggest an almost pathological, almost demoniacal state of antagonism to spiritual values which can have most serious consequences for your development as an individual.

It's much the same here. It's perhaps not such a serious matter if there's disharmony between you and other ordinary people, but if there is discord between you and someone whom normally you look up to as more spiritually experienced than yourself, that is a very serious matter indeed, because you are disrupting something that is of vital importance to you, closing yourself off from that which you most need. Here Milarepa is speaking very seriously to Rechungpa, because the fact is that on account of Rechungpa's pride and conceit there is some discord between him and Milarepa – not from Milarepa's side, obviously, but from Rechungpa's side. In the Pāli scriptures, the Buddha, speaking about ideal conditions in any given country, mentions that the *arhants* – that is to say, those who are Enlightened – come and go freely. They're not subject to any hindrance or restriction, and people have respect for them. The Buddha mentions this as indicating a very desirable state of affairs: that people in a country look up to those who are spiritually more developed, that there is harmony between them. If that state of harmony and respect is disrupted, it is quite unfortunate, quite disastrous in fact, for the people of that country.[184]

It's as if 'father' here represents the spiritual tradition itself. When there is discord between you and your 'father', you cut yourself off from the living spiritual tradition. This need not mean open hostility: it can be just carelessness and indifference, as perhaps was the case with Rechungpa. In this verse Milarepa is almost saying that if you get on well with your spiritual father it will counter-balance the fact that you don't get on well with anybody else, because that relationship is more important than any other.

Notice the emphasis, not only from the spiritual but from the cultural point of view, that according to Milarepa, and Buddhism generally, the most important relationship is the vertical relationship. In modern times in the West, by contrast, what do we consider the most important relationship? Is it your relationship with your local vicar? Most people don't even know who he is – and most people would say that the most important and meaningful relationship was between husband and wife. Milarepa is speaking within a purely Vajrayānic context, and as we have seen, for the Vajrayāna, the guru is all-important – more important even than the Buddha. But although that emphasis is strongest in the Vajrayāna, in Buddhism generally it is considered that your most important relationship is with whoever you regard as your source of spiritual inspiration, and that all other relationships, whether with husband or wife, with children, with blood relations or with ordinary friends, are secondary. Consider the difference that makes to one's whole outlook. If the most important relationship in your life is with your guru (to use the Tantric term), that indicates that the most important thing is your life is the spiritual ideal, spiritual growth. And if the most important relationship in your life is with your wife or husband, one could surmise that for you pleasure is the most important thing in life, and everything else is built up around that.

To take another pattern, the medieval one, where your most important relationship was with your feudal superior, your liege lord, that tells us that in those times the most important thing in life was protection. In a very dangerous world you wanted someone to protect you, so you swore to serve him in return for his protection. Of course serving him could have involved becoming a soldier, because he couldn't protect his dependents without an army, and he would need supplies for the army, so he would tax you as well.

Another important pattern of relationships that colours one's whole attitude towards life is friendship. Friendship in general is not a completely horizontal relationship, but nor is it completely vertical; it can tend either towards the horizontal or towards the vertical. It is your relationship with your friends in the broadest sense that gives you a sense of being part of the positive group – and the positive group has affinities with the not-so-positive group on the one hand and with the spiritual community on the other.

The parent–child relationship is obviously also very important. There are some cultures in which the relationship between biological father and son is considered to be the most important relationship in life. In that case, as the son you would tend to be submissive to authority, conservative and traditionalist, because the strength of your relationship with your father would give you a tendency to do things in his way, in other words to continue doing things in the old way. This was very characteristic of ancient Chinese Confucianist culture, for example.

If it seems surprising that Milarepa is talking about spiritual relationships in terms of father and son, we could consider that perhaps for Tibetans, as for many ancient peoples, the relationship between father and son in the ordinary sense is a very positive one, with none of the authoritarian overtones that it may have for us. The male and female Buddha figures represented in sexual union in Tantric iconography are called *yab-yum*, meaning 'father-mother', which suggests that the attitude of the ancient Tibetans towards father and mother was very positive. Similarly, in the Tibetan tradition it is suggested that you should regard all living beings as having been your mother or father in some previous existence. That might be rather difficult for us to contemplate – some people might be horrified to consider that their best friend had once been their mother – so should we just discard that sort of symbolism? It's a question of what you find positive. If your experience with friends is very happy, you can think, 'Everybody I meet might have been my best friend in a previous life, so why should I not have positive feelings towards them in this life?'

This mode of approach of course suggests a very strong belief in the reality of rebirth. If you have that belief, you could say, 'In the course of numberless previous existences, I must have stood in every conceivable relationship to all the people that I meet now. They must have been my best friend in some life or other. So why should I not try to continue that kind of relationship in this life? We've been best friends in the past; why can't we be best friends in this life too?' You could look at it in that way, rather than reflecting that they have all been your mother or father, if that is not very positive or inspiring for you.

Another very important relationship, one which is perhaps nowadays the most important of all, even rivalling that between husband and wife, is that between master and servant, or employer and employee, as we would say today. If that is the most important relationship in your life, what does that tell you about your attitude towards life? All these relationships which are horizontal from the spiritual point of view have one thing in common: they're all based on power. In a way they all involve protection and indulgence. But since the Industrial Revolution, since the growth of the capitalist type of economy, the relationship between employer and employee has become much more important than it was before. It has even been invested with, not to say glorified by, a particular kind of ideology. I was reading an article in the *Economist* a few days ago about the way in which young executives are trained, especially in the United States. They're sent on special courses and groomed to be 'young executives'. One of the points made on these courses is that family life is quite inconsistent with the life of a young executive. He is not encouraged to get married or enter into relationships in a serious way, because that will take up too much time and energy, limit his mobility and impede his career. One gets the impression that a sort of capitalist asceticism is expected of him. You've got to give yourself up completely to that life, dedicate yourself completely to getting on in your firm or even hopping from one firm to another, rising higher and higher all the time. Mammon is your God, in a way, and you are prepared to sacrifice yourself on his altar.

This whole question of the most important relationship in one's life is itself very important. People have sometimes asked me, 'Does your Buddhist movement encourage relationships?' but it's an absurd question because relationships are inevitable. To be a human being is to relate, to have relationships. The only question is, relationships with whom, and of what kind? One of the distinguishing characteristics of Buddhism is that it places such emphasis on the vertical relationship, but one mustn't look at that in a one-sided way; it also puts emphasis on horizontal relationships which are themselves vertically related. The horizontal relationship you have with other people whose vertical relationship is the same as yours is of a quite different kind from other horizontal relationships you may have. It has something of the quality of a vertical relationship; it is not a horizontal relationship pure and simple. That relationship – which is of course the relationship you have with fellow members of the sangha – is just as important as your relationship with the guru or teacher, because you go for Refuge not only to the Buddha, but also to the Sangha. And among those with whom you have that kind of horizontal relationship, some are more horizontal than others, one might say. There may be some who are not 'gurus', but are rather like elder brothers or sisters, or older friends.

Is it impossible to have a spiritual friendship with someone who hasn't got the same teacher as you? No. You can perhaps have the most intense kind of spiritual friendship only with someone who has the same vertical relationship, i.e. the same teacher, but you can certainly have a spiritual friendship with someone who has some kind of vertical commitment, even though not with the same teacher as you. As to whether the same could apply to artists and poets who don't have the same conception of the ideal as you, but who do have a higher ideal, that depends on whether it is a genuine ideal. If there is some kind of ideal in his or her outlook, implicit in his or her life and work, you would be able to strike up a spiritual friendship, at least to some extent, because a broad common base would be there.

The key points are that Buddhism emphasizes the spiritual community in a way that modern Western life does not, and that the nature of your most important relationship affects your whole attitude towards life. To take the case of the rising young executives being discouraged from getting married, there cannot be two full-time commitments. If you are married and then you're offered a promotion that would take you to a foreign country, away from your wife and family, you have to face up to the question: 'Which is more important? My career, or my relationship with my wife and family?' Which is going to be sacrificed to which?

In Hinduism they sometimes distinguish between *vidyā-guru* and *dīkṣā-guru*. The *vidyā-guru*, literally 'the guru who imparts knowledge', is the teacher in the ordinary educational sense, and the *dīkṣā-guru* is the guru who imparts initiation or spiritual inspiration. The same person could fulfil both functions, but the two roles are distinct. Indians and Tibetans tend to have respect for teachers of all kinds, whether secular or spiritual. They retain respect all through their lives for the teacher from whom they learned their ABC. Even if you far outstrip the old teacher who taught you to read, you still retain your respect for him or her, because he or she laid the foundation.

The question 'What is the most important relationship in my life?' is very important. If you ask yourself, 'If I had to sacrifice one relationship to another, which would I sacrifice?' your response will tell you a lot about yourself and your outlook on life. If you think that your relationship with your spouse or partner is the most important relationship in your life, and if it came to the crunch, you'd sacrifice everything else to that, you can't be a Buddhist, not in the full sense. That doesn't mean that a Buddhist can't be married or have a partner, but if you are a Buddhist who has gone for Refuge, that particular relationship cannot be the primary relationship in your life. It doesn't mean you can't give it any place at all – it will have its place in the mandala of your life – but it won't be right at the centre. That place is reserved for the Buddha. From the Buddhist point of view, it's a question of a sense of proportion and priority.

> Good it is to maintain harmony with one's father by
>   right deeds,
> Good it is to repay one's mother's kindness and bounties,
> Good it is to act in concord with all.

Here Milarepa seems to be talking more about the positive group than about the spiritual community. 'Father' seems to be intended in a quite literal sense, because mother is also mentioned. But why especially should one maintain harmony with one's father by 'right deeds'? Perhaps we can't take the translation too literally; perhaps it means behaving properly, particularly by treating your father well. And 'Good it is to repay one's mother's kindness and bounties'. Perhaps, having spoken so highly about the vertical relationship, the relationship with the spiritual teacher, Milarepa wants to make it clear that he is not denigrating one's relationship with one's ordinary father, or with one's mother, and he ends up by saying, 'Good it is to act in concord with all.'

It is well known that nowadays people are often out of harmony with their parents, on account perhaps of cultural and historical developments. Things are changing very rapidly. Children learn things that their parents have never heard of, and this tends to create a difference. In the old days, if you were having trouble with your school homework, you asked your father or your mother to help, and usually he or she could. But nowadays at school children learn subjects that their parents know nothing about. As a young person, if you're not careful, you start thinking that your father's an old fogey who doesn't know anything about anything. You don't feel there's anything that you can talk to him about, you are quite remote from him, and this leads to a certain degree of alienation. Likewise in the field of ethics, moral ideas have changed very much in recent years, and your values may be very different from those of your parents. They may feel that you are leading a wicked life, while you may feel that you're leading a quite ordinary life for a young person. There have been such rapid changes over the last few years that the generations are further apart than they were before, and this can lead to disharmony. It requires a special effort to maintain harmony with one's father and mother and with other members of the family; formerly very small changes occurred from generation to generation, but now the differences are tremendous. That certainly imposes stresses which aren't always easy to cope with, and it raises the whole question whether these changes add up to real progress.

That question is not easy to answer, but the fact is that these days, at least in western Europe and North America, children have to make a special effort to remain on positive terms with their parents. It is important psychologically that one should do this. The relationship with your parents goes very deep, and there is an inevitable tie; the only question is whether it's going to be positive or negative. Unfortunately, very often it's negative, at least to some extent, but you can't therefore decide just to break off the relationship. Even if you never go to see your parents, you're still connected with them, so the only choice you have is between a negative attitude towards them and a positive one. You can discontinue your dependence on them by growing up and adopting a more mature attitude towards them, but you can't behave or live as though you had never had any parents. You may never see them, you may never think about them, but you can still have a positive attitude towards them in the sense that you make sure you are are free from resentment towards them and you wish them well. You don't have to live with them or go and see them every weekend or write them long letters. You may not have any physical contact with them at all. But nonetheless your relationship with them can be positive, and it should be, because if there's a residue of negativity towards your parents, that will go quite deep into your nature and have a general effect on your life. If you find that you actually hate your parents, clearly that is something that you have to overcome. It may be that from an ordinary human point of view they deserve your hatred – they may have brought you up very badly, or have made a terrible mess of your early life – but that is no reason for continuing to have a negative attitude towards them. If you do, that will only hold you back, so you have to forgive your parents, if necessary.

> One's wish can be fulfilled
> If he is on good terms with his brothers.

The context seems to have been changed slightly. We're back with a spiritual community, not a family; these are brothers in the spiritual sense, fellow disciples of the same teacher. But what does this mean? One's wish in this context is spiritual growth, but how can being on good terms with your spiritual brothers affect your growth and development? Well, if you're on good terms with them, you're more likely to be in communication, there is more *kalyāṇa mitratā*, and *kalyāṇa mitratā* is highly conducive to growth and development.

> To please one's Guru is to gain his blessings.

Presumably you please your guru by showing him that you're progressing. If you do your bit, he will do his. In a sense, he's doing his bit all the time. It's as if the tap is constantly flowing, but you've got to put your cup underneath it. If you please him, you automatically get his blessings.

> To be humble is to succeed.

The English translation given is 'humble'; I don't know what the Tibetan is. But how do you succeed by being humble? If you're humble, there's less ego, more patience, and that in itself shows that you've made spiritual progress, so to that extent you succeed. But the word 'humble' has all sorts of undesirable, even unBuddhistic connotations for us: 'umble Uriah Heep and so on. Of course it's pseudo-humility in his case; he makes out that he's very lowly and unimportant and that he doesn't have any power to put people off their guard so that he can take advantage of them all the more. That is not real humility.[185] But 'humble' is not a very appropriate word in any case. As we have seen, the Buddha said that one shouldn't think of oneself as being either superior, inferior or even equal to others. That's real humility – when you don't think in those terms at all. If you're humble in that way, you really do succeed. Well, you have succeeded already, because you're not egoistic, not competitive.

> A good Buddhist is one who conquers all bad dispositions.

'Bad dispositions' is not a very precise term – perhaps it represents the Sanskrit *kleśas*, defilements – but anyway, the good Buddhist is one who conquers all negative or unskilful mental states. That's pretty obvious, but perhaps we need to be reminded of it. What you are concerned with as a Buddhist is the transformation of your state of mind, the transformation of your consciousness, and that means the elimination of all unskilful mental states, as well as the production of skilful mental states in an uninterrupted flow. That's the basic thing. It's all right to circumambulate and make prostrations and chant, but the basic thing you're concerned with is the transformation of your mind from a stream of skilful and unskilful, or even entirely unskilful, mental states, into a stream of wholly skilful mental states. As the Buddha says in the *Dhammapada, Sabbapāpassa akaraṇaṃ, kusalassa upasampadā*, 'The non-doing of all evil, the causing to arise of all good, the purification of the mind, this is the teaching of the Buddhas.'[186] It's as simple as that. That's all you need to know. And it's all here in Milarepa's statement.

The meaning of this goes far beyond the cultivation of *śamatha* mental states. All unskilful mental states are rooted ultimately in craving and ignorance. Without insight, you couldn't be positive indefinitely and under all circumstances. Sooner or later you would come up against a situation that would put an end to your positivity. Suppose someone appeared and threatened to shoot you – what would happen to your skilful mental state then? If you had just come out of a *dhyāna* state, it's possible that at first you wouldn't react in any way, but after a few minutes, if the person was still holding the gun, you would start feeling fear – in other words, an unskilful mental state would arise. But if your stream of consciousness was imbued with insight, you would see the situation for what it was without any unskilful mental state arising in consequence. You can ensure the uninterrupted production of skilful mental states only by developing insight. You have that flow of skilful mental states in *śamatha* meditation, but it's very precarious, it can be disturbed. *Śamatha* is like a picture drawn with coloured chalks or oil pastels. It's very delicate, and can easily be brushed off or smudged, so you need to fix it by spraying it with some kind of fixative. Insight fixes the picture, one might say. That's not a very good analogy because in fact nothing is fixed, it's all flowing, but it's useful up to a point.

And how does one develop insight? Is the only way through *vipaśyanā* meditation? Well, all meditation practices have their *śamatha* and *vipaśyanā* aspects. Visualizations are not necessarily *vipaśyanā* practices, but they have an element of *vipaśyanā*. First of all there is the visualization of the Buddha or bodhisattva, and that can be a purely *śamatha* experience. Reflecting on the significance of what that figure represents is what makes it possible to develop insight. You can develop insight even through visualizing an abstract geometrical figure. For instance, you can visualize a red disc and concentrate upon it, and that is a *śamatha*-type meditation. But then you can start reflecting that the red disc you can see has arisen on dependence on certain conditions – for instance, on the fact that you have concentrated your mind. Then you can go on to reflect that all mental states whatsoever arise in dependence upon the appropriate conditions. There is nothing that arises independent of conditions. In that way, using that red disc as a basis, you start developing insight into the conditionality of all mundane existence. And you visualize a Buddha or bodhisattva in the same way. To begin with, it's just a pretty picture, something beautiful and attractive, so it's a *śamatha* experience. But if you start reflecting that this is your spiritual ideal, that this is what you must wholly devote your life to, that compared to this nothing else is of any value, all such reflections are of a *vipaśyanā* nature.[187] There are many other *vipaśyanā* practices. For instance, there's the recollection of the *nidāna* chain – 'in dependence upon ignorance arises craving' and so on. And there's the six element practice, in which you think of all the solid matter in your body as being given back to the earth element in the universe, all that is fluid in your body being given back to the water element and so on; this too can become the basis of understanding, even of insight, the truth being that there is nothing solid or fixed in human personality, whether materially or mentally.[188]

In this way we progress, via one method or another, from the *śamatha*-type, *dhyāna*-type experience to the *vipaśyanā*-type experience. All Buddhist systems of meditations which are in any way comprehensive contain a *śamatha* element and a *vipaśyanā* element. It's generally held, at least in the Theravāda, that the *mettā bhāvanā* is a purely *śamatha* practice, but this can be doubted. If you practise the *mettā bhāvanā* deeply enough it merges with *vipaśyanā* practice, because if you develop *mettā* for all living beings equally, you're cultivating an equal attitude towards all and that means seeing them as all essentially non-different.[189] You thus have an appreciation of *śūnyatā*, and that involves the element of *vipaśyanā*. So the *mettā bhāvanā* cannot really be restricted to the *śamatha* level in the way that it very often is in the Theravāda. Some Theravādin monks say patronizingly of the *mettā bhāvanā*, 'Oh yes, that's a very good little practice – that's OK for the lay people', as though it was just a trifling practice that anybody is capable of at the drop of a hat, but that is very far from being the case.

Is *vipaśyanā* only possible through formal meditation practice? *Vipaśyanā* is extremely penetrating and powerful; in order for it to be really *vipaśyanā* and not just an intellectual understanding you need behind it the combined energies of your whole being, and you usually only achieve that sort of union of energies through the systematic practice of *śamatha* meditation, which will unify and mobilize your energies to such an extent that they can give enough impetus to your intellectual understanding to transform it into insight. You may not necessarily be sitting and meditating formally when insight arises; it may come at some other time when your energies are all in harmony, all unified, all integrated, all flowing in the same direction. But the principle is that no insight can arise without the virtually total unification of your energies behind the intellectual activity which results in insight, and for most people that sort of integration comes only by the systematic practice of what we call meditation.

> *Kindness is toleration of slanders.*

It could be that 'kindness' here refers to the *pāramitā* of *kṣānti*, patience – otherwise, it is difficult to see how kindness in the strict sense is simply toleration of slanders.

> *To be modest is to gain fame and popularity.*

Perhaps Milarepa is being a little old-fashioned here. I don't think this works any more, not in the days of the modern media. In a very limited social environment, a small village, for example, where everybody knows everybody else, it would be possible to be known for your modesty, and it might be possible within a Buddhist movement, but it wouldn't be likely to happen among the public at large. Modesty – not overstepping the mark, not pushing yourself forward – seems somewhat more positive than humility.

To maintain pure discipline
Is to do away with pretense and concealment.

This is considered very important in the Buddha's teaching: that you should profess to be no other than what you are. It isn't an easy thing to achieve. If you're hypocritical, if you indulge in pretence and concealment, you become divided, because you're behaving in two incompatible ways, one when people are watching you and the other when you are not being observed. You're leading a double life, and that can't be psychologically healthy.

This is a bit different from just not knowing yourself very well. Hypocrisy involves an element of conscious and deliberate deception, which is why it is such a serious matter. It's like the Theravāda *bhikkhus* who deny that they eat after twelve o'clock, even though they know that they do it, and they're quite conscious that it is against the rule. In Buddhism great importance is attached to not concealing any thought, and of course if you practise the precepts wholeheartedly, if you 'maintain pure discipline', you do away with pretence and concealment, because you have nothing to hide, no need to lie or conceal anything, and no fear of being found out. You can be perfectly open, which is a great thing, a wonderful opportunity.

If you think it over, you will probably find that you are completely open, completely free from pretence and concealment, in very few situations and with very few people. You're always thinking about what people will think of you. You like to appear in the best possible light and you don't want people to think less of you, so almost insensibly, almost without intending to, you hide certain aspects of yourself, or play them down, or make them out to be less important to you than they are. You make out that they occupy just a corner of your mandala when perhaps they occupy a place very near the centre. You might say, 'Oh, yes, I have the odd drink occasionally' – but the truth might be that you go to the pub every night of the week. If in your relationship with anyone you have to resort to pretence and concealment it means that you're not being yourself with that person, and therefore no full and open relationship is possible between you because you're not allowing them to know you or to see you or to experience you as you are. That's what happens in most relationships, even those we consider to be our closest.

It doesn't have to be that way. You can be completely open with people even if you sometimes break the precepts; if you break a precept, you can be open about that. But what makes it possible to be open? It is only possible with somebody who has the same ideals as you. If you attach importance to being open, you can be open about even your non-observance of precepts with your spiritual friends because you know that they are not going to use that as an opportunity to attack you. They're not going to think worse of you, because they recognize that even though you've broken the precept and fallen by the wayside to that extent, nonetheless you continue to cherish the ideal, so your admission to them that you have broken a precept can be a positive thing and can help you. But if you feel that by breaking a precept you have put yourself beyond the pale, you may be quite reluctant to speak about it even to your spiritual friends, and that is very unfortunate, because it closes the avenues of communication and makes it still more difficult for you to pick yourself up and carry on again. It is a very positive and helpful thing to have at least one or two friends, if not three or four, to whom you feel you can say absolutely anything. Whatever you tell them, they're not going to reject you. They're going to accept what you say and try to understand it. But that sort of spiritual friendship is quite rare.

As Milarepa says here, there's no necessity for pretence and concealment if you maintain pure discipline. But perhaps we shouldn't take this word 'discipline' too literally. It means observing the precepts, adopting a lifestyle that enables you to give full expression to your ideals.

> *To live with a sage is to gain improvement.*

In fact you don't necessarily gain improvement even if you do live with a sage. In the *Dhammapada* the Buddha says, 'The spoon does not detect the taste of the soup.'[190] In the same way, a fool may live with a wise man but he won't learn anything from him. It's only someone who is himself to some extent wise who can learn from a wise man. You might not even know that you are living with a sage; you have to be a bit of a sage yourself to be able to recognize that it's a sage you're living with. So Milarepa's statement requires a little qualification. He is of course speaking to Rechungpa and referring presumably to Rechungpa's staying with him, which would certainly mean that Rechungpa would gain improvement.

To be indifferent is to stop all gossip.

If there's gossip about you, it's best not to say anything at all. If you try to reply or to rebut what is being said, it'll only blow the whole thing up still further. It's best just to say nothing. Then it will die down.

To be good and compassionate is to advance one's Bodhi-mind.

By the Bodhi-mind is meant the *bodhicitta*. I'm not sure what 'good' means here, but it's quite clear what 'compassionate' means. 'Good' perhaps means observing the precepts, in which case Milarepa is simply saying that if one observes the precepts and one develops compassion towards all living beings, that will advance one's *bodhicitta*, one's aspiration towards Supreme Enlightenment for the benefit of all. This is very straightforward Mahāyāna teaching.

> *These are the things a wise man should do,*
> *But a fool can ne'er distinguish friend from foe.*

Milarepa is no doubt saying this to Rechungpa because Rechungpa can't see that Milarepa is his best friend, but regards him almost as an enemy, a rival. And then Milarepa says:

> *Where the (actual practice of the) Path is concerned,*
> *The Formless Ḍākinī Dharmas do not mean too much.*

This in a way is an extraordinary statement. The Formless Ḍākinī Dharmas are these precious, esoteric Tantric teachings which Rechungpa has brought from India. Surely they are concerned with the practice of the path? What is Milarepa really saying? His point is that as far as Rechungpa is concerned, they are not the actual practice of the Dharma. They're just intellectual knowledge from books. They don't represent the next step that he needs to take. For him, therefore, those Dharmas are not Dharmas. They're not relevant to his needs, and perhaps they pertain to a stage of the path far in advance of the stage that he has reached.

It's very important to be able to discern what is relevant to oneself. There can be a sort of spiritual snobbery in some Buddhist circles. People think that because they are to some extent intellectually developed, they are qualified to practise whatever they are able to understand intellectually. Whether they even understand it intellectually is another question, but they think they do. People don't understand to what extent their intellect is divorced from their being. You can have an understanding of a teaching intellectually, but not be ready to practise it at all. This is what people often don't understand. They go for what their intellect recognizes as the most abstruse and advanced teaching and they think that that's what they ought to practise. Only the best is good enough for them. They don't have time for elementary things, the ABC of Buddhism: the five precepts, the *mettā bhāvanā* – that's all kids' stuff! They're spiritually mature people. They are capable of understanding Zen and the Mahāmudrā and Bhakti Yoga and all the rest of it, capable of giving lectures about it, writing books on it. But their being is utterly remote from it. They don't understand it, and yet they become authorities on it.

When I returned from India to England in 1964, some real shocks awaited me in this respect. When I went along to the Buddhist Society summer school, I sat in on one or two of the things that were happening, including a Zen class run by a woman whom I got to know better later. There was a silent meditation for five minutes while she adjusted her thoughts, and then she gave her talk on Zen: 'Well, you look out of the window and you see the flowers and then you hear the birds singing ... it's all one! And that's Zen.' I'm afraid I thought it was really pathetic, and some years later when I had a talk with her about it, she admitted as much herself. But she has read a lot of books about Zen since then, and she has even written and broadcast about Zen, and what she doesn't seem to realize is that she hasn't got any further than that. She certainly hasn't practised meditation, or gone any deeper. She has just acquired more and more information about Zen, so she can waffle on about it in a somewhat more sophisticated fashion. If we're not careful, that is what happens. We don't achieve a deeper understanding; we just become better informed, which is quite another matter.

> *My relationship with you is much deeper and more important*
> *Than the Tantric staff of Dipupa.*

Rechungpa has brought back from India the staff of some special wood which belonged once upon a time to the great Dipupa (more correctly called Tiphupa). He thinks he's done a great thing in bringing this back to Tibet and giving it to Milarepa, but Milarepa isn't at all impressed. He's trying to turn Rechungpa's attention from external things to internal things. It's nice that Rechungpa has brought him back this present, but what is really important is their relationship. It must be deep and genuine, not a superficial matter of presents. He is suggesting that Rechungpa is attaching more importance to this staff than to his relationship with Milarepa, which is the basis of everything.

> *Of the accomplished Mother Magi,*
> *There is no better disciple than I.*

Rechunpga may be full of his meeting with this Mother Magi, but there's no better practitioner of her teachings than Milarepa. 'I'm Mother Magi,' he's saying, as it were. 'Don't try to impress me by telling me that you've met a famous *yoginī*. Whatever she has to teach, I've realized it, I've experienced it.'

> *If Ḍākinīs keep their secret teachings from me,*
> *To whom will they impart them?*

'You're going on about these Ḍākinī Dharmas, but to you they are only books, whereas to me they are actual realizations. Why can't you see that?'

> *In the golden Mandala*
> *I have enjoyed many sacramental festivals.*
> *With the Patron Buddha, Dorje Paumo,*
> *I have had much longer acquaintance than you.*
> *There is not a land of Ḍākinīs and Bha Wos*
> *That is unfamiliar to me.*

'Dorje Paumo' is more usually spelled 'Dorje Pagmo' or 'Dorje Pakmo'; her Sanskrit name is Vajravārāhī. What Milarepa is really saying is that Rechungpa has gone in search of the very things that are near at hand and available to him in the person of Milarepa. It's like someone who is involved with the London Buddhist Centre but thinks they ought to go off to India and learn about meditation and meet some proper

Buddhists. It's extraordinary that people sometimes don't appreciate what they've got in their own hand, practically, immediately available to them. They want it in some far-off mysterious exotic form, so they go haring off to India, and the chances are that they don't find it and they come back. I was hearing about someone who visited a Theravādin monastery in England, and was quite impressed by the sheer fact of seeing people in yellow robes. It was apparently impossible to convince him that it's possible to practise the Dharma seriously without a special costume. If you didn't do it in a yellow robe, apparently it didn't count. That is unfortunate, and it is totally opposed to the Buddha's teaching. The Pāli scriptures, more than any other Buddhist texts if anything, insist on the real thing, not the outward trappings.[191]

Presumably people expect some sort of magic to transform them, without being prepared to work on themselves. They may try a bit of meditation for a while, but when nothing much happens, they think, 'This must be wrong. I'd better go off to India where the real magic is.' Also, there is a tendency to project spiritual life onto other people and in effect expect others to lead your spiritual life for you, while for your part you just worship and respect them. If people wear colourful robes and shave their heads and all that sort of thing, it's easier to believe that they are different from you, superior to you, not in the sense that they are showing you what you can do, but they are doing something that you can't do. Theravāda lay people tend to say, 'No, I can't meditate. That's for the *bhikkhus*. The *bhikkhus* are very holy!' If you project the demands of the spiritual life onto these other special people, that excuses you from the need to practise the spiritual life yourself. This pattern is found almost everywhere in the Buddhist world, unfortunately. People support the *bhikkhus* so that they can follow the spiritual path on their behalf. This is why if the *bhikkhus* deviate from perfect practice the lay people get very upset about it, because they feel that they're being cheated and their salvation is being compromised. Likewise, in the Middle Ages in Europe lay people became very upset about 'wicked' priests, fearing that if the priests were wicked that might interfere with the efficacy of the sacraments, and thus their salvation would be put at risk. In response, the Church promulgated the teaching that the sacraments were still fully efficacious even if they were administered by a priest who was guilty of all sorts of sins and crimes. That led to a very external conception of religion indeed, and it was against this that Martin Luther eventually protested.

It's an example of group thinking: the group being led by priests who specialize in religion on behalf of the whole community. This is very much the situation in most Theravāda countries. The *bhikkhus* live your Buddhism for you, and you support them in that, as you might support research scientists to do research. Obviously there is an element of something genuine; sometimes you may sincerely recognize that someone is capable of greater effort than you, and you may support them while they are making that effort. But that is quite different from expecting somebody else to practise the Dharma for you.

> *Much more than yourself,*
> *I am concerned about the things you are doing*

This is the most significant thing that Milarepa says in this song. He is saying, 'I am taking better care of you, Rechungpa, than you are taking care of yourself.' This is characteristic of the spiritual friend. He has your best interests at heart more than you yourself sometimes have, so he's a better friend to you than you are to yourself. Very often you are your own worst enemy. It's as though your spiritual friends are your conscience, your own 'better self'. Your friends represent you as you are in your better moments, so they give you an objective standard against which you can measure yourself. At moments when you're at a low ebb, you can be reminded of what you're like at your best. When you become miserable, or angry, or aggressive, or petty, or mean, or childish, your spiritual friends can say to you, 'You're not really like that. You're quite capable of being different from that. This is just a passing phase. It's not the real you.'

This reminds us of a very important point: people often don't love themselves. They aren't really good friends to themselves, they don't have *mettā* for themselves. When we do the *mettā bhāvanā*, we start off with ourselves, and this shouldn't be a formality, because goodwill towards ourselves is the basis of goodwill towards other people. But it isn't easy to be kind to yourself. Very often people are very unkind to themselves for one reason or another. They don't do what is best for themselves. It's easy enough to blame your parents for not doing their best by you, but what about you? You yourself don't do the best that you can for yourself, so how can you blame other people? Perhaps your parents didn't give you what you really needed, but do you give yourself what you really need? You may blame mother and father for not knowing the best way to bring you up, but do you know the best way to bring yourself up to a higher level of maturity now?

> *Rechungpa, do not be proud and go astray!*
> *Let us go into the mountains and meditate in solitude!*

Milarepa is always bringing Rechungpa back to the main point, which for him is definitely meditating in solitude. That is what he really needs. But is there any special reason for this advice in Rechungpa's case? Meditating in solitude is good for everybody, at least from time to time. Why is Milarepa so insistent that *Rechungpa* should do so? Presumably because Rechungpa gets distracted very easily by external things, and meditation works to counteract that tendency. But why does one get distracted? What is distraction? It's really lack of integration. Maybe one part of you wants to lead a spiritual life, but another part of you wants to do something else. Meditation in solitude counteracts that, pulling all the different bits of yourself together. Among the more well-known meditation practices, the Mindfulness of Breathing especially makes a whole out of all the different bits and pieces. You might be a jumble of elements and attitudes and ideals, but meditation creates a mandala out of all those disorganized elements, helps you to put all the bits of the jigsaw in the right places to give you a picture. In fact you get the mandala itself; you become the mandala. You can't have a mandala unless you have a centre, and meditation helps you to establish that. You find what you really want to do, what is really of most importance to you. You clarify that, and then you organize all the rest of your personality, the rest of your being or your other interests, around that. In that way you create the mandala.

If Rechungpa goes into retreat, if he starts meditating, he is going to have to ask himself, 'What really is most important to me? Is it collecting these religious curios – somebody's staff, somebody's hat? Is that really important? Or is it all these intellectual studies: learning, logic, travelling, meeting people, performing ceremonies for lay people? Is this what I really want to do? Is this what I want to build my life around? Or is it meditation? Is it Enlightenment? What is it?' If he follows this line of thought, he will come to the realization that what he really wants to do is to grow spiritually – in traditional Buddhist language, to gain Enlightenment. Everything has to fall into place around that. In that way the mandala is created. You put the thing that is of greatest importance in the centre of your mandala and you group everything around that. You don't have to deny your other interests. There is a place for them, whether relatively near the centre of the mandala or relatively closer to the edge. You may have an interest in music, or painting, or sport. Whereabouts in the mandala are you going to put those interests? What position do you assign to them? That is what you have to sort out, so that your life is a living mandala, instead of just a mishmash of interests and whims, as first one aspect of your being becomes uppermost and then another.

You could imagine this quite literally. You might start by thinking, 'Tārā represents Enlightenment for me, and the most important thing in my life is to develop Tārā-like qualities, so I will put her right in the middle. Then, what else is of importance to me? There's my friends; I'll put them in a circle here. Then there's my painting – I'll put my brushes and paints there. And there's my guitar – that's quite important, I'll put that there.' In this way you build up the mandala. Does travel have a place? Yes, even travel has its place, provided it's not aimless and purposeless. How about making money? Yes, right down at the bottom of the mandala you can see the bodhisattva Jambhala, squeezing a mongoose from whose mouth jewels are popping out. Even making money has its place, provided it's for the sake of the Dharma and under conditions of right livelihood. The image of the mandala is important because it's a rich and diverse and complex symbol, and also a concrete one. It's not bare and abstract. It makes it clear that there's a place for everything, at least for everything in its purified and refined form. It isn't a question of excluding things from one's life but more a question of giving them the place that represents their true importance.

It might be a good idea to draw two mandalas. In the first, the mandala as it actually exists, the so-called mandala, put in the centre what really and truly is the most important thing in your life. If you're honest, right in the middle might be your wife or husband, or your guitar – or even something else that you would rather not even think about or admit to. But you have to force yourself to think about it: 'I'm afraid that's in the centre of my mandala at the moment.' When you group all the other things around it, you might find that puja and meditation occupy just a little corner. Then you could draw the second mandala as it should be, your mandala as reorganized, putting the most important thing in the centre and the less important things toward the periphery, and see what sort of difference there is between the two. If you are really committed to the spiritual life, you will genuinely have at the centre Avalokiteśvara or Śākyamuni or whichever figure represents Enlightenment for you, and then you might have squash or yoga or D. H. Lawrence or sex or travel, or whatever it is, around the edges. Money would be there somewhere. Beethoven might even be there somewhere. The aim is to to include and arrange all your main interests in a harmonious way around the thing which is objectively of the greatest importance. But first of all, draw the mandala as it actually is. It might not even be round. Perhaps it has two centres; perhaps it's an ellipse or a sort of peanut shape, or even quite amorphous, like an amoeba with lots of different little centres. Sometimes it's good to think in visual terms instead of in abstract conceptual terms. You have to ask yourself just how important such and such a thing is in your life. You could start with concrete material things rather than attitudes – things like your guitar or your piano, your books, your bank account, your friends, your parents.

If there's something in the middle of your mandala which isn't so good, how do you go about putting the Buddha in the centre instead? You have to ask yourself what is objectively of greatest importance in human life, even if you don't feel it at the moment. What must you try to make the centre of your mandala? You might find that the Buddha is tucked away in a remote corner, almost pushed out by other things. You might find that only one foot of the Buddha is inside in the mandala and the rest is right outside. Maybe playing with model trains has a more important place in your mandala than the Buddha. Maybe your car is in the centre; I'm sure that would be true for some people.

Of course there will be things that you will have to exclude from your mandala altogether. It's true that everything finds a place in its more purified and refined form, but there are some things that, once they are purified or refined, just cease to exist: things like hatred. There's no place for hatred within the mandala. You could say that there is a place for anger, in the form of a fiery energy that encounters and deals with obstacles and hostile forces and factors. But there's no place in the mandala for thoroughly unskilful activities. So a sorting out process is required. In your heap of jigsaw puzzle pieces, there may be pieces that don't belong to that particular jigsaw at all, and have to be thrown away. But the point must be emphasized that in Buddhism, according to the Vajrayāna, anything that is of genuinely human value and significance finds a place within the mandala. The four elements are included within the mandala. Earth, water, fire, and air all have their place. The senses are included within the mandala. There's nothing wrong with the senses just as senses, as perceiving apparatuses. Food and drink find a place. Beauty of course finds a place. There is very little that can't find a place within the mandala: only attitudes that are complete perversions of human instincts and activities that are utterly negative and unskilful.

You have to make sure that you place at the centre of the mandala what really, essentially, objectively is the most important thing – not just in your life subjectively, but in human existence as such – and establish that very firmly. Otherwise the tendency will be for other things to gravitate towards the centre of the mandala and displace that object or figure or whatever it is. What you need to concentrate on is establishing at the centre of the mandala the figure that belongs there. Get that right and everything else will come right.

There are two great symbols for the spiritual life in Buddhism: the path and the palace or temple. The palace is of course the mandala, a three-dimensional mandala. If you think of the spiritual life in terms of the path, you are thinking of it in terms of progression in time, and if you think of it as the palace, you are thinking in terms of position in space. At the centre of a palace there is the throne room, in the centre of the throne room is a throne, and on the throne sits the king or queen. All the other rooms and all the other people are arranged around that central point. A still more rarefied form of the same symbol is the Pure Land, in which the Buddha is seated in the middle on his lotus throne, surrounded by *arhants* and bodhisattvas, or (in the Tantric version), by gurus, *ḍākinīs*, *devas* and so on.

These two symbols are both useful in different ways. If you are of a dull and sluggish temperament, it can help to think of the spiritual life in terms of following the stages of the path and being active and vigorous, but if you are overactive and restless and need calming down, it might be better to think of the spiritual life in terms of the more static symbol, think in terms of rearranging the contents of your mandala.

There is a lot to be said for keeping one's mandala fairly simple, but there's no theoretical objection to its containing a lot of elements.

If you can, it's best to keep it simple at first so that its main lines are preserved. The mandala mustn't be cluttered. The objects must be arranged beautifully and harmoniously, and there must be enough space between them; it shouldn't be crowded. There's a lot of space in the mandala. Things don't usually touch; they're separate. They're part of the mandala but they retain their own distinct individuality, even their own uniqueness.

The section closes with the comment:

Thereupon, the Jetsun and Rechungpa set out together on their journey. This is the first of Rechungpa's meetings with the Jetsun at Yaug Ru.

Milarepa has quite a time of it with Rechungpa. He's not a very easy or comfortable disciple to deal with. Having a disciple like that might be stimulating, but does someone like Milarepa needs that kind of stimulation? While Rechungpa was away, was he feeling dull and unstimulated, just meditating on his snow mountain? Of course not. It doesn't matter to Milarepa. Dull disciples, brilliant disciples, good disciples, bad disciples, no disciples: it's all the same to him. He'd be just as happy without them, but he doesn't mind if they come; he doesn't mind even if they are troublesome. That's his attitude, as far as we can tell.

One might think that someone with an attitude of compassion would actively seek out people to teach, but it seems that Milarepa, who was after all instructed by his guru Marpa to meditate in solitary places, attracted people by his compassion. People seem to have flocked around him wherever he went, however inaccessible the place where he was living. Apparently if people heard of a yogi meditating alone in a mountain cave, they'd go up into the mountains to find him. That was the way to attract people in Tibet in those days. Nowadays perhaps no one would take any notice; you could live and die up there without anybody knowing about it.

5

STRONG THOUGHTS, FULL OF INFIDELITY

As the Jetsun and Rechungpa proceeded along the road,
Rechungpa again thought, 'Had this been another Guru, I would
have had a good reception and been most hospitably treated
upon my return from India. But my Guru lives under such poor
conditions himself, naturally it would be impossible for me to
expect any comforts or pleasures from him! I have been in India
and have learned so many of the Tantric teachings! A man like me
should not practice his devotion as an ascetic but should practice
it with pleasure and enjoyment.' With these arrogant and evil ideas
in his mind, strong thoughts, full of infidelity toward the Jetsun,
arose within him.

As we know, Rechungpa has been expecting a magnificent reception on
his return from India. He's even been thinking that perhaps Milarepa
ought to receive him as an equal now that he's been to India and achieved
so many things. But he's been disappointed, and now he is in a very
sour and disgruntled mood. In short, he's got hold of the wrong end of
the stick, the 'stick' being the Vajrayāna attitude towards pleasure. The
Buddhist teaching about pleasure is closely connected with the teaching
about craving. In the chain of *nidānas*, in dependence upon *vedanā* –
feeling, especially pleasurable feeling – arises craving.[192] Usually in our
experience pleasure and craving are closely associated, and we find it
very difficult to distinguish between them, because it seems to us that

craving inevitably arises whenever there is an experience of pleasure. But although craving may seem to follow so quickly upon pleasure that it's as though they're one and the same thing, actually they're two quite different things, because pleasure is a *vipāka*, a fruit of previous action, and craving is a *karma*, a volition. Pleasure in itself is therefore ethically neutral. The terms 'skilful' and 'unskilful' do not apply to pleasure as such. If you experience a sensation of pleasure, there is nothing ethically skilful or unskilful about it, because you're in a passive state, not a state that is exercising volition. Pleasure in this sense is a *vipāka*, the result of something that you have done, not the doing of that thing. For example, the eye exercises its faculty of seeing and sees a visual object, perhaps a beautiful visual object – say a red flower. As a result of that visual perception, the sensation of pleasure arises. The experience of that sensation of pleasure is ethically neutral. If in dependence upon that pleasurable sensation, craving arises, then that is unskilful, but if pleasurable sensation does not become the basis of craving, there is nothing wrong with it. There's nothing wrong with pleasure as such, or with the senses as such. They're merely perceiving apparatuses. There's nothing wrong with the mind as a sense, the sixth sense, as it's called in Buddhism. The unskilful element comes in when in dependence on pleasure there arises craving.

In the Theravāda, and even in the Mahāyāna to a great extent, the close association between pleasure and craving is considered so dangerous that it is thought that in order to get rid of craving you must disassociate yourself from pleasure. Pleasure can exist without craving, but usually the two things go together, and in order to be free from craving, the Theravāda, and the schools of Early Buddhism generally, are quite prepared to give up pleasure: not the pleasure that comes in meditation, but certainly worldly pleasure, sense-pleasure. But the Vajrayāna view is different. Maintaining that the experience of bliss, the experience of pleasure to the highest degree of intensity, is an integral part of the spiritual life, the Vajrayāna, while agreeing that craving is completely unskilful and must be got rid of, says that it is a mistake to throw away pleasure in order to get rid of craving. While we should get rid of craving, we should continue to experience pleasure – pleasure that does not become an occasion for craving – because according to the Tantric teachings, the experience of pleasure or bliss has to be united with the experience of illumination.

Rechungpa seems to got a bit muddled about this. He has understood that the spiritual life is not just a matter of getting rid of craving but involves learning to experience pleasure free from craving. But he seems to think that asceticism can be dispensed with altogether and that the spiritual life is a kind of profession whereby you can satisfy your cravings and enjoy pleasure by becoming a famous scholar, going to India and learning a lot of Tantric teachings.

There are two important aspects of the spiritual life from the Vajrayāna point of view: the experience of pleasure and bliss, especially through the *dhyānas*, and the experience of illumination or clarity. It's a bit like the connection between *śamatha* and *vipaśyanā*, bliss representing the more 'saṃsāric' principle and illumination representing the more spiritual, transcendental, 'nirvāṇic' principle. These two are not an ultimate duality. The bliss that is usually associated with *saṃsāra* has to blend with the illumination that is usually associated with *nirvāṇa*. The Vajrayāna takes a non-dualistic approach, so its practice is non-dualistic too.

The Vajrayāna would agree with the earlier forms of Buddhism that craving is to be got rid of, but it does not agree that the way to do this is by eliminating pleasure, because pleasure is an essential part of the spiritual life – pleasure disassociated from craving and united with illumination. The Vajrayāna's position is difficult, even dangerous, because it is so open to rationalization. It is important to remember that according to the traditional procedure you first of all practise the teachings of the Pāli canon, then the Mahāyāna, and then the Vajrayāna. It's not something that you take up straightaway. You have to prepare yourself for it. But from the Vajrayāna point of view you don't prepare by cutting off pleasure under the impression that you are thereby getting rid of craving. You have to learn to separate the two. We hardly ever have an experience of pleasure free from craving, but it is possible. For example, if you can just contemplate nature, just see it, just enjoy it for what it is, without wanting to do anything with it, or make any use of it, or appropriate it for yourself in any way, then this is a pleasurable experience free from craving. Of course, even then craving might arise: you might see a beautiful flower and then desire to pick it.

One method of separating pleasure and craving recommended by the Vajrayāna is to practise the limited or provisional asceticism of giving up something pleasurable so that you can experience your craving apart from the pleasure. Suppose you get a great deal of pleasure from chocolate biscuits. Maybe you're almost addicted to them; maybe you like to have a few every day. And then suppose you go on a solitary retreat and you don't take any chocolate biscuits with you. You will experience the continued craving for them, but without the pleasure of actually eating them, so you have separated the craving from the pleasure, at least temporarily. If you can experience craving apart from the pleasure with which it has been connected, there is also the possibility of experiencing the pleasure without the craving. 'Provisional asceticism' is a very difficult path, but in the long run you cannot get rid of craving simply by giving up pleasure. You have to conquer craving so that you can experience pleasure, even intense pleasure, without experiencing the corresponding craving.

It's very easy to fool oneself about this. To go back to the text, Rechungpa has gathered that the Vajrayāna does not require the renunciation of pleasure, and he interprets that as recommending leading a professionally religious life as a way of having a good time. In other words, he has almost completely misunderstood. He gives the game away when he says to himself, 'A man like me should not practise his devotion as an ascetic, but should practise it with pleasure and enjoyment.' And thus, 'with these arrogant and evil ideas in his mind, strong thoughts, full of infidelity toward the Jetsun, arose within him'. This shows his complete misunderstanding about the Dharma, especially the Vajrayāna teaching, and his misunderstanding of Milarepa too. He feels he isn't being appreciated. He thinks that his guru isn't on the 'right path', that he shouldn't follow him, that he's meant for better things. From his thoughts, we can tell that he clearly hasn't been able to separate pleasure from craving. He craves position and recognition and social contacts and ease and comfort and a good time, and he wants to use his so-called 'knowledge' of Tantric Buddhism as a means of securing these things. That is not what the Vajrayāna means at all when it speaks of the importance of bliss.

At once, Milarepa read Rechungpa's mind. He then pointed to a yak's horn lying along the side of the road, saying, 'Pick up this yak-horn and bring it with you.' Rechungpa thought, 'Sometimes my Guru wants nothing as he always claimed, but at others "his hatred is much stronger than that of an old dog, and his greediness is greater than that of an old miser", as the proverb says. After all, what is the use of this torn-out yak-horn?' He then said to the Jetsun, 'What good can this piece of waste do us? – leave it alone!' The Jetsun replied, 'To take a small thing like this will not increase one's greediness, and sometimes these discarded things are very useful.' Saying this he picked up the yak-horn and carried it himself.

In attributing hatred and greed to Milarepa, Rechungpa is clearly projecting. The hatred and a greed are in his own mind and he sees Milarepa in a very distorted way. When Milarepa says, 'To take a small thing like this will not increase one's greediness, and sometimes these discarded things are very useful,' there's quite a lot of meaning in what he says, but Rechungpa does not realize that. He's so blinded by his own hatred and greed, his own delusions, that he can't see that Milarepa is trying to tell him something, trying to teach him a lesson. Perhaps there is some significance in his asking Rechungpa to pick up this yak-horn, but Rechungpa is quite incapable of seeing that.

When they reached the central part of Balmo Baltang Plain where no hiding-place could be found for even a small mouse, the heretofore clear sky suddenly became darkened by gathering clouds. Then a great storm, accompanied by violent hail, arose. In the midst of this onslaught Rechungpa covered his head in such haste and confusion that he completely forgot even to look at his Guru. After a while, when the hail began to abate, Rechungpa started to search for Milarepa, but could not find him. For a time he sat upon the ground and waited. Then he seemed to hear the Jetsun's voice coming from the yak-horn which had been left beside the road. He walked towards the place and saw it was undoubtedly the same yak-horn which the Jetsun had taken a few moments before. Rechungpa then tried to pick it up, but it was so heavy that he could not move it, even an inch. Then, he bent down and looked into it, and saw Milarepa seated comfortably within with ample room to spare; his body was no smaller, and the horn no larger than before, just as the reflection of a large image may be seen in a small mirror.

What has happened here? Clearly Milarepa is teaching Rechungpa a lesson, but how literally can one take this? A hailstorm comes on and Milarepa takes shelter within the yak-horn. This is reminiscent of the incident in the *Vimalakīrti-nirdeśa* when Vimalakīrti's house becomes very large, suggesting the relativity of space and time.[193] But I don't know whether that is the sort of lesson that Milarepa is trying to teach here. You can either take it literally – that this is actually what Milarepa did – or you can take it that it appeared to happen. In either case the question remains: what lesson is Milarepa teaching, in plain simple terms? The lesson is simply that he has mastered a great deal, and certainly more than Rechungpa, who has apparently got wet in the storm while Milarepa was quite snug inside the yak-horn. Rechungpa seems to think that he is equal to, or even higher than, his guru, and Milarepa is showing him that he's nowhere near him.

You can take it literally – in terms of ordinary magic, Milarepa can perform this sort of feat and Rechungpa can't – but surely it goes beyond that, even if that did literally happen. It suggests that Milarepa is beyond space and time, and that suggests that Rechungpa cannot comprehend him. He's trying to make Rechungpa aware of his own limitations in the broadest sense. I don't think he is pointing out Rechungpa's conceit and pride by becoming very small. He has become small only in a manner of speaking. The illustration is 'just as the reflection of a large image may be seen in a small mirror', so it isn't that Milarepa has reduced his size; a large object doesn't have to become small for its reflection to be seen in a small mirror. If he hasn't had to reduce his size in order to enter into the yak-horn, that is part of the miracle. Anyway, he's inside the yak-horn, but Rechungpa is too big to get in.

Another thing the incident shows is that something that Rechungpa thought was useless is in fact of great value. He couldn't see the value of the yak-horn, and this is also perhaps an expression of his pride and arrogance and conceit. But however one interprets the incident, Milarepa is baffling Rechungpa. He is forcing him to realize his limitations, his arrogance, and the fact that he is far from being the spiritual equal of Milarepa. Milarepa, in every sense, can do things that Rechungpa can't do, because he is what Rechungpa is not.

And then Rechungpa hears Milarepa singing from inside the yak-horn:

The grace of my Guru enters into my body.
If one's body remains like a commoner's
He is not a great yogi.
Rechungpa, you should pay homage to my miraculous body.

The grace of my Guru enters into my mouth.
If one makes nonsensical remarks
He is not a great yogi.
All Pith-Instructions are found in my song.
Rechungpa, you should bear them in your heart.

The grace of my Guru enters into my mind.
If any unfaithful thought ever arises in one's mind
He is not a great yogi.
Rechungpa, you should pay homage to my power of telepathy.

Oh, son Rechungpa, your mind is like a nimble bird;
Now it flies high, and now it swoops low.
You should observe this unstable change,
Stop thinking so much,
And devote yourself to the Repa's practice!

If you think you can match your Guru,
Now you may come into this horn.
Come in right now –
Here is a spacious and comfortable house!

Rechungpa, your Enlightenment is like the sun and moon;
Sometimes they shine bright, but sometimes they are darkened
    by clouds.
You should observe this unstable change,
Stop thinking so much,
And devote yourself to the Repa's practice!

If you think you can match your Guru,
You may come into this horn.
Come in right now –
Here is a spacious and comfortable house!

Son Rechungpa! Your behavior is like the mountain wind;
Now it blows fast and violent,
And now it blows gentle and slow.
You should observe this unstable change,
Stop thinking so much,
And devote yourself to the Repa's practice!

If you think you can match your Guru,
You may come into this horn.
Come in right now –
Here is a spacious and comfortable house!

Son Rechungpa, your accomplishments
Are like the crops in the field.
Sometimes they grow badly, and sometimes well.
You should observe this unstable change,
Stop thinking so much,
And devote yourself to the Repa's practice!

If you think you can match your Guru,
You may come into this horn.
Come in right now –
Here is a spacious and comfortable house!

If one's mind can master the domain of space,
He can enter this horn and enjoy it.
Come in right now, my son, your father is calling!

It wouldn't be nice
If a son refuses to enter his father's house.
I am a sick and worn-out old man
Who has never been in India in all his life;
His insignificant body is frightened
By the dangerous road outside,
Therefore inside this horn he stays!
Son Rechungpa, you are young, and have been in India.
Also, you have studied under many learned and accomplished
    Gurus.

You should now step into this horn
With your splendid and prominent body.
Of little value is this rotten yak-horn;
Surely it will not inflate one's egotism and desire.
Come in, Rechungpa, come and join your father inside!

Let's look at this bit by bit.

> *The grace of my guru enters into my body.*
> *If one's body remains like a commoner's*
> *He is not a great yogi.*

By a 'commoner' here is meant the non-*āryan*, the *pṛthagjanas*, the many-folk, as it's sometimes translated. Milarepa is suggesting that as a result of one's spiritual practice, one's development of insight, one's experience of the Transcendental and of 'the grace of the guru', which is of course a transcendental influence, there is an actual change, a transformation, in one's physical body. This is quite an important aspect of Vajrayāna teaching. The Vajrayāna is concerned with total transformation. It is not satisfied simply with transforming the mind; it insists also on transformation of speech and even transformation of body. It makes the point that if there's a great change in the mind, that will be reflected or echoed in speech and body, not just in terms of the body's actions and behaviour, but in terms of the actual constitution of the body.

In Buddhism generally it is believed that if you have been a great yogi and you have gained Enlightenment, when you die and are cremated, among your ashes will be found relics – not just fragments of bone but pearl-like objects (the name for these is *śarīra*) which are crystallizations on the physical level of your spiritual practice. The Vajrayāna believes that as a result of the most advanced practice of meditation, the body can be transformed into a body of light, into what is called the 'rainbow-body'. Sometimes this is taken quite literally, sometimes just symbolically, but it is a general belief in Buddhism, especially in the Vajrayāna, that if you practise meditation, physical changes take place in the body. I think one can say that there is some truth in that, because we know that there is such a thing as psychosomatic illness. A certain mental state can cause you to become ill, and in the same way, presumably, because of a certain mental state you can become well. For instance, there is the meditation practice of *tummo*, the generation of so-called psychic heat. This heat isn't just a subjective experience. There is an actual change in the temperature of the physical body, a change that can be perceived by other people. So here physical change is brought about by mental change.

At present, Milarepa is concerned with change in the physical body as the result of yogic attainment in a purely magical sense. He's able, as it were, to shrink his physical body so that it is small enough to enter into the yak's horn, and this is something that Rechungpa has not yet learned to do. But whether we take that literally or not, we should not lose sight of the general principle that the physical body as well as the mind is transformed as a result of one's practice. You may have experienced yourself that if you have a good meditation you feel physically better as well as mentally better, so that you can see the truth of this, even though you may think that you can't transform your body to the extent of being able to make it bigger or smaller as you please. Perhaps anyway this episode in which Milarepa creeps into the yak-horn is not to be taken literally. But nonetheless, the Vajrayāna attaches great importance to the transformation of the physical body.

Rechungpa, you should pay homage to my miraculous body.

The point here is that Milarepa's body should not be regarded as an ordinary body. It is the body of a Buddha, a *nirmāṇakāya*. It appears to be an ordinary physical body, but actually it has been completely transformed. There's a reminder of this in the five-coloured Buddhist flag. The five colours are red, white, orange or saffron, yellow, and blue, and then there's a section of the flag which has all five colours together. The human body consists principally of five things: blood, bones, water, flesh, and marrow. Blood is red, flesh is saffron or orange-coloured, bone is white, water is blue, and marrow is yellow. (Sometimes bile is cited instead of marrow as being represented by yellow.) It's said that the Buddha's aura is made up of light of these five colours, plus a sixth, indescribable light which blends all five. The Buddha's aura represents the purified, refined, and sublimated physical body; in other words, as a result of the Buddha's meditation and attainment of Enlightenment, his gross physical body of blood, bone, etc. has been transformed into a subtle body of light of those six colours. His halo represents the fact that the Buddha's nature, even on the level of the physical body, has been thoroughly transformed by the Enlightenment experience. That's an expression of the same sort of idea within the Theravāda tradition.

Buddhism generally speaks in terms of transformation, but usually we think of transformation of mind or consciousness, which is obviously the most important. The transformation of speech and body is usually thought of as referring to the transformation of action, not the body itself. You may commit no unskilful action with the physical body, but it's still the same old physical body. But the Vajrayāna says it's not enough to transform your actions. The body itself has got to be transformed, and we can see the possibility of that in the fact that as a result of meditation experience, subtle physical changes do occur in the body.

This is the background to this little episode. We can take it literally or not, but the principle being stressed is the transformation of the physical body. Some teachers go so far as to say that if you are a great yogi you'll never fall ill. Sometimes, of course, great yogis do fall ill but it's usually explained by saying they have taken upon themselves the sufferings or the defilements of other people. It's very difficult to know whether that is the case or not.

The phrase 'the grace of my Guru' refers to something very different from the Western idea of 'the grace of God'. The Tibetan word translated here as 'grace' is *jinlap*, which renders the Sanskrit *adhiṣṭhāna*. Setting aside the etymology of this word for the moment, what is grace? Even in the Theravāda you get the conception of grace, *ānubhāva*, which can also be translated as 'influence'. It's as though coming from every object, whether material or mental, there is an influence; every object propagates itself in the form of an influence, if you like, a vibration. If someone is in an angry mood, you feel it; they may not give any sign of anger but you can pick it up. It affects you. Sometimes you can sense it even if you're not in the same room as the angry person. Every mental state is perceptible, and exerts an influence over other living beings. They feel it, they perceive it, they're affected by it. Animals are sometimes more sensitive to these things than human beings. So if someone is in a highly positive, meditative, insightful state, this will surely have an effect on other living beings, especially on those who are receptive to the person who is in that highly positive state. This is what is meant by 'grace'. It comes, as it were, from above, in the sense that it pertains to a vertical relationship, it comes from a mind more highly developed than one's own, a mind with which one is in tune and to which one is receptive. One feels the influence of that mind, and that is what is called grace.

That grace cannot transform you against your will. You have to cooperate with it. It's only an influence; it is not decisive. You can resist it, close yourself to it, block it off. But if you are open to it, you can allow it to have an effect on you. This is what is meant by grace in the Buddhist context, especially the Tibetan Buddhist context. In Christianity, by contrast, the 'grace of God' sometimes seems arbitrary, as though God is like a king who is endowed with tremendous power and can do anything he likes. Just as if the king has a fancy to give you a title or a large sum of money he can do it, by his grace, if God wants to grant you salvation, he can do so, and if he doesn't want to, well, he doesn't. The grace of God tends to be presented in this way, as the purely whimsical act of someone with arbitrary power. Grace in that sense is something that you have not done anything to earn. It's freely bestowed. But why is it freely bestowed upon some and not upon others? This is where the element of arbitrariness come in. This is carried to its logical conclusion in Calvinism, in which God predestines some people to hell and some to heaven before they're even born. Calvinist theology even has the expression 'irresistible grace'.[194] But there is no such thing as 'irresistible grace' in Buddhism. Grace, even in the sense that I've described it, is not irresistible; you certainly can resist it. The freedom of the individual is fully maintained. And indeed, Rechungpa is being pretty resistant to Milarepa here. He's closing himself to Milarepa's influence, just as Devadatta closed himself to the Buddha's influence.[195]

> The grace of my Guru enters into my mouth.
> If one makes nonsensical remarks,
> He is not a great yogi.
> All Pith-Instructions are found in my song.
> Rechungpa, you should bear them in your heart.

In other words, a great yogi's speech is thoroughly transformed. He never makes nonsensical remarks. He never indulges in meaningless talk. Whatever he says is 'right speech'. It is truthful, it is affectionate, it is useful, and it is uttered at the right time and in the right place.

Milarepa hardly ever speaks except to instruct. Everything he says is a continual 'Pith-Instruction', because his speech principle has been completely transformed. This is quite an easy test to apply, because the extent to which your mind has been transformed will show itself in your speech. What are the things you usually talk about? Following the idea of the personal mandala described earlier, you could have a sort of speech mandala, putting right in the middle the things you like talking about the most. Some people find that their favourite football team is in the centre of their speech mandala, some find that the Dharma is there, while some like talking about meditation more than anything else. Some have talking about other people in the centre of their mandala, while others find that their favourite topic is their own health, all their aches and pains.

> *The grace of my Guru enters into my mind.*
> *If any unfaithful thought ever arises in one's mind,*
> *He is not a great yogi.*
> *Rechungpa, you should pay homage to my power of telepathy.*

Earlier on we heard what was going on in Rechungpa's mind: 'With these arrogant and evil ideas in his mind, strong thoughts, full of infidelity toward the Jetsun, arose within him.' It seems that Milarepa has had a sense of what Rechungpa has been thinking, and here he is in effect telling Rechungpa that because he has had these unfaithful thoughts, his mind has not been completely transformed. Milarepa's grace has not entered into his mind; he has been resistant to it. But what is meant by 'thoughts full of infidelity'? Rechungpa has been thinking of going to another guru who can give him more than he can get from Milarepa. He has also been thinking that Milarepa is no better than he is himself. He simply doesn't have the attitude of faith and devotion that one would naturally have towards someone whom one recognizes as spiritually superior. If one does not see them as spiritually more developed than oneself, one will feel no faith and devotion. One's attitude is thus one of infidelity, and that is Rechungpa's position.

> *O son Rechungpa, your mind is like a nimble bird;*
> *Now it flies high and now it swoops low.*
> *You should observe this unstable change,*

Stop thinking so much,
And devote yourself to the Repa's practice!

This is the keynote. Rechungpa is very unstable, almost bipolar, as we would say, and he thinks too much. We saw that when he was approaching Milarepa. When they were about to meet, he was thinking, 'What's going to happen? How is Milarepa going to salute me? Will he return my obeisance?' So now Milarepa says, 'Stop thinking so much and devote yourself to the Repa's practice' – that is, solitary meditation.

If you think you can match your Guru,
Now you may come into this horn.
Come in right now –
Here is a spacious and comfortable house!

If you think you are as great as I am, you should be able to do the things that I can do. This is what Milarepa in principle is saying.

Rechungpa, your Enlightenment is like the sun and moon;
Sometimes they shine bright, but sometimes they are darkened
    by clouds.
You should observe this unstable change,
Stop thinking so much,
And devote yourself to the Repa's practice!

Milarepa is acknowledging that Rechungpa has some spiritual realization, but it isn't constant, it comes and goes. This is not true of *vipaśyanā*, of insight, but it is certainly true of *dhyāna* experiences, and even of some *samāpattis*, or higher spiritual attainments. They come and they go. Rechungpa is like that. When they come, he's a spiritual sort of person, but when they go, he's quite different. This kind of oscillation between spiritual states of mind and very mundane states is quite common. There was a famous French preacher in the seventeenth century who used to preach wonderful sermons in the morning and then really live it up by night. There was a little rhyme about him that went something like this: 'Preach like an angel in the morning. Live like a devil at night!' That is the state of quite a lot of people. You can experience tremendous changes even in the course of a single day. In the morning you can be really inspired by the spiritual life: 'I'm going to be a real bodhisattva, sacrifice everything for the sake of the Dharma and spend all my time meditating and studying and giving talks and lectures and working in a right livelihood business.' But by the evening you can be thinking of giving it all up, not meditating any more, going and having a good time, getting drunk. You can think and feel that in the evening of the very same day when in the morning you were so inspired with such beautiful aspirations and lofty ideals, and so genuine and devoted. It's not that you're pretending – in both cases, it's genuine, because you're genuinely divided.

It is like that for a long time. You enjoy spiritual experiences but they don't last. This is why William James, the great psychologist, once said that anyone can have religious experiences but a religious man is one who makes those religious experiences the centre of his existence. In other words, he places them in the centre of his mandala. He cherishes them. He tries to preserve them, safeguard them, make sure he doesn't lose them.

One useful way of handling these oscillations is to put yourself in stable surroundings which encourage positive mental states and give you access to the experience of more definitely spiritual attainments. Also, don't take on too much at a time. You mustn't force the pace, otherwise there will be a reaction in the opposite direction. You must proceed wisely and circumspectly. In the Pāli scriptures, there are quite a number of cases of followers of the Buddha who were *bhikkhus* for a while, then gave it all up and went back to the household life. They got fed up with that after a while, so they came to the Buddha again and were ordained again, only to tire of the *bhikkhu's* life again, disrobe and return to the household life. Over time a tradition arose that *bhikkhus* did not disrobe and go forth again more than seven times. Look at the oscillations there: people going forth, then sliding back, then going forth again. So this is by no means a modern development. At all times of Buddhist history people have sometimes felt full of faith in the morning and by the evening have been full of doubt. In the morning you can be completely sure that Buddhism is what you want to devote your life to, but by the evening you're thinking, 'Maybe it's all a bit of a will-o'-the-wisp. Maybe it would be better to devote myself to my career and my family.' The next morning you're full of inspiration for the Dharma again. Having contact with the spiritual community, where all the conditions help you to maintain your genuine interest in the Dharma, therefore becomes very important.

It's reassuring to realize that it's likely that you will experience these oscillations; otherwise you might think that there's something wrong with you, and that maybe you're not suited to spiritual life after all. It's an experience that a lot of people go through. You don't settle down all at once. The *Dhammapada* gives the image of a fish floundering on the bank, twitching from side to side.[196] It's nearly always the case that your head decides that you're going to commit yourself to the spiritual life, and then it takes time for the rest of you to catch up. People can sometimes see and understand quite clearly what they ought to do long before they're able to do it. Sometimes they may force themselves to do it by an act of will, but if they're not ready, a greater part of their being rebels, and they backslide rather dramatically for a while, then pick themselves up and try again. These ups and downs are only to be expected, and they need not present a real setback so long as you press on nonetheless.

> Son Rechungpa! Your behavior is like the mountain wind;
> Now it blows fast and violent,
> And now it blows gentle and slow.
> You should observe this unstable change.
> Stop thinking so much,
> And devote yourself to the Repa's practice!

You find this with some people with regard to spiritual practice. Someone can 'blow fast and violent' and try to chivvy everybody along and get them all doing lots of extra meditation, but a few days later that same person has slackened off dramatically and now just 'blows gentle and slow'. These oscillations tend to happen much more quickly when you're living with other Buddhists. If you get a bigger dose of spiritual life, sometimes you get a stronger reaction against it. If you're living at home with your family, you've got a job, and you just come along to the Buddhist centre once a week, it's unlikely that you're going to get a strong reaction against that, because there's not very much to react against. Your life is pretty safe; it doesn't feel threatened in any way. But if you're living in a community and meditating twice a day and there are no distractions – no family, no television, no newspapers, nothing but the Dharma – under those conditions you can start reacting very strongly and very quickly.

So again he says:

> If you think you can match your Guru,
> You may come into this horn.
> Come in right now –
> Here is a spacious and comfortable house!

We've had this refrain several times, but perhaps Milarepa says 'Come in right now' as a teasing challenge. If Rechungpa really is as great as Milarepa, whatever Milarepa can do, he ought to be able to do too, on the spot. It's like if you tell me you can speak French, and I say, 'OK then! Let me hear you speak it now!' Now Milarepa comes up with another simile:

> Son Rechungpa, your accomplishments
> Are like the crops in the field.
> Sometimes they grow badly, and sometimes well.
> You should observe this unstable change,
> Stop thinking so much,
> And devote yourself to the Repa's practice!

The similes that Milarepa is giving all tell the same story, illustrate the same fact: that Rechungpa's spiritual life is rather a patchy, intermittent affair. He's got to stabilize his spiritual experience, and start treading the path of regular steps.[197] He's too clever, too sure of himself, too conceited, too mixed up. Although he's very gifted as regards to the Dharma, it's still only one interest among many. He hasn't solidly committed himself to it. He still swings back and forth too much.

In traditional Buddhist terms, to say that someone is spiritually gifted can only mean that as a result of practice in previous lives they have outstanding spiritual qualities. They haven't inherited them from their parents; they've carried them over from previous lives, though in this life they may not have found circumstances that encourage those gifts. Sometimes you come across people who don't have strong cravings, experience pleasure in a detached, healthy way, and are naturally kind, helpful, and unselfish – 'naturally' in that they don't have to make much of an effort, they don't have to behave like that as a discipline, whereas other people can behave in that way only after a severe struggle with themselves. Some people are naturally generous. As to whether some people find insight easier than others, some people are more intelligent than others, but whether that makes it easier for them to develop insight is rather difficult to say. You can meet people who are very good scholars of Buddhism and have a remarkable understanding of Buddhist doctrine on an intellectual level, but no insight. And at the other extreme there was Huineng, who had an insight experience upon his first hearing of the Dharma even though he was illiterate.[198] Capacity for insight is not necessarily associated with intellectual understanding.

> If one's mind can master the domain of space,
> He can enter this horn and enjoy it.
> Come in right now, my son, your father is calling!

You master space by realizing that space is in mind, not mind in space, that – in Abhidharma terminology – space, like time, is only a concept. Space is not a thing, it's only a particular way in which you perceive or experience things. You can go beyond that because you can modify your experience, you can modify your consciousness. But starting to come to terms with realizing that space is only a concept isn't easy. There is a method described in the *Śūraṅgama Samādhi Sūtra* (which is contained in Dwight Goddard's *Buddhist Bible*).[199] You first of all start off with the common-sense idea that the mind is inside the body, inside the head, and looking out through the eyes. You would think that just as you see the inside of a window and then you look out to the view beyond, if your mind is inside your head looking out through your eyes, you should see the inside of your eyes first, or even the inside of your head, and then look out through your eyes to see the external world. It doesn't happen like that, though, so it seems that the mind isn't inside your head in that way. So is the mind outside of you? Well, if it was, you ought to be able to see your own face, but you can't. So is the mind in between the two? Well, the *sūtra* goes on, that also is not possible. In the end it brings you to the conclusion that mind does not stand in any relationship to space at all because space is not, so to speak, a thing outside the mind, but an idea in the mind.

This is a philosophical approach, but there are other, simpler approaches to give you at least some idea of the relativity of time and space. For instance, when you come out of a meditation, or even while you are meditating, you can do a little exercise. Keep your eyes closed, and if you are meditating in London, say to yourself that you're actually in, say, Norfolk. After all, the subjective experience is the same, whether you're meditating in London or in Norfolk. With a bit of practice, you can actually feel that you are meditating in Norfolk, and you can become at least doubtful as to whether you're in Norfolk or London. You can even travel about in time; you can imagine to yourself that you aren't in the present century. You're in the sixth century BCE. You're in India and here you are with your closed eyes just meditating. You're in the forest and not far away there's the Buddha's vihara. You can get an actual feeling of being there, at that time – and then of course you can switch back to the present century. If you practise this, you can start feeling that the mind can switch back and forth; that time and space are inside the mind – not the mind inside time and space.

As to whether that is a *vipaśyanā* experience, one must proceed cautiously. Just as it's often difficult to point to the moment when intellectual understanding passes over into insight, in the same way, this juggling about with space and time at a certain point does pass over into an actual insight into the relativity of space and time, but you can have an experience of it, though not a very strong one, before reaching that point. One can't say that if one has an experience of this sort, it is sure to amount to insight; it depends on how strong and vivid the experience is and whether it has a permanent effect on you. But our consciousness of things isn't fixed in the way we usually think it is. This is what Milarepa is showing Rechungpa. Space and time are relative. A little yak-horn can contain a man's body.

We may feel that the mind is somewhere around the head, because the brain is in the head and we think of the brain as the seat of consciousness, but it doesn't have to be. There is an exercise in which one pulls the consciousness down, as it were, to the region just below the stomach. You can be sitting meditating, looking down from the head to the stomach, and then you can close your eyes and imagine yourself pulling your consciousness down so that you feel that you are there, in that stomach area, rather than looking down to the stomach from the head. Sometimes this has a very relaxing effect; you can feel very warm and comfortable and sleepy, and it can help to get rid of excessive mental activity. There are Vajrayāna exercises where you practise locating your consciousness in different parts of the body, or even interchanging senses – seeing with your ears or hearing with your eyes. It may sound ridiculous, but these things sometimes spontaneously occur. It all goes to show that things we think of as fixed aren't so fixed as all that. It's interesting to consider this with regard to two consciousnesses in communication. If you're having a really good communication you might ask yourself, 'Where's the consciousness? Who am I? Which am I?'

> Rechungpa thought, 'There seems to be plenty of room there; can I also get in?' Thinking this, he tried to enter the horn, but he could not even get his hand and head in (let alone his whole body). Then he thought, 'The Jetsun's miraculous power may or may not be genuine, but he can surely produce hail.'

Rechungpa misses the irony completely. He thinks that Milarepa is seriously inviting him in, and thinks there may be room for him; he doesn't recognize his own limitations. This is quite symbolic. 'He couldn't even get his hand and head in, let alone his whole body.' He isn't really like Milarepa at all. He doesn't have Milarepa's powers, doesn't have Milarepa's realization, but he still doesn't completely accept the situation.

> Putting his mouth close to the horn, Rechungpa sang in a quavering voice:

> Oh, my father Jetsun Guru, please listen to me!
> Whether the View, Practice, Action, and Accomplishment
> Of your servant and son, Rechung Dor Draug,
> Be high or low, bright or dim, great or small,
> Better or worse, it makes no difference;
> He shall continue to pray to you.
> Whether his cotton robe be dry or wet,
> He shall continue to pray to you.
> He may or may not match his father,
> But he shall continue to pray to him!

Rechungpa seems to be melting a little bit. Recognizing at least the possibility that Milarepa may in fact be more highly developed than he is, he is beginning to realize that perhaps he isn't Milarepa's equal after all.

Milarepa came out of the horn. He gestured toward the sky, and at once the storm began to abate, the clouds to disperse, and the sun to break through. Immediately the air became very warm, and before long, Rechungpa's clothes were dried.

That makes it clear that Milarepa had brought on the hailstorm by his magical power. He staged the whole thing to give himself an opportunity of slipping into the yak's horn and teaching Rechungpa a good lesson.

6

I AM STARVING TO DEATH RIGHT NOW

After resting a while, the Jetsun said, 'Rechungpa, I knew from the beginning that your trip to India was unnecessary. Being quite satisfied with the teaching of Mahāmudrā and the Six Yogas, I did not go to India. I am very glad that you have now returned with the teaching you wanted.'

When Milarepa says, 'I am very glad you have now returned with the teaching you wanted,' he is probably referring to the Formless Ḍākinī Dharmas, but it may be a reference to the science of logic, the study of which was Rechungpa's reason for going away. In either case, it seems that the statement is a bit ironical, because he says that the trip to India was unnecessary, but anyway, 'I'm glad that you have now returned with the teaching you wanted.' Rechungpa has done what he wanted to do. He got his own way in the end. All right, never mind!

'Dear Lama, I am very hungry and cold,' said Rechungpa, 'let us go to the tents over there and beg some food.'
'But this is not the time to beg alms,' replied Milarepa.
'I do not know whether it is the time to beg alms or not, but I know that I am starving to death right now. By all means let us go.'
'Very well, we shall go. I think perhaps it would be better to go to the first tent.'
'But in begging alms one must not look only for rich people, and

neglect the poor,' said Rechungpa. 'Therefore let us go to that small brownish tent near the lower end (of the terrace).'

So they went toward the small tent. When they reached its entrance to ask the host for alms, a fearful old woman came out and said, 'A yogi should stick to poverty all the time. Good yogis always refuse our offerings, even when brought to them. But greedy people like you, never content with what they already have, always come after others' belongings. All the things that I had to spare for charity, I already gave to some beggars this morning. Nothing is left now. You had better go somewhere else to beg.' Upon hearing these malicious remarks, the Jetsun said, 'The sun is about to set; it makes no difference whether we get food or not this evening, so let us find a place to sleep.'

Rechungpa's remark about which tent they should go to tells us that he is very keen on observing the rules. In suggesting that Milarepa wants to avoid the small brownish tent because someone poor lives there, he is surmising that Milarepa wants to go to the first tent because apparently that's a bigger one and maybe the people there are richer, and he is rebuking Milarepa for not observing the rule of begging from everybody equally, whether they are rich or poor. But just a minute before Milarepa said, 'But this is not the time to beg alms'! Rechungpa doesn't bother about that rule because he is starving to death, he says, but he's very quick to try to trip Milarepa up about some other rule. He's clearly still in a rather disagreeable state of mind.

There's another point: he doesn't realize that perhaps Milarepa knows better. He still hasn't got complete faith in Milarepa. Milarepa probably says, 'I think perhaps it would be better to go to the first tent' because he knows what sort of reception they are likely to receive at the small brown tent, but Rechungpa can't take the hint. He wants to put his guru in the wrong. So Milarepa just shrugs his shoulders and goes along with Rechungpa, as he always does.

You do come across lay people like this fearful old woman who are very strict with monks and yogis, always advising them and rebuking them and saying that they're not good enough. She says, 'Good yogis always refuse our offerings, even when brought to them.' It must be very convenient for lay people that 'good' yogis and monks won't accept their offerings. It certainly saves on expense. Whether she really has already given everything away we don't know. But anyway, they've lost time going to that small brown tent, and it's too late to go to the other tents now, but Milarepa doesn't mind. He says, 'It makes no difference whether we get food or not this evening, so let us find a place to sleep.' You can imagine how Rechungpa felt then. He really has a very hard time with Milarepa.

Perhaps there is some symbolic significance to the whole thing. Rechungpa is very aware of his physical hunger, but he isn't aware of his spiritual needs, and furthermore he is aware of his physical needs but not of the best way of satisfying them, so he goes to the wrong place. Similarly, he's not aware of where to go for his spiritual needs and goes off to India when in fact what he needs is at home. Both things happen for the same reason: he doesn't listen to Milarepa. Milarepa hints, 'I think perhaps it would be better to go to the first tent,' but Rechungpa is so closed to any suggestions from Milarepa that he doesn't take any notice. Again he wants to do things his own way, and thus he gets into difficulties. That's typical of his whole attitude towards Milarepa. He's not receptive to any advice or suggestion or hint or anything of that kind, so he gets into trouble.

That night the Jetsun and Rechungpa slept nearby. About midnight, they heard a noise in the tent. Then it subsided and all became quiet again. The next morning when the sun arose, the Jetsun said to Rechungpa, 'Go over to the tent and take a look inside.' Rechungpa did so, but he found nothing left in the tent except the corpse of the old woman who had refused to give them alms the evening before. Rechungpa then informed Milarepa of what he had seen. The Jetsun said, 'The food and other things must be hidden somewhere underground,' and they went over to the tent together.

The fact was, that regardless of her malicious talk, the hour had come for the old woman – the land was full of epidemics at that time. (They found that) her jewelry had all been stolen by the nomads. Left behind on the ground was nothing but a small bag of butter, some cheese and barley flour, and a pail of yogurt. The Jetsun said to Rechungpa, 'Son, all things are like this. Last evening this old woman was full of stinginess and worry, but now

she is dead. Oh, in sooth one should give alms to those in need.'
Thereupon, Milarepa and Rechungpa prepared a sacramental
offering for the dead woman with the things that were left.
Rechungpa then packed up the remnants of the edible food and
was about to carry it away with him, when the Jetsun said, 'It is
not good for one to eat the food of a corpse without benefiting
it. The proverb says, "The old men should eat the food and the
young men should produce it." Now, carry the corpse upon your
shoulder and I'll go ahead to lead the way!'

With misgivings that he might be contaminated by the filth of the
corpse, Rechungpa unhappily carried it upon his shoulder while
the Jetsun went ahead to guide them on the road. When they
reached a marsh, the Jetsun said, 'Now put the corpse down.' He
then placed the point of his staff at the heart of the corpse, and
said, 'Rechungpa, like this woman, every sentient being is destined
to die, but seldom do people think of this fact. So they lose many
opportunities to practice the Dharma. Both you and I should
remember this incident and learn a lesson from it.' Whereupon, he
sang the 'Song of Transiency and Delusion,' having six parables.

The old woman had food to give, although she said that she didn't have
anything. She had had the opportunity of giving alms, of practising *dāna*,
but she didn't realize that she was about to die and she didn't do it.
Milarepa is saying that if one realizes that the hour of death can come
at any time and that after that one will not have the opportunity for
creating merit, one will take advantage of every opportunity that one
has here and now. In this way, the recollection of death helps one to lead
the spiritual life.

Oh, the grace of the Gurus is beyond our comprehension!

When the transiency of life strikes deeply into one's heart
His thoughts and deeds will naturally accord with Dharma.
If repeatedly and continuously one thinks about death,
He can easily conquer the demon of laziness.
No one knows when death will descend upon him –
Just as this woman last night!

Rechungpa, do not be harsh, and listen to your Guru!
Behold, all manifestations in the outer world
Are ephemeral like the dream last night!
One feels utterly lost in sadness
When he thinks of this passing dream.
Rechungpa, have you completely wakened
From this great puzzlement?
Oh, the more I think of this,
The more I aspire to Buddha and the Dharma.

The pleasure-yearning human body is an ungrateful creditor.
Whatever good you do to it,
It always plants the seeds of pain.
This human body is a bag of filth and dirt;
Never be proud of it, Rechungpa,
But listen to my song!

When I look back at my body,
I see it as a mirage-city;
Though I may sustain it for a while,
It is doomed to extinction.
When I think of this,
My heart is filled with grief!
Rechungpa, would you not cut off Saṃsāra?
Oh, the more I think of this,
The more I think of Buddha and the Dharma!

A vicious person can never attain happiness.
Errant thoughts are the cause of all regrets,
Bad dispositions are the cause of all miseries.
Never be voracious, oh Rechungpa,
But listen to my song!

When I look back at my clinging mind,
It appears like a short-lived sparrow in the woods –
Homeless, and with nowhere to sleep;
When I think of this, my heart is filled with grief.
Rechungpa, will you let yourself

Indulge in ill-will?
Oh, the more I think of this,
The more I aspire to Buddha and the Dharma!

Human life is as precarious
As a single slim hair of a horse's tail
Hanging on the verge of breaking;
It may be snuffed out at any time
Like this old woman was last night!
Do not cling to this life, Rechungpa,
But listen to my song!

When I observe inwardly my breathings
I see they are transient, like the fog;
They may vanish any moment into nought.
When I think of this, my heart is filled with grief.
Rechungpa, do you not want to conquer
That insecurity now?
Oh, the more I think of this
The more I aspire to Buddha and the Dharma.

To be close to wicked kinsmen only causes hatred.
The case of this old woman is a very good lesson.
Rechungpa, stop your wishful-thinking
And listen to my song!

When I look at friends and consorts
They appear as passers-by in the bazaar;
Meeting with them is only temporary,
But separation is forever!
When I think of this, my heart is filled with grief.
Rechungpa, do you not want to cast aside
All worldly associations?
Oh, the more I think of this,
The more I think of Buddha and the Dharma.

A rich man seldom enjoys
The wealth that he has earned;

This is the mockery of Karma and Saṃsāra.
Money and jewels gained through stinginess and toil
Are like this old woman's bag of food.
Do not be covetous, Rechungpa,
But listen to my song!

When I look at the fortunes of the rich,
They appear to me like honey to the bees –
Hard work, serving only for others' enjoyment,
Is the fruit of their labor.
When I think of this, my heart is filled with grief.
Rechungpa, do you not want to open
The treasury within your mind?
Oh, the more I think of this
The more I aspire to Buddha and His teachings.

> *Oh, the grace of the Gurus is beyond our comprehension!*

No doubt he says this at the beginning of his song because this event is so timely as far as Rechungpa is concerned. It's as though it's due to the grace of the gurus that they've just had this experience with the old woman and seen her stinginess just before her death. It has been a good lesson, and Milarepa is saying that it is due to the grace of the gurus, which can work in all sorts of mysterious ways. If the gurus themselves are beyond our comprehension, clearly their grace will also be beyond our comprehension.

> *When the transiency of life strikes deeply into one's heart*
> *His thoughts and deeds will naturally accord with Dharma.*

When the 'transiency of life strikes deeply into one's heart', one has an insight, and when one has a real insight into the transiency of life, then one's 'thoughts and deeds will naturally accord with Dharma'. There won't be any question of effort or discipline. If you realize something, if you have a genuine insight, your being is transformed in accordance with that insight, and your thoughts and deeds naturally accord with the Dharma. That is the criterion of insight: that it does actually transform you, it does actually make a difference.

If repeatedly and continuously one thinks about death,
He can easily conquer the demon of laziness.

This almost suggests that in order to overcome the demon of laziness, you need a degree of insight. It is suggesting that laziness is a very deep-rooted and terrible thing. It's not just a mild, superficial weakness; it is a manifestation of the effect of the gravitational pull, and requires drastic treatment. It's a sort of inertia with regard to the spiritual life. And of course Milarepa thinks that Rechungpa has been lazy in going to India. Laziness from a spiritual point of view has got nothing to do with how much effort you put into ordinary activity. Sometimes in the evening people say they're too tired to meditate or do a puja, but if a few minutes later you say, 'Let's go and see a film', they brighten up extraordinarily. They're ready to go out straightaway – no trace of tiredness at all. The energy was there; they were just being lazy.

If you think you're too tired to meditate, but you go ahead and meditate anyway, very often you will break through to another level of energy. It isn't very often that you are genuinely too tired to meditate or do a puja. In fact, if you're feeling tired and it isn't yet time to sleep, you probably need to meditate, to refresh yourself.

No one knows when death will descend upon him –
Just as this woman last night!

You just don't know how much time you've got left. You may be young and healthy but you could have an accident tomorrow, or fall victim to a fatal disease. You just don't know, so you should make the best use of your opportunities, not postpone things.

Rechungpa, do not be harsh, and listen to your Guru!
Behold, all manifestations in the outer world
Are ephemeral like the dream last night!
One feels utterly lost in sadness
When he thinks of this passing dream.

The dream he is talking about is the dream of life itself. While you're dreaming, the dream may be very vivid, and your experience of it can be very intense, but when you wake up, it's gone as though it had never been. Very often one feels the same way about experiences during the waking state, even good experiences. You might have a very good retreat, but only a few weeks later, when you try to think about it, it's almost like a dream. You ask yourself, 'Did I really have that experience?' It's not long ago, but you're now so out of tune with it that it's as though it had never been. All worldly experiences can be like that. In retrospect, they seem so unreal. In that respect, without going into more metaphysical considerations, everything seems like a dream. It's here today, gone tomorrow. Today it's so vivid – you're so immersed in it, it's so intense, so clear, so enjoyable – but a few days or weeks later, you can't recapture it at all, it's so faint, dim, indistinct. It's as though it had never been. Milarepa says that when one thinks of all the experiences of one's life as a passing dream, 'one feels utterly lost in sadness'. It's a salutary sadness, one can say.

> Rechungpa, have you completely wakened
> From this great puzzlement?
> Oh, the more I think of this,
> The more I aspire to Buddha and the Dharma.

The suggestion is that just as you awaken from the dream into the waking state, so you wake up from the dream of life itself into the state of 'awakening', the state of Enlightenment. The puzzlement is that of transitory worldly existence. As an observer, you can see the emptiness and insignificance of all Rechungpa's actions, but he doesn't have that vision, which is quite a desperate situation to be in. He doesn't feel sad in this positive way. He simply feels depressed, which is a quite different state.

I wonder if this kind of emptiness and despair is felt very much these days? Perhaps people feel more or less happy and satisfied with their job, their home life – the pub in the evening, football matches, and television. And if they feel dissatisfied, perhaps it is disgruntlement rather than disillusionment – thinking they won't get what they want rather than not really wanting it even if they could get it. They'd like to be able to enjoy the good things of life, but they think that they probably won't get them. They don't really see through things in a way that leads to true disillusionment. There's a lot that people do that they find quite enjoyable, and quite a lot of people find it difficult to believe that there is some other way of life, even when it is presented to them. They've become so set in their ways, so convinced that life is just something they have to put up with. You enjoy it when you can but you mustn't expect to enjoy it all the time. And there's no other way to live – that's your life and you're stuck with it. That's true of a lot of people in England, at least; it may be different in other countries and other cultures.

It isn't easy to go from disgruntlement into the spiritual life. You have to develop genuine disillusionment first. People who find worldly life satisfactory – who are successful and reasonably happy – usually also find it very difficult to make the transition. It's very difficult to go from the *devaloka* – the world of the gods – onto the spiritual path. But on the other hand, if life has been very painful and you've become disgruntled, bitter, and resentful, then also you may find it very difficult. As tradition says, it's very difficult to find a path from the world of the gods and it's also difficult to find it from the hell state. It's easiest to find it from the human state, where pleasure and pain are mixed.[200] Perhaps someone who has had a reasonable experience of life – who has experienced so little happiness that he's bitter and resentful, but has experienced enough suffering to make him think – most easily makes the transition to the spiritual path. If your starting point is a basis of disgruntlement, you should aim to develop real disillusionment. If for instance you would like to be successful but you're not, you're likely to be disgruntled, and to believe that if you could be successful, you would be happy, but if you managed to become disillusioned, you will realize that even if you were successful, that wouldn't give you happiness.

> *The pleasure-yearning human body is an ungrateful creditor.*
> *Whatever good you do to it,*
> *It always plants the seeds of pain.*

Perhaps 'yearning' should be understood in the sense of craving, but it isn't the body that craves for pleasure; it's the mind that does the craving, and one has to be careful to make that distinction. But why is it that whatever good you do to the body, 'it always plants the seeds of pain'? It is because to be associated with the body is to be associated with the permanent possibility of pain. You may look after your body – you may bathe it and wash it and smooth it and perfume it – but all the same, sooner or later it is going to get a stomach ache or a headache and you suffer because you are identified with the body, at least to some extent; your mind is bound up with it in some mysterious way. You may do good to the body, but it only does harm to you, because it brings with it the possibility of suffering; in fact, it does suffer, which means that you suffer.

Milarepa's line of approach here is of course a one-sided view for a particular purpose, rather like Śāntideva's special pleading in the Bodhicaryāvatāra.[201] The body also plants the seeds of pleasure, you could say, because through the body comes pleasurable sensation, but that's not the side of the matter that Milarepa wants Rechungpa to see.

> This human body is a bag of filth and dirt;
> Never be proud of it, Rechungpa,
> But listen to my song!

Don't forget that Rechungpa has been burdened with the corpse of the old woman on his shoulder, so he's in a position to appreciate what Milarepa is saying. This is one aspect of the human body, but it isn't the whole story. It's also through this body that you gain Enlightenment, and that is also a Vajrayāna emphasis. But if you are attached to the body – if you try to make use of it for selfish, egoistic purposes, and if you are attracted to and crave the bodies of others – you need to be reminded of the other side of the picture, reminded that the human body is a heap of filth and dirt. The corpse of this old woman is not a very attractive object at all. This sort of contemplation is generally used to counteract craving and attachment – especially craving and attachment to the physical body, whether one's own or those of other people or both.[202]

> When I look back at my body,
> I see it as a mirage-city;
> Though I may sustain it for a while,
> It is doomed to extinction.

In the previous verse Milarepa spoke of the manifestations in the outer world as being like dreams, but now he is comparing his body itself to a 'mirage-city', a city that you see but isn't there. It's an optical illusion, a reflection due to the particular condition of the atmosphere. One moment it's there, the next it's gone, like a dream, but more dramatic, because you see the 'mirage city' in your waking state: you can see the towers and spires and walls, and the next instant, it disappears. Milarepa is saying that the human body is like that. Not only experiences in the world are transitory and dream-like; bodies too come and go in the whole process of birth, death, and rebirth.

> *When I think of this, my heart is filled with grief.*
> *Rechungpa, would you not cut off Saṃsāra?*
> *Oh, the more I think of this,*
> *The more I think of Buddha and the Dharma!*

Saṃsāra is the succession of these dream experiences and mirage-city-like bodies, one after the other – constantly coming, constantly going. So Milarepa asks Rechungpa whether he would not like to end this process. In effect he's saying, 'Wake up!'

> *A vicious person can never attain happiness.*
> *Errant thoughts are the cause of all regrets,*
> *Bad dispositions are the cause of all miseries.*
> *Never be voracious, oh Rechungpa,*
> *But listen to my song!*

A 'vicious person' means a person who has many unskilful mental states and acts in accordance with them. Such a person can never attain happiness because unskilful mental states are painful and lead to painful experiences. One only torments oneself in the long run. But in what way are 'errant thoughts' – that is, wandering thoughts – 'the cause of all regrets'? It is because they carry you away from your true interest. You miss what really matters, and that is a cause of regret. The old woman was the victim of errant thoughts – thoughts of greed and miserliness – and if she knew that, she would have cause for regret because due to those thoughts she deprived herself of the opportunity of practising *dāna* and to that extent leading a spiritual life. 'Bad dispositions' probably means *kleśas*, defilements, and 'voracious' means greedy, particularly perhaps with reference to food. Don't forget that Rechungpa has been very hungry and very concerned about getting almsfood.

Milarepa is trying hard to bring Rechungpa to a genuinely serious state of mind, to confront him with the facts of life and try to induce some genuine insights to arise in his mind. He is giving him a very serious object lesson. Consider what Rechungpa has been through: first the hailstorm and the strange happening with the yak-horn, then being refused food by the old woman, and then going back into the tent in the morning and finding the old woman's dead body. At least they had something to eat at this point but then Milarepa made Rechungpa shoulder the corpse of the old woman and carry it quite a distance until they found themselves in the middle of a marsh and Rechungpa put the corpse down. Milarepa pointed his staff at the heart of the old woman and sang Rechungpa this song. The treatment is very drastic indeed.

Rechungpa has been immersing himself in the material world in a one-sided way, and now Milarepa is presenting the other side of worldly existence. Rechungpa has seen the colourful side of religious life: meeting famous teachers and collecting mementoes and being welcomed everywhere, performing Tantric rites and mingling with the lay people. It's as though that has been the religious life, so far as he is concerned. He gave himself away earlier on when he said, 'A man like me should not practise his devotion as an ascetic – one should practise it with pleasure and enjoyment.' Well, he's not getting much pleasure and enjoyment now – with a corpse in the middle of a marsh and Milarepa giving him these drastic teachings. Rechungpa is a good person, he has some genuine spiritual aspiration and genuine devotion to Milarepa, but there's a lot of worldliness still mixed up with it and that has to be purged away. That is what Milarepa is doing in this drastic manner. He manages to make the most of every opportunity. He started with advice and exhortations, but they don't do the trick.; they were just words so far as Rechungpa was concerned. It's life itself that has got to teach him. He has to be involved in actual happenings and to some extent, according to the story, Milarepa creates those happenings, or if he doesn't create them, he foresees what is going to happen or realizes what has happened and makes the fullest use of it.

It's just like when you first get interested in Buddhism. You read books about it and you can quite appreciate a good lecture on transitoriness and maybe even give one yourself, but it doesn't really strike home. But when someone who is near and dear to you dies suddenly or is killed, that's quite a different matter; life itself has started teaching you. Something like that, with the help of Milarepa, has started happening to Rechungpa. He had almost a playboy's conception of religion apparently, even though it was mixed up with a great deal that was genuine. We mustn't overlook the fact that he is quite a spiritually gifted person; he just has a very uneven, unstable personality, and needs to get right down to the bedrock of things, spiritually speaking, needs to develop some real insight. He needs to develop some constancy in his spiritual life, to stop oscillating and gyrating in the way that he has been doing.

He does seem particularly susceptible to worldly temptations. He seems to be a 'greed type', in terms of the usual classification,[203] hence all this emphasis on transitoriness and impermanence, death and decay and the filthiness of the body. That kind of emphasis is meant for that kind of temperament. It's not the whole truth of the matter, but it's the particular aspect to which the attention of people like Rechungpa needs to be drawn, because they're inclined to overlook that side of things. In *The Life of Milarepa* there's an exchange between Milarepa and his rather worldly-minded sister. She says in effect, 'Well, religion is OK but you ought to make something out of it. I don't mind you being a yogi or a hermit or a guru, but you should be like those gurus who have lots of disciples and fine temples and palatial apartments where they can put up their relations.' But Milarepa says, 'I could have these things if I wanted – the beautiful temple and the crowd of attentive disciples, and tea or wine to drink whenever I wanted it – but I do not choose to live that way.'[204] Rechungpa to some extent has had Milarepa's sister's conception of the spiritual life, a successful 'ecclesiastical career', but Milarepa is not having any of that. He doesn't think of spiritual life in those terms.

In the Buddhist East still, a successful monk is one who manages to establish his own vihara, who is well-known to all the local nobility and gentry and received with respect everywhere, who is given a seat of honour on public occasions, has a number of disciples and prominent lay supporters and wears beautiful silk monastic robes. People do know the difference between ecclesiastical success and spiritual attainment, but there's a lot of confusion. Very often nowadays the measure of success for a monk is to become a professor of Pāli in a university. But Milarepa sees the spiritual life in very different terms.

Even the present Kagyupas would find it a little uncomfortable if Milarepa were to come back. There are analogues in the Christian tradition. For example, when Francis Xavier (he wasn't Saint Francis Xavier yet) arrived at Goa, the local ecclesiastics and administrators had laid on a splendid reception and were going to lead him to the governor's palace or somewhere like that, but he just wouldn't go. He went straight to the nearest leper colony and started looking after the lepers. The dignitaries of the church were quite scandalized when they saw him because he was dressed practically in rags, not at all like a respectable priest. They had one idea about the religious life and he had quite another.[205]

I had a similar experience myself in a small way when I once went down from Kalimpong to Calcutta to stay at the Maha Bodhi Society. I was wearing an old robe – perfectly clean, but old and a bit faded, maybe with a patch or two here and there. The head monk, or 'high priest' as he called himself, of the Maha Bodhi Society was quite scandalized. He said, 'Haven't you got a better robe than that to wear?' I said no – it was quite all right as far as I was concerned. He said, 'You shouldn't wear robes like that! What will people think of us?' And he promptly gave me a new robe and insisted I wear it.[206] This is what can very easily happen; you start to evaluate people, even from an ostensibly spiritual point of view, in quite worldly terms: whether they're well-dressed, whether they're educated, whether they're well-spoken, whether they're attractive. It is very easy to be influenced by such factors.

> When I look back at my clinging mind,
> It appears like a short-lived sparrow in the woods –
> Homeless, and with nowhere to sleep;
> When I think of this, my heart is filled with grief.

Here Milarepa is comparing his clinging mind – the mind that has a natural tendency to attach itself to objects and cling on to them – to a short-lived sparrow in the woods, 'homeless and with nowhere to sleep'. But in what sense is the clinging mind homeless? In what sense has it nowhere to sleep? It has no fixed abode, there is nowhere it can settle down safely and comfortably, and anyway, it doesn't live very long. Mental states don't last long, and even while they last, they don't manage to settle down on anything. Presumably Milarepa says 'when I look back at my clinging mind' because he hasn't got a clinging mind any more, but Rechungpa still has. Of course, often the clinging mind thinks it has found its true home and settles down in particular interests or attachments, but it soon discovers that it is not able to settle down for long. It has, in fact, nowhere to sleep.

'When I think of this, my heart is filled with grief.' This has the flavour of insight into *duḥkha*, and there is also a suggestion of compassion for those who are still deluded in this way, and especially Rechungpa.

> *Rechungpa, will you let yourself indulge in ill-will?*
> *Oh, the more I think of this,*
> *The more I aspire to Buddha and the Dharma!*

In this verse there is perhaps an echo of a verse in the *Dhammapada* in which the Buddha says that if one recollects that one is heading for death, one will compose one's quarrels with other people.[207] Milarepa is saying that as the mind is of such a nature that it cannot really settle down in anything, and so short-lived, it isn't worth cherishing ill will or continuing to quarrel with people.

Most religions would seem to offer the mind a fixed abode; that is why one must be careful not to think of the Buddhist refuges as a sort of 'home'. Even the translation 'refuge' has the wrong connotation. The refuges are a refuge only in the way that the top of a mountain is a refuge for the man who is trying to climb the mountain. 'Refuge' translates the Pāli and Sanskrit word *śaraṇa*, and that does literally mean 'refuge'. It is a word in general use, not a specifically religious term, just like our own word 'refuge'. Just as we say 'I found refuge from the storm under the tree', the word *śaraṇa* is used in exactly the same way in Pāli and Sanskrit. As far as we can tell from the Pāli scriptures, when someone was deeply impressed by something that the Buddha had said, and felt complete confidence in the Buddha and wanted to follow his teaching and join his community, he said *Buddhaṃ saraṇaṃ gacchāmi* – 'To the Buddha for refuge I go'. Because people took refuge in the Buddha, the Dharma, and the Sangha – the Three Jewels, as we call them – they came to be called refuges. I prefer to speak of committing oneself to the Three Jewels rather than taking refuge in them because 'commitment' seems closer to the real meaning of *śaraṇa*. 'Refuge' is a literal translation but 'commitment' gives much more of the spirit of the term. The expression 'going for Refuge' sounds as though it's an act which is performed once and for all, whereas to speak in terms of commitment, to say, 'I commit myself to the Buddha, Dharma, and Sangha', makes it much clearer that it is an ongoing process.

The mind has an inveterate tendency to try to settle down somewhere, to try to find some permanent satisfaction, and it usually tries to find it in some kind of mundane object or activity, which means that it doesn't really find it at all. It may find it for a short while, and it may start thinking, 'This satisfaction is going to last for ever', but it doesn't. It very quickly comes to an end – circumstances change.

> *Human life is as precarious*
> *As a single slim hair of a horse's tail*
> *Hanging on the verge of breaking;*
> *It may be snuffed out at any time*
> *Like this old woman was last night!*
> *Do not cling to this life, Rechungpa,*
> *But listen to my song!*

This is a vivid comparison – that human life is as precarious as a single slim hair of a horse's tail hanging on the verge of breaking. A horse has long coarse hairs in its tail and as they rub against one another they may become frayed, so it is only a matter of time before a particular hair detaches itself. Milarepa is saying that human life is just like that – it is hanging by a thread all the time, or less than a thread. Almost everything you come into contact with could kill you. You could trip over a stone; you could choke when eating your lunch; you could be knocked down by a car. Human life is precarious, like the slim hair of a horse's tail on the verge of breaking, and sooner or later it will break. It's not a question of if – it's only a question of when and how. Milarepa is asking Rechungpa just to be aware of the precariousness of human life, reminding him about the old woman who in the evening was so obstreperous and malicious, but who by the next morning was dead and now is going to be buried in the middle of the marsh. Again Milarepa is trying to bring Rechungpa up against the facts of life in the deepest sense.

He continues in the same way:

> *When I observe inwardly my breathings*
> *I see they are transient, like the fog;*
> *They may vanish any moment into nought.*
> *When I think of this, my heart is filled with grief.*

The breath comes in, it goes out, it comes in, it goes out; and at any moment you could breathe out and not breathe in again. Our whole life depends upon this process. It's as frail, as insubstantial as that.

> *Rechungpa, do you not want to conquer*
> *That insecurity now?*

Here Milarepa is referring to the insecurity of life itself. Does Rechungpa not want to overcome that, transcend that, by becoming Enlightened?

> *Oh, the more I think of this*
> *The more I aspire to Buddha and the Dharma.*

When Milarepa sings in this simple but profound way, there is very little to say about it. It's very straightforward, very obvious – there is not even very much of Buddhism, in the technical sense, in it. All you can do with it is remember it and practise it. Sometimes Milarepa sings almost in the language of the Pāli canon, of fundamental things like transience and suffering. There is very little of the Mahāyāna here, and nothing of the Vajrayāna. It's plain straightforward basic Buddhism, as one might call it. Well, it's hardly even Buddhism; it's just common sense. Buddhism, after all, doesn't have a monopoly on transitoriness; it just makes a point of trying to see deeply into it.

> *To be close to wicked kinsmen only causes hatred.*
> *The case of this old woman is a very good lesson.*

Why has Milarepa taken up this topic now? Perhaps it's just that he is singing or speaking to Rechungpa about very basic things. He has reminded him that life is like a dream, that the human body is a bag of dirt and filth, and that it is like a 'mirage-city', doomed to extinction.

He has reminded him that a vicious person can never attain happiness, that the clinging mind is short-lived and homeless and with nowhere to sleep, that human life is precarious and depends upon the breath. And now, in speaking about wicked kinsmen, he is bringing in another basic principle – attachment to those who are near and dear to you, even when they are wicked. You may be attached to your father and mother and your brothers and sisters, but they may not be following the Dharma. They may be just like that old woman. If you live with those who are supposedly near and dear to you, but they are not following the Dharma, what is the good of that? It will only cause hatred in the end. So the case of this old woman is a very good lesson. In a way, she is a typical worldly person.

> Rechungpa, stop your wishful-thinking
> And listen to my song!

The wishful thinking is Rechungpa's desire to go on practising the Dharma in pleasure and enjoyment, his wish to believe that you can practise in a happy-go-lucky sort of way, without truly detaching yourself from the world.

> When I look at friends and consorts
> They appear as passers-by in the bazaar;
> Meeting with them is only temporary,
> But separation is forever!
> When I think of this, my heart is filled with grief.
> Rechungpa, do you not want to cast aside
> All worldly associations?
> Oh, the more I think of this,
> The more I think of Buddha and the Dharma.

Milarepa has spoken about kinsmen, and now he goes on to talk about friends and consorts. 'Consorts' doesn't seem to be a very good translation; perhaps it should be 'friends and companions'. One doesn't usually have more than one 'consort'. The bazaar is a very typical scene in Eastern countries. It's the shopping centre of the town, where people set up their stalls on market days and everybody goes to shop once or twice a week. As you wander from stall to stall you meet friends and usually you stop and have a chat for a minute or two and then pass on. Milarepa is saying that your friends and companions are just like that. The world itself is like a bazaar, or a sort of Vanity Fair.[208] You go there, buying and selling, exchanging this for that, and you happen to meet people, but it's only for a minute or two and then you don't see them again. Life is like that. While you're with people you tend to think it will be forever, but sooner or later you part and it's as though you've been together a very short time. Milarepa therefore asks Rechungpa, 'Do you not want to cast aside all worldly associations?' It's no use getting attached to people and trying to settle down with them. You can be with them for only a very short time, and after that you will never see them again. They may die, or they may go away. 'Oh, the more I think of this, the more I think of Buddha and the Dharma.'

Milarepa is speaking of worldly associations, but the same thing can be applied to spiritual friendships, though in a different way. You don't know how long you will be able to be with your spiritual friends, and it may be for only a very short time, so make the best use of the opportunity. Make sure that your communication with your spiritual friends is clear and honest, and that you develop as positive a relationship as possible, because you may be parted at any time. You shouldn't think that your spiritual friend is going to be around for ever, so there is no need to worry if you haven't seen him for a few weeks. Before you know what has happened he may have gone away to another country, or he may have died.

With regard to 'worldly friends', you can realize that you should not be too attached to them, because you aren't going to have them forever, and if you have been very attached, when you lose them you are going to suffer, quite apart from the fact that if you are attached to worldly friends they may influence you in a way that may hinder your growth and development. But even spiritual friends are not going to be friends forever, in the sense that they will die or go away or you will be separated in some way or other. We need to make the best use of the time that we are able to spend with our spiritual friends. We don't know if we will ever have the opportunity again. What a pity to waste the time talking about trivial things! It's better to try to deepen one's communication and have genuine contact with them.

A rich man seldom enjoys
The wealth that he has earned;
This is the mockery of Karma and Saṃsāra.

A man may be very rich, but there's a limit to what he can eat. He can only drive around in one car at a time. He can only live in one house at a time. He can only swim in one swimming pool at a time. So 'a rich man seldom enjoys the wealth that he has earned'. It's more often than not enjoyed by other people – those who depend on him, those he employs, those who serve him. 'This is the mockery of Karma and Samsāra.'

Money and jewels gained through stinginess and toil
Are like this old woman's bag of food.
Do not be covetous, Rechungpa,
But listen to my song!

In the world people devote a great deal of time and energy to accumulating wealth or getting on in various ways. You might succeed, but when you get there, you find that it's not really what you wanted. It's not as good as you thought it would be; it's as though you've been cheated. Maybe you get to the position that you've been aiming at for many years, but after so much effort and worry and trouble, you're not able to enjoy that position. The old woman denied that she had that bag of food; she thought she'd like to enjoy it herself, perhaps, but she died before she could do that. So Milarepa warns, 'Do not be covetous, Rechungpa, but listen to my song!' Rechungpa has of course shown himself to be covetous in going to India for spiritual 'acquisitions' rather than for opportunities for practice.

When I look at the fortunes of the rich,
They appear to me like honey to the bees –
Hard work, serving only for others' enjoyment,
Is the fruit of their labor.
When I think of this, my heart is filled with grief.

Nowadays you can work very hard and earn a lot of money, but the taxman takes the greater part of that, so you're working for somebody else, not for yourself. You're just like the bee: you work hard all day, flying back and forth, collecting pollen, making honey, but in the end somebody comes along and robs your hive, or at least you may think it's robbery, although the government calls it taxation. So what's the use of it?

> Rechungpa, do you not want to open
> The treasury within your mind?
> Oh, the more I think of this
> The more I aspire to Buddha and His teachings.

Milarepa is sounding quite a different note now, almost a Mahāyānistic note. From speaking about riches, gains, acquisitions, which usually one thinks of in external terms, Milarepa is now reminding Rechungpa that there is a treasury within one's own mind in the form of all the possibilities of spiritual development. It's very strange that people think in terms of developing land, investing their money, even decorating their house, but they don't think in terms of developing themselves. They're concerned about getting the highest possible rate of interest for their money, but what about their own potential? They don't think so much in terms of that. In fact, very often people aren't even aware that they've got potential; the whole idea of human potential for development is quite new to a lot of people. Even if you have an ideal, it has to be an ideal that you recognize as a possibility for you, something that you can actually achieve, actually realize. Enlightenment may be an ideal, but if you don't feel that Enlightenment is something that you can develop, it isn't an ideal for you. It's more like an abstract idea, a theoretical ideal, which is really a contradiction in terms.

> The corpse of the old woman was buried (in the swamp), and
> her soul was delivered to the Dharmadhātu. Thereupon the
> Jetsun and Rechungpa took the edible food with them and set
> out for Betze Duyundzon. This is the second chapter, the story of
> the yak-horn.

How is one to understand that? It could mean that they performed the Tibetan funeral rites, as described in the *Tibetan Book of the Dead*, as we call it. By his spiritual powers Milarepa could have guided her through the *bardo*. There is one thing we shouldn't overlook: the old woman came into contact with Milarepa. She may have been a wicked old woman, she may have been angry and malicious and mean, but she did come into contact with Milarepa. A Tibetan Buddhist might say that she had tucked away somewhere some good karma, on account of which she came into contact with Milarepa, even though she didn't make the best use of the opportunity. Also, by her death she has been the means of enabling Milarepa to teach Rechungpa a good lesson, so perhaps she has earned some merit. Buddhism, especially Mahāyāna Buddhism, takes a charitable view of such cases.

It's true that the idea behind merit is that it is the attitude behind your action that is important, and her attitude wasn't very positive, but she has come into contact with Milarepa, and that must be due to something. Milarepa is a highly developed yogi, maybe he's even Enlightened, and she has come into contact with him. If you take it literally, it seems quite unjust. Here's this wicked old woman – she does seem a quite dreadful character – but she has been delivered to the *dharmadhātu*. I don't know whether we can take this literally or whether it is just a pious hope on the part of the compiler, but Milarepa has performed her funeral ceremony, so we can hope that even the consciousness of a wicked old woman like her can be guided in the direction of the *dharmadhātu*.

The *Tibetan Book of the Dead* suggests that after death one has an experience of the clear light of the Void. If you can recognize it and merge with it, then you gain Enlightenment. It's a crucial opportunity, and the purpose of the lama who performs the ceremony is to remind you of things you perhaps learned in your lifetime, or perhaps which are new to you, to point out to you that the light that you are experiencing is the clear light of your own mind. One should not be afraid of it or shrink back from it; one should allow oneself to enter into it. Under the guidance of the lama, one is able after death perhaps even to achieve Enlightenment. So it is possible that this happened at the moment when the old woman's consciousness was liberated from the physical body. Everybody, according to the Tibetan tradition, has this experience. It's instantaneous in the case of most people, and they can't do anything with the opportunity, they recoil from it and forget it, but subsequently there are experiences of lower degrees of intensity symbolized by the different Buddhas and their families or their mandalas, and if one is able to stay with the experience and not shrink back from it, one can be united with whatever those forms or symbols represent.

It would be possible, according to this teaching, for Milarepa to have guided the old woman's consciousness in this way. Perhaps it was due to past meritorious action that she met Milarepa, died under these circumstances, and was able to be guided by him. Whether one can take it that she gained final deliverance is another matter; perhaps she just had a very positive experience, with Milarepa's help, which helped her in her next incarnation. But anyway, this is the general background of belief.

7

AN EXPERIENCE POWERFUL
LIKE A SHARP KNIFE

Later, while the father Jetsun and the son Rechungpa were resident
at Betze, Rechungpa gained great improvement in his meditation.
In an Experience of great joy, numerous thoughts appeared in
his mind. Being aware of this, the Jetsun said, 'Rechungpa, what
have you experienced in your meditation lately?' In relating his
Experiences, Rechungpa sang:

Living with my Guru, I had
An Experience powerful like a sharp knife;
With it I have cut inner and outer deceptions.
Because of this I am happy and gay!

In the midst of many manifestations,
I felt as if I were a radiant lamp;
All instructions thus became clearer than ever before.
Because of this, I am happy and gay!

When I sat on the peak of a snow mountain,
I felt like a white lioness,
Predominating and surpassing all others in the world.
Because of this, I feel happy and gay!

When I dwelt on the hillside of Red Rock,
I felt as if I were a majestic eagle;
Forever have I conquered
The fearful expanse of the sea.
Because of this, I am happy and gay!

When I roamed from country to country
I felt as if I were a tiger cub, or a bee –
Non-attached to all and utterly free.
Because of this, I am happy and gay!

When I mingled with people in the street,
I felt as if I were an immaculate lotus
Standing above all filth and mud.
Because of this, I am happy and gay!

When I sat among crowds in the town,
I felt as if I were like rolling mercury –
It touches all but adheres to nought.
Because of this, I feel happy and gay!

When I sat among faithful disciples,
I felt as if I were the Jetsun Mila;
With cheer and ease I gave instructions through songs!
It is the blessing of my Guru
That brings me this joy.
It is through resting one's mind at ease
That Buddhahood is realized.

Now at last the lesson given to Rechungpa by Milarepa has really sunk in.

> In an experience of great joy, numerous thoughts appeared in his mind.

What sort of experience does Rechungpa seem to be having? Perhaps the translation 'thoughts' may not be very accurate; maybe they are not just thoughts but actual insight experiences. Milarepa raises this question indirectly. Clearly there is an experience of great joy and exuberance, as a result of which there are all sorts of reflections, ideas, and possibly insights. There's a great rush of intuitions, one could say, which may be discursive thoughts of a refined kind or insights. In any case, Milarepa asks Rechungpa to tell him about them, and the first thing he says is:

> *Living with my Guru, I had*
> *An Experience powerful like a sharp knife*

He seems to be claiming that insight has arisen. To describe it as being powerful like a sharp knife suggests a definite, tangible, clear-cut experience – we might even say a sharp experience, an unmistakable experience. Some experiences are vague, hazy, dream-like, misty, but this one is very definite. There can be no mistake about it.

> *With it I have cut inner and outer deceptions.*
> *Because of this I am happy and gay!*

The inner deceptions are all sorts of unskilful mental attitudes, unskilful passions, whereas the outer deceptions are the deceptions of so-called external objects, as when you think of external objects as ultimately real, fixed, unchanging, and so on, so perhaps Rechungpa is saying that he has realized that there is no permanent unchanging soul within, and no permanent unchanging thing without.

> *In the midst of many manifestations,*
> *I felt as if I were a radiant lamp*

The image of the radiant lamp is reminiscent of the Pāli scriptures' description of the fourth *dhyāna*, in which you are insulated from all outside influences.[209] You are influencing external things, but they are not influencing you. Usually we are bombarded by all sorts of influences which all too often have an unfortunate effect on us, but when we meditate, we generate very powerful, positive, skilful states, on the basis of which we start taking the initiative, we become active rather than passive. We become not only positive but bright; not only bright, but clear. We are no longer under the influence of the things that surround us; they, in a manner of speaking, are under our influence. We are like the radiant lamp dispelling the darkness. In the light of that radiant lamp, there is a heightened positivity, a stronger experience of individuality. You don't feel so crushed and overwhelmed by the world. You feel more powerful than your surroundings. The lamp is not overwhelmed by the darkness.

It is not possible to function in the world while in the higher *dhyānas* in the sense of walking about and talking with other people. You may not even be conscious of the physical body in that state. What you have to do, on the basis of your *śamatha*, is develop transcendental insight. This nsight does not come and go; it is permanent, and once you have gained it, you don't need to retain the *dhyāna* state, and you can move about in the world without being affected by it. Even *dhyāna* experience, highly developed state though it is, doesn't protect you from outside influence in that way because it is dependent upon favourable conditions. Insight permanently destroys unskilful mental states, whereas the *dhyānas* only temporarily suspend them. That is the difference. Insight cuts at the very roots of greed, hatred, and ignorance. When you are in the *dhyānas*, you have temporarily removed yourself from those unskilful mental states, but when you are again in contact with very powerful stimuli, they can return. Insight is another kind of state altogether – a higher state, one could say – and it permanently affects your character regardless of the experiences that befall you. If you have insight, a painful experience may still happen to you, but you will not react to that experience with anger, hatred or impatience, so you will remain in a higher state of consciousness. You feel the pain or suffering but it's quite peripheral; you're not disturbed by it because you are so strongly centred that it can't throw you off balance. The experience of suffering will not give rise to unskilful mental states, and that is all you are really concerned about. If the insight is sufficiently developed, you become incapable of allowing unskilful mental states to arise. The root has been entirely destroyed. So if you want to be able to move about in the world without succumbing to its various temptations and stimuli, you need to develop insight. *Dhyāna* states are not enough, because they can protect you only so long as you are living under those conditions which enable you to develop them.

It is true that the greater one's insight, the easier it is to get into *dhyāna* states, because according to tradition you are prevented from entering *dhyāna* states by the five hindrances,[210] and they essentially amount to craving and aversion. The more insight you have, the less craving and aversion you have. Once insight has arisen, you can go into the *dhyānas* whenever you have the opportunity, when you're not having to concern yourself with practical matters or talk to people, when you are just quiet and by yourself. An Enlightened person like the Buddha or Milarepa will spontaneously go into a *dhyāna* state whenever chance allows, because there's nothing to prevent them. Even in a quite ordinary way, if you have nothing to do and no one to see and you are in a calm, peaceful state of mind, as soon as you are left to yourself, you can just enjoy that calm, peaceful state of mind. Insight is the fundamental thing, and *dhyāna* states are secondary, but if you have developed insight, the *dhyāna* states will come naturally when conditions permit, almost without your making an effort.

Is it easier to gain insight having had some experience of *dhyāna*? Well, what enables one to have transcendental insight, and in what way does this insight differ from ordinary intellectual understanding? The only difference is that when insight arises, all the energies of one's being are behind it, which suggests that those energies have been unified; and that kind of unification is most likely to take place as a result of meditation. Meditation, in the sense of *śamatha*, is the bringing together of all the mundane energies, so that when you start reflecting upon, say, impermanence, you understand it with your whole being, and because you understand it with your whole being, your whole being is transformed.

It isn't a matter of course for someone who can get into the *dhyānas* to gain insight, because they may not know that there is such a state to be developed, but within the Buddhist tradition it is very well-known indeed. It is said that having experienced the *dhyānas*, you apply your mind to the development of insight by reflecting upon such topics as impermanence or no-self or *śūnyatā*, or the Buddha, which provides a base, an object, for the development of insight. In order to do that, you have to come down to the first *dhyāna*, where mental activity is possible. But the mental activity that you take up is of quite a different nature from that which is not preceded by an experience of the *dhyānas*. It's not scattered or undirected. It isn't necessary to go right through the four *dhyānas* and back before you work on developing insight, but that is the best way. Usually in a complete practice of meditation you alternate between trying to develop insight and experiencing the *dhyānas*. You experience the *dhyānas* for a while, or at least you have a good meditation; then you reflect on impermanence, on no-self or the *nidānas*, and try to develop insight. After a while your mind may become tired or you may feel that your reflections are becoming just intellectual; you may sense that the *dhyāna* experience is fading away and your attention is becoming scattered. At that point you go back to the practice of *śamatha*, and then, having established *śamatha* again, you go back to the *vipaśyanā*. This is the usual procedure.

There might be a resistance for someone who is in a higher *dhyāna* state to come back and start reflecting. You might not want to start up the mental activity which becomes a basis for the development of insight because *dhyāna* experiences are very pleasurable and one can become attached to them. A teacher like Milarepa would warn someone like Rechungpa not to linger in the *dhyānas*. If you have achieved the *dhyāna* experience, it's time you started developing insight, even though in order to do that you have to come down a little in the *dhyāna* scale.

It is said that greed types find it harder to gain insight than hate types because hate types have an affinity with wisdom – wisdom being more or less the same thing as insight. A greed type is more inclined to linger over or become attached to any pleasurable experience, including that of the *dhyānas*. Of course, hate types might not be able to get into the *dhyānas* at all because their minds are so disturbed by hatred. And deluded types sometimes behave like the greed type and sometimes like the hate type – that's why they're deluded, they're not fixed. In some ways they have the best of both worlds, and in some ways the worst. They find it difficult to get into the *dhyānas* and once they get into them, they find it difficult to get out![211]

There are insight-type reflections to be applied to the *dhyānas* themselves. One starts reflecting that these *dhyānas* are not the ultimate attainment. They arise in dependence on conditions and cease when those conditions are no longer there. You can reflect: 'It is not *dhyāna* experience that I am after. I am concerned with Enlightenment, and in order to gain Enlightenment, I will have to develop insight.' In that way one can make the transition from the *dhyānas* to insight: by reflecting on the *dhyānas* themselves and their limitations. You may be able to initiate some reflection of this kind even in the high *dhyāna* states, or you may need some external help in the sense of the teacher or the tradition reminding you. It may be that before entering into the *dhyāna* state you understood very clearly that such states are not the be-all and the end-all of spiritual life, so after you've been in the *dhyāna* state for a while, the thought may occur to you, based on your previous reading and understanding, 'Perhaps I should now be developing insight'. There is a sort of interruption, a positive distraction, if one can use that expression.

A serious ideal for every Buddhist is to become a Stream Entrant. Your experience of insight will build up depending on the strength of the meditation behind it, but once you've developed insight, you never lose it. If you die a Stream Entrant, you will be reborn as a Stream Entrant. And a Stream Entrant is someone who has broken the first three fetters – well, they are enumerated as three fetters, but they are really three different aspects of the same experience. To begin with, your insight might not be powerful enough to break the first three fetters. It's like when you start saving money to buy a new car. Even when you haven't saved enough to buy the car, you have the money you've saved so far. In the same way, your insight may not yet be powerful enough to break through the three fetters, but some degree of insight is there. It is building up, and the time will come when it will be strong enough to have that sort of effect. Or – to change metaphor – it's like sawing through a branch of a tree. You may have sawn through a few inches and nothing happens, the branch doesn't fall, but after you've sawn three-quarters of the way through, the branch starts falling under its own weight. Similarly, you can't fall back from a limited experience of insight. Even if you don't add to it for the time being, it's still there and you can add to it in the future.

There is quite a discussion in the medieval Buddhism of the Sarvāstivādin school about this intermediate state. You're not a complete worldling, but on the other hand, you're not definitely an *ārya*. The technical term is *gotrabhū*, which literally means 'one who has entered the lineage (of the Noble Ones, *āryas*)'[212] – because you have to some extent determined your spiritual family. You are definitely going to be a Stream Entrant because you have already accumulated some insight, but it isn't yet fully operative to the extent of breaking those first three fetters, so as actually to make you a Stream Entrant. The general position is that insight, once developed, cannot be lost, even though it hasn't been developed to the point where it can break those first three fetters.

It is said that before becoming a Stream Entrant, one can still fall back; that is, to the extent that unskilful mental states have not been permanently eliminated, they can reappear at any time. Even once you have broken the three fetters, there are still the subtle unskilful mental states to be removed. But once you've developed some insight, even if you haven't yet broken the first three fetters, your unskilfulness will not go beyond a certain point. You have already started to limit it, and there has been a permanent change in your being. The comparison sometimes given is that once the banana plant has been cut, it doesn't sprout again. Once you've cut the root of craving, it doesn't spring up again.

'Cutting the root of craving' means seeing through it so clearly and definitely that you can't be fooled any longer. For instance, you might have a sexual partner to whom you are very attached, and then one day you might hear that he or she has been unfaithful to you. Your attachment is disturbed a bit, but your lover tells you some story and you see no reason not to believe it, so the relationship persists. But then one day you may see clear evidence of infidelity with your own eyes, and then you see through the situation and your attachment completely ceases. You've seen through all the lies and pretence of affection, and you can never again be affected by that person in the way you used to be. It's rather like that. We say 'in-sight', which suggests seeing into, but it is more like seeing through – seeing through something so completely that you can no longer be taken in by it. That does sometimes happen, even in everyday life. Maybe you believe that someone is honest and then he cheats you a few times and after that you never trust him again. It's like that with existence. You've seen through it. It might appear to be permanent, but really it's impermanent, and once you've seen through it in that respect, once you've had insight into the truth of impermanence, you are no longer fooled by it, and you don't place your trust in it any more. In that way, your being is transformed by your insight.

It isn't absolutely the case that insight can only arise during meditation. Insight arises in consequence of all one's energies being united, and this usually happens in the course of what we call meditation, but one must be careful to distinguish the reality from the name. When all your energies are united, you are meditating. You may not have adopted the formal meditation posture; you may not be sitting with closed eyes in the shrine-room. You could be just sitting under a tree somewhere, not even thinking of meditating, but you could be very concentrated. All your energies are unified and flowing together, and then you start thinking about something seriously. Under those conditions, insight can develop. Insight can arise in dependence upon intellectual activity, and sometimes it happens that if your energies are naturally unified, even apart from formal meditation, and there is a high degree of concentration behind your intellectual activity, you see things as they really are. Some people are drawn into the spiritual life as a result of an understanding of that sort, almost amounting to a degree of insight. Alternatively, you might be driven blindly by the experience of suffering, without any understanding or intellectual sense of direction at all. Some people walk away from *saṃsāra* and bump into *nirvāṇa*, and other people walk towards *nirvāṇa*. There is the faith type, who is attracted by the beauty of the ideal especially as embodied in the Buddha, rather than repelled by the ugliness of *saṃsāra*. He turns his back on *saṃsāra* and, attracted by the ideal, hardly realizes he is leaving *saṃsāra* behind. Somebody else tries very hard to get away from *saṃsāra* and in doing so 'backs into' the ideal, and then turns around and recognizes it. One could say that the type that is attracted to the Unconditioned is the greed type, and the type that is repelled by *saṃsāra* is the hate type. But you're repelled by *saṃsāra* because you see its imperfections. You see through it, and that is insight.

All instructions thus became clearer than ever before.

When one is immersed in the *dhyānas*, one's experience is of intense positivity, clarity, and awareness, on account of which one understands the Dharma, 'all instructions', better and more clearly than before. It's as though a *vipaśyanā*-like element starts entering into the experience.

> *When I sat on the peak of a snow mountain,*
> *I felt like a white lioness,*
> *Predominating and surpassing all others in the world.*
> *Because of this, I feel happy and gay!*

This verse seems to suggest that Rechungpa has had a spiritual experience and now his ego is grabbing onto it. When he says, 'I felt as if I were a radiant lamp', that seems to be a completely genuine experience. There doesn't seem to be anything of ego there. But when he says, 'I felt like a white lioness, predominating and surpassing all others in the world', that does suggest a kind of ego. In a way it's natural. He has developed a clearer mind than people usually have, and he can't help being conscious of that, and a subtle ego-sense has become attached to the experience. We'll find Milarepa having something to say about that a little later on.

If your experience is very positive, if you become very exuberant and joyful, if you start having all sorts of brilliant ideas, there is a tendency to become intoxicated and get carried away, and then you start losing your mindfulness. We used to notice this on our early retreats. Sometimes people would arrive quite stiff and blocked and then in the course of a few days they would start relaxing, become more at ease, more open, more communicative, more talkative, and things would start to get a bit out of hand, especially at mealtimes. There would be a lot of shouting and loud conversation and a lot of general hilarity and fooling around, people racing up and down the corridors. Silence would be imposed for a day or two and things would calm down, but then people tended to go back to their original blocked state. We learned that we had to maintain a careful balance, so that people's energies were freed but didn't get out of hand. When people become happy and cheerful, for some of them it's such a new experience that it rather goes to their heads. They become almost intoxicated and their mindfulness starts slipping. One has to watch this very carefully. You can even get carried away by your meditative experience: 'Oh, what good meditations I'm having! I'm really happy! Life is so good!' You can make too much of it and start thinking, 'I'm in this state and other people aren't. I'm doing better than they are. I'm so much more positive. All these people haven't got much energy, but look at me, look at all the energy I've got....'

Rechungpa seems to have got into a refined form of this kind of egoistically tinged state. His happiness and gaiety have taken on not exactly a hysterical note, but an over-emphatic note, one might say. One has to watch that. One has to remain calm, and not allow even highly positive blissful experiences to 'lay hold of one's mind', as the Buddha puts it.[213] Don't let them throw you off balance. It's the same with negative states. If you don't feel very well or very cheerful, if you feel a bit depressed, you can start feeling as though it's the end of the world. On the other hand, you can feel positive and elated, and start saying to yourself, 'I'm practically there, spiritually speaking.' In both cases, you're exaggerating, over-dramatizing.

This isn't just a temperamental thing. Most people go through these experiences in their own way. If your normal experience has been that life is rather miserable, when you start feeling happy and cheerful it will tend to go to your head. If you're the sort of person who usually experiences himself as rather weak and powerless then when, as a result of practising meditation, you start feeling more energetic, that sort of experience may go to your head. Or if you have been someone who doesn't like other people very much, when you start feeling *mettā* you might start feeling sentimental and lovey-dovey, and almost swamping people with your love.

> *When I dwelt on the hillside of Red Rock,*
> *I felt as if I were a majestic eagle;*
> *Forever have I conquered*
> *The fearful expanse of the sea.*
> *Because of this I am happy and gay!*

By 'the fearful expanse of the sea' Rechungpa is probably referring to *saṃsāra*, the sea of birth and death and rebirth. But to have 'conquered' *saṃsāra*, he would have to be Enlightened, which he may or may not be: we shall see what Milarepa has to say. Perhaps it's an overstatement on his part. He is beginning to get on top of things, but probably not quite to that extent. Again, this is a common experience. You overcome one or two obstacles and you feel you've overcome them all; but there may be further obstacles awaiting you on the path.

> *When I roamed from country to country*
> *I felt as if I were a tiger cub, or a bee –*
> *Non-attached to all and utterly free.*
> *Because of this, I am happy and gay!*

Is this how Rechungpa really roamed from country to country – 'non-attached to all and utterly free'? Apparently not, from what we've gathered from this and other chapters. He's painting a rosier picture of his spiritual life to date than is really justified, it seems. And then he goes even further:

When I mingled with people in the street,
I felt as if I were an immaculate lotus
Standing above all filth and mud.
Because of this, I am happy and gay!

You sometimes find when you come off a retreat and go back into the city that this is very much how you feel. You feel quite insulated – quite apart, quite separate, quite different in a positive way. It usually doesn't last long, because it's based on a *dhyāna* experience, or a diffused *dhyāna* experience as one might call it, not on insight, but it lasts for a while – some days, even a few weeks. It can be notable for the lack of any element of compassion. You find the simile of the lotus blooming in the midst of the mire even in the *Dhammapada*,[214] and this is to some extent one's experience sometimes, but one has to be careful not to start looking down on other people as the 'filth and mud'.

When I sat among crowds in the town,
I felt as if I were like rolling mercury –
It touches all but adheres to nought.
Because of this, I feel happy and gay!

One would guess that this probably wasn't quite how Rechungpa behaved when he was among crowds in the town, but anyway, that's how he feels now, on his mountain peak, in his cave. He is in a way antedating the experience. From these verses we can tell that he is experiencing something, there's no doubt about that, but he's tending to be somewhat taken over by it, a bit intoxicated by his own experience.

When I sat among faithful disciples,
I felt as if I were the Jetsun Mila;
With cheer and ease I gave instructions through songs!
It is the blessing of my guru
That brings me this joy.

In these lines he is almost claiming – or at least suggesting – that he's pretty near Buddhahood. He feels as though he's like Milarepa himself; he's practically attained whatever Milarepa has attained.

> *It is through resting one's mind at ease*
> *That Buddhahood is realized.*

'Resting one's mind at ease', as if it's not a struggle, is an important aspect of the Mahāmudrā teaching or practice: one aims to relax completely, which is a very difficult thing to do. It's analogous to the 'just sitting' practice.[215] You don't try, you don't make any effort, because in a sense there's nothing to make an effort for. It's all there – you have it already. People are so far from even the ordinary experience of relaxation that talking about ultimate spiritual experience in terms of relaxation becomes almost meaningless. We can generally only think of following the path in terms of struggle and effort and overcoming obstacles, and all those comparisons hold good, but only to the extent that we take time as real. All effort takes place within time. From the standpoint of the Mahāmudrā all craving is of the nature of tension and non-craving is of the nature of relaxation, so as you get rid of craving, you get rid of tension, you relax. One could therefore speak not so much in terms of getting rid of craving as of just relaxing. Don't go in pursuit of pleasure or gain; don't go in pursuit of ambition. Don't go in pursuit of anything. Relax! This is very much the approach of the Mahāmudrā.

This emphasis is not one that most people need: many people are in a sluggish state most of the time and need to get their energies moving. Had I spoken of relaxing in the early days of our movement, this would have been the very thing that people wanted to hear, and they would have relaxed in the sense of subsiding into sloth and torpor and laziness. I can remember the days when I walked into the Pundarika centre in Balmore Street and I had to step over the bodies of people lying around on the floor. Many of our friends were hippies and thought that taking drugs was the quick and easy way, and that you didn't have to bother meditating. When people are making an incredible effort, that is the time to emphasize relaxation, but not before. But one does need a balance. It's good to think of the spiritual life in terms of both of the two great images of the Buddhist tradition: the path, which implies time, and the mandala, which implies space. The 'just sitting' practice is very important in this respect, if you can do it. It's very difficult; most people, when they're supposed to be 'just sitting', fall back on some particular meditation practice. They know that if they try to 'just sit' – well, of course you can't try to do it, that's the point – their minds go wandering, so they fall back on the Mindfulness of Breathing or reciting a mantra. It's best to have a period of 'just sitting' after a couple of sessions of some specific meditation practice; it isn't really possible to go straight into it.

The introduction before the song says that 'Rechungpa gained great improvement in his meditation' and it's clear from his song that he has been making great progress – but there are some unskilful elements nonetheless.

8

AWAKENED FROM A GREAT DREAM

The Jetsun commented, 'If not brought out by pride, these
Experiences are fine; and you have truly received your Guru's
blessings. Toward such Experiences, however, one needs certain
understandings, in which you still seem to be lacking. Now listen
to my song.'

By pointing out that Rechungpa lacks certain understandings towards
his experiences, Milarepa is suggesting that there is no depth of insight,
and it is this that Rechungpa now needs to develop. So Milarepa sings
this song, which is very important:

From the depths of my heart, when the great Compassion arose,
I felt that all beings in the Three Realms
Were enslaved in a prison of fire.

When the Instructions of the Lineage
Were imbibed in my heart,
As the dissolving of salt into water,
I experienced thorough absorption.

When the Wisdom shone bright from within,
I felt as if awakened from a great dream –

I was awakened from both the main and ensuing Samādhis;
I was awakened from both 'yes' and 'no' ideas.

When one secures the great bliss through Viewing,
He feels all Dharmas spontaneously freed
As mists of rain vanish into air.

When one comes to the Essence of Being,
The shining Wisdom of Reality
Illumines all like the cloudless sky.

When both pure and impure thoughts are cleared,
As in a silver mirror,
The immanent bright Wisdom shines forth.

When the Ālaya consciousness dissolves into the Dharmakāya,
I feel my body and soul break forth
Like the crushing of an egg when stamped upon.

When the rope of clinging is cut loose,
I feel the existence of Bardo disappear
Like the uncoiling of a snake.

When I act without taking or leaving,
My mind is always at ease and non-doing.
I feel as if I were a lion,
With the power of the Three Perfections.

The Illuminating Voidness, the Illuminating Wisdom,
And the Illuminating Manifestations
Are my three inseparable friends;
Like the sun shining from a cloudless sky,
I am always in the Great Illumination.
Like dividing the horses from the yaks,
The (outer) world and the senses are clearly distinct (from
    the inner).
The string of mind and Skandhas is forever cut!

Having fully utilized this human form,
I have now completed all Yoga matters.
Rechungpa, do you also have these Experiences?
Oh, my son, do not be proud and presumptuous!

> From the depths of my heart, when the great Compassion
>   arose,
> I felt that all beings in the Three Realms
> Were enslaved in a prison of fire.

The difference between Milarepa's song and Rechungpa's is made clear
in the very first verse, in which Milarepa's compassionate awareness of
others is made plain. He feels not just compassion, but great compassion,
compassion in the transcendental sense, united with or inseparable from
transcendental wisdom, compassion which is the emotional counterpart
of wisdom.

In the *Perfection of Wisdom in Eight Thousand Lines*, one of the
questions raised is how one can know an irreversible bodhisattva.[216] On
the Mahāyāna path, the bodhisattva path, irreversibility is equivalent
to Stream Entry on the Theravāda path, and in order to become an
irreversible bodhisattva, you have to develop wisdom in the distinctively
Mahāyāna sense. So how is one to recognize an irreversible bodhisattva?
Various answers are given, but one of them is that if an irreversible
bodhisattva is asked a question about the Dharma, in his reply he will
always bring in compassion. If he left compassion out, it would indicate
that his wisdom was not true wisdom in the Mahāyāna sense, and he
was not in fact an irreversible bodhisattva. From the Mahāyāna point
of view, compassion must be there all along the way. To the extent that
there is wisdom, there will be compassion. The one is the counterpart of
the other. Putting the matter in conceptual terms, one speaks in terms
of wisdom; putting the thing in emotive terms, one speaks in terms of
compassion. They are one and the same thing, looked at from different
points of view.

The image in this verse reminds one of the *White Lotus Sūtra*, but
here it's not only a house on fire, but a prison of fire.[217] In the light
of his wisdom and compassion, Milarepa sees all beings in the three
realms as being in a pitiable state of slavery. The three realms are the
kāmaloka or *kāmadhātu*, the *rūpaloka*, and the *arūpaloka*: that is to

say, the world or plane of sensuous desire, the world of form, and the formless world or formless plane. The *rūpaloka* and the *arūpaloka* are comparatively refined, but in comparison with Enlightenment, they're painful, because they are conditioned. One way to understand this is that they are potentially painful because you can lose them. But also, even while you are experiencing their blissful nature, in comparison with the bliss of Enlightenment that bliss is painful. How can that be? Put it this way: if you are a child playing with your toys, it can be an intensely blissful experience, but if a grown man was made to go back and play with those toys, how would he feel? It's the same with someone who is Enlightened. Every comparison has its limitations, obviously, but if it was at all possible for him to go back and just play around with the *dhyānas*, that would be a painful and limiting experience for him because he has experienced so much more. Any conditioned experience in comparison with the Unconditioned is unsatisfactory. Perhaps 'unsatisfactory' is a better term than 'painful', or at least more acceptable to us. You can even get tired of *dhyāna* experiences after a while. Even in an ordinary way, pleasant worldly experiences start to pall after a while.

Milarepa hits the nail on the head straightaway, bringing in compassion and by implication bringing in wisdom as well. There's a reference to the unsatisfactory nature of the whole of conditioned existence, to all sentient beings and their unsatisfactory condition, and by implication to the bodhisattva ideal. There's a lot in this little verse. Milarepa is in a sense referring to the arising of the *bodhicitta*, because when with compassion one sees beings suffering in this way, one will want to do something about it, one will want to help. Unless one has something of that feeling, one won't really want to do anything to help people. You won't try to bring the Dharma to people's notice unless you see and feel they really need it. If you think, 'They're getting on all right without it. It would be a pleasant optional extra', you're not going to be very strongly motivated to bring it to their attention. There's another song of Milarepa's about how young men need the Dharma, old men need the Dharma, young women need the Dharma, old women need it, children need it, and so on.[218] Everybody needs the Dharma. They need the Dharma because they're in a very difficult existential position. Their lives are very cramped, very unrewarding, without possibility of development. People need the Dharma very badly, whether they realize it or not, and if one really feels that, one will do everything that one possibly can to make it available to them.

Is it possible to see all beings as living in a 'prison of fire', but then for no compassion to arise? It depends what one means by 'seeing'. You can open your newspaper any day of the week and see that people have been killed in plane crashes, earthquakes, floods, and wars, so you are aware of what has happened, but that can't be described as really seeing that all those people have died in that way. If you really see, you really feel. The two things are inseparable. Really seeing what is going on has an intellectual aspect and also an emotional aspect – a *prajñā* aspect and a compassion aspect. Perhaps 'seeing' is not quite the right word, because seeing is associated with the eyes, but this is really about feeling. Milarepa doesn't say, 'I *saw* that all beings in the three realms were enslaved in a prison of fire'; he sings, 'I *felt* that all beings ...' It's not just an objective understanding, it's something very much more than that. By using the expression 'from the depths of my heart' he suggests that his whole being is involved in the experience. A distinction is usually made between great compassion and compassion, or great love, great *maitrī*, and *maitrī*. *Mahā*, great, indicates an experience of *śūnyatā*, of the Void or reality or insight – wisdom along with the emotional experience of compassion. This is where 'great compassion' differs from compassion in the ordinary sense. There is an element of insight there as well; in fact it goes even further than that. What one speaks of as the great compassion from one point of view is from another point of view the great wisdom.

It is said that a bodhisattva feels compassion but at the same time he realizes that there's no one to feel compassion towards. So what does his compassion consist in? Surely he won't feel compassionate towards beings if he sees that they don't really exist? It's not that beings are not actually there. He sees them – but how is one to describe the bodhisattva's experience? We've only got the words that have been developed to refer to purely mundane experience. You could say that a bodhisattva sees beings, but not in the way that we see them, or you could say that he doesn't see beings at all. Both statements would be equally true. You could say that he sees suffering but doesn't attribute it to any beings, but suffering is something felt or experienced, and from our point of view at least there can't be an experience without someone who experiences it.

In this little verse we see where in principle the 'growth movement' differs from Buddhism,[219] participation in the growth movement tending to be concerned with individual development without that consciousness of other people's needs, that element of compassion. We mustn't be too growth-oriented in a one-sided, subjective or precious way. You can become precious about your own development. It can even become a bit of a rationalization: 'Oh, I don't think I want to do that – it'll get in the way of my development.' In the end, your development comes to mean something like 'whatever you find agreeable', and you start saying that holidays abroad and cultural expeditions to museums and art galleries are all part of your spiritual development, and in that way justified. Sometimes they are, but you have to be vigilant. The growth movement, though useful in some ways, has also been responsible for a lot of intellectual confusion and some very one-sided emphases. Of course, one is not necessarily genuinely altruistic in the Mahāyāna sense just because one is concerned with other people. Doctors are often very altruistic people, but it's possible to regard even becoming a doctor like entering into any other kind of business: you become a doctor to earn money, not to alleviate human suffering.

This raises the whole question of one's motive for engaging in Dharma activities. There can really be only one motivation: compassion, a desire to help, a desire to make the Dharma available to those who need it. Sometimes one hears people say, 'I think one day I'll start up a Buddhist centre. I think it would be good for me to have that responsibility. It would stretch me and help me in my personal development.' There is a danger of coming to see helping others primarily as a way of helping yourself. Of course you have to have a genuine concern for yourself and do the best you can for yourself, but you also have to think in terms of helping others, seeing the two as inseparably interconnected. You must help yourself both for your own sake and so that you can help others, and help others for their own sake – not just so that by helping others you can be helped. Helping others so that you can help yourself is a way of getting started, but you can't really help others unless you make them an end in themselves. For instance, if someone is very upset and they need a listening ear, but it's late at night and you realize that if you stay up talking to them you may miss your meditation in the morning, you may have to let go of the meditation. You can't really help people if you're going to think exclusively in terms of your own interests, even the interests of your personal development. Helping others may help you as well, but that shouldn't be your motivation for helping. So long as you are within the subject–object framework, the object – the other person – is as real as the subject – that is to say, you. The more you forget about yourself the better, though if you've got a Christian background you have to watch out for the danger of latching on to a sense of martyrdom, self-sacrifice, or 'do-gooding'. You cannot help others as a substitute for helping yourself. But when you do help others, you must help them, not do it just as an indirect way of helping yourself. That is the main point. At least for the time being, you completely forget about yourself. At the same time, you're not helping others in order to avoid having to work on yourself. Within our own movement as a whole we are probably still too growth-oriented and not sufficiently other-oriented. We don't think sufficiently yet in terms of going out and helping others, especially in the sense of making the Dharma available to them by setting up more centres, bringing out more publications, organizing more lectures. People tend to think in terms of doing these things provided they fit in with the things they find personally agreeable or useful.

It's true that you need a solid base, but if you think that, are you working on creating that solid base? If you are not careful, you'll tend to settle down in a reasonably comfortable community, working for a not particularly demanding right livelihood business, and in your spare time engaging in some agreeable cultural activities, but not really either working on yourself in a radical way or committing yourself to helping others in a radical way. For a lot of people it could be a useful practice to suspend thoughts of their own development and try objectively to put themselves at the disposal of others, provided that is genuine, and not simply a way of escaping from the demands of self-development. Not many people think in terms of giving themselves completely to the situation. Sometimes people are reluctant to attend a meeting or class at the Buddhist centre or to circulate and talk to new people; they'd rather spend the evening quietly somewhere, or go to see a film, because their feeling for the needs of others is not yet sufficiently strong. If you are spending the evening getting on with your meditation, that's different, but even then, if you're a regular meditator, you could sometimes sacrifice your extra meditation for the sake of making contact with people who could be helped. If you have a strong sense of all the people around who haven't heard of the Dharma and could be benefited by it, you will be strongly motivated to try to make it available to them, and in that way the Buddhist movement will spread very rapidly. If it isn't spreading as rapidly as it could, it's a sign that people aren't motivated enough. There are thousands of people almost on your doorstep who could benefit from contact with Buddhism. You have time for so many things, why not for this?

You have to be discriminating. You can feel sorry for people who come along, realizing that their needs are very great, but you don't always have the skills to be able to meet those needs. It is a question of whether what people need is really the Dharma. People have a lot of needs and one would like to meet them all, but that may not be possible. In some places there are people who are starving, and we'd like to alleviate that suffering but we don't have the resources. Sometimes people come along to a Buddhist centre in need of psychological or even psychiatric help, and we're not in a position to provide that. Since we have a limited amount of time and energy, we have to invest it, so to speak, where it will really do some good – not expend it trying to help people who are beyond our power to help.

To find out whether you are involving yourself with other people's needs as a way of escaping from the demands of your self-development, ask your spiritual friends. If they know you well, and know what meditation and other spiritual practices you are doing, and they say, 'Look, it would be really useful if you could spend the evening helping out', you can follow their advice. If it's the suggestion of your own mind, you are right to be a bit suspicious.

> When the Instructions of the Lineage
> Were imbibed in my heart,
> As the dissolving of salt into water,
> I experienced thorough absorption.

The Instructions of the Lineage are the Pith-Instructions of the Kagyu tradition, given to Milarepa by his guru Marpa personally, so he's saying in effect that the words of the guru were imbibed in his heart. When you put salt into water, because the salt consists of tiny granules, it is dissolved instantly. This simile for the way in which Milarepa imbibed the guru's instructions suggests that he was very receptive, very open. As soon as he heard the guru's instructions he received them into his heart and assimilated them, and that is quite an extraordinary thing. Usually people offer up initial resistance that might last for some time. You mull things over, turn them over in your mind, think about the teachings and gradually absorb them. Milarepa's experience seems to have been quite different. He was a quite extraordinary man, even as a disciple. Probably absorption stands for the *dhyānas*, though this isn't made explicit, or perhaps there's a touch of insight experience, but whatever it is, Milarepa was so receptive to the guru that he assimilated the teachings instantly and as a result he experienced a powerful spiritual state. The image of the salty water rather reminds one of the 'taste of freedom'.[220] Just as the salt is now part of the water, in the same way Milarepa's whole being has been transformed by the instructions he has imbibed. Here Milarepa appears as almost the ideal disciple. He was completely open to the guru's instructions and straightaway imbibes them in his heart, just like salt being dissolved in water, and he apparently instantly experienced a very deep meditative or contemplative state.

> When the Wisdom shone bright from within,
> I felt as if awakened from a great dream –
> I was awakened from both the main and ensuing Samādhis;
> I was awakened from both 'yes' and 'no' ideas.

Milarepa's being 'awakened from both the main and ensuing Samādhis' suggests that even they are a state of sleep, part of the great dream, because even *dhyāna* states are still mundane, though incredibly refined. But 'when Wisdom shines bright from within', you awaken from conditioned existence as such, even in its most refined form. You awaken therefore even from the *samādhis*. Lofty states though they are from the mundane point of view, in comparison with wisdom they seem no more than dreams. Though *samādhi*, *dhyāna*, is indispensable as the basis for the development of transcendental wisdom, wisdom infinitely transcends it. 'I was awakened from both 'yes' and 'no' ideas' suggests that he was awakened from the duality of existence and non-existence, being and non-being, affirmation and negation, and from all intellectual, conceptual limitations, from the taking of concepts as ends in themselves. In other words, all limitations, whether intellectual or emotional, were removed by the experience of wisdom.

The 'ensuing Samādhi' is the *samādhi* you continue to experience after the cessation of your main meditation practice, in the midst of the activities of daily life. It's not just an after-effect, because you try to keep it up even though you are now in more difficult conditions. Say you sit in the shrine-room for an hour doing the Mindfulness of Breathing practice, and you have an experience of a *dhyāna* state. When the period of meditation comes to an end and you get up from your cushion to do something else – perhaps you go and chop some wood – even though you're chopping wood, there is some trace of the *dhyāna* experience persisting, and you can try to keep in contact with that experience. The experience of *dhyāna* you have sitting on your cushion is called the main *samādhi*, and the experience of the trace of *samādhi* that you have as a result, while you're chopping wood, is called the ensuing *samādhi*. The function of the ensuing *samādhi* is to link up main *samādhis*. If you're practising meditation seriously, you have periods of practice sitting on your cushion and in the periods in between sitting practice you try to maintain the experience you had while sitting on the cushion as long as you possibly can. In that way, when you have another period of sitting meditation, you're not starting from scratch, because you haven't completely lost the benefits from last time. If you're taking meditation seriously, even when you're not actually meditating you're careful to see that you don't stray too far away from the *dhyāna* experience that you had when sitting on your cushion.

You will probably only be able to practise in this way on retreat. In the course of ordinary life, you might have a good meditation in the morning, but even if you stay positive during the day, you probably won't have any trace left of the specific *dhyāna* consciousness, so you will have to start all over again. But if you sit to meditate a number of times during the day and you're very mindful about what you do in between, especially if you're engaged in very simple physical activity and you aren't talking very much, you can keep the *dhyāna* experience practically the whole day. It just fluctuates: it goes up a bit when you sit and down a bit at other times Our usual experience is that we achieve meditative concentration in the morning and then we lose it completely, and in the evening we have to start again. It can make quite a difference if you introduce a third sitting meditation halfway through, perhaps just before lunch, to give your sagging *dhyāna* line a hoist in the middle of the day. You can do things in the first *dhyāna*, in which state discursive mental activity is still continuing, but it is quite difficult, and may not even be desirable. You shouldn't try to stay in two worlds or two mental states at the same time; you'll get splitting headaches. If you're doing a task that involves a simple repetitive physical movement you can do that while remaining in a *dhyāna* state, but if your job involves thinking things out, it becomes virtually impossible. You can chop wood in a *dhyāna* state but if you have to think in terms of selling the wood and calculating the price and finding a buyer and making arrangements for transport, that is incompatible with the *dhyāna* state.

> *When one secures the great bliss through Viewing,*
> *He feels all Dharmas spontaneously freed*
> *As mists of rain vanish into air.*

The great bliss is presumably *mahāsukhā*, to use the Sanskrit term. It's a Vajrayāna way of looking at the Goal, the ultimate experience. One secures the great bliss through viewing in the sense of 'seeing things as they really are', *yathā-bhūta-jñāna-darśana,* which is the eighth of the positive *nidānas.*[221] One awakens to transcendental bliss, one 'enters the stream', as the Early Buddhist tradition put it, as a result of seeing things as they really are, and when one has that experience, one 'feels all Dharmas spontaneously freed as mists of rain vanish into air'.

'All Dharmas spontaneously freed' refers to the Theravāda way of looking at existence. According to the Theravādin tradition, the so-called 'person' can be analyzed into a number of different material and mental factors which the tradition calls *dharmas* or ultimate phenomena. That way of seeing things was taken over by the Mahāyāna, but it doesn't regard it as expressing ultimate truth, maintaining that these *dharmas* are not in fact ultimate, but conceptual constructions which should also be dissolved. In the same way that the so-called 'person' is dissolved into *dharmas*, the *dharmas* have to be dissolved into the Void. Reality can no more be explained in terms of a fixed number of irreducible *dharmas* than in terms of fixed unchanging ego-entities. So after resolving the so-called person into *dharmas*, one resolves the so-called *dharmas* into the Void. In other words, one recognizes the purely relative validity of all conceptual constructions, even those of the Abhidharma.

Different schools came up with different lists of these *dharmas*. For instance, the eleven positive mental states are regarded as *dharmas*; and on the material side, so are the great elements, earth, water, fire and air. Some schools regard all *dharmas* as manifestations of mind, so they recognize only mental *dharmas*, but the Theravāda and the Sarvāstivāda recognize the existence of *dharmas* which are material as well as mental. The Sarvāstivādins had a list of seventy-five *dharmas*, most of which made up conditioned existence and three of which were unconditioned *dharmas*. So you had a short list of unconditioned *dharmas*, including two kinds of Nirvāṇa, and a long list of conditioned *dharmas*, and this list of *dharmas*, both conditioned and unconditioned, was held to include the whole content of reality.

The Mahāyāna maintains that existence cannot be broken down in this way because the so-called '*dharmas*' are not things in themselves, not ultimate entities, but only intellectual constructions. It's similar to the way modern physics talks in terms of particles and waves. Is there really a particle or is there really a wave? It's useful to think so for certain purposes, but one shouldn't think that there are such things as particles or waves actually existing out there. In the same way, the Mahāyāna says it's useful to think of existence as consisting of permutations of different *dharmas*, but that is just a useful way of thinking. It doesn't represent the nature of reality itself, which is beyond thought, beyond expression, *śūnyatā*.

So therefore, 'he feels all Dharmas spontaneously freed as mists of rain vanish into air'. When one has the realization of *śūnyatā* – and that is implied in the realization of the great bliss, because great bliss is bliss which has been thoroughly purified by the experience of *śūnyatā*, as the prefix 'great', *mahā*, always implies – one sees all intellectual constructions, even those of the Abhidharma, even those of Buddhism itself, just dissolving, just melting away. They are 'spontaneously freed' because they go away by themselves. You don't have to take any further steps. When you see the nature of reality, you are freed from the limitations of all provisional, relatively valid constructions about it.

Then he says:

> *When one comes to the Essence of Being,*
> *The shining Wisdom of Reality*
> *Illumines all like the cloudless sky.*

I'm not sure what term 'essence of being' translates, but the 'Wisdom of Reality' is the wisdom of the *dharmadhātu*. According to the Mahāyāna, especially the Yogācāra teaching, there are five wisdoms or five knowledges, as represented by the mandala of the Five Buddhas. Each Buddha is the embodiment of a particular wisdom, and at the centre of one popular form of the mandala you have the figure of Vairocana, who represents wisdom itself, the wisdom of reality, the wisdom of the *dharmadhātu*, as it is called. The other four Buddhas, at the four cardinal points of the compass, represent the four main aspects of that central wisdom. The term for 'wisdom' here, by the way, is *jñāna*. Some translators translate them as the five wisdoms, some the five knowledges, and to make it still more difficult, Guenther translates them as the five Awarenesses. When Guenther speaks of Awareness, with a capital 'A', he means *jñāna*, not mindfulness.[222]

In the east there's Akṣobhya with his 'mirror-like wisdom', the wisdom that simply reflects. It's purely objective. It doesn't distort. It reproduces things just as they are. If there's a red object in front of the mirror, the mirror reflects it red. If it's green, it reflects it green. If it's square, it reflects it square – that is, if it's a flat mirror. Most people's minds are distorting mirrors, one could say, but the mirror-like wisdom is the mirror that reflects or that sees things just as they are, with no element of subjective distortion. Another relevant feature of the mirror is that things don't stick to it. The mind that has developed this mirror-like wisdom isn't attached to anything any more than the mirror is attached to the reflections. When the object is in front of the mirror, the mirror reflects it, but when the object is no longer there, the reflection doesn't leave any trace on the mirror. In the same way, if you have the mirror-like wisdom, when you see a beautiful sunset your mind reflects that, but when the sunset has gone you don't think about it any more; you're not attached to it. The image of the sunset doesn't stick to your mind. The mirror-like wisdom thus resembles the mirror in these two respects: it reflects with complete faithfulness and objectivity and it doesn't allow the reflections to stick. This mirror-like wisdom is embodied in the figure of Akṣobhya, the dark blue Buddha of the east, whose *mudrā* is the *bhūmisparśa*, the 'earth-touching' or 'earth-witness' *mudrā*.

One could say that Akṣobhya represents overcoming the ego, overcoming the self, in that a mind that reflects things as they are in reality reflects no separate unchanging self. If it did reflect a self, that would be an element of distortion, and it would not then be the 'mirror-like wisdom'. One would express this mirror-like quality in ordinary life by being objective, not being swayed by subjective feelings, not projecting. The 'mirror-like wisdom' is the 'non-projecting wisdom', the wisdom that truly sees things as they are, without any element of subjective distortion.

If the image of the mirror suggests something a bit cold to you, it's important to take the point of the comparison and not let other irrelevant associations enter in. Also, don't forget that the 'mirror-like' wisdom is only expressing one aspect, one side, of Enlightenment. Enlightenment can't really be split into different aspects, but we have to do that in order to get any understanding of it at all on the intellectual level. On the level of Enlightenment itself, the four are one, and that one is what is called the 'wisdom of Reality', the 'wisdom of *dharmadhātu*', the wisdom embodied in the central Buddha. We split this one central wisdom into four different aspects just to give ourselves a fuller and clearer and in a way richer idea of it.

Moving round the mandala, we come to Ratnasambhava, the Buddha of the south, the yellow Buddha who makes the gesture of supreme giving and embodies the wisdom of equality or sameness. One mustn't forget that from the Mahāyāna point of view, to see things as they really are is to see them all as *śūnyatā*. *Śūnyatā* is usually translated as 'voidness' or 'emptiness', but perhaps it would be better to render it as 'inexpressible'. A tree is *śūnyatā*, a flower is *śūnyatā*, a house is *śūnyatā*, a person is *śūnyatā*, the moon is *śūnyatā*, the stars are *śūnyatā*, the sun is *śūnyatā*; all things are *śūnyatā*, all things are the same. The wisdom of sameness is the wisdom that sees all things equally in terms of *śūnyatā* or, if you like, in terms of the One Mind.

Going on round the circle, we come to Amitābha, the red Buddha of the west. He is represented in the *dhyāna mudrā*, the gesture of meditation, and he represents, he embodies, the discriminating wisdom, the wisdom that sees things in their particularity, in their uniqueness. In a sense it balances the wisdom of equality, because when you see things in terms of equality, it does not mean that differences are all wiped out. You aren't left with a featureless, blank monism, a sense that all things are one undifferentiated consciousness. You see all things as equally *śūnyatā*, but you continue to see the unique features of every individual thing, and that seeing is called the discriminating wisdom. Even if you can see that a rose and a daffodil are equally *śūnyatā*, you don't cease to see their distinctive qualities. In the vision of reality, sameness does not swamp difference, difference does not swamp sameness, and reality cannot be expressed exclusively in terms of either.

Travelling further round the mandala, in the north we encounter the green Buddha, Amoghasiddhi. Amoghasiddhi means 'Infallible Success' and he is represented as having the gesture of fearlessness, the *abhaya mudrā*. He represents or embodies the all-performing wisdom, the wisdom that gets things done or, if you like, practical wisdom, the wisdom that overcomes all obstacles or the irresistible wisdom.

And Vairocana, the Buddha in the centre, is white in colour, of course. His hands are in the *mudrā* of teaching the Dharma, and he embodies knowledge or awareness itself. He represents all those four wisdoms blended into one, the wisdom of reality, as Milarepa calls it here. Vairocana is sometimes called the 'Sun Buddha'. The word Vairocana itself, which means the brilliant or shining one, in pre-Buddhist times was a name of the sun.

When it comes to visualizing the mandala of the Five Buddhas, usually you start in the east and go clockwise from there. The east is where the sun rises, where things begin, so you enter the mandala at the eastern gate. When the mandala is depicted, the east is at the bottom, because it is organized in relation to yourself at the point of entry. So you start off visualizing, right in front of you, Akṣobhya and then on your left, Ratnasambhava, then opposite to you, Amitābha, and on your right, Amoghasiddhi, and in the middle, Vairocana. Alternatively, you can start off by visualizing Vairocana in the middle. You can consider the symbolism of these Buddhas in all sorts of ways, for example according to their *mudrās* and colours. In the case of the *mudrā* of Akṣobhya, his hand is pointing down to the earth, in the case of Ratnasambhava, the palm of his hand faces outwards, in the case of Amitābha's *dhyāna mudrā*, the two palms are facing up, and in the case of Amoghasiddhi, his palm is also facing outwards. If you look at them in pairs, the palm of Amoghasiddhi, who is in the north, is facing out, and that of Ratnasambhava in the south is also outward, but one is the 'out' of keeping fears at bay and the other is the 'out' of giving. Amitābha's palms are facing up to the heavens, while Akṣobhya's right palm and fingers are pointing down to the earth. Playing around with all these significances helps you to get a more concrete feeling of these five Buddhas and their wisdoms. One gets a definite feeling for them by acquainting oneself in a factual way with their names, their positions in the mandala, their colours, their *mudrās*, and then, if you want to go further than that, the knowledges or wisdoms they're associated with, their consorts, their elements, their *skandhas,* and so on.

But how important is it to do that? Does one 'have to' have a feeling for these Buddhas? Well, if you are going to relate to them at all, you can't have a nebulous idea about them. Your sense of them has got to be concrete. That means, to begin with, gathering the factual information, and then, through the concrete details, getting a feeling for the *Dhyāni* Buddhas, as they are sometimes called. The term '*Dhyāni* Buddhas', incidentally, is not really a Buddhist term at all. It was used by someone who wrote about Nepalese Buddhism in the last century, and then taken up by Theosophists. Buddhist texts never mention '*Dhyāni*' Buddhas; they refer to the five Jinas, the five Conquerors, or the five Tathāgatas.

One mustn't forget that the four Buddhas, plus the central Buddha, represent an attempt to communicate something of the nature of Buddhahood or Enlightenment. To speak of the wisdom of reality is very vague, very general, so considering it in terms of four principal aspects – the mirror-like wisdom, the wisdom of equality, the discriminating wisdom, and the all-performing wisdom – gives you a fuller and richer idea of what Buddhahood is like. And then each Buddha can be seen as having a masculine aspect and a feminine aspect, the feminine aspect being the consort. If you had any feeling that these wisdoms are a bit cold, the consort will counteract that. The attendant bodhisattvas bring out further, more specific aspects of the activity of the Buddhas, and the *dharmapālas*, the guardians of the Dharma, bring out further aspects still. In some mandalas, there are wrathful Buddhas as well as peaceful Buddhas. In that way, more and more aspects are brought out. I sometimes make the comparison to a precious stone. A beautiful precious stone in the form of a sphere might be complete and perfect, but because it's a sphere, it doesn't reflect very much, it's not very colourful. If you cut it into facets, these facets catch and reflect the light and you get rainbows, so the beauty of the precious stone is brought out more by being cut and faceted in that way. In the same way you bring out the content of Buddhahood more fully by splitting it up into so many aspects and embodying each aspect in a particular Buddha or consort or bodhisattva or *dharmapāla* form. The Buddhas and *ḍākinīs* and bodhisattvas and *dharmapālas* of the mandala are all aspects of the one Buddha, and that mandala represents that one Buddha in his totality of aspects.

But why is the central Buddha not Śākyamuni? Why is a new archetypal form chosen? This is because the mandala depicts an ideal level, free from ordinary limitations. Śākyamuni is the human historical Buddha and as such is limited by time and space to a particular spot on the earth's surface in a certain epoch of history. But the ideal Buddha, the *sambhogakāya*, is not limited in that way. It's the ideal that the Buddha Śākyamuni also represents, but liberated from the limitations under which Śākyamuni realized that ideal. The fact that he lived in India 2,500 years ago has nothing to do with Buddhahood itself. The ideal Buddha figure, the *sambhogakāya* Buddha, represents Buddhahood emancipated from all the particular conditions under which it may be realized. It is not Buddhahood at a particular time or in a particular place. It's just Buddhahood itself, under ideal conditions. The *nirmāṇakāya* is Buddhahood realized under certain specific historical conditions but the *sambhogakāya* is Buddhahood as eternally realized under absolutely ideal conditions. That's why the *sambhogakāya* Buddha sits enthroned in a world which is a Pure Land. And the *dharmakāya* is Buddhahood free from all limitations whatsoever, even ideal limitations. The five Buddhas of the mandala are all *sambhogakāya* Buddhas, aspects of the one ideal Buddha, or, as he's sometimes called, the universal Buddha, the eternal Buddha. It's this Buddha who is very often represented as teaching the Mahāyāna *sūtras*, though not always – sometimes Śākyamuni teaches them.

Vairocana is not always in the centre; any Buddha can occupy the centre because any aspect can be considered as central. If you've got a faceted jewel, you can turn it in such a way that any facet becomes the central one. If you have a particular devotion to Amitābha, put him at the centre of the mandala and put Vairocana in the west. Historically either Vairocana or Akṣobhya has tended to be in in the centre of the mandala, but this is just because those two figures seem to have been more appealing to most people. Sometimes a bodhisattva like Avalokiteśvara can be put in the centre of the mandala, or a *ḍākinī* like Vajrayoginī. Sometimes it's a peaceful Buddha, sometimes a wrathful one; sometimes a single Buddha, sometimes a Buddha in *yab-yum* form – that is to say, in male-female form in sexual union. Which figure you put in the centre of the mandala depends on the Buddha or bodhisattva who so far as you are concerned is at the centre of your practice. Most people respond quite strongly to this or that Buddha or bodhisattva or *ḍākinī*, so the tradition goes along with that. If you find yourself especially attracted by Tārā, do the Tārā *sādhana* and recite the Tārā mantra, and if you visualize the mandala, let Tārā be in the centre of it. There's even a mandala of twenty-one Tārās; you can have all the figures of the mandala in Tārā form – different Tārās with different *mudrās* and different colours.

It's worth noticing that the verse says that this shining wisdom 'illumines all like the cloudless sky' – not 'like the sun in the cloudless sky'. The reason for that is that the sun would be a particular point in the sky, the light would have a particular point of origin, but wisdom isn't like that. It isn't as if the light comes from a particular point in reality; it is all equally luminous. Analogies tend to break down, because light as we know it always originates from a certain source, but it isn't like that in the case of the light of the wisdom of reality. It shines everywhere equally, not from any particular point.

> When both pure and impure thoughts are cleared,
> As in a silver mirror,
> The immanent bright Wisdom shines forth.

The point of the comparison here is that when objects are taken away from the mirror, what is left is just the mirror. It's as though the mind in its purity is just like the mirror. Different objects are put in front of the mind, some pure and some impure. In other words, at one time the mind is skilful, at another time it is unskilful. But when all objects are taken away, when it is behaving neither skilfully nor unskilfully, the mind manifests its natural purity, just as when no objects are in front of it – if that were at all possible – the mirror just reflects the light. You could see mind and mental events like that. It's not only impure thoughts that are cleared away, it's pure thoughts too. The mind is completely free from thoughts. There are no objects at all in front of the mirror, and it is not reflecting anything. It's shining by its own light, so to speak. 'The immanent bright Wisdom shines forth' – there's nothing to cloud it, nothing to obstruct it. This is not quiescence as opposed to action. It's a state beyond quiescence and action, beyond passivity and activity, beyond pure and impure. But one mustn't be misled by anything in the comparison itself. The mind isn't really passive, although the image of the mirror might suggest that. Don't forget that wisdom is also an active, all-performing wisdom.

> When the Ālaya consciousness dissolves into the Dharmakāya
> I feel my body and soul break forth
> Like the crushing of an egg when stamped upon.

The Sanskrit word for consciousness is *vijñāna*, and the word for wisdom or knowledge, as in the five wisdoms or knowledges, is *jñāna*. In both cases the *jñāna* comes from the root *jñā*, 'to know'. *Vijñāna* is knowledge or consciousness which is split up, divided, whereas *jñāna* is knowledge which is not split up. Or, to put it another way, *vijñāna* represents dualistic knowledge, or dualistic consciousness, whereas *jñāna* is non-dualistic knowledge, non-dualistic consciousness. *Vijñāna* represents consciousness of an object, but in the case of *jñāna* there's no distinction between subject and object.

The Yogācāra lists eight *vijñānas*. First there are the five sense *vijñānas* – eye-consciousness, ear-consciousness, nose-consciousness, touch-consciousness, and taste-consciousness. When the eye, for instance, comes into contact with a visual object, eye-consciousness arises from the contact between these two, and it's similar with the other four sense-consciousnesses. Then sixthly there is the mind-consciousness, mind in this sense meaning the organ that perceives ideas, just as the five sense organs perceive their corresponding sense-objects. Just as the eye is conscious of forms, in the same way the mind is conscious of ideas. The word for 'ideas' which is generally used here is *dharmas*; it's another sense of the term *dharma*.

The sense-consciousnesses can operate without the mind-consciousness being present. You can open your eyes and see a red round object, and all that your eye-consciousness sees is a red round object. It's your mind-consciousness that tells you that it is a tomato. But then there's a seventh consciousness which is called the *kliṣṭamano-vijñāna*, the soiled, defiled, or even suffering mind-consciousness. This is the consciousness that says 'that tomato is mine'. It is 'soiled' by the ego-sense: by the sense of mine and yours, me and you. This consciousness has an emotional content, and it is of course unskilful, to the extent that it is ego-based. The eighth *vijñāna* is the *ālaya* consciousness. There are many different teachings about this, but it is usually said to be divided into two: the relative *ālaya*, where the seeds of all impressions and experiences are stored, and the absolute *ālaya*, which is usually considered to be identical with reality itself.

Milarepa's statement that 'when the Ālaya consciousness dissolves into the Dharmakāya, I feel my body and soul break forth/ Like the crushing of an egg when stamped upon' refers to the way that, on the gaining of Enlightenment, the relative *ālaya* consciousness dissolves into the absolute *ālaya*, into the *dharmakāya*. To look into this in a little more detail, we've got on the one hand eight consciousnesses, and on the other hand five knowledges, and the spiritual life consists in the transformation of the one into the other. In the simplest terms, the unenlightened human being is transformed into an Enlightened human being, the ordinary human being is transformed into a Buddha. From one point of view, the ordinary human being consists of eight *vijñānas*, and Buddhahood consists of five wisdoms; so the process of Enlightenment consists in the transformation of your eight consciousnesses into the five *jñānas* or knowledges.

This can be worked out in detail. It is said that the five sense-consciousnesses are transformed into the all-performing wisdom, because you function through the senses, and the all-performing wisdom is the functioning wisdom, as it were. So your five senses are transformed into Amoghasiddhi. Not all the accounts agree, but usually it is said that the mind-consciousness, the *mano-vijñāna*, is transformed into the discriminating wisdom, because the mind sees the differences between things, and the discriminating wisdom likewise sees things in their particularity, though it is a particularity that does not exclude sameness. So your mind is transformed into Amitābha. The 'soiled mind-consciousness', which sees things in terms of me and you, mine and yours, in other words dualistically, is transformed into the wisdom of equality, which sees things in terms of sameness, which doesn't discriminate between self and others. So the soiled mind is transformed into Ratnasambhava. And the relative *ālaya*, which contains all the seeds deposited by the actions of all beings throughout time, including yours, is transformed into the mirror-like wisdom of Akṣobhya. Just as the mirror contains all the reflections, the *ālaya* contains all the seeds deposited, as a result of our functioning through our senses, our mind, and our defiled mind-consciousness. The *ālaya* is like a mirror, but a mirror to which reflections stick, whereas in Akṣobhya's mirror-like wisdom, the reflections do not stick to the mirror. Akṣobhya thus represents the relative *ālaya* in its transformed state. The teachings differ here, but it is as though when you come to the relative *ālaya* you go beyond individuality in the ordinary sense. It is something like a collective consciousness, or collective unconsciousness, on the Jungian model, as though underlying the individual consciousness there is this wider consciousness. One could look at it as being like race learning, though it's much wider, and even much deeper, than that. It is similar to the archetypal, the source of myth, at least from the Jungian point of view. The Yogācāra system says nothing about that. One can identify the relative *ālaya* with Jung's collective unconscious to some extent if care is taken not just to conclude that they are really the same thing.

The absolute *ālaya* doesn't require any transformation; it is all the time identical with the wisdom of the *dharmadhātu*, the wisdom of reality. The absolute *ālaya* is thus represented by Vairocana in the centre of the mandala, by the wisdom of reality. Remember, though, that all the four wisdoms are aspects of the wisdom of reality, they're not separate from it. All of this is simply trying to make more concrete the whole process of transformation.[223]

The previous verse said that the bright wisdom is immanent. In other words, it is somehow already contained within the ordinary human being. If you are tempted to ask in what way, you have to remember that strictly speaking it isn't contained at all. This is metaphorical language, which if one isn't careful one can mistake for literal language. Can you really speak in terms of something mental – that is, non-spatial – being contained within something else? To speak of something being contained in something else is to speak in spatial terms; it's a metaphor. We must be careful not to think of Enlightenment as being literally contained within, as though it's already there. It's just a way of saying that if you make sufficient effort, you can realize it. For example, when you are feeling *mettā*, although you still have the potential for hatred, that doesn't mean that hatred is within you as a feeling but you are unconscious of it. That is self-contradictory nonsense. It just means that even though now you are experiencing *mettā*, on some other occasion, under other circumstances, it would be possible for you to experience hatred. Even the idea of the unconscious mind is only a metaphor, and if you think of it as something spatial, it's a metaphor that you're taking too literally. The unconscious mind is just those things of which you could be conscious, but of which you are not conscious now. For instance, at this moment you may not be conscious of the telephone number of a certain friend. So where is that knowledge of your friend's telephone number when you're not actually thinking of it? We say that it's in your unconscious, but that only means that if you so wish, you can bring the telephone number of your friend to consciousness. We don't know how it happens. Similarly, in some schools of Buddhism they say that Buddhahood is within you, that you are Enlightened already, which is all right speaking poetically, but taking it literally it's nonsense. What it really means is that if you make the necessary effort, you can attain the experience represented by the word Buddhahood. It doesn't mean that you're like a box containing all sorts of things and Buddhahood is at the bottom, so if you take the other things out of the box, you'll find Buddhahood. The danger of this sort of language is that if Buddhahood is already there, supposedly, you don't need to do anything about attaining it. This idea of something being there even though you don't experience it is very dangerous because it encourages a feeling of alienation.

It's very difficult for us to think in non-spatial terms. If we speak in terms of understanding something, 'under' is a spatial term, so do we take it that 'understanding' is standing under something? We speak of having a 'penetrating mind', another spatial term, but how can you penetrate something if it isn't in space? When we speak of a 'thorough understanding', we think in terms of considering a subject from every point of view, of going all round it, having a comprehensive understanding of it. These are all spatial terms. Insight, even, is a spatial term. We have to remember that in the beginning, when we human beings started talking, our experience was entirely sense experience, and language was formed under the influence of sense experience. We've gradually extended its scope to include mental states and mental operations, and we continue to use space- and time-bound language to describe them, but we get into difficulties when we start speaking – and even thinking – about mental states and mental operations as though they were actually conditioned by space and time.

The *ālaya vijñāna* represents the notions of potentiality, availability, accessibility, a sort of collective memory. It is not really like a sort of box in which we keep mental states and memories until we need them, although our experience may suggest something like that. It's better to use the sort of terminology that the Buddha himself seems to have used. He never spoke in terms of Enlightenment or Buddhahood being within you all the time, but he did say that if you made the necessary effort, Enlightenment could be realized. You are potentially Enlightened in the sense that the experience called Enlightenment is within your reach but it's dangerous and unnecessary to translate that into the static notion that 'Enlightenment is there within you all the time'. We should all the time be aware of the limitations of language; otherwise we get caught up in problems of language, problems which are artificial, not real.

Even the idea of people having certain emotions 'within' them is quite limiting. It doesn't encourage a complete breakthrough, because you are liable to think 'there's a certain amount of hatred in me and I can't just break through that', but it isn't really like that at all. You have a capacity for hatred in the sense that in dependence on certain conditions, hatred would arise, but it's not as though it's been kept in a little box somewhere in the meantime, or that it is actually there in you. Thinking in those terms creates all sorts of artificial, unreal difficulties. You may think, 'I don't feel angry at all, I feel quite friendly.' If someone then says to you, 'Ah no, the anger is there, deep inside you. You're not in contact with it – it's very deep – but it's there,' that puts you in a strange position, as though a feeling is there and you have it, even though you don't feel it. Then you might be told, 'Well, you must be very alienated from it. You're just not in touch with your feelings.' But is it really correct to speak in terms of not feeling a feeling? Surely if it's a feeling, you are aware of it. If you are angry you feel angry. To say that you're angry but you don't feel angry is language run wild, as it were.

The term alienation is sometimes tossed around very lightly, but what does it really mean? Let's take a starting point from the dictionary. It says: 'alienation: (1) a turning away, estrangement. (2) the state of being an outsider or the feeling of being isolated, as from society. Psychiatry: a state in which a person's feelings are inhibited so that eventually both the self and the external world seem unreal.'[224] The crux of the definition is 'inhibited'; it's a state in which a person's feelings are inhibited. So how do you know that a feeling is being inhibited?

What happens when you're alienated from feelings is that you have the beginnings of a feeling, but it's very faint. You don't want that feeling to become stronger, so you take steps to prevent it from fully emerging into consciousness. When you inhibit a feeling, you're hindering the natural process of that feeling becoming stronger because for one reason or another you don't want it to become too strong. Using the word 'inhibition' introduces another spatial metaphor – putting the lid on something. But let's take a concrete example. Think of a feeling and then imagine what happens when you become conscious of that feeling, or rather when you have that feeling (because if we say 'become conscious of it' it suggests it can exist apart from your being conscious of it, which is self-contradictory). Suppose you have a slight feeling of some kind or other, and then you think that it wouldn't be good if this feeling was to become stronger, so you take steps to prevent it from becoming stronger. Mental states and bodily states are very closely bound up together. You can inhibit in all sorts of ways – for example intellectually, by force of intellectual conviction. You might for instance feel angry, and then you might think, 'Who am I feeling angry with? I'm feeling angry with my father. I hate my father.' But then you might feel unwilling to acknowledge that you hate your father, so you inhibit: you prevent the feeling from becoming stronger by saying to yourself, 'No. I don't hate my father, of course I don't. I'm very fond of my father. I ought to love my father, so I do.' In this way, by force of intellectual argument, you prevent the feeling of being angry with your father from becoming any stronger, and you are said to inhibit it.

The feeling may then emerge in some other form. The natural thing, given your nature, would be for you to hate your father, but you have taken steps to suppress that feeling, so the energy in the feeling becomes displaced and you have another kind of feeling instead – depression, say, or anxiety. If the feeling of hatred goes, it hasn't become unconscious. The energy that had started to produce the feeling of hating your father is now producing another feeling – anxiety, fear, or whatever it is. Perhaps one should speak in terms of inhibiting particular expressions of energy rather than inhibiting emotions, if by inhibiting emotions is meant thrusting emotions back into the unconscious.

But isn't the idea of pushing the emotions back down into a box, say, useful in that you can see that later on they're going to have to come back up again? Not really. It's more useful to ask what has caused the energy to move in that direction, to start expressing itself as an emotion of hatred towards your father? It's the whole situation. Because there is that situation, there is that tendency for your energies to find their way into consciousness in that particular way. If you block that, those energies have to find another outlet, and they do so in the form of some other emotion. The whole process should be envisaged in quite dynamic terms. Alienation, one could say, is the replacement of primary emotions by secondary or even tertiary emotions. An alienated person doesn't feel no emotions; he feels inappropriate emotions. A stage can be reached where you don't feel any emotions at all, because the energy has been pushed further and further back, but most alienated people feel emotion in the form of a dull discomfort, unease, and anxiety. They haven't allowed their energies to take their natural course and express themselves straightforwardly as primary emotions, so those energies have taken another turning and expressed themselves as a secondary emotion, which will be a weaker expression of emotion and possibly more painful, because if your energies are not allowed to express themselves directly, it is painful, whereas the direct expression of emotion is generally pleasurable. It's an unskilful pleasure, but it is still a pleasure. If you dislike or hate someone for a certain reason, it can be a great relief to say so, because the energy has found its authentic expression.

The skilful way of dealing with this energy, experiencing this negative emotion, is first to acknowledge it, and to recognize that your energies have taken that direction due to a certain complex of causes and conditions. Then you can start altering that complex of causes and conditions, and even setting up a complex of counter causes and conditions. If somebody has a lot of energy but continually alienates himself from it, he could one day have a great outburst. That's why the poet John Dryden said, 'Beware the fury of a patient man.'[225] It suggests that you should be very careful to allow your emotions their primary expression. If someone hits you, the natural reaction of your energies is in the form of anger, and if they keep on hitting you, the anger will turn to hatred. At least one must acknowledge one's primary emotional responses, not try to divert them into secondary or even tertiary channels. But there's a big difference between acknowledging your emotions and expressing them. You have to consider whether or not it is skilful to express them, and if you decide that it is not skilful, you have to consider how to transform those emotions. You may in the end have to do that by changing the whole situation. For instance, it may be that certain irritations arise from your job, and when you understand that, you may have to conclude that you should change your job.

Sometimes you do need to suppress emotions, if expressing them would clearly have unskilful consequences. If you wanted to kill somebody, you would certainly have to suppress that emotion. You would acknowledge to yourself that that was how you felt and then you would take steps to deal with the emotion by trying to change it, by seeing things differently, so that the emotion didn't have even a tendency to arise, so it didn't need to be suppressed or inhibited. Inhibition is always negative; if you're having to inhibit any emotions, it's a sign that your energies are wrongly organized, or are being wrongly influenced, wrongly conditioned.

These emotional shifts can be triggered by a shift in the flow of physical energy, as when, for example, you are being massaged, or some event happens that has no apparent link with these energies and suddenly they come pouring forth. When energy flows in a certain direction or finds a certain outlet there is an appropriate emotional feeling, and when the direction of the energy is shifted, or even reversed, there is another, different, appropriate emotion. During massage sometimes the flow of energy is shifted back into its original channel and you get the emotional response or experience appropriate to energy flowing in that particular channel. For example, if someone is suffering from anxiety, a massage may shift the energy from the channel that expresses itself in terms of anxiety back into another more basic channel which expresses itself in terms of sex, so the emotion of anxiety is replaced by a sexual feeling. To speak of energy flowing in channels is still to use spatial terms, and one mustn't take even that too literally, but inasmuch as the emotions are acted on through the body and the body occupies space, perhaps that isn't altogether illegitimate. It shows how careful we have to be with language. We need to use language and not let language use us.

To sum up, at least one should acknowledge the direction one's energy is taking and the feeling that one experiences. Then one has to ask oneself if it is skilful not only to acknowledge it but also to allow it expression. If it is unskilful to allow it expression, it is equally unskilful to block it, so you have to change the causes and conditions that were causing your energy to take that direction. If you find, for example, that your job is making you angry, first of all you need to acknowledge that you are growing angry and that it is your job that is making you feel that way. Then ask yourself, is it skilful for me to express this anger in a destructive manner? If you conclude that it is not skilful, one of the things you can do is to change the conditions that are causing your energy to take the direction it is taking and express itself in the form of the emotion that you are experiencing. You might change your job, or you might decide that you can't change your job, so you must set up conditions that will enable you not to feel angry despite all the provocations. You might say, 'I will make sure that every morning and evening I will do an hour's *mettā bhāvanā*. That will counteract the effect on me of my work.' What you mustn't do is acknowledge the situation and decide you can't give the emotion expression, then just leave it at that. Then you will be forced sooner or later to displace the energy and, as we say, inhibit the emotion, which may then become anxiety, depression, or whatever it is.

If you were in a situation where you felt a lot of hatred towards somebody but you saw that it would be unskilful to express that hatred, you might have to move away from that person, or, if you couldn't avoid them, you could try to introduce other factors into the situation in such a way that your energy was not going in that particular direction, and you were not experiencing that particular emotion. It's a question of the economics – or dynamics if you like – of human energy.

All this has emerged from this verse in which Milarepa describes how, when the *ālaya* consciousness dissolves into the *dharmakāya*, 'I feel my body and soul break forth like the crushing of an egg when stamped upon'. His statement amounts to saying: 'The eight *vijñānas* have been destroyed, they've been replaced by five wisdoms. I'm not an ordinary human being any more. I'm a Buddha, an Enlightened being. Energy now flows in other channels.'

> When the rope-of-clinging is cut loose
> I feel the existence of Bardo disappear
> Like the uncoiling of a snake.

The *bardo*, the 'intermediate state', is intermediate between death and rebirth. It's due to clinging, to attachment, to craving, that, in a manner of speaking, people take up one human body after another, i.e. they are reborn. It's not so much like a rope; it's more like a thread on which different beads are strung. Your continued craving is the connecting thread from birth to birth, from life to life. So when the rope of clinging – when that thread – is cut, the *bardo* disappears like 'the uncoiling of a snake'. No doubt there's a point to this comparison, but it isn't obvious. A snake doesn't disappear when it uncoils. Maybe it's just the coil that disappears. Instead of being in a coil, the snake becomes more of a spiral perhaps, or is completely straightened out. Maybe it's something like that.

'Coil' gives an impression of pent-up energy, energy turning round and round on itself. In all these verses Milarepa gives the impression of something happening instantaneously – a sudden transformation, a sudden breakthrough: the smashing of the egg, the uncoiling of a snake, bright wisdom shining forth, Dharma spontaneously freed, waking up, salt dissolving into water. When there's no more clinging, no more attachment, there's no more rebirth. The round of birth and death and rebirth suddenly comes to an end, just like a snake suddenly uncoiling.

In this song, Milarepa starts off recalling what he experienced, then goes on to speak in the third person, then reverts to the first person. If he went into the third person to prevent what he is saying from being too personal, perhaps now he has gone back into the first person because he doesn't want it to become too impersonal in an abstract, alienated way. In terms of language what he says has to be either personal or impersonal, but in real terms it's neither. Perhaps he can only convey that by sometimes speaking in personal terms, sometimes in impersonal terms, in that way giving a feeling or an idea of that which is neither personal nor impersonal. Similarly, it's neither past nor present. It's almost as though it happened at a certain point, but it's still happening; it's a continuous process, though not a process that is taking place in time.

> When I act without taking or leaving,
> My mind is always at ease and non-doing.
> I feel as if I were a lion,
> With the power of the Three Perfections.

The Three Perfections are probably the perfections of body, speech, and mind.[226] But how does one act without taking or leaving? 'My mind is always at ease and non-doing.' It's not 'non-doing' in the ordinary sense; it's absence of the egoistic, absence of strain, absence of tension. Tibetans seem very fond of the comparison with the lion, especially the snow-lion.

The Illuminating Voidness, the Illuminating Wisdom,
And the Illuminating Manifestations,
Are my three inseparable friends.

The whole of Milarepa's life and experience is reduced to these three things: reality itself (represented by the illuminating voidness), the realization of reality, and the whole of existence as seen in the light of reality. In reality there is no division of subject and object, but if one is going to speak about reality, the nature of language is that one has to turn it into a subject and an object. So first of all Milarepa mentions the illuminating voidness, beyond subject, beyond object. Next he mentions the illuminating wisdom, which is illuminating voidness appearing as a subject – that is to say an Enlightened being, an Enlightened consciousness. And then he speaks of the illuminating manifestations, the objective universe, as seen in the light of ultimate reality, as seen by illuminating wisdom and lit up by illuminating voidness. When he says these 'are my three inseparable friends', he means that subject and object are suffused by the light of reality, and this is his constant experience. He has this experience of reality all the time. In fact, he says:

Like the sun shining from a cloudless sky,
I am always in the Great Illumination.
Like dividing the horses from the yaks,
The (outer) world and the senses are clearly distinct (from
    the inner).

Our idiom for dividing the horses from the yaks would of course be separating the sheep from the goats. In that way, 'The (outer) world and the senses are clearly distinct (from the inner)'; in other words, you don't project, though even that non-projection is only relatively real, because that suggests a subject and an object, and the distinction between subject and object is not ultimately valid.

The string of mind and Skandhas is forever cut!

I think this means the string tying together mind and *skandhas*. If we take the mind as mundane, it must be included in the *skandhas*; but presumably 'mind' here is not included in the *skandhas*, in which case it has to be transcendental, and presumably the 'string' is the rope of clinging that has already been referred to. One's mind – so to speak – has been dissociated from the *skandhas*, to become perfectly free.

> *Having fully utilized this human form,*
> *I have now completed all Yoga matters.*

I've made full use of the opportunity of human birth. I've carried my human development to the limit. I am in fact Enlightened. 'I have now completed all Yoga matters' – I have no need to meditate any more.

> *Rechungpa, do you also have these Experiences?*
> *Oh, my son, do not be proud and presumptuous!*

Rechungpa's song relating his experiences was pretty good, but Milarepa's song goes far beyond it, and indeed it is very difficult truly to understand. One can only get a glimpse of the meaning. In essence, it's the difference between the *dhyānas* and transcendental insight. Rechungpa is describing the *dhyānas* and certain side effects and reflections based upon them, but in Milarepa's song you get the impression of something issuing directly from insight itself. There's a whole new dimension present. Previously he talked about wisdom itself as illuminating all like the cloudless sky, but he is now saying that he himself is a Buddha, the embodiment of that illumination.

9

RECHUNGPA'S MIND WAS
STRAIGHTENED OUT

Hearing this song, Rechungpa's mind was straightened out.
Then Milarepa said, 'Now let us, father and son, go to Di Se or
Lashi, those remote mountains, to meditate.' Rechungpa replied,
'I am very tired – my physical strength has reached the point of
exhaustion. I think it best that I go to a near-by monastery to
recover (my strength), otherwise I will not be able to meditate or
travel at all.'

'If a determination is made from the bottom of one's heart, one
can practice his devotion under any circumstances, at any time,'
countered the Jetsun. Thereupon, he sang a song called 'The Six
Sufficiencies'.

O Son, one's own body suffices as a good temple,
For the vital points within are Heavenly Paradise.
One's own mind suffices as the Guru,
For all true understanding comes from it.
The outer phenomena suffice as one's Sūtras,
For they are all symbols of the Liberation Path.
The Food-of-Samādhi is sufficient to sustain one,
For the Father Buddhas will come and bless him.
The Dumo-heat suffices for one's clothing –
The warmth and blissful dress of the Ḍākinīs.

To cut off all ties is the best companion;
To live alone is to become a friend of deities;
To regard all enemies as passers-by on the road
Is to avoid hatred.
The best remedy for all obstacles
Is to meditate on Voidness,
For they are all magic-like plays of the mind.
This is the right way for you to follow –
Against it, you will go astray!

I am an old man close to death,
Who has no time for chatting.
You are young, vigorous, and healthy
And would not listen to my helpful advice.
To talk with honesty and straightforwardness
To prideful and greedy persons would be a sheer waste.
If you want to meditate, you may come along with me;
If you do not, you may do whatever you please.

Hearing this song, Rechungpa's mind was straightened out.

This is quite an expressive way of putting it. There has already been a reference to the uncoiling of a snake, and now it's as though Rechungpa's mind also uncoils. But all the same, he says he is too tired to meditate or travel, though Milarepa questions that. It is difficult to say whether Rechungpa has really reached the point of exhaustion. Perhaps he has, but Milarepa is saying that if you're sufficiently determined there is another level of energy to which you can break through. Your resources are always far greater than you think. Usually if we feel a bit tired, we just stop, but it's rare to reach a point of exhaustion. Whether it's advisable to carry on depends very much on the circumstances, but it is good at least sometimes to be stretched. Sometimes the objective needs of the situation may demand that you carry on. If someone's life is at stake, you go all out to do whatever you can. We tend to give ourselves a fairly easy time. People tend not to stretch themselves very much, either because they don't feel sufficiently inspired or because they don't see the objective needs of the situation. But Milarepa is quite uncompromising:

'If a determination is made from the bottom of one's heart, one can practice his devotion under any circumstances, at any time,' countered the Jetsun.

That's the crux of it. It isn't always easy to make such a determination; that's where will comes in. Milarepa is presumably not talking about will in an alienated sense. It's real determination; you really want to put all your energies into what you are doing, which suggests that you're quite an integrated person. It's true that operating on will power tends to have a limit after which you do just stop, whereas with inspiration you can carry on. If you're keeping going by strength of will, there's quite a large part of you that doesn't want to get involved, whereas when there is a determination made from the bottom of your heart, your whole being is involved and it is therefore easier to keep going.

We may have to use willed effort sometimes. I would say, for example, that you should go to your morning meditation under virtually any circumstances, even if you feel very tired, but probably until you start getting real benefit from meditation there will always be some initial resistance to be broken through. Of course you can use willed effort either sensibly or foolishly, based on a genuine understanding of the situation and your own need for discipline or based on foolish pride, just wanting to be successful or wanting to show other people you can do it, even though your heart isn't completely in it.

Rechungpa says that he thinks it best that he goes to a nearby monastery, but Milarepa replies:

Oh Son, one's own body suffices as a good temple,
For the vital points within are Heavenly Paradise.

He's saying that you don't need a monastery or temple in which to rest. Your own body is sufficient, because it's your own mind that is the decisive factor. Just as within the temple there is the Buddha image, so within the temple of your body there is your own Buddha mind, and that's all you need.

These vital points are presumably the chakras – it isn't altogether clear. They are the heavenly paradise because it's within those chakras, those lotuses, those wheels, that higher spiritual realizations take place. There seems to be an implied comparison with the mandala. It's all allied symbolism: the temple, the chakra, the wheel or lotus, the heavenly paradise, the Pure Land. Milarepa is saying that all these are within you. You don't need an external temple or monastery; you've got everything within your own body.

The Hindu and Buddhist chakras correspond to an extent, although in the Hindu system there are seven chakras whereas most Buddhist systems make use of three, four, or five. The most commonly found in Buddhism are those of the head, throat, and heart, which correlate with body, speech, and mind, or with the three *kāyas*. In some practices the head centre is located at the forehead; in others at the crown of the head, and in yet others you visualize chakras at both these places. Sādhanas usually specify that the topmost centre is 'at the crown' of the head. Sometimes the fourth, the navel centre, is brought in, but the two lowest centres are not usually made use of in Buddhist systems, though occasionally they are. One could say that the lower emotions are those that are more crude or more tinged with selfishness, more closely related to our animal needs, our bodily needs, and so on – the more self-centred emotions. The higher emotions are, as it were, the more spiritual emotions, those of faith and devotion, *mettā*, *karuṇā*.

Then he goes on:

> *One's own mind suffices as the Guru,*
> *For all true understanding comes from it.*

He's going so far as to say that in the last analysis you don't need an external guru. Your true guru is your own mind. I don't know whether it is significant that at the beginning of this song he doesn't invoke Marpa as he usually does. Here he says that all true understanding comes from your own mind. This is true, but sometimes you need an external guru or teacher to help your mind to develop that true understanding, a point which Rechungpa is about to make.

> *The outer phenomena suffice as one's Sūtras,*
> *For they are all symbols of the Liberation Path.*

It's a bit like Shakespeare's 'books in the running brooks, sermons in stone and good in everything'.[227] But it's not a question of just learning something. Milarepa is saying that all things are symbols of the

Liberation Path, but is that true? For whom? Is it easy to see all things as the symbols of the Liberation Path? Most people don't. In what way is a tree, for example, a symbol of the Liberation Path? It isn't enough to reflect that it is impermanent. That's not seeing it as a symbol, but just using it as a reminder of a certain abstract truth. On the other hand, if you look at the earth and reflect that the earth bears all, supports all, is patient, the earth could then become for you a symbol of patience. All things could be symbols of the Liberation Path, but only if you can see them in that way, which isn't so easy.

Milarepa is adopting a totally uncompromising stance, and perhaps it is good occasionally to hear such a statement, prone as we are to compromise, make allowances, let ourselves off lightly, make things easy for ourselves, make excuses.

> The Food-of-Samādhi is sufficient to sustain one,
> For the Father Buddhas will come and bless him.

Don't bother about eating and drinking. You can sustain yourself on *samādhi*, you can live on your meditation, because if you meditate, the 'Father Buddhas' will come and bless you. That is to say, in the course of your meditations you will have visions of Buddhas and bodhisattvas, and their blessing will strengthen and nourish you; you won't need ordinary food. So don't bother about it, just get on with your meditation. That will solve all problems. Again he takes this totally uncompromising position. And then:

> The Dumo-heat suffices for one's clothing –
> The warm and blissful dress of the Ḍākinīs.

Practising the *tummo*-heat meditation (as we usually transliterate it in English) makes you feel as though you're enveloped in very soft, warm garments. You don't need to bother about clothes – just meditate to develop this *tummo* heat. That's all you have to do.

So far Milarepa has said you don't need a place to stay, you don't need a guru, you don't need sacred books, you don't need *sūtras*, you don't need food or clothing. You can get everything from your own spiritual life, everything from your meditation. That's all you should be bothering about.

> To *cut off all ties is the best companion;*
> To *live alone is to become a friend of deities.*

Don't even bother about *kalyāṇa mitras*, just cut off all ties. That, paradoxically, will be your best companion. If you want spiritual companionship, just live by yourself and practise meditation; then you will see all the Buddha and bodhisattvas, and that's the best companionship that you could have.

> To *regard all enemies as passers-by on the road*
> Is *to avoid hatred.*

Even if someone upsets you or acts inimically towards you, don't worry about it; think that they're just like passers-by on the road. They're here for a minute or two and then they're gone. Don't disturb yourself, don't worry, don't become angry.

> *The best remedy for all obstacles is to meditate on Voidness.*
> *For they are all magic-like plays of the mind.*

If there's any obstacle, remind yourself that it is not absolutely real; it's only relatively real. It has arisen in dependence on causes and conditions, and when those causes and conditions are no longer there, the obstacle itself will no longer be there.

> *This is the right way for you to follow –*
> *Against it you will go astray!*

Is Milarepa being reasonable? Perhaps, having taken all kinds of approaches to Rechungpa, there isn't much else he can do. He seems to be getting tougher and tougher as the chapter proceeds. At first he's apparently just going along with Rechungpa, but he becomes more and more strict. Perhaps if he'd been strict right away, either Rechungpa would not have listened, or he would have taken what he heard the wrong way. He had so much pride, thinking that his own body was as good as a temple, and that he didn't need a guru. It's only now that he's been straightened out that he can receive this. When Milarepa says things like 'The outer phenomena suffices for one's Sūtras', one mustn't forget that Rechungpa has been over-valuing the written scriptures. And when Milarepa says, 'The Food-of-Samādhi is sufficient to sustain one', it's a reminder that Rechungpa has neglected his meditation in order to go off to India.

It is natural to feel that this sort of passage is so far away from your own experience that you can't identify with it very strongly. It's hard to imagine living without food, for example. But the principle is: don't do less than you can. It's not a question of all or nothing. If you can meditate all day, then, other factors being equal, you should. And if you can't meditate for more than an hour a day, whether for objective or subjective reasons, you must be uncompromising about that one hour a day. It's as though Milarepa is saying to Rechungpa, 'You are now capable of this, so you should not settle for less.' I don't think that what he means is that everybody should disregard the need for a temple or monastery, that nobody should have a guru, that everybody should look to his own mind, that nobody should ever read the *sūtras* or eat, but that we should all just get on with our meditation. He's saying it to Rechungpa presumably because he's convinced that Rechungpa has reached the point at which he can consider acting with this total uncompromisingness. With regard to others, or perhaps even with regard to Rechungpa earlier on, Milarepa would not adopt this sort of attitude, but he would certainly tell you to do the utmost of which you are capable, and that you are capable of doing more than you think. This is the basic point.

I don't think Milarepa is just trying to destroy any attempt at rationalizations. He wouldn't say it unless he really thought it applied to Rechungpa at that particular moment. In advising Rechungpa to act like this, he is expecting him to do so, or at least urging him to try. It may seem very *arhant*-like to focus on your own practice, but Milarepa will not have forgotten about compassion, on which he placed such an emphasis earlier on.

Milarepa seems to know much better than Rechungpa himself what Rechungpa is capable of, and it is often true that your spiritual friend has a much better idea of your capabilities than you do yourself, assuming that he has roughly the same intelligence as you, and that he really is your spiritual friend, he really does know you. When you are rationalizing or making excuses, your friend is much more likely to be able to see that than you can – not because he is wiser than you but because he is not personally involved, so he can see more clearly. You would therefore be at least well advised to consider very seriously what your friend says, especially if you are convinced he knows you and wishes you well, and especially when his advice goes against your own inclinations. You still have to decide whether or not to accept that advice, of course.

Looking at it the other way round, as a spiritual friend you have to be very careful about giving advice. You have to ask yourself whether you have really entered into the situation of the other person. You might advise someone who is very attached to his books to go and burn the lot, even his books on Buddhism, but that might be because, even though you mean well, you just don't realize what those books mean to him, and you can't see the positive side of his possessing them. Maybe books aren't very important to you, so you can say very lightly, 'Burn your books, you're too attached to them.' You don't, in a sense, realize what you are saying to him. If you give someone advice of that sort you must really have entered into the situation and have tried to experience it as he does, and to see it as it affects him, not as it would affect you if you were in that position yourself.

That's why when people ask me, 'Shall I give up my job?' or 'Shall I leave college?' I'm very reluctant to say anything other than, 'Consider the situation very carefully, and listen to what everybody else has to say.' Especially if I don't know somebody well, I certainly don't apply an automatic yardstick: it's good for everybody to give up their job and join a co-op, so yes, give up yours. I find myself being used as a sounding-board, but that's all right. I usually just point out the factors that the person needs to take into consideration. If I feel that I know somebody quite well, and if I can see clearly what the situation is, and if I feel they need to be advised, I don't hesitate to advise them, but I'm not in a hurry to give anybody any advice, especially when they could make up their own minds. One should encourage people to make their own decisions and confine oneself to drawing their attention to factors in the situation or possible consequences which they may have overlooked.

You have to be very sure of your ground before you give advice in a way that puts pressure on somebody to act in a particular way. It's always best to put your advice, if you have any, in the form of a suggestion: have you ever thought about doing such and such? Just plant that seed. Leave them to think about it. One should adopt this attitude especially with younger people, who may be impressionable, or emotionally under your influence, and very ready to do exactly what you tell them to do. If someone has considered all the different factors involved and genuinely isn't able to come to a decision, you can tell them what you think would be best. If you are in a position to see that, then you have to say so if you're asked. But otherwise, be quite cautious about giving advice, especially with regard to crucial decisions, otherwise you're playing around with people's lives in a quite irresponsible way. If it's some relatively neutral matter, if they're asking your advice about whether they should have their holiday in Spain or in Portugal, it doesn't matter much what you say, but when it comes to more vital matters one should be very careful and very conscientious.

Then Milarepa says:

> *I am an old man close to death,*
> *Who has no time for chatting.*
> *You are young, vigorous, and healthy*
> *And would not listen to my helpful advice.*

From what Rechungpa has just said about having reached the point of exhaustion you wouldn't have thought that he is 'young, vigorous, and healthy', but Milarepa is refusing to give him any false sympathy. It's very easy to weaken people by indulging them in their feelings of self-pity. If someone says, 'Oh, my knees are really aching, I've been meditating for three hours this morning,' it might seem sympathetic to respond, 'You've been doing really well, you've been doing so much meditation. Better take it easy for a bit. Don't strain yourself, don't overdo it.' But that's not real sympathy. Real sympathy would be to say, 'Knees aching? Yes, I suppose that's natural after three hours, but it'll soon pass, especially if you sit and meditate again.' Very often people welcome an opportunity of showing pseudo-kindliness and being indulgent rather than bracing.

If someone is a bit down and you think they need some encouragement, make sure that you offer real encouragement and inspiration. Don't say things like, 'Oh yes, you're really hard done by. Life is very difficult for you. I sympathize, I understand.' If someone has a lot of self-doubt, don't indulge them in that. If they say, 'I'm very weak, I can't do very much,' say, 'You can do more than you think you can. Come on, you've been doing quite well.' The principle is the same but the approach is quite different. Your sympathy should be bracing, not weakening, with no element of indulgence. If someone says, 'I'm feeling really sleepy this morning, I don't think I'll meditate,' if you say, 'Ah well, I don't suppose it'll matter much if you miss just this once. Go and have a nice sleep,' that is not real sympathy. Real sympathy would be to say, 'Come on, you've had enough sleep. You'll feel better as soon as you get up. Let's go and meditate in five minutes' time.' Perhaps if you're lucky someone might do the same sort of thing for you.

Perhaps, wanting to present an image of being a very kindly person, you're more concerned that they should think how kind and sympathetic you are than with really being kind and sympathetic. Sometimes when you're genuinely kind, people may not experience it as that, but feel that you're not very sympathetic, or that you haven't understood the position they're in, whereas you might have understood it very well indeed, but you're trying to have a bracing effect on them rather than a relaxing and enervating effect. To be able to strike the right note you have to be very much in tune with somebody, very genuine within yourself, and very clear about what you're doing. Are you really being sympathetic, or are you just trying to present the image of a sympathetic big brother, or daddy, or mother? If you indulge and pamper them, you're not taking them seriously, you're not treating them as an adult. Your concern is to make them feel good, rather than to do what is best for them.

> To talk with honesty and straightforwardness
> To prideful and greedy persons would be a sheer waste.
> If you want to meditate, you may come along with me;
> If you do not, you may do whatever you please.

Milarepa has now brought the situation to a climax. The talking has to stop. Rechungpa has to decide what he's going to do. Is he going to come with Milarepa or not? This is sometimes what you have to do with people, with more or less rigour: you have to bring them to the point of decision. Sometimes when one gets a copy of the minutes of a meeting, there's a lengthy record of a detailed discussion, but one looks at the end in vain for the decision. People say things like 'it would be good if somebody did such-and-such', and everybody agrees 'oh yes, it would be great if such-and-such happened', but no decision is taken as to what should be done and who is going to do it. Everybody goes away under the impression that something is going to be done, but of course nothing happens, and next time they meet they're surprised to discover that nothing has happened since the last meeting. In the end decisions have to be taken, even if it's only a decision to postpone taking a decision. Things shouldn't be left hanging in the air. Something needs to be done. So Milarepa is forcing Rechungpa to decide. Otherwise he may dither endlessly.

10
WHEREVER YOU GO, I WILL GO

The Jetsun was about to set out on his way, when Rechungpa grasped his clothing in time (to stop him), and sang this song called 'The Eight Needs'.

Though the best temple is one's own body,
We need a place for cover and sleep;
Without mercy, the wind and rain attack all.
Because of this, we always need a temple.

Though the best Guru is one's own mind,
We need a teacher to illustrate our Mind-Essence –
We cannot neglect for a moment to pray to him.
Because of this, we always need a Guru!

Though outer phenomenon may substitute for the Sūtras,
Hindrances and doubts in any case will arise.
To clear them up,
A lucid reference to the Sūtras is necessary.
Because of this, we always need the Sūtras!

Though the food of Samādhi may be sufficient,
Provisions for nourishment are necessary;

On food this delusory body must live.
Because of this, we always need food!

Though the best clothing is the Dumo-heat,
Something to cover the body is necessary,
For who is not afraid of shame and disgrace?
Because of this, we always need clothing.

Though the best thing is to cut off relations with all,
To get support and aid is ever necessary;
Good or bad, who has not some friends?
Because of this, we always need friends.

Though to avoid one's enemies is sufficient,
Sometimes one meets them on the road –
For who can be immune from hostility?
Because of this, we always need protection.

Though the best remedy is to view all hindrances as void,
The demons and ghosts are malignant and powerful;
To conquer the demon of ego
Is even more difficult.
Because of this, we always need safeguards.

To stay with my Guru brings happiness.
To return to you brings joy.
Wherever you go, I will go.
But I beseech you, by all means,
To stay in the valley for a short time.

> Though the best temple is one's own body
> We need a place for cover and sleep;
> Without mercy, the wind and rain attack all.
> Because of this, we always need a temple.

It's quite difficult to live without a house, without shelter, certainly in a place like Tibet. You might just about manage in some parts of India at certain times of the year, but even in the Buddha's day, though the

Buddha and his disciples wandered from place to place for eight or nine months of the year, for three or four months of the year, during the rainy season, they had to take shelter. It seems that the Buddha and his disciples normally meditated in the open air – in the forest, at the foot of trees. It's strange that we should find that difficult. I suppose it's because indoors you are sheltered from the wind and draughts, insects and noise, or it may just be what we're used to. If you're not used to living outdoors, you may find it distracting to hear breezes or birds, and in England it's cooler outside than in India. Tibet of course is cooler still. But we have to make sure that we don't demand more than we need. You need very little in the way of shelter really – just four walls and a roof to give you somewhere weatherproof and sufficiently comfortable and sufficiently warm (or cool) to be able to get on with your meditation without being distracted. When I lived in India I didn't find meditating out of doors difficult. What did make things difficult at one stage was walking from place to place. I don't know whether that was because I was not in very good physical condition or because it was exhausting, especially in that climate, but I found that adopting the wandering lifestyle made meditation very difficult. But I didn't find meditating in the open air difficult; in fact, I rather liked it. It can be very conducive to meditation, especially when you're sitting at evening time on the banks of a broad, slow river, and it's very still, and the sun is setting. You get quite a different experience when you meditate under those conditions. I've never done it, but I'm quite sure it would be very different also to meditate in the open air high up in the mountains, as Milarepa did.

We should at least be aware that we meditate under rather special conditions, that is to say almost always indoors. What you may think of as an essential part of the meditation experience may just be due to the fact that you're meditating indoors; it may not have anything much to do with the meditation. It might be a good idea to experiment gently and try meditating under different conditions, especially in the open air if you get an opportunity – if you're out hiking, or you are living in the country and can sit outside without disturbance. The real aspects of meditation are what meditations in different conditions have in common. For instance, when you meditate you might experience a feeling of security, but that may not be because of the meditation, but because you're safe and secure inside a house. When you're meditating in the open air, depending on your character and temperament, you may feel very different. You may even feel threatened, not because of the meditation, but because you are out in the open instead of being tucked away safely in your shrine-room. You should be quite clear what is due to the meditation and what is due to the circumstances under which you are meditating, and not associate your meditation too exclusively with any one set of circumstances. That may be necessary at first, but gradually you should acclimatize yourself to meditating under different conditions. Some people can meditate only in the shrine-room, or only in their own room, or only at a particular time of day, and to begin with these limitations have to be accepted – you have to start somewhere – but after a while you should try to overcome them. A friend of mine in India had a number of disciples, and he used to encourage them to meditate at whatever time of the day they found most difficult, which was usually of course in the early hours, just when they felt most sleepy. Don't take up this sort of practice prematurely, but as time goes on, try to make your meditation independent of conditions, even your own bodily conditions. Some people think that if they're a bit unwell, they can't meditate, and this might be true for the beginner, but as you become more established in meditation you shouldn't give it up just because you're not feeling very well. You should be able to break through that after you've had a certain amount of experience.

In principle Milarepa is right. He's telling Rechungpa not to allow his meditation, his spiritual life, to depend on any special set of circumstances – on the fact that he is well fed, or healthy, or not tired. In the end it mustn't depend on any circumstances or conditions. By agreeing to stay in the valley he recognizes that Rechungpa isn't yet able to follow his instructions to that extent, but nonetheless he has stated the principle involved without any compromise. Rechungpa keeps saying that we always need a temple, but we don't. You certainly need one at the beginning, but in the end you should be able to meditate under almost any conditions. Some of the members of our sangha in India are very good at this. I heard about one woman who had to sleep at night in a room she shared with twenty-two other people, and she had her bed on a shelf on the wall, but she still managed to meditate every day. Quite a number of people in India meditate in what we in the West would regard as intolerably crowded conditions, just sitting in a corner of the room while family life is going on all around them, people talking and cooking and getting on with their homework. Their meditation is usually quite good, and it shows on retreats, when they really get deeply into their practice. When I was there, they sat on through a violent hailstorm when we were on retreat. Hailstones as big as marbles came bouncing in through the door amongst them, and there was thunder and lightning, but no one took any notice.

It's a relative thing. We should accustom ourselves gradually to being less dependent on external conditions in every way; otherwise we become the slaves of external conditions. We become quite precious: we can't meditate unless we've got a quiet shrine-room and a decent cushion, and unless people are not fidgeting. It made me smile on my return to England to hear all the fuss and bother about cushions. All the time I was in India I never had a cushion to sit on when I was meditating. All I had at the very most was a folded blanket, or a piece of cotton cloth.

> *Though the best Guru is one's own mind*
> *We need a teacher to illustrate our Mind-Essence –*
> *We cannot neglect for a moment to pray to him.*
> *Because of this, we always need a Guru!*

This verse and the next refer to a Mahāmudrā teaching on the four kinds of teacher: (1) The human teacher with a transmission; (2) The Buddha's words; (3) Appearances; (4) Ultimate reality. In a sense it's true that 'the best guru is one's own mind', but it's not one's ordinary mind, it's a higher mind, so to speak, and you need a teacher to point that out, to put you in touch with it, or to help you to put yourself in touch with it. It isn't as though your own mind can be a guru to you from the very beginning. You need a considerable amount of spiritual experience, and you don't get that without the help of someone else. So 'because of this, we always need a guru'. And in the same way:

> *Though outer phenomenon may substitute for the Sūtras,*
> *Hindrances and doubts in any case will arise.*
> *To clear them up,*
> *A lucid reference to the Sūtras is necessary.*
> *Because of this, we always need the Sūtras!*

A tree or a flower may be a wonderful symbol, but it cannot speak. If you have difficulties or doubts, the tree or the flower cannot clear them up. For that you need to refer to the Buddha's teachings, to the *sūtras*, and even they may not always be able to clear up your specific questions; you may need a teacher as well. The *sūtras* are the records of the Buddha's teachings, an Enlightened human being in communication with unenlightened or less enlightened human beings, so the teachings contained in the *sūtras* are certainly more helpful to us than 'outer phenomena'.

Such rationalizations are quite common, though. You hear people saying, 'Life is my teacher – I don't need to meditate,' or 'You mustn't depend on anyone else,' or 'Buddhism teaches you to be independent. I'm an individual. I'm free.' This used to be Krishnamurti's approach, at least in theory – but in practice it doesn't work like that. Krishnamurti's followers used to go eagerly to listen to his lectures and buy his books and in effect regard him as a guru.[228] There seemed to be an element of intellectual dishonesty involved. They looked down on other people who had gurus, but they looked up to Krishnaji as he criticized foolish people who had gurus and looked outside themselves for help and so on and so forth. I heard him speak once – he was quite a good speaker – and I remember him looking round at his audience, mostly Hindus, and saying, 'There you are, rotting under your *Bhagavad Gītā*!' There was a great deal of truth in what he said, but you can also get people rotting underneath their copies of Krishnamurti's talks, though he didn't seem to be able to see that. I had a discussion about this with one of his followers, and asked why he said that sort of thing about scriptures, but at the same time he seems to encourage people to read his books. The reply was that his books aren't books, they're slices of experience. I said, 'Well, aren't scriptures also slices of experience?' and he had no answer to that. One could even say that that is what distinguishes Buddhist scriptures from Christian or Hindu scriptures – they are slices of experience rather than revealed knowledge.

Another way to think about it is to bear in mind that the *sūtras* are themselves outer phenomena. Sri Ramakrishna told a little story about someone who had been studying the Advaita Vedanta in a one-sided sort of way and believed, in a muddle-headed fashion, that everything was one, it was all the same. Everything was God. One day he was walking through the bazaar when there was a sudden shout of alarm – a mad elephant had escaped! He saw this elephant coming towards him with its trunk upraised, and he thought, 'Well, everything is God, why should I get out of the way?' The mahout on the back of the elephant was shouting, 'Get out of the way, the elephant's gone mad!' But the man didn't take any notice, and the elephant picked him up with its trunk and tossed him aside. Luckily he was only slightly concussed, and when he came to, people were scolding him, saying, 'Why on earth didn't you get out of the elephant's path, you fool?' He said, 'Well, the elephant is God. It's all one, it's all the same.' So they said, 'The elephant may be God, but what about the mahout? Is he not God too? And he was telling you to get out of the way!' In the same way, books are not distinct from outer phenomena. Books are *included* in outer phenomena. Why should you make a point of paying attention to things like trees and flowers but ignore what books have to say?

People might say that books are from somebody else's point of view, they're biased, whereas trees are completely objective, but are they really? Can a tree tell you anything? No, it can say nothing at all. Any 'lesson' you learn from it, any message you glean from it, any symbolism you attribute to it, comes from your own mind, and may or may not be useful. At least in the case of the book, especially the *sūtra*, you are genuinely in contact with another mind, but in the case of the outer phenomena of nature, you may be in contact with something, but it is something so to speak less developed than yourself. Perhaps you teach yourself by projecting your own thoughts or reflections onto the tree or the flower, but they don't say anything at all – or rather, they can say anything you want them to say. So we always need the *sūtras*.

> Though the food of Samādhi may be sufficient,
> Provisions for nourishment are necessary;
> On food this delusory body must live.
> Because of this, we always need food!

Even Milarepa used to gather nettles and make soup. If he could really live on the food of *samādhi* and only that, why should he have bothered to do that? But no doubt you can get more nourishment from your *dhyāna* experience than you think. At least part of your dependence on food may be neurotic. You don't really need that chocolate bar, or that bag of peanuts. As you get more into meditation you feel less need for food, even a sort of distaste for it. It seems a coarse, crude thing to do, to put lumps of matter into your mouth and chew them and swallow them. It seems almost unnatural. But you may feel hungry after meditating because your senses have not received any satisfaction for some time. You've been out of contact with the sense-world, and the senses are reasserting themselves. After you've been in a somewhat different state of consciousness, the senses start to get a bit restless; they're not getting any attention, and there's a tendency to want to make up for that afterwards.

> Though the best clothing is the Dumo-heat,
> Something to cover the body is necessary,
> For who is not afraid of shame and disgrace?
> Because of this, we always need clothing.

If they're going to be meditating up in the mountains and there's no one around, the question of shame and disgrace probably doesn't arise, but should shame and disgrace arise at all in relation to being naked? The considerations are partly climatic, of course, but some people can't be in the nude in a natural, healthy, unselfconscious way. They become a bit exhibitionist, they do it quite self-consciously almost for the kick that they get out of it and the consciousness that they are offending somebody. A lot of things that people do in the name of the arts come under this sort of heading. People want to see whether they can provoke Mrs Whitehouse, for instance, to loud screams of horror and outrage, and if they do, they feel they've succeeded.[229]

If that's a stage of necessary reaction, the reactions sometimes seem to last a very long time. It seems rather self-indulgent. People seem to be exploiting something subjective and not very pleasant in the name of freedom of expression. If a play requires someone to be naked, that's fair enough, but sometimes people introduce nudity onto the stage just for its own sake. When you've got a number of people together, when the weather permits and it seems desirable, no one need feel any self-consciousness about not having any clothes on, though very often people do feel quite self-conscious in that sort of situation. It's a question of what is appropriate to the circumstances and your own genuine feelings. So perhaps we need not agree with Rechungpa that we always need clothing. It reminds me of a story about a nun who was asked why nuns took a vow that in the bathroom they always kept on their shift. So she said, 'Oh dear, we couldn't be naked in front of the Good Lord!' – as though the Good Lord was able to see through the wall of the bathroom but not through a shift. Nudity, if it occurs, should be natural and unselfconscious. It shouldn't be something that you feel a need to flaunt or inflict on other people.

> Though the best thing is to cut off relationships with all,
> To get support and aid is ever necessary;
> Good or bad, who has not some friends?
> Because of this, we always need friends.

Rechungpa was probably thinking in the first place of material aid and support, food and clothing from lay patrons, but perhaps he is also thinking of spiritual support, protection from difficulties and dangers. When Milarepa said in his song, 'To cut off all ties is the best companion. To live alone is to become a friend of deities', he was saying is that if you can have the company of Buddhas and bodhisattvas, that's better than having the company of ordinary human beings. That's true, but it's a big if. Most people are not capable of enjoying the company of Buddhas and bodhisattvas, so they need spiritual friends, or even ordinary friends. If in meditation you can conjure up all around you the presence of Buddhas and bodhisattvas, who would not want to do that? But very few people can do it; most people are dependent on spiritual friends in the flesh. Milarepa is not against companionship. He is only saying that if spiritual companionship in the form of Buddhas and bodhisattvas is available to you, why not avail yourself of that?

It seems that Rechungpa hasn't fully grasped the point. He is probably right in saying, 'Good or bad, who has not some friends?' Whether you like it or not, you will be in contact with people, so it's good to have the best friends that you possibly can, whether on the human level or even on some higher level.

> Though to avoid one's enemies is sufficient,
> Sometimes one meets them on the road –
> For who can be immune from hostility?
> Because of this, we always need protection.

Here, presumably, our friends come in. One can't always avoid one's enemies as Milarepa has suggested. They don't always just pass by; sometimes they hang around. Sometimes they even try to get at you and finish you off. We always need protection from them; it's not as simple as just waiting until they've passed by.

If we take Milarepa's words in the fullest possible sense, in the end our enemies pass by in the sense that they die, or we die. But it isn't necessarily true that if you keep quiet, in the end people will leave you alone. In some cases their hatred is so virulent that it continues indefinitely and you may have to take steps to guard yourself against it. Not that you should retaliate, but you may have to take measures to protect yourself from the other person's attempts to harm you. In enmity of this sort, when people just don't give up, there's something almost demoniacal, almost crazy, about it. You may occasionally come across people who've really got it in for you. You can't see why but they keep at it, year after year, even though as far as you know you have done nothing to upset them. They've taken an unreasoning dislike to you, or even actually hate you. Sometimes there is some reason for their being annoyed with you, but not to that extent. That sort of anger and hatred seems quite pathological.

> Though the best remedy is to view all hindrances as void,
> The demons and ghosts are malignant and powerful;
> To conquer the demon of ego
> Is even more difficult.
> Because of this, we always need safeguards.

If you can view all hindrances as void, that's best, but very often you can do this only in a purely theoretical, intellectual way, so you need practical safeguards. (Perhaps 'safeguards' isn't quite the right word here. I don't know what the original Tibetan or Sanskrit word was.) For instance, take the question of the ego. You are perhaps conscious that your ego is very strong, but just contemplating the Void won't be enough to get rid of that feeling of ego, because your experience of the Void may be very weak, or perhaps amounts just to an intellectual understanding. You need actual practices, 'safeguards', that will help you to weaken your ego. You need to engage in unselfish work for the benefit of other people, perhaps, or to practise the *mettā bhāvanā*, or communicate with other people, even teach other people the Dharma. You are not in a position directly to apply the remedy of *śūnyatā*. It seems that Milarepa is insisting almost on the path of no steps at all, just going straight to the top of the stairs with one tremendous leap, but not everybody is able to make that leap. Rechungpa is right to insist on the path of regular steps.

When it comes to how we should view the hindrances that come up in meditation, which can seem very real, there are traditionally various ways of dealing with them. If for instance the hindrance of anger comes up, you can deal with it by cultivating the opposite of anger – that is to say, *mettā*. You can deal with it by reflecting on the unpleasant or undesirable consequences of indulging in your anger. You can deal with it by reflecting that your anger is just a passing mental state and that if you watch it carefully it will eventually dissolve. But the ability to view all hindrances as void is the prerogative only of a person who is very highly gifted, spiritually speaking. Most people have to accept the hindrances as real and deal with them on that level. They can't directly see their unreality, their voidness. Nonetheless, what Milarepa says is true. The hindrances are void. That is the ultimate answer to them. That is in a way the approach one is taking if one uses the antidote of Going for Refuge, of trying to transcend the whole thing.[230]

One could say that the difference between the two approaches is that you can get rid of the unskilful with the help of the skilful and then go beyond even the skilful; or, as Milarepa is saying, you can get rid of the unskilful straight away, without going via the skilful – but the ability to do that is very rare. The saying in this connection is that you use one thorn to get rid of another.[231] If there's a thorn sticking in your flesh, you take another thorn and use it to loosen the first thorn, and in that way pull it out. Similarly, you use the skilful mental state to get rid of the unskilful mental state, but even the skilful mental state is still mundane, and you need to go beyond the mundane, so in the end you abandon even the the skilful mental state.

Rechungpa concludes:

> To stay with my Guru brings happiness;
> To return to you brings joy.
> Wherever you go, I will go.
> But I beseech you, by all means,
> To stay in the valley for a short time.

It's as though he's saying, 'I really am exhausted. Wherever you go, I will go, but please, if at all possible, let me have a little rest.'

> Milarepa replied, 'If you have confidence, to follow my way will be quite sufficient; otherwise, there will always be a need for something. Well, if by all means you are unwilling to go to no-man's mountain now, let us go to Bouto to preach the Dharma.'

So in the end Milarepa gives in, in a sense. Perhaps Rechungpa really is tired. Milarepa has put the ideal to him in all its uncompromisingness. He has considered it necessary to do that. But Rechungpa has in effect said that some concessions need to be made to human weakness. He doesn't deny that the path that Milarepa has pointed out is the best, but he says that for most people it is just not possible to follow it, and Milarepa seems to accept that.

It seems important that the ideal is always pitched somewhat beyond people's reach; otherwise they won't push themselves as much as they could. It's a sort of bargaining. Someone says, 'I can meditate for an hour a day.' The guru says, 'What? Only an hour a day? No, you need to do at least ten hours.' The disciple says, 'I couldn't possibly manage ten hours. Maybe I could manage two, but certainly not ten.' The guru says, 'I'm sure you could manage ten hours a day.' The disciple says, 'Well, perhaps I could manage three or even three and a half, but not ten' – and so on. In the end they may settle on five hours a day, but if the guru was to give in straightaway, the disciple would not be stretched. He would not do what in fact he was capable of doing.

> Thereupon the Jetsun and Rechungpa went to Bouto of Red Rock.

Milarepa gives way, but not entirely. The fact that you relax a little doesn't mean that you give up effort altogether. They're going to stay a little while to preach the Dharma and then carry on with further solitary meditation. Milarepa has had his say, Rechungpa has had his, and they've come to an agreement. Milarepa has unambiguously stated the ideal in all its integrity, and Rechungpa has pleaded for some concessions to be made to ordinary human weakness. What he says is not unreasonable, but it is so easy to make excuses and rationalize that it's not a bad thing that someone like Milarepa holds up spiritual principles in a totally uncompromising way. There are very few people around who are totally uncompromising, and it's very good that there should be at least a few. Otherwise there's no end of compromise. You can compromise your spiritual life out of existence if you're not careful. At some point you have to make a stand. Sometimes when you're uncompromising, people are more amenable than you think they are going to be. Perhaps it's not such a big deal after all, or perhaps they don't mind all that much. Sometimes you've made it a big thing in your own mind, or they're more reasonable than you've feared. Maybe the fact that you are firm and decisive means that there's not as much need for discussion as there would be if you were uncertain yourself.

This is the end of the story of the yak-horn. It wasn't all about the yak-horn, but perhaps that's the title because that is the highlight of the whole chapter – Milarepa's creeping into the yak-horn and Rechungpa's being unable to follow him. In a sense the whole episode is about pride. Pride is so obviously an unskilful mental state that one has to find a way of getting over it or doing something about it or transcending it, so perhaps there isn't very much to say about it, but inasmuch as pride is the basic error from the spiritual point of view, all spiritual practices, especially *vipaśyanā* ones, are meant to tackle it, directly or indirectly. If you meditate, or if you engage in right livelihood, in the long run what you're trying to do is break down your idea of yourself as a fixed stable ego. In a metaphysical sense you're trying to transcend the existing limits of your consciousness. Pride or egotism is settling down at a particular level and refusing to go beyond it, refusing to change, refusing to grow. The spiritual life consists in growth, which is the complete antithesis of pride and conceit, so everything that helps you to grow is inimical to egotism, inimical to pride and conceit. How can you be proud of what you are now if you realize that it must be transcended as quickly as possible?

Rechungpa's conceit was more specific – for example, he was expecting approval from his guru – but there's no need to look for a specific way of overcoming your desire for approval. If you are keeping up with your spiritual practices they will all have that effect, because the desire for approval is really desire for approval for yourself as you are now. Probably the best practical way of dealing with that is remaining in contact with spiritual friends, who will give you genuine encouragement but who will not just approve of you as you are now, who will not allow you to settle down in what you now are.

Ultimately your aim is to get rid of the very distinction between subject and object, but you can't do that immediately. You can't reduce them immediately to the Void; you have to purify and refine them until in the end you get a tenuous, even diaphanous, subject–object distinction that you can begin to see through. Sometimes change is thought of in quite external, peripheral terms. External changes help to bring about internal changes, but they are not the same thing. Even if you make changes in your way of life, you still have to take advantage of those external changes and change internally as well. You don't necessarily change just because you join a spiritual community. Externally speaking, you just exchange one roof for another. It's what you do under that roof that counts. You don't necessarily change just because you give up your job, or give up going to college. It only gives you an opportunity to change.

NOTES

1 Sir Humphrey Clarke (trans.),
   *The Message of Milarepa:
   New Light upon the Tibetan
   Way*, John Murray, London
   1958, p. 80; now available
   as *Songs of Milarepa*, Dover
   Publications, Mineola NY
   2003.

2 Ibid., p. xiv.

3 W. Y. Evans-Wentz, *Tibet's
   Great Yogī Milarepa*, Oxford
   University Press, Oxford 1928.

4 Sangharakshita, *The Rainbow
   Road from Tooting Broadway
   to Kalimpong* (*Complete
   Works*, vol. 20, p. 151).

5 Garma C. C. Chang, *The
   Hundred Thousand Songs
   of Milarepa*, Shambhala
   Publications, Boston and
   London 1999, p. ix.

6 Sangharakshita, *Moving
   Against the Stream*, Windhorse
   Publications, Birmingham
   2003, p. 42 (*Complete Works*,
   vol. 23).

7 Chogyam Trungpa, *Milarepa:
   Lessons from the Life and
   Songs of Tibet's Great Yogi*,
   edited by Judith L. Lief,
   Shambhala Publications,
   Boulder 2017, p. xv.

8 Edited seminars in the
   Complete Works include
   Mahāyāna commentaries
   Wisdom Beyond Words
   (vol. 14), *Know your Mind*,
   Living Ethically, and *Living
   Wisely* (all vol. 17), and
   commentaries on Pāli texts
   Living with Awareness and
   Living with Kindness (vol. 15).
   Seminar material also appears
   woven into text gathered from
   talks in vol. 4 (*The Bodhisattva
   Ideal*, *The Endlessly
   Fascinating Cry*), vol. 5 (*The
   Purpose and Practice of
   Buddhist Meditation*), vol. 13
   (*Creative Symbols of Tantric
   Buddhism*), and vol. 16
   (throughout).

9   An account of how Rechungpa came to tell Milarepa's life story is given in chapter 1 of 'Rechungpa's Journey to Weu'; see Sangharakshita, *Milarepa and the Art of Discipleship II* (*Complete Works*, vol. 19, pp. 304–7).

10   Andrew Quintman (trans.), *The Life of Milarepa*, Penguin 2010, p. 169.

11   See Sangharakshita, *Milarepa and the Art of Discipleship II* (*Complete Works*, vol. 19, pp. 249–51).

12   Lama Kunga Rinpoche and Brian Cutillo (trans.), *Drinking the Mountain Stream: Songs of Tibet's Beloved Saint, Milarepa*, Wisdom Publications, Boston 1995, p. 30.

13   See Sangharakshita, *Milarepa and the Art of Discipleship II* (*Complete Works*, vol. 19), the commentary on 'Rechungpa's Repentance', pp. 5–168.

14   See *Milarepa and the Art of Discipleship II* (*Complete Works*, vol. 19), pp. 22, pp. 394–5.

15   'Is a Guru Necessary?' appears as chapter 14 of *What is the Sangha?* (*Complete Works*, vol. 3, pp. 545–62). 'My Relation to the Western Buddhist Order', originally published in booklet form, is included in *Complete Works*, vol. 2.

16   'It has been said that a guru should consider that he has not been successful as a guru unless his disciples do better than him. If in each generation the disciples fall below the guru, in a few generations what will be the state of affairs? The guru should therefore not be thinking in terms of keeping his disciples as disciples, or even of his disciples doing as well as he has done himself. He'll be thinking in terms of his disciples doing even better; otherwise the chances are that the whole tradition will degenerate very quickly.' Sangharakshita, *Milarepa and the Art of Discipleship II* (*Complete Works*, vol. 19), chapter 2 of 'Heartfelt Advice to Rechungpa'.

17   My second gift is a golden net.
     Can you recognize it?

     'Four Gifts', written in 1975; see *Complete Poems 1941–1994*, (*Complete Works*, vol. 25).

18   Unless otherwise stated, quotations in chapters 1 and 2 are taken from Garma C. C. Chang (trans.), *The Hundred Thousand Songs of Milarepa*, Shambhala Publications, Boston and London 1999, pp. 1–7.

19   *Majjhima Nikāya* 10. See I. B. Horner (trans.), *The Collection of the Middle Length Sayings*, vol. i, Pali Text Society, Oxford 1995, pp. 70–82; or Bhikkhu Ñāṇamoli and Bhikkhu Bodhi (trans.), *The Middle Length*

Discourses of the Buddha, Wisdom Publications, Boston 1995, pp. 145–55. See also Sangharakshita's commentary, *Living with Awareness* (*Complete Works*, vol. 15).

20 Section 6.7 of the *Mahāparinibbāna Sutta, Dīgha Nikāya* 16 (ii.156); see M. Walshe (trans.), *The Long Discourses of the Buddha*, Wisdom Publications, Boston 1995, p. 270; or T. W. Rhys Davids (trans.), *Dialogues of the Buddha*, part 2, Pali Text Society, Oxford 1977, p. 173.

21 *Makhadeva Jātaka, Jātaka* 1.9. *The Jatāka*, volume 1, trans. Robert Chalmers, Cambridge University Press 1895, pp. 31–2.

22 The story of the Buddha, Māra, and the earth goddess seems first to have been introduced to the accounts of the Buddha's journey to Enlightenment in the Mahāyāna tradition's *Lalitavistara Sūtra*. For a translation, see Gwendolyn Bays (trans.), *The Voice of the Buddha*, vol. ii, Dharma Publishing, Berkeley 1983, pp. 481–2.

23 *Mahāparinibbāna Sutta, Dīgha Nikāya* 16 (ii.87). See T. W. & C. A. F. Rhys Davids (trans.), *Dialogues of the Buddha*, part 2, Pali Text Society, Oxford 1995, p. 92; or M. Walshe (trans.), *The Long Discourses of the Buddha*, Wisdom Publications, Boston 1995, p. 237–8.

24 *Udāna* 4.4. See John D. Ireland (trans.), *The Udāna and the Itivuttaka*, Buddhist Publication Society, Kandy 1997, pp. 56–8.

25 This seems to be a reference to Matthew 12:26. 'And if Satan cast out Satan, he is divided against himself; how shall then his kingdom stand?'

26 *Mahāsaccaka Sutta, Majjhima Nikāya* 36 (i.246). See Bhikkhu Ñāṇamoli and Bhikkhu Bodhi (trans.), *The Middle Length Discourses of the Buddha*, Wisdom Publications, Boston 1995, p. 340; or I. B. Horner (trans.), *The Collection of the Middle Length Sayings*, vol. i, Pali Text Society, Oxford 1995, p. 301.

27 This is a reference to the Old Testament's account of the exile of the prophet Elijah: 'And the ravens brought him bread and flesh in the morning, and bread and flesh in the evening; and he drank of the brook.' (1 Kings 17:6)

28 *Nivāpa Sutta, Majjhima Nikāya* 25 (i.151–60). See Bhikkhu Ñāṇamoli and Bhikkhu Bodhi (trans.), *The Middle Length Discourses of the Buddha*, Wisdom Publications, Boston 1995, p. 246–52; or I. B. Horner (trans.), *The Collection of the Middle Length Sayings*, vol. i, Pali Text Society, Oxford 1995, pp. 194–203.

29 Unless otherwise stated, quotations in this chapter are taken from Edward Conze (ed.), *Buddhist Texts Through the Ages*, Oneworld

Publications, Rockport 1995, p. 258 and pp. 266–7.

30 For Sangharakshita's commentary on this parable, see chapter 7, 'The Jewel in the Lotus', in *The Drama of Cosmic Enlightenment* (*Complete Works*, vol. 16, pp. 169–74); also the address 'The Priceless Jewel', ibid., pp. 213–23.

31 Sangharakshita (trans.), *Dhammapada*, Windhorse Publications, Cambridge 2008, verse 200 (*Complete Works*, vol. 15).

32 For an account of the seven *bodhyaṅgas*, see Sangharakshita, 'Mind – Reactive and Creative', in *Buddha Mind*, Windhorse Publications, Birmingham 2001, pp. 55–61 (*Complete Works*, vol. 11).

33 *Ariyapariyesanā Sutta, Majjhima Nikāya* 26 (i.168). See I. B. Horner (trans.), *The Collection of the Middle Length Sayings*, vol. i, Pali Text Society, Oxford 1995, p. 212; or Bhikkhu Bodhi (trans.), *The Connected Discourses of the Buddha*, Wisdom Publications, Boston 2000, p. 261.

34 Unless otherwise stated, quotations in this chapter are taken from Garma C. C. Chang (trans.), *The Hundred Thousand Songs of Milarepa*, Shambhala Publications, Boston and London 1999, pp. 161–3.

35 *Saṃyutta Nikāya* v.283, in Bhikkhu Bodhi (trans.), *The*

Connected Discourses of the Buddha, Wisdom Publications, 2000, p. 1741.

36 A famous quotation from the Smaragdine Tablet, an ancient alchemical document ascribed to Hermes Tresmegistus, states the 'Hermetic correspondence' between higher and lower levels of reality: 'That which is above is like that which is below and that which is below is like that which is above, to accomplish the miracles of one thing.'

37 Kate Crosby and Andrew Skilton (trans.), *The Bodhicaryāvatāra*, Windhorse Publications, Birmingham 2002, chapter 5, verse 13.

38 Unless otherwise stated, quotations in this chapter are taken from Garma C. C. Chang (trans.), *The Hundred Thousand Songs of Milarepa*, Shambhala Publications, Boston and London 1999, pp. 164–70.

39 *Sāmaññaphala Sutta, Dīgha Nikāya* 2 (i.76). See T. W. Rhys Davids (trans.) *Dialogues of the Buddha*, part 1, Pali Text Society, Oxford 1995, p. 86. See also M. Walshe (trans.), *The Long Discourses of the Buddha*, Wisdom Publications, Boston 1995, pp. 103–4.

40 See page 171.

41 There are various versions of this story. See, for example, Lu K'uan Yü, *Ch'an and Zen Teaching*, Samuel Weiser, Maine 1993, vol. i, p. 31.

42 *Dhammapada* 203. See Sangharakshita (trans.),

Dhammapada, Windhorse
Publications, Cambridge
2008, p. 72 (*Complete Works*,
vol. 15).

43 For an account of the
seven *bodhyaṅgas*, see
Sangharakshita, 'Mind –
Reactive and Creative', in
Buddha Mind, Windhorse
Publications, Birmingham
2001, pp. 55–61 (*Complete
Works*, vol. 11).

44 A version of the traditional
guru yoga practice is described
in chapter 4, 'The Cosmic
Refuge Tree and the Archetypal
Guru', in Sangharakshita,
*Creative Symbols of Tantric
Buddhism*, Windhorse
Publications, Birmingham
2002, pp. 102–5 (*Complete
Works*, vol. 13).

45 The story of Śāriputra and
Aśvajit is told at *Vinaya Piṭaka*
i.39 (*Mahāvagga* 1.23); see I.
B. Horner (trans.), *The Book
of the Discipline*, part 4, Pali
Text Society, Oxford 1996, pp.
52–4.

46 *Dhammapada*, verse 204.
See Sangharakshita (trans.),
Dhammapada, Windhorse
Publications, Cambridge
2008, p. 73 (*Complete Works*,
vol. 15).

47 W. Y. Evans-Wentz (ed.),
Tibet's Great Yogī Milarepa,
Oxford University Press, 1928,
p. 96.

48 For a further description of
the six perfections, see, for
example, the section titled
'The Six Perfections' in
Sangharakshita, *A Survey*

of Buddhism, Windhorse
Publications, Birmingham
2001, pp. 466–90 (*Complete
Works*, vol. 1).

49 William Blake, in his preface to
Milton.

50 *Pātimokkha*, Suddhapācittiyā
50.

51 Unless otherwise stated,
quotations in this chapter
are taken from Garma C. C.
Chang (trans.), *The Hundred
Thousand Songs of Milarepa*,
Shambhala Publications,
Boston and London 1999,
pp. 171–2.

52 *Bhagavad Gītā*, vii.2.

53 See Sangharakshita, *Wisdom
Beyond Words*, Windhorse
Publications, Birmingham
2000, pp. 95–102 (*Complete
Works*, vol. 14).

54 Lobsang P. Lhalunga (trans.),
The Life of Milarepa, E. P.
Dutton, New York 1977,
pp. 134–9.

55 The three lamas were Chattrul
Rimpoche, Jamyang Khyentse
Rimpoche, and Dudjom
Rimpoche, as Sangharakshita
explains in the preface to
Precious Teachers, Windhorse
Publications, Birmingham
2007 (*Complete Works*,
vol. 22). He goes on to say,
'For my part, I have never
tried to find out how my
teachers compared with one
another, spiritually speaking.
Indeed, I never thought in
such terms. It was enough that
they were vastly superior to
me in wisdom and compassion
and that, by a strange

combination of circumstances, I had come to be in contact with them and could benefit from their teaching and spiritual influence.'

56 Lobsang P. Lhalungpa (trans.), *The Life of Milarepa*, Penguin Books, 1995, p. 48.

57 Sangharakshita tells the story of this meeting in his volume of memoirs *In the Sign of the Golden Wheel*, Windhorse Publications, Birmingham 1996, pp. 318–9 (*Complete Works*, vol. 22).

58 Unless otherwise stated, quotations in this chapter are taken from Garma C. C. Chang (trans.), *The Hundred Thousand Songs of Milarepa*, Shambhala Publications, Boston and London 1999, pp. 172–83.

59 The offering of the mandala practice is one of the four foundation practices (*mūla yogas*) of Tantric Buddhism. It is described in more detail in chapter 6, 'Offerings and Self-Sacrifice' in Sangharakshita, *Creative Symbols of Tantric Buddhism*, Windhorse Publications, Birmingham 2002, pp. 143–9 (*Complete Works*, vol. 13).

60 Kate Crosby and Andrew Skilton (trans.), *The Bodhicaryāvatāra*, Windhorse Publications, Birmingham 2002, chapter 2, verse 61.

61 *Etadaggavagga, Aṅguttara Nikāya* 1.14 (i.24–7). See Bhikkhu Bodhi (trans.), *The Numerical Discourses of the Buddha*, Wisdom Publications 2012, pp. 109–113; or F. L. Woodward (trans.), *The Book of the Gradual Sayings*, vol. i, Pali Text Society, Oxford 1995, pp. 16–25.

62 Lobsang P. Lhalungpa (trans.), *The Life of Milarepa*, Penguin Books, 1995, pp. 120–1.

63 Unless otherwise stated, quotations in this chapter are taken from Garma C. C. Chang (trans.), *The Hundred Thousand Songs of Milarepa*, Shambhala Publications, Boston and London 1999, pp. 184–6.

64 *The Moment*, fourth instalment, 1855.

65 *Dhammapada* 5. See Sangharakshita (trans.), *Dhammapada*, Windhorse Publications, Cambridge 2008, p. 14 (*Complete Works*, vol. 15).

66 'The Sermon of the Plowers', 18 January 1548.

67 *Alagaddūpama Sutta, Majjhima Nikāya* 22 (i.133–4). See I. B. Horner (trans.), *The Collection of the Middle Length Sayings*, vol. i, Pali Text Society, Oxford 1995, p. 172; or Bhikkhu Ñāṇamoli and Bhikkhu Bodhi (trans.), *The Middle Length Discourses of the Buddha*, Wisdom Publications, Boston 1995, pp. 227–8.

68 William Shakespeare, *As You Like It*, Act II, Scene i.

69 Constituent Assembly of India, November 1948: 'What is the village but a sink of

localism, a den of ignorance, narrow-mindedness and communalism?' Dhanajay Keer, *Dr Ambedkar: Life and Mission*, Popular Prakashan, Bombay 1981, p. 409.

70 Trevor Ling, *The Buddha*, Penguin Books, Harmondsworth 1976, p. 117.

71 For a detailed description of these eleven positive (*kuśala*) mental states, see chapter 7, 'The Creative Mind at Work', in Sangharakshita, *Know Your Mind*, Windhorse Publications, Birmingham 2002, pp. 117–55 (*Complete Works*, vol. 17).

72 *Dhammapada* 62.

73 This much loved extended metaphor is from verse 6 of the *Bhagavad Gītā Mahātmya* ('The Glories of the *Bhagavad Gītā*') by Adi Shankaracharya, an eighth-century CE philosopher who consolidated the teachings of Advaita Vedanta.

74 *Etadaggavagga*, *Aṅguttara Nikāya* 1.14 (i.24–7). See Bhikkhu Bodhi (trans.), *The Numerical Discourses of the Buddha*, Wisdom Publications 2012, pp. 109–113; or F. L. Woodward (trans.), *The Book of the Gradual Sayings*, vol. i, Pali Text Society, Oxford 1995, pp. 16–25.

75 For more about the *ālaya vijñāna*, see chapter 4, 'The Turning About', in Sangharakshita, *The Meaning of Conversion in Buddhism*, Windhorse Publications,

Birmingham 1994, p. 68 (*Complete Works*, vol. 2).

76 *Dhammapada* 33. The *Cittavagga* is the third chapter of the *Dhammapada*.

77 Sangharakshita explains this distinction in a talk, 'The Path of Regular Steps and the Path of Irregular Steps', published in *The Taste of Freedom*, Windhorse Publications, Birmingham 1997, pp. 27–48 (*Complete Works*, vol. 11).

78 See chapter 4, 'The Heroic Ideal in Buddhism', in Sangharakshita, *Who is the Buddha?* (*Complete Works*, vol. 3, pp. 57–71).

79 'There is a book, who runs may read, / Which heavenly truth imparts': John Keble (1792–1866), *The Christian Year: Septuagesima*.

80 For example, see the extract, 'Twofold Agelessness and Emptiness', quoting from the *Laṅkāvatāra Sūtra* in Edward Conze et al (trans.), *Buddhist Texts Through the Ages*, Shambhala, Boston and Shaftesbury 1990, pp. 211–2.

81 In his glossary to the *Laṅkāvatāra Sūtra*, D. T. Suzuki translates *anāboghacaryā* as 'effortless, purposeless, not being aware of conscious strivings'. See D. T. Suzuki, *Studies in the Laṅkāvatāra Sūtra*, Routledge & Kegan Paul, London and Boston 1972, pp. 378–9. Suzuki describes it as 'one of the very significant conceptions of Mahāyāna Buddhism' (ibid.,

p. 379) and 'the quintessence of Bodhisattvahood' (ibid., p. 226).

82 Garma C. C. Chang, *The Hundred Thousand Songs of Milarepa*, Shambhala Publications, Boston and London 1999, pp. 225–40.

83 Ibid., pp. 374–96.

84 Ibid., pp. 563–9.

85 For example, 'The Preaching on Mount Bonbo', ibid., p. 545.

86 Ibid., p. 550.

87 Ibid., p. 103.

88 Ibid., p. 475.

89 Peter Alan Roberts, *The Biographies of Rechungpa: The Evolution of a Tibetan Hagiography*, Routledge, London and New York 2007, p. 210.

90 Garma C. C. Chang, *The Hundred Thousand Songs of Milarepa*, Shambhala Publications, Boston and London 1999, p. 434.

91 In the Early Buddhist conception of the path to Enlightenment, it is said that the 'point of no return' is reached at the stage called 'knowledge and vision of things as they really are'. Up to this point there is still the danger of regressing, but beyond it, one's spiritual momentum is unstoppable. This point is synonymous with what is also called 'Stream Entry'. This point corresponds to the eighth of the ten stages (*bhūmis*) of the bodhisattva path taught in Mahāyāna Buddhism. At this stage the bodhisattva 'is now in possession of all the qualities of a Buddha, in consequence of which the possibility of retrogression is permanently precluded'. Sangharakshita, *A Survey of Buddhism*, Windhorse Publications, Birmingham 2001, pp. 498–9 (*Complete Works*, vol. 1).

92 The story of how Milarepa built, tore down, and rebuilt a tower, again and again, at his guru Marpa's instruction is told in part 2, chapter 2, 'Ordeals' of the autobiography of Milarepa as told to Rechungpa. There are various translations; see, for example, Lobsang P. Lhalungpa, *The Life of Milarepa*, E. P. Dutton, New York 1977, pp. 49–56.

93 Aristotle's account of the four causes he identified is to be found in his *Physics* II.3 and *Metaphysics* V.2.

94 *Dhammapada* 154.

95 A two-dimensional drawing or painting of a mandala is in a sense an architect's plan of what is 'really' a three-dimensional structure. Three-dimensional models of mandalas, which indeed take the form of a house or palace, are sometimes made by artists, especially in the Tibetan tradition, and some Buddhist temples are constructed in the form of mandalas, notably Borobudur in Java and Angkor Wat in Cambodia.

96 Canto 60 of *The Life and Liberation of Padmasambhava* (Yeshe Tsogyal, *The Life and*

Liberation of Padmasambhava, Dharma Publishing, Emeryville 1978, p. 370 ff.) describes how Padmasambhava subdued the demons of Tibet and they became *dharmapālas*.

97 This distinction between the reactive and the creative process is considered in detail in Sangharakshita's lecture 'Mind – Reactive and Creative', in Sangharakshita, *Buddha Mind*, Windhorse Publications, Birmingham 2001, pp. 35–66 (*Complete Works*, vol. 11).

98 The Mahāyāna teaches six *pāramitās* or perfections to be practised by the aspiring bodhisattva: giving (*dāna*), ethics (*śīla*), vigour (*vīrya*), patience (*kṣānti*), meditation (*dhyāna*), and wisdom (*prajñā*). For a detailed exploration of the six *pāramitās*, see Sangharakshita, *The Bodhisattva Ideal*, Windhorse Publications, Birmingham, pp. 87–170 (*Complete Works*, vol. 4).

99 W. B. Yeats, 'An Acre of Grass', published in *Collected Works*, Macmillan, London 1940.

100 The sequence of the positive *nidānas*, also sometimes called the spiral path, begins when in dependence upon unsatisfactoriness (*duḥkha*) arises not craving (*tṛṣṇā*) but faith (*śraddhā*). A detailed description of this process is to be found in chapter 7, 'The Spiral Path', in Sangharakshita, *What is the Dharma?* (*Complete Works*, vol. 3).

A canonical reference to the twelve positive *nidānas* occurs in the *Upanisa Sutta* of the *Saṃyutta Nikāya* (ii.29–31). See Bhikkhu Bodhi (trans.), *The Connected Discourses of the Buddha*, Wisdom Publications, Boston 2000, p. 554; or C. A. F. Rhys Davids (trans.), *The Book of the Kindred Sayings*, part 2, Pali Text Society, Oxford 1997, pp. 25–7.

101 The terms 'faith follower' (*saddhānusārin*) and 'doctrine follower' (*dhammānusārin*) have their origin in the Pāli canon; for example, in the *Cūḷagopālaka Sutta*: 'Just as that tender calf just born, being urged on by its mother's lowing, also breasted the stream of the Ganges and got safely across to the further shore, so too, those bhikkhus who are Dharma-Followers and faith-followers – by breasting Māra's stream they too will get safely to the further shore.' *Majjhima Nikāya* 34 (i.227). See Bhikkhu Ñāṇamoli and Bhikkhu Bodhi (trans.), *The Middle Length Discourses of the Buddha*, Wisdom Publications, Boston 1995, p. 321; or I. B. Horner (trans.), *The Collection of the Middle Length Sayings*, vol. i, Pali Text Society, Oxford 1957, p. 279. Sangharakshita introduces the two terms at the beginning of his talk 'A Vision of Human Existence', published in *Buddhism*

for Today and Tomorrow, Windhorse Publications, Birmingham 1996, pp. 24–5 (*Complete Works*, vol. 11).

102 B. Alan Wallace (trans.), *The Life and Teaching of Geshe Rabten*, George Allen and Unwin, London 1980, pp. 3–11.

103 For more on subject–object dualism, see Sangharakshita, *Know Your Mind*, Windhorse Publications, Birmingham 1998. pp. 53ff. (*Complete Works*, vol. 17).

104 The Higher Evolution is one of the ways Sangharakshita has chosen to frame the process of spiritual development. For an outline, see Sangharakshita, *What is the Sangha?*, Windhorse Publications, Birmingham 2000, chapter 9, 'The Evolution of the Individual' (*Complete Works*, vol. 3).

105 One might cite the importance of the Prajñāpāramitā tradition as expressed in, for example, the *Heart Sūtra*, so called because it is at the heart of spiritual life as conceived by the Mahāyāna: 'All Buddhas of past and present, Buddhas of future time, using this *prajñā* wisdom, come to full and perfect vision.'

106 Blake expressed his view about the casting out of error in notes meant to accompany a painting, *The Last Judgement*, which was intended to be shown in an exhibition in 1810. (The exhibition was cancelled and the painting has since been lost.) In the catalogue, Blake wrote: 'Error is Created; Truth is Eternal. Error or Creation will be Burned Up, & then & not till then Truth or Eternity will appear. It is Burnt up the Moment Men cease to behold it.'

107 *Gestalt* is a German word literally meaning form or shape, which began to be used in a particular way in the context of psychology in the early twentieth century. *Collins Dictionary* gives the definition: 'In psychology, a gestalt is something that has particular qualities when you consider it as a whole which are not obvious when you consider only the separate parts of it.'

108 Florence Nightingale was famous for her pioneering nursing work, developing her methods while tending injured troops in the Crimean War. This statement is from the preface to her book *Notes on Hospitals*, published in 1863.

109 SOCRATES: Surely you're following, Theaetetus; it's my impression at any rate that you're not inexperienced in things of this sort.
THEAETETUS: Yes indeed, by the gods, Socrates, I wonder exceedingly as to why (what) in the world these things are, and sometimes in looking at them I truly get dizzy.

SOCRATES: The reason is, my dear, that, apparently, Theodorus' guess about your nature is not a bad one, for this experience is very much a philosopher's, that of wondering. For nothing else is the beginning (principle) of philosophy than this.

Plato, *Theaetetus*, trans. Seth Bernardette, University of Chicago Press, Chicago 1986, 155c–d.

110   For more, see chapter 4, 'The Turning About', in Sangharakshita, *The Meaning of Conversion in Buddhism*, Windhorse Publications, Birmingham 1994, pp. 63–76 (*Complete Works*, vol. 2). See also Sangharakshita, *A Survey of Buddhism*, Windhorse Publications, Birmingham 1999, p. 408 (*Complete Works*, vol. 1).

111   This is the story of the farmer Kasi-Bhāradvāja, told in *Sutta-Nipāta* 1.4.

112   Herbert V. Guenther, *The Tantric View of Life*, Shambhala Publications, Berkeley and London 1972, p. 150.

113   The three *āsavas* (Sanskrit *āsrava*) are listed in many places in the Pāli canon. For example, section 43 of the *Mahāsaccaka Sutta*, *Majjhima Nikāya* 36 (i.249). See Bhikkhu Ñāṇamoli and Bhikkhu Bodhi (trans.), *The Middle Length Discourses of the Buddha*, Wisdom Publications, Boston

1995, p. 342; or I. B. Horner (trans.), *The Collection of the Middle Length Sayings*, vol. i, p. 303. A few sources list a fourth *āsava*, *diṭṭhāsava*, the mental poison of wrong views; for example, section 1.12 of the *Mahāparinibbāna Sutta*, *Dīgha Nikāya* 16 (ii.81). See M. Walshe (trans.), *The Long Discourses of the Buddha*, Wisdom Publications, Boston 1995, p. 234; or T. W. Rhys Davids (trans.), *Dialogues of the Buddha*, part 2, Pali Text Society, Oxford 1977, pp. 327–37.

114   For more about this classification, see Sangharakshita, *Know Your Mind*, Windhorse Publications, Birmingham 1998, p. 13 (*Complete Works*, vol. 17).

115   Plato, *Theaetetus*, 150 b–c:

I am so far like the midwife that I cannot myself give birth to wisdom, and the common reproach is true, that, though I question others, I can myself bring nothing to light because there is no wisdom in me. The reason is this. Heaven (Jowett: 'the god') constrains me to serve as a midwife, but has debarred me from giving birth. So of myself I have no sort of wisdom, nor has any discovery ever been born to me as the child of my soul. Those who frequent my company at first appear, some of them, quite unintelligent, but, as we go further with our discussions, all who are favored by heaven make progress at a rate that seems surprising to others as well as to themselves, although it is clear that they have never learned anything from me. The many admirable truths they bring to birth have been discovered by themselves from within. But the delivery is heaven's work and mine.

116   For more about the four grades or levels of Tantras, see Sangharakshita, *Tibetan Buddhism*, Birmingham 1996, p. 108 (*Complete Works*, vol. 13).

117   Raoul Birnbaum, *The Healing Buddha*, Shambhala Publications, Boulder 1979, pp. 3–24.

118   For an account of the three esoteric refuges – the guru, the *yidam*, and the *ḍākinī* – see Sangharakshita, *Creative Symbols of Tantric Buddhism*, Windhorse Publications, Birmingham 2002, pp. 83–90 (*Complete Works*, vol. 13).

119   For what Sangharakshita means by 'the greater mandala', see Sangharakshita, *Wisdom Beyond Words*, Windhorse Publications, Birmingham 2000, pp. 183–194 (*Complete Works*, vol. 14).

120   This is a reference to the third of the 'ten fetters' that bind us to the wheel of life, and which are progressively 'broken' in the course of the spiritual life. (At the point of Stream Entry the first three fetters have been broken.) 'Grasping ethical rules and religious observances as ends in themselves' is the traditional version of the third fetter; in *The Taste of Freedom*, Windhorse Publications, Glasgow 1990, Sangharakshita terms it 'superficiality', and recommends 'commitment' as its antidote. The ten fetters are enumerated in, for example, the *Saṅgīti Sutta*, *Dīgha Nikāya* 33 (iii.234). See M. Walshe (trans.), *The Long Discourses of the Buddha*, Wisdom Publications, Boston 1995, p. 495; or T. W. Rhys Davids (trans.), *Dialogues of the Buddha*, part 3, Pali Text Society, Oxford 1991, p. 225. See also *Saṃyutta Nikāya* v.61; Bhikkhu Bodhi (trans.), *The Connected Discourses of the Buddha*, Wisdom Publications, Boston 2000, p. 1565; or F. L. Woodward (trans.), *Kindred Sayings*, part 5, Pali Text Society, Oxford 1979, p. 49.

121   See 'An Evocation of Prajñāpāramitā' in Edward Conze et al., *Buddhist Texts Through the Ages*, Shambhala Publications, Boston and Shaftesbury 1990, pp. 252–4.

122   The scriptural *locus classicus* for the 'eight worldly claims', more usually known as the eight worldly winds or the

eight worldly conditions, is the *Lokavipatti Sutta, Aṅguttara Nikāya* iv.157–9: see Bhikkhu Bodhi (trans.), *The Numerical Discourses of the Buddha*, Wisdom Publications 2012, pp. 1116–9; or E. M. Hare (trans.), *The Book of the Gradual Sayings*, vol. iv, Pali Text Society, Oxford 1995, pp. 107–9. They are also enumerated by Buddhaghosa at *Visuddhimagga* 683. See Buddhaghosa, *The Path of Purity*, trans. Pe Maung Tin, Pali Text Society, London 1975, p. 838. See also Sangharakshita, *What is the Dharma?*, *Complete Works* vol. 3, pp. 159–60.

123 Uriah Heep is a character in Charles Dickens' novel *David Copperfield*. While constantly claiming to be 'umble, Heep in fact has ambitions to become rich and powerful by entirely deceitful and unscrupulous means.

124 The yogi's name was Mother Lakshmi. See Sangharakshita, *The Rainbow Road*, Windhorse Publications, Birmingham 1997, p. 359 (*Complete Works*, vol. 20, pp. 366–7).

125 Sangharakshita describes his acquaintance with Dr Dinshah Mehta in his memoir *In the Sign of the Golden Wheel*, Windhorse Publications, Birmingham 1996, pp. 268 ff. (*Complete Works*, vol. 22).

126 A *sāmaṇera* (fem. *sāmaṇerī*) is someone who has taken initial ordination vows but not yet the *upasampadā*, the full ordination of the *bhikkhu*.

127 Sangharakshita describes this incident in his memoir *Facing Mount Kanchenjunga*, Windhorse Publications, Glasgow 1991, pp. 408–9 (*Complete Works*, vol. 21).

128 T. S. Eliot, 'Ash Wednesday' section 6.

129 'Erastianism: doctrine that the state is superior to the church in ecclesiastical matters. It is named after the sixteenth-century Swiss physician and Zwinglian theologian Thomas Erastus, who never held such a doctrine. He opposed excommunication as unscriptural, advocating in its stead punishment by civil authorities. The state, he held, had both the right and the duty to punish all offences, ecclesiastical as well as civil, wherever all the citizens adhered to a single religion. The power of the state in religious matters was thus limited to a specific area. Erastianism acquired its present meaning from Richard Hooker's defence of secular supremacy in *Of the lawes of ecclesiasticall politie* (1593–1662) and as a result of debates held during the Westminster Assembly of 1643.' *Encyclopaedia Britannica*.

130 Lobsang P. Lhalunga (trans.), *The Life of Milarepa*, E. P. Dutton, New York 1977, p. 120.

131 See Sangharakshita's talk, 'Is a Guru Necessary?', in *What is the Sangha?* (*Complete Works*, vol. 3, pp. 548–9).

132 Samuel Butler, *Hudibras*, canto 3, lines 547–8. Butler was a Royalist and an Anglican, and wrote *Hudibras*, a long satirical poem, between 1660 and 1680, to poke fun at those on the opposing side, the Cromwellians and the Presbyterian Church, who had ruled Britain after the Civil War but were vanquished with the restoration of the monarchy in 1660.

133 The verse is *Dhammapada* 183. This story of the encounter between the sage and the man of worldly power has been variously attributed. According to Dōgen, this exchange took place between Haku Kyo-i, the governor of Hangzhou, and the Zen master Choka Dorin. See Master Dogen, *Shobogenzo Book 1*, trans. Gudo Nishijima and Chodo Cross, Windbell Publications, Woking 1994, pp. 106–8. Also quoted in Thomas Cleary (trans.), *Rational Zen: The Mind of Dōgen Zenji*, Shambhala Publications, Boston 1995, pp. 91–4.

134 Lobsang P. Lhalunga (trans.), *The Life of Milarepa*, E. P. Dutton, New York 1977, pp. 48–71.

135 See Thomas Cleary (trans.), *The Sutra of Hui-Neng*, Shambhala Publications,

Boston and London 1998, p. 43: 'I have a formless hymn: if you can memorize it, the impact of the words can cause your accumulated eons of confusions and errors to dissolve away all at once.'

136 *Meghiya Sutta, Udāna* 4.1 in John D. Ireland (trans.), *The Udāna and the Itivuttaka*, Buddhist Publication Society, Kandy 1997, pp. 50–4.

137 The *bhikkhu*'s name was Vakkali. The story of Vakkali is told in different ways in the Pāli literature. The central message of each of the stories is the same – that he who sees the Dhamma sees the Buddha – but the context varies. It is the *Dhammapada* commentary that describes Vakkali's fascination with the Buddha's form. See Eugene Watson Burlingame (trans.), *Buddhist Legends, Translated from the Original Pali Text of the Dhammapada Commentary*, Harvard University Press 1921, part 3, xxv.11, pp. 262–3. In this version, the Buddha's advice is not enough to satisfy Vakkali; when forbidden to keep following the Buddha around he threatens suicide, and is only pacified when the Buddha creates an image of himself specially for Vakkali. After the Buddha says a few more words, Vakkali attains *arhantship*. In the *Saṃyutta Nikāya* (iii.120) the story is rather different. Vakkali is ill, and the Buddha visits him. It

is when Vakkali says how he has wanted for a long time to set eyes on the Buddha, that the Buddha tells him that 'he who sees the Dhamma sees me'. The Buddha reassures Vakkali that he will have a good death. The text says that after the Buddha's departure, Vakkali 'used the knife' (Bhikkhu Bodhi's translation). The Buddha, seeing a swirl of black smoke in the distance, says that this is Māra looking for Vakkali's consciousness, but he won't find it, because Vakkali has attained *nibbāna*. See Bhikkhu Bodhi (trans.), *The Connected Discourses of the Buddha*, Wisdom Publications, Boston 2000, pp. 938–41; or F. L. Woodward (trans.), *The Book of the Kindred Sayings*, part 3, Pali Text Society, London 1975, p. 101–6.

138 Nāgārjuna, *Mūlamadhyamakakārikā*, trans. Kenneth K. Inada, Hokuseido Press, Tokyo 1970, p. 93 (chapter 13, verse 8): 'The wise men (i.e. Enlightened ones) have said that *śūnyatā* or the nature of thusness is the relinquishing of all false views. Yet it is said that those who adhere to the idea or concept of *śūnyatā* are incorrigible.'

139 The story of Nanda's ordination on what would have been his wedding day is told in the *Dhammapada Commentary*: see Eugene Watson Burlingame (trans.), *Buddhist Legends (Dhammapada Commentary)*, part 1, Pali Text Society, Luzac, London 1969, pp. 218–9. The better known sequel, in which Nanda, now ordained, is pining for his wife and wants to leave the order of monks, is told in the same volume, pp. 220–3, also at *Udāna* 3.2; see John D. Ireland (trans.), *The Udāna and the Itivuttaka*, Buddhist Publication Society 2007, pp. 35–9.

140 The language of near and far enemies is derived from *Visuddhimagga* 319–20, in which Buddhaghosa identifies the near and far enemies of emotions such as loving-kindness and compassion. A far enemy is clearly opposite and inimical to the positive quality one wishes to cultivate, thus ill will is the far enemy of loving-kindness. A near enemy, by contrast, is sufficiently like the desired quality to be mistaken for it: thus, sticky or needy affection (*pema*) is said to be the near enemy of loving-kindness. See Bhikkhu Ñāṇamoli (trans.), *The Path of Purification*, Buddhist Publication Society, Kandy 1991, pp. 311–2.

141 For Sangharakshita's account of the journey of the sacred relics, see chapters 10 and 11 of his memoir, *Facing Mount Kanchenjunga*, Windhorse Publications, Glasgow 1991 (*Complete Works*, vol. 21).

142 William Shakespeare, *Hamlet*, Act II, Scene ii.

143 Herbert V. Guenther (trans.), *The Life and Teachings of Nāropa*, Oxford University Press, Oxford 1963, pp. 50–93.

144 For an account of the love mode and the power mode, see Sangharakshita, *The Ten Pillars of Buddhism*, part 2, section 1, on the first precept (*Complete Works*, vol. 2).

145 This is in the story 'Rechungpa's Repentance': 'In his pride, Rechungpa thought, "My Guru has now become very bitter and egoistic."' See Garma C. C. Chang, *The Hundred Thousand Songs of Milarepa*, Shambhala, Boston and London 1999, p. 443. For Sangharakshita's commentary, see *Complete Works*, vol. 19.

146 'About the Workers', essay 28 in G. K. Chesterton, *As I Was Saying*, Methuen, London 1936, pp. 169–74.

147 *Dhammapada* verse 168: 'Get up! Don't be heedless! Live practising the Dhamma, (the Dhamma) which is good conduct.' (trans. Sangharakshita.)

148 '"Gross laziness" means being attached to nonvirtues like destroying enemies, accumulating wealth, and so forth. These are the direct causes of suffering and, therefore, should be avoided.' Gampopa, *The Jewel Ornament of Liberation*, trans. Khenpo Konchog Gyaltsen Rinpoche, Snow Lion Publications, Ithaca 1998. p. 215.

149 This is the 56th of the 60 *pācittiyas*; see Vinaya Piṭaka iv.115; I. B. Horner (trans.), *The Book of the Discipline*, part 2, Pali Text Society, Oxford 1997, pp. 398–400.

150 'The Little Birds Who Won't Sing' in G. K. Chesterton, *Selected Essays*, Collins, London 1939, pp. 123–8.

151 Taverns and brothels are among the 'places of wrong resort' listed in the Vinaya; see, for example, Ven. Somdet, *The Entrance to the Vinaya, Vinayamukha* II (the Thai Vinaya commentary), Mahamakut Rajavidyalaya Press, Bangkok, 1969–83, pp. 178–80.

152 This is perhaps a reference to the story 'Rechungpa's Repentance', at the beginning of which Rechungpa is keen to 'stay in Drin tonight and meet the patrons', but Milarepa says, 'Let us first go to Bouto without the knowledge of our patrons, disciples or the monks.' See Garma C. C. Chang, *The Hundred Thousand Songs of Milarepa*, Shambhala, Boston and London 1999, p. 442. For Sangharakshita's commentary, see *Complete Works*, vol. 19, p. 7.

153 For example, the Chinese hermit Hanshan wrote:

I look far off at Tianti's summit,
alone and high above the

crowding peaks.
Pines and bamboos sing in
the wind that sways them;
sea tides wash beneath the
shining moon.
I gaze at the mountain's
green borders below
and discuss philosophy with
the white clouds.
In the wilderness, mountains
and seas are all right,
but I wish I had a
companion in my search for
the Way.

This is the 60th of the 101
poems translated by Burton
Watson and published in
Cold Mountain. Shambhala
Publications, Boston 1997.

154 The four *śūnyatās* are
described in Sangharakshita,
What is the Dharma?, chapter
5, 'The Mystery of the Void'
(*Complete Works*, vol. 3,
pp. 233–8).

155 This much-loved extended
metaphor is from verse 6 of
the *Bhagavad Gītā Mahatmya*
('The Glories of the *Bhagavad
Gītā*') by Adi Shankaracharya,
an eighth-century CE
philosopher who consolidated
the teachings of Advaita
Vedanta.

156 *Mahāparinibbāna Sutta, Dīgha
Nikāya* 16 (ii.156). See M.
Walshe (trans.), *The Long
Discourses of the Buddha*,
Wisdom Publications, Boston
1995, p. 270; or T. W. Rhys
Davids (trans.), *Dialogues of
the Buddha*, part 2, Pali Text
Society, Oxford 1977, p. 173.

157 The hymn began life as a poem
published by the American
poet Julia Abigail Fletcher
Carney in 1845; this is the first
verse.

158 *Dhammapada*, verse 121.

159 See, for example, 'What
Meditation Really Is' in
Sangharakshita, *Human
Enlightenment*, Windhorse
Publications, Glasgow 1993,
pp. 45–50 (*Complete Works*,
vol. 11); or 'A Method of
Personal Development' in
Sangharakshita, *Buddhism
for Today and Tomorrow*,
Windhorse Publications,
Birmingham 1996,
p. 17 (*Complete Works*,
vol. 11).

160 Traditionally, the duration of
a *kalpa* is illustrated by the
following simile: suppose that
every hundred years a piece of
silk is rubbed once on a solid
rock one cubic *yojana* in size;
when the rock is worn away
by this, one *kalpa* will still
not have passed. See *Saṃyutta
Nikāya* ii.181; Bhikkhu
Bodhi (trans.), *The Connected
Discourses of the Buddha*,
Wisdom Publications, Boston
2000, p. 654. A *yojana* is the
distance covered by a pair of
oxen in one day, about seven
or eight miles.

161 Sangharakshita describes his
time working at Parkes' Coal
Company in Torquay in *The
Rainbow Road*, Windhorse
Publications, Birmingham
1997, pp. 54–6 (*Complete
Works*, vol. 20).

162 For more about the two accumulations, see Sangharakshita, *Know Your Mind*, Windhorse Publications, Birmingham 1998, p. 32 (*Complete Works*, vol. 17).

163 For the cherub with his flaming sword is hereby commanded to leave his guard at the tree of life, and when he does, the whole creation will be consumed and appear infinite and holy whereas it now appears finite & corrupt. This will come to pass by an improvement of sensual enjoyment.

William Blake, *The Marriage of Heaven and Hell*, verses 112–3.

164 This idea is familiar from the *Heart Sūtra*: form is no other than emptiness, emptiness no other than form. For Sangharakshita's commentary on this line of the *sūtra*, see Sangharakshita, *Wisdom Beyond Words*, Birmingham 2000, pp. 27–8 (*Complete Works*, vol. 14).

165 I wander thro' each charter'd street,
Near where the charter'd Thames does flow.
And mark in every face I meet
Marks of weakness, marks of woe.

From William Blake's poem 'London', one of his *Songs of Innocence and Experience*, first published in 1794.

166 At the time this seminar was given, no biography of Rechungpa had been translated into English, but since then various volumes have been published. Two volumes by Thrangu Rinpoche are available: *Rechungpa, a biography of Milarepa's Disciple*, Namo Buddha Publications, Glastonbury (Connecticut) 2011, and *A Spiritual Biography of Rechungpa*, Sri Satguru Publications, Delhi 2001. The latter was translated by Peter Roberts, who has also published an illuminating account of the various biographies of Rechungpa produced in Tibet over a period of 300 years, in the course of which the life story evolved; see Peter Alan Roberts, *The Biographies of Rechungpa: The evolution of a Tibetan hagiography*, Routledge, Abingdon 2007.

167 The *yoginī* is better known as Machig Labdron; see Tsultrim Allione, *Women of Wisdom*, Routledge and Kegan Paul, London 1985, pp. 142–204, especially pp. 145–9.

168 See Sangharakshita, *Precious Teachers*, Windhorse Publications, Birmingham 2007, p. 103 (*Complete Works*, vol. 22).

169 The five *nīvaraṇas*, or hindrances to meditation, are sensuous desire, ill will, restlessness and anxiety, sloth and torpor, and doubt. They

are listed in many places in the Pāli canon; for example, the Mahāvagga of the *Saṃyutta Nikāya* (v.91–8) has a whole section on them; see Bhikkhu Bodhi (trans.), *The Connected Discourses of the Buddha*, Wisdom Publications, Somerville 2000, pp. 1591–4; also F. L. Woodward (trans.), *The Book of the Kindred Sayings*, part 5, Pali Text Society, London 1979, pp. 76–81. For more about the poisons and their antidotes, see Sangharakshita, *What is the Dharma?*, chapter 11, in *Complete Works*, vol. 3, pp. 340–51.

170 For example, the *Bhayabherava Sutta, Majjhima Nikāya* 4 (i.22). See Bhikkhu Ñāṇamoli and Bhikkhu Bodhi (trans.), *The Middle Length Discourses of the Buddha*, Wisdom Publications, Boston 1995, p. 105; or I. B. Horner (trans.), *The Collection of the Middle Length Sayings*, vol. i, Pali Text Society, Oxford 1957, p. 29.

171 The mandala offering practice is one of the four foundation practices (*mūla yogas*) of Tantric Buddhism. It is described in chapter 6, 'Offerings and Self-Sacrifice' in Sangharakshita, *Creative Symbols of Tantric Buddhism*, Windhorse Publications, Birmingham 2002, pp. 143–9 (*Complete Works*, vol. 13).

172 For more about the five *kleśas*, see Sangharakshita,

Know Your Mind, Windhorse Publications, Birmingham 2002, p. 161 (*Complete Works*, vol. 17).

173 The idea of five methods of meditation as antidotes to the five poisons or *kleśas* identified in the Mahāyāna tradition was first suggested to Sangharakshita by his teacher C. M. Chen, whom he knew in Kalimpong. For Mr Chen's own account, see C. M. Chen, *Buddhist Meditation, Systematic and Practical*, published by Dr Yutang Lin, El Cerrito 1989, chapter 8, 'The Five Fundamental Meditations to Cure the Five Poisons', pp. 326–30. See also Sangharakshita, *The Purpose and Practice of Buddhist Meditation*, Ibis Publications, Coddington 2012, pp. 29–35 (*Complete Works*, vol. 5). For an account of the meditations themselves, see chapter 8, 'The "Death" of the Buddha', in Sangharakshita, *Who is the Buddha?*, in *Complete Works*, vol. 3, pp. 123–138.

174 The three *āsavas* (Sanskrit *āsravas*) are listed in many places in the Pāli canon. For example, the *Mahāsaccaka Sutta, Majjhima Nikāya* 36 (i.249). See Bhikkhu Ñāṇamoli and Bhikkhu Bodhi (trans.), *The Middle Length Discourses of the Buddha*, Wisdom Publications, Boston 1995, p. 342; or I. B. Horner (trans.), *The Collection of the Middle Length Sayings*,

vol. i, p. 303. A few sources list a fourth *āsava*, *diṭṭhāsava*, the mental poison of wrong views; for example, the *Mahāparinibbāna Sutta*, *Dīgha Nikāya* 16 (ii.81). See M. Walshe (trans.), *The Long Discourses of the Buddha*, Wisdom Publications, Boston 1995, p. 234; or T. W. Rhys Davids (trans.), *Dialogues of the Buddha*, part 2, Pali Text Society, Oxford 1977, pp. 327–37.

175 For more about the *āvaraṇas* see Sangharakshita, *A Survey of Buddhism*, Windhorse Publications, Birmingham 2001, p. 303 (*Complete Works*, vol. 1, p. 270).

176 For example, *Saṃyutta Nikāya* iii.49. See Bhikkhu Bodhi (trans.), *The Connected Discourses of the Buddha*, Wisdom Publications, Boston 2000, p. 887; or C. A. F. Rhys Davids (trans.), *The Book of the Kindred Sayings*, part 3, Pali Text Society, Oxford 1997, p. 43. Another example is found at *Sutta-Nipāta* verse 855; see K. R. Norman (trans.), *The Rhinoceros Horn and other early Buddhist poems*, Pali Text Society/ Routledge and Kegan Paul, London 1985, p. 142.

177 This is the last line of the second verse of William Cowper's poem 'The Solitude of Alexander Selkirk'. Alexander Selkirk (1676–1721) was a privateer (a sort of pirate) who was marooned on an uninhabited island in the South Pacific with nothing but a musket, a hatchet, a knife, a cooking pot, a Bible, bedding, and some clothes. He managed to survive for more than four years before being rescued. It was observed by one of his rescuers, impressed by Selkirk's evident peace of mind, that 'one may see that solitude and retirement from the world is not such an insufferable state of life as most men imagine, especially when people are fairly called or thrown into it unavoidably, as this man was.' Daniel Defoe's *Robinson Crusoe* was inspired by Selkirk.

178 The four *mūla yogas* or foundation yogas of the Tantric Buddhist tradition are the generation of the *bodhicitta*, the Going for Refuge and Prostration practice, the Vajrasattva visualization practice, and the offering of the mandala. See chapter 6, 'The Four Foundation Yogas', in Sangharakshita, *Tibetan Buddhism*, Windhorse Publications, Birmingham 1999, pp. 87–102 (*Complete Works*, vol. 13).

179 These two terms are sometimes translated as 'sense of shame' and 'fear of blame'. In a section on these two mental events in *Know Your Mind*, Sangharakshita translates them as 'self-respect' and 'respect for wise opinion': 'In the Pāli canon

they are jointly referred to as the two *lokapālas*, the two guardians of the world: *hiri* and *ottappa* in Pāli or *hrī* and *apatrāpya* in Sanskrit. They are the guardians of the world because there would be no social order, no civilized existence, without them. The idea that they are the only restraint on our evil actions is perhaps hyperbole, but they are mentioned in all schools of Buddhism and considered very important indeed.' Sangharakshita, *Know Your Mind*, Windhorse Publications, Birmingham 2002, p. 125 (*Complete Works*, vol. 17). For a reference in the Pāli canon, see, for example, *Itivuttaka* section 42, in John B. Ireland (trans.), *The Udāna and the Itivuttaka*, Buddhist Publication Society, Kandy 1997, pp. 179–180, in which context they are described as 'two bright qualities that safeguard the world'.

180 The French nun appears many times in Sangharakshita's memoirs of his Kalimpong days. See, for example, chapters 12 and 15 of *In the Sign of the Golden Wheel*, Windhorse Publications, Birmingham 1996, pp. 182–3 and pp. 207–11 (*Complete Works*, vol. 22); also chapter 2 of Sangharakshita, *Precious Teachers*, Windhorse Publications, Birmingham 2007 (*Complete Works*, vol. 22).

181 For example, see C. A. F. Rhys Davids, *Gotama the Man*, Luzac and Co., London 1928, p. 78.

182 These four crimes – to murder one's father intentionally, to murder one's mother intentionally, to kill an *arhant*, and to wound a Buddha, along with causing a schism in the sangha (Pāli *saṅghabheda*) were named in the Early Buddhist tradition as the five 'heinous crimes', actions that are said to bring immediate and disastrous karmic consequences (Sanskrit *ānantarika-karma*, Pāli *ānantarika-kamma*), with no possibility of any other mitigating karmic factors. In the *Bahudhātuka Sutta*, *Majjhima Nikāya* 115 (iii.64–5), the Buddha is recorded as saying that it would be impossible for someone possessing right view to commit any of these five acts. See Bhikkhu Ñāṇamoli and Bhikkhu Bodhi (trans.), *The Middle Length Discourses of the Buddha*, Wisdom Publications, Boston 1995, pp. 928–9; or I. B. Horner (trans.), *The Collection of the Middle Length Sayings*, Pali Text Society, London 1967, p. 108.

183 This incident is described at Vinaya Piṭaka ii.193–5 (*Cullavagga* 7.3). See I. B. Horner (trans.), *The Book of the Discipline*, part 5, Pali Text Society, Oxford 1992, p. 271. The boulder did not

harm the Buddha except that a splinter injured his foot.

184   This may be a reference to the Buddha's remarks, recorded at the beginning of the *Mahāparinibbāna Sutta*, concerning the conditions under which the Vajjian people may be expected to prosper, which includes the condition 'that proper provision is made for the safety of Arahants, so that such Arahants may come in future to live there, and those already there may dwell in comfort'. *Mahāparinibbāna Sutta, Dīgha Nikāya* 16 (ii.76). See M. Walshe (trans.), *The Long Discourses of the Buddha*, Wisdom Publications, Boston 1995, p. 232; or T. W. Rhys Davids (trans.), *Dialogues of the Buddha*, part 2, Pali Text Society, Oxford 1977, p. 80.

185   Uriah Heep is a character in Charles Dickens' novel *David Copperfield*. While constantly claiming to be 'umble, Heep in fact has ambitions to become rich and powerful by entirely deceitful and unscrupulous means.

186   *Dhammapada*, verse 183.

187   This visualization of a disc is called the *kasiṇa* practice. For details, see Sangharakshita, *The Purpose and Practice of Buddhist Meditation*, Ibis Publications, Ledbury 2012, pp. 559–64 (*Complete Works*, vol. 5).

188   Sangharakshita describes the recollection of the *nidāna*

chain in, for example, *What is the Dharma? (Complete Works*, vol. 3, pp. 346–8). There are many references to the twelve cyclical *nidānas* in the Pāli canon, for example, *Mahātaṇhāsaṅkhaya Sutta, Majjhima Nikāya* 38 (i.261–4). See Bhikkhu Ñāṇamoli and Bhikkhu Bodhi (trans.), *The Middle Length Discourses of the Buddha*, Wisdom Publications, Boston 1995, pp. 353–7; or I. B. Horner (trans.), *The Collection of the Middle Length Sayings*, vol. i, Pali Text Society, Oxford, pp. 318–9. Also the *Mahānidāna Sutta, Dīgha Nikāya* 15 (ii.55–9). See M. Walshe (trans.), *The Long Discourses of the Buddha*, Wisdom Publications, Boston 1995, pp. 223–4; or T. W. Rhys Davids (trans.), *Dialogues of the Buddha*, part 2, Pali Text Society, Oxford 1977, pp. 50–5. Sangharakshita describes the six element practice in, for example, *What is the Dharma? (Complete Works*, vol. 3, pp. 346–8). A canonical reference to the 'six element practice' is found in the *Mahārāhulovāda Sutta, Majjhima Nikāya* 62 (i.421–4). See Bhikkhu Ñāṇamoli and Bhikkhu Bodhi (trans.), *The Middle Length Discourses of the Buddha*, Wisdom Publications, Boston 1995, pp. 528–30; or I. B. Horner (trans.), *The Collection of the Middle Length Sayings*, vol. ii,

Pali Text Society, Oxford 1957, pp. 92–5.

189 This is a reference to the fifth and final stage of the *mettā bhāvanā* meditation, in which, having developed loving-kindness towards oneself, a friend, a 'neutral person', and an 'enemy', one cultivates *mettā* towards each of the four people equally.

190 *Dhammapada*, verse 64.

191 See, for example, *Dhammapada* chapter 26, 'The Brāhmaṇa', which discourses at length on the characteristics of the true *brāhmaṇa*, as distinct from someone with the outward trappings of one: 'What use (your) matted hair, (you) man of evil understanding; what use your deerskin garment? Within, you are a dense jungle (of passions), (yet) you touch up the outside.' (verse 394, trans. Sangharakshita).

192 A chain of twelve *nidānas* or links is depicted around the edge of the Tibetan wheel of life, and in that context *vedanā*, feeling, is represented by a man with an arrow in his eye (intended to show the immediacy of feeling, not necessarily painful experience), while craving (Sanskrit *tṛṣṇā*, Pāli *taṇhā*) is illustrated by a woman offering a man a drink. The importance of breaking the link is brought out in, for example, Sangharakshita, *What is the Sangha?*, chapter 2, 'The Dynamics of Being',

(*Complete Works*, vol. 3, pp. 202–3). The teaching of the twelve cyclical *nidānas* has its origin in the Pāli canon; for example, sections 17–21 of the *Mahātaṇhāsaṅkhaya Sutta*, *Majjhima Nikāya* 38 (i.261–4). See Bhikkhu Ñāṇamoli and Bhikkhu Bodhi (trans.), *The Middle Length Discourses of the Buddha*, Wisdom Publications, Boston 1995, pp. 353–7; or I. B. Horner (trans.), *The Collection of the Middle Length Sayings*, vol. i, Pali Text Society, London 1976, pp. 318–9. Alternatively see sections 1–9 of the *Mahānidāna Sutta*, *Dīgha Nikāya* 15 (ii.55–9); M. Walshe (trans.), *The Long Discourses of the Buddha*, Wisdom Publications, Boston 1995, pp. 223–4; or T. W. Rhys Davids (trans.), *Dialogues of the Buddha*, part 2, Pali Text Society, London 1977, pp. 50–5.

193 See Robert A. F. Thurman (trans.), *The Holy Teaching of Vimalakīrti*, Pennsylvania State University Press, University Park and London 1976, p. 51. For Sangharakshita's commentary on this incident, see chapter 6 of Sangharakshita, *The Inconceivable Emancipation* (*Complete Works*, vol. 16, pp. 535–7).

194 Of 'irresistible grace' John Calvin said, 'It is not violent, so as to compel men by external force; but still it is a powerful impulse of the

Holy Spirit, which makes men willing who formerly were unwilling and reluctant.' That is, in the Calvinist view, those who are 'elected' by God to be saved are brought to hear the call of the Gospel through the irresistible grace of God, which overcomes whatever reluctance they may feel.

195 Devadatta, who was a cousin of the Buddha, became a monk when the Buddha first returned to Kapilavatthu after his Enlightenment. His practice was exemplary and the Buddha praised it (*Udāna* 3.4). But then, having begun to develop psychic powers as a consequence of his diligent meditation, Devadatta became proud, and began to feel that the Buddha was not strict enough in teaching ascetic practices. He demanded that the Buddha should insist on five specific forms of asceticism, and when the Buddha refused, on the basis that the middle way should be followed rather than going to an extreme of asceticism, Devadatta and his followers separated from the Buddha and his followers, thus bringing about a grievous split in the Sangha. This story is told at Vinaya Piṭaka ii.188 (*Cullavagga* 7.3); see I. B. Horner (trans.), *The Book of the Discipline*, part 5, Pali Text Society, Oxford 1992, p. 264. For the full story and all its sources, see Reginald A. Ray, *Buddhist Saints in*

India, Oxford University Press, New York and Oxford 1994, pp. 162–8.

196 *Dhammapada*, verse 34.

197 See Sangharakshita, 'The Path of Regular Steps and the Path of Irregular Steps', in *The Taste of Freedom*, Windhorse Publications, Birmingham 1997, pp. 27–48 (*Complete Works*, vol. 11).

198 Philip B. Yampolsky (trans.), *The Platform Sutra of the Sixth Patriarch*, Columbia University Press, New York 1967, includes a biography of Huineng (pp. 58–88).

199 See Dwight Goddard (ed.), A *Buddhist Bible*, Beacon Press, Boston 1970, pp. 114–5.

200 For an account of the potential for spiritual development of the beings in each of the six realms of the wheel of life, see chapter 1, 'The Tibetan Wheel of Life', in Sangharakshita, *Creative Symbols of Tantric Buddhism*, Windhorse Publications, Birmingham 2002, pp. 23–8 (*Complete Works*, vol. 13).

201 In chapter 8 of the *Bodhicaryāvatāra,* 'The Perfection of Meditative Absorption', verses 43–71, Śāntideva goes to town on the horrible aspects of the human body: for example, verse 52:

If you have no passion for what is foul, why do you embrace another, a cage of bones bound by sinew, smeared with slime and flesh?

Śāntideva, *The Bodhicaryā-vatāra*, trans. Kate Crosby and Andrew Skilton, Windhorse Publications, Birmingham 2002, p. 122.

202 Sangharakshita describes various forms of this meditation in chapter 11, 'The Threefold Path: Meditation', in *What is the Dharma?* (*Complete Works*, vol. 3, pp. 344–6).

203 At *Visuddhimagga* 102–110, Buddhaghosa identifies six 'kinds of temperament'. As well as 'greedy' and 'hating'; the other four are 'deluded', 'faithful', 'intelligent', and 'speculative'. See Bhikkhu Ñāṇamoli (trans.), *The Path of Purification*, Buddhist Publication Society, Kandy 2010 (fourth edition), pp. 102–111; or Pe Maung Tin (trans.), *The Path of Purity*, Pali Text Society, London 1975, pp. 118–28.

204 Lobsang P. Lhalunga (trans.), *The Life of Milarepa*, E. P. Dutton, New York 1977, pp. 134–5.

205 Francis Xavier (1506–1553) was a Spanish Jesuit priest who first arrived at Goa in 1542. His missionary work also took him to Malaysia and Japan. His body is preserved in a silver casket in the Basilica of Bom Jésus in Goa.

206 Sangharakshita describes this incident in his memoir *Facing Mount Kanchenjunga*, Windhorse Publications, Glasgow 1991, pp. 408–9

(*Complete Works*, vol. 21). The 'high priest' was the Venerable Jinaratana.

207 *Dhammapada* 6.

208 Vanity Fair is the name given by John Bunyan in his *Pilgrim's Progress* for the fair selling every kind of temptation through which the pilgrims have to pass on their way to the Celestial City:

> It is kept all the year long.... At this fair are all such merchandise sold as houses, lands, trades, places, honours, preferments, titles, countries, kingdoms, lusts, pleasures; and delights of all sorts, such as harlots, wives, husbands, children, masters, servants, lives, blood, bodies, souls, silver, gold, precious stones, and what not.

209 The image the Buddha used to describe the fourth *dhyāna* was that of a man who, having bathed, wraps himself in a pure white sheet. See Sangharakshita, *Complete Works*, vol. 3, p. 307; for a canonical reference see *Mahā-Assapura Sutta*, *Majjhima Nikāya* 39 (i.279); Bhikkhu Ñāṇamoli and Bhikkhu Bodhi (trans.), *The Middle Length Discourses of the Buddha*, Wisdom Publications, Boston 1995, p. 369; or I. B. Horner (trans.), *The Collection of the Middle Length Sayings*, vol. i, Pali Text Society, Oxford 1957, p. 332. See also the *Mahāsakuludāyi*

Sutta, *Majjhima Nikāya* 77
(ii.17); Bhikkhu Ñāṇamoli
and Bhikkhu Bodhi (trans.),
*The Middle Length Discourses
of the Buddha*, Wisdom
Publications, Boston 1995,
pp. 642; or I. B. Horner
(trans.), *The Collection of the
Middle Length Sayings*, vol. ii,
Pali Text Society, Oxford 1957,
p. 217.

210 The five *nīvaraṇas* or
hindrances to meditation,
are sensuous desire, ill will,
restlessness and anxiety, sloth
and torpor, and doubt. They
are listed in many places in the
Pāli canon; for example, the
Mahāvagga of the *Saṃyutta
Nikāya* (v.91–8) contains a
whole section about them. See
Bhikkhu Bodhi (trans.), *The
Connected Discourses of the
Buddha*, Wisdom Publications,
Somerville 2000, pp. 1591–4;
or F. L. Woodward (trans.), *The
Book of the Kindred Sayings*,
part 5, Pali Text Society,
London 1979, pp. 76–81. They
are described (in Woodward's
translation, p. 81) as 'the
five hindrances which cause
blindness, loss of sight and
ignorance, which obstruct
insight, consort with pain and
conduce not to Nibbāna'.

211 At *Visuddhimagga* 102–110,
Buddhaghosa identifies six
'kinds of temperament'. As
well as 'greedy' and 'hating';
the other four are 'deluded',
'faithful', 'intelligent', and
'speculative'. See Bhikkhu
Ñāṇamoli (trans.), *The Path*
of Purification, Buddhist
Publication Society, Kandy
2010 (fourth edition), pp. 102–
111; or *The Path of Purity*,
trans. Pe Maung Tin, Pali
Text Society, London 1975,
pp. 118–28. For more about
the affinity between hatred and
wisdom, see Sangharakshita,
*Creative Symbols of Tantric
Buddhism*, Windhorse
Publications, Birmingham
2002, pp. 20–1 (also *Complete
Works* vol. 13).

212 For more about the term
gotrabhū, see Nyanatiloka,
Buddhist Dictionary, Buddhist
Publication Society, Kandy
1988, pp. 71–2; see also Bimala
Charan Law, *Designation
of Human Types*, Pali Text
Society, London n.d., pp. 4–5.

213 For example, this is
Woodward's translation of the
Buddha's description of his
own experience of the *dhyānas*
just before Enlightenment: 'the
blissful feelings that arose failed
to lay hold of and control my
mind' (F. L. Woodward, *Some
Sayings of the Buddha*, Oxford
University Press, Oxford 1973,
p. 19). For other translations,
see the *Mahāsaccaka Sutta*,
Majjhima Nikāya 36 (i.249);
Bhikkhu Ñāṇamoli and
Bhikkhu Bodhi (trans.), *The
Middle Length Discourses
of the Buddha*, Wisdom
Publications, Boston 1995,
pp. 340–1; or I. B. Horner
(trans.), *The Collection of the
Middle Length Sayings*, vol. i,
pp. 302–3.

214 The *Dhammapada* (verse 58) in fact refers to lotuses growing from 'a heap of rubbish thrown in the highway', but the image of the lotus growing out of the mud occurs many times elsewhere in the Pāli canon, most famously in the Buddha's vision of humanity prompted by Brahmā Sahāmpati's request that he should teach the Dharma, which is told in various places in the scriptures, for example in the *Ariyapariyesanā Sutta, Majjhima Nikāya* 26 (i.167–70). See Bhikkhu Ñāṇamoli and Bhikkhu Bodhi (trans.), *The Middle Length Discourses of the Buddha*, Wisdom Publications, Boston 1995, pp. 260–2; or I. B. Horner (trans.), *The Collection of the Middle Length Sayings*, vol. i, Pali Text Society, London 1967, pp. 211–3.

215 As we find elsewhere in this commentary on the *Songs of Milarepa*, the 'teaching of relaxing and sitting at ease is very important for the Kagyupas, and for the Vajrayāna generally'. The 'just sitting' practice, as it was called, also forms an important aspect of Sangharakshita's 'system of meditation', which he first outlined in a talk given on the Order Convention in 1978. Since then, other Order members have elaborated on the 'just sitting' practice; see, for example, Kamalashila, *Buddhist Meditation*, first published in 1991 and republished by Windhorse Publications in 2012 with a new section on Just Sitting (pp. 32–44).

216 See Edward Conze (trans.), *The Perfection of Wisdom in Eight Thousand Lines*, Four Seasons Foundation, San Francisco 1983, p. 227. This translation has 'skill in means' rather than 'compassion', but the sense is the same.

217 This is a reference to the parable of the burning house, chapter 3 of the *Saddharma Puṇḍarīka Sūtra*. For Sangharakshita's commentary on the parable, see chapter 3, 'Transcending the Human Predicament' in *The Drama of Cosmic Enlightenment* (*Complete Works*, vol. 16, pp. 67–84).

218 This, sung by Milarepa in response to the request to 'give us some Buddhist teaching that is easy to understand', is the first song in chapter 59 of *The Hundred Thousand Songs of Milarepa*, 'The Song of the Good Companions'. See Garma C. C. Chang, *The Hundred Thousand Songs of Milarepa*, Shambhala Publications, Boston and London 1999, pp. 653–4.

219 This could be a reference to the Human Potential Movement or its offshoot, 'est' training (Erhard Seminars Training), which was very popular at the time this commentary was given.

220 'Just as in the great ocean there is but one taste – the taste of salt – so in this Doctrine and Discipline (*dhammavinaya*) there is but one taste – the taste of freedom.' This is the sixth of the eight qualities of the great ocean described by the Buddha in the *Uposatha Sutta, Udāna* 5.5. See John D. Ireland (trans.), *The Udāna and the Itivuttaka*, Buddhist Publication Society, Kandy 2007, p. 68. See also Sangharakshita's talk 'The Taste of Freedom' (*Complete Works*, vol. 11).

221 *Yathābhūta-jñānadarśana* means 'knowledge and vision of things as they really are'. It is the eighth of the twelve positive *nidānas* or links, and represents the point of Stream Entry, or the arising of Insight. Chapter 7 of Sangharakshita, *What is the Dharma?*, 'The Spiral Path', gives a detailed account of the positive *nidānas*; see *Complete Works*, vol. 3, pp. 258–79, and for 'knowledge and vision of things as they really are' see pp. 274–5.

222 See, for example, Herbert V. Guenther, *The Tantric View of Life*, Shambhala Publications, Berkeley and London 1972, p. 54; or Gampopa, *The Jewel Ornament of Liberation*, trans. Herbert V. Guenther, Rider, London 1970, p. 268 (in which context, incidentally, Dr Guenther directs the reader to Vasubandhu's *Vijñaptimātratasiddhi* for a detailed discussion of these awarenesses).

223 For more about the *ālaya vijñāna*, see chapter 4, 'The Turning About', in Sangharakshita, *The Meaning of Conversion in Buddhism*, Windhorse Publications, Birmingham 1994, p. 68 (*Complete Works*, vol. 2).

224 *Collins English Dictionary*.

225 This is a line from John Dryden's poem 'Absalom and Achitophel', (part 1, line 1005) published in 1681.

226 See Hajime Nakamura, *Indian Buddhism*, Motilal Banarsidass, Delhi 1980, p. 330.

227 William Shakespeare, *As You Like It*, Act II, Scene i.

228 Jiddu Krishnamurti (1895–1986) was born in India and brought to the West by Theosophists in 1911. He distanced himself from the Theosophists around 1930 and began teaching his own philosophy in Europe and latterly California.

229 In the 1960s and 1970s Mrs Mary Whitehouse was a vocal critic of the British media and the arts, especially the BBC. Her campaigns against swearing, obscenity, and other causes of concern, especially on television, were fiercely criticized by some, who accused her of demanding censorship, and approved by others who saw her as a force for the prevention of moral decline.

230 For a canonical account of how
to deal with the hindrances,
see *Vitakkasaṇṭhāna Sutta,
Majjhima Nikāya* 20 (i.119–
122). See Bhikkhu Ñāṇamoli
and Bhikkhu Bodhi (trans.),
*The Middle Length Discourses
of the Buddha,* Wisdom
Publications, Boston 1995,
pp. 211–4; or I. B. Horner
(trans.), *The Collection of the
Middle Length Sayings,* vol. i,
Pali Text Society, Oxford 1957,
pp. 152–6. Sangharakshita
discusses antidotes to the
hindrances in part 5, section 4
of *The Purpose and Practice
of Buddhist Meditation,* Ibis
Publications, Ledbury 2012,
pp. 346–58 (*Complete Works,*
vol. 5).

231 The idea that a thorn may be
removed by another thorn is
found in the Tantric text called
the *Cittaviśuddhiprakaraṇa,*
as quoted in Edward Conze
et al. (trans.), *Buddhist Texts
Through the Ages,* Shambhala
Publications, Boston and
Shaftesbury 1990, p. 221:

> Just as water that has
> entered the ear may be
> removed by water and just
> as a thorn may be removed
> by a thorn, so those who
> know how, remove passion
> by means of passion itself.'

INDEX

animals (*cont.*)
  effect on human psyche 23, 453–4
  sensitivity to mental states 537
animism 21–2, 54
anubhāva 98, 537; *see also* grace
anxiety 609, 611–12
apatrāpya 486, 661n
appamādena sampādetha 12
appreciation 42, 493–4
approval
  desire for 639–40
  rationalization and 366
  seeking 363–4, 368, 404
archetypal, the 606
argument
  best entered into as a game 360
  conceptual, and self-delusion 168
  creativity, and reactivity in 355
  different to discussion 459
  ego-propelled 170
  and friendship 354
  individuals and 353
  transcended by the quality of being
    357
arhant, killing an 503–4
arhants 172, 268, 295, 504, 525
Aristotle 269, 287, 648n
Ariyapariyesanā Sutta 644n, 667n
artists 119, 508
arts 43, 130, 132, 281, 372, 634
  as means of arousing energies 412
  and the refinement of consciousness
    158
  religious 158
  secular 414
  works of 132
arūpaloka 171, 448, 588–9
āryas 578
Āryasaṅgha 297
'As above, so below' 77
āsavas, see āsravas
asceticism 177, 199, 222, 527, 529–30,
    560, 664n
  capitalist 507
  dangers of 104
  and joy 129
  provisional 529–30
Aśoka 223
aśraddhā 207
āsravas 295, 449, 651n
Aśvajit 93
Atiśa 3
ati-yoga compared to Mahāmudrā 243
attachment 128, 331–3
  and the *bardo* 612

to the body 557
and conceit 399
to family and friends 215, 566
and fear 139
and non-attachment 337
to our own community 139
to a particular means 352
to places 336–7
to reputation 461
attachments, worldly 13, 124, 128, 142,
    154, 176
attainments, spiritual 43, 44–5
  behaving as though one has 473
  conditions to support experience of
    541
  and credibility to teach 414
  different to ecclesiastical success 561
  individual, and the survival of the
    Dharma 497
  and renunication 116
  should never be used 119
  surpassing those of your guru 112
  no way to prove beyond doubt 108–9
  as wealth 96
attitude, *see also* views
  creative and reactive 363
  of an ideal disciple 62–3, 594
  to life, affected by relationships 508
  right and wrong 353–4
aura 98, 244
avadhūtī 76
Avalokiteśvara 602
āvaraṇas, two 449–50, 660n; *see also*
    veils
Avataṃsaka Sūtra 161
aversion 448–9
avidyā 451
awareness 44
  aesthetic 132, 158
  appreciative 53
  and communication 205
  and *dhyānas* 580
  and faith 207, 274
  and fear 52
  in first precept 183
  and freedom 489
  of the goal 165
  of impermanence 155
  and individuality 215, 301
  jñāna as 598
  mind- 300–1
  mindful 50
  and non-duality 344
  as one of two accumulations 415
  of purpose 411

supported by *prāṇa* or active energy
322
of the unconditioned nature of reality
143
Vairocana as embodiment of 600
Awarenesses
five (*jñānas*) 451, 598

Bahudhātuka Sutta 661n
balance
of attainment and skilful means 414
of effort and relaxation 584
of energies on retreat 581
of intellect and imagination 145, 344,
372–3
Milarepa and 179
of qualities in a teacher 145
Rechungpa's need for 372
sahaja and 344
of scriptural knowledge and practice
486
Balkhu 432, 437–8
Balmo Baltang Plain 531
bardo 30, 65, 83, 612; *see also* state,
intermediate
definition of 30
of the dream state 83
of everyday life 83–4
of meditation 83
training in after-death experience of
65
vision of reality in 30
battle, as metaphor for spiritual life
103–5
Beatles 153
beauty
added to the world by Enlightenment
447
ancient Indian definition 159
capacity to appreciate 42–3
of the ideal, embodied in the Buddha
580
as intermediary between unreality and
reality 158
and the mandala 525
and refinement of consciousness 157
bee colony, as metaphor for *bodhicitta*
227
Belsen 312
Benares 116
Betze 572
Betze Duyundzon 437
Bhagavad Gītā 108, 220, 408, 632,
647n, 657n
Bhante, meaning of word 315

Bhāradvāja Sutta 294
Bhari Lotsawa 157
Bharima 431, 432
bhāva 98
Bhayabherava Sutta 659n
bhikkhus, see also monks
and lay people 315, 347, 387, 390,
520–1
Milarepa as 196
ordination 653n
and precepts 105, 487, 515
and projection 520–1
and re-ordination 541
and robes 333
and state 339
bhūmis, ten 268, 648n
bhūmisparśa 598
biases 295–6; *see also āsravas*
bindu 89, 91
*Biographies of Rechungpa: The
Evolution of a Tibetan
Hagiography, The* 261
'Bird with Five Families, The' 401
Blake, W. 103, 277, 416, 424, 438,
650n, 658n
blame 111
by the wise, fear of 486
blessings xiv, 48, 92, 95
and approval 363, 405
food 430
of guru 315, 511, 573, 586
in guru yoga 92
Tantric initiation as 175
through visions 620
bliss
and communication 419–20
distinct from ease and comfort 530
and emptiness/illumination, non-
duality of 90–1, 299, 528–9
great 65, 400, 415, 596–7
and Vajrayāna 529, 596
as highest and most sublimated level of
saṃsāra 415
and insight 133
mundane and transcendental 129,
589
and *śamatha* meditation 416
tummo and 90
blueprint, psychological-cum-spiritual
279; *see also* gestalt, pattern
Bodh Gaya 365
bodhi leaves 25
bodhicarya 254
Bodhicaryāvatāra 80, 131, 558, 664n

bodhicitta 52, 102, 296–7, 463, 517;
    see also Enlightenment, will to
  arising of 161, 589
  bee colony as metaphor for 227
  and the bodhisattva 297
  and *brahma vihāras* 103
  as companion 225–6
  practice 660n
  and Tantric initiations 136
  Tibetan expression for 226
  and yab-yum symbolism 296
Bodhidharma 360
bodhi-heart 102, 225–6, 253, 517; *see*
    also bodhicitta
bodhisattva
  ideal 37, 172
    Milarepa and 216, 589
    and pride 463
    and skilful means in teachings 414
    in the Vajrayāna 374, 463
  vow 161, 488
    devaluation of 488
    Milarepa's 26
    and positive pride 82
    and whole human race as family
      215
  of wisdom 19, 104
bodhisattvas 172, 463
  archetypal 19, 86–8
  attendant on the Five Buddhas 601
  and the *bodhicitta* 297
  career 414
  and compassion 590
  as esoteric refuge 317
  irreversible 588
  and knowledge of arts and sciences
      463–4
  in mandalas 125, 601–2
  sixteen years old, significance 238
  and Stream Entry 648n
  and ten *bhūmis* 268
  visualization of 319–20, 418, 513,
      603
  and weapons 104
  worship of 425
  wrathful 601
bodhyaṅgas, seven 53, 90, 644n
bodies
  multiplicity in one mind 227–8
  three, of the Buddha, *see trikāya*
body
  as *ālaya-vijñāna* 226–7
  between the conscious and unconscious
      state 236–7
  created, *see nirmāṇakāya*

essential to awakening 48–9, 74,
    75–6, 89, 227, 558
  as a good temple 618
  as house 227–8
  human 39, 46, 49
    constituents 536
    like a mirage-city 558
    as painful and unattractive 557–8,
      664n
  illusory or subtle 65, 76, 536
  magic 87; *see also nirmāṇakāya*
  in Mahāyāna 86–7
  of mutual enjoyment, *see*
      sambhogakāya
  in Pāli canon 86–9
  precious human 39, 46, 49
  rainbow- 535
  relationship to mind 227–8
  and suffering 558
  transformation, into *nirmāṇakāya* 293
  of truth, *see dharmakāya* 68, 86–7
  Vajrayāna and, transformation of
      74–5, 535, 535–7
  Vajrayāna understanding of 74–5, 76,
      415, 535, 558
Bong 62
book learning 14, 185, 308
books, as outer phenomena 632–3
boots 79–81
boredom 452–3
Borobudur 648n
Bouto 638
Brahmā 25
brahmacarya 127
brāhmaṇa, true 663n
Brahmā Sahāmpati 57, 667n
brahma vihāras 103
breath 76, 119, 566; *see also prāṇa*
  of the *ḍākinīs, see ḍākinīs'* breath
bride 206
The Buddha (Trevor Ling) 203
Buddha 602
  and blessing of food offerings 429–30
  description of bliss before
      Enlightenment 666n
  and *dhyāna* 31
  and earth goddess 19
  embodiment
    of the beauty of the ideal 580
    of illumination 615
  eternal 602
  families, five, and Ḍākinī Dharmas
      401
  first depictions of 25
  historical, and transcendental 88

chanting (*cont.*)
  Milarepa's singing as 48
  Tibetan 4–5, 157
Chattrul Rimpoche 645n
Chen, C.M. 22, 75, 659n
cheno 98
Chesterton, G. K. 390, 392
chhaang 403
childhood 130–1, 140
children 130, 200, 209–11, 288, 330,
    505, 510, 589
  Milarepa's metaphorical 300–1
chinlap 98
chöd 432
chokidar 347
Christianity 24, 120, 149–50, 161, 163,
    313, 538, 562, 592
  scriptures 632
chung 307
citta 207
cittata 338; *see also* Mind-Essence
'Cittavagga' 231, 647n
Cittaviśuddhiprakaraṇa 669n
Clarke, H. xi, xvi, 641n
clinging 48
  ego- 242
  mind 262, 345, 552, 562–3, 566
  and non-duality 344
  to possessions 10, 13, 139
  and rebirth 612–13
  as rope or string 587, 612, 615
  self- 139
  subtle 27
  to views 172
clothes 13, 121, 134, 198, 221, 313,
    321–2, 326, 330, 620, 628, 634
  and heat yoga 322, 616, 620
Coleridge, S. T. 167
collective unconscious 606
colours, symbolism of 59, 536
commitment 115
  as antidote to third fetter 652n
  and the bodhisattva ideal 172
  communication and effect of one's
    153
  disagreement about nature of 171
  effect of not honouring 487–8
  and going for Refuge 563
  to helping others 592
  importance of honouring 487–8
  and marriage 212
  Milarepa's 33
  money and 113–16
  and offering material wealth 113–14
  ordination as recognition of 176

oscillation in 541–2
quarrelling with your own 15
seeking acknowledgement of 165
as translation of *śaraṇa* 564
communication 17, 58, 115, 152–3,
    169–70, 178, 216
  across difference 169–70
  bliss and 419–20
  and the bodhisattva ideal 374
  conditions for effective 205, 357, 422,
    476, 477–8
  and cultural flotsam 153
  ḍākinīs as 373, 424
  of different facets of one reality 182
  effective 57–8
  energy and 478, 482
  highest form of 418
  horizontal and vertical 418–19
  human, versus technical debate 353–4
  as initiation 495–6
  and *kalyāṇa mitratā* 511
  lowest form of 318
  need for intensity in 380
  need for means other than the Dharma
    itself 414
  need to create conditions for 205
  and openness 354
  openness and fearlessness in 420
  and 'secret feasts' 424–5
  by seeing directly 216
  and seeing the pattern of another
    person 285
  and singing 462
  skilful means in 377, 414, 418
  no spiritual community without 497–8
  of spiritual experiences, forcing 476
  with spiritual friends 567
  and spiritual friendship 16, 516
  and study groups 478
  through enactment 377–9
  through working together 391
  two consciousnesses in 546
  Udānas as heightened 6
  with and without speech 216
communities, residential 34
community 303; *see also* spiritual
    community
comparison 450
compassion xiii, 33, 517, 588–90
  arising of 52
  as *brahma vihāra* 103
  and demons 27
  and engaging in Dharma activities 591
  great 26, 354, 586, 588, 590
    compared with mundane 590

and leading people onto spiritual path
357
Milarepa and 33, 268, 526
path of 102
and wisdom, non-duality of, *see*
wisdom, and compassion, non-
duality of
withdrawal and 52
in yab-yum symbolism 296–7, 373
competition
Rechungpa and 372
in the spiritual community 17–19, 418
concealment 515
conceit 103, 442, 448, 450
and attachment 399
not dispelled by *śamatha* practices 449
and growth 639
intellectual 168–9
inverted 82
self- 489
concentration
mandala as image of 125
meditative 90
and heat 89–90
in real communication 478
concepts
and imagination 238
intelligence as creative manipulation
of 238
as a necessary provisional framework
397–8
operational 396–8
as 'playwords' 66
as symbols 399
conditionality 149
benefit of awareness of 155
foundation for Mahāmudrā 243–4
and meditation 513
path as understanding of 243–4
and realization of *śūnyatā* 85
conditioned, and unconditioned,
perspectives on 85
conditioning
goes beyond logic 356
reinforced by reference to the past 204
conditions
for communication 477
for Dharma practice 34, 342, 504,
595, 630
making best use of one's 42
Milarepa and effect of external 45–6,
89, 631
safeguarding positive 34
to support spiritual aspirations 36
worldly 652n; *see also* winds, worldly

confidence
and approval 165
danger of over- 34
effect of vows on 161
loss of false 144
conflict 170–1
in guru-disciple relationship 365–6
Confucianism 506
Conquerors, five 601
consciousness 11–12, 44, 224, 226,
242, 604–7
ālaya, see ālaya
archetypal 606
and art 132
and the body 237
cannot raise level by force 358
collective 606
in communication 546
ḍākinīs and 59
and death 65, 154, 361, 570
in *Dhammapada* 231
effect of one's companions on 152
of a goal or vision 443
illumination of 74, 90, 143
and insight 512, 545
integration of 77
irruption of *ḍākinī* into 59
levels of 156, 173, 290, 298, 358,
359, 381, 396, 499, 575
practice of relocating 545–6
refinement of 157
six groups of 344
and skilfulness 207
soiled-mind 291
transformation of 77, 512, 537, 544,
639
universal seed 224, 226–7, 235
and writing 453
and Yogācāra 604–6
consciousnesses, eight of Yogācāra
schools 289, 604
consorts 126–7, 566, 601
consumerism 134
contact, spiritual 15
contentment 90–1, 95
as wealth 96
convention, social 101, 133, 135–6, 152
Conze, E. 319, 643n, 647n, 652n,
667n, 669n
Cordelia 211
correspondence, Tantra and idea of 77
covering of defilements (*kleśa āvaraṇa*)
449
covering of knowables (*jñeya āvaraṇa*)
449

delight, importance of 129

delights 47, 54, 59, 129–30, 151, 159
  three, of Milarepa 407, 417, 419

deluded types 577

Dem Chog 65, 159

demons 21–7, 29, 31, 270
  Buddhist attitude towards 24
  Christian usage of term 24–5
  doubts and xv
  as emanation of Milarepa's state of
    mind 27
  hindrances as 628, 636
  and house building 276
  and the integration of energies 25–30
  King 32
  of laziness 555
  local 24, 26
  Marpa and 28
  miser's 217–18
  Padmasambhava and 271, 649n
  possession by 441–2
  pride 442
  seeing through 27, 31–2
  and storms 12
  subduing 24–7, 29, 32, 37
  taught by Milarepa xiii
  unskilful mental states as 276
  of worldly clinging 12

dependence 73, 387–8
  on rites and rituals... 319

depression 53, 609, 612

desire 171–2, 329
  to gain Enlightenment 371
  and the kleśas 449
  plane of, see kāmaloka
  for the pleasures of the Buddhist path
    (dharma-chanda) 129
  and samādhi 142
  sense 147, 159, 171, 658n
  and vision 443
  for worldly pleasures (kāma-chanda)
    129

detachment 331–3

Devadatta 504, 661n, 664n

devaloka 25, 557; see also god realm,
    heaven realm

devas xiii, 418, 469, 496, 525

development 18, 122, 217, 273, 384,
    444, 593
  awareness as first fruit of 300–1
  and coercion 488
  conditions for 485–6
  Dharma and 589
  duty to your own 184
  friends and 567

and growth as basis of spiritual life
    396
  human potential for 569
  individual, and compassion 591–3
  and kalyāṇa mitratā 511
  and lifestyle 213
  personal 31
    and work 391
  preciousness about one's own 591
  a result of own volition 358
  suspending thoughts of own 592

devil, Māra as 27, 149

devotion 117, 182, 185, 319, 539, 616,
    618–19
  as adornment 96
  as bootlaces 81
  as a cotton belt 117
  developing 447
  development of 447
  to the guru 14, 539
  Milarepa's song of 14
  as practice 319

dhammānusārin 649n

Dhammapada 50, 90, 96, 219, 231,
    411, 563, 583, 654n, 656n, 663n,
    667n
  and Enlightenment 370

dhara 474

Dhardo Rimpoche 109, 492

Dharma 196
  books 167, 459
    one page enough 495
  as the breath of the Buddha/ḍākinīs
    180
  brothers 7, 15
  cannot be bought 188
  communicated individually 97, 162,
    362–3
  corruption and contamination of 174
  and dāna 113, 219–20
  danger of approaching wrongly 180
  danger of making livelihood from
    174–6
  difference between reading and
    practising 166
  disappearance of 255, 497
  Essence 400–1, 407, 411
    differs from Pith-Instruction 413
  etymology 474
  everything a natural expression of 340
  experience of, and worldly advantage
    173–4
  -followers 492, 649n; see also doctrine
    follower
  gift of the 116

Milarepa's 55, 58–9, 62, 144
and receptivity 58
and six yogas of Nāropa 65
Drin 156
Drinking the Mountain Stream xvii
Dryden, J. 610, 668n
duality
above and beyond 85, 415–16
fear and 49
freedom from 43–4, 131, 594
no ultimate 86, 529
Dudjom Rimpoche 645n
duḥkha
insight into 563, 649n
and the spiral path 649n
dveṣa 449
dynasty 3

eagle, golden, as symbol of
Enlightenment 30
Eagle Castle 9
earth goddess 19
earth-touching *mudrā* 598
education 182, 285, 419
ego 74, 241, 253, 432
Akṣobhya represents overcoming 598
appropriation of knowledge 167
appropriation of spiritual practice
174–6, 580
and argument 170
at death 250
exhaustion of 189–90
and going for Refuge 241–2
as neurotic individuality 219
non-, *see* non-ego
practices to weaken 636–7
and receptivity to the Dharma 188
and relative mind 242
ego-clinging (*see also* self-view, fetter of)
10, 27, 81–2, 131, 165, 170, 242,
245, 253, 636
freedom from 54, 83
and guru's role 111, 368
and identifying with religious group
27
and loneliness 16, 54
metaphors for 10, 12, 81
mindfulness and 12
and praise 111
and pride 459, 463
seeing through 27
egoism, different to self-confidence 464
Eightfold Path, Noble 168
'Eight Worldly Claims' 325; *see also*
worldly winds, eight

elements 66, 525, 597
six, practice 513, 662n
elephant 50, 420, 633
Elijah 643n
Eliot, T. S. 337, 653n
Elizabeth I 95
emotional energies 59, 88, 157–8,
273–5, 284
emotions 159, 443, 608–11, 619
assumptions in Pāli Canon about 417
near and far enemies 158n
negative, repeated patterns of 276,
610
positive 90, 98, 103, 105, 168; *see
also* positivity, emotional
at the root of *micchā-diṭṭhis* 158n
employer-employee relationship 506–7
empowerment, Tantric 75
emptiness, *see śūnyatā*; voidness 10,
179, 247
enactment 377–9
enemies 80, 209, 211, 217, 472, 617,
621, 635–6, 656n, 663n
near and far 655n
energy 74–9
and *bodhyaṅgas* 90
the Buddha and 417
and communication 476, 478
ḍākinīs and 59, 178, 371–2, 424
discrimination in investing 593
and emotions 609–12
lineage as current of spiritual 93
literalism and the language of 611
of local culture 25
of the mind 236
and pleasure 129
in pursuit of the good 106; *see also
vīrya*
reflection and 53
rousing by the arts or sports 412
in study groups 479–80
symbolized by horse 72
and talking 482
unification of 25, 67, 77–8, 90–1,
125, 322, 411–12, 443, 514, 576,
609–10
Vajrayāna and 74–5, 371–2, 411–12,
415; *see also* Tantra
and visualization 320
enjoyment 52, 130, 133, 158–9, 448
Enlightenment (*see also* Nirvāṇa) 30,
51, 58, 61, 68, 90, 164, 221, 296,
314, 370–1, 447, 569, 599, 648n
in the *bardo* 85–6
and *bodhicitta* 52

Enlightenment (*cont.*)
  Buddha's use of terminology about 608
  ḍākinīs, as aspect of 59
  and karma 84–5
  not a possession 314–15
  Pure Land as a 'social experience' of
    303–4
  and suffering 47
  timeless 94
  Vajrayāna view of path to 86, 296,
    416
  will to 136, 280, 296; *see also*
    bodhicitta
envy 103, 168, 448–9
equanimity 39, 48, 53, 103
Erastianism 339, 653n
Eros 158
escapism 34
Etadaggavagga 646n
ethics 79, 83–4, 100, 649n
  conditions for practising 84
  and conventional morality 135
  and energy 79
  and freedom from concealment 515
  and Going for Refuge 100–1
  and shame 486
  three stages of, in Kagyu school 84
ethnic, integration with universal 25
Evans-Wentz, W. Y. xii
evocation 319–20
evolution 120
  higher 275, 292, 650n
  lower 275, 301
exemplification 33
exhaustion 338, 617
exoticism 519–20
experience
  direct 61, 75, 77, 87, 125
  knowing the Dharma in our own
    166–7
  Milarepa's emphasis on personal 228
  sense-, and language 607
  trusting one's own 19–20
  visionary 88
eye
  inner 23
  of veneration 93

factors of Enlightenment, seven, *see*
    bodhyaṅgas 53, 90
faculties
  bodhicitta 102
  reasoning or intellectual 78, 359
  spiritual 106, 233
  visionary or imaginal 88, 438, 528

failure
  blaming teacher 111
  of communication 461
  does not apply to the spiritual battle
    104
  to honour commitments 488
  and insight 189
  of nerve and vision 135
  patterns of 276
faith (*śraddhā*) 19–20, 207, 272–5
  in the bond 181
  and energy 274–5
  -follower 129, 154, 272, 308–9, 580,
    649n
  as foundation 207, 243, 272–5
  in the guru 306–7, 410
  and insight 67, 71, 88, 90, 512,
    513–14
  and joy 33, 143, 188
  oscillation with doubt 541
  in principles 473–4
  and reason 64, 185
  and the spiral path 649n
  tests of 61
  transcendental 33
  unshakable 219
  and vision 273–4
fame 461
family 215, 330–1, 410, 477, 484–6
  duties towards 150
  giving up for a while 215
  life 455–7, 485
  whole of humanity as 214
fantasy 373
farming 202–3, 288–9, 291, 293–4
father 210, 298, 315, 609, 661n
  harmony with 503, 509
  as metaphor for guru 502
  and son relationship 506
  as the spiritual tradition itself 504
'Father Buddhas' 620
fear 48–52
  of annihilation 46
  arising from insight 71
  and attachment 138–9
  of death 341
  of future suffering 128
  of loneliness 49, 128
  and possession 334
fearlessness 49, 52
  in facing death 245
  and generosity 115
  gesture of 600
  and Mahāmudrā teaching 245
  and spiritual friendship 420

happiness
   and craving 452
   and dependence on others 388
   evenmindedness as 343
   and faith 143
   of Milarepa 328–30
   must be created for yourself 208
Happy Valley 327
harmony 15, 130, 136, 501–4, 510
   of complete integration 299
   effect of being out of 483
   of energies and understanding 322
   of experience and reason 416
   with fellow disciples 511
   with guru, *see* guru, harmony with
   horizontal and vertical 502
   living in, with surroundings 41
   with local deities 43
   with one's parents 500, 509
   and spiritual hierarchy 504
hat 92
hate types 577, 580
hatred 103–4, 138, 183, 290, 524, 531,
   566, 575, 577, 606, 608, 609, 636
   and anger 610
   anger and 524
   and inhibition 609
healing, spiritual 313
Heart Sūtra 650n, 658n
heat, inner 65, 90, 536; *see also tummo*
Heat Yoga 307–8, 322
hell 61, 385, 538, 557
   fear of 71, 97, 128
Hermes Tresmegistus 644n
Hermetic correspondence 644n
hermitage, Milarepa's 51
hermits 33, 177, 395, 656n
   Milarepa as 48, 110, 487, 561
heroic ideal 104–5, 245–6, 647n
   and kindness 105
Herrick, R. 151
heruka 373
Hevajra Tantra 14, 65
hierarchies 17, 19
hierarchy, spiritual
   and harmony 504
   and literalism 176
   not readily apparent 18
Higher Evolution 275, 292, 650n
'Hīnayāna' 172–3
   and Mahāyāna 497
hindrances
   antidotes to 637
   five 11, 442, 448–9, 575–6, 637,
      658n, 666n, 669n

Hinduism 25, 249, 312, 363, 417, 429,
   508, 619, 632
home 201–6
Homer 71
honesty 137, 140, 184
horse 70–3
   metaphorical 321–2
   as pride 71
house, symbolism of 269–72, 276
hrī, shame 486, 660n
Hudibras 360
Huineng 364, 544
hūm 293
human life 24, 503, 553, 564
humbug 429
humiliation 143
humility 62, 165, 243–4, 480, 483,
   511, 514
   as foundation for Mahāmudrā 243
Humphreys, C. 347
*Hundred Thousand Songs of Milarepa,
   The* xii, 3, 259, 308
hungry ghosts 27; *see also pretas*
hypocrisy 460, 515

ideal 273–5, 279–82, 443–4
   embodied 111, 503–4
   and the mandala 446
   manifests differently in people 221–3
ignorance 31, 103–4, 179–80, 295,
   448–9, 451, 512–13, 575
   and effect of *śamatha* practices 449
   as 'Housebuilder' 269
illimitables, *see brahma vihāras*
illness 535, 537
illumination
   and bliss, non-duality of 528
   of consciousness 74
   in experience of voidness 91
   metaphorical 285
   mind and 229–31
   synonym for insight into emptiness
      528
   as synonym for *samādhi* 432
   wisdom as 615
ill will 11, 104
images, and literalism 88
imagination
   balance with intellect 372–3
   and concepts 238
   and Enlightenment 372
   fantasy as near enemy 373
   and freedom from group 135
   and the rational mind 88

intellectual understanding
  compared to *ḍākinīs'* breath 180, 475
  of Dharma need not be perfect 359
  different to experience 233, 399
  and imagination 372
  important but not enough 360, 409,
    514, 518, 636
  and insight 359–60, 544–5, 580
  linear road of 287
  more common than actual practice
    107
  and wisdom 118, 439
interconnectedness, and gratitude 93
intoxication, through positive experience
  581
intuition 69
invocation 319–20
irreversibility 268, 295, 588; *see also*
  Stream Entry

Jambhala 523
James, W. 541
Jamyang Khyentse Rimpoche 645n
jar, initiation with the 65
Jātaka tales 13, 643n
jealousy 103, 449
'Jerusalem' 103–4
Jetsun, meaning xvi
Jewel Ornament of Liberation, The xv,
  433
jewels 20, 45, 295; *see also* Three
  Jewels
  four, of Milarepa 294
  seven inexhaustible 50
  whole body of *ḍākinī* teachings as
    401
jhāna 499; *see also dhyānas*
Jidun 431
Jinas 601
jinlap 537–8
jñā 604
jñāna 415, 598, 604
  and *puṇya* 415
jñānas, five 451, 605; *see also*
  knowledges, five
jñeya āvaraṇa 449; *see also* veils
Johnson, S. 16
joy 33, 41, 43, 45, 53, 254, 451
  asceticism and 129
  Buddha's experience as a boy 31
  in contemplating beauty 157
  essential in spiritual life 133
  and faith 33, 143, 188
  'faith follower' and 129
  Milarepa not attached to 54

often more difficult than negative
    energy 78
  rooted in bodily experience 46
  serene 90; *see also prīti*
  and suffering not separate 47
  sympathetic (*muditā*) 103
  transcendence of 49, 85
judgement
  of other people 111–12
  using one's own 408
Jung, C.G. 145, 606
just sitting practice 584–5, 667n

Kadampa tradition 261
Kagyu school 4, 14, 84, 94, 96, 168,
    176, 462, 667n
  emphasis on guru-disciple relationship
    186
  founders of 243
  highest teaching 65
  lineage of the oral transmission 380
  and Mahāmudrā 243
  meditation and study 359
  robes 462
Kalimpong 75, 99, 109, 116, 301, 337,
    339, 432–3, 487, 492, 498
  effect of beauty of 158
kalpas 414
  simile to illustrate 657n
kalyāṇa mitras 369
  and *apatrāpya* 486
  being out of harmony with 483
  ceremony 379
kalyāṇa mitratā 207, 300, 367, 393,
    511
kāma-chanda 129
kāmadhātu 588
kāmaloka 171, 448, 588–9
karma 11, 60, 81, 85, 146, 306, 528
  after Enlightenment 84–5
  of breaking a vow 161
  and connections through lifetimes
    146, 255, 303, 306
  -exhausted 60, 71
  joy of freedom from 46
  Milarepa's weighty negative 60
  and rebirth 60
  vipāka 146, 292, 528
Karmapa 429
karuṇā 103, 357, 619; *see also*
  compassion
  mahā 354
kaupin 199–201
kāyas, three, and chakras 619
Khambas 99

in thinking about spiritual life 287
lobha 449
logic
  attachment to 352
  limits of 356–7
  and science 352
  versus experience, in argument 360–1
Lokavipatti Sutta 653n
loneliness 15–17, 42–3
  cold as representing 49
  and depression 53
  fear of 49, 128
  and sense of separate selfhood 17, 54,
    128
  and solitude 42
lotus
  flowers 84
    as symbols for *cakras* 76, 618
  as metaphor for heart 58
  thousand-petalled 76
Lotus Sūtra 45, 161, 172
love
  mode
    functioning passively in 385
    and power mode 354–5, 363, 411,
      656n
    receptivity and 384–5
    and relationship with guru 385
  and quarrelling 208
lust 11
Luther, M. 428

Machig Labdron 432, 658n
Madhyamaka 417
madness, yogic 177
Magi 432
magic
  black 362
    as skilful means 361
  expectation of 520
  love 432
  need for 321
mahā 65, 243, 590, 597
Mahā-Assapura Sutta 665n
Maha Bodhi Society 333, 562
Mahāmudrā 10, 65
  compared to *ati-yoga* 243
  definition of 65
  description of 243
  foundations for practice of 61, 243–6
  and Kagyu tradition 243
  Milarepa's initiation into 159
  and path of irregular steps 237
  and pointing out 243
  and spontaneity

importance of 253
  of non-duality 231
  and Zen 13
Mahānidāna Sutta 662n
Mahāparinibbāna Sutta 643n, 651n,
    657n, 660n, 661n, 662n
Mahārāhulovāda Sutta 662n
Mahāsaccaka Sutta 643n, 651n, 659n,
    666n
Mahāsakuludāyi Sutta 665n
mahāsukha 415, 596
Mahātanhāsankhaya Sutta 662n, 663n
Mahāvagga 659n, 665n
mahāvana 23
Mahāyāna
  and *bodhicitta* 102
  development of 497
  Milarepa and 33, 569
  and non-duality 102
  and pleasure 528
  sūtras 86, 161, 172, 414
    Buddha in 602
  view of the *dharmakāya* 86
maitrī 590
Majjhima Nikāya 642n, 643n, 644n,
    646n, 649n, 651n, 659n, 661n,
    662n, 663n, 665–6n, 669n
mālā 116, 168
mandala 125–6, 446–7, 525–6, 584,
    603, 618
  creating a 522–6
  of Dem Chog 65
  of the Five Buddhas 446, 570–1,
    598–603
  greater 318, 652n
  as a higher pattern 279
  multi-dimensional models of 648n
  offering practice 125–6, 446–7, 646n,
    659n, 660n
  of Padmasambhava 217
  and path images compared 525, 584
  personal 265, 435, 509, 523–4, 539,
    541
  of speech 539
  the, and the *trikāya* 293
  of twenty-one Tārās 603
  'Mandala of the Whole' 446
Mañjughoṣa 104
Mañjuśrī 19
mano-vijñāna 605
mantras
  Buddhaṃ saraṇaṃ gacchāmi as 239
  and concentration 458
  and dissolving negativity 78–9

mantras (*cont.*)
  and healing 311
  and sacramentalism 428–9
Māra 19, 27, 34, 149, 150, 153, 177,
    367, 655n
Marpa 60–1, 64–5, 110, 113, 145, 185,
    400–1
  and the Formless Ḍākinī Dharma
    Series 364–5, 402, 463
  lifestyle of 110
  Milarepa's attitude to 14, 19–20, 28,
    61, 65, 92, 249, 328, 379–80, 383,
    385, 406, 488
  and towers 269, 648n
  and trials of Milarepa 352, 362
  visions of, by Milarepa 19, 32
  visualization of, by Milarepa 13, 92
  wife of 14
marriage
  and choice 457
  compatibility with the spiritual life 212
  and gurus 410
  in India 457
  and patterns of rejection 276
  as a sacrament 428
  taken for granted 334
  unrealistic expectations of 208
Marriage of Heaven and Hell, The 78,
    416, 658n
Mary 105
mātṛkās 469
Maudgalyāyana 25, 375
Mayas 3
median nerve 73, 76, 91, 411
meditation 23, 130, 275, 293, 359,
    423, 462, 496, 498, 512–13, 576,
    620, 649n
  bardo of 83
  brahma vihāras 103
  conditions for 142, 477, 629–31
  danger of speaking of 421–2
  doing different practices 167, 326,
    392–3, 473
  effect on others of 355
  giving up 356, 419, 484
  and insight 75, 398, 449, 579, 659n
  just sitting practice 584–5, 667n
  on a mandala 125, 522–3
  and merit 343
  as preparation for death 154
  a process of natural growth 31
  resistance to 618
  on retreat 595
  in solitude 522, 621
  systematic practice of 247

system of 322, 667n
talking about experiences in 476
in Tantric practice 302–3
teaching 228, 412–13, 498
and tiredness 555, 617
Meghiya 367, 654n
Mehta, Dinshah 332, 653n
memory xiv, 289
mental function (*caitta*) 207
mental objects, recollection of 10
mental states 42, 53–4, 164, 207–8,
    309, 312, 361–2, 428, 441, 512–13,
    535, 537, 607, 637, 647n
  all are perceptible 537
  eleven positive (*kuśala*) 596, 647n
  negative, as demons 441
  skilful 207, 343, 423, 512, 637
  skilful and unskilful 207–8
  transformation of is the basic Buddhist
    practice 512
  unskilful, and insight 575
merit 146
  description of 244
  field of 186
  gratitude as receptivity to guru's 93
  making use of 71
  meditation and 343
  as seeds 291
  transference of 102
Message of Milarepa, The xi–xii
metaphors
  care needed in using 286
  of clear light, for the Void 43
  effect of elaboration 288
  inherent in language 607
  limitations of 283
  and metaphysics 285, 289, 291–2,
    320, 341
  Milarepa's use of 10, 12, 80, 302
  speaking in spatial terms as 606
  for spiritual life 80, 103–5, 136–7
  use of 282–3, 285
mettā 103, 619
  in cooking 82
  self- 521–2
mettā bhāvanā 80, 168
  and anger 612
  and family 214
  as insight practice 513–14, 663n
  and resentment 444
  self-*mettā* as basis 521
micchā-diṭṭhis (wrong views) 295, 439,
    449–51, 473, 651n
middle way 35, 51
midwife 301, 651n

state 48, 58
  samādhi 90
two-in-one-ness, coursing in 128
non-duality 43, 51, 66, 72, 102
  of bliss and illumination 528–9
  ḍākinīs, as experience of 66
  enlightened and unenlightened
    perspectives on 85
  and fearlessness 49
  and guru-disciple relationship 58
  at the highest level 130
  and integration 66
  and the Mahāyāna 86
  and the mandala 126
  Milarepa's joy in 49
  and 'practice of two-in-one' 43, 51
  purpose of Mahāmudrā 65
  realization of 462
    and joy 462
  of 'two-in-one' path 102
  in Vajrayāna 529
  of wisdom and compassion 51
non-ego 247
  in Hīnayāna and Mahāyāna 246,
    246–7
no-self 576–7
nuns 42, 661n
Nyams 299
Nyingmapas 243, 498

objectification, of thoughts and feelings
  278
objects
  inanimate 21
  mental 10–11
  respect for 70–1
Obstacle-Maker 32
offerings 430
  of the mandala, *see* mandala, offering
    practice
  and merit 186
  motivation for giving 188
  oneself 125–6
old woman 549–51
oṃ 293
One Mind 44, 599
openness
  with spiritual friends 516
  and spiritual friendship 420
  the Void as 44
oral tradition
  disadvantage of 402
  distinguishing authentic/inauthentic
    470

Order
  being out of harmony with the 483
  Triratna Buddhist
    (formerly Western Buddhist) 709
    and precepts 487
  Western Buddhist xviii, 151
  as a whole, relating to 385
  ordination 176
    ceremony, as enactment 378
    in Kagyu and Nyingma schools
      176–7
    Milarepa and 180, 196, 333
    monastic, and Vajrayāna 417
    name taking of new and 150
    pride and 176
    request
      to Milarepa 97–8
      and reorganization of life 97–8
    sāmaṇera 653n
    of women 42
  oscillation, and integration 540–1
  Oujen 217, 301, 304
  'own being' (*svabhāva*) 84

pācittiyas 656n
Padmaloka 23
Padmasambhava 24–5, 223
  teachings 469
painting 119, 260, 277, 523, 650n
Pāli canon
  on *bhikkhus* disrobing 541
  on bliss 90
  on comparison 450
  and the *dharmakāya* 86
  on factors of Enlightenment 90
  on faith follower and doctrine follower
    649n
  on going for Refuge 563
  language of, Milarepa and 565
  and language of energy 417
  on meditation 75
  Milarepa's use of language of 565
  parable in 34
  and path of renunciation 128
  on qualities of disciples 132
  spirits and demons in 22, 25
parables
  of the burning house 667n
  of deer 34
  of jewel in cloak 44–5
paradox 86, 106, 479, 489
pāramitās 271, 275, 295, 514, 649n;
  see also perfections
parents 505
  harmony with 509–10

and renunciation 54
through engaging our energies 158
Vajrayāna view of 528
poems, compared to prose 262
poets, and spiritual friendship 508
pointing-out 243
ceremony 233
point of freedom 456–8
poisons
five 103, 442, 448–9, 659n
and five hindrances 448–9, 669n
and 'insight' practices 449
three 449
Polonius 382
positivity, emotional 50; see also
emotion, positive
and freedom 489
and having a goal 272–5, 449
and insight 449, 512
spiritual community 277
possessions 72, 124, 138–9, 156, 187,
218–20, 296, 342
clinging to 11, 13
Milarepa's metaphorical 288
pot, as metaphor for receptivity 117
power
calling on a 320
-mode 110
and advice-giving 623–4
and love mode 354–5, 363
in sangha 488
in relationships 506
and spiritual community 110
spiritual, Milarepa's 31
practice, spiritual 3, 153, 157, 212,
250, 323, 326, 428, 542, 639
beautifies the mandala 447
and breaking down ego 639
and complacency 164
crystallizations of 535
danger of becoming end in itself 164
different to knowledge 107, 166
external and internal 302–3
giving as 115
how to make effective 167–8
and individual teaching 393
and lifestyle 133
making all activities into 153–4
and passivity 422
putting off 473
reaction against 542–3
ritual as crucial intermediate stage of
157
selecting 392
and 'shopping around' 110, 473

of wandering musician yogis 5
weaving as metaphor for 136
practice. visualization, see visualization
practice
prajñā 66, 90, 233, 252, 649n
prajñā pāramitā 649n
Prajñāpāramitā tradition 650n
prāṇa 72, 76, 322, 400, 407, 411, 466;
see also energy
Prāṇa-Mind 72, 322
pranāyāma 177
prārthana 319
prasad 312
prayer 48, 71, 138, 239, 247, 265, 319,
380, 427, 429
precepts 342, 487; see also ethics
better to have a small number 487
of guru, betraying 483
individual applicability 338
in the Kadam sense 393
as mirror 324
observing effectively 487–8
as part of effective practice 167
personal 162, 166, 393–4, 408; see
also 'pith teachings'
putting them into practice 183
ten 487
as vow 325
Precious Teachers 645n
preferences 35–6, 131–2, 187
and spiritual progress 130–1
presence, sense of 22, 71
pretas 27, 220; see also hungry ghosts
pride 103, 142, 437–8, 440–3
and altruism 463
the basic error 639
Buddha- 82
in Dharma knowledge 480
and following the guru's precepts 483
and growth 639
horse as 71
of learning 470
positive form of 82
and receptivity the Dharma 141
renunciation of 73
unawareness of 464
principle of the conservation of moral
effort 290
prīti (rapture) 50, 90
problems, psychological and spiritual
443
progress, and regression 397
projection 614
and craving 309
of spiritual life onto others 520

property 217–18
　respect for 335
protection 628, 635–6
　and lineage 181
　Milarepa's song of 79–80
　spiritual 49, 81, 98, 100, 138–9
　worldly 187, 505–6
Protestantism 428
prthagjanas 535
pseudo-equality 441
psychic, forces, non-human 22–4
psychic heat 49, 89–90, 536
pudgala-nairātmya 246
pudgala-śūnyatā 246
puja 320–1
　beginners and 412
　and mental state 428
　as part of effective practice 167
　preparation for 477
　Sevenfold 319
　Tantric 320
Pundarika centre 584
punya 146, 244, 415; see also merit
　and jñāna 415
punya karma 244
Pure Land
　as a higher pattern 279
　as a mandala 525
　of Padmasambhava 217, 303–4
　and sambhogakāya Buddha 602
　as 'social experience' of Enlightenment
　　303–4
　spiritual community as 34, 121
purification 360, 640
purity, of attitude 353

Ragma 196, 221, 254
rainbow-body 535
Rainbow Road, The 328, 641n, 653n,
　657n
rakṣasas 304
Ramakrishna Mission 363
rapture 50, 90; see also prīti
rasanā 76
rationalizations 366
rational mind, imagination and the 88
Ratnasambhava 599–600, 605
ravens 33, 53–4, 643n
reactivity
　and creativity 279, 355, 649n
　incorporation of into creativity 298
　preferences and 131
reading 458–9
　and experience 382
　as hindrance to practice 168

reality
　approached via imagination 88
　different facets of one 182, 216
　encountering non-temporal 69
　not a target in time and space 103
　ultimate 87, 614, 631; see also
　　dharmakāya, Enlightenment,
　　Nirvāṇa, śūnyatā, Void, the
　vajra as symbol of 94
　vision of, sameness/difference 600
　wisdom of 598–9
realms
　archetypal 87–8, 171, 217
　　receptivity to 89
　　Urgyen as 217
　human 60
　manifestation of a different 63
　six
　　and potential for spiritual
　　　development 664n
　　of the Tibetan wheel of life 220
　three 588–9
　three lower 220
　transcendental 30
reason
　and emotion 77
　faculty that restrains energy 78
　and faith 64, 185, 273
　and following the scriptures 416
　giving up 189
　and meditation 359
　and power-mode 354
　and the subject-object problem 231
rebirth 85, 269, 559, 582
　ālaya and 290, 292
　and the bardo 83, 85, 612
　conscious direction of 146
　and craving 612–13
　and the creation of a 'gestalt' 282
　end of 613
　karma and 60
　like building a house 269
　in lower realms 251
　pleasure and 129
　process of 30
　and relationships 144, 146–7, 506
　and store-consciousness 290
　vows and 144, 147–8
receptivity
　an active state 456
　to archetypal forms 89
　changes with age 382
　complete, to someone else 383–6
　to the Dharma and pride 141
　of disciple to guru 110–11, 115

relationships
  benefit of a network of 336
  Buddhist emphasis on vertical 507
  disruption of positive 336
  employer-employee 506–7
  father and son 506
  with guru, as initiation 495
  guru-disciple 55, 58, 61, 65, 94,
    110–11, 181, 261, 317–18, 388,
    393–4, 418–19, 495, 504–9,
    518–19
    as basis of everything 519
    horizontal and vertical 418–19
    most important 504–8
    need for a higher principle in 214
    parent-child 505–6
    unconditioned 386
    vertical 504
  relatives 213–15
    and change 204–5, 485
  relativity, of time and space 544–5
  relaxation, Mahāmudrā teaching of
    451–2, 584
  relics 535, 655n
  renunciation 10, 36, 55–6, 133, 183,
    185–7, 245, 316
    after full-blooded worldly life 159
    care in use of language of 215
    as inner boots 80
    an inner experience 36
    in the Kagyu tradition 176, 183
    and non-material wealth 50, 80–1, 96
    path of 128
    and pleasure 54, 130
    sexual 127
    of worldly attachments 128
  repa 462
  repression, of energy 77–8
  reputation, attachment to 461
  resentment 103
    and family life 455
    and mettā bhāvanā 444
    and passivity 457
    in sexual relationships 208–9
  resistance, mental as demons 270–1
  restlessness
    and anxiety 11
    freedom from 341
    hindrance 448
  retreats 303
    Māra and 177
    as means of creating a mandala 522–3
    returning from 34, 72, 583
    and silence 482
    solitary 53, 391, 530

reverence 14, 167
Rhys Davids, C. 499
right livelihood, see team-based right
    livelihood
rites and rituals as ends in themselves
    378, 428
ritual
    as first level of Tantric practice 302
    Tantric 157
Roberts, P.A. 261, 648n, 658n
robes 333, 562
roots 336
    need for 332
roots of unskilfulness, three 449, 575
rTogs 299
rumours 461
rūpa 102, 416
    and śūnyatā 416
rūpaloka 171, 448, 588–9
    painful compared to Enlightenment
    589
Ryōkan 105

saddhānusārin 308–9, 649n
Saddharma Puṇḍarīka 45
sādhana 87, 603, 619
sage 68, 77, 516, 653n; see also guru
sahaja 249, 344
Sahajayāna 417
sahajiya 91
Sahle Aui 437
Saint Francis 562
Śākyamuni 315, 504, 602; see also
    Buddha
samādhi 84, 106, 594
    after meditation 595
    awakening from 594
    bliss and emptiness 90
    conditions to deepen 141–2
    ensuing 595
    as food 321, 620, 627, 633
    illumination as synonym for 432
    main and ensuing 595
    on meeting guru 305
    perseverance in, as food 321, 321–2
    and prajñā 90
    as spiritual faculty 106
    spontaneous 305
Samādhi of Guru-Union 63
sāmaṇera 333, 653n
samāpattis 540
śamatha meditation 299, 398–9, 416,
    449, 512, 512–13, 529, 575–7
samaya 325
sambhogakāya 86–9, 222

saṃsāra 47, 559
  freedom within 45
  and *nirvāṇa* 396
    as concept to be transcended 396
    going beyond 395–6
    Mahāyāna view 396
    need to discriminate between 85,
      179, 399, 405
    non-duality and 51, 84, 102, 395,
      415
    as operational concepts 396–7
    Theravāda view 395–6
    Vajrayāna perspective on 415
saṃvara 65
Saṃyutta Nikāya 75
sangha xv, 35–6, 175, 281, 496, 661n,
  664n; *see also* spiritual, community
  and Āryasaṅgha 297
  being out of harmony with 483
  blame of 111
  direct contact with 496
  distribution of labour in 390
  economic basis of 175, 339
  horizontal and vertical relationships
    in 507
  as important condition for practice
    152
  receptivity to 385
  relating to 385, 507
  schism in 661n, 664n
  seen as separate to oneself 475
  and state control 339
  working with other people in 277
saṅghabheda 661n
Sangharakshita
  Library xi
  reflection on study group 480
  seminars xii, xiii–xiv, 259, 641n
  teachers, compared to each other 645n
Saṅgīti Sutta 652n
Sang Jye Jhab 187, 239
Śāntideva 80, 131, 664n
śaraṇa, meaning of 563–4
Śāriputra 25, 93, 375, 496
śarīra 535
sarvadharmaśūnyatā 247
Sarvāstivāda, on *dharmas* 597
Sarvāstivāda school 207, 295, 578, 597
sarva-śūnyatā 246
Satan 27
Satipaṭṭhāna Sutta 10–11
Sautrāntika school 407
scholasticism 496–7
science, attachment to 352
Scott, Walter 276

scriptures
  all elaboration of same message 370,
    495
  Buddhist, compared to Christian or
    Hindu 632
  and individualized teachings 394
  reasoning, to be balanced with
    following 416
seeds 290–2
  in relative *ālaya* 605
  teaching as 293
seed syllables 293
seeing
  real, and feeling 590
  things as they really are 596
  through, and true disillusionment 556
self
  -awareness, illuminating 65
  -conceit 489
  larger, contacted through myth 318
  new, as castle 275
  -respect 82, 134, 136, 660n
  -view, fetter of 11; *see also* ego
    clinging
selfhood, sense of separate 17; *see also*
  ego
  and loneliness 17
Selkirk, A. 660n
semantics 356
sems nyid 338
sense
  bases, six 10–11
  -consciousnesses, five 345, 605
  desire 147, 156, 159
  -pleasure, refinement of 129–30
  vijñānas, five 604
senses 129
  and the mandala 525
sensitivity 129, 132
  hierarchy of spiritual 132
  psychic 311–12
sensuality 160–1
  purifying and refining 157
seven factors of Enlightenment, *see*
  bodhyaṅgas
sex, as analogue for inspiration 425
sexual relationships, resentment in 208
Shakespeare, W. 619, 646n, 656n, 668n
shame 459, 486, 660n; *see also hrī*
Shankaracharya 647n
Shepherd's Search for Mind, The xv,
  224–55
Shindormo 375
'shopping around' 110, 381
Siddhartha 19

tradition, as the 'father' 504
values, *see* values
spiritual, community, not always real
27, 497
spiritualism 412
spiritually gifted 543–4
spontaneity 130, 253, 253–4, 344
sports 412, 523
śraddhā, *see* faith
Sri Krishna 108
Sri Ramakrishna 632
Stagg, C. xiii
state
alienated 337–8, 442
elephantine 420
Enlightened 217
facets of in different people 216,
222
and unfettered energy 73
hell 557
insight as a higher 575
intermediate 30, 83, 85–6, 612; *see
also bardo*
before stream entry 578
meditative 31, 398, 423
dhyāna 31
mental, *see* mental states
non-dual 48, 58
status 101, 440
St Augustine 160
St Francis xi, xvi, 160
store-consciousness 289–90; *see also
ālaya vijñāna*
Stream Entry 295, 578–9, 588,
596, 648n, 652n, 668n; *see also*
irreversibility
study groups, and communication
478–9
subject–object 231, 640, 650n; *see also*
non-duality
success, worldly 101–2
suffering 47, 102, 128, 151, 565, 593,
656n
bodhisattva and 172, 589–91
and the body 235–6, 558
as drive to practise 580
and the Enlightened mind 47
and insight 575
and joy not separate 47
sukha 90; *see also* serene joy
Sukhāvatī 121, 304
śūnyatā (emptiness) 43, 65–6, 74, 127,
599; *see also* voidness
alive with energy 74
as armour 81

aspect of *mettā bhāvanā* practice
513–14
balanced by 'Mind Only' teaching 74
mahā as a prefix denoting 597
mind as clear light of 65
misunderstanding of 179
and *prajñā* 66
realization of 597
and *rūpa* 416
sky as symbol of 59
twofold 246
as warehouse 294
śūnyatās, four 398, 657n
Śūraṅgama Samādhi Sūtra 544
Survey of Buddhism 347
Sūtra of Huineng 364, 654n
sūtras
Mahāyāna 86, 161, 172, 414, 602
need for 633
as outer phenomena 632–3
Sutta-Nipāta 294, 651n, 660n
Suzuki, D. T. 254, 647n
svabhāva 84
Swat valley 304
sword, as metaphor for wisdom 102,
104
symbol, great (*mahāmudrā*) 65
symbolism 59, 63, 272, 296, 601
symbols 49, 72, 88, 373, 399, 425,
427–8, 525, 619–20, 632
sympathy 624–5
Symposium 158
system of meditation 667n

Tale of Red Rock Jewel Valley, The xv,
10
talking, and energy 482
Tantra 74–9, 177
and ethics 79
Hevajra 14
and idea of correspondence 77
integration of ethnic magical rites
174
practices can destabilize the mind
177–8
Tantras, four grades or levels of 302–3,
652n
Tantric practice
discussing 476
levels of 302–3
Tārā 311, 603
taste 131–2
'taste of freedom' 594
Tathāgatas, five 601
tea ceremony, Japanese 426

trees
    angry 23
    effect of loss of on human psyche 23
trikāya doctrine 86–9
    and body, speech, and mind 87, 293
    as 'three inseparable friends' 614
Triratna Buddhist Order 487
trousers 133, 137
tṛṣṇā 451, 649n, 663n
Trungpa, Chögyam xiii
truth
    absolute and relative 85
    body of, see dharmakāya
    resistance to 262
truthfulness 139–40
Tsangnyön 261
Tsongkhapa 52, 223
tulku 100
tummo 49, 65, 89–91, 620
'two-in-one,' (yuganaddha) 51, 299
two-in-one path 102
types
    deluded 577
    greed 561, 577, 580
    hate 577, 580
    and insight 577, 580

Ucchuṣma 426
Udāna 6
Uddiyāna or Urgyen, see Oujen
Unconditioned, the, and the conditioned
    51
unskilfulness, three roots of 449, 575
upadeśa 394, 408
Upanisa Sutta 649n
upāsaka ordination 98
upasampadā 653n
upāyamarga 407
upekkhā 103; see also equanimity
Uposatha Sutta 667n
Urgyen, as archetypal realm 304
Uriah Heep 511, 653n
usefuless and uselessness 120–2
utpatti 320

Vairocana 401, 598, 600, 602, 606
vajra 94
vajra bell 94
vajrācārya 15
Vajradhara 92, 94, 380, 383
vajra-gīta 5
vajra guru 15, 61
vajrāsana 19
Vajrasattva visualization practice 660n
Vajravārāhī 519

Vajrayāna 74–5, 361, 408, 417, 496–7,
    529, 596
    and bodhicitta 102, 374, 463
    and body, see body, Vajrayāna and
        75, 377, 415
    career 60
    communication 380
    and early Buddhism 529
    and energies 371–2, 411–12, 415,
        416–17
    and expression 377
    hidden teachings 469
    and Hinayana 172–3
    and initiations 498
    intellectual elaboration of 496–7
    and just sitting 666n
    and Mahāyāna 74, 408, 415, 463
    and mandala 525
    path 408
    and philosophy 408
    and pleasure 528–9
    practice, importance of preparation
        for 529
    three refuges and 418, 496
    and trikāya 87
    on union of bliss and emptiness 415–16,
        528–9
    visualization practices 87
    yab-yum symbolism of 65, 296, 506
Vajrayoginī 260, 602
Vakkali 654n
values 135, 161, 301–2, 504, 509
    and generosity 103, 376
    of group 101, 134
    hierarchy of 130
    and hypocrisy 460
    spiritual, conditions to nurture 34–6
    Three Jewels represent transcendental
        252
    worldly 34, 36
Vanity Fair 567, 665n
Vasubandhu 223
vedanā, in nidāna chain 663n
veils
    and the trikāya 88
    two 449–50
veins, three 30
vicar of Hampstead 347
vidyā-guru 508
views, see also attitude
    fixed 53–4, 163
    rarely changed for logical reasons 360
    right 415
    wrong (micchā-diṭṭhis) 295, 439,
        449–51, 473, 651n

vigour 106, 478, 649n; *see also vīrya*
vijñāna 289; *see also* consciousness
vijñānas, eight 604–6
Vimalakīrti Nirdeśa 161
Vinaya 105, 187, 339, 390, 487, 656n
Vināyaka 32
vipāka 146, 528
vipaśyanā (*see also* insight) 299, 359–60,
    398, 449, 512–13, 514, 529, 540,
    577, 639
Vipulakirti xi
vīrya 106, 275, 649n
vision 30, 57, 122, 126, 272, 280–1,
    620
  as central point of spiritual life 280
  in childhood 30
  of the *Dharmakāya* 253
  effect of lack of 556–7
  embodying one's 277
  failure of 135
  and faith 272–3, 279–81
  and gestalt or pattern 279–81
  and insight 88
  as irruption of another element 280
  lost by listening to others 30
  of reality in bardo 30
  Rechungpa's lack of 556
  and *sambhogakāya* 88
  transcendental 279
  and transformation 173
  and unblocking energy 443
  of world, mandala as 125
visions
  Milarepa's 19, 32, 126, 437–8
  as nourishment 620
visualization, practice 496, 660n
  and esoteric Dharma refuge 418
  and evocation 319
  getting a feel for concrete details 601
  of guru 15
  of the inner fire 89
  and insight 513
  and the mandala of the Five Buddhas
    600–1
  and mantra recitation practice 317
  role of beauty in 158
  as unification of mundane bliss and
    emptiness 416
Vitakkasaṇṭhāna Sutta 669n
vocation xii, 119
Void, the, *see śūnyatā* 30, 43, 74, 242,
    570
voidness 43, 84, 247
  of absolute being 49
  and bliss 299

of both subject and object 246
and clarity 91
of hindrances 637
illuminating- 614
intuition of 90
as protection 49
as translation of *śūnyatā* 294, 599
twofold 246
wisdom of the 242
volition 362, 410, 412, 423, 528
  karma, distinct from fruit (*vipāka*) 528
  and spiritual development 358
vows 65, 81, 161–2, 172
  bodhisattva 172
  effect of not keeping 487
  mutual 146–7
  as oath or *samaya* 325
  precepts as 325, 487
  and rebirth 144, 146–8

Wala Tsandra 326
warrior, spiritual 103–6
Wayman, A. 494
wealth 13, 94–6, 218–19
  Dharma as 96, 334
  from renunication of 50
  spiritual qualities as 50
weapons 98, 104
Wesley, C. 120
West, M. 479
Wheel of Life 172, 396, 663n
'whispered,' transmission 14, 65, 96–7,
    181
Whispered Lineage 96
Whitehouse, M. 634, 668n
White Lotus Sūtra 588
winds, worldly, eight 329, 343, 652n;
    see also 'Eight Worldly Claims'
wisdom
  all-performing 600
  bodhisattva of 19
  and compassion
    non-duality of 51, 77, 102, 296–7,
      299, 373–4, 588, 590
    symbolized by *ḍākinī* and *heruka* 373
    two-in-one path 102
    and yab-yum symbolism 296
  conceptual 68
  as cornerstone 275
  of the *dharmadhātu* 599, 606
  discriminating 599–600, 605
  in distinctively Mahāyāna sense 588
  of equality 599, 605
  as illumination 614–15
  innate-born 248–9

A GUIDE TO THE COMPLETE
WORKS OF SANGHARAKSHITA

Gathered together in these twenty-seven volumes are talks and stories, commentaries on the Buddhist scriptures, poems, memoirs, reviews, and other writings. The genres are many, and the subject matter covered is wide, but it all has – its whole purpose is to convey – that taste of freedom which the Buddha declared to be the hallmark of his Dharma. Another traditional description of the Buddha's Dharma is that it is *ehipassiko*, 'come and see'. Sangharakshita calls to us, his readers, to come and see how the Dharma can fundamentally change the way we see things, change the way we live for the better, and change the society we belong to, wherever in the world we live.

Sangharakshita's very first published piece, *The Unity of Buddhism* (found in volume 7 of this collection), appeared in 1944 when he was eighteen years old, and it introduced themes that continued to resound throughout his work: the basis of Buddhist ethics, the compassion of the bodhisattva, and the transcendental unity of Buddhism. Over the course of the following seven decades not only did numerous other works flow from his pen; he gave hundreds of talks (some now lost). In gathering all we could find of this vast output, we have sought to arrange it in a way that brings a sense of coherence, communicating something essential about Sangharakshita, his life and teaching. Recalling the three 'baskets' among which an early tradition divided the Buddha's teachings, we have divided Sangharakshita's creative output into six 'baskets' or groups: foundation texts; works originating in India; teachings originally given in the West; commentaries on the Buddhist scriptures; personal writings; and poetry, aphorisms, and works on the arts. The 27th volume, a concordance, brings together all the terms and themes of the whole collection. If you want to find a particular story or teaching, look at a traditional term from different points of view or in different contexts, or track down one of the thousands of canonical references to be found in these volumes, the concordance will be your guide.

1. FOUNDATION

What is the foundation of a Buddhist life? How do we understand and then follow the Buddha's path of Ethics, Meditation, and Wisdom? What is really meant by 'Going for Refuge to the Three Jewels', described by Sangharakshita as the essential act of a Buddhist life? And what is the Bodhisattva ideal, which he has called 'one of the sublimest ideals mankind has ever seen'? In the 'Foundation' group you will find teachings on all these themes. It includes the author's *magnum opus, A Survey of Buddhism*, a collection of teachings on *The Purpose and Practice of Buddhist Meditation*, and the anthology, *The Essential Sangharakshita*, an eminently helpful distillation of the entire corpus.

2. INDIA

From 1950 to 1964 Sangharakshita, based in Kalimpong in the eastern Himalayas, poured his energy into trying to revive Buddhism in the land of its birth and to revitalize and bring reform to the existing Asian Buddhist world. The articles and book reviews from this period are gathered in volumes 7 and 8, as well as his biographical sketch of the great Sinhalese Dharmaduta, Anagarika Dharmapala. In 1954 Sangharakshita took on the editing of the *Maha Bodhi*, a journal for which he wrote a monthly editorial, and which, under his editorship, published the work of many of the leading Buddhist writers of the time. It was also during these years in India that a vital connection was forged with Dr B. R. Ambedkar, renowned Indian statesman and leader of the Buddhist mass conversion of 1956. Sangharakshita became closely involved with the new Buddhists and, after Dr Ambedkar's untimely death, visited them regularly on extensive teaching tours.

From 1979, when an Indian wing of the Triratna Buddhist Community was founded (then known as TBMSG), Sangharakshita returned several times to undertake further teaching tours. The talks from these tours are collected in volumes 9 and 10 along with a unique work on Ambedkar and his life which draws out the significance of his conversion to Buddhism.

3. THE WEST

Sangharakshita founded the Triratna Buddhist Community (then called the Friends of the Western Buddhist Order) on 6 April 1967. On 7 April the following year he performed the first ordinations of men and women within the Triratna Buddhist Order (then the Western Buddhist Order). At that time Buddhism was not widely known in the West and for the following two decades or so he taught intensively, finding new ways to communicate the ancient truths of Buddhism, drawing on the whole Buddhist tradition to do so, as well as making connections with what was best in existing Western culture. Sometimes his sword flashed as he critiqued ideas and views inimical to the Dharma. It is these teachings and writings that are gathered together in this third group.

4. COMMENTARY

Throughout Sangharakshita's works are threaded references to the Buddhist canon of literature – Pāli, Mahāyāna, and Vajrayāna – from which he drew his inspiration. In the early days of the new movement he often taught by means of seminars in which, prompted by the questions of his students, he sought to pass on the inspiration and wisdom of the Buddhist tradition. Each seminar was based around a different text, the seminars were recorded and transcribed, and in due course many of the transcriptions were edited and turned into books, all carefully checked by Sangharakshita. The commentaries compiled in this way constitute the fourth group. In some ways this is the heart of the collection. Sangharakshita often told the story of how it was that, reading two *sūtras* at the age of sixteen or seventeen, he realized that he was a Buddhist, and he has never tired of showing others how they too could see and realize the value of the '*sūtra*-treasure'.

5. MEMOIRS

Who is Sangharakshita? What sort of life did he live? Whom did he meet? What did he feel? Why did he found a new Buddhist movement? In these volumes of memoirs and letters Sangharakshita shares with his readers much about himself and his life as he himself has experienced it, giving us a sense of its breadth and depth, humour and pathos.

6. POETRY, APHORISMS, AND THE ARTS

Sangharakshita describes reading *Paradise Lost* at the age of twelve as one of the greatest poetic experiences of his life. His realization of the value of the higher arts to spiritual development is one of his distinctive contributions to our understanding of what Buddhist life is, and he has expressed it in a number of essays and articles. Throughout his life he has written poetry which he says can be regarded as a kind of spiritual autobiography. It is here, perhaps, that we come closest to the heart of Sangharakshita. He has also written a few short stories and composed some startling aphorisms. Through book reviews he has engaged with the experiences, ideas, and opinions of modern writers. All these are collected in this sixth group.

In the preface to *A Survey of Buddhism* (volume 1 in this collection), Sangharakshita wrote of his approach to the Buddha's teachings:

> Why did the Buddha (or Nāgārjuna, or Buddhaghosa) teach this particular doctrine? What bearing does it have on the spiritual life? How does it help the individual Buddhist actually to follow the spiritual path?... I found myself asking such questions again and again, for only in this way, I found, could I make sense – spiritual sense – of Buddhism.

Although this collection contains so many words, they are all intent, directly or indirectly, on these same questions. And all these words are not in the end about their writer, but about his great subject, the Buddha and his teaching, and about you, the reader, for whose benefit they are solely intended. These pages are full of the reverence that Sangharakshita has always felt, which is expressed in an early poem, 'Taking Refuge in the Buddha', whose refrain is 'My place is at thy feet'. He has devoted his life to communicating the Buddha's Dharma in its depth and in its breadth, to men and women from all backgrounds and walks of life, from all countries, of all races, of all ages. These collected works are the fruit of that devotion.

We are very pleased to be able to include some previously unpublished work in this collection, but most of what appears in these volumes has been published before. We have made very few changes, though we have added extra notes where we thought they would be useful. We have had the pleasure of researching the notes in the Sangharakshita Library at 'Adhisthana', Triratna's centre in Herefordshire, UK, which houses his own collection of books. It has been of great value to be able to search among the very copies of the *suttas*, *sūtras* and commentaries that have provided the basis of his teachings over the last seventy years.

The publication of these volumes owes much to the work of transcribers, editors, indexers, designers, and publishers over many years – those who brought out the original editions of many of the works included here, and those who have contributed in all sorts of ways to this *Complete Works* project, including all those who contributed to funds given in celebration of Sangharakshita's ninetieth birthday in August 2015. Many thanks to everyone who has helped; may the merit gained in our acting thus go to the alleviation of the suffering of all beings.

Vidyadevi and Kalyanaprabha
Editors

THE COMPLETE WORKS OF SANGHARAKSHITA

IV COMMENTARY

WINDHORSE PUBLICATIONS

Windhorse Publications is a Buddhist charitable company based in the UK. We produce books of high quality that are accessible and relevant to all those interested in Buddhism, at whatever level of interest and commitment. We are the main publisher of Sangharakshita, the founder of the Triratna Buddhist Order and Community. Our books draw on the whole range of the Buddhist tradition, including translations of traditional texts, commentaries, books that make links with contemporary culture and ways of life, biographies of Buddhists, and works on meditation.

To subscribe to the *Complete Works of Sangharakshita,* please go to: windhorsepublications.com/sangharakshita-complete-works/

THE TRIRATNA BUDDHIST COMMUNITY

Windhorse Publications is a part of the Triratna Buddhist Community, an international movement with centres in Europe, India, North and South America and Australasia. At these centres, members of the Triratna Buddhist Order offer classes in meditation and Buddhism. Activities of the Triratna Community also include retreat centres, residential spiritual communities, ethical Right Livelihood businesses, and the Karuna Trust, a UK fundraising charity that supports social welfare projects in the slums and villages of India.

Through these and other activities, Triratna is developing a unique approach to Buddhism, not simply as a philosophy and a set of techniques, but as a creatively directed way of life for all people living in the conditions of the modern world.

For more information please visit thebuddhistcentre.com